Understanding Enterprise

Entrepreneurs and Small Business

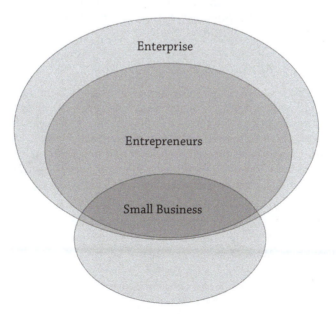

Praise for the fifth edition:

'This is a very timely new edition of what I see as a classic in the small business and entrepreneurship literature. The authors draw on their substantial knowledge to provide a critical review of the essential concepts, their overlap, and the implications for policies. An excellent volume and definitely a must-read for students, but also for those researching and supporting small businesses and entrepreneurs.'
– **Friederike Welter**, *Managing Director at Institut für Mittelstandsforschung Bonn (IfM) & Professor of SME Management and Entrepreneurship at University of Siegen, Germany*

'An authoritative text which will delight teachers and students. In particular, Part 3 on Enterprise Policy and Government Intervention is a classic and should be mandatory reading for Enterprise policy makers worldwide.'
– **David Storey OBE**, *Professor of Enterprise at the University of Sussex, UK*

'If I were to write a book about smaller enterprise, this is the book I would like to write. *Understanding Enterprise* wonderfully contextualizes smaller enterprise for readers with entirely different perspectives and needs. It offers useful (and well-documented) material to the student, instructor, policy-maker and even the casual reader who might wish to obtain realistically positive, but non-hyped material about small enterprise and its opportunities. In fact, one of the great virtues of *Understanding Enterprise* is that it counters much common wisdom that in end proves more fiction than fact. I like this volume very much and highly recommend it.'
– **William J. Dennis, Jr.**, *Former Senior Research Fellow at NFIB Research Foundation Washington, USA*

'Bridge and O'Neill's fifth edition delivers an accessible outlook into the fundamental characteristics at the interface of enterprise, entrepreneurs, small business, and its consequences for policymaking. This book offers a practical resource for ardent scholars, readers, lecturers and policymakers responsible for the design and implementation of enterprise strategies, enabling us to expressively engage with and challenge distinct entrepreneurial theoretical and practical scientific debates. Building on previous editions, this three-part interactive volume is packed with contemporary illustrations, case studies and paradigms that transmit the wide-reaching and often fleeting tendencies of entrepreneurial value systems in transitioning towards more sustainable social entrepreneurship economies.'
– **Lorraine Johnston**, *Senior Lecturer in Urban Entrepreneurship, Newcastle Business School, UK*

'This is not a book in how-to-start-your-own enterprise, but an up-to-date book on entrepreneurship, enterprise and small business. After introducing the basics, the authors turn to new developments, e.g. effectuation and the capital's approach, in Part 2. The third part is on policy and its implications and the effects of government interventions. Theory meets practice, students (and lecturers) will love this book. I recommend this book for both undergraduate and graduate courses on entrepreneurship.'
– **Peter van der Sijde**, *Professor of Organization, Entrepreneurship & Technology, Vrije Universiteit, The Netherlands*

Praise for the fourth edition:

'The fourth edition of this book is a wonderful example of continuous innovation as it builds upon previous editions by adding additional layers of depth and knowledge. It is also evident throughout the book that the authors utilize their vast experience as practitioners and academics to bring the reader excellent insights into the varying perspectives held by different stakeholders. My recommendation is based upon my actions - I have already ordered the book for my forthcoming classes.'
– **Thomas Cooney**, *Academic Director of Institute for Minority Entrepreneurship, Dublin Institute of Technology, Ireland, and President of the International Council for Small Business*

'This volume is a welcome new edition of a highly successful and well acclaimed text, written by authors who combine a strong academic pedigree with practical application. As such, it represents one of the best foundation texts for students of small business and entrepreneurship and an excellent building block for subsequent specialised study. At the same time, its clarity of organisation and uncluttered style makes it accessible to all.'
– **David Smallbone**, *Professor of Small Business and Entrepreneurship and Associate Director of the Small Business Research Centre at Kingston University, UK*

UNDERSTANDING
ENTERPRISE
Entrepreneurs & Small Business

Simon Bridge / Ken O'Neill

Fifth edition

 macmillan education   palgrave

First edition 1998
Second edition 2003
Third edition 2009
Fourth edition 2013
This edition published 2018 by
PALGRAVE

Palgrave in the UK is an imprint of Macmillan Publishers Limited, registered in England, company number 785998, of 4 Crinan Street, London, N1 9XW.

Palgrave® and Macmillan® are registered trademarks in the United States, the United Kingdom, Europe and other countries.

ISBN 978–1–137–58454–0 paperback

This book is printed on paper suitable for recycling and made from fully managed and sustained forest sources. Logging, pulping and manufacturing processes are expected to conform to the environmental regulations of the country of origin.

A catalogue record for this book is available from the British Library.

A catalog record for this book is available from the Library of Congress.

Contents

List of Illustrations vi

List of Figures viii

List of Tables ix

About the Authors x

Preface xi

Acknowledgements xiii

1   Introduction: Understanding Enterprise 1

PART 1   The Evolution of Enterprise Understanding 9

2   A Brief History of Enterprise Understanding 10

3   Enterprise and Entrepreneurship: Their Meanings and Variations 33

4   Enterprise and Entrepreneurs: Understanding Their Nature 56

5   Small Businesses: Their Characteristics and Variety 77

6   Small Businesses: Understanding Their Dynamics 108

7   Social Enterprise and the Third Sector 136

PART 2   Challenges to the Traditional View 151

8   Rethinking Small Business 153

9   Rethinking Entrepreneurs and 'Entrepreneurship' 172

10   Enterprise and Life 191

11   Becoming an Entrepreneur 205

12   Running a Small Business 227

13   Social Capital and the Enterprise Mix 242

PART 3   Enterprise Policy and Government Intervention 261

14   Why Governments Intervene: The Aims of Enterprise Policy 263

15   Enterprise Policy: Approaches and Implementation Methods 289

16   Does the Policy Work? 320

17   What Might Work? 341

18   Afterword: The Impact of Change 357

Index 363

List of Illustrations

2.1	The position of entrepreneurship as a field of study	21
2.2	The entrepreneurial economy	27
3.1	Types of business owner	44
3.2	Enterprising acts	45
4.1	Three models of entrepreneurial potential	72
5.1	Some official definitions of a small business	86
6.1	Starting a business	113
8.1	Conventional wisdom	155
8.2	A case study of a policy based on a false perspective?	168
9.1	The assumption of individual risk/return analysis	180
9.2	Behavioural economics and the 'social brain'	181
9.3	The Global Entrepreneurship Monitor's assessment of influences	184
10.1	What is the aim of enterprise?	191
10.2	Christopher Columbus: a case study of an entrepreneur?	198
10.3	The right to a job	201
11.1	Some reflections on effectuation and causation	207
11.2	You start – and you keep going	209
11.3	Business plans are advocated	210
11.4	Who advocates business plans?	210
11.5	Business plan scepticism	212
11.6	The limitations of market research	215
11.7	The failed plan	216
11.8	Left- and right-brain thinking	216
11.9	Risk and uncertainty in enterprise	217
11.10	The 'Beermat' plan	221
11.11	The establishment of a small consultancy business	223
12.1	Aspects of growth	229
12.2	Motivation and the theory of planned behaviour	234
12.3	Criteria for assistance	235
12.4	Why business owners might not want to grow their businesses	237
12.5	How owners learn	238
13.1	The power of social capital – a single-dimension view	245
13.2	The power of social capital – a multi-dimensional view	248
13.3	Identifying different forms of social capital	249
13.4	An example of the influence of social group norms	254
13.5	Some thoughts on networking from the 1980s	256
13.6	Accessing social capital through the Dragons' Den	257
13.7	Social capital in ethnic networks	258
14.1	An example of outputs and outcomes	267
14.2	Distinguishing between small business, entrepreneurship and enterprise policy	268
14.3	Arguments for and against targeting growth businesses	273
14.4	Policy rationale: an OECD view	279
14.5	'Small business growth stunted by reluctance to seek advice'	282
15.1	Initiatives for high-tech businesses	294
15.2	Policy analysis: an example from Denmark	298
15.3	The Cruickshank Review	302

15.4	The Grameen Bank	307
16.1	Economic appraisals	322
16.2	Two guides to evaluation	325
16.3	The McNamara fallacy	328
16.4	Why workers in smaller businesses are less likely to receive training	334
17.1	The contribution of GEM	346
17.2	A study in government enterprise policy	352

List of Figures

1.1	The transition route from data to wisdom	4
1.2	A summary of the scientific method	4
1.3	Bygrave's hierarchy of sciences	5
2.1	UK unemployment 1950–2015	18
3.1	Three types of small business owner	44
3.2	E-numbers: a categorisation of enterprise and entrepreneurship	51
4.1	Intentions model of entrepreneurial potential (simplified)	65
4.2	Attributes and resources model	66
4.3	Mechanisms through which genetic factors might influence entrepreneurship	70
4.4	Nature or nurture?	73
5.A1	Size distribution of UK family businesses (in 2012)	96
6.1	Small business paths from conception to death	110
6.2	Growth process as reflected in possible growth paths	110
6.3	The Greiner growth model	111
6.4	Entrepreneurial success	113
6.5	Early-stage small business finance	119
6.6	Management factors and stages	121
6.7	Types of business termination	128
6.8	The ingredients of failure	131
7.1	The sectors of an economy	140
8.1	The DFID model of development capital	162
8.2	The influences on a business	163
8.3	The supposed effect of the provision of growth support	163
8.4	A hierarchy of needs model	165
9.1	A possible model of the level of entrepreneurs	183
9.2	The layers of the small business support network	183
9.3	Alternative pictures of the entrepreneur	185
10.1	A journey through life?	195
10.2	What you see is not everything	200
11.1	Business start-up: the strategic planning process	212
13.1	The perceived key business start-up needs (circa 1985)	246
14.1	A diagram of a policy framework	265
14.2	The sequence from inputs to impacts?	267
14.3	The interface between entrepreneurship policy and SME policy	268
15.1	(repeated) A diagram of a policy framework	290
15.2	Enterprise policy map	291
15.3	Simple form of the OECD Framework for Entrepreneurship Indicators	299
15.4	Aspects of enterprise policy implementation in the UK	312
15.5	Applying limited resources to maximise the benefit returned	313
16.1	Possible evaluation stages	321
17.1	Model of factors leading to entrepreneurial activity	348
17.2	Institutional and cultural dimensions	348
17.3	Levels of observation	351

List of Tables

2.1 Bolton's eight 'important economic functions of the small business' 15
2.2 Reasons for the re-emergence of small-scale enterprise 16
2.3 Fordism and post-Fordism 26
2.4 Features of the new economy 27
2.5 Differences between 'managed' and 'entrepreneurial' economies 28
3.1 Summary of approaches for describing entrepreneurs 40
3.2 Entrepreneurial behaviours, attributes, skills, values and beliefs 43
3.3 The focus of learning 44
3.4 E-numbers: interpretation and some comparable uses 51
4.1 Traits associated with entrepreneurs 59
4.2 Attributes and resources, and how they are acquired 66
5.1 More benefits of small businesses 79
5.A1 Different criteria by which family businesses have been defined 97
6.1 The five stages of business growth 109
6.2 New technology adoption rate 112
6.3 Approaches to starting a business 114
6.4 The four dimensions of management development 114
6.5 Some of the benefits which can be obtained from networks 115
6.6 Analysis of a start-up business 116
6.7 Economies ranked on their ease of doing business 118
6.8 Obstacles to the success of business 123
6.9 Percentages of businesses in 2007 surviving after one, two
    and three years 127
7.1 Organisations and activities not in the public or the private sector 137
7.2 Comparison of market sector and social economy characteristics 144
7.3 Autonomous and community entrepreneurs compared 147
8.1 Owners' motivations 157
9.1 Entrepreneurial v. corporatist management – some contrasts 175
9.2 A process definition of entrepreneurs 175
10.1 Barrett's seven levels of consciousness and Maslow's hierarchy of needs 193
10.2 Some of the means by which people can obtain resources for life 195
10.3 Some different kinds of entrepreneurs 199
10.4 How enterprise might be viewed from people and venture perspectives 202
11.1 The five key principles of effectuation 207
11.2 What effectuation is not 208
11.3 Comparison of accept-uncertainty and business-plan approaches 218
12.1 Yardsticks for business growth 230
12.2 The roles needed for business development at different stages 233
13.1 The 'Conscise' project and the elements of social capital 248
14.1 The possible components of a policy framework 266
14.2 Market imperfections, their causes and the actions needed 278
15.1 UK government SME policies 301
15.2 Barriers and incentives to training 309
15.A1 Taxonomy of enterprise initiatives 315
16.1 Major UK enterprise policy questions 323
18.1 Some of the challenges to conventional enterprise wisdom 359

About the Authors

SIMON BRIDGE For over 30 years Simon Bridge has been involved in exploring aspects of enterprise and in formulating, delivering, assessing and/or commenting on enterprise policy. He has been the enterprise director of a small business agency, then an enterprise and economic development consultant, and is now a visiting professor at Ulster University. Much of his varied experience and learning is reflected in his books which, in addition to this one, include *Rethinking Enterprise Policy: Can Failure Trigger New Understanding?* (Palgrave Macmillan, 2010), *Beyond the Business Plan: 10 Principles for New Venture Explorers* (Palgrave Macmillan, 2013) co-written with Cecilia Hegarty, *Understanding the Social Economy and the Third Sector* (Palgrave Macmillan, 2014) co-written with Brendan Murtagh and Ken O'Neill, and *The Search for Entrepreneurship: Finding More Questions Than Answers* (Routledge, 2017).

KEN O'NEILL is Professor Emeritus of Entrepreneurship and Small Business Development at Ulster University and spent much of his career as Director of the Northern Ireland Small Business Institute developing and delivering business and management development programmes for small business owners and their advisers.

He is Chair of the School for Social Enterprises in Ireland, a director of The Genesis Initiative, the International Small Business Congress and other not-for-profits and SMEs. Previous roles have included President of the International Council for Small Business and of the UK's Institute for Small Business Affairs (now ISBE) as well as a Board member of Young Enterprise Ltd.

He is the first person to be awarded The Queen's Award for Enterprise Promotion – Lifetime Achievement Award (2005). Other published works include *Understanding the Social Economy and the Third Sector,* which he co-authored with Simon Bridge and Brendan Murtagh.

Preface

For the last 30 years or so enterprise, entrepreneurs and small business have been popular concepts – not least because they are seen as being economically beneficial. The world is always changing, but it is now apparent that since the last decades of the last century there has been a significant economic shift in which the dominance of big businesses has lessened and individual enterprise is becoming ever more necessary for economic success.

Throughout history many people have been enterprising and many businesses have been small. Recently enterprise and small businesses have been seen as the answer to economic problems like unemployment, and this process, or aspects of it, has been referred to variously as the development of an enterprise culture and of an entrepreneurial economy – and its benefits have been widely sought. Enterprise and its associated concepts of 'entrepreneurship' and small business have been widely promoted therefore and their development supported.

As a result, in many developed countries a new industry of enterprise promotion and support has arisen and been developed and/or fostered by government departments, by local economic and enterprise agencies, by community organisations, by private organisations and by academic institutions. This process is also being repeated in other countries, such as those of Central and Eastern Europe, which have had less well-developed market economies and where enterprise development is seen as a key route to economic growth.

It is in that context that this book endeavours to provide an introduction to the different aspects of this subject. It aims, not so much to tell people how to be enterprising or how to start a business, but instead to inform them about enterprise, entrepreneurs and small business. It describes what they are, how they are related and what is currently known about them. It also looks at areas where some of the learning about them may need to be re-assessed because it now appears to be based on false assumptions. Such re-assessments have policy implications so they are considered also.

Readers familiar with the earlier editions will still find, in Part 1, introductions to the concepts of enterprise and small business, what they are and how they are variously defined and also to what we appear to know about their make-up, their impact and the influences upon them.

Part 2 then introduces relatively new thinking and identifies where it challenges some of what has become received wisdom. It also uses some of this new thinking to suggest alternative ways of understanding the processes of small business formation and growth, and also how better to become an entrepreneur, to run a small business and/or to help either of those activities.

Part 3 looks at this from a government and policy perspective. It considers why and how governments have enterprise policies and intervene to encourage and/or assist enterprise, entrepreneurs and small business. It explores how effective these interventions appear to have been and, based on the new thinking now emerging, suggests alternatives which might be more successful.

Who should read this book

This book is targeted at students of enterprise at universities, business schools and further and higher education establishments; at researchers and teaching staff; at policy-makers and staff of business support organisations; and at the informed public. It provides a foundation text for those who are studying enterprise and 'entrepreneurship' and who want a perspective appropriate for those who might want to do it by starting a business as well as for those who might want to work with, but not in, such businesses or with the broader aspects of enterprise. It has been written in the UK, but much of its content should be relevant in all countries where people, for whatever reason, wish to know more about enterprise. It seeks to present them with an introduction to the key concepts and issues as a basis for understanding and working in this area, and as a starting point for further explorations. Aspects of the book have been specifically written for students who need a broad introduction to the whole field of enterprise, such as those doing an enterprise or 'entrepreneurship' option on a Bachelors or Masters course. It also provides students and lecturers with cases and questions, summaries and suggestions for further reading.

Changes in the fifth edition

This is the fifth edition of the book, written some 20 years after the first edition. In those intervening years there has been much further research into enterprise, entrepreneurs and small business – leading to new conclusions and also to re-assessments of earlier ideas and conclusions. Because of that new learning and its implications, the fourth edition was extensively rewritten in order better to reflect changes to the state of knowledge in this area.

The fifth edition builds on that re-assessment. It updates some of the information and reflects some of the more recent thinking. In particular it acknowledges the concept that in almost every subject (maths may be the exception) the available knowledge may have a half-life: the period of time over which half of it will be found to be wrong, irrelevant or otherwise not useful. This area is no exception – and the process should be expected to continue.

One concept particularly questioned in this edition is that of 'entrepreneurship' itself. The word appears to have been coined about 80 years ago by English speakers adding the suffix 'ship' to the word 'entrepreneur' which originally came from the French. Possibly because the word then existed and because they wanted there to be such a phenomenon, many people appear subsequently to have believed it did indeed exist as the discrete, identifiable and deterministic phenomenon they had supposed it to be. What therefore, the book considers, would be the implications if that is not actually the case?

Thank you

As in the earlier editions, this one has benefited a lot from the help of other people and we are conscious of the many who have encouraged and assisted us. We owe them considerable thanks. We would like especially to highlight the continuing patience and support shown by our wives who have again had to put up with our application to this instead of to other tasks, and who have tolerated the many phone calls and interruptions. We are very grateful to them.

Simon Bridge and Ken O'Neill, Belfast

Acknowledgements

The authors and publisher gratefully acknowledge permission from the following to reproduce copyright material in the fifth edition of this book.

Paul Cowie for permission to reproduce the diagram in Figure 16.1.

Emerald Publishing Group Ltd for permission to reproduce from A. A. Gibb, 'Enterprise Culture – Its Meaning and Implications for Education and Training', *Journal of European Industrial Training* (1987).

Allan Gibb for permission to reproduce from *Creating The Leading Edge*, Allan Gibb and Judi Cotton, Durham Business School, 1998; *The Focus of Learning* from 'Enterprise Culture – Its Meaning and Implications for Education and Training', *Journal of European Industrial Training*, 1987, p. 17; 'Towards the Building of Entrepreneurial Models of Support for Small Business', paper presented at the *11th (UK) National Small Firms Policy and Research Conference*, Cardiff, 1988; and 'Towards the Entrepreneurial University: Entrepreneurship Education as a Lever for Change', **National Council for Graduate Entrepreneurship Policy Paper 003**, May 2005.

Harvard Business Publishing for permission to reproduce *The Greiner Growth Model* from L. E. Greiner, 'Evolution and Revolution as Organisations Grow', *Harvard Business Review*, July/August 1972.

HMSO under the Open Government License for extracts from a number of publications.

Ji-Hee Kim for permission to reproduce from J. Kim, A. G. Weinstein, S. E. Shirley and I. Melhern, 'Toward a Comprehensive Model of Global Entrepreneurship', a paper presented and the **ICSB Conference at Seoul**, Korea, in June 2009 – and with acknowledgement of the wish of these authors to contribute to global enterprise understanding.

Norris Krueger for permission to reproduce *Intentions Model of Entrepreneurial Potential* from *How Communities Can Create Potential for Entrepreneurs* (Washington, DC: Small Business Foundation of America, Working Paper 93-03, 1995).

Anders Lundström for permission to reproduce from L. Stevenson and A. Lundström, *Beyond the Rhetoric: Defining Entrepreneurship Policy and Its Best Practice Components* (Stockholm: Swedish Foundation for Small Business Research, 2002).

OECD for permission to reproduce from N. Ahmad and A. Hoffman, 'A Framework for Addressing and Measuring Entrepreneurship', *OECD Statistics Working Papers*, 2008/2.

Palgrave Macmillan for permission to reproduce material from:

S. Bridge, *Rethinking Enterprise Policy: Can Failure Trigger New Understanding* (Basingstoke: Palgrave Macmillan, 2010).
S. Bridge, B. Murtagh and K. O'Neill, *Understanding the Social Economy and the Third Sector*, 2nd Edition (Basingstoke: Palgrave, 2014).
P. Burns, *Entrepreneurship and Small Business*, 3rd Edition (Basingstoke: Palgrave Macmillan, 2011).

Taylor and Francis for permission to reproduce from:

J. Curran and R. A. Blackburn, 'Youth and the Enterprise Culture', *British Journal of Education and Work*, Vol. 4, No. 1, 1990.
H. H. Stevenson, 'Intellectual Foundations of Entrepreneurship' Chapter 1 of H. P. Welsch (ed.), *Entrepreneurship* (London: Routledge, 2004).
D. J. Storey, *Understanding the Small Business Sector* (London: Routledge, 1994).
UEAPME for permission to reproduce material from G. Carnazza, *The Role and the Main Developments of SMEs in the European Economy* (Brussels: UEAPME).

John Wiley & Sons Ltd for permission to reproduce from:

W. D. Bygrave, 'The Entrepreneurship Paradigm (I): A Philosophical Look at Its Research Methodologies', *Entrepreneurship Theory and Practice*, Vol. 14, No. 1.

J. B. Cunningham and J. Lischeron, 'Defining Entrepreneurship', *Journal of Small Business Management*, Vol. 29, No. 1, 1991.

W. J. Dennis, 'Entrepreneurship, Small Business and Public Policy Levers', *Journal of Small Business Management*, Vol. 49, No. 1, 2011.

R. W. Hornaday, 'Dropping the E-words from Small Business Research', *Journal of Small Business Management*, Vol. 28, No. 4, 1990.

Introduction: Understanding Enterprise

CONTENTS

- Why do people want to understand enterprise?
- What are enterprise and entrepreneurship?

- The evolution of enterprise knowledge
- The layout of this book

KEY CONCEPTS

This chapter covers:

- Why people want to understand enterprise.
- The difficulty sometimes encountered in knowing what enterprise and entrepreneurs – and associated concepts such as entrepreneurship and small business – are because these words can have different uses.
- The way our knowledge about this area might be expected to evolve, and the questions we might now have about it.
- The layout this book adopts in trying to answer such questions.

LEARNING OBJECTIVES

By the end of this chapter the reader should:

- Appreciate the different motivations people might have for wanting to learn about enterprise, 'entrepreneurship' and small business.
- Realise that the terminology used can cause confusion.
- Understand how knowledge can be developed and, despite the research which has taken place, the sort of questions that still remain.
- Understand the sequence in which the book seeks to address this subject.

WHY DO PEOPLE WANT TO UNDERSTAND ENTERPRISE?

This book, called *Understanding Enterprise, Entrepreneurs and Small Business*, is now in its fifth edition. Since it was first published it has been joined by many other books on this subject which often have a selection of the words 'enterprise', 'entrepreneurship' and 'small business' in their titles. While many of these books recognise that there is more to enterprise than starting, running or growing small businesses, nevertheless it is its application in a business context that is still the focus of much of the 'enterprise' literature.

This book tries to correct that impression and, by looking at what enterprise can mean to people's lives rather than considering it to be limited only to aspects of starting a business, to acknowledge it in its broader context. The true spirit of enterprise, this book suggests, is having the inclination and the ability to make one's own choices in life instead of having to follow a path which is in some way predetermined, whether because of tradition, social pressure, lack of other perceived opportunities or apparent lack of appropriate skills. If you don't want to choose for yourself in such matters, then you will not be enterprising. If you haven't got the ability to see or to follow other courses, then that too will severely limit any enterprising ambitions. As Peter Drucker has suggested, you will be a bystander:

> Bystanders have no history of their own. They are on stage but play no part in the action. They are not even audience. The fortunes of the play and every actor in it depend on the audience whereas the reaction of the bystander has no effect except on himself.[1]

This is a book for people who want to understand something about enterprise in a broad context including, but not limited to, its application in business through its associated components of entrepreneurs and small business. There are many reasons why people might seek such an understanding, for instance because they are:

- Studying the subject for an academic course.
- Teaching and/or researching in the field.
- Wanting to influence enterprise, to advance it and/or to develop more of it.
- Being employed to advise and/or assist those involved in enterprise.
- Wishing to be more enterprising themselves.

Thus there are people with different interests in enterprise, depending on whether they want:

- To know about enterprise, for instance about its history or what it means.
- To know how to be enterprising.
- To know how to be an entrepreneur and how to start and/or grow an enterprise.
- To know how to encourage and/or support enterprise, and to know about policy in this area.

This book explores different views of enterprise, both because of those different requirements for knowledge and because knowing about different aspects of a subject can help any understanding of it. But, before that exploration can start, it may be helpful to consider what enterprise is, how it relates to the concept of entrepreneurship, and how knowledge about such a subject can be developed.

WHAT ARE ENTERPRISE AND ENTREPRENEURSHIP?

Enterprise – Undertaking, esp. bold or difficult one; readiness to engage in such undertakings; enterprising, showing courage or imaginativeness.
Entrepreneur – Person in effective control of commercial undertaking; one who undertakes an enterprise, with chance of profit or loss.

(The Oxford Handy Dictionary)

It is difficult to be precise about the meanings of enterprise, entrepreneurs and entrepreneurship, not only because, over time, words change their meaning, but also because, in particular in the case of enterprise and entrepreneurship, these words have come simultaneously to have a variety of different uses and definitions – despite any apparent clarity in the Oxford definition quoted above.

The word 'enterprise' can have a broad meaning, being applied, for instance, to any goal-directed, non-routine action carried out in a dynamic and adventurous manner.

However, enterprise can be used more narrowly when it refers specifically to the field of small business or is used as an alternative word for a (small) business. There is probably less confusion about the term 'small business'. Although there have been a variety of attempts to set quantified limits to what can be considered a small business, these are generally measurable proxies for the essence of those businesses which, because of their small size, behave differently from large businesses. (For more on the essence of a small business and some definitions of it see Chapter 5.)

In contrast the word entrepreneur was originally used in economics to refer to a particular form of economic participant. However, it was then turned into a wider but ill-defined concept by adding a suffix – and the word 'entrepreneurship' now has some very varied, and sometimes conflicting, uses. In its early use it seemed to be applied almost exclusively to the process of starting and/or running some sort of business, and an 'entrepreneur' was anyone so engaged. But 'entrepreneurship' is now sometimes given a wider meaning and is even, on occasion, used interchangeably with 'enterprise'. Despite that, recently there have been instances of it being used in a very narrow context to refer only to high-tech and/or high-growth start-ups and, similarly, the label entrepreneur is sometimes used to refer only to 'stellar' or 'heroic' business proprietors like Richard Branson or Bill Gates. (For a fuller exposition of the variety of uses of enterprise and entrepreneurship see Chapter 3.)

In the field of policy the label 'entrepreneurship' is sometimes applied to those policies designed to increase the number of people wanting to start and/or grow businesses, and the label 'small business' or 'SME' (small and medium-sized enterprise) is applied to those policies designed to encourage and/or support the start-up and growth of those businesses – while 'enterprise' has been the label used to encompass both 'entrepreneurship' and 'small business' policy. However, this distinction has not been consistently applied so, without checking, it is often not possible to know when this distinction is being made.

With such a wide variety of meanings, anyone working in this field will have to expect some confusion and uncertainty in the common vocabulary and needs some understanding of the varieties of meanings and definitions which they might encounter. Because of this, and because it introduces, and quotes from, other material which has a variety of meanings, this book does not set out to limit itself to applying and using only one single definition in each case. Instead it tries, when necessary, to indicate the different possible definitions and to make the meanings clear when the words are used.

However, a particular caution is urged in the use of the word 'entrepreneurship'. Although it has been widely used for many years, there isn't a single common definition and/or a clear explanation of it, and it has been suggested that this is because it does not exist as the condition it has been supposed to be. Consequently, as indicated in Chapter 9, it has also been suggested that its use should now be dropped. Nevertheless, because the word has been used, where this book reflects on that usage it still sometimes uses the word.

THE EVOLUTION OF ENTERPRISE KNOWLEDGE

Enterprise has many aspects, although people seeking to understand it may be more interested in developing their knowledge about some aspects of it than others. Nevertheless an understanding of one aspect may be helped by some knowledge of others. Developing an understanding of enterprise is complicated as our knowledge about it is itself still evolving. It might seem that we should know a lot about enterprise because, as Chapter 2 indicates, it has been extensively researched in the last quarter of a century, but converting research output into knowledge, or even wisdom, is not automatic. Frequently several stages of thinking are required, as Figure 1.1 suggests.

Even when data is converted into information and that information into knowledge, the knowledge thus produced is not immutable. New data, and/or a revised understanding of relations or patterns, may produce different results, suggesting that what had been accepted as knowledge is wrong. In science it is not only accepted, but even expected, that current theories will eventually be replaced by better

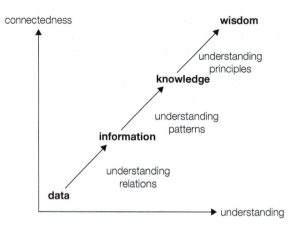

Figure 1.1 *The transition route from data to wisdom*

Source: G. Bellinger, D. Castro and A. Mills, *Data, Information, Knowledge and Wisdom*, 2004. Available at www.systemswiki.org/index.php?title=Data,_Information,_Knowledge_and_Wisdom (accessed 15 April 2010).

theories. Being formulated by an acknowledged genius, and elevated to the rank of scientific laws, as exemplified by Newton's inverse square law of gravitational attraction, is no guarantee of infallibility, as Einstein showed.

In science the generally accepted process for developing knowledge is the scientific method. This is summarised in Figure 1.2. It indicates that if a theory passes initial inspection, it might be thought to be correct; therefore, it might be widely used, but it can never finally be proved. It should last only until such time as it is disproved by being shown to be inconsistent with the then available evidence, whereupon a new theory should be sought to take its place.

According to 'best practice' in scientific method, no theory or explanation should be accepted as an incontrovertible fact, but should instead constantly be checked against any new, or old, evidence which might disprove it. That should stimulate new thinking, in turn leading, it is to be hoped, to a better theory. In this way understanding in any subject should be expected to evolve, and to go stale if it does not evolve – which is likely to happen if it is not challenged. But in reality, even in mainstream science, the evolution of knowledge is rarely as straightforward or as ordered as diagrams of the scientific method suggest.

Bygrave[2] refers to entrepreneurship and has suggested that, if it is a science, then it is an applied science which comes very low on the accepted hierarchy (see Figure 1.3). It is in the basic sciences higher up the hierarchy in which general theories such as those of Newton and Einstein can be expected, and where the scientific method can be rigorously applied and formalised. It is in the lower-level sciences,

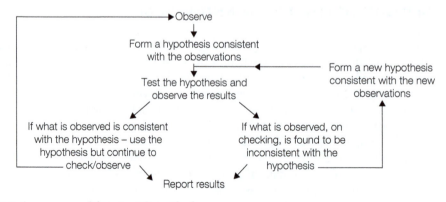

Figure 1.2 *A summary of the scientific method*

	'BASIC'	'APPLIED'

                    'BASIC'   'APPLIED'

                  Mathematics
                   Physics
                                     Engineering
                  Chemistry
                   Biology
                                     Medicine
                  Psychology
                  Sociology   Economics
                                     Business
                              Entrepreneurship

Figure 1.3 *Bygrave's hierarchy of sciences*

Source: W. D. Bygrave, 'The Entrepreneurship Paradigm (I): A Philosophical Look at Its Research Methodologies', in *Entrepreneurship Theory and Practice*, Vol. 14, No. 1, p. 10 (reproduced with permission from John Wiley & Sons Ltd).

especially on the applied side, where, in practice, there seems to be less acknowledgement of theory and more reliance on what amounts to no more than custom and practice.

Thus, in the enterprise literature, there are very few general theories to be found, although some 'models' are advanced. Instead what often seems to be reported as fact appears sometimes to be no more than passed-on assumptions, the origins of which it is hard to identify. Although many enterprise research papers purport to identify and then test hypotheses, as the scientific method would require, that does not appear to extend to the wider corpus of received enterprise wisdom. There it seems, not infrequently, that assumptions have been made which, instead of being acknowledged as such, have, over time, been absorbed as accepted truth into conventional learning, without actually having been properly put to the test. It might be relevant to note that, in still being based to a significant extent on assumptions, rather than on tested theory, enterprise is not unique. Almost any history of medicine will indicate the tensions that have arisen between long-established practice, such as bleeding patients to cure a variety of ills, and new discoveries and ideas which suggest that a different approach is needed. Therefore it is now being recognised that in almost every field, the generally accepted knowledge is not all everlasting but has a half-life as, over time, some will be found to be no longer relevant (as further discussed in the Introduction to Part 2).

At times the scientific method may be taken to imply that scientific knowledge is a new type of knowledge which can only be discovered by trained scientists, but that is not so. It has a much wider application and, as a method for continually improving knowledge, its principles have not been bettered. While it might be applied more widely to some advantage, in the field of enterprise that may not happen until the need for better knowledge is accepted.

According to the scientific method, understanding will always be evolving as the cycle is repeated, and there is never a time when the final answer is known. Understanding at a point in time is based on past learning and is still liable to change. Also different aspects of the subject will be interdependent. This means that in considering any particular contribution to enterprise understanding, it may be helpful to know what the contribution was and why it was made; what its context was and whether any policy has been based on it; what its antecedents were and whether there have been any consequent developments from it; and whether it still appears to be valid or whether there is any reason to question the assumptions on which it is based. However, these different lines of thinking cannot all be followed simultaneously.

So where is the current understanding of enterprise? As described in Chapter 2, the role of the entrepreneur was first highlighted in the 18th century, but it was not until towards the end of the 20th century that small businesses as a particular category of business really began to receive a lot of attention – because they were identified as the main source of the new jobs which were being sought to reduce unemployment. That identification triggered a lot of research into small businesses, and into the entrepreneurs behind them, leading in turn to new ideas about them and how and/or why they appear.

Thirty years later there are many books and seemingly innumerable papers on aspects of this subject. There are many, mainly complementary, ideas about how enterprise and small businesses develop and, consistent with those ideas, a sort of conventional wisdom has emerged. 'Entrepreneurship' is widely taught in universities, business schools and other institutions, sometimes as a subject area together with enterprise and/or small business and sometimes as a useful supplement to other disciplines. In parallel with this, many governments have introduced enterprise, entrepreneurship and/or small business policies apparently informed by this wisdom.

But what has been the outcome of this learning? Has our wisdom, or even just our knowledge, about this area increased, and has its application in policy worked? Today should we be celebrating the culmination of our knowledge, or contemplating challenges to it? Among the questions relevant to this are:

- Have our questions about enterprise and entrepreneurship been answered or have they multiplied instead?
- How much do we appear to have learned about enterprise, entrepreneurs and small business?
- How much of that is useful and how much is instead questionable?
- Has our learning informed relevant government policy and has this policy resulted in significant change?
- Or, alternatively has this whole area of study actually been dreamt up to address fears and/or hopes about the future of the small business sector which appear to be groundless?

THE LAYOUT OF THIS BOOK

To try to answer such questions, this book presents the various and varying aspects of enterprise, entrepreneurs and small business. It explains the current understanding of these aspects and where that may need to change in the light of new thinking. In doing so it observes the following sequence:

What we think we know. **Part 1** presents the current thinking about enterprise, entrepreneurship and small business. It summarises the main sequence of contributions to knowledge in this area and the main understanding which seems to have evolved from these contributions, and/or from other assumptions, to form our current accepted thinking about enterprise. This part describes the present 'default' or received view, therefore, and its evolution.

Challenging the traditional view and assumptions. **Part 2** indicates where emerging ideas and/or a re-assessment of earlier contributions are challenging aspects of this received view. It suggests reasons why aspects of the current received wisdom might need to be re-assessed and indicates areas where a new understanding is emerging. It seeks to highlight areas therefore where applying the 'scientific method' might suggest that changes are needed in our understanding. It also suggests the practical relevance of some of this new thinking both for those practising enterprise by starting, running or growing businesses, and for anyone seeking to assist them.

Implications for policy. **Part 3** reviews the motivation for, and the methods used by, government policy interventions in this area. It considers the evidence for the effectiveness of such interventions before exploring the possibilities for future policy in the light of such evidence and the emerging new understanding as reviewed in Part 2.

☞ THE KEY POINTS OF CHAPTER 1

- People seek to know more about enterprise, entrepreneurs and small business for a number of different reasons.
- The terminology used can cause confusion because the words enterprise and entrepreneurship can each be used with a variety of different meanings.
- Knowledge in this area is evolving, but the development of lasting wisdom is not guaranteed and many questions still appear to remain unanswered.

- This book seeks, therefore, in successive parts to present:
  - The current thinking which forms the conventional wisdom about enterprise, entrepreneurship and small business.
  - The reasons for supposing some of that thinking may be wrong.
  - The application of such supposing in the field of enterprise policy, and how it, too, might need to be re-thought.

REFERENCES

[1] P. Drucker, *Adventures of a Bystander* (New York, NY: Harper Colophon, 1980) p. 1.
[2] W. D. Bygrave, 'The Entrepreneurial Paradigm (I): A Philosophical Look at Its Research Methodologies', in *Entrepreneurship Theory and Practice*, Vol. 14, No. 1, 1989, pp. 7–26.

Companion website

Please visit the companion website at www.palgravehighered.com/Bridge-UE-5e for access to additional learning and teaching materials.

PART 1:
THE EVOLUTION OF ENTERPRISE UNDERSTANDING

The first management course attended by one of the authors took place over 40 years ago. The course covered 'the environment and organisation of the business enterprise' and the main textbook, which had first been published some years earlier, was entitled *Business Enterprise*.[1] Revisiting this book today is interesting, in particular for what it doesn't say. For instance, although the word 'enterprise' appears in the book's title, it does not feature in its index, and neither does 'entrepreneur' or 'entrepreneurship'. There is an index entry for 'small organisations' but only with reference to 'advantages of, ease of co-ordination; ... high morale; ... [and] opportunities for junior executives'. In the text the existence of small firms is acknowledged, for instance in the context of the birth of firms and, when describing the merits of large organisations, where reference is made also to their disadvantages. However, nowhere is there a reference to small firms as a separate category of business which have their own distinct features, which make a particular economic contribution, and which are worthy of special study.

Today it would seem incredible for a book which purports to be 'a study of the economic and political organisation of British industry' not to have a section on the particular role, features and contribution of small businesses and to make reference also to the entrepreneurs who create and grow them. Entrepreneurs and small businesses were around when *Business Enterprise* was written, but they weren't recognised as being significant. In the last 40 years or so that position has changed, and

Part 1 of this book recognises that by describing how the regard for entrepreneurship and small business (sometimes jointly or severally referred to as enterprise) has arisen and by outlining some of the key points in our current understanding of them.

Chapter 2, therefore, presents a historical review of some of the main contributions to our evolving regard for, and understanding of, enterprise, entrepreneurship and small business. Chapter 3 then explores what enterprise and entrepreneurship now means to us, including the various ways in which these terms have been used and/or defined. Chapter 4 follows this with a summary of the main theories about the origins and effects of enterprise and entrepreneurs and the key factors which are thought to influence them.

Then, doing the same thing for small businesses, Chapter 5 reviews the characteristics and definitions of small businesses and their variety before Chapter 6 describes the main possible stages in their life cycles from gestation to termination. Finally, in this part, Chapter 7 provides an overview of the enterprise and entrepreneurs who are to be found in the third sector and the social economy because their economic contribution is now starting to receive greater recognition, as was that of private sector small businesses about 40 years ago.

Reference

1 R. S. Edwards and H. Townsend, *Business Enterprise: Its Growth and Organisation* (London: Macmillan, 1958).

A Brief History of Enterprise Understanding

CONTENTS

- Introduction: the origins of enterprise and of business
- Identifying the entrepreneur (Cantillon and Say)
- The fruits of enterprise (in the Industrial Revolution)
- The rise of big business (and the emergence of Fordism)
- The decline of small business (and the Bolton Report)
- A better understanding of entrepreneurs and small business
- 1970s and rising unemployment
- Identifying the source of new jobs (Birch)
- The 1980s: the enterprise decade (Thatcherism and Reaganism)
- The 21st century and a focus on entrepreneurship
- The new economy (Toffler, Handy and others)
- Where are we now?

KEY CONCEPT

- This chapter summarises some of the key contributions to the current understanding of enterprise, entrepreneurship and small business. It also explains the reasons for the emerging interest in these areas.

LEARNING OBJECTIVES

By the end of this chapter the reader should:

- Understand why our interest in enterprise, entrepreneurship and small business has arisen.
- Understand how our understanding of them has evolved.
- Appreciate the main reasons why they are thought to be a key factor in a thriving economy today.

INTRODUCTION: THE ORIGINS OF ENTERPRISE AND BUSINESS

Can animals be enterprising or is it a quality only exhibited by humans? If a chimpanzee uses a stick to fish termites out of their mound, is it being enterprising or is it just copying another chimp? If it is just copying others, then which chimp was the first to do it and was it being enterprising? Some birds drop shellfish onto rocks to break their shells so that they get to the flesh inside. Is that enterprising? And what about the first fish to climb out of the water and start to explore dry land: was that enterprise or just the result of an accidental mutation which enabled the fish to do that? Can something accidentally or instinctively be enterprising, or does it have to be the product of deliberate action?

Debating the origins of enterprise in that way may produce a good argument but it is unlikely to be conclusive. It does suggest, however, that enterprise is at least as old as humankind and that, while humans may not all have been enterprising, there has always been an element of enterprise in the actions of at least some humans.

The concept of enterprise is now closely associated with business, and indeed businesses are frequently referred to as enterprises. But being enterprising does not necessarily mean running a business, and although enterprise may be as old as humankind, businesses aren't. When did businesses, as organised efforts on a sustainable basis to generate goods or services to trade, first appear?

Our understanding of pre-history suggests that, in the early stages of their existence as a distinct species, human beings were all nomadic hunter-gatherers moving around in family bands in search of food. They worked directly to use their resources, such as their time and skills, to provide the food, shelter, warmth and other things that they wanted. This work was probably undertaken on an 'all for one and one for all' basis and, while it might be supposed that individuals would vary in their relative ability to undertake different tasks, there would have been little specialisation and all organised activity most likely happened within the family context. There may have been some enterprising people, such as those who contributed to innovation in tool making. They may even have exchanged some of the tools they made for food or other goods, but there was nothing beyond the family circle which might be considered to have been a business.

Recent observations of surviving hunter-gatherer societies indicate that, although occasionally more food may be obtained than can be consumed in the short term, such surpluses are of little use. They cannot be stored and/or protected for any length of time either as an investment for the future or for exchange with others. In such societies, there are few or no full-time specialists and almost everyone is engaged in all the work of the society. The concept of getting a job, or of having a choice of employment, scarcely exists.

A big stage in economic evolution was the advent of farming, and although it seems that hunter-gatherers may have needed to work for fewer hours a day than farmers, farming, nevertheless, could support a greater population density. With the change from hunter-gathering to agriculture, societies became more settled and surpluses could be stored and, if necessary, guarded. For instance grain could be stored in barns and animals kept in fields. With this, hierarchies and non-food-producing specialists began to emerge. Families may have grouped together as tribes, and agriculture led to larger, denser and stratified societies,[1] but the kinship basis for groups may have persisted with no significant human organisation existing outside the extended family or tribe.

Eventually, even tribes grouped together as larger units and, once the superior authority of kings and other rulers became established, it meant that some activity of, or for, government clearly took place outside the family. This activity of government could be described as work to provide for some of society's needs which was undertaken separately from the work of providing goods, such as food, for consumption. It is here that the beginnings of distinct public sector activity might be found.

Another feature of agriculturally based societies was the emergence of craft workers with the establishment of activities such as smithing, carpentry and leather work producing goods for others to use. This is probably where the establishment of specialised businesses started. Initially many of these would have been family businesses, but there were also examples of early non-family organisations, such as monasteries, producing goods such as beverages for their own consumption but with a surplus which could be traded with others. Once such ventures grew bigger than the family, or had a regular surplus to trade, they too might be distinguished as a separate economic activity, and thus as distinct businesses. Researching such early ventures is not easy, however, as they left few, if any, records of their existence. It tends only to be when bigger businesses were formally created that records are found, such as that of the East India Company, which derived its powers from a Royal Charter of 1600. Nevertheless there are some exceptions, and the Company and Fraternity of Free Fishermen and Dredgermen of Faversham claims to be the oldest company in the UK on the basis that there is evidence that it was in existence as early as 1189.[2]

Thus, in England at least, there is evidence for specific non-family businesses as early as the 12th century and a presumption of family businesses existing long before that. However, the rate of economic change and innovation was then still relatively low, so many business people would have continued to operate in the way that their predecessors did. New businesses, in new formats, with new processes and/or for new markets must have been comparatively rare and therefore, according to some definitions, entrepreneurs were rare also.

IDENTIFYING THE ENTREPRENEUR (CANTILLON AND SAY)

Although businesses existed from an early stage, the application of the label 'entrepreneur' to those who started and/or ran businesses came much later. There have been examples of entrepreneurs and entrepreneurial behaviour from very early times. As Bolton and Thompson point out,[3] one type of entrepreneur who has appeared consistently throughout history has been the merchant entrepreneur, some of whom made the Great Silk Road into the market-driven highway it became. They did not describe themselves as entrepreneurs though; nor did they appear to have had a concept of entrepreneurship.

The introduction of the word entrepreneur to our economic vocabulary is attributed to Richard Cantillon: an Irishman who lived much of his life in France but apparently died in London in 1734. In France he had been an entrepreneur and a banker, earning a lot of money from stock market trading. He recorded his observation of the economic system of his day in his *Essai sur la nature du commerce en général*,[4] which was not published until 1755, some time after his death. As a work on economics, it has been ranked alongside classics such as Adam Smith's *Wealth of Nations*.[5]

Cantillon did not invent the word 'entrepreneur' but in his *Essai* he used it to describe people who were an important component in the economic system. According to Cantillon there were three such components: there were the landlords who owned the land, from the proprietors of large estates to those who only had smallholdings; there were the labourers who worked, often for the landowners, for a wage; and there were the entrepreneurs. Both the landowners and the labourers, Cantillon suggested, had incomes which were agreed in advance, whether from renting out their land or hiring out their labour. In contrast the entrepreneurs had fixed costs, such as the rent for the land they used or the wages of the people they employed, but income was uncertain because it depended on factors beyond the entrepreneur's control. Thus a farmer promises to pay to the landowner a fixed sum for the land of his farm which is then used to grow crops the price of which will be determined by factors such as the weather and the level of demand at the time the crops are ready to be sold. Because these variables cannot be foreseen, the farmer 'consequently conducts the enterprise of his farm at an uncertainty'.[6] As well as farmers, merchants, wholesalers, shopkeepers, manufacturers and many other artisans are all entrepreneurs who operate 'at risk' in this way.

Cantillon's *Essai* was published in French, although there has been some speculation that it might have been a translation from a lost English original.[7] And although the French verb 'entreprendre' might be translated as 'to take between', it may be of interest that when the *Essai* was translated into English by Higgs in about 1930 he used the English word 'undertaker' as the nearest English equivalent of 'entrepreneur'. This suggests that, even though Cantillon in the 18th century is credited as being the source of our use of the word, around 200 years later it was still not in common use in England.

Cantillon's implicit concept of the entrepreneur is a broad one, and it is based on the entrepreneur as a person with the foresight and confidence, or possibly the need, to operate in conditions when costs may be known but rewards are uncertain. Jean-Baptiste Say (1767–1832) produced a narrower definition of the entrepreneur that focused on the combination and co-ordination of the factors of production to accommodate the unexpected and overcome problems.

Having been a publicist and an industrialist, Say was made professor of political economy at the Collège de France in 1831. He is perhaps most commonly identified with Say's Law, which states that supply creates its own demand, although it seems he did not discover it. His main work was *Traité d'économie politique* (translated into English as *A Treatise on Political Economy*[8]) in which he indicates that he saw the entrepreneur as someone who can effectively manage all of the factors of production such as materials, labour, finance, land and equipment. This type of entrepreneur, who has mastered the art of administering and organising work and is capable of managing the growth of a larger organisation, does not include those who are self-employed with no, or very few, employees. Thus many people, who might now be described as entrepreneurs, would not necessarily have the capabilities identified by Say.

THE FRUITS OF ENTERPRISE (IN THE INDUSTRIAL REVOLUTION)

Even before Say came to prominence, the capitalist concept had been described as a relatively complete theory by Adam Smith in his book *The Wealth of Nations*.[9] This work was the foundation of the classical capitalist economic theory and it identified the capitalist as the owner or manager who, from basic resources of land, labour and capital, constructed successful industrial enterprises. Later, however, and following Cantillon's example, the word 'entrepreneur' was being used to indicate the owner-manager of an industrial enterprise.

Cantillon's list of entrepreneurs included many people engaged in manufacturing such as hatters, coppersmiths, pastry cooks, shoemakers, carpenters and wigmakers, some of whom operated on their own or just with their families and some of whom were 'master craftsmen' who employed journeymen to help them. Nevertheless it is very unlikely that any master craftsman would then have had a business which would not be described today as small. That, however, was to change, largely as a consequence of the Industrial Revolution, which, coincidentally, might be said to have started in Britain at about the time that Cantillon was writing.

One of the effects of the Industrial Revolution was to concentrate many volume production facilities near arteries of transport, such as rivers and canals and later the railways, and around sources of power, which were often initially water 'mills' and later steam engines. The new enhanced output machines, such as power looms and spinning jennies, were not suitable for home production. Also, since a water wheel or especially a steam engine could drive many such production machines, and needed the output of many such machines to justify their investment, the economics of power production led to the establishment of bigger businesses. Another development which had a similar effect was the emergence of the technology for the consistent production of standard items which were thus interchangeable. This was seen, for instance, in the production of firearms where a big manufacturer could produce many arms built to one specification all of which could use the same ammunition and be repaired with the same parts. Before that many small armourers would have worked to equip a large force, but they produced arms of somewhat different dimensions necessitating a variety of different sizes of ammunition and spare parts.

THE RISE OF BIG BUSINESS (AND THE EMERGENCE OF FORDISM)

The Industrial Revolution thus changed much industry from craft production to mass production. Before the Industrial Revolution it would seem that almost all businesses were small ones, but the advent of the revolution could be said to have started a trend towards bigger businesses which had its apogee in Fordism. This was apparent from the 1930s to the 1970s and was named after Henry Ford, the American industrialist who lived from 1863 to 1947 and was the founder of the Ford Motor Company and developer of the assembly line technique of mass production.

The essence of Fordist production was standardised products produced on assembly lines using the technology of the day to produce special tools and equipment which could be used by relatively unskilled labourers who were paid good wages to ensure their recruitment and retention. This, combined with a centralised controlling administrative system, enabled manufacturers like Ford to produce relatively complicated products such as cars very cheaply, provided they were produced in standard forms and in sufficiently large quantities to justify the capital investment needed. Some, such as Ford himself, also integrated their businesses vertically thus making them bigger but also giving them greater control over the whole process and further economies. Fordism therefore played a key part in the drive for economies of scale which meant that, for much manufacturing and even some service businesses, bigger was better.

Whyte in his book *The Organization Man* suggests that the American experience of the Depression followed by the military training of the Second World War created a belief in bureaucracies, or at least an obedience to them.[10] America had thus become conditioned to believe in the large corporation as the major, and as the preferred, source of employment. In 1967 John Kenneth Galbraith published *The New Industrial State*, in which he highlighted the benefit of economies of scale in production, as evidenced by Henry Ford's assembly lines.[11] As production organisations become larger, the theory went, greater specialisation of labour and machines was possible, which in turn reduced the unit cost of production. Large firms therefore have lower costs of production than small ones and, as there are no theoretical limits to their size, they will dominate society. Galbraith thus believed that large corporations would work with government and large unions and, based on a shared view of organisation life, they could in effect run the state.

The idea of economies of scale fitted in well with neo-classical economic theory, and evidence for their existence appeared to be provided by management information and by plant engineers' calculations. The fact that researchers had difficulty in documenting real examples did not impinge on mainstream economic thought. Big business ruled, and the dominant perception of entrepreneurs was summed up in the saying that 'Entrepreneurs are people who start their own business to avoid getting a job'.

THE DECLINE OF SMALL BUSINESS (AND THE BOLTON REPORT)

So inevitable did this trend towards bigger businesses seem to have become that there were worries for the survival of the small business sector. Thus, in the UK in 1969, the Committee of Inquiry on Small Firms was set up under the chairmanship of J. E. Bolton (the Bolton Committee) with the following remit:

> To consider the role of small firms in the national economy, the facilities available to them and the problems confronting them; and to make recommendations. For the purpose of the study a small firm might be defined broadly as one with not more than 200 employees, but this should not be regarded as a rigid definition. In the course of the study it will be necessary to examine in particular the profitability of small firms and the availability of finance. Regard should also be paid to the special functions of small firms, for example, as innovators and specialist suppliers.[12]

The resultant 'Bolton Report' was published in 1971. In its preface it noted that:

> It is a reasonable presumption that the decision to set up the Committee was influenced partly by short-term considerations: 1969 was a very difficult year for business generally and for small firms in particular, and this gave rise to considerable pressure for an investigation of the immediate position of the small firm. But it was made clear to us that the major purpose of the Inquiry was a long-term one – the collection of information on the place of small firms in a modern economy as a basis for recommendations about future policy towards them. Prior to the appointment of this Committee there had never been a comprehensive study, official or otherwise, of the small firm sector in the United Kingdom. This important area is little researched and poorly documented, and the formulation of industrial policy has inevitably proceeded without adequate knowledge of the functions performed by small firms, of their efficiency and of the likely effects upon them of the actions of government. It was hoped that we should be able to throw light on all these matters and at the same time form views on the controversial issues which were giving rise to anxiety in 1969.[13]

This introduction makes it clear that small businesses were still then something of an unknown quantity (and quality) as far as economic development considerations were concerned. However, the report did much to change this, concluding, as it did, that:

- The small firm sector is of substantial importance to the UK economy.
- Despite this it is in a state of long-term decline.
- The contribution of small businessmen to the vitality of society is inestimable.

and:

> On balance we believe that the small firm sector is at present, and will remain for the foreseeable future, vigorous enough to fulfil the 'seedbed function', given a fair crack of the whip, and is not therefore in need of special support. This is a finely balanced judgement which should be kept under constant review by Government, and we have suggested means by which this might be done. There is no cheap or easy way of insuring against an excessive decline in the sector; if there were, we should unhesitatingly have recommended it. Any action by Government would have to be on a massive scale to offset the enormous market forces which are bringing about the decline and would necessarily lead to inequities and distortions. Such action could only be justified if the sector were clearly unable to fulfil its proper role in the economy. This is not demonstrably so at present.[14]

The Bolton Report did list a number of important functions that small businesses provided in an economy (see Table 2.1) but did not include the creation of jobs in this list because that aspect of the contribution of small businesses was not then appreciated (see Birch below). In addition the report made observations about the nature of small businesses, noting, for instance, that they are heterogeneous:

> When we come to look at the human social factors affecting them we can see that firms are, in fact, as varied and individual as the men who founded them. Although true of all forms of business this is particularly true of the small firm which ... is usually not only the creation of one man but directly managed by him or his family, and therefore bears the stamp of an individual personality.[15]

Despite this reference to the founders of small firms (indicated in this quote only as men) it is also noticeable in retrospect that, in examining the small firm sector, the prime focus of the Committee had

Table 2.1 *Bolton's eight 'important economic functions of the small business'*

The eight important economic functions performed by small firms which, according to the Bolton Report of 1971, comprise their special contribution to the health of the economy:

i.   The small firm provides a productive outlet for the energies of that large group of enterprising and independent people who set great store by economic independence and many of whom are antipathetic or less suited to employment in a large organisation but who have much to contribute to the vitality of the economy.

ii. In industries where the optimum size of the production unit or the sales outlet is small, often the most efficient form of business organisation is a small firm. For this reason many important trades and industries consist mainly of small firms.

iii. Many small firms act as specialist suppliers to large companies of parts, sub-assemblies or components, produced at lower cost than the large companies could achieve.

iv. Small firms add greatly to the variety of products and services offered to the consumer because they can flourish in a limited or specialised market which it would not be worthwhile or economic for a large firm to enter.

v.   In an economy in which ever larger multi-product firms are emerging, small firms provide competition, both actual and potential, and provide some check on monopoly profits, and on the inefficiency which monopoly breeds. In this way they contribute to the efficient working of the economic system as a whole.

vi. Small firms, in spite of relatively low expenditure on research and development by the sector as a whole, are an important source of innovation in products, techniques and services.

vii. The small firm sector is the traditional breeding ground for new industries – that is, for innovation writ large.

viii. Perhaps most important, small firms provide the means of entry into business for new entrepreneurial talent and the seedbed from which new large companies will grow to challenge and stimulate the established leaders of industry.

Source: Bolton Report, *Report of the Committee of Inquiry on Small Firms* (London: HMSO, 1971) p. 343.

been on the firms themselves, rather than on the people behind them. Later thinking has suggested that it can be much more enlightening to focus on these people as it is their emotions and motivations which drive the businesses, rather than the other way around, but it was the firms which were specified in the remit given to the Bolton Committee.

It is interesting to note that, just as the Bolton Committee was appointed in the UK because of worries about the decline of small businesses, the Small Business Administration was created in the USA in 1953 as a government agency to help to preserve the small business sector there. In both administrations at that time what small business policy there was tended to be preservationist, not expansionist.

A BETTER UNDERSTANDING OF ENTREPRENEURS AND SMALL BUSINESSES

Although the Bolton Committee was appointed because the small firm sector was thought to have been shrinking, in retrospect it is clear that, in the UK and in other economies, by that time this decline had already been reversed. Indeed it is now clear that the share of small firms in manufacturing employment, which had been falling for most of the 20th century, started to rise again dramatically from about 1970[16] and the small business sector started to re-emerge (for reasons such as those given in Table 2.2). However, before that reversal is explored in more detail, it is relevant to introduce some other contributors to our understanding of entrepreneurship and small businesses.

Table 2.2 Reasons for the re-emergence of small-scale enterprise

Supply	Demand
Technological changes	Structural changes
• New products	• Demand for service
• New industries	• Demand for variety
Fragmentation/cost advantage	Uncertainty of demand
• Subcontracting	• Individual customer requirements
Labour force/unemployment	Macro-economic conditions
• Redundancy	• Unemployment
• Education	Economic developments
Government	• Services
• Privatisation	• Just-in-time
• Deregulation	• Niches
• Tax benefit	

Source: Based on D. J. Storey, *Understanding the Small Business Sector* (London: Routledge, 1994) p. 35 (used with permission of Cengage Learning EMEA Ltd).

By the start of the 20th century a refinement in the theory of the capitalist economy had been developed by the neo-classical school, in particular by Leon Walras and Alfred Marshall. Its key component is that of market equilibrium: when supply equals demand in a perfectly competitive market. This theory does not have a place, however, for the 'entrepreneur' as a cause of economic activity. Suppliers should instead respond to market pressures: if prices rise they should supply more, and if they fall, less. They should not upset this equilibrium by introducing innovative products or services. Classical economists, and in particular a group in Austria, objected to this absence of entrepreneurialism. One of their students was Joseph Schumpeter (1883–1950) who, in Austria, worked as a professor of economics and government, as the Austrian Minister of Finance and as the president of a bank. In 1924 the bank collapsed and he then held a chair at the University of Bonn. However, in 1932, due to the rise of Nazism, he moved to the United States where he taught at Harvard until his death in 1950. Among his contributions to economics were theories of entrepreneurship and the role of entrepreneurs, and in particular the popularisation of the term 'creative destruction'. Schumpeter didn't invent this term but, in *Capitalism, Socialism and Democracy*,[17] he described how it led to advances in economic development. He noted that old established methods and businesses will not normally change themselves but will continue as they were until they are destroyed by the creation of new ones. Further he suggested that it is entrepreneurs who apply the new methods, often starting new businesses to do so. These new businesses can take markets away from the old businesses and lead to their demise, often with unfortunate consequences such as job losses by people whose skills may no longer be needed as, for example, the development of the motor car reducing the need for businesses in horse breeding, harness-making, blacksmithing and carriage building and for people with those skills. Nevertheless, it has been argued, it is because of such creative destruction that, overall, the accumulation of successful innovation should move an economy forwards.

Schumpeter believed that the concept of innovation, described as the use of an invention to create a new commercial product or service, was the key force in creating new demand and thus new wealth. Entrepreneurs were the owner-managers who, in this way, started new businesses to exploit invention. If successful, they thus created wealth for themselves and employment for others from their ability and ambition, rather than only from ownership of land or capital. Harvey Leibenstein, whose first theoretical observations on entrepreneurship were published in 1968,[18] distinguished between two activities: the activity of the entrepreneur who introduces innovation in product, process or service, and the activity of the manager who establishes or runs a business in traditional ways. Schumpeter argued in 1934, in *The Theory of Economic Development,* that entrepreneurs were different from those who solely managed businesses without innovating, and it was these entrepreneurs who were the key to wealth creation and distribution in capitalism.

Accompanying such developments in the perception of entrepreneurs, Edith Penrose (1914–1996) looked at businesses and the characteristics of the small business. She was born in Los Angeles and was for many years a university lecturer and research associate at Johns Hopkins University. Then, after working for a while in Australia and Baghdad, she and her British-born husband moved to London where she was eventually appointed to a chair in economics. While in Johns Hopkins University, Penrose studied the growth of firms, which led her to realise that firms did not in reality grow as theory supposed. She explored this in her second book, *The Theory of the Growth of the Firm,*[19] in which, among other issues, she reflected on the changes of management and administration needed as a firm grew in size. Thus she described how small firms are structured and behave very differently from big ones. As firms grow larger, she said, it is 'likely that their organisation will become so different that we must look on them differently; we cannot define a caterpillar and then use the same definition for a butterfly'.[20] She also considered the comparative advantages of small and large firms concluding, for instance, that larger firms did not always have an advantage, as there were activities in which small firms had their 'own peculiar place'.[21]

1970S AND RISING UNEMPLOYMENT

On 20 January 1972 Prime Minister Edward Heath faced angry protests in the House of Commons when it was announced that, for the first time since the 1930s, the number of unemployed in the UK had risen to over one million.

Thus, at a time of the apparently irresistible rise in economic importance of larger businesses and their corporate world, Schumpeter highlighted the importance of the entrepreneur and Penrose pointed out that small businesses were in many ways different from big businesses, that they had a competitive advantage in some areas, and that they were not going to disappear. Nevertheless to a considerable extent the focus on larger businesses continued throughout the 1960s, and small businesses were rarely mentioned as a distinct and/or important part of an economy. As indicated in the Introduction to Part I, the first business 'enterprise' textbook[22] used by one of the authors dates from this time and has no section on small businesses and nowhere does it indicate that they are in any way special, different or otherwise worthy of separate treatment.

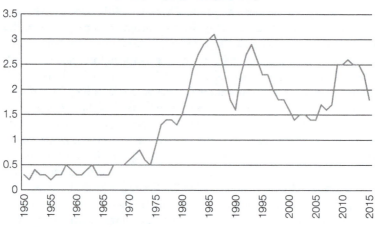

Figure 2.1 *UK unemployment 1950–2015*

Source: Office for National Statistics, Labour Market Statistics.

This attitude started to change, however, in the 1970s when a number of factors combined to upset the economic *status quo* and/or to challenge the theory behind the mechanisms which appeared to have controlled it. Among these were the condition known as 'stagflation' which seemed to affect economies in the early 1970s, the dramatic oil price increase in 1973 and the rise in unemployment, which, it was becoming increasingly apparent, was a new trend and not a minor fluctuation. It had been thought that, since the war, in the UK and in other economies, the lessons of the earlier depression had been learnt. Keynesian economic policies were being applied, with the result that unemployment had remained relatively low and steady for about 25 years. However, from about 1970 it started to rise (see Figure 2.1), and by the end of the decade, when it was clear that this was not just a temporary fluctuation, new approaches were sought as the then-accepted methods for economic control, and especially for the maintenance of full employment, no longer appeared to work.

IDENTIFYING THE SOURCE OF NEW JOBS (BIRCH)

There is no such thing as an American economy, at least not in the way the term is usually employed. Rather there are about 7 million companies, close to 90 percent of which employ fewer than 20 workers. Taken together, these small companies create more jobs than the giants comprising the *Fortune 500*, grow more rapidly, run greater chances of failure and show more adaptability.

This is an important concept requiring elucidation because the facts run contrary to the conventional wisdom.

Source: D. L. Birch, *Job Creation in America: How Our Smallest Companies Put the Most People to Work* (New York, NY: The Free Press, 1987) p. 7.

Thus an urgent issue for many governments, and others, at the end of the 1970s was where new jobs might be found to replace the jobs then being lost so as to halt, or reverse, the seemingly irresistible rise in unemployment. It was in this situation that, in 1979, David Birch released the results of his research into employment in the USA.[23] He concluded that it was small firms which created the most jobs:

Of all the net new jobs created in our sample of 5.6 million businesses between 1969 and 1976, two-thirds were created by firms with twenty or fewer employees and about 80 percent were created by firms with 100 or fewer employees.[24]

Net new jobs is the difference between the total of new jobs created and the total of jobs lost during the same period. Birch found that all areas of the USA were losing jobs at more or less the same rate but that some areas were growing economically because they were creating jobs faster than they were losing them. What distinguished higher-growth areas from the others, therefore, was not the rate of job losses but the rate of job replacement by new job creation. As this job creation requires innovation, which involves risk taking and consequently some failures, he concluded that the most successful areas were those with the highest rates of innovation and failure, not the lowest.[25] Net new jobs is sometimes used as a reasonable indicator of economic growth and, because of Birch's finding that it was small firms which were the prime source of this employment creation, the implication was that they were thus responsible for much of the economic growth – at least in the USA. Many people discounted Birch's work when it was first published, as his conclusion was contrary to the perceived wisdom of that time, which was still influenced by Fordism and the supposed economic primacy of big corporations. Nevertheless, the issue was important enough to stimulate others to try to replicate his work.

One of the problems is that a dynamic analysis is required. It is not sufficient just to count the number of jobs in businesses categorised as small (for instance with fewer than 100 employees) at the start of the period under review and compare that with the number of jobs in businesses in the same category at the end of the period. That is because the jobs created in a business in the small category might be enough to take that business's total employment to over 100 and so move it to the bigger category by the end of the period. Consequently all the jobs in that business would then be credited to the bigger category, rather than to the smaller category which was where they were created. Some questions have been raised, therefore, both about the methods Birch used to produce his analysis and about the appropriateness of the database he used, which was that of the Dun and Bradstreet credit company.[26] Attempts have been made to check and improve Birch's methods and the database, apparently with mixed results: some seeming to confirm his findings and some to challenge them. More recent studies, however, highlighted by Van Praag and Versloot[27] seem to confirm most of Birch's initial results (for more detail see Chapter 5).

Nevertheless, despite the lack of overall agreement over Birch's findings, the importance of the entrepreneur and the relevance of Schumpeter's theory were at last becoming established, and it does now seem to be accepted that small businesses do create, and maintain, significant numbers of jobs and that they are a very significant component of many economies. Further, back in the 1980s, when governments first heard of Birch's work and its implications, they did not wait for full and final confirmation but, because they were keen to find sources of new jobs, latched onto small businesses as a possible answer to their economic prayers. Moreover, for some governments, the findings were also welcomed as being supportive of their championing of laissez-faire capitalism and 'petit bourgeoisie' values. Thus they instigated programmes to stimulate the creation of more small businesses: a process which was often labelled as enterprise policy.

THE 1980S: THE ENTERPRISE DECADE (THATCHERISM AND REAGANISM)

The 1980s thus became the decade in which an enterprise culture emerged as a central objective in government policies, not least in the UK. There, following the election in 1979 of a Conservative government under Margaret Thatcher, what had been 'a steady stream of measures to assist the small firm sector, turned into a torrent'.[28] Thatcher became Prime Minister in 1979 at a time when economic policy-makers were searching for new methods of economic control to replace the post-war Keynesian policies that no longer seemed to be working, together with new sources of jobs to stem the rising level of unemployment. Thus Birch's message that small businesses created jobs came at an opportune time and, when this was combined with economic monetarism and an emphasis on conservative ideals such as free markets and self-help, it led to a drive for what was often referred to as an 'enterprise culture'.

The idea of an enterprise culture seems to have emerged rather than being deliberately created with a single purpose and definition. In the UK, the Thatcher government led what has been described as a 'radical programme of economic and institutional reform ... couched primarily in the rediscovered language of economic liberalism, with its appeals to the efficiency of markets, the liberty of individuals and the non-interventionist state'.[29] The Centre for Policy Studies, which had been established in 1974 with official Conservative Party approval, in a joint policy document with the Institute for Policy Research (described as another right-wing think-tank), offered the following definition of enterprise culture:

> Enterprise culture is defined as the full set of conditions that promote high and rising levels of achievement in a country's economic activity, politics and government, arts and sciences, and also the distinctive private lives of the inhabitants.[30]

In 1985 Lord Young became Thatcher's Secretary of State for Employment in which position he pushed the enterprise message explaining why more enterprise was needed and, *inter alia*, why there should be more enterprise education. In 1988, at the Department of Trade and Industry (DTI) he unveiled plans in a White Paper which indicated that one of the major goals was the encouragement of enterprise and that a keynote of DTI policy was to foster business and personal enterprise. After that the DTI launched a series of 'enterprise initiatives' including the Enterprise Allowance Scheme and the Private and Business Enterprise Programmes. The White Paper also sought a partnership between the DTI and commerce and industry, in order to create 'a climate for enterprise'.[31]

In his speeches and the various papers and other documents for which he was responsible, Lord Young indicated a view that enterprise involves 'generating and taking ideas and putting them to work, taking decisions and taking responsibility, taking considered risks, welcoming change and helping to shape it [and] creating wealth';[32] that enterprise is a natural quality that only has to be 'set free';[33] and therefore that 'our approach is not to preach, and not to meddle'.[34] Because of this and his key role in the Thatcher government's approach to enterprise, Lord Young has been described as 'the architect of the enterprise culture'.[35]

In the USA much of this approach was mirrored in the policies pursued under Ronald Reagan, who became president in 1981. Thus both 'Thatcherism' in the UK and 'Reaganism' in the USA encompassed a belief in supply-side monetarist economics, free markets, limiting state control, reducing regulation and encouraging enterprise/entrepreneurship (and, in the UK, privatisation while in the USA a tougher anti-trust approach).

THE 21ST CENTURY AND A FOCUS ON ENTREPRENEURSHIP

Government support

The end of the Thatcher and Conservative era in the UK did not mean an end to government support for enterprise. On the contrary, the Labour government which took over in 1997 continued to promote enterprise and in 2000 set up the Small Business Service (SBS) 'to drive progress towards the government's aim to make the UK the best place in the world to start and grow a business'.[36] In 2004, the Foreword to the Small Business Service's Action Plan stated:

> This government recognises that enterprise is a vital contributor to the health of our economy and to diversity of opportunity in our society. Enterprise boosts productivity, increases competition and innovation, creates employment and prosperity, and revitalises our communities.

and that:

> It is the dynamism of individual entrepreneurs that drives small business success, but government, through its actions, can do much to stimulate and support enterprise and help businesses overcome barriers to growth.[37]

Thus, albeit with slight variations in language, the focus on enterprise and small businesses, supported by the Conservatives in the 1980s and 1990s, continued into the new century under Labour. This government agenda, and the budgets that went with it, were influential and encouragement and funding were available, not just for organisations and programmes to promote enterprise, but also for associated activities such as research. The result, according to Allan Gibb, was that:

> Since the 1980s and particularly into the 1990s there has been an explosion of research into entrepreneurship and the small and medium enterprise. This is reflected in a substantial growth in both the academic literature and in the grey literature of the press, journals and consultant reports. Combined with ease of access to information through the new international information technologies the growth in 'knowledge' has been exponential.[38] (See more on this topic from Gibb in the introduction to Part 2.)

A similar rush to introduce entrepreneurship, small business and/or SME policies also happened in other countries, and one manifestation of this is in the widespread interest in, and support for, the Global Entrepreneurship Monitor (GEM) initiative (see below).

ILLUSTRATION 2.1 – THE POSITION OF ENTREPRENEURSHIP AS A FIELD OF STUDY

While the summaries presented in this chapter indicate entrepreneurs and entrepreneurship have been studied for some time, it was only in the 1980s that the increase in government interest in entrepreneurs, and a consequent search for information about them, led to a meaningful growth in academic interest. Since then, increasing numbers of researchers have pursued entrepreneurship as a legitimate field of study.

A paper by Shane and Venkataraman has been credited with being one of the first to make a succinct case for such legitimacy. Their starting point was that:

> For a field of social science to have usefulness, it must have a conceptual framework that explains and predicts a set of empirical phenomena not explained or predicted by conceptual frameworks already in existence in other fields. To date, the phenomenon of entrepreneurship has lacked such a conceptual framework. Rather than explaining and predicting a unique set of empirical phenomena, entrepreneurship has become a broad label under which a hodgepodge of research is housed. What appears to constitute entrepreneurship research today is some aspect of the setting (e.g. small businesses or new firms), rather than a unique conceptual domain. As a result, many people have had trouble identifying the distinctive contribution of the field to the broader domain of business studies, undermining the field's legitimacy. Researchers in other fields ask why entrepreneurship research is necessary if it does not explain or predict empirical phenomena beyond what is known from work in other fields. Moreover, the lack of a conceptual framework has precluded the development of an understanding of many important phenomena not adequately explained by other fields.[39]

In response to such concerns Shane and Venkataraman explain why they see entrepreneurship as an important and relevant field of study lying within the domain of business studies and being concerned with the existence and discovery of entrepreneurial opportunities and decisions by some people to exploit them. Thus Shane in his later book, *A General Theory of Entrepreneurship*, seeks to develop a conceptual framework for entrepreneurship, taking as his central premise that it 'can be explained by considering the nexus of enterprising individuals and valuable opportunities and by using that nexus to understand the process of discovery and exploitation of opportunities; the acquisition of resources; entrepreneurial strategy; and the organising process'.[40]

Does this approach, however, look at entrepreneurship differently from earlier writers, such as Cantillon, who identified the entrepreneur through his/her place in an economy and by what he or she did? Is it necessary to define a field in order to study it – or does studying it help us to define it? Also can study be useful even if it doesn't have academic legitimacy? The policy-makers behind the mainly government-led drive for more entrepreneurship were more interested in output than process and did not seem to mind what field of study informed, or at least supported, their policy efforts – only that it was relevant and helpful.

Further Bridge has suggested that a tendency to be an entrepreneur may be socially determined and that only in some cases does it lead to the establishment of a recognised business. In that case, he suggests, the study of entrepreneurship may be closer to the social sciences than it is to the field of business studies with which it is often associated.[41]

Global Entrepreneurship Monitor (GEM)

An influential development in the field of entrepreneurship research was the creation in 1997 of the Global Entrepreneurship Monitor (GEM), which came to prominence in the 2000s. It was a joint initiative by Babson College, Massachusetts, USA, and the London Business School, UK, and is concerned with 'improving our understanding of the relationships between perceptions of entrepreneurship, entrepreneurial activity and national economic growth'.[42] GEM initially planned to explore three questions about entrepreneurship:[43]

1. Does the level of entrepreneurial activity vary amongst countries and, if so, to what extent?
2. Does the level of entrepreneurial activity affect a country's rate of economic growth and prosperity?
3. What makes a country entrepreneurial?

GEM was designed as a long-term longitudinal research study involving international comparisons amongst the G7 countries (Canada, France, Germany, Italy, Japan, UK and USA) and initially three others (Denmark, Finland and Israel). Subsequent additions have raised the total number of economies involved: over 100 different economies have participated at one time or another, and 62 participated in the 2015 survey.[44] For the purposes of its study, GEM now defines entrepreneurship as 'Any attempt at new business or new venture creation, such as self-employment, a new business organization, or the expansion of an existing business, by an individual, a team of individuals, or an established business'.[45] It suggests that such a definition allows for the inclusion of, for example, employees within organisations who behave entrepreneurially (also known as intrapreneurship or corporate entrepreneurship).

Over time not only has GEM changed this definition, but it has also changed the questions it has tried to address, not least, it suggests, because some questions have been answered by earlier surveys.[46] The current objectives are not stated clearly in the 2015/16 report but in the 2014 report they are given as:

- Determine the extent to which entrepreneurial activity influences economic growth within individual economies.
- Identify factors which encourage or hinder entrepreneurial activity, especially the relationships between the National Framework Conditions, social values, personal attributes and entrepreneurial activity.
- Identify policy implications for enhancing entrepreneurial capacity in an economy.[47]

However, in the order indicated by its earlier questions, GEM's approach might be summarised as follows.

Levels of entrepreneurial activity

To indicate differences in levels of entrepreneurial activity amongst countries, GEM developed a measure called the Total (Early-Stage) Entrepreneurial Activity (TEA) index. The index value shows for each country the percentage of the adult population (18 to 64 age group) who are actively involved in setting up a business they will own or co-own (but which has not yet paid salaries or wages for more than three months) or who are the owner-managers of an active business less than 3.5 years old. This value is therefore made up of two measures:

- The nascent start-up rate (those taking some steps towards the creation of a business).
- The new firm rate (those actually running early-stage businesses).

In 2001 the GEM study was widened to explore two sub-sets within entrepreneurship: opportunity entrepreneurs and necessity entrepreneurs. As the 2006 report stated:

> The GEM study allows for differentiation according to the reasons that motivate entrepreneurial behaviour. In the GEM framework, individuals start a business for two main reasons:
>
> - They want to exploit a perceived business opportunity (opportunity entrepreneurs).
> - They are pushed into entrepreneurship because all other options for work are either absent or unsatisfactory (necessity entrepreneurs).[48]

However the usefulness of categorising entrepreneurship as either necessity or opportunity has been questioned.[49] It may be relevant therefore that GEM itself became possibly less dogmatic on this issue and, in later reports, indicated that some people might fall into both categories. Despite this, an additional category within TEA has been introduced more recently entitled 'Improvement-driven opportunity early-stage entrepreneurial activity', which it defines as the percentage of individuals involved in total (early-stage) entrepreneurial activity (TEA), as defined above, who (1) claim to be driven by opportunity as opposed to finding no other option for work; and (2) indicate that the main driver for being involved in this opportunity is being independent or increasing their income, rather than just maintaining their income.

Since 2011 GEM has also introduced a new measure called Entrepreneurial Employee Activity (EEA) which occurs where, in the past three years, an employee has been actively involved and had a leading role in either the idea development, or the preparation and implementation, for a new activity.

The relationship between the level of entrepreneurial activity in a country and its rate of economic growth

In the first three years of its work GEM's reports indicated that a statistically significant association had been found between entrepreneurial activity and national economic growth (as indicated by a growth in GDP) although 'the strength of the association tends to vary depending on the countries included ... and the nature of the entrepreneurial activity'.[50] In 2001, when GEM for the first time looked separately at opportunity and necessity entrepreneurship, it reported that 'the prevalence rate of necessity entrepreneurship was positively associated with national economic growth and that this association was strongest when countries highly dependent on international trade (Belgium, Hungary, Ireland, the Netherlands, and Singapore) were excluded', but that 'the prevalence rate of opportunity entrepreneurship was not associated with any measure of national economic growth'.[51]

In 2004 GEM began reporting a different relationship. Instead of comparing rates of entrepreneurship and economic growth, GEM compared levels of early-stage entrepreneurship (its TEA rate) with per capita GDP and produced what is essentially a U-shaped curve in which:

- For low/middle-income countries the level of early-stage entrepreneurship is relatively high but it reduces as income levels rise.

- For high-income countries necessity entrepreneurship is low but opportunity entrepreneurship starts to increase as income levels rise.

More recently still GEM has been dividing counties into three categories of factor-driven economies, efficiency-driven economies and innovation-driven economies. In its 2014 report it indicated that TEA levels were high in some factor-driven economies (although very low in some others) and low in innovation-driven economies – thus producing a sort of L shape when TEA rates are plotted against GDP per capita. However, in contrast EEA rates are highest in innovation-driven economies.

GEM thus argues that entrepreneurial activity can be carried out in different forms, and in order to evaluate the level of entrepreneurial capacity of an economy, it is necessary to combine both indicators (TEA and EEA). GEM accepts that the link between general firm creation rates and economic development remains unproven. It states that 'It is unquestionably the case that business creation rates fall as economic development increases in low-income countries. More questionable is whether higher rates of enterprise creation in middle- and higher-income countries are either associated with, or lead to, increased wealth.'[52] Nevertheless it supports the link between entrepreneurial activity and economic development noting that 'surveys also confirm that entrepreneurial activity, in different forms (nascent, start-up, intrapreneurship), is positively correlated with the economic growth, but that this relationship differs along phases of economic development'.[53] GEM thus stops short of claiming causal relationships between firm creation, entrepreneurial activity and economic growth.

The factors that make a country entrepreneurial

GEM's research programme was derived from a conceptual model summarising the main causal mechanisms thought to affect national economies and their entrepreneurial activity, but the issue of what makes a country entrepreneurial appears to be the original question on which GEM now says least. It indicates that different countries have different rates of entrepreneurship, and it does now suggest that the stage of economic development might influence the rate of entrepreneurship rather than the level of entrepreneurship influencing economic growth. (For some further comments on GEM see Illustration 17.2.)

GEM's research programme was derived from a conceptual model summarising the main causal mechanisms or conditions thought to affect national economies. It now talks about an entrepreneurial ecosystem as 'the combination of conditions that shape the context in which entrepreneurial activities take place'.[54] However the conclusions and policy recommendations drawn from its finding seem rather pedestrian as they include recommendations such as reforming the regulatory environment, developing innovation capacities and introducing entrepreneurship through the education system.

Overall, despite the data collected across countries for up to 17 years, there is little which has been demonstrated on an evidence basis to support a particular array of policy interventions at any point in time. Instead GEM states that its 'surveys confirmed that the level of entrepreneurial activity varies among countries at a fairly constant rate, thus additionally confirming that it requires time and consistency in policy interventions in order to build factors that contribute to entrepreneurial activity'.[55] It may also be relevant to note that, in the main, it is at national and regional, but not sub-regional, levels at which GEM assesses TEA and EEA in the economies to which they relate. There is no attempt made to examine the significant variations which may occur within parts of an economy and how such variations come about, never mind their impact upon economic development.

Social enterprise

One aspect of enterprise which, by the beginning of the 21st century, had become the subject of increasing interest is social enterprise. There are many enterprises which are formed, or run, at least in part for social purposes but which, because they are not part of the government system and paid for by taxes, are not considered to be in the public sector. Although these enterprises have to generate income in order to survive, usually they are not formed primarily to make a profit for their members and/or founders nor are they considered to be in the private sector. Because they have a social purpose, many of these organisations are often referred to as social enterprises and are said to form part of the social economy. They are also considered to be a part of that sector of the economy sometimes called the third sector because the organisations in it belong in neither the public nor the private sector. Third sector organisations are many and varied and include, for instance, charities and churches, associations and amateur dramatic clubs, foundations and fair trade companies, co-operatives and community bodies, mutuals and trades unions, voluntary organisations and professional bodies.

From the time that the private and public sectors first emerged as separate parts of an economy, there have been organisations which belonged to neither of those sectors. Churches are obvious early examples, as also are the first schools and hospitals, which were often based on religious bodies. To some extent this part of the economy had been overlooked, not least because there has not been a suitable vocabulary to use when referring to it. However, in 1830 the term *économie sociale* was first used by the French economist Charles Dunoyer, and this was the origin of the term social economy.

It would seem that recognition of the economic contribution of the social economy, and the social enterprises within it, was a long time coming and that it was this contribution, more than any other factor, which stimulated official interest in it. Nevertheless, for whatever reasons, by end of the 20th century and into the 21st, government attention was being paid to the social economy in many of the EU member states, including the UK.

(For more detail and further comments on social enterprise and the social economy see Chapter 7.)

The factors of production

Traditionally the three key factors of production have been considered to be land, labour and capital. They were supposed to be the main commodities or services which are used to produce goods and services. This concept can be traced back to Adam Smith, although he referred to the 'component parts of price', which he considered to be land or natural resource, labour, and 'capital stock' such as tools, machinery and buildings.[56] However, by the end of the 20th century other terms were being used and factors recognised.

For instance, in keeping with Adam Smith's ideas, the 'capital stock' in the traditional three factors has been interpreted as physical capital and so financial capital has been added as separate factor. The term 'human capital' was introduced to cover not just labour but also those things that people needed to have in order to labour effectively. These include skills and knowledge, and the latter has been increasingly recognised as sufficiently important, especially for technology-based businesses, to be listed as a capital in its own right. A product of the application of this knowledge capital sometimes is intellectual capital, which covers patents and other forms of idea protection.

Another capital increasingly recognised is social capital, which has been variously defined but which, in economic terms, covers the connections between people which facilitate doing business. There is now a significant body of literature linking social capital to entrepreneurship and suggesting that social capital is a necessary component in the enterprise mix. However, Audretsch and Keilbach, while acknowledging this literature, suggest that this aspect of social capital may be a more specific sub-component which they have called entrepreneurship capital.[57] Thus it is claimed by some that, while the traditional factors such as financial capital, physical capital, land, labour and knowledge are often all still necessary, entrepreneurship capital is also needed to bring them together into a productive mix. (For more on social capital and the possible link between it and entrepreneurship capital, see Chapter 13.)

THE NEW ECONOMY (TOFFLER, HANDY AND OTHERS)

Alvin Toffler suggested that there have been three waves of change in human affairs.[58] The first was the agricultural revolution, which took thousands of years to spread as far as it did but which changed most of us from nomadic bands of hunter-gatherers to settled stratified societies. Others[59] have suggested that it was that stratification which facilitated innovations such as writing, metal-working and explosives. The second wave was the rise of industrial methods, which has happened only in the last

300 years but which has given us civilisation as we know it today. However, according to Toffler, in 1980 the third wave had already started to affect us and it was bringing a new way of life based on diversified renewable energy sources, production methods that replace factory production lines, and institutions which are not centralised, standardised or bureaucratic.

If the height of the second wave was Fordism and its emphasis on mechanisation and economies of scale which led to the seemingly irresistible dominance of large corporations, then it is only very recently that there have been signs that it may have peaked. Toffler was writing over 30 years ago and he seems to have been remarkably prescient because, in retrospect, the peak may have been only a few years before that. He was accompanied by others such as Charles Handy who, writing just after Toffler, suggested in his book *The Future of Work*[60] that what was happening economically in the 1970s and 1980s amounted to a fundamental re-structuring of work. For millennia of human history the major source of jobs had been agriculture and, in the timescale of human development, industry had only taken over relatively recently, and not in all societies. But, in his introduction, Handy pointed out that it was during the 1970s that visible changes began to appear in what had by then become the normal working life. Large organisations had begun to decline and concepts such as redundancy and long-term unemployment became more familiar. Britain, along with other countries such as the USA and France, was no longer primarily an industrial nation. Since the early 1970s the aggregate profits from the service sector had exceeded those from manufacturing, and similar changes had taken place throughout the industrialised world.

If the change from craft production to mass production under Fordism was the first major production transformation in the 20th century, then the change to flexible production has been said to be the second.[61] The switch by many businesses towards flexible production has been driven by reductions in the cost of communication, of logistics, and of information processing – which have, for instance, facilitated computer-aided design and manufacturing, which can make short-run production competitive. Thus, writing in 1990, Curran and Blackburn were already able to list the key features of post-Fordism businesses (see Table 2.3).

Table 2.3 *Fordism and post-Fordism*

Fordism	Post-Fordism
Slow innovation	Fast innovation
Dedicated production technology	Flexible production technology
Mass production of homogeneous products	Small batch production of differentiated products
Mass marketing	Niche marketing
Large inventories	Low inventories
Vertical and horizontal integration	Vertical and horizontal disintegration
Mechanistic organisation	Organic organisation

Source: J. Curran and R. A. Blackburn, 'Youth and the Enterprise Culture', *British Journal of Education and Work*, Vol. 4, No. 1, 1990, Table 11.4.

As a result, smaller businesses can often offer as good and as cheap a product or service as larger businesses, and often quicker and/or more flexibly. So, instead of small businesses either trying to gain the scale needed for mass production, being taken over or going out of businesses – three processes which had led to declining numbers of small businesses – now larger businesses are hiving off non-core work and then shrinking their cores to be able to respond as flexibly as small businesses.

The rules of the new economy

In this new economy many of the rules as applied to our economies by traditional economists appear to have changed. In the old economies, convergence within and across countries was possible as, in the longer term, capital migrated to lower-wage areas. But there is no such convergence in a knowledge economy. Knowledge doesn't spread so easily. It tends to stay 'regional' as evidenced by what some have alluded to as the knowledge 'black holes' of Silicon Valley, Route 128, Atlanta and Austin in the USA and of Cambridge in the UK. Knowledge develops within and through close personal networks which are facilitated by geographical proximity. Indeed it is also now well known that 'business angels', who are important to high-growth start-ups, concentrate their investments within easily accessible distances. It is an apparent paradox that in an era in which data and information can be transmitted globally in fractions of a second, knowledge is relatively immobile and still requires geographic proximity for its spread (see Table 2.4).

Table 2.4 Features of the new economy

Factor	New economy	Old economy
Unit of analysis	The entrepreneur	The plant/business
Policy instrument	Knowledge infrastructure	Interest rates
Entry criteria	Knowledge (available to all)	Financial capital (available to a few)
Growth drivers	Entrepreneurs	Managers
Source of competitiveness	Knowledge and value added	Economies of scale and cost reduction
Infrastructure required	Knowledge infrastructure	Transport infrastructure. Labour supply
Convergence	Knowledge stays regional	Capital moves to lower-wage areas

It is interesting to note that in this context countries can be placed within one of three categories:

- *Creators of knowledge:* about 30 countries are, according to the number of patents filed, significant creators of knowledge.
- *Users of knowledge:* many countries, such as the former Soviet Bloc countries, use knowledge but do not appear to create a lot of it.
- *Others:* those countries which are neither creators nor users of knowledge, such as parts of Africa and Latin America.

To convert from a 'user' to a 'creator' it is necessary to have an infrastructure that both generates and applies knowledge. As well as universities and research institutes, that also requires, for example, market researchers and marketing organisations as well as knowledge-based businesses.

ILLUSTRATION 2.2 – THE ENTREPRENEURIAL ECONOMY

Audretsch *et al.* have explored the difference between what they call the *entrepreneurial economy* and the *managed economy* which preceded it. According to them 'the *managed economy* is defined as an economy where economic performance is positively related to firm size, scale economies and routinized production'. In contrast, the *entrepreneurial economy* is defined as 'an economy where economic performance is related to distributed innovation and the emergence and growth of innovative ventures'.[62]

During the first three decades after the turmoil of the Second World War the 'managed' economy seemed to be performing very well, 'providing the engine for jobs, growth, stability and security'[63] as it 'seemed that all countries were converging towards economies dominated by a handful of powerful enterprises, constrained only by the countervailing powers of the state and workers'.[64] However, they suggest, two main factors then triggered the emergence of the entrepreneurial economy: globalisation and information and communications technology (ICT).

In the 1950s and 1960s the economies of Western Europe and North America gained comparative advantage through low-cost production facilitated, not by low wages, but by exploiting scale economies of large-scale production. However, the emerging economies of Japan and Asia and the transforming economies of central Europe then started to offer bases from which to do this with lower wages, partly because they had an educated but nevertheless relatively cheaper workforce. Combining this with the fast information-carrying capacity provided by ICT led to a very significant geographic redistribution of production, which put the old 'managed' economies at a significant disadvantage when it appeared that they could then have high wages or high employment, but not both.

One response to this development was the emergence of what Audretsch and Thurik refer to as an 'entrepreneurial' economy based on knowledge and ideas rather than economies of scale. They recognise that, while ICT can transmit information very far and very quickly, knowledge is different from information and, being subjective, uncertain and hard to write down, it is much better developed through face-to-face contact. Thus a knowledge-based entrepreneurial economy, which can create and sustain high-wage jobs, has emerged in localised areas such as Silicon Valley in the USA and Cambridge in the UK. The differences between 'managed' and 'entrepreneurial' economies are illustrated in Table 2.5.

Table 2.5 *Differences between 'managed' and 'entrepreneurial' economies*

Managed economy	Entrepreneurial economy
Globalised	Local
Characterised by continuity	Characterised by change
Jobs or high wages	Jobs and high wages
Seeks stability	Accepts turbulence
Specialisation leads to greater efficiency	Diversity leads to spillovers and more innovation
Based on homogeneity	Based on heterogeneity
Command and control matter	Motivation matters
Compete or co-operate	Compete and co-operate
Scale matters	Flexibility matters

Source: Based on D. B. Audretsch and A. R. Thurik, 'What's New about the New Economy? Sources of Growth in the Managed and Entrepreneurial Economies', *Industrial and Corporate Change*, Vol. 10 No. 1, 2001.

One outcome is that, while a managed economy favours large businesses and corporate managements, an entrepreneurial economy offers more advantages for small businesses and more opportunities and rewards for entrepreneurs.

WHERE ARE WE NOW?

Looking back, as the chapter does, over the last 300 or so years reveals how the perception of enterprise and the role of entrepreneurship and small businesses have evolved. From the perspective of the 18th and 19th centuries it might have seemed that the economic future lay in Toffler's second wave, which was launched by the Industrial Revolution and climaxed in the middle of the 20th century in Fordism and the consequential apparent superiority of the bigger business. However, it now appears that it too is succumbing to a third wave in which entrepreneurship and smaller businesses are recognised for the key part they play.

That recognition has not arrived steadily. As views on the key issues in business have changed from those of Cantillon's era, via Fordism, to today's search for technology- and knowledge-driven growth, so the prevailing view of the importance of the entrepreneur has altered from little recognition, via insignificance, to being the key to economic growth in entrepreneurial economies. Appreciation of small businesses has also changed from no specific recognition because they were so predominant, via a worry that they might be an endangered species, to a belief that they hold the key to generating employment and other benefits.

That interest in entrepreneurs and small businesses continues. For instance in the UK in 2012 Lord Young, once Margaret Thatcher's Secretary of State for Employment and in 2012 again the Prime Minister's adviser on small business and enterprise, produced a report on 'supporting the start-up and development of small business' which described itself as 'the first comprehensive report on small and medium-sized enterprises since the Bolton Report of 1971'.[65] However, as Lord Young's report indicates, much interest in small businesses and the entrepreneurs who create them is still apparently based more on their supposed potential to deliver jobs and other economic benefits and less on their more social benefits such as choice, stability, and personal self-actualisation. But it should be expected that thinking on such matters will continue to evolve, although not always smoothly or in the same direction.

This chapter has presented a brief indication of how the current view has developed, the route taken in its development and some of the choices made in the context of the events, agenda and issues summarised above. The result could be said to be that there is a received 'wisdom' about enterprise, entrepreneurship and small businesses which is summarised in Chapters 3 to 6. However, like many, if not all, received wisdoms, it too is likely to be found wanting, and Part 2 suggests some of the areas in which, in a direct continuation of the journey of understanding described in this chapter, that may already be happening.

☛ **THE KEY POINTS OF CHAPTER 2**

- Our understanding of entrepreneurship and its relevance to economic activity has been evolving since Cantillon first introduced the entrepreneur in this context over 250 years ago.
- Although the role of the entrepreneur has thus been recognised for some time, the Industrial Revolution and subsequent development in economies of scale and Fordism seemed, by the mid 1900s, to be leading to the demise of the small business.
- However, interest in small businesses was revived when, at the end of the 1970s at a time of rising unemployment, Birch showed that they were the major creators of both gross and net new jobs.
- For the last 30 years or so entrepreneurs have been encouraged and supported, not least because it is they who create small businesses.
- Other key economic contributions of small businesses have also been recognised and, with the emergence of 'third wave' entrepreneurial economies, the economic value of enterprise and entrepreneurship has received further emphasis.

✓ **QUESTIONS, EXERCISES, ESSAY AND DISCUSSION TOPICS**

- Who do you think have made the three most significant contributions to the evolution of our understanding of enterprise and entrepreneurship? What are the reasons for your selection?

- Why have so many small businesses been started in the past 30 years?

- Why is entrepreneurship thought to be so important to a modern economy?

- Governments are only interested in entrepreneurship because entrepreneurs create new businesses. Discuss.

- Entrepreneurship is more important now than it has been at any time in the past. Discuss.

REFERENCES

[1] For further discussion of such implications of farming see J. Diamond, *Guns, Germs and Steel* (London: Vintage, 1998) pp. 85–104.

[2] According to information on www.faversham.org (accessed 29 April 2007).

[3] W. K. Bolton and J. L. Thompson, *Entrepreneurs: Talent, Temperament, Technique* (Oxford: Butterworth-Heinmann, 2000) p. 261.

[4] R. Cantillon, *Essai sur la nature du commerce en général*, edited with an English translation and other material by H. Higgs (London: Frank Cass & Co Ltd, 1959 – reissued for the Royal Economic Society).

[5] For instance by A. E. Murphy in the Foreword to A. E. Murphy (ed.), *Economists and the Irish Economy from the Eighteenth Century to the Present Day* (Dublin: Irish Academic Press, 1984) p. 9.

[6] R. Cantillon, Op. Cit. p. 49.

[7] See for example H. Higgs, 'Life and Work of Richard Cantillon', in R. Cantillon, Op. Cit. p. 383.

[8] J-B. Say, *A Treatise on Political Economy* (translated by C. R. Prinsep and edited by C. C Biddle) (Philadelphia, PA: Lippincott, Grambo & Co, 1803).

[9] A. Smith, *An Inquiry into the Nature and Causes of the Wealth of Nations* (New York, NY: Modern Library, 1937) (first published in 1776).

[10] W. H. Whyte, *The Organization Man* (Garden City, NY: Doubleday Anchor Books, 1957).

[11] J. K. Galbraith, *The New Industrial State* (Boston, MA: Houghton Mifflin, 1967).

[12] J. E. Bolton (Chairman), *Report of the Committee of Inquiry on Small Firms* (London: HMSO, 1971) p. xv.

[13] Ibid.

[14] Ibid. p. 344.

[15] Ibid. p. 22.

[16] J. Stanworth and C. Gray (eds), *Bolton 20 Years On: The Small Firm in the 1990s* (London: Paul Chapman Publishing Ltd, 1991) p. 3.

[17] J. A. Schumpeter, *Capitalism, Socialism and Democracy* (New York, NY: Harper, 1975) originally published 1942.

[18] H. Leibenstein, 'Entrepreneurship and Development', *American Economic Review*, Vol. 58, No. 2, May 1968, pp. 72–83.

[19] E. T. Penrose, *The Theory of the Growth of the Firm* (New York, NY: John Wiley and Sons, 1959 and Oxford: Basil Blackwell, 1959).

[20] Ibid. p. 19.

[21] Ibid. p. 228.

[22] R. S. Edwards and H. Townsend, *Business Enterprise: Its Growth and Organisation* (London: Macmillan, 1967).

[23] D. L. Birch, *The Job Generation Process*, unpublished report prepared for the Economic Development Administration (Cambridge, MA: MIT Program on Neighborhood and Regional Change, 1979).

[24] D. L. Birch, 'Who Creates Jobs?' *The Public Interest*, Vol. 65, 1981, p. 7.

[25] Ibid. pp. 5–7.

[26] For an account of some of these queries see D. J. Storey and S. Johnson, *Job Generation and Labour Market Change* (Basingstoke: Macmillan Press, 1987) Ch. 3.

[27] M. Van Praag and P. Versloot, 'The Economic Benefits and Costs of Entrepreneurship: A Review of the Research', *Foundations and Trends in Entrepreneurship*, Vol. 4, No. 2, 2008, pp. 65–154.

[28] J. Stanworth and C. Gray (eds), *Bolton 20 Years On: The Small Firm in the 1990s* (London: Paul Chapman Publishing Ltd, 1991) p. 16.

[29] R. Keat, 'Introduction', in R. Keat and N. Abercrombie (eds), *Enterprise Culture* (London: Routledge, 1991) p. 1.

[30] Quoted in P. Morris, 'Freeing the Spirit of Enterprise', in R. Keat and N. Abercrombie (eds), *Enterprise Culture* (London: Routledge, 1991) p. 23.

[31] Quoted in Ibid. p. 32.

[32] Quoted in Ibid. p. 30.

[33] Quoted in Ibid. p. 30.

[34] Quoted in R. Selden, 'The Rhetoric of Enterprise', in R. Keat and N. Abercrombie (eds), Op. Cit. p. 67.

[35] P. Morris, 'Freeing the Spirit of Enterprise', in R. Keat and N. Abercrombie (eds), Op. Cit. p. 28.

[36] Small Business Service, *Enterprise Britain: A Modern Approach to Meeting the Enterprise Challenge*, HM Treasury (London: HMSO, November 2002) p. 2.

[37] Small Business Service, *A Government Action Plan for Small Businesses*, Department of Trade and Industry (London: HMSO, 2004) p. 2.

[38] A. A. Gibb, 'SME Policy, Academic Research and the Growth of Ignorance, Mythical Concepts, Myths, Assumptions, Rituals and Confusions', *International Small Business Journal*, Vol. 18, No. 3, 2000, p. 13.

[39] S. Shane and S. Venkataraman, 'The Promise of Entrepreneurship as a Field of Research', *The Academy of Management Review,* Vol. 25, No. 1, 2000, p. 217.

[40] S. Shane, *A General Theory of Entrepreneurship* (Cheltenham: Edward Elgar, 2003) p. 9.

[41] S. Bridge, *Rethinking Enterprise Policy: Can Failure Trigger New Understanding?* (Basingstoke: Palgrave, 2010) p. 220.

[42] N. Bosma, K. Jones, E. Autio and J. Levie, *Global Entrepreneurship Monitor 2007 Executive Report* (Wellesley, MA: Babson College and London: London Business School, 2008) p. 4.

[43] A. L. Zacharakis, W. D. Bygrave and D. A. Shepherd, *Global Entrepreneurship Monitor United States of America 2000 Executive Report* (Kansas City, MO: Kauffman Centre for Entrepreneurial Leadership at the Ewing Marion Kauffmann Foundation, 2001) p. 5.

[44] D. Kelley, S. Singer and M. Herrington, *Global Entrepreneurship Monitor 2015/16 Global Report*. Taken from www.gemconsortium.org (accessed 18 April 2016).

[45] Taken from www.gemconsortium.org/wiki/1149 (accessed 13 January 2016).

[46] S. Singer, J. E. Amorós and D. Moska Arreola, *Global Entrepreneurship Monitor 2014 Global Report* (London Business School, 2015) p. 17.

[47] Ibid. p. 21.

[48] N. Bosma and R. Harding, *GEM 2006 Results* (Wellesley, MA: Babson College and London: London Business School, 2007) p. 18.

[49] For instance P. Rosa, S. Kodithuwakku and W. Bakunywa, 'Reassessing Necessity Entrepreneurship in Developing Countries', paper presented at the *29th ISBE Conference*, Cardiff (2006) p. 12.

[50] P. R. Reynolds, S. M. Camp, W. D. Bygrave, E. Autio and M. Hay, *Global Entrepreneurship Monitor: 2001 Executive Report* (Kansas City, MO: Kauffman Centre for Entrepreneurial Leadership at the Ewing Marion Kauffmann Foundation, 2001) p. 12.

[51] Ibid. p. 5.

[52] S. Singer, J. E. Amorós, and D. Moska Arreola, Op. Cit. p. 68.

[53] Ibid. p. 20.

[54] D. Kelley, S. Singer and M. Herrington, *Global Entrepreneurship Monitor 2015/16 Global Report*. Taken from www.gemconsortium.org (accessed 18 April 2016) p. 30.

[55] S. Singer, J. E. Amorós and D. Moska Arreola, Op. Cit. p. 20.

[56] A. Smith, Op. Cit.

[57] D. B. Audretsch and M. Keilbach, 'Does Entrepreneurship Capital Matter?', *Entrepreneurship Theory and Practice*, Fall 2004.

[58] A. Toffler, *The Third Wave* (London: Collins, 1980).

[59] See, for instance, J. Diamond, *Guns, Germs and Steel* (London: Jonathan Cape, 1997).

[60] C. Handy, *The Future of Work* (Oxford: Basil Blackwell, 1984) p. ix.

[61] *Fordism, Post-Fordism and the Flexible System of Production*. Taken from www.willamette.edu (accessed 2 September 2010).

[62] D. B. Audretsch, A. R. Thurik and E. Stam, *Unraveling the Shift to the Entrepreneurial Economy* (Zoetermeer: EIM, December 2011) p. 3.

[63] D. B. Audretsch and A. R. Thurik, 'Capitalism and Democracy in the 21st Century: From the Managed to the Entrepreneurial Economy', *Journal of Evolutionary Economics*, Vol. 10, No. 1–2, 2000, p. 18.

[64] D. B. Audretsch and A. R. Thurik, 'What's New about the New Economy? Sources of Growth in the Managed and Entrepreneurial Economies', *Industrial and Corporate Change*, Vol. 10, No. 1, 2001, p. 268.

[65] Lord Young, *Make Business Your Business – Supporting the Start-up and Development of Small Business* (London: Department for Business, Innovation and Skills, 28 May 2012).

Companion website

Please visit the companion website at www.palgravehighered.com/Bridge-UE-5e for access to additional learning and teaching materials.

Enterprise and Entrepreneurship: Their Meanings and Variations

CONTENTS

– Introduction

– The enterprise vocabulary

– Broad and narrow meanings of enterprise and entrepreneurship

– Even narrower meanings of entrepreneurship

– Categorising the uses

– In conclusion

KEY CONCEPTS

This chapter covers:

- The spectrum of meanings of the words 'enterprise' and 'entrepreneurship', which, judging from the contexts in which they are used, range from the narrow to the very broad.
- The 'narrow' meanings refer specifically to business and in this context can refer to starting a business, being in business or developing a business; the word enterprise can even refer to a business itself.
- The 'broad' meanings refer to attitudes and skills which, when possessed by individuals, lead them to exhibit innovative behaviour, including business entrepreneurialism.
- The attempted introduction of narrower meanings referring to only the creation and growing of the high-tech/high-value-added businesses.
- A possible categorisation of the different interpretations and meanings.

LEARNING OBJECTIVES

By the end of this chapter the reader should:

- Be aware of how the words enterprise and entrepreneurship are used, and the range of meanings they can have.
- Understand the distinctions between the 'narrow' and 'broad' ranges of meaning.
- Be aware of the potential for misunderstanding when it is not clear with which meaning either or both of the words are being used.
- Be aware of the possible confusion that attempts to introduce narrower meanings might cause.

INTRODUCTION

Chapter 2 presents a brief summary of some of the key inputs to, and triggers for, our current understanding of enterprise and entrepreneurship. That review indicates that it was Cantillon who is credited with first identifying the entrepreneur as an important component in an economy: the person who runs a business 'at risk' because, while the costs might be known in advance, any future income is likely to be uncertain as it will be subject to market fluctuations. The importance of the entrepreneur was then further enhanced by the insight of Schumpeter and the concept of creative destruction. Here, it might be said, the emphasis should be on the 'creative' aspect: entrepreneurs create new businesses to avail of new opportunities in technology, markets, fashions or other development and, by doing so, bring about the destruction of older businesses which can no longer compete. As with the natural world, a combination of new births and deaths is necessary if evolution is to happen, and entrepreneurs are directly responsible for new business births.

After Schumpeter, however, the focus might be said to have turned to businesses and, after Birch identified their job creation potential, in particular to small businesses. Although Storey confirmed that it is only a small proportion of all new businesses that, over time, account for a disproportionate numbers of jobs, nevertheless, in a time of high unemployment, government tended to view small businesses collectively as a possible answer to the problems of unemployment. Later the contribution of small businesses to innovation, and other economic benefits such as supply chains, was also recognised as a further reason to encourage them.

It seems to have been around the time that Schumpeter moved to America that the word 'entrepreneurship' was coined, apparently to refer to the concept associated with being an entrepreneur. Its early users do not appear to have suggested a definition of it but, possibly because it was used, people came to accept it as the label for the condition of being an entrepreneur and, as such, the key to economic strength. Since then its use has slowly spread. For instance when, in the 1980s, governments wanted more jobs and thus more small businesses and more entrepreneurs, they tended to call what they wanted 'enterprise' but now they seem to refer more often to 'entrepreneurship'. Governments were prepared to allocate budgets to this quest, and those budgets were in turn used to fund programmes to stimulate the creation of more start-ups, supporting existing small businesses and associated research into all things 'enterprise'. Enterprise and then entrepreneurship became popular labels to attach to policies, programmes and people, as well as to concepts, cultures and organisations – culminating in the entrepreneurial economy.

One result of this increased interest and budget largesse has been described as 'an explosion of research into entrepreneurship and the small and medium enterprise'.[1] However there has also been a sometimes confusing evolution of the terminology used. The term entrepreneurship, in particular, is applied on occasion with a broad meaning, overlapping that of enterprise, and on other occasions with a much narrower intent.

Like the chicken and egg debate, it is pointless to argue which came first: the terminology or the interest. Sometimes increasing interest in a subject has led to new words and phrases and new uses of existing words, whereas some subject areas have remained relatively ignored until a vocabulary has been developed for them. Language does evolve, but the speed with which some enterprise vocabulary appears to acquire new uses means that different definitions are used at the same time, with a consequent danger of mis-communication and confusion.

This chapter starts therefore with a discussion on this vocabulary. It considers the evolving use of the words enterprise and entrepreneurship and the varied, and even conflicting, definitions they have acquired. It then offers a 'map' of what the words enterprise and entrepreneurship can mean in different contexts, as an understanding of their different possible uses is likely to be helpful in making sense of any debate about them.

THE ENTERPRISE VOCABULARY

That most noble centoure Publius Decius so hardie an entreprennoure in the bataile.

Source: Oxford English Dictionary record of the use of the word entreprennoure in 1475.[2]

Although the word 'entreprennoure' had apparently been used in English as early as the 15th century it was not in a business context (see box above), and the use of the word entrepreneur to describe a particular economic agent appears to have come from France where its introduction is attributed to Cantillon in the 18th century. The words enterprise, entrepreneur and entrepreneurship are all believed to be derived from the French word *entreprendre* meaning 'to take between' (also sometimes given as 'to undertake'), and the word *entrepreneur* referred originally to a 'go-between' or broker (see also the section on Cantillon in Chapter 2).

From the word entrepreneur we also get entrepreneurship and, also from the same root, enterprise. These words may be related, but trying to pin down their current multi-dimensional meanings is not an easy task. At one time it seemed that enterprise had a wider meaning whereas entrepreneur and entrepreneurship were applied more narrowly and almost exclusively to a business context. That distinction, however, can no longer be assumed, as the following paragraphs show.

Examples of 'entrepreneurship' usage

'Entrepreneurship is the pursuit of opportunity beyond the resources you currently control.'[3]

'Entrepreneurs are, like elephants, easier to recognise than to define.'[4]

Kilby[5], however, has likened the entrepreneur, not to an elephant, but to a 'Heffalump': the much sought after, but never quite found, animal in *Winnie-the-Pooh*.

While (a) generally accepted definition of entrepreneurship is lacking, there is agreement that the concept comprises numerous dimensions.[6]

The field of entrepreneurship is 'an intellectual onion. You peel it back layer by layer and when you get to the centre, there is nothing there, but you are crying.'[7]

'Entrepreneurship is "I've earned it", not "I deserve it".'[8]

For a while, and consistent with Cantillon, the word entrepreneurship was used mainly to refer to the process of starting or running a business. This usage is, for instance, that of the Global Entrepreneurship Monitor (GEM) initiative (see Chapter 2), which initially defined entrepreneurship as 'any attempt to create a new business enterprise or to expand an existing business by an individual, a team of individuals or an established business'.[9] It is also the basis of Shane's approach: 'Entrepreneurship is an activity that involves the discovery, evaluation, and exploitation of opportunities to introduce new goods and services, ways of organising, markets, processes, and raw materials through organising efforts that previously had not existed.'[10]

The concept of entrepreneurship has, however, been moving away from one which is just concerned with the act of new venture creation, or growth. Thus a Scottish Enterprise paper on enterprise and economic growth has stated that 'entrepreneurial and enterprising behaviour is not confined to the creation of new businesses … and can also be found in organisations of all sizes in both private and public sectors'.[11] Additionally, the Northern Ireland government's *Entrepreneurship and Education Action Plan*, produced in 2003, offered as its definition of entrepreneurship 'the ability of an individual, possessing a range of essential skills and attributes, to make a unique, innovative and creative contribution in the world of work, whether in employment or self-employment'.[12] This approach is also used by Gibb who has said that 'Entrepreneurship relates to ways in which people, in all kinds of organisations behave in order to cope with and take advantage of uncertainty and complexity and how in turn this becomes embodied in: ways of doing things; ways of seeing things; ways of feeling things; ways of communicating things; and ways of learning things.'[13]

These two, somewhat different, approaches to the meaning of entrepreneurship were picked up by the EU Working Group, which looked at entrepreneurship education in preparation for the Lisbon Strategy. The Group's definition of 'education and training for entrepreneurship' therefore included two components:

- A broader concept of education for entrepreneurial attributes and skills, which involves developing certain personal qualities and is not directly focused on the creation of new businesses, and
- A more specific concept of training in how to create a business.[14]

Thus entrepreneurship now seems to have a range of meanings. Whereas it was used primarily to refer to the process of business formation or growth, it now sometimes has a wider application which is similar to a broader meaning of enterprise.

Examples of 'enterprise' usage

The word enterprise appears in many contexts, but mainly in the context of economics and business and it is often used alongside, or even interchangeably with, entrepreneurship. Smaller businesses are almost universally referred to as small and medium-sized enterprises, which is usually abbreviated to SMEs, and many bodies with an economic remit have an enterprise policy which is often focused on the needs of business. Nevertheless there are sources which recognise that enterprise can have a much broader application.

In the European Union

The EU recognised the importance of enterprise by having a Directorate-General for Enterprise and Industry (although this was re-structured as the Directorate-General for Internal Market, Industry, Entrepreneurship and SMEs) and a specific enterprise policy:

> EU enterprise policy aims to ensure we keep up with our rivals while also creating jobs. It pays particular attention to the needs of the manufacturing industry and small firms. ... The focus of EU enterprise policy is on creating the right environment for investment – not just for strategically important sectors like aerospace and biotechnology, but also more traditional industries, such as textiles and cars.[15]

By the UK government

Governments have wanted to encourage the creation and growth of more small businesses. Because it was entrepreneurs who were understood to be the people who created and grew small businesses, and because that process had been labelled entrepreneurship, many government initiatives sought to promote more entrepreneurship through a process which was, in turn, often labelled enterprise. Thus in the UK, pronouncements in favour of enterprise and entrepreneurship have been made by both main political parties:

> In 1993 Lord Young, the Secretary of State for Employment, said that 'We must have an enterprise culture, not a dependency culture.' When he was asked what he meant by enterprise, he described it as 'Get up and go – not sitting back and accepting it. Think positive and things can happen; if you are passive and think negative then nothing happens. It's a mental attitude.'[16]

> In 2004 Gordon Brown, as Chancellor of the Exchequer, declared that 'Working together we can do more to enhance Britain's great entrepreneurial culture – ensuring that there is no no-go area for enterprise in any part of Britain.'[17]

In 2014, as the Prime Minister's Adviser on Enterprise, Lord Young produced a report entitled *Enterprise for All* which states that 'Enterprise is more than the creation of entrepreneurs, it is about a can-do and positive attitude and equipping people with the confidence to develop a career and vocational interests'.[18] The report led, *inter alia*, to the creation of Enterprise Passports for young people as well as to a network of Enterprise Advisers.

In the UK in 1988 the Department of Trade and Industry (DTI) (later the Department of Business, Enterprise and Regulatory Reform [BERR], the Department for Business, Innovation and Skills [BIS] and now the Department for Business, Energy and Industrial Strategy) launched its Enterprise Initiative, which brought together many of the schemes of support provided by the DTI for industry and commerce. At its launch the DTI considered whether its plans were 'an industrial policy', but concluded that:

the phrase itself is unfortunate, because it appears to concentrate on industry rather than consider all the factors which affect the ability of industry and commerce to create wealth; it also carries the flavour of the DTI taking responsibility for the fortunes of individual industries and companies. It will be obvious that neither is consistent with the philosophy of this paper ... But the government has a coherent set of policies towards industry and commerce. That set of policies is better described as an enterprise strategy than an industrial policy.[19]

The DTI also said that:

We will encourage the transfer of technologies and co-operative research, the spread of management education and the growth of links between schools and the world of work. Our objective will be to produce a climate which promotes enterprise and prosperity.[20]

and:

Enterprise is fundamental to a dynamic and growing economy. Lack of enterprise played a major part in the relative decline of the British economy; its return has played a major role in the recent economic revival. The key to continued economic success lies in the further encouragement of the enterprise of our people ... The change of approach is reflected throughout DTI's activities. DTI will be the Department for Enterprise.[21]

These examples all relate to the UK Conservative government of the 1980s and 1990s. In 1997 the Labour government took over and it declared also that one if its priorities was to create an environment conducive to stimulating entrepreneurship. It later reported that, since its arrival, it had taken steps to tackle barriers to enterprise and entrepreneurship by addressing economic, political, legal and cultural issues in order to boost rates of entrepreneurial activity.[22] The subsequent Conservative government has continued this and, for instance, when Lord Young was appointed at the Prime Minister's Enterprise Adviser he reported that he was asked 'to write a report on how the Government supports enterprise and small firms and what needs to change'.[23]

In regional and local enterprise organisations

Many enterprise organisations have been formed as a result of regional and local initiatives. Examples include:

Scottish Enterprise is Scotland's main economic development agency, funded by the Scottish Government. It is the successor to the Scottish Development Agency and its mission is 'to help the people and businesses of Scotland succeed'. In doing so, it aims 'to build a world-class economy'.[24]

Enterprise Northern Ireland is the organisation formed to represent the network of local enterprise agencies (LEAs) in Northern Ireland which are 'independent locally-based not for profit companies which have been established, often in partnership with local councils, to support local business and enterprise development. By working together through Enterprise NI, LEAs can offer a service of consistent standard across Northern Ireland.'[25]

In England, Local Enterprise Partnerships (LEPs) are voluntary partnerships between local authorities and businesses set up in 2011. They were established by the Department for Business, Innovation and Skills to help determine local economic priorities and lead economic growth and job creation within the local area (carrying out some of the functions of the Regional Development Agencies which were formally abolished in 2012).

In enterprise and education

Education is another area where governments have been keen to introduce more enterprise, or at least more preparation for it later in the students' lives (and see the later section in this chapter on enterprise education). In the UK, for instance, the Enterprise in Higher Education (EHE) initiative was introduced in 1987 by the Secretary of State for Employment and the aim of its application in one university was described as being:

> to provide the opportunity for all full-time undergraduate students to acquire enterprise competencies, without compromising academic and intellectual standards. Students will be afforded the chance to develop both personal skills, such as leadership, creativity, problem analysis and solving, self awareness and flexibility; and interpersonal skills such as team building, negotiation and persuasion, conflict resolution and all forms of communication including IT.[26]

After the Enterprise in Higher Education initiative, another attempt made by the UK government was the Science Enterprise Challenge introduced in 1999. Its aim was 'to establish a network of centres in the UK universities, specialising in the teaching and practice of commercialisation and entrepreneurialism in the field of science and technology'.[27] In the first round of funding 12 Science Enterprise Centres were established in UK universities. By 2008, under its new name of Enterprise Educators UK, this initiative supported almost 80 institutions 'to develop their practice, network with peers, and collaborate in enterprise and entrepreneurship teaching and research across all curriculum areas'.[28]

Following Lord Young's report *Growing Your Business*,[29] the Small Business Charter was launched to encourage staff and students in business schools to work more closely with business and entrepreneurs to deliver support for small businesses and drive local economic growth. Delivered through the Association of Business Schools, Small Business Charter Awards are made to business schools based on their track record across various activities in support of students, start-ups and small businesses.

A non-governmental initiative to introduce more enterprise into education has been Young Enterprise, which had its origins in the Junior Achievement programme in the USA. In the UK it is a national educational charity, founded in 1963, with the mission of providing young people aged 5 to 25 with an exciting, imaginative and practical business experience, enabling them to develop their personal and interpersonal skills, knowledge and understanding of business objectives and the wealth creation process. It does this by, *inter alia*, giving young people the chance to learn from setting up and running their own businesses during one academic year. By 2016, over 200,000 students from schools and colleges were participating each year in the UK, supported by businesses and volunteers. The benefits it seeks to deliver to its participating 'Achievers' include improving their business knowledge, influencing their career and study preferences, improving their attitudes and skills (such as self-confidence and the ability to work in a team) and supporting qualifications in business core skills.

Young Enterprise sees 'enterprise' therefore primarily in the context of business, but within that context it is concerned with the acquisition of attitudes and skills that involve discovery, confidence and achievement, as well as the specific business skills of marketing, finance, communication and organisation.

In conclusion

> The mission of the Starship *Enterprise* is 'to boldly go where no man has gone before'.

These examples demonstrate that the word 'enterprise' has, in normal usage, a wide variety of meanings. In some cases its meaning is limited to the business context, but in others, for instance when applied to the Starship *Enterprise*, it is an attitude to life, an attitude of exploring, of developing, of leading and of taking initiatives, which, while it may help in the business context, has much wider relevance.

Social enterprise and entrepreneurship

Other uses of the words enterprise and entrepreneurship which have become noticeable recently are in the terms social enterprise and social entrepreneurship. In the private sector, enterprises are formed primarily to make money for their founders and/or owners. In the third sector, social enterprises and other organisations, while they have to generate financial income to pay for their costs, are formed primarily to achieve other purposes, which are often social in nature. Nevertheless the process of starting or growing third sector organisations still requires entrepreneurs, and those who do it are referred to as social entrepreneurs. Like private sector entrepreneurs, they are being enterprising in the achievement of personal objectives, and if they differ, it is only in the extent to which their objectives are focused on personal enrichment. (For more, see Chapter 7.)

BROAD AND NARROW MEANINGS OF ENTERPRISE AND ENTREPRENEURSHIP

> *Endeavour to be firm (10 letters)*
>
> (Crossword clue)[30]

The evolution of the concepts of enterprise and entrepreneurship has been traced in Chapter 2. Although the central role of the entrepreneur, and therefore also of entrepreneurship, in business and economics is now accepted, this does not now mean that there is a single accepted definition of what an entrepreneur is. On the contrary, there are a range of possible meanings, some derived from different ways of looking at the entrepreneur (see Table 3.1) and how he or she operates. Thus it is possible for two people to talk about entrepreneurship yet mean somewhat different things. Just as it is possible for one person to use the word 'enterprise' and another 'entrepreneurship', and yet be talking about more or less the same thing.

In many of the examples examined above, the implication is that enterprise and entrepreneurship are seen, at least primarily, as connected with the promotion of business generally or of smaller businesses and/or business starts in particular. Some of the examples, however, suggest that, on occasion, enterprise, and even sometimes entrepreneurship, can have a wider meaning. Writing on 'enterprise culture', the author of an OECD monograph indicated that

> There are, in effect, two definitions of, or approaches to, the word 'enterprise' and the practice of it. One, which can be termed a 'narrow' one, regards enterprise as business entrepreneurialism, and sees its promotion and development within education and training systems as an issue of curriculum development which enables young people to learn, usually on an experiential basis, about business start-up and management. The second approach, which can be termed the 'broad' one, regards enterprise as a group of qualities and competencies that enable individuals, organisations, communities,

Table 3.1 – Summary of approaches for describing entrepreneurs

Entrepreneurial model	Central focus or purpose	Assumption	Behaviour and skills	Situation
'Great Person' School	The entrepreneur has an intuitive ability – a sixth sense – and traits and instincts with which he or she is born	Without this 'inborn' intuition, the individual would be like the rest of us mortals, who 'lack what it takes'	Intuition, vigour, energy persistence and self-esteem	Start-up
Psychological Characteristics School	Entrepreneurs have unique values, attitudes and needs that drive them	People behave in accordance with their values; behaviour results from attempts to satisfy needs	Personal values, risk-taking, need for achievement and others	Start-up
Classical School	The central characteristic of entrepreneurial behaviour is innovation	The critical aspect of entrepreneurship is in the process of doing rather than owning	Innovation, creativity and discovery	Start-up and early growth
Management School	Entrepreneurs are organisers of an economic venture; they are people who organise, own, manage and assume the risk	Entrepreneurs can be developed or trained in the technical functions of management	Production planning, people organising, capitalisation and budgeting	Early growth and maturity
Leadership School	Entrepreneurs are leaders of people; they have the ability to adapt their style to the needs of people	An entrepreneur cannot accomplish his or her goals alone, but depends on others	Motivating, directing and leading	Early growth and maturity
Intrapreneurship School	Entrepreneurial skills can be useful in complex organisations; intrapreneurship is the development of independent units to create, market and expand services	Organisations need to adapt to survive; entrepreneurial activity leads to organisational building and entrepreneurs becoming managers	Alertness to opportunities and maximising decisions	Maturity and change

Source: J. B. Cunningham and J. Lischeron, 'Defining Entrepreneurship', *Journal of Small Business Management*, Vol. 29, No. 1, 1991, p. 47 (used with permission of John Wiley & Sons Ltd).

societies and cultures to be flexible, creative, and adaptable in the face of, and as contributors to, rapid social and economic change.[31]

In answer to the question, 'What do we mean by enterprise?', another commentator replied:

> Two schools of theory and practice are evident, each based on different although not contradictory answers to the question. They can be called the 'economy school' and the 'education school'. The 'economy school' says that enterprise is what entrepreneurs do and entrepreneurs create business and jobs and wealth and those things all contribute to, indeed they comprise, the economy … The 'education school' says that enterprise has a broader meaning and application than that … It says that many types of initiative which need to be taken, many types of responsibility which need to be discharged and many types of problems which need to be resolved require the individual to act in an 'enterprising' manner. Thus this school sees business-type entrepreneurialism as just one context in which people act in 'enterprising' ways. It says that enterprise involves using the imagination, being creative, taking responsibilities, organising, identifying ideas, making decisions, dealing with others in a wide range of contexts. It says that as society becomes more complex and as it changes towards greater complexity, people need to be more and more enterprising. At the heart of this approach is, therefore, personal development and, in particular, the development of self-confidence.[32]

The narrower (economy) view of enterprise and entrepreneurship: business start-up and growth

> 'The carrying out of new combinations (of means of production) we call "enterprise"; and the individuals whose function it is to carry them out we call "entrepreneurs".'[33]
>
> 'In this paper we will use the terms business ownership and self-employment as equivalent to entrepreneurship.'[34]
>
> 'Most definitions of the word "entrepreneur" will take into account the individual aspect, the innovative aspect, the commercial organisation aspect and business behaviour. … However … (only) a small fraction of new starters are really innovative (and) if such a criterion is used … the level of entrepreneurial vitality will be fairly low. … We use an approach to define entrepreneurs (as) mainly people in the pre-start-up, start-up and early phases of business ownership.'[35]

Used in their narrow sense, enterprise and entrepreneurship are closely associated with the act of starting up or running smaller businesses, although some take the view that not all small businesses are entrepreneurial. Nevertheless when governments have funded programmes to encourage more enterprise and/or entrepreneurship, they have done so not primarily because they wanted enterprise and/or entrepreneurship for themselves, but because they wanted the economic benefits which were expected from the businesses which they supposed entrepreneurs would create and/or grow. Thus, where enterprise and entrepreneurship had to be defined, it tended to be in terms of businesses' creation and growth. These were the entrepreneurial outputs which were intended to lead to the desired economic outcome.

The word 'enterprise' can be used to refer to a unit of business, the processes of business start-up, and the process of being in business and of business growth and development. In other words, it is used to refer to the various elements that contribute directly to economic development and to job creation. As some of these elements, such as business start-up, are also referred to as entrepreneurship, these are areas in which the meanings assigned to the words enterprise and entrepreneurship can be synonymous. They are, however, the 'narrow' meanings of enterprise and of entrepreneurship and they refer to a form of behaviour devoted to the successful development of business.

The broader (education) view of enterprise (and entrepreneurship): attributes and resources

> An enterprising individual has a positive, flexible and adaptable disposition towards change, seeing it as normal, and as an opportunity rather than a problem. To see change in this way, an enterprising individual has a security, born of self-confidence, and is at ease when dealing with insecurity, risks, difficulty and the unknown. An enterprising individual has the capacity to initiate creative ideas ..., develop them, and see them through into action in a determined manner. An enterprising individual is able, even anxious, to take responsibility and is an effective communicator, negotiator, influencer, planner and organiser. An enterprising individual is active, confident, purposeful, not passive, uncertain and dependent.
>
> OECD/CERI[36]

Rather than referring exclusively to the realm of business, the broader view of enterprise, and sometimes of entrepreneurship, relates to a way of behaving and a set of attributes which can be applied in a number of situations. Enterprise, claims Gibb, is the exercise of such a set of attributes, while the entrepreneur is someone who demonstrates a marked use of these attributes in a particular task or context, usually in business or commerce. Thus entrepreneurial behaviour is underpinned by entrepreneurial attributes – and also by entrepreneurial skills and informed by relevant values and beliefs (see Table 3.2).

If entrepreneurs are defined solely in terms of a form of behaviour, underpinned by a set of attributes and skills, it follows that there are entrepreneurs in all kinds of organisations, for the relevant attributes and skills are displayed and developed by a wide variety of people working in many different circumstances – these are 'enterprising' people. There is, for example, much scope for entrepreneurial behaviour within bureaucracies, although when this behaviour is perceived as dysfunctional and difficult to contain within the organisation, it can be adjudged undesirable. This is in line with the idea of the entrepreneur as a 'marginal man': put simply, this is someone who does not fit easily into the conventional organisation. Within the conventional employee role, there may be more or less scope for exercise of entrepreneurial attributes, depending on the structure and purpose of the organisation (or parts of it) and the amount of individual freedom. Motivation to develop and exercise entrepreneurial approaches, whatever the nature of the work or location, is important. It is clear that, in some organisations, such will be seen as 'desirable'; in others it will be labelled as 'deviant'. The issue of 'desirability' of entrepreneurial behaviour is an important one not confined only to the culture of the work place, but also clearly of importance in terms of society as a whole.[37]

Within the debate on enterprising attributes and culture it has been pointed out that the characteristics that are required for the wider application of enterprise are also those needed for the narrower one. Being enterprising is not limited only to business contexts. If someone has these attributes and skills, then he or she is liable to use them wherever they appear to be appropriate, whether it be for economic, social, political, environmental or other purposes. These attributes, it has been suggested, can be acquired during upbringing and at least in part through education, although the focus of education may not encourage it (see Table 3.3). To get more enterprise in business, therefore, it would appear to be necessary to try to develop more enterprise for all contexts.

Table 3.2 Entrepreneurial behaviours, attributes, skills, values and beliefs

Entrepreneurial behaviours
Opportunity seeking and grasping
Taking initiatives to make things happen
Solving problems creatively
Managing autonomously
Taking responsibility for, and ownership of, things
Seeing things through
Networking effectively to manage interdependence
Putting things together creatively
Using judgement to take calculated risk

Entrepreneurial attributes
Achievement orientation and ambition
Self-confidence and self-belief
Perseverance
High internal locus of control (autonomy)
Action orientation
Preference for learning by doing
Hardworking
Determination
Creativity

Entrepreneurial skills
Creative problem solving
Persuading
Negotiating
Selling
Proposing
Holistically managing business/projects/situations
Strategic thinking
Intuitive decision-making under uncertainty
Networking

Values and beliefs – entrepreneurship is embodied in sets of values and beliefs
relating to:
Ways of doing things
Ways of seeing things
Ways of feeling things
Ways of communicating things
Ways of organising things and, importantly for education
Ways of learning things

But not.   Entrepreneurial behaviours, skills and attributes are not synonymous with interpersonal, transferable or core skills as set out in GNVQ literature. Problem solving is very different from creative problem solving. Communication, presentation skills, numeracy, and so on, underpin entrepreneurial skills but are not identical with them and can be utilised in 'bureaucratic' occupations. Without clearer thinking it is therefore possible to end up confusing entrepreneurship with:
Industrial awareness
Financial awareness
Economic awareness
Business management skills
Small business management
Work experience
Project work in industry
Start-up simulations
Transferable skills
Key skills

Source: Based on Allan Gibb and Judi Cotton, *Creating The Leading Edge*, Durham Business School, 1998 and Allan Gibb, 'Entrepreneurship in Schools and Colleges: Insights from UK Practice', *International Journal of Entrepreneurship Education*, Vol. 6, No. 2, 2008, pp. 48–96.

Table 3.3 *The focus of learning*

Education focus on	Entrepreneurial focus on
The past	The future
Critical analysis	Creativity
Knowledge	Insight
Passive understanding	Active learning
Absolute detachment	Emotional involvement
Manipulation of symbols	Manipulation of events
Written communication and neutrality	Personal communication and influence
Concept	Problem or opportunity

Source: A. A. Gibb, 'Enterprise Culture – Its Meaning and Implications for Education and Training', *Journal of European Industrial Training* (1987) p. 17.

ILLUSTRATION 3.1 – TYPES OF BUSINESS OWNER

Enterprise and entrepreneurs are closely associated with business. But, just as enterprise, and some would say entrepreneurship also, can be exercised in contexts other than business, so too not all business action is enterprising – and this is recognised in some categorisations of different types of business owners and/or managers.

Various writers have developed a range of owner typologies built on the presumption that not all business owners are the same. Several studies have identified three main types of owner, typically labelled craftsman, professional manager and entrepreneur. Craftsman owners run rigid, stable firms often with few if any employees. Professional manager types grow adaptive firms over time while the entrepreneur creates and develops a firm 'not as an end in itself' but as a mechanism to facilitate invention and the presentation of new products (see Figure 3.1).

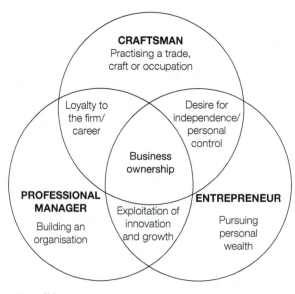

Figure 3.1 *Three types of small business owner*

Source: R. W. Hornaday, 'Dropping the E-words from Small Business Research', *Journal of Small Business Management*, Vol. 28, No. 4, 1990, pp. 22–33 (used with permission of John Wiley & Sons Ltd).

Work by Miner et al. in the 1990s served to confirm the existence of this tripartite typology.[38] Such a categorisation helps to make the point that not all business owners are equally entrepreneurial or may not be entrepreneurial at all. For example, a craftsman practising the same trade as his/her parents in the same way may start and run a business but may not be entrepreneurial. To the extent that most business owners are not exceptional in demonstrating 'stellar' innovation and/or growth, is it reasonable to assume that they can be 'made' rather than 'born'? (See also Chapter 4 for the 'born' v 'made' debate.)

ILLUSTRATION 3.2 – ENTERPRISING ACTS

The 'broad' or 'education' approach is largely based on the concept of enterprise as something demonstrated in the actions individual people take: actions that can be enterprising in a variety of situations, not just in business. These actions are in turn due to a considerable extent to the make-up of the individuals concerned: and to what are variously referred to as their behaviours, attributes, competencies, attitudes, skills, ideas and resources. The context in which the individuals operate is also of relevance, because enterprise in some aspects and in some contexts seems to be due more to group and societal dynamics than to individual ones. This chapter, however, explores enterprise largely from the perspective of the individual; the group and societal aspects are considered in Chapter 9.

In looking at the personal aspects of the broad definition of enterprise, it is worth considering how far they apply also to the narrow definition and therefore, by implication, whether the two are inconsistent with each other. The narrow definition regards enterprise as synonymous with business founding and development, for which the term entrepreneurship is also often used. The broad definition sees it as the application of an array of adaptable skills to new, unique or complex tasks. Enterprising individuals often initiate and develop projects; they do not sit around and wait for things to happen but take control and see issues through to their conclusion. Although there is an apparent difference between the two aspects of enterprise, the distinction may be more apparent than real. In reality, founding a business can be just as much an enterprising act as any other, and that aspect of enterprise can be seen as one component of a larger domain. The 'narrow' definition is in this case just an example of the 'broad'.

Consider, for example, a welfare officer faced with a serious teenage drugs problem. The officer has ideas about what might be done. She mobilises parents, community groups, doctors, police and others connected with the problem to take action. She communicates with the teenagers and elicits their views on the issue. She lobbies, deals and harangues to obtain the physical and monetary resources to create a day centre manned by advisers with access to medical personnel. One year after her intervention the drug problem has not gone away, but teenage suicides have decreased in the area, fewer teenage pregnancies are reported and large numbers attend group therapy sessions. Was this an enterprising process? The individual concerned displayed many of the qualities usually associated with the business formation process, and the outcome of this project would be regarded by many as reasonably successful, even if the original aim was not achieved. Many would therefore describe the individual concerned as enterprising.

There are innumerable undertakings of this nature in business, social, family and private life that can be described as enterprising and, though it is a relative term rather than absolute, it can be considered appropriate to enumerate the key characteristics of such undertakings. In doing so it can be helpful to distinguish between the nature of the task and the manner in which it is tackled. Broadly, however, the label 'enterprise' might be applied when:

- the task is non-routine;
- the task is somewhat complex;

- the task is goal-directed;
- the goal(s) are demanding but attainable;

also when:

- the task is tackled in an adventurous manner;
- the task is approached in a determined and dynamic manner; or
- the task accomplishes the set goals (or comes near to so doing).

A project has been defined as 'a task requiring considerable or concerted effort'[39] and, in short, it might be considered therefore that an enterprising act is one in which a project is undertaken in an energetic, bold and adaptable manner. This means that there are businesses, and even business start-ups, which would not be considered to be enterprising. This would be the case, for instance, in many forms of self-employment and in some family businesses when a second or third generation takes over without making any significant innovation.

Defining enterprise in this way can accommodate both the narrow and broad approaches and underpins the importance of newness, change and flexibility for enterprise. This definition also emphasises the relevance of success. Bold, dynamic acts that fail to meet predetermined goals may not always be considered to be enterprising. Those goals, however, need not be economic, and success in enterprise is not just limited to commercial success. In addition actions that appear to be, or indeed are, initially successful and would be regarded as innovative, but which then subsequently fail, would usually be regarded as having been enterprising. Enterprising acts take place within a time-frame, and outside it conditions can change radically.

Enterprise and/or entrepreneurship education

A close examination of what is taught under the name of enterprise reveals, however, that instead of the consensus claimed by leading practitioners, the organisations that are teaching this new culture are all working with different lists of the core skills.

Part of the confusion stems from the fact that the word 'enterprise' is used in different ways, sometimes referring to an individual ability considered amenable to improvement and at other times to a form of economic activity, usually in small business.

We are not dealing with a tightly defined, agreed and unitary concept but with a farrago of hurrah words such as creativity, initiative, and leadership.

Professor Frank Coffield[40]

It is also likely that young people in education now will face greater economic uncertainty and more frequent change in their future working lives than did their predecessors. Against that background, all young people will need more enterprising skills and attitudes, not just to set up businesses (or enter self-employment), but also to build their own careers and to stay employable. In addition enterprise may be seen as a set of skills, attributes and capabilities which can help weaken the link between economic uncertainty and social exclusion.

(Sir) Howard Davies in his review of *Enterprise and the Economy in Education*[41]

One area in which different meanings of both enterprise and entrepreneurship have become apparent is enterprise and/or entrepreneurship education. In many countries the desire to develop more entrepreneurs has led to funding being made available for 'entrepreneurship (or enterprise) education' in which 'entrepreneurship' is to be taught, or otherwise introduced, to students at all levels in the education system. This has also led to different interpretations of entrepreneurship, connected to whether such education should be 'about, through, or for' entrepreneurship.

This aspect of education is also an area in which the meanings assigned to words enterprise and entrepreneurship can overlap to the extent that they sometimes appear to be used interchangeably. An example is a paper on evaluating entrepreneurship education which did not distinguish between the words 'enterprise' and 'entrepreneurship' and often used them jointly and treated them more or less as one concept. The paper did point out, nevertheless, that there were three different roles which might be assigned to enterprise and/or entrepreneurship education programmes depending on whether the aim was:

- to learn to understand entrepreneurship (What is entrepreneurship? What do entrepreneurs do? Why are entrepreneurs needed?);
- to learn to become entrepreneurial (I need to take responsibility for my learning, career and life. How to do it.); or
- to learn to become an entrepreneur (Can I become an entrepreneur? How do I become an entrepreneur? Managing the business.).[42]

Despite such clarification, those funding or otherwise promoting entrepreneurship education have not always clearly specified what entrepreneurship means to them in this context. Often they have tended to assume a business start-up 'default' definition based on economic development considerations, while those charged with running the courses sometimes have wanted to use an 'enterprise for life' definition which was more appropriate for their students.[43] The result has been that some approaches have taken a 'narrow' view while others have followed a 'broad' approach. One American commentator, for instance, asserted that 'one of the major objectives of entrepreneurship education is to provide students with the necessary skills to design, create, launch and effectively manage a business'[44] while in the UK some universities have linked their approach instead to 'employability', defined by one as 'enabling students to acquire the knowledge, personal and professional skills and encouraging the attitudes that will support their future development'.[45]

EVEN NARROWER MEANINGS OF ENTREPRENEURSHIP

While the above review of the evolving meanings of enterprise and entrepreneurship may be complex, it can be observed that, having started with a relatively narrow meaning which on occasion has been broadened, the word entrepreneurship is now being used at times with a very narrow meaning. Although the association of entrepreneurship primarily with private sector business has not been universal, the lure of the supposed needs of economic development has proved to be difficult to resist. This drive has led in some areas to a focus in particular on those new businesses which are emerging-technology-based, high-value-added and export-focused, as they are thought to contribute most to economic growth. Sometimes such businesses are classed as HPSUs (high-potential start-ups), and they can be a key component in policies to encourage the provision of jobs in high-value-added sectors in the hope that they will deliver high labour productivity growth. Although the search for such 'high-end jobs' has been likened to that for the Holy Grail, they often appear, nevertheless, to be 'the preferred route to regional prosperity'.[46]

Thus there is a branch of the evolving use of the term entrepreneurship which seems to produce ever narrower definitions, driven, it appears, by such economic development considerations. This aspect of entrepreneurship has been acknowledged by GEM in its reporting on 'High (Job) Expectation Entrepreneurship' but others seem to have gone further in defining entrepreneurship in even narrower terms. For instance when the Danish government set a goal that 'by 2015 Denmark (would be) among the countries with the highest start up rates of high-growth enterprises',[47] it also launched an initiative which defined entrepreneurship specifically as 'the entry and creation of high-growth firms'.[48] Similarly Invest Northern Ireland, in its Corporate Plan for 2008–2011, declared that its Accelerating Entrepreneurship

Strategy 'will increasingly emphasise the acceleration of high-potential existing and start-up companies ... (to) provide the supply line for future exports based on new product and process innovation'.[49]

Ács and Szerb, in constructing a Global Entrepreneurship Index, use as their definition of entrepreneurship: 'a dynamic interaction of entrepreneurial attitudes, entrepreneurial activity, and entrepreneurial aspiration that vary across stages of economic development'.[50] They define entrepreneurial activity as 'the startup activity in the medium or high technology sector, initiated by educated entrepreneurs and launched because of opportunity motivations in a not too highly competitive environment'[51] and entrepreneurial aspiration recognises 'the effort of the early-stage entrepreneur to introduce new products or services and/or new production processes, to penetrate new markets, to increase employment and to finance the business with formal or informal venture capital'.[52] This definition of entrepreneurship may have been designed to facilitate the construction of an index by listing more or less measurable components but it does present different facets of entrepreneurship thus indicating that it is multi-dimensional. However, in its definition of entrepreneurial activity, it does limit it to the specific field of medium- to high-technology businesses.

Observation or wishful thinking?

It is understandable and acceptable that there should be a desire for the activity indicated in the narrower definition of entrepreneurship indicated above. But is it realistic to expect that new definitions introduced unilaterally in this way should then be universally accepted? And what do attempts to insist on such definitions imply? Do such narrow definitions suggest that entrepreneurship in wider applications (enterprise for life) is a different phenomenon rather than a different manifestation of the same phenomenon? Do they mean that all that had previously been written about entrepreneurship, but which did not fit these narrow definitions, was not actually about entrepreneurship? In that case, what was it about and what should that now be called?

Bridge, however, has asked if some agencies are now adopting an aspirational approach.[53] Whereas it seems that Cantillon and others used the term entrepreneur to label an observed component of the venture creation process, others now seem to be trying to define entrepreneurship in terms of the sort of businesses which it is hoped entrepreneurship will produce. For example those definitions of entrepreneurship which refer only to high-tech, high-growth business outcomes are clearly associated with strategies designed to achieve just those outcomes.

This, in turn, raises the issue of whether the form of entrepreneurship covered by the narrower definitions shares the same origins as other forms and, if it does not, what label should be applied to those other forms (some of which may be early-stage ventures which do later develop into the narrower form)? It is understandable that governments would like to see the emergence of more gazelles (Birch's word for high-growth businesses), but to what extent can gazelles alone be encouraged? Is there a specific stream of business creation activity which leads exclusively to the creation of innovative new-technology-based, high-value-added, export-focused businesses? If there is, narrower definitions of entrepreneurship may be justified. If there is not, attempts to impose narrower definitions seem to be a case of basing definitions on what is desired rather that what is observed: on wishful thinking rather than on reality.

CATEGORISING THE USES

Different phases can be discerned in this process of the evolution of the current variety of meanings of the words enterprise and entrepreneurship:

> The first phase was a single-meaning phase in which it was assumed that the words meant the same things to everyone. Entrepreneurship appeared to refer to the process of starting and growing businesses, whereas enterprise appeared to have a wider connotation. Therefore, although each word might have been used sometimes in different ways, those differences were often not perceived and, as a result, little need was seen for more careful definitions.

The second phase could be said to be a multiple-meanings phase. In this phase it became apparent that the meanings of the words had widened and/or changed, that there were different interpretations of them, and that they were not being used in the same way by everyone. Sometimes both enterprise and entrepreneurship were used with quite broad meanings but not always, and it wasn't always clear which meanings were being assumed.

The third phase might be described as the competing-meanings phase. Whereas in the multiple-meanings phase it was generally possible to place meanings in a progression model in which narrower definitions could be seen to be refinements of, or possible developments from, the broader definitions; in this phase some uses seem to be opposed to others. Thus attempts to present entrepreneurship as only encompassing high-tech, high-growth businesses and to focus on them alone, seem to suggest that these businesses, the HPSUs, have separate roots from other businesses the formation of which therefore might no longer be classed as entrepreneurship, or supported through entrepreneurship policy.[54]

Could there soon be a fourth phase in which it becomes accepted that, as is suggested in Chapter 9, entrepreneurship does not exist as it has been conceived?

Other sources of variation have been the different disciplines in which entrepreneurship has been explored, and the different perspectives from which it has been viewed. Naudé, in looking at that role of entrepreneurship in economic development, reported that Wennekers and Thurik had identified thirteen distinct roles of an entrepreneur and suggested that one reason for this multiplicity of definitions/roles is that entrepreneurship is studied in so many different disciplines. He also suggested that, within economics, the entrepreneur is approached most often from an occupational definition, a behavioural definition or an outcomes definition. On the basis that a person can be either unemployed, self-employed or in waged employment, the occupational definition sees entrepreneurs as the self-employed. The behavioural view includes Schumpeter's view of the entrepreneur as the agent of creative destruction and, as such, the entrepreneur is an innovator and/or someone who starts or expands new businesses. The outcomes of 'entrepreneurship' are often seen to be the creation of new firms but can include other results such as corporate entrepreneurship.[55]

Baumol also presents a view of entrepreneurs which is not limited to business situations. His basic hypothesis is that the productive contribution of entrepreneurs to society varies less because of the total supply of entrepreneurs than it does from the way that they apply themselves to productive, unproductive or destructive uses. By looking at historical evidence from ancient Rome, early China, the Middle Ages and Renaissance Europe he shows that the role entrepreneurs play is influenced by the rules of the society in which they operate. In ancient Rome, he suggests, 'people of honourable status had three primary and acceptable sources of income: landholding, usury and political payments'. Productive commerce and industry could generate wealth but not prestige, so those who wanted prestige directed their entrepreneurship to the acceptable applications which helped the individual concerned but were unproductive for society as a whole. In Medieval China also the rules did not favour productive entrepreneurs and instead accorded supreme prestige to high positions in the state bureaucracy, thereby encouraging the application of entrepreneurial tendencies to unproductive activity. In England in the early Middle Ages the institution of primogeniture meant that often the only opportunity for the younger sons of barons lay in warfare, with the result that their enterprise became destructive. Under all these systems, entrepreneurs were not necessarily in short supply but were often directed by society's rules to unproductive or destructive applications. However, in situations like that in England at the time of the Industrial Revolution, when the rules had changed to allow those who engaged productively in industry to accumulate not just wealth but also respect and influence, the engagement of entrepreneurs in productive purposes was encouraged and the economy benefited.[56] Because it is only in the last of these examples that entrepreneurs are engaged in business formation and/or growth, Baumol's concept of entrepreneurs is, necessarily, a wide one.

The result of these varied treatments is a proliferation of uses, interpretations, dimensions and meanings of both enterprise and entrepreneurship such that the current state might be described as one of multiplicity, contradiction and confusion. Both the words now have a range of meanings and those ranges overlap. It is difficult therefore to discuss them without some method of categorising their different meanings so that they can be referred to simply and unambiguously.

It would be nice to think that out of all this, a single meaning for the word entrepreneurship could be agreed and used. But, given the plethora of definitions and meanings currently in use, that does not seem to be a realistic objective. One response to this had been to accept the variety of uses and different meanings of 'entrepreneurship' and to see if some form of categorisation might help – but that is not a simple task. The examples given above indicate that in common usage it does now have a number of different perspectives or dimensions. Three of these might be:[57]

The type of entrepreneurship. Some people refer to different types of entrepreneurship. Baumol for instance, as indicated above, highlighted the potential of entrepreneurship to be productive, unproductive or destructive. He has also suggested that an obvious sub-division is that between 'innovative' and 'replicative' entrepreneurs, with the former being people who do something that has not been done before and the latter being people who organise 'an enterprise of a variety that has been launched many times before'.[58]

The stage of entrepreneurship. Another dimension of entrepreneurship is its stage of development. Some definitions, such as GEM's, apply the label entrepreneurship only to the stages around actually founding or growing a venture. Others, such as Gibb, have extended entrepreneurship further back to include acting entrepreneurially, aided by the possession of essential skills and attributes, and even to having appropriate entrepreneurial attitudes and aspirations which can be found at a pre-start stage.

The focus of entrepreneurship. A further key dimension is what might be termed the focus of entrepreneurship. Some definitions of entrepreneurship are narrow, applying only to private sector businesses or, as described above, even more narrowly to high-technology, high-growth businesses. In contrast, there are relatively broad definitions of entrepreneurship encompassing its realisation in many fields of human activity. Additionally there are other manifestations such as:

- *Social entrepreneurship.* As Chell[59] has pointed out, social entrepreneurship is increasingly being recognised as a branch of entrepreneurship which is often realised in the founding and growth of social enterprises.
- *Various forms of self-employment.* The self-employed include sole owners, lifestyle 'entrepreneurs', trades people and small business owners of whom only a minority will found high-growth, sustainable businesses.[60] To these can be added free-lancing.
- *Women's enterprise.* Many countries have programmes specifically designed to encourage and support more entrepreneurship by women (and also youth, ethnic and/or disabled entrepreneurs).
- *Employability.* The *Entrepreneurship and Education Action Plan* and the *Enterprise for All* report quoted earlier are examples of initiatives for which entrepreneurship is defined in a way which includes its application in employment, implying that one manifestation of it can be to make people more employable.
- *Non-business ventures.* It can also be argued that the launch of a new theatrical production or other artistic venture, a new scientific initiative or a new geographic exploration are all ventures which require a considerable degree of entrepreneurship, even if they are not business ventures.

Bridge[61] has therefore proposed a system of 'E-numbers' to categorise the different uses. It is based on the system used by economists when referring to different measures of the money supply. In this system the base and narrowest measure is called M0, which is the notes and coins in circulation and in bank vaults plus the reserves commercial banks hold with the central bank. The next is M1, which is the funds that are readily available for spending, and then there is M2, which is M1 plus savings and small time deposits. The broadest is M3, which is M2 plus large time deposits, institutional money-market funds, short-term repurchase agreements and other larger liquid assets. On the assumption that it would be helpful to apply a similar system to enterprise and entrepreneurship, the 'E-number' system uses E0 to indicate the base (broadest possible) definition and then higher numbers to indicate narrower interpretations, which are each sub-sets of those E-numbers lower than it. (This is the other way around from the M numbers for money because the interpretation of the money supply starts from the base and then gets broader, whereas in the case of enterprise there has been a tendency to establish a base and then to narrow the definitions.) Descriptions of the possible E-numbers, and possible comparisons with a number of definitions and usages quoted above, are given in Table 3.4 and the system is portrayed diagrammatically in Figure 3.2.

Table 3.4 *E-numbers: interpretation and some comparable uses*

E-number	Interpretation	Comparable uses?
E0	The application of enterprise attributes in any context, for instance in sport, exploration or art.	Broader definitions of enterprise
E1	The application of enterprising attributes for the economic advancement of self and/or others, but not necessarily as a business (for instance in employment or in unproductive or even destructive entrepreneurship).	Baumol NI *Entrepreneurship and Education Action Plan* Social enterprise
E2	The formation of any new economic venture (or its subsequent growth), including self-employment and me-too businesses.	Birch GEM (but with time limits) Social entrepreneurship
E3	The formation and/or growth of novel private sector business ventures (i.e. ventures which are a distinct development from what already exists).	The target of much entrepreneurship policy?
E4	The formation and/or growth of new, innovative, high-tech, fast-growth, high-value-added, knowledge intensive, exporting business ventures.	Gazelles, HPSUs Recent Invest NI and Danish uses
E5	Could there be narrower definitions – for instance with the same focus as E4 but limited only to certain targeted sectors?	

Source: S. Bridge, *Rethinking Enterprise Policy: Can Failure Trigger New Understanding?* (Basingstoke: Palgrave Macmillan, 2010) p. 107.

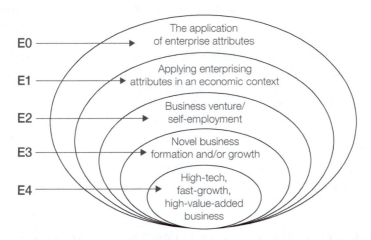

Figure 3.2 *E-numbers: a categorisation of enterprise and entrepreneurship*

Source: S. Bridge, *Rethinking Enterprise Policy: Can Failure Trigger New Understanding?* (Basingstoke: Palgrave Macmillan, 2010) p. 108.

Does entrepreneurship exist?

A further response to the proliferation of meanings of 'entrepreneurship' is to conclude that it does not actually exist as the discrete identifiable and deterministic phenomenon we have supposed it to be – and therefore the application of the word might usefully be terminated. This suggestion is explored further in Chapter 9.

IN CONCLUSION

The words enterprise and entrepreneurship may have a common origin but they have acquired a wide variety of meanings, some very different but some overlapping. So on occasion they can be used interchangeably and on other occasions they are used to refer to separate concepts. This variety of possible meanings can be a source of some confusion which can hinder good communication. Consequently anyone who is not aware of the possible variety of meanings may be confused or even misled if the meaning they assume is not the one intended. And anyone using the words, especially in a narrow way, should make their meaning clear if they wish to be properly understood.

Enterprise and entrepreneurship are therefore varied concepts, both in their application and in their explanation. They remain, nevertheless, the subject of considerable interest.

☞ THE KEY POINTS OF CHAPTER 3

- The words enterprise and entrepreneurship have become popular labels. In the case of enterprise in particular it has often seemed that it has been used more for its cachet as a supposedly desirable label than as the most appropriate word in the particular circumstances.
- The way that the terms 'enterprise' and 'entrepreneurship' are used indicates that they now have a wide continuum of meanings. In some cases the use implies a meaning that is limited to a business context, and enterprise can even be used as a synonym for business. Other uses, however, imply a wider meaning, often associated with an attitude to life: of exploring, of developing, of leading and of taking the initiative. Such an attitude can be very helpful in the business context, but it also has much wider applications.
- Different uses have been described as the narrow and broad meanings. The narrow meaning regards enterprise and/or entrepreneurship as applying business entrepreneurialism, and in that context the words 'entrepreneurship' and 'enterprise' are usually interchangeable. The broad meaning, on the other hand, regards enterprise or entrepreneurship as a set of behaviours, attitudes and skills that enable individuals and groups that possess them to be flexible, creative and adaptable in the face of change. These two approaches to enterprise have also been labelled the 'economy school' and the 'education school': at the heart of the latter is the concept of personal development including the development of self-confidence.
- In recent years even narrower definitions of entrepreneurship have been suggested, restricting it to only the creation and growth of those businesses which are supposed to contribute most to an economy because they are high-tech and/or high-value-added. What these definitions have not shown, however, is how such entrepreneurship is different from the creation and growth of other businesses in a way that can be separately identified and developed at an early stage.
- Enterprise and entrepreneurship are varied concepts, therefore, both in their application and in their explanation. They are, however, the subject of considerable interest. Therefore would understanding and communication in this field be well served by a system of categorisation similar to the categorisation of the money supply in economics?

✓ QUESTIONS, EXERCISES, ESSAY AND DISCUSSION TOPICS

- Distinguish between 'enterprise', 'entrepreneurship' and 'small business'. To what extent do these concepts overlap?
- In the context for the variety of possible meanings, what is an enterprise culture?
- How might the meanings of the words enterprise and entrepreneurship be made clear when they are used in different contexts?
- Is it possible to develop entrepreneurship only in its narrow, or narrowest, sense?

📖	## SUGGESTIONS FOR FURTHER READING AND INFORMATION

W. J. Baumol, 'Entrepreneurship: Productive, Unproductive, and Destructive', *Journal of Political Economy*, Vol. 98, No. 5, 1990, pp. 893–921.

S. Bridge, *Rethinking Enterprise Policy: Can Failure Trigger New Understanding?* (Basingstoke: Palgrave Macmillan, 2010) Chapter 6.

E. Chell, *The Entrepreneurial Personality: A Social Construction* (Hove: Routledge, 2008).

REFERENCES

[1] A. A. Gibb, 'SME Policy, Academic Research and the Growth of Ignorance', *International Small Business Journal*, Vol. 18, No. 3, 2000, p. 13.

[2] The Compact Edition of the *Oxford English Dictionary* (London: Book Club Associates, 1979) p. 879.

[3] The 'Harvard' use reported, for instance, in H. H. Stevenson, 'Intellectual Foundations of Entrepreneurship' in H. P. Welsch (ed.) *Entrepreneurship: The Way Ahead* (New York, NY and London: Routledge, 2004) p. 3.

[4] G. Bannock, *The Economics and Management of Small Business* (London: Routledge, 2005) p. 89.

[5] P. M. Kilby, *Entrepreneurship and Economic Development* (New York, NY: Macmillan, 1971) p. 1.

[6] Z. Ács and L. Szerb, 'The Global Entrepreneurship Index (GEINDEX)', Jena Economic Research Papers 2009–028, p. 14.

[7] Reported in H. H. Stevenson 'Intellectual Foundations of Entrepreneurship' in P. Welsch (ed.), *Entrepreneurship: The Way Ahead* (New York, NY and London: Routledge, 2004) p. 3.

[8] David Hall, in an Institute of Business Advisers breakfast presentation, Belfast 2003.

[9] A. L. Zacharakis, W. D. Bygrave and D. A. Shepherd, *Global Entrepreneurship Monitor United States of America 2000 Executive Report* (Kansas City, MO: Kauffman Centre for Entrepreneurial Leadership at the Ewing Marion Kauffmann Foundation, 2000) p. 5.

[10] S. Shane, *A General Theory of Entrepreneurship* (Cheltenham: Edward Elgar, 2003) p. 4.

[11] Scottish Enterprise, *Enterprise and Economic Growth*, SEBPC(08)01. Taken from www.scottish-enterprise.com (accessed 15 February 2009).

[12] *Entrepreneurship and Education Action Plan* (Northern Ireland: DETI, DE and DEL, published in March 2003) p. 5.

[13] A. A. Gibb, 'SME Policy, Academic Research and the Growth of Ignorance, Mythical Concepts, Myths, Assumptions, Rituals and Confusions', *International Small Business Journal*, Vol. 18, No. 3, 2000, p. 16.

[14] Reported by S-M. Mukhtar and J. Redman in 'Developments in EU/UK Entrepreneurship/Enterprise Education Policy – Current Debate and Implications', a paper presented at the *27th ISBA Conference*, Newcastle, Nov 2004, p. 3.

[15] Taken from http://europa.eu/pol/enter/index_en.htm (accessed 23 July 2012).

[16] In answer to questions during a celebrity lecture in Northern Ireland, May 1993.

[17] Gordon Brown, as Chancellor of the Exchequer, launching 'Enterprising Britain' in 2004.

[18] Lord Young, *Enterprise for All: The Relevance of Enterprise in Education* (No. BIS/14/874) (London: Department for Business, Innovation and Skills/Prime Minister's Office, 2014).

[19] *DTI – The Department for Enterprise*, White Paper presented to Parliament, Cm 278 (January 1988) p. 41.

[20] Ibid. p. ii.

[21] Ibid. pp. 1, 5.

[22] As reported in R. Huggins and N. Williams, *Enterprise and Public Policy: A Review of Labour Government Intervention in the United Kingdom*, The University of Sheffield Management School Discussion Paper No. 2007, 03 August 2007.

[23] Lord Young, *The Report on Small Firms 2010–2015* (London: National Archives, 2015) p. 6.

[24] Taken from www.scottish-enterprise.com (accessed 17 January 2007).

[25] *The Vision*, Enterprise Northern Ireland, 2007, p. 2.

[26] University of Ulster, 'Enterprise in Higher Education', leaflet.

[27] Taken from www.berr.gov.uk (accessed 12 February 2008).

[28] Taken from www.enterprise.ac.uk (accessed 12 February 2008).

[29] Lord Young, *Growing Your Business: A Report on Growing Micro Businesses: The Second Part of the Report on Small Firms* (No. BIS/13/729) (London: Department for Business, Innovation and Skills, 2013).

[30] From the crossword, *Independent*, 8 January 1996.

[31] C. Ball, 'Towards an "Enterprising" Culture: A Challenge for Education and Training', *OECD/CERI Educational Monograph*, No. 4, 1989, pp. 6–7.

[32] 'What Do We Mean by Enterprise?', *Employment Initiatives*, February 1990, pp. 3–4.

[33] J. A. Schumpeter, *The Theory of Economic Development* (New York, NY: Oxford University Press – Galaxy, 1961) p. 74.

[34] I. Verheul, S. Wennekers, D. Audretsch and R. Thurik, *Research Report – An Eclectic Theory of Entrepreneurship: Policies, Institutions and Culture* (Zoetermeer Holland: EIM/Small Business Research and Consultancy, 1999), p. 9.

[35] A. Lundström and L. Stevenson, *Entrepreneurship Policy for the Future* (Stockholm: Swedish Foundation for Small Business Research, 2001) p. 18/19.

[36] OECD/CERI, 'Towards an "Enterprising" Culture', quoted in C. Ball, B. Knight and S. Plant, *New Goals for an Enterprise Culture*, (London: Training for Enterprise, 1990,) p. 21.

[37] A. A. Gibb, 'Enterprise Culture – Its Meaning and Implications for Education and Training', *Journal of European Industrial Training*, Vol. 11, No. 2, 1987, p. 10.

[38] J. B. Miner, N. R. Smith and J. S. Bracker, 'Defining the Inventor-Entrepreneur in the Context of Established Typologies', *Journal of Business Venturing*, Vol. 7, No. 2, 1992, pp. 103–113.

[39] *New Collins Dictionary* (Glasgow: HarperCollins, 1992).

[40] F. Coffield, 'Hunting a Heffalump in the World of the Enterprise Industry', *Independent*, 29 August 1990.

[41] Howard Davies, *A Review of Enterprise and the Economy in Education* (London: HM Treasury/HMSO, 2002).

[42] U. Hytti and P. Kuopusjärvi, 'Three Perspectives to Evaluating Entrepreneurship Education: Evaluators, Programme Promoters and Policy Makers', paper presented at the *EFMD 34th EISB Conference*, Turku 2004, based on *Evaluating and Measuring Entrepreneurship and Enterprise Education*, Small Business Institute, Turku, Finland, 2004 – from a Leonardo funded project.

[43] See, for instance, S. Bridge, C. Hegarty and S. Porter, 'Rediscovering Enterprise: Developing Appropriate University Entrepreneurship Education', *Education + Training*, Vol. 52, No. 8/9, 2010, pp. 722–734.

[44] D. Jasinski, 'A New Approach to Integrated Entrepreneurship Education', paper presented at *the ICSB 48th World Conference*, Belfast, 2003.

[45] S. Brown. 'Enterprise in the Curriculum at Sheffield Hallam University', paper presented at *Institute for Small Business Affairs 27th National Conference*, Newcastle, 2004.

[46] See T. Jackson, 'Beyond Rhetoric', *RSA Journal*, Winter issue, 2009.

[47] National Agency for Enterprise and Construction, *Entrepreneurship Index 2006: Entrepreneurship Conditions in Denmark*, November 2006. Taken from www.foranet.dk (accessed 16 March 2009) p. 5.

[48] H. M. Gabr and A. Hoffmann, *A General Policy Framework for Entrepreneurship*, FORA (Ministry of Economic and Business Affairs' Division for Research and Analysis) Copenhagen, Denmark, April 2006.

[49] Invest Northern Ireland, *Corporate Plan 2008–2011*. Taken from www.investni.com (accessed 11 February 2009) p. 5.

[50] Z. J. Ács and L. Szerb, 'The Global Entrepreneurship Index (GEINDEX)', *Jena Economic Research Papers*, 2009–028, p. 17. Taken from www.jenecon.de (accessed 23 April 2009).

[51] Ibid. p. 18.

[52] Ibid. p. 18.

[53] S. Bridge, *Rethinking Enterprise Policy: Can Failure Trigger New Understanding?* (Basingstoke: Palgrave Macmillan, 2010) p. 108/109.

[54] Based on S. Bridge, C. Hegarty and S. Porter, 'Clarifying Entrepreneurship: Gazelles or Green Shoots', paper presented at *32nd ISBE Conference*, Liverpool, November 2009.

[55] Based on W. Naudé, *Entrepreneurship in Economic Development*, United Nations University – World Institute for Development Economics Research (UNU-WIDER) Research Paper No. 2008/20, March 2008.

[56] Based on W. J. Baumol, 'Entrepreneurship: Productive, Unproductive, and Destructive', *Journal of Political Economy,* Vol. 98, No. 5, 1990, part 1.

[57] Based on S. Bridge, C. Hegarty and S. Porter, 'Clarifying Entrepreneurship: Gazelles or Green Shoots', paper presented at *32nd ISBE Conference*, Liverpool, November 2009.

[58] W. Baumol, 'Entrepreneurs, Inventors and the Growth of the Economy', *Economics Program Working Paper Series* (New York, NY: The Conference Board, 2008) p. 2/3.

[59] E. Chell, 'Social Enterprise and Entrepreneurship', *International Small Business Journal,* Vol. 25, No. 1, February 2007, pp. 5–26.

[60] E. Chell, *The Entrepreneurial Personality: A Social Construction* (Hove: Routledge, 2008) Chapter 2.

[61] S. Bridge, Op. Cit. Chapter 6.

Companion website

Please visit the companion website at www.palgravehighered.com/Bridge-UE-5e for access to additional learning and teaching materials.

PART 1

Enterprise and Entrepreneurs: Understanding Their Nature

CONTENTS

- Introduction
- Economic approaches to entrepreneurs
- Personality approaches
- Sociological and other approaches
- Integrated approaches
- Nature or nurture?
- Conclusions

KEY CONCEPTS

This chapter covers:

- Perceptions on the nature of enterprise.
- Economists' views on the role of the entrepreneur in economic systems.
- Some of the theories about people's internal make-up and experiences which have been suggested to explain why some people are more enterprising than others.
- The arguments advanced for whether entrepreneurial activity is the result of people's nature or nurture.
- A suggestion for an explanation which combines nature and nurture.

LEARNING OBJECTIVES

By the end of this chapter the reader should:

- Be familiar with a range of views on the role of the entrepreneur.
- Have an appreciation of different theories advocated about people's internal make-up which seek to explain why some are more enterprising than others.
- Be able to recognise the key personal traits which are said to distinguish entrepreneurs and enterprising people from other groups in society and have a view on the usefulness of trait theory.
- Be aware of the main points of the sociological approach to explaining entrepreneurial behaviour.
- Be familiar with some integrated and other approaches to explaining entrepreneurial behaviour.
- Understand the possible roles that nature and nurture might play in determining whether someone is likely to behave entrepreneurially.

INTRODUCTION

Chapter 3 explored the various different uses to which the words enterprise and entrepreneurship are currently put, but mapping their different uses and meanings does not explain what makes people enterprising and/or entrepreneurial. As it appears to most observers that some people are more enterprising and/or entrepreneurial than others, various explanations have been advanced to explain why this might be so.

As indicated earlier, in the last 30 or so years there has been a lot of research into enterprise and entrepreneurs in their many guises. The agenda for that research have been varied, but among the issues which it has tried to address have been questions such as:

- What is an entrepreneur and what does being enterprising or entrepreneurial mean?
- Why are some people more enterprising than others, or at least appear to be so?
- Is entrepreneurial behaviour the product of nature or nurture?
- How can enterprise and entrepreneurs be encouraged and supported?

Has this research produced useful answers to such questions? That itself is not an easy question to answer because, although the research has produced many answers, their veracity and/or usefulness is another issue (see, for instance, Part 2). Neither is it possible, in just part of a chapter, to give anything like a definitive guide to the main research findings. Instead, therefore, the following gives a brief introduction to some approaches taken and the resulting theories.

ECONOMIC APPROACHES TO ENTREPRENEURS

The current interest in entrepreneurs, as noted in Chapter 2, has arisen mainly for economic reasons so, in reviewing approaches to understanding entrepreneurs, it may be helpful to begin with economic approaches. Also the starting point for most, if not all, research into entrepreneurs must be some concept of what entrepreneurs are. Although, as Chapter 3 suggests, the perception of the role of the entrepreneur has changed over time, and a number of different perceptions are still current. Nevertheless it was economists who introduced the concept, and the following are some of their contributions:

The speculative trader. Cantillon cites the entrepreneur as any individual who operates under conditions where expenditures are known and certain, but incomes (sales revenues) are unknown and uncertain. The unique characteristic of Cantillon's entrepreneur is foresight and the confidence to operate under conditions of uncertainty. The main qualities of the Cantillon entrepreneur lie in the creation of entrepreneurial income through decision-making and risk-taking rather than orthodox effort.

Managing demand and supply. In the German-Austrian tradition personified by Mengler and Schumpeter, the entrepreneur is characterised as someone who manages the inputs into the process in such a way that the outcome is higher-level outputs: essentially, trying to manage demand and supply. In this the entrepreneur has to cope with uncertainty and is, as a result, a risk-bearer.

Driving the economy through innovation. Schumpeter saw the role of the entrepreneur as driving through 'innovation'. Innovation will lead to the creation of new firms and to the demise of old firms. The survival-of-the-fittest process detailed by Schumpeter leads to the creation of wealth. Schumpeter believed that only large firms would have the resources both to innovate and prevent the competition from new entrepreneurs threatening them. However, we know that small firms continue to be an engine of innovation in any economy and that these firms are led by entrepreneurs.

Acceptor of risk and uncertainty. The Chicago tradition, evidenced in the work of Knight, indicates that the entrepreneur does take risks. This is the fundamental characteristic of the entrepreneur. It is linked to the level of uncertainty that exists within any economy and with which the entrepreneur must deal.

More than a business man. The work of Schultz sought to provide for a bigger role for the entrepreneur in that the entrepreneur should not have a limited role as a business man. This view is also outlined in the work of Mises writing within the modern Austrian tradition.

The entrepreneur as the agent of economic change. The same modern Austrian tradition seeks to portray the entrepreneur as someone who must demonstrate 'great ingenuity' and in so doing reaches the higher level of promoting economic change. This means that the entrepreneur can be someone who can contribute much more to the economy and is much more than just an effective manager.

Alert to opportunity. For Kirzner the entrepreneur is not interested in routine managerial tasks. Kirzner's entrepreneur is concerned to demonstrate qualities of creativity and perception. The entrepreneur is alert to changes in the economy and takes advantage of this.

Combining effective management with innovation. The work of Liebenstein moves towards confirming the more complex profile of the effective entrepreneur. The first is a routine or managerial figure allocating inputs to the production process in a traditional manner. The other is the Schumpeterian entrepreneur who can produce a new product or process through innovation. The effective entrepreneur is one who is capable of playing both roles. Liebenstein observes that such individuals are scarce. This separation moves towards the distinction between an entrepreneurial management/organisation and an alternative organisational form which can be designated as professionally managed.

The multi-skilled entrepreneur. This notion recognises the work of the classicists and particularly of Say, who perceived the entrepreneur as someone who can effectively manage all of the factors of production. For Say the entrepreneur is someone who has mastered the art of administration and superintendence. This type of entrepreneur is a real team player and capable of managing the growth of a larger organisation. Again it can be observed that few entrepreneurs show these capabilities and many have limited or no desire to manage, co-ordinate and combine all of the factors of production.

PERSONALITY APPROACHES

The economic theories may have indicated what an entrepreneur was considered to be but they have not suggested what leads some people to become entrepreneurs. Early attempts to do this included personality approaches which assume that it is the personality of individuals that explains their actions. As personality is also thought to be genetically influenced, such approaches tend to assume that entrepreneurial tendencies are derived more from nature than nurture.

Trait theory

One approach to determining the make-up of entrepreneurs has been based on taking the more obvious 'heroic' entrepreneurs and trying to identify the particular traits, or combinations of traits, possessed by them and which predispose them towards entrepreneurial behaviour.

Traits are assumed to derive from a person's genetic make-up, and the entrepreneurial traits most often proposed are achievement motivation, risk-taking propensity, a desire for control and a need for achievement. Other personal qualities that are purported to predispose people to being enterprising and/or entrepreneurial are also listed in Table 4.1 (see also Table 3.2). Some of the classic traits or attributes linked to entrepreneurs are elaborated upon below.

Achievement motivation

Entrepreneurial people are said to have a strong need for achievement (sometimes referred to as NAch), which stimulates them into action. When they accomplish something which they consider to be worthwhile, their self-esteem is enhanced and they are encouraged to seek other demanding assignments. Thus enterprising people are constantly on the lookout for challenges. It has been suggested that strong-willed children, with parents who make their expectations known and who provide positive feedback, become high achievers, although McClelland also argues that NAch can also be developed in adults.[1]

Table 4.1 *Traits associated with entrepreneurs*

The traits most commonly associated with entrepreneurs:

- Achievement motivation (NAch)
- Risk-taking propensity
- Locus of control
- Need for autonomy

Other personal qualities sometimes associated with entrepreneurs:

- Determination – being persistent and capable of seeing ideas through to fruition.
- Initiative – being purposeful, proactive, dynamic, active and able to take the initiative.
- Innovation and creativity – being innovative, able to identify ideas, imaginative, adaptable, creative, flexible and able to tolerate ambiguity.
- Trusting and trustworthy and being responsible and self-confident.
- Being positive and being able to see change as on opportunity.
- Having an appropriate vision.

The importance of NAch for enterprise is not generally in dispute, but how can an individual with a high NAch be recognised? McClelland argues that such a person

> is more self confident, enjoys taking carefully calculated risks, researches his environment actively, and is very much interested in concrete measures of how well he is doing. Somewhat surprisingly ... he does not seem to be galvanised into activity by the prospect of profit; ... [he] ... works hard anyway, provided there is an opportunity of achieving something.[2]

Although NAch has been widely used as one measure of the entrepreneurial personality, results are not clear-cut. An interesting point also arises in connection with causality. It is generally assumed that achievement-oriented people become entrepreneurs or enterprising individuals. However, it is equally plausible that the sense of mastery and achievement that accompanies a successful enterprising project such as establishing a business might create the need to achieve more.

Risk-taking propensity

The outcomes of enterprising events are less certain than those of conservative ones, and therefore enterprising individuals will need to have the capacity to tolerate risks and the psychological make-up and resources to cope with failure.

While they must be able to countenance risk, that is not to say that enterprising people are high risk-takers. Entrepreneurial research suggests that effective entrepreneurs are moderate risk-takers, while others believe that enterprising people take calculated risks. In this vein Drucker argues that successful entrepreneurs 'try to define the risks they have to take and to minimise them as much as possible'.[3] They search for opportunities, give them serious consideration and if promising, capitalise on them. Drucker goes so far as to say that successful entrepreneurs tend to be cautious and are opportunity-focused, as opposed to risk-focused.

Chell *et al.* point out, however, that there are problems in defining risky behaviour.[4] Risk assessment takes place in context, and behaviour that appears risky to outsiders may not be perceived as risky by those who are fully cognisant of a situation. Enterprising persons may not perceive a course of action as risky because they fully understand the situation, but this can also arise because of cognitive biases. It is argued[5] that entrepreneurs may not perceive a risk in a risky situation because they are overconfident, because they have the illusion that they are in control of a situation and because they tend to associate with optimistic people who do not dwell on failures.

Locus of control

'Locus of control' refers to being in control of events. Enterprising people believe that they personally make things happen in a given situation, and underplay the importance of luck and fate. Rotter was instrumental in assessing this aspect of personality, and he designated those who feel in control as 'internals' and those not in control as 'externals'. 'Internal' declarations emphasise the importance of ability, hard work, determination and planning in achieving outcomes – and an outlook which is epitomised by the statement 'What happens to me is my own doing'.[6]

Locus of control is often regarded as a crucial indicator of enterprising potential but there are concerns about the construct.[7] The concept was not designed for entrepreneurial settings and has been described as a 'distal' measure.[8] That is, it might explain general behaviour but is of little use in predicting how people will behave in specific situations. In addition, entrepreneurial studies which have used the construct have produced inconclusive results. As Chell *et al.* point out, perceptions of control will be influenced by many variables including experience. If individuals have recent successful experience of completing enterprising projects, they might consider themselves to be capable of controlling events. If, however, they have experienced failure, they may blame external factors.

Need for autonomy

'Autonomy' refers to independence from other people, being in control of one's own destiny. This can accompany 'locus of control', which involves control of events beyond the individual, but it is not the same thing. Entrepreneurial people have a strong desire to go it alone. In interviews with enterprising people they constantly refer to a need to control their own lives. Phrases such as 'I want to be in control', and 'I do things my way', are used regularly.[9] Individuals in many groups, organisations and societies are expected to adhere to the norms, rules and regulations of collective social organisms. Conformity is the price of membership. However, independent people often resent these constraints and regard them as counter-productive in developing innovative proposals.

People who do their own thing regardless of others or who disregard with impunity rules that constrain them could be considered as disruptive dissenters who may leave and set up their own ventures. When asked why they wanted to start their own firm, aspiring entrepreneurs in one study most frequently cited autonomy and the need to achieve as the most important factors in their decisions.[10] It should be noted, however, that entrepreneurial experience can cause people to want even more autonomy.[11]

Determination

Entrepreneurial people also possess determination. They normally complete projects, and a degree of persistence is necessary for success. Being in control is important, as is the freedom to exercise ingenuity, but a determination to see a difficult project through is also vital.

Initiative

The entrepreneurial individual may also need to be proactive. A person may have a strong need to achieve, may possess determination, may welcome the chance to do his or her own thing and to exercise control over his or her environment in pursuit of an assigned project, and may, when presented with an opening, exhibit many enterprising qualities. If, however, he or she does not actively take the initiative and seek openings and opportunities, then the enterprise is limited. Therefore entrepreneurial people take bold steps and have a propensity to seek new opportunities.[12]

Creativity

The entrepreneurial person is often concerned with developing new products, processes or markets. Such people tend to have more originality than others and are able to produce solutions that can fly in the face of established knowledge. They are also inclined to be more adaptable and are prepared to consider a range of alternative approaches. They challenge the status quo, which can sometimes bring them into conflict with their colleagues.

Self-confidence and trust

It has been argued that entrepreneurial individuals seek out demanding tasks that produce the intrinsic rewards of achievement, that they act on their environments in uncovering these opportunities rather than responding to changes and that they impose their independent authority to explore creative, risky options for problems or opportunities. It is most unlikely that people who lack self-confidence could undertake these tasks. Often proactivity, creativity and achievement are not accomplished without major change, and enterprising persons have a security born of self-confidence in uncertain situations.

Critiques of trait theory

Simple trait theory implies that the kind of person you are will influence whether you become an entrepreneur, but the short review above of some classic traits suggests that the connection between innate qualities and entrepreneurs is not simple. The traits and qualities described do impact on behaviour, but it is accepted that most entrepreneurs do not possess all the enterprise traits identified, and many of the traits are also possessed by those who would not be described as entrepreneurs. Delmar,[13] for instance, feels that trait theory has serious limitations. He argues that there is little consistency in trait research in that while a large number of traits are linked to entrepreneurs, the same traits are operationalised in different ways. Moreover research evidence linking predisposition, enterprise and performance is at variance. In effect, a particular combination of traits does not predict a particular form of behaviour. Further he has claimed that 'the theory and methods in use are, in relation to modern psychological research, obsolete'.

Shane also distrusts the trait approach:

In general, this school of thought has focused on explaining entrepreneurship as a function of core human attributes, such as willingness to bear uncertainty, tolerance for ambiguity, or need for achievement which differentiate entrepreneurs from the rest of society. Unfortunately, this approach has proved largely unsuccessful, perhaps because entrepreneurial activity is episodic. Because people engage in entrepreneurial behavior only at particular points in time, and in response to specific situations, it is impossible to account for entrepreneurship solely by examining factors that should influence all human action in the same way all of the time.[14]

In theory personality traits, which might be defined as relatively enduring behavioural dispositions, should help to predict behaviour in a variety of different situations. However, traits which seem to apply in some situations do not seem to apply in others (see for instance Illustration 12.2). Additionally, personality traits might be supposed to be related to attitudes; however, when attitudes are assessed through questionnaires, they do not seem to correlate closely with observed behaviour.

The entrepreneurial trait argument, Chell suggests, has to some extent swayed to and fro,[15] and there are questions about traits which still need to be addressed. For instance, if actions are trait based, is there a single trait of 'entrepreneurialism' or is there instead a relevant profile or constellation of traits? Also do all entrepreneurs have the same trait or traits and is everyone with those traits an entrepreneur? Does behaviour influence traits as well as vice versa? Do traits vary over time and is the behaviour it is claimed they predict not context specific? All these questions pose a challenge to trait theory.

A development of the trait approach had considered whether traits, if they do not predict single actions very well, could nevertheless predict actions in aggregate, or whether other factors could be identified which moderated the consistency between dispositions and actions. However, neither aggregating behaviour nor a search for moderating variables seems to help link dispositions to actions. In any case, personality traits are inferred from behaviour and so do not help to explain that behaviour. Suggesting that someone has a trait or traits for entrepreneurship because they behave entrepreneurially, does not help to predict entrepreneurial behaviour before it occurs.

Psychodynamic and social-psychological approaches

As well as trait theory, other personality theories include psychodynamic approaches, which view the entrepreneurial individual as someone who is 'deviant' in society, and social-psychological approaches, which also consider the context in which the individual operates.

Psychodynamic approaches

Psychodynamic approaches are the product of Freud's psychoanalytic theory of personality. Freud considered that individuals have instinctive drives (the *ID*), and that a part of the personality seeks instant gratification for these desires. However, the pursuit of instant gratification can get people into trouble, and as people develop their *ego* emerges to constrain instinctive behaviour. This controlling mechanism protects the individual from the unpleasant consequences of pursuing innate desires. With further development, the individual realises that behaviour can meet with the approval or disapproval of significant others and a *superego* develops to limit behaviour to that which is in keeping with the moral code of parents and society. Freud argues that there are many conflicts amongst these forces, and that the resolution of these conflicts is instrumental in creating the personality. If instinctive behaviour is severely constrained, then it can lead to frustration, and psychodynamic approaches to entrepreneurs consider that this frustration is the source of much entrepreneurial motivation.

Psychodynamic approaches are based on three basic premises: that most behaviour is goal-directed and is caused by a force within the person, that much behaviour originates from the unconscious mind and that early childhood experiences are crucial in the development of the personality. One of the leading advocates of this approach in the entrepreneurial field is Kets de Vries, who suggests that early frustrations are the product of unhappy family backgrounds.[16] Fathers, in particular, are seen as controllers and manipulators who are remote. In addition they are often seen as deserters who place an unwarranted burden on heroic mothers. These negative images of fathers may have little basis in reality, but perception is all-important. As a result of these experiences or perceptions, individuals can develop an intense dislike of authority figures and develop suppressed aggressive tendencies towards persons in control. This leads such individuals to be classified as 'deviant' or 'marginal' people who, if they engage in employment, change jobs on a regular basis. Thus they may get a variety of job experiences, which provides them with a range of skills that are indispensable for running a business. As a consequence of their behaviour, these individuals make a determined effort to start their own business. In this milieu they are in control, are answerable to no one and are 'at the centre of action'.

However, psychodynamic theories have been criticised because of their subjective nature and the lack of empirical evidence. Their ability to explain entrepreneurial activity has been found wanting because they do not cover all situations, such as a business start prompted through unemployment; because not all deviants start businesses and many characteristics associated with deviancy are not typical of successful entrepreneurs; and because entrepreneurs tend to create their ventures in their 30s or later when many of life's experiences, not merely childhood ones, will influence their behaviour.[17]

Social-psychological approaches

Trait approaches depict behaviour as being determined by innate qualities but it is widely recognised by social psychologists that behaviour is constrained by contextual factors. Behaviour is influenced by social realities and is also interpreted in a given context. The work of Chell and her colleagues, already mentioned, notes that behaviour which is classified as risky and innovative can only be categorised as such in a given context. Those who observe entrepreneurial individuals, and indeed the entrepreneurs themselves, classify given behaviour as entrepreneurial only in certain circumstances. Thus context is important and some writers[18] argue that individuals who find it difficult to make progress in mainstream careers become marginalized and become entrepreneurs as a means of escape. This has, for instance, been used to explain the emergence of women and ethnic entrepreneurs.

SOCIOLOGICAL AND OTHER APPROACHES

Personality approaches are concerned with the innate qualities which are presumed to motivate individuals to act in certain ways, although social-psychological approaches also allow for the impact of social structures on behaviour. Other approaches to entrepreneurs give more weight to factors external to the individual and thus tend to suggest the influence of nurture at least in addition to, if not instead of, the inherent nature of individuals.

Sociological approaches

Some sociologists consider that individuals are seriously constrained in making career choices by the limitations of experience and by the expectations that individuals face in the social world. Indeed, Roberts goes so far as to say that careers follow patterns that are 'dictated by the opportunity structure to which individuals are exposed first in education, and subsequently in employment'.[19] He contends that ambition is moulded by 'the structures through which' people pass. Others, who would not deny that individual choice plays a part in career decisions, still emphasise contextual awareness.

Different opportunity structures expose people not only to different possibilities but also to different expectations from other people. Individuals are socialised to behave in ways that meet with the approval of their role set. For example, a young person with a business-owning parent may well be expected to join the family business, and not to do so would create a vacuum in the business. The son of an unemployed labourer may well be socialised quite differently. The dominant values of close associates will translate into expectations which strongly influence individual behaviour. In the UK at least, it appears, for instance, that individuals whose parents or other close relations have had their own business appear generally much more likely to have businesses themselves, and certain social groupings, such as ethnic minorities, produce proportionately more entrepreneurs than others. As evidence of parental influence, Stanworth and Gray describe research results for persons employed in selected service sectors:

> Overall some 43.5 per cent … had fathers and/or mothers who had been self-employed ranging from 56 per cent for the owners of free houses, wine bars and restaurants down to 33.3 per cent for the owners of both advertising, marketing and design companies and computer services business. This finding thus strongly supports the contention that parental experience of self-employment in general, and small business ownership in particular, is the best single predictor of the propensity to enter into small business ownership, although this propensity will clearly differ across different types of small enterprise.[20]

The implication of this approach is that enterprising individuals differ from others in at least some of their values and beliefs and these are derived from many sources including the family, peers, community activists and the media.

In general, sociological approaches recognise the importance of social structures on individual decision-making and are a counter to those who might extol the virtues of rugged individualism as the sole determinant of becoming an entrepreneur. However, while they do tell us quite a lot about the kind of people who become entrepreneurs, they do not tell us much about the process by which social factors actually influence decision-making.

Cognitive approaches, behavioural theories and competencies

An approach which does appear to have found favour is that of cognitive psychology. A cognitive approach considers that whilst the personal characteristics of individuals may play a part in determining who becomes an entrepreneur, it is more important to examine the decision-making process by which individuals choose to act entrepreneurially. Delmar has produced a useful analysis of cognitive models in which he argues that becoming an entrepreneur, and other career choices, have a major interpretative element and that behaviour 'is heavily based on how individuals perceive the situation or environment and how it is presented to them'.[21] For a person to decide to become an entrepreneur, he or she will have to believe that this is a viable career option. The intending entrepreneur will form an opinion about the 'job' – the requisite attributes, knowledge, skills and resources needed for success – and about self – the perceived attributes, knowledge, skills and resources that are possessed by the person before expending energy in the pursuit of this career. The individual, on the basis of these assessments, which may not be worked out in a precise manner, will decide on his or her level of potential.

Beliefs and attitudes can influence behaviour, but it is suggested that the link between these variables is mediated by intentions. Boyd and Vozikis[22] argue that intentions are indicative of a person's willingness to engage in a behaviour and are influenced by personal factors such as personality, experience and perceived ability and by contextual factors such as social and economic structures. Delmar argues that more is needed to elicit planned behaviour. A second condition is that perceived social norms must be supportive of the intended behaviour. In other words, the potential entrepreneur must believe that significant others will approve of the chosen course of action. However, supportive attitudes and societal norms are necessary but not sufficient conditions, and the belief by a person that he or she has the capability to succeed will also strongly influence behaviour. This concept of 'self-efficacy' is defined by Boyd and Vozikis as 'a person's belief in his or her capability to perform a given task'.[23] These authors argue that self-efficacy is crucial in determining whether a person will pursue a goal and is equally important in maintaining motivation once action is taken. In short, if people firmly believe that they have what it takes to set up and complete enterprising projects, this will strongly influence their intentions to attain this outcome. These ideas lead to the development of a theory of planned behaviour (see below) which illustrates how people behave in situations which are not entirely within their control, as is the case with the intending entrepreneur.

Cognitive theories emphasise the individual decision-making process and the impact of perceived competence on the decision to become an entrepreneur. The behavioural approach to studying entrepreneurs, however, focuses on the behaviours they display in a context, rather than on what they themselves are. One approach with particular relevance to this theory is the examination of individual 'competencies' relevant to a specific event.

Cognitive approaches have been highlighted by psychologists, but other writers have also commented on the role played by competencies, attributes and resources – ideas that are closely linked with issues such as perceived behavioural control and self-efficacy in the entrepreneurial decision-making process.

An individual will not be in control of an enterprising event if he or she is not competent, and there is now considerable interest in enumerating the key competencies of successful entrepreneurs. Competence has been described as the modern terminology for ability. However, there is still considerable confusion around the concept, in particular with regard to what the term 'competency' actually means. There are two broad approaches to the question. Boyatzis considers that competency relates to the 'personal characteristics' of individuals, while the Management Charter Initiative in the UK adopts a work-functions approach. The former focuses on the person and on the characteristics that make people competent, while the latter looks at the job and details those job functions that competent people can perform effectively.[24]

In general, a major problem with the competency approach, as with some other approaches, is that it is not definitive. There appears to be no competency that is possessed by all entrepreneurs, and many examples exist of non-entrepreneurs who appear to possess more entrepreneurial competencies than do some people who clearly are entrepreneurs. Lists of competencies are more general than domain-specific concepts such as self-efficacy. However, if individuals could be convinced of their self-efficacy with respect to key entrepreneurial competencies, this may, it is argued, increase their motivation to become an entrepreneur.

Gender and ethnicity

Two other prominent aspects of individuals are also perceived, at least in some circumstances, to be relevant to the extent to which people become entrepreneurs or engage in wider aspects of enterprise. They are the individual's gender and ethnicity. Theories have therefore been advanced as to why historically most entrepreneurs have been men and why people in some ethnic groups seem to be more predisposed to being entrepreneurs than others. These are considered further in Chapter 9.

INTEGRATED APPROACHES

Each of the theories so far considered has drawbacks, not least because no single theory seems to cover all aspects of enterprise. Therefore attempts have been made to amalgamate parts of two or more theories to produce an integrated approach with more general application.

Planned behaviour

The thinking behind the planned behaviour approach was not that traits are irrelevant but that there are other factors which influence behaviour. Ajzen, in developing his Theory of Planned Behaviour,[25] suggested that, of all the behavioural dispositions, it is intentions which are most closely linked to the corresponding actions. According to his theory, a person's intentions are assumed to capture the motivational factors that have an influence on that person's behaviour. Those factors act directly to determine intentions which in turn affect actions and thus, although there is a connection between the factors and the actions, it is indirect. Further, intentions do not necessarily lead to immediate action, and once they are formed, intentions initially remain as behavioural dispositions until, given an appropriate time and opportunity, they translate into actions.

This theory also suggests that there are three independent determinants of intentions: attitudes towards the behaviour in question, subjective norms and perceived behavioural control. Krueger, in developing his model, started with the assumption that much of what is considered to be entrepreneurial activity is planned behaviour and that 'planned behaviours such as starting a business are intentional and thus are best predicted by intentions towards the behaviour, *not* by attitudes, beliefs, personality or demographics'.[26] 'Empirically', he and his colleagues state, 'we have learned that situational (for example, employment status or informational cues) or individual (for example, demographic characteristics or personality traits) variables are poor predictors'.[27]

Krueger's model[28] (see Figure 4.1) argues, like Delmar, that intentions to act entrepreneurially are underpinned by the development of potential, which is in turn built upon credibility. Krueger contends that to be credible to oneself and to others, entrepreneurs must both perceive the probable outcome of their endeavours in a favourable light and believe that they have the wherewithal to succeed. Perception is all-important in this process; indeed it may be more important than reality. The favourable light is a product of personal preference and social approval for entrepreneurs, and the wherewithal comes from experience, from innate and learned attributes that might enhance enterprising propensity, and from skills, knowledge and resources that increase self-efficacy. That light and that wherewithal alone, however, are not necessarily sufficient. A trigger or key event (a situational context) may be necessary to start the individual on an enterprising course of action. It can be seen that this model draws on ideas from trait, cognitive, sociological and behavioural approaches and neatly summarises a range of relevant variables.

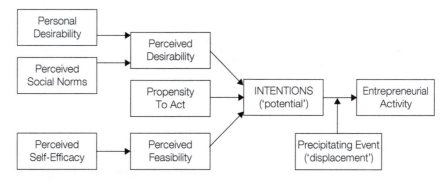

Figure 4.1 *Intentions model of entrepreneurial potential (simplified)*

Source: N. F. Krueger, *Prescription for Opportunity: How Communities Can Create Potential for Entrepreneurs* (Washington, DC: Small Business Foundation of America, Working Paper 93-03, 1995) p. 10.

It may also be relevant to point out that simply because a person took an enterprising decision at one time does not necessarily mean that he or she would automatically do it again. For instance an owner's motivation to expand a business may decline once that business produces a satisfactory level of income or if their personal circumstances change. This can be explained as a change in personal desirability and shows the need to take into consideration more than factors such as attributes and traits.[29]

Attributes and resources

Similar to the Krueger model, the attributes and resources approach offers perceived self-efficacy as an important aspect of cognitive models. It corresponds with a view of enterprise, and of enterprising behaviour, that is based on the attributes and resources an individual may possess at any point in time. Attributes may include self-confidence, diligence, perseverance, interpersonal skills and innovative behaviour. Resources may include finance, experience, knowledge, skills, a network and a track record. It is suggested that it is the interaction between these factors that produces a rational response, on the basis of available information, when the opportunity occurs for a business start-up.

This view, however, also acknowledges that there is inertia in individual behaviour and that it may take a discontinuity in work, or in life, to trigger a review of an individual's situation. Whether this review will lead to people trying their own enterprises will then depend on the attributes and resources they have accumulated, together with their perceptions of environmental factors such as the availability of encouragement and forms of support such as advice, grants and training. This is illustrated in Figure 4.2 and Table 4.2.

The implications of this view are that the start-up decision will be affected by the attributes and resources acquired prior to the trigger for taking the decision, and that there is scope for initiatives to enhance the acquisition of those attributes and resources. It does not deny that, at the time of the decision, the availability of support such as grants and training is influential on that decision. It does, however, indicate that, whether or not grants and training are available, more people are likely to decide to try a business start-up, and with more chance of success, if they are in possession of the relevant attributes and resources. There should be economic benefits to be gained therefore from enhancing relevant individual attributes and resources.

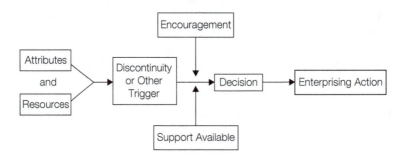

Figure 4.2 *Attributes and resources model*

Table 4.2 *Attributes and resources, and how they are acquired*

Attributes	Resources
Attitude	Ideas
Self-confidence	Technical skills
Enthusiasm	Interpersonal and communication skills
Diligence and perseverance	Information, and access to it
Initiative	Network
Independence	Finance
Persuasiveness	Experience (e.g. of small business, of marketing and of planning)
Positive outlook	Track record and credibility
Perception	
Attitude to risk	
Direction	
How acquired	
Attributes can be acquired from both nature and nurture. The nurture influences can include family, education, culture, work experience, role models, peers, economic structure, lifestyle and stages of life.	Resources are acquired through many of the processes of working and living. They will, however, be more readily acquired if this acquisition is planned and targeted.

Delmar argues that this approach is more useful than trait theories in that it more clearly reflects the complexity of the entrepreneurial decision-making process. It also highlights some factors which are amenable to change through intervention. However, he concedes that the connection 'between intentions and actual behaviour is still an uncharted area'.[30]

NATURE OR NURTURE?

Do the theories of entrepreneurs indicate that their activity is the result of nature or nurture? Are entrepreneurs born that way or are they made into entrepreneurs as a result of environmental influences? Different theories and approaches would seem to suggest different answers. For instance trait theory would seem to suggest that inherited characteristics are important, but sociological theories emphasise the influence of other people. The theories are not therefore consistent on this point, but to some extent the answer also depends on what is meant by 'entrepreneurship'. If the question what makes some people more entrepreneurial than other refers only to those people such as Richard Branson or Oprah Winfrey, who seem to launch venture after venture and who might be classed as 'heroic' or 'stellar' entrepreneurs, the answer might be different than if it refers to all self-employed people. (This distinction is also seen in the different types of business owner shown in Figures 3.1 and 4.4.)

The case for nature

> Some people maintain that becoming an entrepreneur is genetic:
>
> > No real entrepreneur actually believes entrepreneurial skills are learnable or transferable. You're either an entrepreneur or you're not. It's a state of being, not a trade or a vocation.[31]
> >
> > Young entrepreneurs are often born, rather than bred.[32]
> >
> > The study found that almost half a person's propensity to be self-employed was due to genetic factors. Family environment and upbringing had little bearing, it said.[33]

The argument that entrepreneurs are born not made tends to rely on observations such as those quoted above and on explanations such as the trait approach, which tends to assume that traits are inherited and determine behaviour. Thus Deakins, in his discussion of the trait approach, comments that:

> From this approach it is possible to argue that the supply of potential entrepreneurs is limited to a finite number of people with innate abilities, that they have a set of characteristics that mark them out as different, and have particular insights not possessed by others. This has led to some controversy and, in terms of policy, has significant implications. Obviously, if entrepreneurial characteristics are inherent, then there is little to be gained from direct interventions to encourage new entrepreneurs to start new businesses, although interventions to improve the infrastructure or environment may still have an effect. Whether an 'entrepreneurial personality' exists, however, is the subject of controversy and, despite attempts to provide prototypical 'lists' of characteristics of the entrepreneurial personality, this author remains sceptical of such approaches.[34]

For the trait approach to demonstrate that entrepreneurs are born not made it is necessary to show both that traits do determine the entrepreneurial personality and that they are genetically determined, presumably because they can be linked to specific genes. However, there is considerable doubt about both these points. Chell, for instance, suggests that more sophisticated research is required to provide more convincing evidence that any traits are prototypical of entrepreneurs and predictors of entrepreneurial behaviour and that, while entrepreneurs may be born with the psychological apparatus to behave entrepreneurially in later life, the strong social component suggests that there is a role for social learning and personal development.[35]

Despite such conclusions, many people will assume, often intuitively, that stellar entrepreneurs were not influenced or taught to behave like that and that their entrepreneurial tendency is therefore to a large extent the result of genetics – possibly also with some early-stage influences before conscious learning takes place.

The case for nurture

Some people argue that the environment influences entrepreneurial tendency:

> At the heart of the matter is whether the psychological and social traits are either necessary or sufficient for the development of entrepreneurship. ... While many authors have purported to find statistically common characters of (the) entrepreneur, the ability to attribute causality to these factors is seriously in doubt.[36]

> Social psychologists have claimed that an individual's attitudes and traits are not inherited but are developed in interaction with the social environment.[37]

> There is clear evidence that entrepreneurship can be learned.[38]

A counter-argument to the trait approach is that being an entrepreneur is about 'doing' (i.e. behaviour) and not 'being' (trait characteristics). 'Such a line of argument does not itself negate the possible influence of personality, as behaviour and personality are related. However, the theoretical position that behaviour is solely a function of personality may not hold up in the case of becoming an entrepreneur. Instead, it could be argued that behaviour is a function of personality and situation, and their interaction.'[39]

If doubts about the case for nature might be seen to support a nurture or environmental approach, Shane does not think that works either:

> Another group of researchers has sought to explain entrepreneurship by reference to the environment in which entrepreneurs have been found. In general, this school of thought has sought to identify situations in which entrepreneurial activity, often measured as new firm formation, is more likely to occur. Key situational factors that have been argued to lead to entrepreneurial activity have included competence-destroying technological change, industry dynamics, and market structure. Unfortunately, this approach, too, has failed to provide an adequate explanation for entrepreneurship, largely because it does not consider the human agency. Entrepreneurship is a self-directed activity that does not occur spontaneously from the presence of technological or industrial change. Rather, it requires the action of individuals who identify and pursue opportunities. No amount of investigation of the environment alone can provide a complete explanation for entrepreneurship.[40]

The nurture argument does not necessarily deny personality traits but stresses the influence of the social environment, for instance in forming or developing those traits. Nevertheless sometimes the case for nurture seems to be based more on the failure of, or lack of proof for, the case for nature than on any hard evidence in favour of nurture. That sort of reasoning, however, presupposes that if it is not one then it must be the other, and some commentators, such as Shane in the quotes above, seem to suggest that neither side has convincing arguments on its own.

Both nature and nurture?

> Entrepreneurs may well be born with the psychological apparatus to behave entrepreneurially in later life, but the strong social component suggests that there is a role for social learning and personal development.[41]
>
> Entrepreneurship is the result of the interaction between individual attributes and the surrounding environment.[42]

Bridge, in his examination of the origins of entrepreneurial tendency, points out that that this issue of nature versus nurture has been debated in the context of other aspects of human behaviour and that various attempts have been made to resolve it.[43] For instance, what has been described as the 'gold standard' for nature versus nurture studies has been to compare the development of identical twins adopted and raised by different parents. In this way, it is supposed, it should be possible to assess the extent to which a trait such as aggression seems to be due to influences from the family, and how much to biology alone.

Initially such studies seemed to indicate that certain traits were largely due to genes, but it now appears, on closer examination of more carefully collected data, that the situation could be more complicated. One example given is that:

> While parents naturally cuddle babies who flirt and hug back, testy and indifferent babies get less cuddling. In the worst case, when a child's genetics lead him to be irritable, aggressive and difficult, parents tend to respond in kind, with harsh discipline, tough talk and their own criticism and anger. That route worsens the child's difficult side, which in turn provokes more of the parents' negativity in a vicious spiral.[44]

Thus the child's behaviour is mainly the result of nurture, although that nurture may initially have been provoked by something in the child's nature.

Such evidence does not suggest that there is no genetic basis to behaviour, but that nurture, and especially early year influences, can often change initial behaviour because it would seem that the human brain can be 're-wired' by appropriate conditioning. For instance a baby's reaction to novelty has been shown to be a reliable predictor of whether it will grow up to be particularly timid and shy. If, however, children thus shown to have a tendency to timidity are encouraged, and even pressured, to spend time with other outgoing children who they might normally have avoided, the timid children can often overcome their genetic predisposition towards shyness.[45] Indeed the science of epigenetics has shown that there are biological mechanisms which can switch genes on or off and thus change characteristics thought to be fundamentally inherited.[46]

Recently, Nicolaou and Shane have suggested some arguments specifically for the possible influence of genetic factors on entrepreneurs:

> We propose that genetic factors may influence the tendency of people to engage in entrepreneurial activity in four complementary ways. First, genes may affect chemical mechanisms in the brain to increase the likelihood that people will engage in entrepreneurial activity. Second, genes may influence individual differences, such as extraversion and internal locus of control, that predispose people to engage in entrepreneurial activity. Third, genes may make some people more sensitive than others to environmental stimuli that increase the likelihood of engaging in entrepreneurial activity. Fourth, genes may affect the tendency of people to select into environments that are more favorable to entrepreneurship.[47]

Nicolaou and Shane illustrate this with the diagram in Figure 4.3 which includes both genes and environment. They also explain that they are not proposing that individuals are born with a gene or genes for entrepreneurship, but rather that there are four complementary mechanisms through which genetic factors might affect the tendency of people to engage in entrepreneurial activity. They point out that, at present, their proposals have yet to be tested so there is no direct empirical evidence that genetic factors affect people's propensity to engage in entrepreneurial activity in the ways they suggest.[48] Nevertheless it is posited that, whilst entrepreneurs may not be born with traits that lead them to behave entrepreneurially regardless of other influences, it could be that their genes might predispose them to develop entrepreneurial characteristics, given a suitable environment.

A further issue within the case for nurture is the possible difference between the impact of early-stage upbringing and later environmental influences. The saying 'give me the child until he is seven and I will show you the man' is attributed to the Jesuits and it highlights the importance of childhood influences

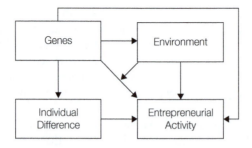

Figure 4.3 *Mechanisms through which genetic factors might influence entrepreneurship*

Source: Based on N. Nicolaou and S. Shane, 'Can Genetic Factors Influence the Likelihood of Engaging in Entrepreneurial Activity?', *Journal of Business Venturing*, Vol. 24, 2009, p. 2.

and suggests that they can be more important than any later instruction. The implication therefore might be that, if some aspects of behaviour are due to nurture, the timing of that nurture may be crucial. Thus promoting some aspects of behaviour may be much more effectively done when people are young and much harder to do when they are adults.

In the debate on entrepreneurial influences, Drakopoulou Dodd and Anderson also raise what they describe as the agency or structure issue: is it the entrepreneur or entrepreneurship which is being considered? Much of the early entrepreneurial literature, they report, included individualistic explanations that were seen as *a priori* true; 'entrepreneurs were different from other people so that difference must explain what they do'.[49] The same sort of argument, they indicate, has been applied to unemployment. If it is viewed through an individualistic lens, then it might appear that only some people cannot get jobs so unemployment must the caused by individuals' lack of skills or of motivation. However, unemployment can also reasonably be explained by structural changes, industrial developments and even political considerations. The problem is to try to achieve a balanced explanation involving the action of individual agents in the context of the social environment.

Such studies and proposals suggest that debating nature against nurture is the wrong approach because it is not one or the other which leads to what might be perceived to be traits, but a combination of both. Sometimes it seems that nature can be reinforced by nurture, sometimes it can trigger certain aspects of nurture, and sometimes it can be countered by nurture. It may be wrong therefore to ignore nature in seeking the source of entrepreneurial traits, but it would also be wrong to ignore nurture. It may not be either one or the other, but both.

Indeed White *et al.* suggest that taken together a combination of nature and nurture help us to better understand entrepreneurial behaviour. Although they acknowledge that the relevant research is in its infancy, they challenge what they see as primarily a nurture approach. They 'do not argue that biological determinism should replace sociological determinism' and their case 'is not for nature to the exclusion of nurture; rather that nurture and nature work together, hand-in-glove'. 'Upon reflection' they suggest, 'most social science researchers accept this basic premise of co-determination'.[50]

The persistence of the 'heroic' myth?

One of the great myths of entrepreneurship … (is) the notion of the entrepreneur as a lone hero, battling against the storms of economic, government, social and other environmental forces.[51]

A complicating factor in this consideration of nature and nurture is the case of those individuals who seem to be so predisposed towards becoming entrepreneurs that they appear to have a different make-up from others though subject apparently to the same environmental factors. Thus the concept persists of the 'heroic' or 'stellar' entrepreneur as an individual who somehow stands out from the rest of society. As Drakopoulou Dodd and Anderson comment:

> The popular vision of the entrepreneur has been shown to be profoundly individualistic; people may have difficulty in understanding the concept of entrepreneurship, but they readily identify with an entrepreneur.[52]

In his contribution to a book on *Mastering Enterprise*, Kets de Vries suggested that many entrepreneurs are 'misfits' who are unable to accept authority and organisational rules and who need therefore to create their own environment. He suggests that:

> The heroic myth begins with the hero's humble birth, his rapid rise to prominence and power, his conquest of the forces of evil, his vulnerability to the sin of pride and finally his fall through betrayal or heroic sacrifice.
>
> The basic symbolic themes here – of birth, conquest, pride, betrayal and death – are relevant to all of us. Some entrepreneurs act out the same myth, as we have seen, with a Greek chorus in the background applauding their achievements but warning them about pride.
>
> Perhaps the myth explains why so many entrepreneurs live under a great amount of tension. They feel they are living on the edge, that their success will not last (their need for control and their sense of distrust are symptomatic of this anxiety) but they have also an overriding concern to be heard and recognized – to be seen as heroes.[53]

Drakopoulou Dodd and Anderson suggest that the persistence, despite considerable evidence to the contrary, of this idea of the entrepreneur 'operating as an atomised individual – sometimes maverick, often non-conforming, but single-handedly relentlessly pursuing opportunity – is an ideological convenience', the endurance of which is an example of 'mumpsimus': 'someone who sticks obstinately to their old ways, despite the clearest evidence that they are wrong'.[54] They have examined the 'individualistic myth' and suggest that it is underpinned both by the popular image, often reinforced by newspaper journalism, of the entrepreneur as a solitary battler and by academic studies which echo the individualistic explanations of psychology and economics,[55] using the individual as the unit of analysis. Such studies, they also suggest, 'remain superficially attractive because of the conflation, perhaps even confusion, of description of entrepreneurial behaviour and cause'.[56]

Perhaps it depends on what is meant by an entrepreneur and whether the perceived heroic or stellar entrepreneur is in the same category as anyone else who starts a business. Many people believe that they know a 'heroic' entrepreneur when they see one and can probably name some famous examples, but those judgements appear to be subjective and not susceptible to scientific measurement. In contrast, the act of starting a business is relatively easy to measure and so is often what is reported in statistics on the levels of 'entrepreneurship'. Then there is also a distinction between the process and the end result. Should an activity be classified as entrepreneurial because of the way it is done or because of its result, such as a new business? True entrepreneurial activity, it has been said, often results in failure. Among entrepreneurs, according to Handy, the successful ones have nine failures for every success but it is only the successes that you will hear about, and the failures they credit to experience. Oil companies, he reports, expect to drill nine empty wells for every one that flows, and thus getting it wrong is a key part of getting it right[57] (see the exploration approach in Chapter 11).

A combination

One way of representing the three possible explanations of nature alone, nurture alone or a combination of both nature and nurture might be represented by the three models in Illustration 4.1. If becoming an entrepreneur is due to nature alone, it might be supposed that people are born either entrepreneurs or not entrepreneurs and that their potential to be an entrepreneur can be shown as black or white.

The nurture case is easier to represent because, if becoming an entrepreneur is due solely to environmental factors, then everyone must be born with the same potential, represented by a uniform shade of grey.

However, it can be argued that nature should not necessarily be shown as black or white because entrepreneurial potential might be like height, which clearly has a strong hereditary basis, and people don't have to be either tall or short but can be somewhere in between. This is shown in Model C. It suggests that some people are strongly predisposed towards entrepreneurial behaviour, whether for reasons of their genetic make-up or early-stage influences, and some people have very little such potential, for the same reasons. It further suggests that many people will lie in the middle with some potential which will be realised or not depending on environmental factors. Model C thus has the attraction of being consistent both with the belief that there are some 'heroic' entrepreneurs while also allowing for an environmental influence on many people. (See also Figure 9.2, which further develops Model C.)

ILLUSTRATION 4.1 – THREE MODELS OF ENTREPRENEURIAL POTENTIAL

Model A presents a black and white perspective, consistent with the case for nature. It assumes that people are either entrepreneurs or they are not. Another underlying assumption is that very many more people fall into the 'non-entrepreneur' category than the 'entrepreneur' category.	Entrepreneurs Non-entrepreneurs
Model B is consistent with the nurture argument. It suggests that, instead of things being either black or white, everything is a uniform shade of grey. Everyone has an equal capacity to be an entrepreneur: all they need is the right development experience.	Everyone
Model C suggests that entrepreneurial potential lies in a spectrum with some people having little or no potential and others having so much potential as to be instinctive entrepreneurs, but with most people being somewhere in between with at least some potential.	Instinctive Entrepreneurs Potential Entrepreneurs Non-entrepreneurs

CONCLUSIONS

In his book on entrepreneurship, Shane explains that:

> A central premise of this book is that the failure of academics to offer a coherent conceptual framework for entrepreneurship has resulted from a tendency of researchers to look at only one part of entrepreneurial process – the characteristics of the entrepreneurs themselves, the opportunities to which they respond, their strategies, their resource acquisition or their organizing processes – without consideration for whether the explanations that they offer have any explanatory power for, or even relationship to, the other parts of the entrepreneurial process examined by other researchers.

> Perhaps the largest part of this problem lies with the division of the field of entrepreneurship into two camps: those who want the field of entrepreneurship to focus exclusively on individuals and those who want the field of entrepreneurship to focus exclusively on external forces.[58]

The summary above indicates that the discussion about whether becoming an entrepreneur is due to nature or nurture may have been stimulated by a focus on individuals and the suggestion that entrepreneurial tendency could be the result of genetically determined traits. Despite some considerable investigation, that hypothesis does not seem to have been conclusively demonstrated, but neither has it been entirely disproved. Nevertheless some people appear to have concluded that if it isn't clearly nature, it must be nurture, presumably on the basis that it has to be one or the other. Others, presumably thinking primarily of 'heroic' entrepreneurs, still insist that entrepreneurs are born like that.

This review of the nature versus nurture argument suggests that it would be reasonable to conclude that entrepreneurial behaviour is not exclusively genetically determined. (Although, particularly in the case of apparently 'heroic' entrepreneurs, genetics may play a part as many doubt that their actions can be learned – but that is a very limited category.) That implies that nurture also has a part to play and that, for some people at least, their environment can have an impact on the likelihood of them engaging in entrepreneurial behaviour. Therefore a reasonable working hypothesis does seems to be that, while some people may become entrepreneurs despite any environmental discouragement, and some people may never engage in it despite considerable encouragement, for some people, possibly many people, environmental factors will have an influence on whether they become entrepreneurs or not. It does not indicate, however, what particular environmental factors might have such an influence or how strong their influence might be. This issue is considered further in Chapter 9. In conclusion it should be noted that, despite all of the research and other work carried out in this field, none of it produces a confident prediction of who will, or will not, become an entrepreneur, or of their success in such endeavours.

It is also relevant to this debate to consider what sort of entrepreneurs are being discussed. As indicated above, some people, when they refer to entrepreneurs or to engaging in entrepreneurship, have in mind archetypical 'heroic' or 'stellar' entrepreneurs such as Bill Gates or Richard Branson and the sort of career paths they have followed. Thus, because they don't think that approach can be learnt, they argue for a genetic predisposition. However, that is a very limited category of entrepreneurs, and this book generally takes being an entrepreneur to be the application of enterprising attributes for the economic advancement of oneself and/or others, and even their application in contexts such as sport, exploration or art (i.e. E1 or even E0 in Table 3.4 and Figure 3.2).

Stellar entrepreneurs are not a separate E number within the Table 3.4 categorisation as, instead, they can be found in many categories. Those entrepreneurs who sometimes seem to be the most different from stellar entrepreneurs, the self-employed, can also be found in all categories at least up to E3. To show how stellar entrepreneurs and the self-employed might be seen in a born or made spectrum, and how they might compare to professional managers, Figure 4.4 is suggested – it links five attributes across that spectrum (see also Hornaday's three types of owner in Figure 3.1).

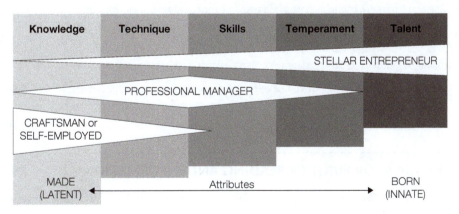

Figure 4.4 Nature or nurture?

With thanks to W. K. Bolton and J. L. Thompson, *Entrepreneurs: Talent, Temperament, Techniques* (Oxford: Butterworth-Heinemann, 2000).

☛ THE KEY POINTS OF CHAPTER 4

- Enterprise is generally recognised in the outcomes of acts by enterprising individuals. They can be called enterprising outcomes. They can be seen in the narrower definition of enterprise, synonymous with being an entrepreneur, or small business formation, and in the wider approach of enterprise, which applies to any task that is non-routine and goal-directed and is accomplished in a determined and adventurous manner.

- Enterprise activity is dependent on enterprising individuals. There have been many studies and approaches to analysing what makes some individuals more enterprising than others. They include:
  - Economic theories.
  - Personality theories considering traits in individuals that predispose them to enterprise, psycho-dynamic approaches that look at the enterprising personality, social-psychological approaches that allow for the context in which an individual operates.
  - Sociological approaches which consider the opportunities for and constraints on career choices.
  - Behavioural theories, including the competencies approach.
  - Integrated approaches which combine a number of different factors.

- All these approaches offer some insight into what makes an individual act in an enterprising way. The integrated approaches offer potentially the most useful models for examining the process of enterprise. No approach has yet proved to be helpful in predicting future enterprise or entrepreneurial success.

- Some observers have suggested that genetic make-up plays a large part in determining whether an individual behaves entrepreneurially. Others have suggested that it is largely due to nurture and environmental factors. A possible model of entrepreneurial potential is suggested which combines both these influences.

✓ QUESTIONS, EXERCISES, ESSAY AND DISCUSSION TOPICS

- Critically evaluate the usefulness of trait theory in predicting who will become an entrepreneur.

- Critically evaluate the usefulness of cognitive theories of motivation for those persons charged with increasing the degree of enterprise in a community.

- According to some observers, 'enterprise can't be taught'. So what is the role of academic schools of 'enterprise' and 'entrepreneurship'?

- Based on Krueger's model, what would you do to encourage more entrepreneurial activity? How would this differ from an approach based on the attributes and resources model?

- Using either Krueger's model or the attributes and resources approach, suggest a programme to help individuals to prepare themselves for eventual self-employment.

- If nurture plays a key role in the development of entrepreneurial potential, what is it in the upbringing of 'heroic' entrepreneurs which makes them behave like that?

📖 SUGGESTIONS FOR FURTHER READING AND INFORMATION

W. K. Bolton and J. L. Thompson, *Entrepreneurs: Talent, Temperament, Techniques* (Oxford: Butterworth-Heinemann, 2000).

E. Chell, *Entrepreneurship: Globalisation, Innovation and Development* (London: Thompson Learning, 2000).

E. Chell, *The Entrepreneurial Personality: A Social Construction* (Hove: Routledge, 2008).

S. Carter and D. Jones-Evans, *Enterprise and Small Business* (London: Pearson Education, 2nd edition, 2005) Chapters 8, 10 and 11.

R. Branson, *Losing My Virginity* (London: Virgin Books, 1999).

A. Roddick (with R. Miller), *Body and Soul* (London: Ebury Press, 1991).

www.dyson.com – the website for James Dyson and the innovatory Dyson appliances.

REFERENCES

[1] D. C. McClelland, 'Achievement Motivation Can Be Developed', *Harvard Business Review*, Vol. 43, November–December 1965, pp. 6–24.

[2] Ibid. p. 7.

[3] P. F. Drucker, *Innovation and Entrepreneurship* (London: Heinemann, 1985) p. 128.

[4] E. Chell, J. Haworth and S. Brearley, *The Entrepreneurial Personality: Concepts, Cases, and Categories* (London: Routledge, 1991).

[5] M. Simon, S. M. Houghton and K. Aquino, 'Cognitive Biases, Risk Perception and Venture Formation: How Individuals Decided to Start Companies', *Journal of Business Venturing*, Vol. 15, 1999, pp. 113–134.

[6] One of the statements used in a questionnaire designed by J. Rotter, 'Generalised Expectancies for Internal Versus External Control of Reinforcement', *Psychological Monographs*, Vol. 80, 1966, pp. 1–27.

[7] For a recent review of research on locus of control see S. Cromie, 'Assessing Entrepreneurial Inclinations: Some Approaches and Empirical Evidence', *European Journal of Work and Organisational Psychology*, Vol. 9, 2000, pp. 7–30.

[8] See F. Delmar, 'The Psychology of the Entrepreneur', in S. Carter and D. Evans-Jones (eds), *Enterprise and Small Business* (London: Pearson Education, 2000) for a discussion on this concept.

[9] See comments by respondents in S. Cromie, 'Motivation of Aspiring Male and Female Entrepreneurs', *Journal of Organisational Behaviour*, Vol. 8, 1987, pp. 251–261.

[10] Ibid.

[11] Ibid.

[12] D. Miller, 'Strategy Making and Structure: Analysis and Implications for Performance', *Academy of Management Journal*, Vol. 38, 1987, pp. 7–32. See p. 32 for a scale to measure proactivity.

[13] F. Delmar, 'The Psychology of the Entrepreneur', in S. Carter and D. Jones-Evans (eds) *Enterprise and Small Business* (London: Pearson Education, 2000) pp. 132–153.

[14] S. Shane, *A General Theory of Entrepreneurship* (Cheltenham: Edward Elgar, 2003) pp. 2–3.

[15] E. Chell, *The Entrepreneurial Personality: A Social Construction* (London: Routledge, 2008).

[16] M. Kets de Vries, 'The Entrepreneurial Personality: A Person at the Crossroads', *Journal of Management Studies*, Vol. 14, 1977, pp. 34–57.

[17] A. MacNabb, *Entrepreneurial Profiling* (Belfast: Institute for Enterprise Strategies, 1993).

[18] M. J. K. Stanworth and J. Curran, 'Growth and the Small Firm – An Alternative View', *Journal of Management Studies*, Vol.13, 1976, pp. 95–110.

[19] A. K. Roberts, 'The Social Conditions, Consequences and Limitations of Careers Guidance', *British Journal of Guidance and Counselling*, Vol. 5, 1977, pp. 1–9,

[20] J. Stanworth and C. Gray (eds), *Bolton 20 Years On: The Small Firm in the 1990s* (London: Paul Chapman Publishing Ltd, 1991) p. 174.

[21] F. Delmar, Op. Cit. p. 139.

[22] N. C. Boyd and G. S. Vozikis, 'The Influence of Self-efficacy on the Development of Entrepreneurial Intentions and Actions', *Entrepreneurship: Theory and Practice*, Vol. 18, 1994, pp. 63–78.

[23] Ibid.

[24] See R. Boyatzis, *The Competent Manager* (New York, NY: Wiley, 1982) and *Management Charter Initiative, Management Standards Implementation Pack* (London: MCI, 1991).

[25] See, for instance, I. Ajzen, 'Attitudes, Traits, and Actions: Dispositional Prediction of Behaviour in Personality and Social Psychology', *Advances in Experimental Social Psychology*, Vol. 20, 1987, pp. 1–63.

[26] N. Krueger and A. Carsrud, 'Entrepreneurial Intentions: Applying the Theory of Planned Behaviour', *Entrepreneurship and Regional Development*, Vol. 5, No. 4, 1993, p. 315.

[27] N. Krueger, M. Reilly and A. Carsrud, 'Competing Models of Entrepreneurial Intentions', *Journal of Business Venturing*, Vol. 15, No. 2, 2000, p. 411.

[28] N. F. Krueger, *Prescription for Opportunity: How Communities Can Create Potential for Entrepreneurs* (Washington, DC: Small Business Foundation of America, Working Paper 93-03, 1995).

[29] See, for instance, D. Smallbone and P. Wyer, 'Growth and Development in the Small Firm', in S. Carter and D. Jones-Evans, Op. Cit. p. 413.

[30] F. Delmar, Op. Cit. p. 147.

[31] M. Brown, 'Risky Business', *Holland Herald* (the in-flight magazine of KLM).

[32] From an article entitled 'Encouraging Youthful Enterprise', *RSA Journal*, Vol. 1,No. 6, 2002, p. 28.

[33] *The Independent*, 6 June 2006.

[34] D. Deakins, *Entrepreneurship* (London: McGraw-Hill, 1999) p. 18.

[35] E. Chell, Op. Cit. pp. 101, 200.

[36] Ibid. p. 87.

[37] E. Stam, 'Entrepreneurship, Evolution and Geography', *Papers on Economics and Evolution*, edited by the Evolutionary Economics Group, Max Planck Institute, Jena, 2009, p. 8.

[38] NESTA, *Creating Entrepreneurship: Entrepreneurship Education for the Creative Industries*. Written and published by the Higher Education Academy Art Design Media Subject Centre and the National Endowment for Science, Technology and the Arts, 2007, p. 26.

[39] E. Chell, Op. Cit. p. 83.

[40] S. Shane, *A General Theory of Entrepreneurship* (Cheltenham: Edward Elgar, 2003) p. 3.

[41] E. Chell, Op. Cit. p. 200.

[42] E. Stam, Op. Cit. p. 2.

[43] S. Bridge, *Rethinking Enterprise Policy: Can Failure Trigger New Understanding?* (Basingstoke: Palgrave Macmillan, 2010) Chapter 7.

[44] D. Goleman, *Social Intelligence* (London: Arrow, 2007) p. 156.

[45] See, for instance, D. Goleman, Op. Cit. p. 154–161.

[46] See for instance T. Spector, *Identically Different: Why You Can Change Your Genes* (London: Weidenfeld & Nicholson, 2012).

[47] N. Nicolaou and S. Shane, 'Can Genetic Factors Influence the Likelihood of Engaging in Entrepreneurial Activity?' *Journal of Business Venturing*, Vol. 24, 2009, p. 2.

[48] Ibid. p. 17.

[49] S. Drakopoulou Dodd and A. Anderson, 'Mumpsimus and the Mything of the Individualistic Entrepreneur', *International Small Business Journal*, Vol. 25, No. 4, August 2007, p. 342.

[50] R. E. White, S. Thornhill and E. Hampson, 'A Biosocial Model of Entrepreneurship', *Journal of Organizational Behavior*, Vol. 28, No. 4, 2007, p. 461.

[51] T. Cooney, 'Editorial: What Is an Entrepreneurial Team?', *International Small Business Journal*, Vol. 23, No. 3, pp. 226–235.

[52] S. Drakopoulou Dodd and A. Anderson, Op. Cit. p. 352.

[53] M. Kets de Vries, 'Creative Rebels with a Cause', in S. Birley and D. Muzyka (eds), *Mastering Enterprise* (London: Financial Times Prentice Hall/Pearson Education, 1997) p. 8.

[54] S. Drakopoulou Dodd and A. Anderson, Op. Cit. p. 341–342.

[55] Ibid. p. 349.

[56] Ibid. p. 349.

[57] C. Handy, *The Age of Unreason* (London, Arrow, 1990) p. 55.

[58] S. Shane, Op. Cit. p. 2.

Companion website

Please visit the companion website at www.palgravehighered.com/Bridge-UE-5e for access to additional learning and teaching materials.

Small Businesses: Their Characteristics and Variety

CONTENTS

- Introduction
- Why small businesses are important
- The distinctive characteristics of small business
- Issues of definition
- The variety of small businesses
- In conclusion
- Annex – Family, women-owned and ethnic businesses

KEY CONCEPTS

This chapter covers:

- The reasons why small businesses are of interest, including the economic and social benefits they can provide.
- The distinctive characteristics of small businesses, the implications of being small and the key areas of difference between small and big business.
- The main definitions of a small business.
- The variety of small businesses, including family firms, women-owned firms, ethnic firms and other categorisations.

LEARNING OBJECTIVES

By the end of this chapter the reader should:

- Know why interest in small businesses has grown.
- Be aware of the distinguishing features of small businesses and understand the main ways in which they differ from big businesses.
- Appreciate the variety of small businesses and the particular issues relevant to them.

INTRODUCTION

Chapter 2 presents a brief summary of some of the key inputs to, and triggers for, our current understanding of enterprise, entrepreneurship and small business. Chapters 3 and 4 explore the enterprise and entrepreneurship aspect of this understanding, including the vocabulary used in talking about them. Although it is entrepreneurs who create and run small businesses, and so are the crucial factor in determining small business actions, it is upon small businesses that attention often focuses as they are thought to be the source of many economic and other benefits. This chapter considers therefore a number of key aspects of small businesses, including their importance and their characteristics, definitions and variety. Chapter 6 then reviews the stages of their development as enterprises.

WHY SMALL BUSINESSES ARE IMPORTANT

> Small and medium-sized enterprises (SMEs) are the backbone of Europe's economy. They represent 99% of all businesses in the EU. In the past five years, they have created around 85% of new jobs and provided two-thirds of the total private sector employment in the EU. The European Commission considers SMEs and entrepreneurship as key to ensuring economic growth, innovation, job creation, and social integration in the EU.
>
> European Commission[1]

Although, as Chapter 2 indicates, the role of the entrepreneur does not seem to have been specifically recorded until the writing of Cantillon in the 18th century, it is clear that entrepreneurs have been around for a long time before that. Businesses also have been part of economic life for a very long time – Chapter 2 reports one surviving business which is known to be over 800 years old – and throughout history most businesses have been small businesses.

The current interest in small businesses as a specific category of business is much more recent, however. At the same time as Cantillon was writing about entrepreneurs, the Industrial Revolution was getting under way in Britain. One of its results was a trend in business towards bigger units which provided economies of scale and led, in the 20th century, to the integrated operations of Fordism and the consequent and seemingly inevitable decline of the small business. It was because of worries about their survival as a sector that, in 1969 in Britain, Bolton was tasked to investigate their role and special functions.

The Bolton Committee reported that small businesses were in a state of long-term decline but were of inestimable value to the vitality of society. It became clear subsequently that, by the time Bolton was appointed, the decline of small businesses had actually halted. It is also relevant to note that Bolton focused on businesses rather than entrepreneurs, not least because the remit he was given was to consider the role of small firms. Nevertheless the appointment of Bolton represents the beginning, at least in the UK, of government interest in small business which was reinforced ten years later when, at a time of rising unemployment, Birch reported that in the USA small businesses were the main source of net new jobs.

Bolton identified eight important economic functions of small businesses (see Table 2.1), although this did not include employment creation. Subsequent research has identified other benefits, such as those summarised in Table 5.1. In consequence, there now seems to be general agreement that small businesses offer significant benefits for an economy. Other research appears to show that it is new or young businesses, rather than small businesses per se, which create most net new jobs but, as most new or young businesses are small, that does not lessen the need to understand them.

An early contribution to the understanding of small businesses, as a category distinct from big businesses, came from Edith Penrose. Before the Bolton Committee was appointed she had already published her work on the growth of the firm in which she pointed out that small businesses are structured and behave very differently from big ones. Subsequently the interest triggered in particular by Birch's findings led to a resurgence of interest in small businesses, to their 'rediscovery' as a significant component of economies, and to the funding of support programmes for them and of research into them.

That interest and research has, in turn, produced much information about the nature of small business. This includes identifying distinguishing characteristics and common factors inherent to their size – and these are summarised in the chapter. Nevertheless as a category they are more heterogeneous than homogeneous so some of their different varieties are also described.

Table 5.1 *More benefits of small businesses*

The recent recognition given to small businesses might have been at first for the employment they create, but other benefits of small businesses have been recognised:

Competition:	In an economy in which even larger, multi-product businesses are emerging, small businesses provide competition, both actual and potential, and provide some check on monopoly profits and on the inefficiency which monopoly breeds. In this way they contribute to the efficient working of the economic system as a whole.
Consumer choice:	The small business sector, by generating competition, widens choice for consumers. This is particularly true for products or services tailored to the desires of small groups of consumers, since larger businesses tend to look for opportunity for large-scale production and ignore specialist niches.
Developers of local economies:	Small businesses frequently employ local people and use local services and suppliers. Moreover the owners may well live locally and so feel an allegiance to their areas, being thus less likely to relocate jobs as well as providing other social benefits to the local community. Small businesses can provide jobs in areas where few big businesses operate, such as very rural areas, and in this way they can distribute jobs more widely.
Individual outlet:	Small businesses provide a productive outlet for the energies of those enterprising people who want economic independence. Many of them are antipathetic or not suited to employment in a large organisation but have much to contribute to the vitality of the economy.
Personal services:	Small businesses supply a range of personal and community services, such as those of restaurants, window cleaning, household repairs and local corner shops. Most artists are, in effect, small businesses, as also are legal and medical practices, and they and similar ventures are essential to the way of life many people enjoy.
Seedbed for new industries:	The small business sector is the traditional breeding ground for new industries – that is for innovation writ large. Small businesses provide the means of entry into business for new entrepreneurial talent and the seedbed from which new large companies will grow to challenge and stimulate the established leaders of industry.
Source of innovation:	Until recently the prevalent view was that large businesses dominate in the process of innovation. Over the last 25 years, however, various empirical studies have revealed that 'small firms can keep up with large firms in the field of innovation', albeit to varying extents in different sectors.[2]
Source of stability:	The sector is also perceived as contributing to economic and social stability, not only through its employment-creating capacity, but also by offering a means of social and community cohesion. Indeed in the United States, when the Small Business Administration was being created over 50 years ago, the sector was described as vital 'to the security of the nation'.
Specialist supplier:	Many small businesses act as specialist suppliers to large companies of components or sub-assemblies, produced at lower cost than the large companies could achieve. Small firms add greatly to the variety of products and services offered to the consumer because they can flourish in a limited or specialised market which it would not be worthwhile for a large firm to enter.

Small businesses and job creation

Although other benefits of small businesses have been highlighted (see Table 5.1) their potential role in job creation is still a key reason for interest in them. Birch's report in 1979 that it was small, rather than big, businesses which were the major net creators of new jobs is summarised in Chapter 2. However, as that chapter also indicates, Birch's findings have not been universally accepted. Two questions in particular are still debated: first, what is the extent of the overall contribution of small businesses to job creation; and second, does this contribution come, in the main, from all small businesses or from only a few of them? The first question is about the validity of Birch's work and its application to other countries such as the UK, and the second is about which small businesses create most jobs. These questions are very relevant to the targeting of government intervention to promote employment, but the answers are not always clear – not least because of the insight sometimes needed if small business statistics are to be interpreted properly.

The validity of Birch

Birch's original work concluded that about 80 per cent of all net new jobs in the USA between 1969 and 1976 were created by firms with 100 or fewer employees (and two-thirds by firms with 20 or fewer employees).[3] Armington and Odle subsequently looked at job creation results for 1978–1980 using a database specially created by the US Small Business Administration (SBA) and found that less than 40 per cent of net new jobs were created by businesses with fewer than a hundred employees. They had no explanation for the discrepancy with Birch's figures, but speculated that Birch may have made errors. Subsequently, Armington and Odle have been cited as experts who found Birch to be in error, but, according to Kirchhoff, what is less commented on is that their subsequent research validated Birch and showed that percentages calculated in their way were cyclical.[4] Subsequent work appears to show that fluctuations in the economy of the USA reveal themselves mainly through job changes in larger firms and that small businesses are consistent net creators of jobs.

Sixteen years after Birch, Kirchhoff stated that, 'It seems safe to say that, on average, firms with less (sic) than 100 employees create the majority of net new jobs in the US economy.'[5] However, the debate still continues. While in 2014 an OECD paper based on a database across 18 countries reported that 'only young businesses – predominately small – create a disproportionate number of jobs',[6] in 2013 Haltiwanger *et al.* had reported that using data from the US Census Bureau they had found no systematic relationship between firm size and growth.[7]

In the UK the position seems to be broadly similar. One analysis indicated 'that during the 1987–9 period, 54 per cent of the increase in employment was in firms with fewer than 20 workers'.[8] In the UK, however, all components of employment change are of lower magnitude than in the USA, and job change in the latter is more strongly influenced by births and deaths, especially of large businesses, whereas in the UK job change 'is more influenced by expansions and contractions'.[9]

More recently Anyadike-Danes *et al.* returned to the theme and, in an attempt to answer the question 'what types of firms create the most jobs in the UK economy?', found that:

> The majority of jobs in the UK were created by small firms (i.e. less [sic] than 50 employees and including micro-enterprises); and these firms also recorded the most churn – the sum of job creation and destruction – which has intensified since 2008. Since the late 1990s smaller firms have been increasing their share of total employment year on year and in 2010 their share was triple that of 1998.[10]

Other analysis issues

Dynamic versus static analysis. One reason why Birch's findings were surprising was that they were contrary to previous thinking on job creation. They were also based on a dynamic analysis, while the previous research was carried out using static analysis. The difference may be illustrated by considering a business employing 70 people which over a period grows by 50 per cent to employ 105 people. At the beginning it would have been classified in the 1 to 100 employee size range, but at the end it is in the 100-plus size range. The effect of its growth is thus to reduce by 70 the number of jobs in businesses in the 1 to 100 size range, and increase by 105 the number of jobs in businesses in the higher size range. Hence the static statistics will show a reduction of jobs in businesses in the lower size range and an increase in the higher size range, but the reality is that the net increase came from a business that was in the lower size range. Static analysis assumes implicitly that the net inter-class movement of businesses is negligible, which may not be the case.

Cohort analysis. Cohort, or dynamic, analysis, in which a class of subjects is tracked as it changes over time, will avoid the problem of static research analysis. It will also reveal other interesting features of growth. For instance dynamic analysis of US small businesses has indicated that survival rates of businesses improve exponentially with, for an original group founded at the same time, a smaller proportion terminating in each successive year. It has also indicated that less than half of the surviving businesses show any growth in the first six years, but that at between six and eight years of age the number of businesses that show growth increases significantly: a result that confirms suggestions of the 'seven lean years' of business development and indicates that observing business survival and growth over a lesser period may be misleading.

Linked ownership. Another factor which is relevant when looking for growth is highlighted in the work of Rosa and Scott on multiple business ownership. They suggest that if the unit of analysis is the business, which it often is, then this will not provide a full picture. Instead they suggest that the unit of analysis should be the entrepreneur, or team of entrepreneurs, who may start several businesses. They talk of clusters of businesses with linked ownership in which 'diversifying into additional businesses may not only be common but may also be associated with positive growth strategies'.[11] This means that growth by an entrepreneur already in business can occur through new business creation rather than through the growth of already established businesses – and that would not be picked up by an analysis focused on business units.

Business age. A further source of challenge to Birch's findings lies in attempts to explore the relevance of the age of businesses as a factor in employment creation. This issue was raised, for instance, by Storey and Johnston[12] and more recently by Haltiwanger *et al*. The latter used US data and claim to have found that 'once we control for firm age there is no systematic relationship between firm size and growth'.[13] But even if it is young firms that create the most jobs then, because most young firms are also small, this still means that most new jobs are created by small firms. Also Anyadike-Danes *et al*. point out that 'UK data suggests that even though age might be critical, size still plays an important role in accounting for job creation'.[14]

Which small businesses create jobs?

Because small businesses are believed to create significant proportions of net new jobs, governments and others trying to increase employment want to support them. However, there are very many small businesses, and support would be spread thinly if it went to all of them. Also research indicates that it is a relatively small proportion of new starts which, over time, create a disproportionate share of the jobs. In the UK in 1994, Storey asserted that 'out of every 100 [new] small firms, the fastest growing four firms will create 50 per cent of the jobs in the group over a decade'.[15] The implication of this is that if support could be focused on those four businesses, or on the few businesses that had the potential for such growth, it would be applied much more effectively than if all 100 businesses were to be supported. These high-growth businesses are those that Birch called 'gazelles'.

Storey's statement needs to be examined with some care, however. He himself pointed out that the data it was based on were rather old. He also acknowledged that the data referred only to manufacturing businesses and then only to new ones. Further his statement does not mean that 4 per cent of small businesses create 50 per cent of the jobs, just 50 per cent of the jobs still existing in a cohort of businesses ten years after they were started – so the total number of jobs created in the ten year period will also include the jobs in the businesses which did not survive that long. Also if the seven lean year theory holds (see above), then by taking only new business starts and looking at their employment after ten years, Storey and others may be missing from their 'high-growth' business category those businesses which do not start to grow until after six years or more.

Nevertheless efforts to identify the key sources of jobs continue, and in 2009 NESTA produced a report which claimed that '6 per cent of UK businesses with the highest growth rates generated half of the new jobs created by existing businesses between 2002 and 2008'.[16] That NESTA report, which was based on work by Anyadike-Danes *et al*. has, however, been criticised by Urwin who notes that it only includes businesses with at least ten employees at the start of the analysis period and businesses which exhibit consistently high growth rates over three years.[17] Botham and Bridge also note specifically in relation to NESTA's 6 per cent that the growth assessed has been systematically exaggerated (by accident or design) for instance by including growth by acquisition.[18] Urwin's conclusion is that in the UK there is 'only a one-in-a-thousand chance that a new firm will become a large firm' and that 'furthermore, it is impossible to predict which firms will become successful'.[19]

Nevertheless the pursuit of growth continues, and further reports continue to be produced from a variety of sources. In this context the following comment by one of those sources may therefore be relevant:

> Throughout the long history of work on job creation and the on-going debates about how the metrics should be defined and used there is a nagging question which does need to be addressed. Namely, what does this methodology actually contribute to our understanding of how a private sector evolves over time, over and above the allocation of jobs to particular types of firms? It is an accounting framework pure and simple and so does not itself provide an explanation of the phenomena it measures. Indeed, that was the view first put forward by Birch 35 years ago. However, where we need to take the 'outputs' from these seemingly simplistic metrics on job creation is to connect them to a theoretical framework which enables us to understand the dynamic processes as the private sector evolves and generates growth over time. Of particular interest is to use the data on job creation (or job flows) and harness theoretical frameworks from labour market economics, macroeconomics and industrial organisation to this end: this appears most readily achievable through the body of literature on employer life-cycle dynamics.[20]

Summary

It is clear that, right or not, Birch's work has been the trigger for much current interest in small businesses and there is evidence that new small businesses do create a disproportionate amount of new employment. However, different researchers vary in their estimates of how much, and there appear to be variations over time and across countries. It is not yet clear whether this employment over longer time periods is due mainly to only a small proportion of that small business population or to all of it. This lack of clarity may be due to different researchers measuring different things and to their findings being misinterpreted or misrepresented.

Care needs to be taken therefore in interpreting figures. Differential results are, in large part, built into the methodologies. For instance how the category of 'high-growth firms' is defined affects results. Definitions based on sales growth will differ from those based on employment growth. Definitions based on employment growth rates as opposed to absolute employment growth will favour smaller firms but credit less employment to the category than if absolute employment growth at the level of the individual firms was measured. Also, while on average net new jobs may come from small businesses, the performance of the large firms sector and the fluctuations in its employment will also have a significant impact on the overall employment position.

THE DISTINCTIVE CHARACTERISTICS OF SMALL BUSINESSES

> The differences in the administrative structure of the very small and the very large firms are so great that in many ways it is hard to see that the two species are of the same genus. ... We cannot define a caterpillar and then use the same definition for a butterfly.
>
> Dame Edith Penrose[21]

Small businesses may be defined by their size (see next section) but, as Penrose points out, their distinctive characteristics lie not in that size, but in the manner in which they behave differently from larger businesses. Although there are many varied categories of small businesses they do share a set of characteristics which distinguish them from other businesses. They are in many respects a separate category, not mini versions of large businesses. As such they behave differently and need to be treated appropriately. For instance:

Organisation structure and management

Top-down. In a small business the dominant position of the owner-manager can create a person-centred culture. Consequently the strategy, or absence of one, for the business will correspond to that of this person. This top-down approach can be attractive in a stable environment if the owner articulates a vision that motivates others. Increasingly, however, even in small businesses, it is intelligent employees, more than the owners, who are in touch with the latest technological, economic and sociological developments. Considerable decision-making discretion, even at the strategic level, may have to be delegated to these individuals, but entrepreneurs are notoriously reluctant to share their power. In a world of discontinuous change, that is a drawback.[22]

Organisational structures. In large organisations much of the work is highly specialised, but an extensive division of tasks, especially at management level, only makes sense when there is a large volume of work: it is not economic to hire experts if they are under-employed. By definition, small businesses do not have large volumes of output and work must be done by generalists. Furthermore, organisations tend to perpetuate the fruits of their learning and standardise regularly recurring activities; although this is sensible only when conditions are stable. In the turbulent environment so characteristic of the small business, change is the order of the day and problem solving is a higher requirement of organisations than efficiency.[23] Because of this, small businesses tend to have simple, flexible, non-differentiated structures and work practices.

Informal systems and procedures. Many businesses start with one person, for whom formal systems and procedures will seem unnecessary. They will grow by taking on new employees, one or two at a time, and it would seem strange to introduce formal systems for just a few people, who will learn what is going on quickly enough through their direct involvement. In any case the owner-manager is probably too busy to introduce more formal systems for running the business. Control of issues such as production, quality, finance, customer service and employee performance is often informal and done by 'feel' rather than procedure. This state of affairs is likely to continue until a crisis arises because the business has grown too big to be run informally. As many small businesses never get to that stage, informality in systems and procedures is a characteristic that they share.

Control. If the standardisation, performance measurement, bureaucratic structures and/or all-pervasive control mechanisms of large organisations are absent, how do managers in small businesses exercise control? Often the close presence of the owners, or their representatives, will mean that control is exercised by direct supervision. However, this often leads to much speedier decision-making and shorter reaction times, which in turn can mean an improved competitive edge.[24]

Strategy and decision-making

Ambition. In terms of their behaviour, however, the biggest difference between small and big businesses is likely to be that which results from the ambition and goals of their owners and managers. The larger the business, the more likely it is to be run by a professional management trying to maximise its value. The converse is that the smaller the business, the more likely it is that it will be run by an owner-manager with an aim based on personal values. (This issue is explored further in Chapter 8.)

A lack of objectivity. A key feature of small businesses is the inability, or unwillingness, of their owners to be objective about them. Instead they frequently identify closely with their businesses, seeing them almost as extensions of themselves. As indicated above, a big business is more likely to be run by a professional management trying to maximise its value, whereas in a small business decisions are influenced more by the needs, desires and abilities of the entrepreneur than by reason. For this reason, many observers will regard the entrepreneur as a critical influence on the growth prospects of the business.

Decision-making. In a bigger business, strategic, administrative and operational decision-making can each happen at different levels and involve different people. In small businesses they are often all done by the same person – risking a lack of clarity about the type of decision being taken, with little distinction in thought between strategic and tactical decisions. In small businesses the omnipresence of the owner(s) can mean that everyone in the business can hear a clear articulation of the goals and objectives, but a lack of managerial skills can also mean that goals are not articulated at all. Moreover a lack of resource in small businesses, and their heavy reliance on information gleaned from personal contacts, often means that the information available to decision-makers may be even more inaccurate, incomplete and time-bounded than in other organisations.[25]

Lack of planning. Typically there is a lack of time devoted to planning, especially medium-to long-term planning, whereas large organisations can have whole departments devoted to it. Short planning horizons dominate, with the emphasis often being on survival as opposed to growth. The result tends to be a reactive, not proactive, approach sometimes described as opportunistic as opposed to strategic in nature. In effect, change, where it occurs, is likely to be the response to short-term need rather than the result of long-term strategy.

Limited knowledge of the business environment. Small businesses, labouring under heavy time constraints with small management teams and a lack of specialist staff, can display limited knowledge of changes in the business environment which may impinge on their competitiveness.

Operations/production

Discontinuities. There are thresholds and discontinuities in a small business that do not occur in a bigger business. In the latter, for instance, increasing capacity by 10 per cent in a key department to cope with a 10 per cent increase in turnover may be relatively straightforward. In a small business, however, that function may be carried out by just one or two people or machines. Then taking on an extra person or machine would be a 50 per cent increase, which may not be justified by the likely extra return.

Economies of scale. The opportunities to benefit from scale economies are few. Production runs are likely to be short and varied, less mechanised and more labour-intensive. Smaller businesses are less able to take advantage of bulk buying and discounts or to carry additional stock. It is for this reason that smaller businesses sometimes specialise in niches where the absence of scale economies is less likely to be felt and where speed of change offers advantages.

Human resources

An absence of functional managers. Often the management of a small business resides with one person. The advantage of this can be that he or she takes an overall view of the organisation, including production, finance and marketing, instead of there being a conflict between the different functions. On the other hand, knowledge of such functions may not be evenly developed and in some areas may be lacking.

A lack of training. There may be little or no capacity, or willingness, to develop staff. The time needed for formal 'training' or review is seen as both an unaffordable distraction from work and as earning a return that is more theoretical than practical. Indeed the entrepreneurs themselves may have acquired most of their business knowledge on the job. They will often have been in the job a long time and may have a deep experience, but not necessarily a broad one, or an objective and informed view.

Financial resources

A lack of resources. It is almost invariably the case that small businesses lack sufficient resources. Most of them are started on a financial shoestring and few get cash-rich subsequently. They may have little credibility with funders especially at the start-up stage, few assets to provide guarantees and limited knowledge of assistance and support available. There can also be a tendency towards poor cash-flow management. Thus financial resources can be limited and may not be available to carry them through a lean period or to utilise a sudden opportunity for expansion.

Personal capital. The money that is invested in the business is often personal money not that of impersonal investors. There can be a reluctance to spend this money, therefore, on anything except the bare essentials for short-term obvious returns. As a result, more formal investment appraisal methods are not seen as being as useful as a 'feel' for what is right.

Market share

Little influence. Small businesses may be able to respond quickly to changes in their environments or markets but, with rare exceptions, they have very little ability to change them. Bigger businesses may be able to dictate terms to distributors, or may be able to acquire their own distribution channels through 'vertical integration'. Small businesses, however, are at the mercy of their distributors, their suppliers and the forces of competition to a very considerable extent – often described as being price-takers as opposed to price-makers.

Small product range and limited customer base. Especially in their early stages, small businesses can be dependent on a very narrow product/service range and a limited number of customers. This makes the businesses very vulnerable to a product weakness or loss of a key client. Unlike the larger business, they cannot spread their risks across different product ranges and markets. A failure to achieve adequate growth in sales can be made worse by a tendency in entrepreneurs to resist change in the product/service offering, often due to an emotional attachment to it as it is their creation.

ISSUES OF DEFINITION

The above summary of the characteristics of small businesses indicates their distinctive features but does not include any definitions of small businesses. The reason is that generally the definitions seek to encapsulate, or at least be consistent with, the distinctions, rather than the other way around. It might be supposed that small businesses could not be studied in detail until they are defined, in order to be clear about what is being studied. However, the reality is that to at least some extent they have to be studied before they can be defined, because before defining them it is necessary to establish what might be their critical defining characteristics. However, when it comes to counting and measuring them, definitions are needed at the beginning if those counts and measurements are to be consistent.

An early definition of a small business is to be found in the Bolton Report in 1971, which defined a small business by reference to an ideal type:

> First, in economic terms, a small firm is one that has a relatively small share of its market. Secondly an essential characteristic of a small firm is that it is managed by its owners or part-owners in a personalised way, and not through the medium of a formalised management structure. Thirdly, it is also independent in the sense that it does not form part of a larger enterprise and that the owner-managers should be free from outside control in taking their principal decisions.[26]

As might be expected most definitions of small businesses are based on size, as smallness is an aspect of size and size can be relatively easy to measure objectively and consistently. Usually size is assessed by the number of employees, but sometimes turnover, net profit or balance sheet values are used, or a combination of these. However, it is important to recognise that definitions based on size are, or should be, using size only as a proxy for other key distinctions. Interest in small businesses, as Chapter 2 shows, did not arise primarily because they were small but because they were economically important yet behaved differently from big businesses. The trouble is that there is no clear cut-off point between those businesses with small and big business modes of behaviour so any division, in practice, must be somewhat arbitrary.

At the extremes it is clear that one-person independent businesses behave as small businesses, and businesses employing 1000 or more people all behave as big businesses. But, if employment is used as the key dimension, where should the boundary be set? There is a point somewhere between these extremes at which it has been found that organisations tend to change.

Dunbar posited that the expected size of social groups in humans should be about 150 based on the relationship between brain size and group size in a variety of primates. This has come to be known as Dunbar's Number, and since at least Roman times the size of fighting units in armies has been about 100 to 150 men.[27] This seems to be the maximum number that would see itself as a unit, without splintering, and thus the maximum number of people that can comfortably be managed on a one-to-one basis by one manager. However, when it comes to defining a precise limit to size categories of businesses, 5, 10, 15, 50, 100, 250 and 500 employees have all been set as the boundary at different times or for different purposes:

5:    The new limit being suggested by some in the UK and the EU for micro-businesses.

10:    The currently accepted size at which a business in no longer considered to be a micro-business.

15:    The legal definition of small business begins at fewer than 15 employees under the Australian Fair Work Act 2009.

50:    In the UK a small firm has been defined as having up to 49 employees.

100:    Used by Birch as the upper limit for small business in his study of net job creation.

250:    The current limit in the EU definition of SMEs.

500:    The upper limit for small businesses in most manufacturing and mining industries in the USA.

ILLUSTRATION 5.1 – SOME OFFICIAL DEFINITIONS OF A SMALL BUSINESS*

United Kingdom

In the UK, for statistical purposes, the Department for Business, Innovation and Skills and its successor have used the following definitions:

- Micro firm   Up to 9 employees
- Small firm   Up to 49 employees (includes micro)
- Medium firm   50–249 employees
- Large firm   250 employees and over

Companies Act

Sections 382 and 465 of the Companies Act of 2006 state that a company is 'small' if it satisfies at least two of the following criteria:

- a turnover of not more than £6.5 million;
- a balance sheet total of not more than £3.26 million;
- not more than 50 employees.

A medium-sized company must satisfy at least two of the following criteria:

- a turnover of not more than £25.9 million;
- a balance sheet total of not more than £12.9 million;
- not more than 250 employees.

Value added tax

In the UK the VAT registration threshold is an annual turnover of £83,000 and the de-registration limit is a turnover of £81,000 (as at April 2016).

The Enterprise Finance Guarantee Scheme (formerly the Small Firms Loan Guarantee Scheme)

The Enterprise Finance Guarantee Scheme (EFG) supports lending to viable businesses with an annual turnover of up to £41m.

British Bankers' Association (BBA)

For BBA statistical purposes, small businesses are defined (Mar 2008) as those having an annual debit account turnover of up to £1 million per year.

EU Commission

In 2003 the EU Commission adopted the following definitions for SMEs for implementation from 2005:

Maximum	Micro-enterprise	Small	Medium-sized
Number of employees	<10	<50	<250
Turnover (million euro)	2	10	50
Balance sheet total (million euro)	2	10	43
Independence criterion[†]	N/A	25%	25%

[†] The independence criterion refers to the maximum percentage that may be owned by one enterprise, or jointly owned by several enterprises, not satisfying the same criteria.

USA

The US Small Business Administration has adopted size standards for each individual North American Industry Classification System (NAICS) coded industry. This variation is intended to better reflect industry differences. Some common size standards are:

- 500 employees for most manufacturing and mining industries
- 100 employees for wholesale trade industries
- $7.5 million of annual receipts for most retail and service industries (but up to $38.5 million for some) and $36.5 million of annual receipts for most general and heavy construction industries
- $14.5 million of receipts for all special trade contractors
- $0.75 million of receipts for most agricultural industries.

The most recent scheme was originally produced in 2002, but has had amendments integrated on a rolling basis.

*As at 2016 unless otherwise indicated.

The summary of definitions in Illustration 5.1 indicates that, although small businesses have been the subject of considerable interest since the Bolton Report, today there is still no single, clear, precise and widely accepted definition of what a small business is. Different definitions exist, often for different purposes: such as the application of support policy, taxation or legislation. Most of the definitions of a small business given above are, in effect, only attempts to provide a proxy for what is the essence of 'smallness' in business units. Many people, however, feel that they know what is meant by a 'small business': it is one that has few employees, a low turnover, little or no formal structure and is usually managed by one person, who is also the business owner (and the influence of the entrepreneur on business behaviour is explored further in Chapter 8); it is about being autonomous yet having limited resources; and it is about having to cope with greater uncertainty and risk while having few opportunities for risk-spreading. It is these characteristics that make a small business behave in the way it does and which present challenges and opportunities different from those in larger businesses. Therefore the key point at which a growing business ceases to be small is when it has to change its organisational and control system from the loose and informal to the structured and formal.

A note of caution

In conjunction with definitions of small businesses it is important to emphasise that a key problem in studying entrepreneurs and small businesses quantitatively is the availability of appropriate data – because often the data that are available will not correspond to the desired definition. For instance, in order to explore entrepreneurial activity in the UK, many people would like to know how many small businesses there are and the rate at which new ones are started and others terminate. However, the data source often used to indicate this is that of business VAT registrations. Registering for VAT is mandatory for businesses whose turnover exceeds a certain level, whereas businesses with a lower turnover are not obliged to register and many do not. Apart from that turnover threshold, no other indicators of size are conveyed in the data. Thus the VAT requirements do not conform to any other definition of small businesses, and VAT statistics cover neither only small businesses nor every small business. Also new registrations may be new starts or existing businesses whose turnovers have crossed the threshold, and de-registrations may be businesses which are terminating or just those whose turnover has fallen below the threshold. A VAT-registered business which changes legal form, for instance a sole-trader forming a limited company, will have to de-register and then re-register, although there may be no actual change in the level of business activity. Nevertheless VAT statistics have often been used as a proxy to the numbers of new small business starts and terminations, because they are available.

Another problem is that the data borrowed may record the right subject but use a different definition in a different context. For instance when researching the characteristics of fast-growth small business, which is a popular area for researchers, making comparisons between different studies is often problematic because of significant variations in the definitions of 'fast growth'. The terms 'small businesses', 'start-ups', 'self-employment', 'owner-managers', 'entrepreneurs' and 'SMEs' are all frequently used, often apparently interchangeably, but they are not the same, and to explore each fully would require different datasets in each case. Often these are not readily available; therefore, in many cases the distinction is lost in those data which are used.

THE VARIETY OF SMALL BUSINESSES

Despite this emphasis on the features which distinguish small businesses from big businesses, it is clear that small businesses are much more heterogeneous than they are homogeneous. For instance the average size of businesses can differ widely in different industry sectors: in relation to other businesses in the same sector, a 10-person window cleaning business would be very large, while a 100-person car manufacturer would be very small. Examples from Europe show some of the ranges: thus in 1995 the average employment in a coal-mining business was 924, in a railway business 996, and in a communications business 376; but in a travel agency 12, in a retail business 4 and in an estate agency 2.[28] The Bolton Committee preferred qualitative definitions of small businesses and, for such reasons, in its Report offered definitions reluctantly – basing them on industrial classifications. As noted in Illustration 5.1, the Small Business Administration in the USA does the same.

One-person businesses and self-employment

In the UK, at the start of 2015, it was estimated that there were almost 5.4 million private sector businesses, of which 4.1 million (76 per cent) had no employees apart from a self-employed owner-manager or single employee director.[29]

The Bank of England reports that data suggests 'that around 15% of the workforce is self-employed. Increases in self-employment have accounted for around a third of the increase in employment since 2010'.[30] However, despite these enterprises being officially categorised as businesses and the people concerned as self-employed, many of them might be closer to being employees of someone else's business than proprietors of their own.

According to Urwin, the distinction between 'employees' and the 'self-employed' can be traced back to the advent of industrial relations at the start of the 20th century. Before this, in the early years of the Industrial Revolution, those supplying labour were essentially self-employed – and the distinction only arose when employers needed to exercise greater control over larger numbers of works and so sought to have contracts of employment instead of contracts of service. In return, groups of employed workers organised to secure things like employment protection, holiday pay and sick leave.[31] While at first glance it might seem straightforward to characterise the difference between those who are self-employed and those working as employees, Urwin suggests that it is still a grey area which the tax authorities in the UK (HM Revenue & Customs) seek to clarify.[32]

Thus among the approximately four million one-person businesses in the UK there will be many people who are much closer to being employees than initiators of new entrepreneurial ventures. There will also be some legitimate businesses operated by people who sell their skills to a number of separate clients but who do not have plans to grow the business by taking on other employees or branching out into new areas, and there are some part-time businesses run by people who are also full-time employees of someone else. Thus the descriptions 'one-person business' and 'self-employed' cover a variety of different forms of enterprise.

Family, women-owned and ethnic businesses

(More information on family, women-owned and ethnic businesses is included in the Annex to this chapter.)

Family businesses

In the UK a 2011 report, using mainly government data, indicated that there are 3 million family businesses in the UK (out of the estimated total at that time of 4.5 million private sector businesses).[33] Research suggests that in the USA one household in ten has a family business.[34]

One distinct type of business that is often small is the family business. In the days when farms and craft businesses were virtually the only businesses in existence it was almost the universal practice for them to be passed on through generations of the same family. It is still widely accepted that family businesses make a major contribution to many economies and therefore their particular characteristics are worth considering.[35]

One of the problems of identifying and describing family businesses is defining them. One researcher identified more than 20 different definitions[36] but with a number of common themes including ownership and control by family members, the degree of family involvement and the intention or practice of transferring ownership and/or control from generation to generation.

Some of the confusion over what constitutes a family business arises because there is such a range of them.[37] For example a micro-business run just by a husband and wife and the Ahlstrom Corporation in Finland, which has 200 family members, may both be considered family businesses, but it is unlikely that they will display similar characteristics of ownership, control, family-to-business interaction or intergenerational transfers. Issues of age, size and numbers of founders and whether family involvement is increasing, stable or declining will influence the business and the way it behaves. One particular type of business which causes problems when attempts are made to identify family businesses is the one-person business. If there is only one owner of a business, then all the ownership is in the hands of one family. Other family members may also help in the business, but more because of convenience than a deliberate attempt to build, or secure, family employment. It is often not possible to determine this from available records, and subjective criteria are sometimes used instead. Consequently there is some doubt about how many one-person businesses should be classed as family businesses, which may explain why there appear to be so many family businesses.

Much family business research seems to have focused on the firm and to have considered that family matters are merely an adjunct to that.[38] However, in line with the suggestion in Chapter 8 that often a focus on the entrepreneur provides a better perspective on business development, it has been argued that for family businesses the focus of interest should be on households[39] and that the two-way interaction between business and family dynamics has been neglected in family business research. There are models, however, which recognise that businesses and families are independent systems with each having resources, processes and goals. In a family business context there are interactions between these systems but 'family issues are seen as disabling the effective working of the (business) system'.[40]

As a result it is often argued that it is good practice to keep family and business affairs separate. The model of a family business often used by business researchers is a rational unit which pursues economic goals, and consequently it is assumed that family feelings, values and dynamics have a detrimental influence.[41] This line of reasoning leads to conclusions that family businesses are less efficient than non-family business. Despite this, there is no general agreement on the relative longevity of family and non-family businesses – also due in no small part to problems of comparison deriving from differing definitions of the family business and because data on many of the criteria important in defining a family business are difficult, if not impossible, to collect.

Women-owned businesses

In the UK, there are approximately 1.5 million self-employed women (10 per cent of women in employment) in comparison to 3.1 million self-employed men (18 per cent of men in employment). In this context self-employment can be as a sole trader, in a partnership or as the owner of a limited company.[42]

Another aspect of business ownership which might be expected to have an influence is the gender of the owner. (See also sections on female entrepreneurs in Chapter 9 and on support for women-owned businesses in Chapter 15.) Carter and Shaw[43] point out that there are three main socio-economic issues that influence women's abilities and prospects as business owners: the gender pay-gap, occupational segregation and unequal employment opportunities, and work-life balance issues. It is their view that one of the key differences between male and female start-ups is the lower levels of capital available to female entrepreneurs. Women, for example, working in a full-time capacity in the UK earn 21 per cent less than men.[44] This reduced ability to accumulate capital both restricts the type of business that women can start and can restrict future business growth and development. Businesses with low barriers to entry may often have poor growth potential and could be a factor in the reported incidence of a faster rate of female business exit. As Carter and Shaw point out, this does not mean that female-owned businesses perform any less well than male-owned businesses; they simply lack the initial resources – which is a clear characteristic of women-owned businesses.

The issue of whether or not women-owned firms have different management styles has moved the research focus on from broad descriptions of personal and business characteristics.[45] Additionally as outlined by Carter and Shaw,[46] recent research review papers have stressed very similar findings on the characteristics of women-owned enterprises:

- women's experiences of business ownership are remarkably similar irrespective of international context;
- women's businesses appear to take longer at the gestation stage;

- they tend to be started by individuals rather than teams;
- they do not demonstrate the same level of business performance as businesses owned by men or co-owned by men and women;
- they exit at a faster rate;
- the presence of dependent children constrains entrepreneurial actions;
- they use about one-third of the starting capital used by men.

In a review of the factors affecting new business creation Reynolds concludes that:

> Virtually every survey of participation in business creation has found that men are more likely to be involved than women; the only variation has been in the relative differences. Yet the detailed assessment of factors affecting participation in business creation, representing the global population of candidates for business creation, finds that women are slightly more likely to be involved in seven types of business creation and men are slightly more likely to be involved in six types of business creation. Gender has far less of an impact than measures of individual age, participation in the labor force, personal readiness for entrepreneurship, educational attainment or household income.
>
> It seems appropriate to conclude that once these other factors are taken into account, the remaining personal features associated with gender have little independent impact. This assessment was able to incorporate measures of these other personal and contextual features that had a more significant association with participation in business creation.
>
> While it is true that when women are compared to men, they are less likely to be involved in business creation, it would appear this is not due to biological differences but to differences in life experiences and context. Women with the same work experience, educational attainment, and access to household income as men of the same age appear to be just as likely to participate in business creation. [47]

Reynolds further contends that 'public policies to increase the participation of women may be most effective if they provide them with the same educational and work experiences as men; in some situations women may benefit from programs that would compensate for the lack of these experiences'.[48] Swedish researchers Dahlberg *et al.* also highlight 'gender socialization', which, they argue, has its impact upon the start-up decisions of nascent women entrepreneurs. They contend that risk perception plays a prominent role in decisions to start a business and that nascent women entrepreneurs perceive more risk than nascent male entrepreneurs. Moreover their view of risk 'partials out' any potential influence of their perceived passion and self-efficacy on their start-up decision.[49]

Ethnic businesses

Another aspect of small business ownership is the ethnicity of the owner(s). In the UK in the second half of the 20th century the proportion of people from minority ethnic groups increased significantly, growing from 2.9 per cent of the total UK population in 1951 to 8.0 per cent in 2001. This led to the development of ethnic enclaves in inner city areas where, it has been suggested, due to the decline in large-scale industrial employment, to the racism and discrimination they faced in the labour market, and to the revival of the SME sector in the 1980s, people were encouraged to create their own businesses.[50] Many of them created enterprises which would be classed as ethnic businesses. (See also sections on ethnic entrepreneurs in Chapter 9 and on support for ethnic minority businesses in Chapter 15.)

But what, if anything, distinguishes an ethnic business from a small business which happens to be run by someone from an immigrant community?

- An ethnic business draws much of its support, including often financial support, from a group socially distinguished by cultural or national origin.
- Ethnic entrepreneurs with the same national origin often engage in similar business activities.
- Ethnic businesses often hire employees from the same ethnic group, and may source their customers there also.

Thus ethnic entrepreneurs frequently rely to a considerable extent on social capital from within their ethnic community. Greene, who has researched ethnic entrepreneurs in the USA,[51] argues that they are influenced by the cultural context within which they function. Many ethnic communities have their particular value systems, transactions are often conducted on the basis of reciprocity, groups often have a sense of belonging and solidarity, and relationships are based on trust. These values and expectations can be a source of tangible benefits such as 'protected markets', sources of labour and financial support but also of less tangible social capital such as values, traditions, ties to one another, group solidarity and networks of information. For example, group solidarity can provide a source of stability for firms as they are established and develop, and those communities with a strong proclivity to be entrepreneurial will have visible role models and an atmosphere generally supportive of business formation. The success of business ventures can be a source of pride throughout the ethnic group. Networks which assist in gaining access to information, capital and support, and tradition can also be a source of stability in a difficult world. Not all ethnic communities use such resources to the same extent, however. Resources only contribute to value when they are utilised, and ethnic communities vary in the extent to which resources are used.

Academic spin-out businesses

The importance of knowledge transfer to economic development has been increasingly recognised by universities, particularly since the 1990s. The present interest in knowledge transfer has been linked to the enactment of the Bayh-Doyle Patent and Trademarks Amendment Act in the USA in 1980 which provided incentives to US universities to patent scientific breakthroughs accomplished using Federal funding.[52] In the UK too, governments have put significant emphasis on stimulating the commercialisation of university knowledge and technology, and in 2001 the Higher Education Innovation Fund (HEIF) was introduced. It is designed to support and develop a broad range of knowledge exchange activities between universities and colleges and the wider world, which result in economic and social benefit to the UK. The government made funding available allocating £150 million per year eventually up to 2016, noting that high priority should be given to activity that can help the country's economic growth.

The university knowledge transfer sector is commonly referred to as the 'third stream' following on from teaching and research. The 'third stream' agenda seeks to encourage four types of university activity:

- Formation of university spin-out companies.
- Licensing of university technology to industry.
- Academic collaborations with industry and contract research (for instance Knowledge Transfer Partnerships – KTPs).
- Knowledge transfer activities including entrepreneurial teaching, student industry placements, encouragement of student start-up companies and university interaction with local SMEs.

Spin-outs and the entrepreneur

In any potentially successful spin-out situation there are a number of key features that need to be in place or put in place if the venture is to succeed. These are:

- Intellectual Property and its evaluation
- Management resources
- Suitable capital structures.[53]

The majority of academic spin-outs are considered to be somewhat different from the typical small business start-up. In a spin-out, instead of just one entrepreneur, the management resources most frequently will comprise the founding scientist(s), a manager recruited to help at the initial stages and a representative from the university. Often the scientist will have no commercial acumen and will not be motivated primarily by any thoughts of financial return. The typical traits of the start-up entrepreneur (e.g. need for achievement, motivation, locus of control, risk-taking) may not be much in evidence.

Instead the founder scientist will be product-driven not business-driven. If it is to succeed, however, a spin-out will need the focus of the research to be on commercial priorities rather than academic priorities:

> Most spinouts, by definition, have unproven or immature business models, combined with inexperienced founders and incomplete management teams with little or no know-how from a commercial perspective.[54]

Vohora *et al.* suggest that each university spin-out must pass through the four different phases of opportunity recognition, entrepreneurial commitment, credibility and sustainability if it is ultimately to succeed.[55] Often, to help this, an experienced chief executive or chairman needs to be brought into the spin-out, usually by the investor(s). Here it is crucial that the scientist and the entrepreneur can understand the other's role in the development of the business and work together. This is the start of the build-up of the management team. If the spin-out is to build to a major business, then other building blocks will be introduced: for instance the creation of a company board, possibly including independent non-executives with relevant experience such as marketing and finance to provide guidance and expertise.

Although easy to describe in terms of the process, this development of an executive team working alongside the scientist(s) and a board representing the interests of investors is not an easy situation, and conflict of some kind is not uncommon amongst the various stakeholders.

Other categorisations of small business

In a population as heterogeneous as that of small businesses there will be many different ways in which firms can be categorised and it is neither practicable nor appropriate to try to list them all here. However, there are some which get quite frequent mention, even if only by policy-makers seeking to target assistance appropriately. Among them are the following.

High-tech/low-tech

High-tech is a category of businesses often favoured by those promoting small business because it is commonly believed that high-tech businesses contribute most to an economy. This depends, however, on what is meant by a high-tech business. Often it seems to be a business based on a new and relatively hard-to-acquire technology and which, as a consequence, is likely to be less vulnerable to competition and so able to earn more, export more and survive longer than businesses based on older technologies. There is, though, more to business success than the technology on which it is based, so while high-tech businesses may have the newness of their technology in common, there is no guarantee that they share the same level of profitability, of exports or of success. They are studied nevertheless as a category because of issues that they are perceived to have in common such as having longer lead times to market, encountering greater difficulty in communicating their potential to other people, needing greater financial resources in order to get started and requiring early access to international markets.

Urban/rural

In places like England and Wales where only 7 per cent of the population live in completely rural areas it might be expected that the urban business is the norm. Yet there is evidence that in recent years many people have left the city and moved to the country, sometimes to start small businesses. Those businesses are often set up in rural areas for environmental and lifestyle reasons,[56] and they would be classed as rural businesses because they are located in a rural area. In practice, that is often the only rural thing about the businesses: they benefit from cheaper property costs and overheads and they have greater distances to go to market, but in other aspects they are just urban businesses which happen to be in a rural setting. Businesses which would have better claims to be rural would be farms and farm diversifications, other primary food producers and rural tourism initiatives.

A distinction which is sometimes made is that between 'accessible' and 'remote' rural areas. Storey[57] points out that 'accessible' rural areas have generally been amongst the most prosperous parts of the

UK and quotes research showing that many businesses there are arts-and-craft based and are started by relatively highly educated individuals who are in-migrants to the area seeking a higher quality of life. It is businesses in the 'accessible' areas which outperform comparable firms in urban areas, whereas firms set up in 'remote' rural areas do not appear to perform as well. Apart from these distinctions there seems to be little evidence that rural businesses are in general significantly distinct from urban businesses.

'Third age' businesses

Age distributions of self-employed people generally show that self-employment becomes increasingly common as middle-age approaches and that it does not cease at the normal retirement age. The reasons given are that middle-age may be a time when capital or knowledge assets have been accumulated, and commitments may be reducing, so a start-up can be attempted. Alternatively it might be a time when people are particularly vulnerable to redundancy or attracted by early retirement offers. Self-employment may persist into the 60s and longer because of a reluctance to let go, although hours can be adjusted to allow for age, and there is no statutory retirement age for the self-employed. Alternatively it may continue because some of those in self-employment may not have adequate pension arrangements.[58]

Whether for these reasons or others, the levels of 'grey entrepreneurship' may be increasing. In the UK the number of over 65s who were self-employed more than doubled in the five years to 2015 to reach nearly half a million.[59] A Bank of England report in 2015 suggests that:

> Much of the rise in self-employment since 2008 is likely to reflect longer-term trends that began before the crisis. These include industrial and technological changes and demographic trends: the ageing of the workforce, for example, can account for around half of the increase since 2004. ... Growing self-employment among female workers, alongside increasing female participation in the labour force, has also contributed to a rising self-employment rate in the population.[60]

Craft businesses

A further classification often used to distinguish different categories of business is that of craft, manufacture, service, technology or agricultural. However, while these categories are in common use, there are no fixed definitions of them and confusion can arise in their use. For instance the distinction between 'craft' and 'manufacturing' is not clear, and there would appear to be some overlap. Indeed in mainland Europe the category 'craft business' depends more on size and ownership than on the type of hand-crafted manufacturing associated with the concept of a UK craft business.

Social enterprises

A classification of business which has recently been receiving significant attention is social enterprise, and many social enterprises are small businesses. They are subject to a wide range of definitions, but one of the defining principles tends to be that their profits are not distributed for personal gain. They are considered further in Chapter 7.

IN CONCLUSION

This chapter has explored not just what is thought about small businesses but also why so much attention is given to them. Interest in them grew at a time of high unemployment when it was revealed that they were a key source of new jobs. They also provide other economic benefits and are now recognised as playing a very significant part in most economies.

Because of this interest in them, there has been a lot of research into small businesses to develop an improved understanding of how they operate. They do not behave like smaller versions of bigger businesses and need to be understood as a distinct and separate category of businesses. Nevertheless they are heterogeneous, not homogeneous, and many sub-sets of small businesses have been investigated, including micro, family, women's, ethnic and craft businesses and, relatively recently, social enterprises.

To a large extent small businesses themselves, rather than the entrepreneurs who start and run them, have become the centre of attention. Because it is the businesses which create jobs, and are the registered entities which can be easily examined and counted, they have become the main unit of analysis. The entrepreneur behind the business is acknowledged but nevertheless the focus is usually on the business. An entrepreneur is seen primarily as the person who starts and/or grows a business instead of a business being seen as a by-product (albeit an important by-product) of the entrepreneur's journey towards his or her life goal(s). Thus, as well as reflecting why and what we think about small businesses, this chapter also reflects how we view them – a perspective which has become something of a default view, and which is explored further in Chapter 8.

☞ THE KEY POINTS OF CHAPTER 5

- Since the end of the 1970s interest in small businesses has grown because they have been identified as the main source of new jobs as well as providing other economic benefits. The statistics on job creation need to be interpreted with some care but they do indicate that significant numbers of jobs are created by small businesses, but not by all small businesses.
- Small businesses are not scaled-down versions of large businesses and do not behave like small big businesses.
- Despite the many differences between different types, sizes, stages or ownership arrangements of small businesses, they have a number of key aspects in common, and many of these aspects distinguish them from big businesses. These aspects include issues of strategic perspective, organisation, management, resources, market position and culture. For many commentators it is these aspects that represent the crucial differences associated with size, and even the description 'small' is only a convenient distinction to serve as a proxy for these real differences.
- There is no single definition of what constitutes a small business. Most definitions use the size of the business as the distinguishing feature, as indicated by turnover, asset value, or profits – or, more commonly, by employment (or a combination of these). It is, however, important to remember that 'small' is often used as a relative term, and what is relatively small in one industry may be relatively large in another.
- The variety of small businesses is not just due to their size ranges or different stages of development. Ownership, location and purpose as well as other considerations can all make a difference.

ANNEX – FAMILY, WOMEN-OWNED AND ETHNIC BUSINESSES

For those readers who are interested, this Annex provides more information on some aspects of family, women-owned and ethnic business issues.

Some family business issues

Family business statistics

Of the 27.2 million firms in the USA, between 3 million and 24.2 million (depending on the definition used and the survey carried out) are said to be family businesses,[61] making a contribution to GDP of between 29 and 64 per cent as well as employing between 27 and 62 per cent of the workforce.

A 2011 Oxford Economics report, using mainly government data, summarised the key statistics on family business in the UK as follows:

- Family businesses account for two-thirds of firms in the UK private sector.
- There are 3 million family businesses in the UK and they are predominantly small and medium-sized enterprises. (For the size ranges see Figure 5.A1.)
- UK family businesses provided 9.2 million jobs, 40 per cent of total private sector employment, or two in five private sector jobs. To place this in context, this is around 50 per cent more than the entire UK public sector and makes family firms the largest source of employment in the private sector.
- Family firms generated revenues of £1.1 trillion in 2010, or 35 per cent of private sector turnover. On these revenues, family firms made a £346 billion value-added contribution to UK GDP, or nearly a quarter of the total.
- Family businesses are estimated to have contributed £81.7 billion in tax receipts to the UK Exchequer, or 14 per cent of total government revenues in 2010.
- The sectors with the highest concentrations of family firms are agriculture and extraction (89%), hotels and restaurants (85%), and wholesale and retail (77%).

Some definitional issues

Table 5.A1 lists some different criteria by which family businesses have been defined, and one report proposes that a firm, of any size, is a family business if it meets the following criteria:[62]

- The majority of decision-making rights are held by the person who established or acquired the firm, or their spouse, parents, child or child's direct heirs.

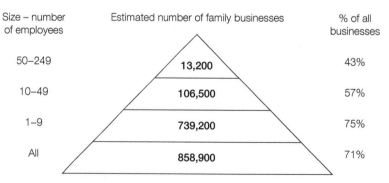

Size – number of employees	Estimated number of family businesses	% of all businesses
50–249	13,200	43%
10–49	106,500	57%
1–9	739,200	75%
All	858,900	71%

Figure 5.A1 *Size distribution of UK family businesses (in 2012)*

(Note: Excludes businesses with no employees.)

Source: P. Braidford, M. Houston, G. Allinson and I. Stone, *Research into Family Businesses – BIS Research Paper No. 172* (London: Department for Business, Innovation and Skills, May 2014) p. 5.

Table 5.A1 *Different criteria by which family businesses have been defined*

Ownership and management	Family involvement in the business	Generational transfer
Ownership and control by a family unit One family member has to own and manage the business Two or more family members must own and manage the business	Transactions and interaction between two systems: the business and the family Interactions involve lots of family members Specific family involvement in business decisions and actions	The actual transfer of ownership and control from one generation to another The intentions to continue transfers between generations

Source: Based on R. K. Z. Heck and E. Scannell-Trent, 'The Prevalence of Family Businesses from a Household Sample', *Family Business Review*, Vol. 12, 1999, pp. 210–211.

- The majority of decision-making rights are indirect or direct.
- At least one representative of the family is involved in the governance of the firm.
- In the case of a listed company, the person who established or acquired the firm, or their family or descendents, possesses 25 per cent of the right to vote through their share capital.

For micro (typically sole traders) businesses, however, subjective criteria are also needed. For instance, in the BIS Annual Business Survey, firms are asked to self-identify as either family or non-family businesses.

The authors of this report also note that although the term 'family business' typically invokes an image of a 'small firm which has been passed down through generations, family businesses vary considerably in terms of their size, the extent of family involvement and age'.[63]

Family business performance

The result of this combination of advantages and disadvantages can be a business that has staying potential, but which does not usually last beyond the tenure of the founder. For instance, UK data[64] has suggested that:

- fewer than 14 per cent of established family businesses will last until the third generation;
- fewer than 24 per cent will make it to the second generation;
- the majority of businesses will fail the first five years.

There appears to be no conclusive evidence about the performance of family versus non-family businesses. Barbara Dunn,[65] drawing on work in the UK and in the USA, argued that publicly quoted family firms were more profitable than non-family businesses in the 1970s and 1980s. Anecdotal evidence from Finland supports this point of view, where it has been suggested that the $3.3 billion Ahlstrom Corporation prospered by combining the benefits of family involvement with the pursuit of sound business principles.[66] A Canadian study examined whether family businesses were typified by high levels of stewardship or of stagnation when compared to non-family businesses, and found far more support for stewardship than stagnation.[67] However, other British researchers have reported no differences 'in the performance and effectiveness of family and non-family firms'.[68]

Similarly comparisons of the survival rates of family businesses and other businesses appear to be ambivalent – and the figures can be misused or misinterpreted. For instance it is often quoted that in the USA 30 per cent of family businesses make it to the second generation, 10–15 per cent make it to the third and 3–5 per cent make it to the fourth generation – but that should be 30 per cent of family businesses make it *through* the second generation, and 3–5 per cent making it to the fourth generation suggests as big, if not a bigger, proportion of long-living businesses to that for other businesses.[69]

The conflict and transition issues in family businesses

Conflict is inevitable in organisations, and it must be managed, but its management presents special problems for family-run businesses. Because the conflict can be intense, and because it is transposed from the business to the personal or family arena, it is often suppressed and not resolved. Therefore open discussion and the challenge of ideas, which can help progress in a changing world, may be avoided. In addition, when disputes do occur, the anger and resentment that occurs may also be transferred to family life, and this makes it difficult for family members to break out of a self-defeating cycle of conflict. All this can make rational business decision-making exceedingly difficult. In family businesses there are often family concerns that override business sensibilities. Incompetent family members may be retained in post as a favour to shore up deteriorating family relationships, and promotion for otherwise eligible non-family managers may be blocked as a result. Business logic and rationale may thus take a back seat in favour of family preference. There is some evidence that this is especially likely in second-generation family businesses. Attempts to improve the business by recruiting professional managers bring other problems: such managers may find that they can never achieve the measure of recognition, such as promotion to the board, and control that their expertise and contribution merit.

Managing the transition of power and control can often be a difficulty in family businesses, especially the transition from one chief executive to another. There is evidence that this is rarely planned and that the transition is, as a result, frequently traumatic. This may contribute to the failure of many family businesses to survive to the second or third generation. This seemingly unprofessional behaviour can come about because owners:

- will not face up to their limited lifespan;
- may unconsciously care little about what happens when they are gone;
- may resent their successor;
- may have an aversion to planning.[70]

Advantages and disadvantages of family businesses

There are both advantages and disadvantages in family businesses. Among the advantages are:

- When a family group strongly influences management and control, a permanent, solid atmosphere and an *esprit de corps* can develop. This can often encourage both a closeness among staff and long-lasting relationships with customers, suppliers and other contacts. Family businesses can as a result often build a reputation for dependability and excellent service.
- Staff in family businesses can have a sense of belonging and strong commitment to the goals of the organisation. When the owning family are justly proud of their venture, their enthusiasm and commitment can enthuse non-family staff.
- This commitment can produce flexibility in terms of working practices, working hours and remuneration. Family members do what is necessary to get a job done and there can be little demarcation of duties. Some of this flexibility can rub off on non-family members, and this can allow the family business to respond rapidly to changing technological, sociological and economic conditions.
- Family businesses are normally free from stock market pressure to produce quick results, because they are not quoted on the market. Also many family members may be reluctant to take money out of the business. They can, as a result, often take a longer-term view and this can be reinforced by the permanent nature of their management teams.

Nevertheless there can also be a number of significant disadvantages. Because of issues such as the following, a stereotypical image of the family firm is of a rather uninspiring working environment which offers little opportunity to non-family personnel and which 'becomes sterile and eventually fails'.[71]

- The pre-eminence of the controlling family, centralised decision-making and long-standing management teams can result in static thinking. It can make it less likely that new ideas which are essential for long-term development will emerge, and family businesses are often reluctant to use outside advisers, preferring instead the counsel of the family when exploring business matters.

- Conflict often emerges between family members, in particular fathers and their children. The father often recognises that he has to let go of the reins and develop his successor, but the business is such an important feature of his life that he fears that the 'loss' of it will damage his self-image and bring his competency into question. Such behaviour can be resented, and tension can build as a result.
- Rivalry between siblings can reach such a level of seriousness that it has an impact on 'every management decision and magnifies the jockeying for power that goes on in all organisations'.[72] Where multiple family members have an interest in the business they may all expect equal treatment but, in the nature of things, this is rarely possible.

Many of the difficulties found in family businesses can be attributed to non-rational behaviour. However, it has been pointed out that values and perceptions play a key part in the succession process and that concepts from behavioural economics can offer insights into the process. The 'endowment effect' can mean that the person handing over control in a family firm's transition 'is likely to place greater value on the business than is the new leader'.[73] It is argued that when people gain assets easily they will not value them highly and will be prepared to gamble with them. In a family business context if a successor is required to display superior performance before succeeding to a position of control, the business will be highly valued and will be treated with discernment. If the succession process is structured in a way which requires successors to invest money and time in the business, and to prove themselves before they are handed the reins, they will assume that the business is worth having.

Some women-owned business issues

In at least some economies the proportion of women-owned business is growing, although in general it seems that men are still almost twice as likely to start businesses as women:

- US Census data[74] reveal that in 2012 there were 9.9 million women-owned businesses up from 7.8 million in 2007, which indicates a 27.5 per cent increase. They made up 36.2 per cent of all non-farm businesses, up from 29.6 per cent in 2007.
- In the UK, according to the BIS Small Business Survey of 2014,[75] 18 per cent of SME employers were majority-led by women, defined as controlled by a single woman or having a management team of which a majority were women. A further 27 per cent were equally-led, with the same number of men and women in director/partner roles. These two figures combined means that 45 per cent of SME employers were majority- or equally-led by women. Nevertheless relative to other high-income countries, particularly the United States, UK rates of female business ownership have been persistently low.
- Carter *et al.*, in noting that the 'global gender gap' debate underpins much of the policy interest in women's enterprise, highlight that:

  > While the number of women engaged in self-employment and business ownership has risen in recent years, much of the growth has been in women working part-time and among those wanting more flexible working hours to complement domestic commitments ... a substantial proportion of self-employed women 'may be working very few hours – as little as an hour per week', fitting in flexible self-employment around family commitments.[76]

The problems experienced by women business owners

In a relatively early piece of research, Cromie[77] examined the problems experienced by male- and female-owned young businesses. He discovered that the problems experienced did not really vary by gender and that men and women both experienced personal problems but women recorded more difficulties. This is especially true with respect to a lack of self-confidence and not being taken seriously, which, when applied by providers of funds, has led to the under-capitalisation of their businesses. However, women respondents did say that once it was clear that they were committed to making a success of their businesses these problems disappeared.

Carter argues that certain problems were perceived by women to be gender-related. These include the 'late payment of bills; a tendency to undercharge; getting business and finding clients; and ... the effect of proprietorship upon personal and domestic circumstances'.[78] It has also been argued that women's life experiences are very different from men's, with the consequence that women do business differently from men.[79] Men are said to aim for profit and growth whilst women focus on relationships and integrate business relationships into their lives. In addition, 'women-owned firms are typically smaller, over-represented within service sectors and more likely to be part-time and to operate from a home-base'.[80]

Access to business finance

In Britain, Carter reviewed recent work on the financing of women-owned firms and suggested that there have been four recurring problems:[81]

- They have difficulty in obtaining start-up finance.
- They are required to provide guarantees when seeking external finance and they are sometimes unable to provide the requisite collateral.
- They find it more difficult to obtain on-going finance.
- Bankers tend to have negative stereotypes of women entrepreneurs and discriminate against them.

Results from a study by Carter and Rosa[82] indicate that there is support for some of these propositions but some differences are accounted for by factors such as firm size and industrial sector. Women do have less start-up finance than men but they use the same sources: personal money, overdrafts and bank loans. There are also gender differences in the use of on-going finance: women are more likely to use loans while men are more likely to use overdrafts and supplier credit. Carter and Rosa found no support for the propositions about the need for guarantees nor the supposed negative stereotypical images of women by bankers. In general there appears to be little evidence of deliberate discrimination against women, a view reinforced by a Women's Enterprise Task Force report in 2009 which:

> dispels the myth that women are charged more for bank loans than men – and in fact shows that women are often charged less, as their businesses may be seen as lower risk. However, there is an issue that women do not access adequate levels of finance from a variety of sources for their businesses.[83]

On the other hand, issues of finance usage most often explained as a product of differences in business size, age and sector, have been critically examined by others. Carter *et al.* draw attention to studies suggesting 'the "gendering" of structure is itself a gender effect'.[84] Indeed, the extent to which structure and gender are coterminous remains an important question for research, and it is suggested that at least some apparent gender effects in business are symptomatic of wider socio-economic gender differences.[85]

The survival of female-owned businesses

There is, however, *prima facie* evidence that female-owned businesses do not survive as long as male-owned businesses, which might be because of the under-capitalisation of female firms at start-up. One British study which investigated this issue argued that research on the performance of women-owned firms is complicated by the different theoretical stances adopted by various authors; by the fact that only sole business owners are investigated; by assumptions that male and female entrepreneurs are homogeneous; and by conflicting ideas on whether biological differences between men and women cause them to adopt different socio-economic roles.[86] It was also pointed out that there were lots of contradictions in quantitative studies of the performance of male- and female-owned firms and that some studies do not allow for the fact that women tend to set up businesses in sectors which traditionally have higher failure rates.

Fairlie and Robb, using census data, report that female-owned businesses in the USA are less successful than male-owned businesses.[87] However, Kalnins and Williams, based on the tax records of one million businesses in Texas, found that, overall, male-owned businesses did not out-survive those owned by women and that women-owned businesses out-survived male-owned businesses in many industries and in large cities.[88]

Some ethnic business issues

The characteristics of ethnic businesses, it has been suggested, include the following:

- A business which draws heavily on a group 'that is socially distinguished (by others or itself) by characteristics of cultural or national origin'[89] for tangible and intangible resources, markets and support constitutes a special kind of small business. Ethnic businesses also develop 'connections and regular patterns of interaction' among people from particular cultural backgrounds.[90] Such ethnic enterprises are commonplace in many parts of the world but problems with definitions and the sheer diversity of these ventures present difficulties for those who try to quantify the phenomenon.

- Ethnic entrepreneurs in different countries may be from different backgrounds. In Britain, Pakistanis, Indian Sikhs, Nigerians, West Indians and East African refugees are common whereas in the USA, Koreans, Mexicans and Vietnamese are found. Nevertheless there is some uniformity in their choice of business activity. For example in North America, studies[91] have revealed that ethnic businesses predominate in the wholesale, retail and service sectors with some presence in light manufacturing, and a recent study in Britain of 82 ethnic minority businesses supports the American finding.[92] However, there were variations amongst the different groups of ethnic business and these can be explained partly by the cultural backgrounds of the respondents, their educational backgrounds and the length of time they have been in the country.

- Educational attainment is another factor in the rate of ethnic enterprise and in the nature of the businesses operated. Li[93] identified that amongst the most poorly qualified (with little formal qualifications) it was the Chinese men (34%) and Chinese women (21%) who were most likely to be self-employed, whereas amongst the best qualified, namely having a first degree or above, it was the Indian and Pakistani/Bangladeshi men who were the most likely to be self-employed. The Chinese tend to predominately operate micro businesses whereas the Indian and Pakistani sample tended to operate small to medium-sized enterprises. It was also noted by Li that Black Africans tended to feature amongst the most qualified yet showed the lowest inclination to be entrepreneurs. Yet this same group, when they did start a business, tended to be amongst the biggest employers with 25 per cent of Black African businesses employing more than 25 people.

- Two aspects in which ethnic businesses rely particularly heavily on others from the same ethnic group are in finding customers and in obtaining labour. Successful businesses must find customers, and it is sometimes argued that firms which fully understand the special needs of ethnic groups, and can thus deliver more appropriate benefits, are at a competitive advantage. In addition, co-ethnic customers may patronise a particular firm because of a sense of ethnic solidarity with the owner. These factors may confer initial competitive advantage, but it has been argued that sustained competitive advantage will only arise when a business has a strategy which no other business is following and when other businesses cannot duplicate the benefits on offer. However, for ethnic businesses located in service and retail areas where barriers to entry are low, there are many competitors who can follow the same strategy and offer similar benefits. In Britain, therefore, the outcome is increasingly 'a mass of ethnic small business owners trapped in a hostile trading milieu'.[94]

- Labour requirements for small ethnic businesses also come largely from co-ethnics in the community and from the extended family. At start-up having a supply of part-time labour allows firms to adjust to the ebb and flow of initial workloads and is cheap and easy to organise. Many of the jobs on offer in the start-up phase are offered to co-ethnics on an informal basis. Indeed, the most noticeable feature of the labour force amongst ethnic businesses is the widespread use of family labour. It is argued[95] that family labour seems attractive in that it helps avoid obstacles to recruitment in the open market; it is also flexible and cheap and problems with the supervision of staff can be avoided. Family members can be loyal and committed to the firm and consequently confer advantages on the firm.

There is, however, another side to the employment of family members which is more contentious. In many ethnic businesses women manage the production processes as well as attending to the administrative and financial aspects of the business. Men tend to handle external relationships whilst women manage the workflow. This division of labour by gender could be a source of competitive advantage, but there is often an exploitative element in the hiring of women. Women manage the work processes and domestic affairs but get little financial or social reward for their endeavours. Men are the official managers, even though women often play 'critical *de facto* managerial roles in running the business'.[96] The domestic subordination of women is reinforced in the work place in many ethnic businesses.

Embeddedness and second generations

Two factors which have particular relevance for ethnic entrepreneurs are embeddedness and second generation entrepreneurs. The concept of embeddedness recognises that economic interactions between people also contain social elements:

> People live out their lives within a spider's web of human relationships: with family, old school friends, former and current business colleagues, competitors, suppliers, customers and neighbours. We also belong to a whole range of formal and informal social groupings, such as religious bodies, ethnic societies, sporting clubs, business associations, local charities, the pub and professional bodies. Our interactions within these relational networks, within which we are 'set' – embedded – shape a whole range of economic transactions, including those specific to the entrepreneur.[97]

Because of the structure of their social relations, early-stage immigrants can often be almost exclusively embedded within an ethnic community – thus, if they are entrepreneurs, linking the nature and success of their entrepreneurial endeavours to that ethnic society. When contacts widen, there can be mixed-embeddedness 'that incorporates both the co-ethnic social networks and ... linkages between migrant entrepreneurs and the economic and institutional context of the host society'.[98] While these are fuzzy concepts they can help to explain entrepreneurial variations of ethnic entrepreneurs[99] as also can second generation effects. Second generation immigrants can be more assimilated than their first generation parents, and that can affect both the type of entrepreneurial activity they consider and even whether or not they engage in it at all.

Problems experienced by ethnic businesses

Just as there are well-known and crucial questions relating to female enterprise, the same pattern exists in relation to ethnic enterprise. The main theories concerning the basis of the disadvantage faced by the ethnic minority population fall under the three main headings of human capital, social capital and economic capital. The human capital approach stresses the role of education, experience, job-related skills and training, and language fluency.[100] The social capital approach emphasises the importance of networks and ties within the community, whereas economic capital explanations are based on the fact that many people in the ethnic minority community came from economically under-developed, war-torn, or former colonial countries. They did not arrive with much in the way of economic capital and have not really accumulated much after their arrival. However, it has been argued[101] that as time has gone by since the first wave of arrival of ethnic minority immigrants into the UK, these groups have had the opportunity to some extent to accumulate both the human and economic capital necessary to seek mainstream employment and possibly self-employment as an effective form of upward social mobility.

Ethnic businesses can also be family or women-owned businesses – and therefore share their problems, possibly compounded by ethnicity. For instance, the lack of prestige afforded to women who manage ethnic family businesses could well have a detrimental effect on economic performance. Another feature of family involvement which is also problematic is the reluctance, also found in non-ethnic family businesses, to recruit non-family managers even when incumbent family managers are less than competent. Family members can be important to ethnic businesses as a means of overcoming the disadvantages of racism and of providing a flexible source of labour, but their over-reliance on the family can also be a source of disadvantage.

✓ QUESTIONS, EXERCISES, ESSAY AND DISCUSSION TOPICS

- Are the arguments about the job creation record of small businesses relevant? In what ways?

- Are definitions based on size meaningful when there is such a variety of small businesses?

- In the absence of a single universally accepted definition, how would you summarise the essence of a small business?

- Of the various characteristics which distinguish a small business from a large one, which do you believe are the most significant? Why?

- What does the Penrose quotation – 'we cannot define a caterpillar and then use the same definition for a butterfly' – mean?

- Is the entrepreneur or the business the more enlightening unit of study in seeking to understand business development and wealth creation?

- In what ways do family businesses differ from non-family businesses?

- What are the implications of studying family businesses from the perspective of the family instead of focusing just on the business?

- Apart from a lack of accumulated capital is there any meaningful argument for saying women-owned businesses are any different from male-owned businesses and should be treated differently?

- Is the case for treating ethnic-owned businesses as a special case any different to that made for women-owned businesses?

📖 SUGGESTIONS FOR FURTHER READING

M. Anyadike-Danes, M. Hart and J. Du, *Firm Dynamics and Job Creation in the UK* (Coventry/ Birmingham: Enterprise Research Centre, 2013).

The BDO Stoy Hayward Centre for Family Business, The Family Business Management Series: Succession Management in Family Companies (2007), www.bdo.co.uk.

P. Braidford, M. Houston, G. Allinson and I. Stone, *Research into Family Businesses – BIS Research Paper No. 172* (London: Department for Business, Innovation and Skills, May 2014).

P. Burns, *Entrepreneurship and Small Business,* 3rd Edition (Basingstoke: Palgrave Macmillan, 2011).

S. Carter and D. Jones-Evans (eds), *Enterprise and Small Business* (London: FT Prentice Hall, 2006) Chapter 9 – Gender and Entrepreneurship, Chapter 10 – Ethnicity and Entrepreneurship, and Chapter 11 – Family and Entrepreneurship.

Leo-Paul Dana (ed.), *Handbook of Research on Ethnic Minority Entrepreneurship: A Co-evolutionary View on Resource Management* (Cheltenham: Edward Elgar, 2007).

Global Entrepreneurship Monitor, www.entreworld.org.

S. Marlow, 'Feminism, Gender and Entrepreneurship', Chapter 5 in K. Mole with M. Ram (eds), *Perspectives in Entrepreneurship: A Critical Approach* (Basingstoke: Palgrave Macmillan, 2012) pp. 59–74.

P. Urwin, *Self-Employment, Small Firms and Enterprise* (London: The Institute of Economic Affairs in Association with Profile Books Ltd, 2011) p. 106.

Women-Owned Businesses in the 21st Century (Washington, DC: US Department of Commerce, Economics and Statistics Administration, for the White House Council on Women and Girls, October 2010).

REFERENCES

[1] European Commission DG Internal Market, Industry, Entrepreneurship and SMEs. Taken from http://ec.europa.eu/growth/smes/index_en.htm (accessed 23 January 2016).

[2] See D. Deakins and M. Freel, *Entrepreneurship and Small Firms* (London: McGraw-Hill, 2006) p. 121.

[3] D. L. Birch, 'Who Creates Jobs?' *The Public Interest*, Vol. 65, 1981, p. 7.

[4] B. Kirchhoff, 'Twenty Years of Job Creation Research: What Have We Learned?', *The 40th Conference of the International Council for Small Business*, 1995, pp. 201–202.

[5] Ibid. p. 202.

[6] C. Criscuolo, P. N. Gal and C. Menon, 'The Dynamics of Employment Growth: New Evidence from 18 Countries', *OECD Science, Technology and Industry Policy Papers, No. 14* (OECD Publishing, 2014). Taken from http://dx.doi.org/10.1787/5jz417hj6hg6-en (accessed 20 April 2016) p. 6.

[7] J. Haltiwanger, R. S. Jarmin and J. Miranda, 'Who Creates Jobs? Small versus Large versus Young', *The Review of Economics and Statistics*, Vol. 95, No. 2, 2013, p. 347.

[8] D. J. Storey, *Understanding the Small Business Sector* (London: Routledge, 1994) p. 165.

[9] Ibid. p. 168.

[10] M. Anyadike-Danes, M. Hart and J. Du, *Firm Dynamics and Job Creation in the UK* (Coventry/Birmingham: Enterprise Research Centre, 2013).

[11] P. Rosa and M. Scott, 'Entrepreneurial Diversification, Business-Cluster Formation and Growth', *Government and Policy*, Vol. 17, 1999, pp. 527–547, at p. 527.

[12] D. J. Storey and S. Johnson, *Job Generation and Labour Market Change* (Basingstoke: Macmillan Press, 1987) p. 44.

[13] J. Haltiwanger, R. S. Jarmin and J. Miranda, Op. Cit.

[14] M. Anyadike-Danes, M. Hart and J. Du, Op. Cit. p. 13.

[15] D. J. Storey, Op. Cit. p. 113.

[16] NESTA, *The Vital 6 Per Cent* (London: NESTA, 2009).

[17] P. Urwin, *Self-Employment, Small Firms and Enterprise* (London: Institute of Economic Affairs in Association with Profile Books Ltd, 2011) pp. 107–108.

[18] R. Botham, and S. Bridge, 'NESTA's Vital (or Not So Vital?) Six Per Cent', a paper presented at the *ISBE Conference*, Dublin 2012.

[19] P. Urwin, Op. Cit. p. 122.

[20] M. Anyadike-Danes, M. Hart and J. Du, Op. Cit. p. 13.

[21] E. T. Penrose, *The Theory of the Growth of the Firm* (Oxford: Basil Blackwell, 1959).

[22] C. Handy, *The Age of Unreason* (London: Arrow Books, 1990).

[23] H. Mintzberg, *The Structuring of Organisations* (Englewood Cliffs, NJ: Prentice Hall, 1979) pp. 305–313.

[24] R. Goffee and R. Scase, 'Proprietorial Control in Family Firms', *Journal of Management Studies*, Vol. 22, 1985, pp. 53–68.

[25] A. Minkes, *The Entrepreneurial Manager* (Harmondsworth: Penguin, 1987) for a discussion of entrepreneurial decision-making.

[26] The Report of the Committee of Enquiry on Small Firms (The Bolton Report) (London: HMSO, 1971).

[27] N. Christakis and J. Fowler, *Connected* (London: Harper Press, 2010) pp. 246–248.

[28] The Third Annual Report of the European Observatory for SMEs (Zoetermeer: EIM Small Business Research and Consultancy, 1995) pp. 50–51.

[29] Department for Business, Innovation and Skills, *Business Population Estimates for the UK and Regions 2015* (Sheffield, 2015) p.1.

[30] S. Tatomir, 'Self-Employment: What Can We Learn from Recent Developments?', Bank of England Quarterly Bulletin 2015 Q1. Taken from www.bankofengland.co.uk/publications (accessed 2 February 2016) p. 56.

[31] P. Urwin, Op. Cit. p. 23.

[32] Ibid. p. 28.

[33] Oxford Economics, *The UK Family Business Sector: Working to Grow the UK Economy* (London: Commissioned by the Institute of Family Business, November 2011) p. 2.

[34] University of Vermont. Taken from https://www.uvm.edu/business/vfbi/?Page=facts.html (accessed 30 January 2016).

[35] Stoy Hayward, *The Stoy Hayward/BBC Family Business Index* (London: Stoy Hayward, 1992).

[36] M. S. Wortman, 'Critical Issues in Family Business: An International Perspective of Practice and Research', Proceedings of the *ICSB 40th World Conference*, 1995, pp. 53–76.

[37] D. Fletcher, 'Family and Enterprise', in S. Carter and D. Jones-Evans (eds), *Enterprise and Small Business* (London: Financial Times/Prentice Hall, 2000) pp. 155–165.

[38] K. Stafford, K. A. Duncan, S. Dane and M. Winter, 'A Research Model of Sustainable Family Business', *Family Business Review*, Vol. 12, 1999, pp. 197–208.

[39] R. K. Z. Heck and E. Scannell-Trent, 'The Prevalence of Family Business from a Household Sample', *Family Business Review*, Vol. 12, 1999, pp. 209–224.

[40] D. Fletcher, 'Family and Enterprise', in S. Carter and D. Jones-Evans (eds), *Enterprise and Small Business* (London: Financial Times/Prentice Hall, 2000) p. 160.

[41] S. Birley, D. Ng and A. Godfrey, 'The Family and the Business', *Long Range Planning*, Vol. 32, 1999, pp. 598–608.

[42] UK Office for National Statistics. Taken from http://www.ons.gov.uk/ons/publications/re-reference-tables.html?edition=tcm%3A77-353568#tab-Employment-tables (accessed 30 January 2016).

[43] S. Carter and E. Shaw, 'Women's Business Ownership: Recent Research and Policy Developments', *Report to the Small Business Service*, November 2000.

[44] Taken from http://www.guardian.co.uk/uk/2010/aug/19/equal-pay-women-2057 (accessed 30 January 2012).

[45] S. Carter, S. Anderson, and E. Shaw, *'Women's Business Ownership: A Review of the Academic, Popular and Internet Literature* (London: Small Business Service Research Report, RR002/01, 2001).

[46] S. Carter and E. Shaw, Op. Cit. pp. 5–8.

[47] P. D. Reynolds, 'New Firm Creation: A Global Assessment of National, Contextual, and Individual Factors', *Foundations and Trends in Entrepreneurship*, Vol. 6, Nos. 5–6, 2010, p. 456.

[48] Ibid. p. 457.

[49] C. Dahlberg, Y. von Friedrichs and J. Wincent, 'Risk Perception Matters: Why Women's Passion May Not Lead to a Business Start-up', *International Journal of Gender and Entrepreneurship*, Vol. 7, No. 1, 2015, pp. 87–104.

[50] A. Phizacklea and M. Ram, 'Ethnic Entrepreneurship in Comparative Perspective', *International Journal of Entrepreneurial Behaviour and Research*, Vol. 1, 1995, pp. 48–58.

[51] For instance P. G. Greene, 'A Resource-Based Approach to Ethnic Business Sponsorship – A Consideration of Ismaili-Pakistani Immigrants', *Journal of Small Business Management*, Vol. 35, No. 4, 1997, p. 58–71.

[52] E. M. Rogers, Y. Yin, and J. Hoffman, 'Assessing the Effectiveness of Technology Transfer Offices at U.S. Research Universities', *The Journal of the Association of University Technology Managers*, Vol. 12, 2000, pp. 47–80.

[53] Quester, 'A Quester Commentary' p. 6, October 2006. Taken from www.quester.co.uk (accessed 6 November 2011).

[54] Ibid. p. 9.

[55] A. Vohora, M. Wright and A. Lockett, 'Critical Junctures in the Development of University High-Tech Spinout Companies', *Research Policy*, Vol. 33, No. 1, 2004, pp. 147–175.

[56] Economic and Social Research Council, *Characteristics of the Founders of Small Rural Businesses* (Swindon: The Council, 1989).

[57] D. Storey, Op. Cit. pp. 272–273.

[58] D. Brooksbank, 'Self-employment and Small Firms', in S. Carter and D. Jones-Evans (eds), *Enterprise and Small Business* (London: Financial Times/Prentice Hall, 2000), pp. 15–16.

[59] Taken from http://www.ons.gov.uk/ons/rel/lmac/self-employed-workers-in-the-uk/2014/rep-self-employed-workers-in-the-uk-2014.html (accessed 2 February 2015).

[60] S. Tatomir, 'Self-employment: What Can We Learn from Recent Developments?', *Bank of England Quarterly Bulletin*, Vol. Q1, 2015, p. 56. Taken from www.bankofengland.co.uk/publications (accessed 2 February 2016).

[61] J. H. Astrachan and M. C. Shanker, 'Family Businesses' Contribution to the U.S. Economy: A Closer Look', *Family Business Review*, Vol. 16, No. 3, 2003, p. 58.

[62] This definition was taken from the final report of the EC Expert Group on Family Business. Taken from http://ec.europa.eu/enterprise/policies/sme/promoting-entrepreneurship/family-business/family_business_expert_group_report_en.pdf (accessed 28 January 2012) p. 4.

[63] Oxford Economics, *The UK Family Business Sector: Working to Grow the UK Economy* (London: Commissioned by the Institute of Family Business, November 2011) p. 4.

[64] BDO Stoy Hayward, Across the Generations: Insights from 100-Year-Old Family Businesses (2004).

[65] B. Dunn, 'Success Themes in Scottish Family Enterprises: Philosophies and Practices through the Generations', *Family Business Review*, Vol. 8, 1995, pp. 17–28.

[66] J. Magretta, 'Governing the Family-Owned Enterprise: An Interview with Finland's Krister Ahlstrom', *Harvard Business Review*, Vol. 76, No. 1, 1998, pp. 113–123.

[67] D. Miller, I. Le Breton-Miller and B Scholnick, 'Stewardship vs. Stagantion: An Empirical Comparison of Small Family and Non-Family Businesses', *Journal of Management Studies*, Vol. 45, No. 1, January 2008, pp. 51–78.

[68] D. Fletcher, Op. Cit. p. 157.

[69] Taken from http://www.thefbcg.com/Family-Business-Survival--Understanding-the-Statistics-/ (accessed 20 April 2016).

[70] H. Levinson, 'Don't Choose Your Own Successor', *Harvard Business Review*, 1974, November–December, pp. 53–62.

[71] S. Birley *et al.*, Op. Cit. p. 598.

[72] H. Levinson, 'Conflicts that Plague the Family Business', *Harvard Business Review*, 1971, March–April, pp. 53–62.

[73] A. Shepherd and A. Zacharakis, 'Structuring Family Business Succession: An Analysis of the Future Leader's Decision Making', *Entrepreneurship Theory and Practice*, Vol. 25, 2000, pp. 25–39.

[74] Taken from http://www.fastcompany.com/3050109/the-state-of-women-owned-businesses-in-the-us (accessed 31 January 2016).

[75] Department for Business, Innovation & Skills, '*Small Business Survey 2014: SME Employers*' BIS Research Paper Number 214 (London: Department for Business, Innovation & Skills, March 2015) p. 31.

[76] S. Carter, S. Mwaura, M. Ram, K Trehan and T. Jones, 'Barriers to Ethnic Minority and Women's Enterprise: Existing Evidence, Policy Tensions and Unsettled Questions', *International Small Business Journal* Vol. 33, No. 1, 2015, p. 56.

[77] S. Cromie, 'The Problems Experienced by Young Firms', *International Small Business Journal*, Vol. 9, 1991, pp. 43–67.

[78] S. Carter, 'Gender and Enterprise', in S. Carter and D. Jones-Evans (eds), *Enterprise and Small Business* (Harlow: Pearson Education, 2000) p. 172.

[79] C. G. Brush, S. Marlow and A. Strange, 'Female Entrepreneurs: Success by Whose Standards?', in M. Taunton (ed.), *Women in Management: A Developing Presence* (London: Routledge, 1994).

[80] K. D. Hughes, J. E. Jennings, C. Brush, S. Carter and F. Welter, 'Extending Women's Entrepreneurship Research in New Directions', *Entrepreneurship Theory and Practice*, Vol. 36, No. 3, 2012, pp. 429–442.

[81] S. Carter, 'Gender and Enterprise', Op. Cit. p. 167.

[82] S. Carter and P. Rosa, 'The Financing of Male- and Female-Owned Businesses', *Entrepreneurship and Regional Development*, Vol. 10, 1998, pp. 225–241.

[83] Women's Enterprise Task Force (WETF) report, *Greater Return on Women's Enterprise* (GROWE), Final Report and recommendations, 2009. Taken from www.womensenterprisetaskforce.co.uk (accessed 28 January 2012) p. 8.

[84] S. Carter, S. Mwaura, M. Ram, K. Trehan and T .Jones, 'Barriers to Ethnic Minority and Women's Enterprise: Existing Evidence, Policy Tensions and Unsettled Questions', *International Small Business Journal*, Vol. 33, No. 1, 2015, p. 57.

[85] Ibid. p. 58.

[86] E. Chell and S. Baines, 'Does Gender Affect Business Performance? A Study of Microbusinesses in Business Services in the UK', *Entrepreneurship and Regional Development*, Vol. 10, 1998, pp. 117–135.

[87] R. Fairlie and A. Robb, *Gender Differences in Business Performance: Evidence from the Characteristics of Business Owners Survey*. Taken from http://citeseerx.ist.psu.edu/viewdoc/download?-doi=10.1.1.226.4580&rep=rep1&type=pdf (accessed 1 February 2016) p. 1.

[88] A. Kalnins and M. Williams, 'When Do Female-Owned Businesses Out-Survive Male-Owned Businesses? A Disaggregated Approach by Industry and Geography', *Journal of Business Venturing*, Vol. 29, No. 6, November 2014, p. 822.

[89] L. M. Dyer and C. A. Ross, 'Ethnic Enterprises and their Clientele', *Journal of Small Business Management*, Vol. 38, 2000, pp. 48–60.

[90] R. Waldinger, H. E. Aldrich and R. Ward, *Ethnic Entrepreneurs: Immigrant Businesses in Industrial Societies* (Newbury Park, CA: Sage, 1990) p. 33.

[91] V. C. Vincent, 'Decision-Making Policies Among Mexican-American Small Business Entrepreneurs', *Journal of Small Business Management*, Vol. 34, 1996, pp. 1–13; Dyer and Ross, Op. Cit.; P. G. Greene, Op. Cit. pp. 57–71.

[92] A. Fadahunsi, D. Smallbone and S. Supri, 'Networking and Ethnic Minority Enterprise Development: Insights from a North London Study', *Journal of Small Business and Enterprise Development*, Vol. 7, 2000, pp. 228–240.

[93] Y. Li, 'Assessing Data Needs and Gaps for Studying Ethnic Entrepreneurship in Britain: A Review Paper', ESRC (URN 07/1052) March 2007.

[94] D. Storey, Op. Cit. pp. 272–273.

[95] M. Ram, 'Unravelling Social Networks in Ethnic Minority Firms', *International Small Business Journal*, Vol.12, No. 3, 1994, pp. 42–53, at p. 44.

[96] Ibid. p. 51.

[97] S. Drakopoulou Dodd, 'An Introduction to Network Approaches and Embeddedness', Chapter 6 in K. Mole with M. Ram (eds), *Perspectives in Entrepreneurship: A Critical Approach* (Basingstoke: Palgrave Macmillan, 2012) p. 75.

[98] E. Razin, 'Conclusion: The Economic Context, Embeddedness and Immigrant Entrepreneurs', *International Journal of Entrepreneurial Behaviour & Research*, Vol. 8, No. 1, 2002, p. 163.

[99] J. Rath and R. Kloosterman, 'The Economic Context, Embeddedness and Immigrant Entrepreneurs', *International Journal of Entrepreneurial Behaviour & Research*, Vol. 8, No. 1, 2002.

[100] G. Borjas, 'Ethnicity, Neighbourhoods and Human Capital Externalities', *American Economic Review*, Vol. 85, 1995, pp. 365–390.

[101] Y. Li, 'Assessing Data Needs and Gaps for Studying Ethnic Entrepreneurship in Britain', URN 07/152, ESRC/CRE/DTI/EMDA, 2007.

Companion website

Please visit the companion website at www.palgravehighered.com/Bridge-UE-5e for access to additional learning and teaching materials.

Small Businesses: Understanding Their Dynamics

CONTENTS

- Introduction
- The stages of development of a business
- Preparing for business start-up
- Getting started
- Growth

- Static phases (survival, consolidation, comfort and maturity)
- Decline
- Termination
- Business success – and failure
- In conclusion

KEY CONCEPTS

This chapter covers:

- Models of the possible stages of the development of a business.
- The process of business start-up and the supply of entrepreneurs.
- Some of the considerations which might influence business start-up.
- How business growth can be interpreted and what influences it.
- The stages of business development after start-up.
- The issues arising in static, declining and terminating businesses.

LEARNING OBJECTIVES

By the end of this chapter the reader should:

- Be aware of the possible development paths for a business.
- Understand the possible stages of business development.
- Be aware of the many varied reasons and attitudes behind business start-up.
- Understand what constitutes small business success and failure.
- Appreciate what growth can mean and understand the range of possible influences on it.
- Appreciate why so few businesses grow to be large.
- Appreciate the main issues which can arise in the static, decline and termination stages.

INTRODUCTION

Part 1 starts with a summary, in Chapter 2, of some of the key inputs and triggers to our current understanding of enterprise, entrepreneurs and small businesses. Chapters 3 and 4 then explore the 'enterprise and entrepreneurs' aspect of this understanding, including the vocabulary used in talking about them, their origins and effects, as well as the influences on them. Often small businesses are the product of entrepreneurs and the reason why they are encouraged and supported, so Chapter 5 explores what small businesses are by examining their characteristics, definitions and variety. This chapter follows on by looking at their life cycles and issues they face in their development from conception to cessation.

THE STAGES OF DEVELOPMENT OF A BUSINESS

It has become customary to recognise a number of stages in the life of a business. However, it is important to recognise that the use of the term 'stage' in relation to the business development process does not mean that businesses develop in discrete phases with clear boundaries between them. Separating the development process into stages is rather like dividing the spectrum of visible light into colours. Traditionally there are said to be seven colours, but in reality there are not only seven distinct colours but a continuing gradation through the colours. We can say that one area is green compared with another area which is yellow, but we cannot say precisely where one changes to the other. Dividing the business development process into stages is helpful, in that there are issues at the heart of each stage that differ from the issues central to other stages; but, while we may be able to indicate broadly the stage of development of a business, we cannot say precisely when it moves from one stage to another.

Like distinguishing colours in the colour spectrum, the number of areas ascribed to the process is a matter of interpretation. However, unlike the colour spectrum, the order of the areas is not necessarily fixed. While a 'pre-start' stage cannot follow 'start-up', and 'termination' has to be the end, businesses do not have to progress through every possible stage in between: they can be static, they can grow and they can decline in any order, they can do these things more than once, and they can reverse their steps. There are many models of the different stages and the sequence in which they occur, but the reality is that very few businesses actually follow the models. Many of the models, in the way they are presented, imply steady growth; however, growth is not the norm and, where there is growth, it is generally achieved through a number of discrete steps, rather than by a steady, even progression. It is also important to recognise that these models do not explain what is happening inside a business: they only describe its situation, and they present symptoms not causes. Therefore they do not help in predicting what will happen next in a business.

Nevertheless some models are presented here to provide a context within which to consider different aspects of business formation and development. One of the simplest models has been that of Churchill and Lewis, which suggests that there can be five stages from early business existence to eventual maturity (see Table 6.1).

Table 6.1 *The five stages of business growth*

- Existence: staying alive by finding products or services and customers
- Survival: establishing the customer base, demonstrating viability
- Success: confidence in its market position, options for further growth
- Take-off: opting to go for growth
- Maturity: the characteristics of a larger, stable company

Source: Summarised from N. C. Churchill and V. L. Lewis, 'Growing Concerns: The Five Stages of Small Firm Growth', *Harvard Business Review*, Vol. 61, No. 3, May–June 1983, pp. 31–40.

Other models have additional stages that come either prior to or after the Churchill and Lewis stages, or show additional features in a progression through the stages. While stages which come before the formation of a business are not strictly stages in the development of that particular business, they are nevertheless relevant to the development of the entrepreneur and to an understanding of the inception of the business. These prior-to-business-start stages can include the following.

- *Culture.* People are more likely to think of starting a business, and that business is more likely to survive, if the underlying culture is one that will help to nurture awareness and interest as well as ideas and embryonic businesses.
- *The idea.* Before they can proceed to start-up, people need to have both the disposition to start a business and have a product or service idea around which the business can be formed.

- *The pre-start phase*. This is the process whereby those thinking of starting a business progress from the business idea to the stage of actually starting the business, infrequently after a revision of the idea.

There are also stages at the end of a business's life when it declines and terminates. So a fuller list of stages is included in the following sequence (which is also presented diagrammatically in Figure 6.1):

- culture and awareness;
- intention – the disposition and intention to start a business;
- idea – a product/service idea for the business;
- pre-start/preparation;
- start-up/inception;
- growth and expansion;
- static – including survival, consolidation, comfort and maturity;
- decline;
- termination.

As well as showing both pre-start and termination phases, this model also recognises the dynamics of business development. Despite the straight lines of most models, businesses very rarely progress steadily onwards and upwards. The diagram in Figure 6.2 recognises this by showing possible paths for

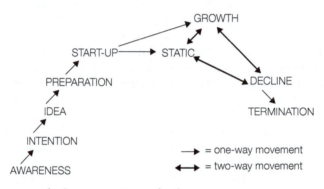

Figure 6.1 *Small business paths from conception to death*

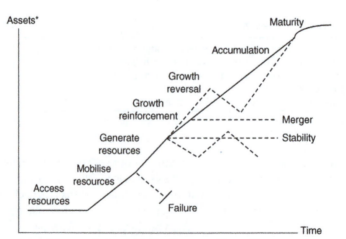

* Businesses, as they grow, accumulate assets, both tangible 'fixed' assets and intangible assets such as expertise and reputation. Assets are therefore used here as an indicator of growth.

Figure 6.2 *Growth process as reflected in possible growth paths*

Source: E. Garnsey, 'A New Theory of the Growth of the Firm', paper presented to the *ICSB 41st World Conference*, Stockholm, June 1996, p. 4.

a business, not only in steady growth, but also in a phase of growth reversal, in stability with possible oscillation, in a merger with another business and in early failure. This model suggests that there may be problems, or at least choices, to be faced by a business as it grows. These are elaborated further in Greiner's model in Figure 6.3.

These models, in effect, present precursors or other aspects of change which can be hard to measure, rather than the effects of change, such as growth, which can be quantified. Consequently, in practice, these aspects are less helpful when trying to identify the extent of development of a business. Nevertheless, their presentation can provide useful insights, and while the stage model approach may have its drawbacks, it helps to divide small businesses into different categories to make them easier to examine.

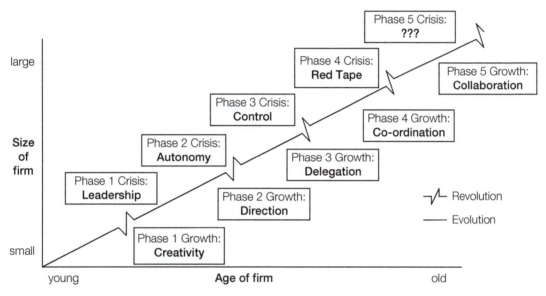

Figure 6.3 *The Greiner growth model*

Source: L. E. Greiner, 'Evolution and Revolution as Organisations Grow', *Harvard Business Review*, Vol. 50, No. 4, July/August 1972.

PREPARING FOR BUSINESS START-UP

The supply of entrepreneurs: the culture stage

What all the listed stages of business development, apart from culture and awareness, have in common is that they are all concerned with people who might be or already are in business. To use a horticultural analogy, they all deal with plants: with sowing the seeds of plants, with growing plants, with pruning plants, with plants flowering and even with plants dying. The culture and awareness stage, however, deals with the preparation of the ground: the preparation of a medium which will encourage, feed and support the seeds and growing plants. Chapter 4 has shown that the surrounding human society or culture is important for business growth, just as the condition and type of the soil are important for plants.

The entrepreneur and the opportunity

Shane has suggested that the components needed for entrepreneurial outcomes are individuals and opportunities:

> The entrepreneurial process begins with the perception of the existence of opportunities or situations in which resources can be recombined for a potential profit. Alert individuals, called entrepreneurs,

discover these opportunities, and develop ideas for how to pursue them, including the development of a product or service that will be provided to customers. These individuals then obtain resources, design organisations or other modes of opportunity exploitation or develop a strategy to exploit the opportunity.[1]

Sarasvathy has found, however, that 'effectual' entrepreneurs (see Chapter 11) often fabricate opportunities from what they do and that they start ventures, not primarily because they see a profit-making opportunity, but because they want to follow an interest or passion.[2] An opportunity thus fabricated can be very profitable but was not the original driver.

A distinction has been made between a small business opportunity and an entrepreneurial business opportunity. Small business people, it has been suggested, typically spot an opportunity to do something they can do, but which does not necessarily have any real growth potential, whereas entrepreneurial opportunities offer something new and different to the market.[3] However. the implications of Sarasvathy's findings are that such distinctions can only be made after the event, as many entrepreneurial opportunities are the result of people developing what they can do.

Drucker[4] suggests that change often provides the opportunity for the new and the different. Therefore, given the rapid pace of change in, amongst other things, consumer tastes and technology, these are areas where there should be business opportunities to exploit. Table 6.2 provides examples of the quickening pace of change in the introduction of new technology, but new technology, as well as opportunity, also involves risk. Many businesses described as being based on 'cutting edge' (i.e. does not yet work!) technology are often found to be based on under-developed technology that runs away with resources and leads to high failure rates.

Table 6.2 *New technology adoption rate*

The time it has taken for new technology to reach 25% of the US population. For example household electricity was first made available in 1873 and it took 46 years for 25% of the US population to get electricity.

The technology	Time in years
Household electricity (1873)	46
Telephone (1875)	35
Automobile (1885)	55
Radio (1906)	22
Television (1925)	26
Video recorder (1952)	34
Personal computer (1975)	15
Cellular phone (1983)	13
Internet (1991)	7
Smartphone (2002)	4

Source: Based on *Wall Street Journal*, in W. Bygrave, 'Building an Entrepreneurial Economy: Lessons from the United States', *Business Strategy Review*, Vol. 9, No. 2, 1998, p. 11 and other sources.

Pre-start preparation

The pre-start stage can be defined as beginning when there is an intention to start a business and initial steps are taken to prepare for it and ending when a business starts. Businesses do not arise fully fledged from even the most positive of enterprise cultures. A time of preparation is still needed and this can be very long. The preparation may include identifying a suitable opportunity (stemming from the idea), acquiring the necessary knowledge and skills, and locating the contacts who will help. Continuing the horticultural analogy, it is the stage of planting and germinating seeds. The growing medium is important, but seeds are also needed to produce plants, and those seeds need the ability to take root and to put out leaves. In business terms, negotiating this stage requires both a willingness to start it and some ideas about what might best be done in it.

If these conditions are met and there is a desire to proceed, then it is important to know how to do so. Various suggestions have been made about the key components of the ideal pre-start process. The formula produced by Peterson and Rondstadt (Figure 6.4) summarises some of the key components that are needed for start-up success, components that by implication might be assembled in the pre-start stage.[5]

$$\boxed{\begin{aligned} \text{Entrepreneurial success} = \;&\text{New venture idea} \\ &+ \text{Entrepreneurial know-how} \\ &+ \text{Entrepreneurial know-who} \end{aligned}}$$

Figure 6.4 *Entrepreneurial success*

Source: R. Peterson and R. Rondstadt, 'A Silent Strength: Entrepreneurial Know Who', *The 16th ESBS/EFMD/IMD Report*, Vol. 86, No. 4, p. 11.

A traditional view of enterprise has been based on the assumption that some individuals are inherently more enterprising than others. Because of that predisposition towards enterprise, it was assumed that, given the right stimulus, such individuals were more likely to try starting a business. Consequently, there could be virtually no pre-start stage in the sense defined above. Another view of enterprise, and of enterprising behaviour, is considered in Chapter 3. It is based on taking advantage of the attributes and resources that an individual may possess, or may believe that he or she possesses. Attributes may include self-confidence, diligence, perseverance, interpersonal skills and innovative behaviour. Resources may include finance, experience, knowledge, skills, a network and a track record. It is suggested that it is the interaction amongst these factors that produces a rational response, on the basis of available information, when the possibility occurs of a business start-up. Illustration 6.1 brings this situation together under a Six Phases of Start-up model (but also see 'effectuation' in Chapter 11).

It is acknowledged that there is inertia in individual behaviour and that it can take a discontinuity in work or in life to trigger a review of an individual's situation. Whether that will lead to an individual trying his or her own enterprise will depend on the attributes and resources he or she has accumulated and his

---

ILLUSTRATION 6.1 – STARTING A BUSINESS

There are many things that can be considered necessities in starting a business. The following list divides them into six phases.

Acquiring motivation. Finding the stimulus and commitment to the notion of starting a business.

Finding an idea. Getting an idea for further investigation. This may involve considering different ways of getting into business such as franchising or buying a business.

Validating the idea. Testing the proposed product/service, both for technical and functional efficiency and for market acceptance as well as protecting the idea.

Identifying the resources needed. Planning the scale of business entry. Identifying in detail the resources required, the timing, and the other support needed.

Negotiating to get into business. Assembling the resources; negotiating for finance, premises and contracts; deciding the name and the legal form of the business and registering them; as well as informing the tax authorities.

Systems and linkages. Developing the on-going business system. Coping with statutory requirements. Establishing ties with customers and suppliers. Developing the workforce.

or her perception of the opportunity and of environmental factors such as the availability of assistance. The acquisition of those attributes and resources, if it is done with a view to a possible business start, is the pre-start stage. It is generally perceived as a stage of individual, or small team, preparation and it is believed that an individual, or a team, can be helped to acquire the components for a start-up. There are many ways in which this can be done, but the following paragraphs illustrate some of the possibilities.

The idea

The 'idea' can cover both the idea of starting a business and the product or service idea for a particular business. The idea of starting a business comes from the issues just explored, and particular business ideas come from the opportunities considered earlier, which may come from a number of sources, such as those listed in Table 6.3.

Table 6.3 Approaches to starting a business

Approach	Source	Key foundation
Turning an interest or hobby into a business	Long-standing passion	Personal connections
Becoming a professional consultant or trainer	Specialised knowledge	Professional contacts
Acquiring an existing business	Managerial and marketing skills	Financial resources
Taking on a franchise	Organisational ability	Financial and marketing resources
Creating a new business	Identifying a potentially profitable opportunity	Enterprising spirit

Source: Based on R. Lessem, 'Getting into Self-employment', *Management Education and Development*, 1984, Spring, p. 31.

Finding an idea can be either deliberate or accidental. In the deliberate search mode the would-be entrepreneur purposefully tries to start a business and actively looks for an idea. This may involve attending business meetings and events of all kinds or getting together with other like-minded individuals to brainstorm ideas. Alternatively, again in purposeful search mode, the entrepreneur, whilst in employment, looks for a business opportunity which is perhaps not being taken up by his or her present employer. In the unforeseen coincidence mode, however, the idea may actually find the would-be entrepreneur. Often business ideas develop because the entrepreneur finds he or she cannot purchase a product or service and decides to start a business to supply the product or service they could not obtain.

Know-how

Know-how covers a number of areas of knowledge and skill, all of which may be needed by the owner-manager of a small business if that business is to be successful. This know-how has been shown to have (at least) four dimensions as shown in Table 6.4.

Table 6.4 The four dimensions of management development

Functional knowledge and skills	Generic management knowledge and skills
The technical knowledge and abilities appropriate to the business. The main know-how typically of 'the butcher, the baker and the candlestick maker'	Planning, organising, managing time, negotiating, co-ordinating resources, solving problems (not functionally specific)
Business and strategic awareness	**Personal competencies**
Understanding the bigger picture, conceptual skills, analysis, synthesis, creativity, opportunity-spotting	Results orientation, initiative, interpersonal skills, enthusiasm, perseverance, commitment, leadership

Source: Based on R. E. Boyatzis, *The Competent Manager: A Model for Effective Performance* (New York, NY: Wiley, 1982).

Small business training is often the means offered for increasing small business know-how. Despite the plethora of courses sometimes offered, it is important to recognise the potential barriers that can make small business owners averse to conventional forms of training, and some of the possible counterbalancing incentives (see Table 7.5). Experience might also be supposed to increase small business owner know-how, but Storey has not found evidence the business owners do learn from their experience[6] (see also Chapter 12).

Know-who and social capital

The expressions, 'it's not what you know, but whom you know' and 'the old boy network' reflect a sometimes popular, but essentially negative, perception of certain social networks. Yet many of those who have examined small business networking are convinced of its importance for the success of the enterprise.

> Credibility is established through personal contact and knowledge of the skills, motivation and past performance of the individual – the bankers call this the 'track record'. Since for an embryonic business there is no trading track record, investors must look to their previous relationship with the individual, whether it be commercial or personal. Thus, for example, a previous employer may agree to be the first customer, a friend may allow use of spare office space, or a relative may be prepared to lend money with little real hope of a return in the short or even the medium term.[7]

What used to be known as networking is an aspect of acquiring social capital – which is considered in more detail in Chapter 13. Information, advice and guidance are often seen as the benefits of a network, and they are the traditional base upon which many small business support agencies have been built. But, while they may be important characteristics of an active network, they are not the only ones,[8] as Table 6.5 suggests.

Networks involving small businesses have a number of particular features. They are usually based on personal contacts, not official links, they are informal and are not openly advertised. They are flexible, being built up and maintained specifically to suit the purposes of their members. It is often these networks that give their member entrepreneurs the potential to react quickly to new developments. As Moensted reveals in his study of high-tech firms, entrepreneurs use networks not only to 'exploit existing opportunities, they use networks to form new relations for creating opportunities'.[9] Having 'know-who' competency, networking skills and/or social capital can be essential therefore for success in dynamic environments.

Table 6.5 *Some of the benefits which can be obtained from networks*

Among the benefits which can be obtained from networks are:

- *Information.* Entrepreneurs use their social networks to signal their intentions and to gather information about potential opportunities.

- *Advice and guidance.* Entrepreneurs also need advice about how or when to do things and guidance in how to do them.

- *Sponsorship and support.* Family and friends will not only provide introductions into appropriate networks, but will also offer emotional and tangible support.

- *Credibility and references.* Family and friends can provide credibility in areas unfamiliar to the entrepreneur and other contacts, former customers, for example, can provide references.

- *Control.* Membership of the network, and assistance from it, require certain standards of behaviour. Owner-managers who do not conduct their business in a way that is acceptable to the community may quickly find themselves, and their businesses, isolated.

- *Business.* There are market networks of customers, suppliers and partners as well as production networks of subcontractors, consultants and service suppliers. In addition, there are networks of businesses that may work in collaboration on projects. This structure can provide all the components necessary for a project without the need for 'vertical or horizontal integration'.

- *Resources.* Friends and family can supply resources. Many businesses are assisted by the informal venture capital market that their owners access through their networks.

And the result

Possessing or acquiring some or all of the possible components of the pre-start stage does not guarantee that a business will be started. The decision still has to be made to do it and this is often triggered by an external event. It has also been supposed that the decision is a choice essentially about the balance of risk – and that while the chances of success increase as relevant attributes and resources are built up, the costs of failure can also increase as personal financial commitments accumulate. However, it is now being suggested that social group encouragement can play a large part (see Chapter 9).

GETTING STARTED

The typical small business start-up is a new business venture; in temporary, small or unusual premises; nearly always financed from within, plus bank borrowings and with little or no long-term borrowing; usually small in terms of employment, often with only family members involved.[10] Table 6.6 presents an analysis of such a business. The reasons for starting a business may vary, but the main values driving the business will be those of the founder(s). The basic skills of the founder will also determine the functional emphasis of the business. Normally, management will be by direct supervision. The main efforts will hinge around developing a commercially acceptable product or service and establishing a niche for it in the marketplace.

Table 6.6 *Analysis of a start-up business*

Aspect of the business	Description
Key issues	Obtaining customers Economic production
Top management role	Direct supervision
Organisational structure	Unstructured
Product and market research	None
Systems and controls	Simple book-keeping Eyeball contact
Major sources of finance	Owner's savings Owner's friends and relatives Suppliers and leasing
Cash generation	Negative
Major investments	Premises, plant and equipment
Product/market	Single line, limited channels and market

Source: Reprinted from M. Scott and R. Bruce, 'Five Stages of Growth in Small Business', *Long Range Planning*, Vol. 20, No. 3, 1987, p. 48.

The result will normally be one working unit operating in a single market with limited channels of distribution. Sources of funds will be haphazard and will place heavy demands on the founder, his or her partner(s) and friends and relatives. With the high level of uncertainty, the level of forward planning is low.[11]

Needs

At the stage of starting up a business, the entrepreneur doing it and/or the business can have many needs. This is one list:

- Capital
- Family support
- Customers
- Suppliers
- Employees
- Premises

- Company formation: a business name, stationery, management procedures
- Infrastructure
- Management skills: provided externally (consultants) or internally (training)
- Information and advice
- Confidence.[12]

Barriers

As well as facing the start-up needs of businesses, which are in the main an inevitable aspect of the process in which they are engaged, entrepreneurs can, at this stage, also face a number of distinct barriers:

- *Building credibility*. This refers to the problem of how to acquire credibility in order to get the resources necessary to prove what you can do.
- *High entry or survival barriers*. The barriers to entry into business will depend on the amount of investment, technology and labour skills required or on the availability of niches or of growing markets. Then, once started, the business may find that there may be barriers to survival. High survival barriers occur when there is intense competition, saturated markets, excess capacity and changing technology or product quality requirements.
- *The burden of government bureaucracy*. Ignorance is no defence when dealing with the legal requirements of officialdom. There are penalties if forms are not returned, or are returned incorrectly; however, full and proper compliance can be costly, even if only in the time it requires, and this is proportionally more costly for small businesses than for large ones.
- *The business plan*. Business plans are often inappropriate (see Chapter 11). When asked for a plan the new entrepreneur feels irritated because producing it takes him or her away from the real work, frightened because he or she is not sure what it means, and confused about how to plan when things change daily.[13]

Business regulation

As indicated many would-be entrepreneurs and those in business often state that 'red tape' is a prime cause of concern and frustration and excessive legislative and regulatory burdens are often thought to be a significant disincentive for those who are thinking of starting a business. The process of registering a business can often differ considerably from country to country where local rules and regulations can either encourage, or deter, entrepreneurship. The 2016 report compiled by the World Bank ranks 'ease of doing business' across 189 economies. A selection of the results, which show that there is a wide variation in the extent of such burdens, is shown in Table 6.7.

The business plan

For the role of the business plan see Chapter 11.

Financing the start-up

The majority of people starting or growing small businesses use funds from one or more of the four Fs: founder, family, friends and foolish strangers. It has been reported that in the UK one third of small businesses do not borrow at all from banks, another third regularly move into and out of an overdraft, and one third are consistent borrowers.[14] It has also been reported by the Federation of Small Businesses that 'Personal savings/inheritance and loans from friends and family are most commonly found among micro businesses and those that have been established within the last five years'.[15] The use of retained profits and bank lending is greatest among small businesses and those that have been established for more than ten years. To some extent small business financing issues vary from country to country. In countries where the banking system has been very undeveloped and unreliable – especially when this is combined with the need to charge very high interest rates in times of high inflation – the result had been that businesses there rarely used bank financing. In almost every country, however, there are claims of

Table 6.7 *Economies ranked on their ease of doing business*

Economy	(benchmarked June 2015)	
	Ease of doing business rank (out of 189 countries)	Ease of doing business score (Scale 0 – 100)
Singapore	1	87.34
New Zealand	2	86.79
Denmark	3	84.40
Korea, Rep.	4	83.88
Hong Kong SAR, China	5	83.67
United Kingdom	6	82.46
United States	7	82.15
Sweden	8	81.72
Norway	9	81.61
Finland	10	81.05
Taiwan, China	11	80.55
Australia	13	80.08
Canada	14	80.07
Germany	15	79.87
Austria	21	78.38
Portugal	23	77.57
Poland	25	76.45
Switzerland	26	76.04
France	27	75.96
Netherlands	28	75.94
Spain	33	74.86
Japan	34	74.72
Bulgaria	38	73.72
Mexico	38	73.72
Belgium	43	72.50
Italy	45	72.07
Russian Federation	51	70.99
Israel	53	70.56
Turkey	55	69.16
Greece	60	68.38
Luxembourg	61	68.31
South Africa	73	64.89
China	84	62.93
Brazil	116	57.67
Argentina	121	56.78
India	130	54.68

Source: World Bank Group. Taken from www.doingbusiness.org/rankings (accessed 15 October 2016).

disadvantage because finding funding is harder for small businesses than it is for bigger ones. There is no doubt that the difficulty of financing small businesses is one of the most frequently heard complaints. The reasons for this difficulty include the following:

- *Small businesses are typically high risk.* Suppliers of business finance, when they exist, want something in return for their money. Usually this is a financial return, either interest or dividends, plus eventually some way of getting back the initial investment or a multiple of it. If the finance sought is a development grant then returning it may not be an issue, but there will still be an expectation by the provider that some benefits will be delivered, such as job creation or other economic benefits. In all cases, if the money is to be provided in advance of the returns, which is inevitably the case, there needs to be some indication that the return will come and that the business will survive to deliver it. Although the often quoted very high failure rates especially for young businesses are not always what they seem to be (see later in this chapter), a significant proportion of small businesses do fail soon after start-up. Small businesses are more vulnerable therefore than larger ones, and will need to provide potential investors with some evidence that, in their particular cases, they will not fail.

- *New small businesses do not have a track record.* It is said that business financiers generally assess a business on three aspects: the management, the management and the management. For a new business with no trading history, and often with untried management, it is very difficult to provide satisfactory evidence that they will not only survive but will also do well enough to provide investors with the returns they seek.
- *It is not cost-effective to provide small amounts of money.* Any commercial source of funds will want to check the business, its backers and its proposals before investing and will want to monitor its investment on a regular basis. This is sometimes known as 'due diligence'. The cost of these checks will have to be recouped from any eventual income from the investments made. It is therefore not cost-effective to check requests for small amounts of money, because the cost of checking will not be significantly lower than for larger amounts yet there will be less interest out of which to recoup it. (However, some steps can be taken to reduce the costs of small amounts of assistance. One example in the USA is the Wells Fargo Bank, which stopped monitoring many of the small businesses to which it had advanced loans because the cost of monitoring was more than the bad debts it incurred – and see also the Grameen Bank in Illustration 15.4.)
- *Small businesses lack security for loans.* Small businesses often lack the security needed to support loans, having few or no significant realisable assets in the business.
- *Small businesses can be equity-averse.* There is evidence that many owners of small businesses can be averse to sharing the equity, and thus the ownership, of the businesses with anyone else. Investors, however, often like to take some equity because it gives them some control over their investments and an opportunity to make greater returns.

The result is that a pattern of small business funding can be as depicted in Figure 6.5, which is based on American experience. Sometimes significant amounts of early-stage funding are also found from credit card funding – often using multiple credit cards. Essentially, however, small business funding can be viewed as falling typically into three levels or stages. In the initial stage the funds come mainly from informal sources, as up to 80 per cent or more of funding at start-up does not involve an equity stake from an outside partner. This funding can be supplemented by a term-based bank loan and overdraft facility and perhaps a small loan or grant from a public body. Second-stage funding might then come

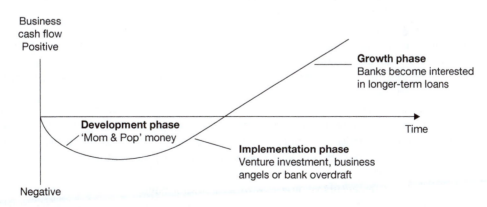

Figure 6.5 *Early-stage small business finance*

Source: Based on author's personal contacts relaying US experience.

from a larger bank loan secured on an asset and perhaps making use of the Enterprise Finance Guarantee (which can underwrite up to 75% of the loan), possibly supplemented by an equity stake from a business angel, and a few businesses might succeed in securing formal venture capital. It is then at the third stage where the funding is more likely to be of the package type, from a number of sources, perhaps combining personal, bank, public sector loans and grants and equity investment. More recently crowd funding has proved another funding option for a growing number of small businesses and start-ups. It enables groups of investors to come together to fund businesses looking for investment. Each investor pledges a small amount in return for a stake in the business, return on their investment or another benefit (such as a discount on products or services).

GROWTH

Influences on business growth

Not all businesses grow. As Chapter 8 indicates, there is no automatic growth imperative in businesses and many businesses, once started, stay the same size. Also those businesses which do grow do not grow steadily and constantly. Nevertheless, for many people, the key stage in a business is when it is growing – not least because that is when it is providing more economic benefits such as employment. Consequently much effort has been put into exploring the factors that influence and/or determine business growth.

The influence of the entrepreneur: motivation and aspiration

It is a characteristic of small business that powers of decision are centralised at the level of the owner-manager, so his or her personality, skills, responsibilities, attitude and behaviour will have a decisive influence on business strategy. One area in which the determinants of business growth have been sought is in the entrepreneur behind the business. Typical of the analysts using this approach is Kirchhoff, who developed a 'dynamic capitalism typology' to explain the relationship between innovation and firm growth.[16] The typology divides businesses into four categories: economic core, ambitious, glamorous and constrained growth.

'Economic core' businesses are the largest single category. Typically they are low on innovation and on growth, but their nature can change after a period. 'Ambitious' businesses achieve high rates of growth with one, or a few, initial innovations but growth cannot be sustained without additional innovations (usually in the product or service or in its marketing). With additional innovations, businesses become 'glamorous'. Glamorous businesses, according to Kirchhoff, can have experienced periods of 'constrained growth' for two broad reasons.[17] First, growth may be self-constrained owing to the owner's reluctance to relinquish ownership and control to generate the necessary resources for growth; and second, it may be constrained where businesses are genuinely limited by a lack of resources. They can often be highly innovative, but still unable to secure early-stage capital.

Kirchhoff concludes that 'what is interesting about these four classes of businesses is that they do not depend upon industrial sector, business size, age nor location'.[18] This typology, he continues, 'identifies the firms' behaviours that indicate the true ambitions and goals of the owners and defines their contribution to economic growth. Aspiring entrepreneurs need to realistically assess their personal ambitions and where they wish to be in this typology.'[19]

For many business owners, however, the growth of their businesses is not an objective. Growth is associated with many unattractive features including loss of management control, reliance on others, sharing responsibilities and decision-making, perhaps relinquishing some ownership stake, and unnecessary risk. A desire to spend more time with one's family or to engage in other forms of social and leisure activity are also valid reasons.

Even among those entrepreneurs who seek growth, significant numbers would appear to seek only moderate or limited growth. They may reach a stage or plateau, described as a 'comfort zone', at which the owner is satisfied with his or her condition and the costs of pursuing continued growth exceed the expected benefits. These perceived costs will dominate over any material or psychological gains that might be expected from growth. As more than one owner has remarked, 'The problems grow geometrically while the firm grows arithmetically.'

The motivation of the owner is undoubtedly a very important ingredient in the growth process and, of course, the motivation can change over time as the business develops and events external and internal to the business occur. It is a dynamic situation. Businesses can appear to be in a steady state for many years and then begin to grow rapidly. Growth is not necessarily a continuous process for many businesses, which is an important consideration for those who rely on recent past performance as a predictor of future performance. One possible reason is a need to establish the business – to build strong roots – before moving on and upwards. The majority of businesses show no growth for their first six years, while more than 50 per cent of surviving businesses show growth after six years. Indeed, rapid growth, when it happens, appears to begin after six to eight years of trading.[20]

It is also worth noting that a significant number of entrepreneurs, instead of managing their established businesses whether in a growth phase or not, may be much more stimulated by, or capable of, generating new business ideas and converting them into new ventures. The excitement and fulfilment for such people may be in creating something new, not in managing an existing operation. In fact while their businesses may essentially be in the early stages of business development, the entrepreneurs themselves can become obstacles to the further development of the business as neither their interest nor competency may be at the appropriate levels. Such people may favour multiple business ownership as habitual entrepreneurs (see Chapter 9).

In conclusion, it is reasonable to deduce that the entrepreneur's (or business leader's) ambition and desire to grow are critical. In addition, the skills of the entrepreneur are particularly important in the early stages of growth. The ability to broaden and adapt to changing circumstances is likely to be of major importance in removing obstacles to growth. Different types of behaviour may be required in different market situations, and different personal competencies are likely to be needed to deal with the different levels of complexity and uncertainty in the business environment. It is important that entrepreneurs are willing to delegate and, by implication, that employees must be capable and willing to accept responsibility. It is also a truism to say that an inability to manage growth, despite a motivation to do so, will prevent growth. It is undoubtedly the case that many businesses fail to grow because of a variety of barriers, including those of a technical, marketing and financial nature, but not least those which are managerial (which may in fact be at the root of most of the other barriers). How some management factors can help or hinder growth at different stages is captured in simplified form in Figure 6.6.

Other influences

A second area in which factors relevant to the growth of a business have been sought is in the characteristics of the business itself such as its structure: its ownership, legal form, age and size; and its management skills and performance, including its access to resources. For instance, studies have examined whether second or subsequent owners are more likely than first owners to grow businesses or whether limited companies grow more than sole traders or partnerships. They have looked at issues such as management ability, market positioning and new product introduction. One factor which seems to have

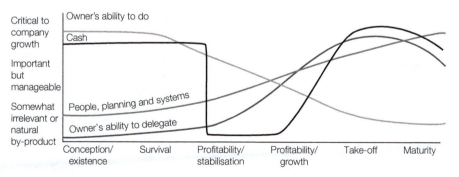

Figure 6.6 *Management factors and stages*

Source: N. C. Churchill, 'The Six Key Phases of Company Growth', 'Mastering Enterprise', *Financial Times*, February 1997, p. 3.

an effect is age, as studies indicate that younger and smaller businesses grow more quickly than older and larger ones. It is important to note, however, that one reason for a correlation between size and growth is that it is easier to achieve a doubling in any growth parameter if the business is smaller to start with. Few large businesses would try a 100 per cent increase in employment at one stroke, but that is just what a previously one-person business does when it recruits its first employee. Additionally, many businesses will grow rapidly initially to reach the 'critical mass' needed to service their market efficiently, but they subsequently 'plateau'.

However, in general, findings about the business's characteristics and growth are of very limited value for policy purposes. As with information about the entrepreneur, either the causal relationship is unclear or no meaningful basis for policy intervention has been identified. Indeed none of the structural factors identified indicates, with adequate clarity, anything about the ambitions or goals exhibited by a business's owners and managers. Delmar *et al.* record that 'research has produced limited knowledge about the key relationships among growth, profitability, and survival for new firms'. Following, over an eight-year period, a panel of knowledge-intensive new firms started in Sweden between 1995 and 2002, they find 'strong support for the notion that profitability enhances both survival and growth, and growth helps profitability but has a negative effect on survival'.[21]

Yet another approach to understanding and explaining growth lies in examining the impact of factors or constraints external to the entrepreneur or the business. These include macro-economic variables such as aggregate demand, taxation, regulations, labour market skills and labour relations, but also embrace sector- and region-specific matters such as product/service and/or market, competition, government assistance, location and the availability (and use) of information. However, as with business characteristics, examinations of external factors have not produced good indicators or predictors of growth.

A theory, however, that links issues such as location, competition and government support to the competitiveness, and hence to the potential growth, of businesses, is based around the cluster effect. This theory is propounded by Porter who, following a four-year study of ten important trading nations, ultimately concluded that nations succeed in particular industries because their home environment is the most forward-looking, dynamic and challenging.[22] These conclusions, he suggests, contradict the conventional wisdom that labour costs, interest rates, exchange rates and economies of scale are the most potent determinants of competitiveness. It is too easy, he says, for governments to adopt policies, such as joint projects for R&D, that operate on the belief that independent research by domestic rivals is wasteful and duplicative, that collaborative efforts achieve economies of scale, and that individual companies are likely to under-invest in R&D because they cannot reap all the benefits. That view, he claims, is flawed and fundamentally misperceives the true sources of competitive advantage.

Porter argues that, while successful businesses will each employ their own strategy, they achieve competitive advantage through acts of innovation. Further, he believes that it is demanding buyers in the domestic market who pressure companies to innovate faster. Why is it, he asks, that certain companies based in certain countries are capable of consistent innovation? The answer, he suggests, is a combination of four main attributes of a region: the availability of appropriate labour and infrastructure; strong home market demand; the presence of supporting industries; and business strategy, structure and rivalry.

How these attributes combine to produce a successful industry is complex, but Porter notes that internationally competitive businesses are usually found in geographically concentrated clusters of related businesses where closeness helps to encourage the attributes to develop. Thus the clusters facilitate the emergence of the conditions which support growth.

The role of chance

Instead of seeking the ingredients for, or predictors of, growth, some observers have emphasised the role of chance. For instance it has been observed that the size distribution of a population of businesses can be derived from a mechanical chance model. Thus, in aggregate, business size follows a 'random walk'. This might suggest that there is some 'iron law' of business growth which determines the size distribution. Indeed, studies suggest that there are many factors influencing firms' growth rates, and while two or three may exert a significant influence relative to the others, they still explain a relatively small proportion of any variance produced within a given sample of firms.

It is possible to conclude, therefore, that chance or luck plays a part in determining which businesses grow. To suggest that all successful entrepreneurs were merely lucky may be to overstate the situation, but as Reid and Jacobsen suggest, 'it is necessary to caution those who would ignore the role of chance in determining the fortunes of the small entrepreneurial firm'.[23] In addition, as Nelson and Winter note, 'luck is the principal factor that finally distinguishes winners from near winners – although vast differences of skills and competence may separate contenders from non-contenders'.[24]

Storey has argued that most theories of business growth are 'one-way bets' because they provide an explanation only for growing businesses and not for declining ones. Instead he suggests that a combination of the role of chance together with the optimism of the business owner can provide an insight, not just into why very few new/small businesses grow continuously, but also into why more individuals in the USA who initially failed in business ultimately became successful compared to their counterparts in Europe.[25] If it is game of chance, then you cannot learn to play the lottery successfully – the only thing you can do is buy more tickets – which reflects access to finance rather than entrepreneurial talent.[26]

Storey points out that many businesses never grow and contraction is much more typical. Further, 'even if [the typical firm] survives – which is unlikely – performance is highly volatile in the short, medium and long run [and] this volatility is extremely difficult to predict'.[27] Thus growth in one period is not a good predictor of growth in the next – so businesses which survive and show net growth over a long period are like gamblers who stay at the table because they have a run of success. Further, if the cost of each bet is low, then they can afford more bets and therefore have more wins – which explains why those who fail in the USA can try again.

There is certainly no lack of anecdotal evidence from successful entrepreneurs about the role of luck, and it is surely undeniable that 'in the presence of uncertainty and bounded rationality, fortune will play a significant if variable role'.[28]

Constraints on growth

Instead of trying to identify the factors which might promote growth, another way of promoting growth might be based on trying to counter those factors which constrain or hinder growth. Table 6.8 shows

Table 6.8 Obstacles to the success of business

Issues reported	Per cent reporting this issue
The economy	59
Competition	56
Red tape	54
Not able to raise prices	52
Regulations	49
Taxation etc.	48
Cash flow	42
Late payment	40
Recruiting staff	33
Shortages of skills generally	31
Obtaining finance	28
Pensions	22
Availability/cost of suitable premises	21
No obstacles	5

Source: BIS Research Paper No. 214, *Small Business Survey 2014: SME Employers* (London: Department for Business, Innovation and Skills, March 2015) p. 82.

the obstacles to meeting business objectives reported in a small firm survey of 4355 UK businesses with fewer than 500 employees carried out in 2014 by the Department for Business, Innovation and Skills. The top issues are all primarily factors external to the businesses themselves.

It may be reasonable to accept these rather typical results at face value, subject to two caveats: first, businesses may tend to blame external, and therefore uncontrollable, factors before internal, controllable factors; and second, there is a tendency to confuse causes and effects. In the latter case, financial constraints may become apparent because of a lack of demand or, in the case of a growing business, because of a reluctance to dilute ownership or control or because of poor financial management skills.

A common-sense approach

It seems that a common-sense approach is to recognise that growth is likely to be dependent upon a combination of chance and the interaction of a number of influences, and that these influences may be important in different combinations for different businesses. This makes generalisations very imprecise and of limited use as guides to action. Given the heterogeneity of entrepreneurs and of small businesses, and the complexity and diversity of the markets in which they operate, any attempt to produce a comprehensive theory or any meaningful analysis of growth may be unrealistic. One may also add that there is no single correct management of a business for growth and that growth itself, as has been noted, is not a simple linear process: rather, if they grow at all, businesses expand, contract and expand again several times and at different rates. As Urwin suggests:

> The group of high-growth firms changes constantly, as we experience high levels of attrition. As such, identifying a group of firms that is growing rapidly at one time and that will continue to grow is more or less impossible. Furthermore, the high-growth firms are likely to be a heterogeneous group. This means that using a public policy approach to incubate and pick winners is more or less impossible.[29]

STATIC PHASES (SURVIVAL, CONSOLIDATION, COMFORT AND MATURITY)

Birch's mice are businesses which stay small, but businesses of any size can remain static for various periods of time. This can be due to coping with issues such as survival or consolidation or for reasons such as comfort or maturity. Such phases of business development are the reality for many businesses; therefore, they are examined next, together with other realities of business life such as decline and, if decline cannot be arrested, termination.

A static, or non-growth, stage in small business development may not sound very exciting, but it is the state of most small businesses. Once they have started their own business, many electricians, plumbers, chimney sweeps and consultants, for instance, rarely grow, and many other one-person businesses are the same. Their businesses are not ailing: operating the businesses may keep the people concerned very busy so the businesses are operating actively and sustainably, but they aren't growing. Remaining at the same size is the normal state for them.

Because, by definition, the static stage is not one that produces results in terms of increased employment, turnover or other benefits, it is often ignored. Growth is a much more attractive stage in those terms, but in many cases it is in the static stage that the growth businesses of the future are to be found. Growth does not often follow immediately after start-up. But even if a static business is not a growth business of the future it can still perform a useful function. Together, static businesses provide significant employment. As noted in Chapter 5 (Table 5.1), they are seen as an essential part of the economic and social fabric; they provide choice and diversity; they provide the necessary infrastructure support for other growth businesses and they can be useful role models.

It is possible to distinguish more than one type of state during which a business does not grow. Survival has been the name given to that period following start-up during which a business may not grow but is nevertheless working hard to maintain its position and struggling to establish itself as a viable enterprise. Once established, a business may have a period of building resources, of consolidation, before the next move. Because a business shows few signs of growth for a relatively long period does not mean that it will never grow. In many cases the growth of a business has been likened to that of bamboo, which can lie dormant for many years before suddenly shooting up in a single season.

There is a large group of businesses whose growth is constrained by their owners' limited ambitions or by their market niche. This state has been labelled comfort or maturity. As noted, there may be many reasons why a business does not expand, such as the desired lifestyle of the owner-manager, the limits of his or her management capability, or even peer pressure not to get too far ahead. In general, however, this phase of development is characterised by a business which has taken up its share of the markets, has reached the limits of its capacity, or for any other managerial, political or social reason remains at the same size either in physical or economic terms.

A categorisation of static businesses can now be summarised:

- *Survival*: This is the stage which comes after start-up. Typically, a 'surviving' business has the potential to be a viable entity, but needs to work at it. It is probably a one-product or one-service business, but is concentrating on short-term issues of survival rather than the longer-term issues of future growth potential.
- *Consolidation*: After winning the struggle to survive or to grow, most businesses need a period of rest to build up the reserves they need to move forward. This may not be a conscious decision or a deliberate strategy. What was happening may only be obvious in retrospect, when subsequent growth can be seen to have been built on the contacts, the credibility and the expertise accumulated at this stage. A period of consolidation following a period of survival may be one during which even businesses which do eventually grow show few indications of their potential.
- *Comfort*: For a business that does not move on to growth, 'consolidation' can easily merge into 'comfort': the state in which a business is doing enough to survive at least into the medium term and is providing enough profits to maintain the owner's desired standard of living. There may be little incentive to do anything different.
- *Maturity*: Maturity is generally seen as coming after some growth, and indeed there may still be slow continued growth. The businesses concerned are no longer in the first stages of their existence. They may be passing the peak of their products' life cycles, or they may be moving out of the category of small businesses because their management structure is facing a transition phase in which personal contact and word of mouth have to be replaced by more formal systems to cope with a larger organisation and more decentralisation. The onset of maturity may be a transition, therefore, either onwards to bigger and better things, or sideways towards an eventual decline.

The issues

Many static businesses are doing what their owners want, and their owners' main requirements are that they continue to do that. The motivation of the owner is critical. A business can just be operating sustainably or be adapting and changing while staying still in terms of turnover or employment, but in the long term staying static is rarely a good strategy. It must always be presumed that competition will change or increase, and in that case not to try to grow may be to invite decline. The needs at this stage are for encouragement and incentive, either to prevent decline or to encourage expansion.

The needs of these businesses include:

- Needs of survival businesses
  - control of the business
  - generating revenues sufficient to cover all expenses
  - supervision of the work
  - both entrepreneurial and administrative management
  - simple structures, systems and controls
  - product and/or market research.

- Needs of mature businesses
  - expense control
  - increased productivity
  - niche marketing, especially if the industry is declining
  - watchdog top management, taking a leadership role
  - product innovation, to replace products towards the end of their life cycle
  - formal systems for objectives and budgets
  - further long-term debt or bridging finance
  - succession planning.

Succession planning may be a key dilemma at this stage of the business. The entrepreneur behind the business may have built it up from its inception and has a keen sense of achievement and ownership. Now it is being suggested that he or she consider who should succeed to the management of the business. This might be advisable because the business needs it, but for the owner concerned it means contemplating giving up the thing that may be the most important part of his or her life.

The longer term

As already explained, the static or survival stage can be seen as the norm for most small businesses. Therefore it is not usually a stage on the way to a different target, but is an end in its own right. It can be preceded by start-up, growth or decline, and be succeeded eventually by growth, decline or termination. It is important to realise that, while this stage is described as static, it may only be so in the short term, and that often in the longer term not to move forward is to risk moving into decline when, because of a business's passivity, others take its market. Survival is not actually compulsory or automatic and there is a natural tendency towards regression. There is no superior power that will intervene to force all businesses to survive and so, ultimately, they must progress or die.

DECLINE

Decline is another of those stages of business development sometimes ignored by government agencies or support organisations when planning assistance, because it appears to offer no benefits. However, decline need not always lead to termination if the problems of the business can be addressed. Helping in the decline stage may result in more surviving businesses or jobs than would otherwise be the case.

Definition

The business is losing its market share, profitability, management skills and the ability to sustain itself at a previous high level. Indeed one can tell sometimes when a business is in trouble by looking at, for example, its staff turnover rate or funding volatility.

Where from and what next

Decline can come after any stage from start-up onwards. If nothing is done then it will in all probability be followed by termination. If it is arrested then it can be followed by a 'static' stage. If it is cured then a 'static' or even a 'growth' stage may follow.

The issues

The needs of the business can include:

- new management and leadership
- key skills

- confidence
- finance
- tolerance
- customers
- suppliers
- a strategic review and plan for a new direction, because the decline may be as a direct result of a market or other relevant business environmental change.

TERMINATION

Many businesses do not survive very long (as Table 6.9 indicates). Yet whilst there is a continuing interest in firm start-up and growth issues, the related issue of termination remains under-explored. The exit or closure of a business is often considered to be a failure. However, just as there are different models of what constitutes the success of a business, so too there are different models of what constitutes its failure. Often there seems to be a propensity to assume that a business closure and a business failure are the same thing. It may seem that the closure, or termination, of a business and it ceasing to exist as a trading entity is *prima facie* evidence that it has failed, but such an assumption presupposes that the purpose of the business could only be achieved if it continued to exist.

Table 6.9 *Percentages of businesses in 2007 surviving after one, two and three years*

Country	Surviving after		
	One year	**Two years**	**Three years**
Czech Republic	79	65	53
France	98	81	70
Germany	77	63	56
Italy	86	75	65
Spain	83	73	66
United Kingdom	97	80	65

Source: Based on G. Carnazza, *The Role and the Main Developments of SMEs in the European Economy* (Brussels: UEAPME) Figures 14, 15 and 16.

This perspective is quite different from that of practising entrepreneurs, who are more likely to be concerned with various types of exit, viewing some options as the ultimate fulfilment of the new venture process. If a business was formed to make as much profit as possible from a market opportunity and if the business has to close while that opportunity continues, it might be legitimate to conclude that the business has failed. If the business owner had other aims in mind, then the closure of the business might be consistent with those aims. For instance a business might be started to provide an income for someone until a pre-planned retirement, and if it does so and is closed when that retirement time arrives, it will have succeeded in its purpose when it is closed. Similarly, if a business is started as an investment and is then sold for a profit to a third party who absorbs it into an existing business, once again the business has achieved its purpose despite being recorded as terminated. This highlights again the need to distinguish between the individual and the firm. As Wennberg and DeTienne observe:

> While scholarly research may see exit as a dichotomous outcome, entrepreneurs are busy examining varying exit routes, developing exit strategies, identifying successors and seeking to understand the best process for achieving their exit.[30]

As noted, often instances of business closure are wrongly described as business failure. Statistics on business failure should therefore be treated warily. The corollary of this is that there are some businesses that do fail, as least in terms of failing to meet their owner-founder's objectives, but which don't close. Such a business may still be kept in existence, for instance, either for possible revival in the future, or because it continues to fulfil at least some needs or to deliver at least some benefit to its owner or employees. The benefit may only be a sop to the owner's pride, but it may be enough to prevent the termination of the business's existence. In such cases, business failure may not lead automatically to business closure.

Nevertheless businesses do terminate, and Figure 6.7 shows some of the ways in which this can happen. In a thriving economy, as in any healthy ecosystem, there will be both births and deaths. Individual business deaths may be deemed regrettable, but some are to be expected in the best of economies. It would be unhealthy to have none, and therefore the policy approach should to be to avoid the unnecessary terminations, but not to prevent them completely.

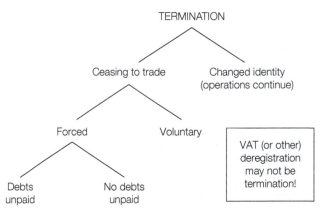

Figure 6.7 *Types of business termination*

The terminology of termination therefore requires care. The word 'failure' should not always be attached to the termination of a business. A business may cease to exist or otherwise change its identification for a number of reasons. A business can terminate if it is sold and its operations are absorbed into another: the operations of the business continue but its separate legal existence disappears. It can terminate when it chooses to cease to trade because those concerned see a better opportunity elsewhere, or it can terminate if it is closed when the owner retires. These are all terminations but they are not all failures. Yet, if the data source used is VAT (Value Added Tax) statistics, a business which declines and de-registers for VAT may be treated as a termination, and even as a failure, although the business is still trading.

Matters of definition

Termination can be any closure of a firm or exit by an entrepreneur from self-employment. As noted, in relation to a firm, the term closure, like failure, can be ambiguous. It might be more accurate to define it as the ending of the separate legal identity of a business and the cessation of trade. That might not be failure, which could be defined as occurring when a business ceases to trade involuntarily and/or when it leaves unpaid debts.

The issues

The need is for excellent legal advice to indicate the best way to handle employees, customers, suppliers and finances.

Intervention

It is not necessarily a waste of resources to help a business to terminate. Compared with a bad termination, too late and with many debts, a properly conducted and orderly termination can save resources. It is important not to pour good money after bad, however difficult the entrepreneur finds it to call a halt to the operation of the business. Voluntary liquidation can also avoid unpaid creditors with the consequent risk to other businesses. This activity can be described as 'ethical entrepreneurship', where the entrepreneur accepts the responsibility of closure without damaging other businesses. This means closing the business while it can still pay its creditors and before it is closed by others. This can save ideas for adoption elsewhere. It can help people to learn and re-apply the valuable lessons they have learnt, instead of being discouraged from ever running their own business again. Assistance, in the form of advice on how to do it well, can also be provided for this stage.

Viewed from a perspective of trying to achieve economic growth, business deaths may seem to be something always to be avoided and, from the perspective of the businesses concerned, there seems to be nothing positive in terminations. However, consider a healthy ecological system such as a forest: if there were no deaths in it, then after a while there would be no space for new growth and no scope for evolution. The death of individual trees might initially leave a hole in the forest, but without it the forest would eventually stagnate. Having some business deaths is inevitable in a healthy economy and, indeed, is necessary for its continued health.

BUSINESS SUCCESS – AND FAILURE

According to Storey,[31] the fundamental characteristic, other than size per se, which distinguishes small businesses from larger ones is their higher probability of ceasing to trade. As already noted, ceasing to trade does not necessarily mean failure, but in some cases at least, business are closed because they have failed to deliver the benefits their owners required. Why small businesses fail, however, is less easy to state with certainty, both because failure itself is not clearly defined and because the precise causes of it are hard to diagnose.

In theory, post-mortems could be carried out on individual business failures but this is rarely done. What is more common is to ask those involved in small businesses which have not yet failed (and so can still be accessed) to indicate what their problems are (which produces results like Table 6.8). However, the stated problems are inevitably linked and it is hard to say which problems are causes and which are symptoms. For example, low turnover can mean it was a poor business opportunity, and/or there was poor marketing/selling or poor quality of the product/service.

Another approach is to look at the businesses which have failed and to try to establish correlations with other factors. Storey[32] presents the following summary of factors which appear to influence the probability of failure of a business:

- *Age.* As businesses get older their chances of survival increase and this is sometimes attributed to the liability of newness. There is a great deal to learn about running a business and expertise grows with time. Other researchers talk about the 'liability of adolescence'.[33] However, most businesses when they start have a stock of resources and energy, which sees them through their early months or years. When this stock is used up, many firms will fail. Thereafter the usual liability of newness arguments apply.
- *Size.* Failure rates are inversely related to the size of the business at start-up. It has been suggested that larger businesses are less likely to fail because if a business is relatively large at start-up then it will quickly benefit from economies of scale. Furthermore, it will probably have sufficient financial resources to see it through its teething problems and it may also be in a good position to raise additional capital.
- *Sector.* Businesses in different sectors of the economy exhibit different failure rates. In Britain, for example, failure rates in manufacturing are greater than in various service sectors, although Storey notes that variations across sectors are not as great as economists would expect. Indeed, differences in failure rates within sectors are greater than across sectors.

- *Past performance.* Those businesses which are able to grow are less likely to fail than those which maintain the status quo. Growth signifies development and perhaps learning, which may be crucial ingredients for survival. Interestingly survival rates are not linked to the rate of growth. Achieving some growth is the determining factor.

Those appear to be the more important factors connected with survival but there are others such as:

- *Ownership.* There is some evidence that the form of ownership can reverse the finding that, other things being equal, smaller businesses have higher failure rates than larger businesses. It has been argued that larger businesses with less personal ownership will more readily divest themselves of non-core interests or leave an industry if demand is falling whilst smaller businesses will struggle on.
- *People/management.* It is likely that the kind of managers and non-managerial personnel who work in a business will influence performance. At the very least there would seem to be a link between competence and success. Storey reviewed a number of studies which attempted to assess how work history (with particular reference to previous business ownership and management experience), education, family background and personal characteristics such as gender, age and ethnic background influenced business performance. He concluded that whilst there is much speculation on the impact of these variables 'it is difficult to draw clear patterns from the results so far'.[34] Also Hayton notes that there is very little evidence showing whether or how skills influence the adoption of management best practices or how they ultimately shape business performance in the SMEs. His research, which sought to address this deficiency, suggests that 'variations in leadership and management skills are associated with variations in SME performance; both directly and indirectly through an increased propensity to adopt management best practices'.[35]
- *Location.* Research reveals that there are *pro rata* many more business failures in urban as opposed to rural areas in the United Kingdom. However, urban areas also have the greatest number of business formations, and since young businesses are vulnerable it is not surprising that high start-up and failure rates are connected. Another finding in this area is that those locations which provide support for SMEs in the form of loans or business advice are likely to have lower failure rates than other areas. Support could be vital for success if crucial resources were being provided, but it might also be that the existence of support agencies is indicative of a supportive climate for business formation. Sometimes support is in essence a subsidy for the SME, and it is interesting to note that there is little association between subsidy and success. A subsidy is no substitute for ability or motivation.
- *Business type.* The final issue investigated by Storey is the connection between the type of business and propensity to fail. Franchise businesses have been found to be less risky ventures than VAT-registered businesses in general, and limited companies are less risky than sole proprietorships or partnerships. Co-operatives on the other hand have similar failure rates to VAT-registered businesses in general.

An understanding of the connection between these factors and failures is very useful for economic planners, but few of the factors are amenable to manipulation by owner-managers. To identify things that owner-managers can do to minimise the chances of failure it is necessary to appreciate the every-day problems that they experience. An analysis carried out in Australia[36] indicated that among those problems were:

- Sales and marketing difficulties were the most common problems encountered. Owners had little appreciation of the marketing concept, had few marketing skills and considered that marketing was synonymous with public relations and advertising. More specifically they had considerable difficulty with market research and promotion. In view of the importance of developing markets for continued business success, interventions to increase marketing awareness and skill seem appropriate.
- The survey also found that the businesses were deficient in general management skills. They found it difficult to produce business plans and manage growth, but one particular area of concern at the time of the study was the need to have appropriate quality assurance systems. With respect to human resources, the biggest problems by far concerned training and development but recruitment and

selection also created dilemmas. Some attempt was made to discover if this varied with the size of the businesses, but for all categories paying wages and benefits, obtaining good people and training were critical issues.

- Several businesses were attempting to grow, and product development difficulties arose. A range of difficulties including pricing and promotion were raised, but the biggest concern was over intellectual property protection. There is legislation in Australia for the protection of these rights, but the high cost of the service means that many new product ideas are not exploited commercially. The businesses also had difficulty in raising start-up finance and in managing cash flows.

Results from this study are largely in keeping with the findings from previous research in the UK and elsewhere, and provide a useful guideline for those whose aim is to support the owners and managers of small businesses. It is possible to develop marketing, management, people and financial skills as well as the technical skills which are specific to a particular business sector, and improving competencies in these areas should improve business performance.

An understanding of the problems that small businesses face and the environmental forces that put pressure on them is useful, but problems can be overcome. Smallbone, North and Leigh[37] argue that a key factor in survival is the adjustments that businesses make to overcome their difficulties. Adjustment requires diagnosis, decision-making and action and depends on effective change management. However, it can be argued that the very characteristics which are needed by entrepreneurs can prevent proper managerial adjustment. For example, high achievers can undertake high-profile but unprofitable projects to feed their egos, entrepreneurs can reject the advice proffered by outsiders and self-confidence can border on the delusional.

There is therefore no simple solution to the problem of failure. Enterprise does have an inherent element of risk, and failure might be reduced but will never be eliminated. The recipe for failure will vary from situation to situation but the ingredients for it are at least known. They are summarised by Burns in Figure 6.8.

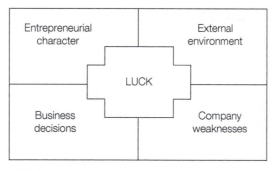

Figure 6.8 *The ingredients of failure*

Source: Slightly modified version of P. Burns, *Entrepreneurship and Small Business*, 3rd Edition (Basingstoke: Palgrave Macmillan, 2011) p. 390. Reproduced with the permission of Palgrave Macmillan.

Business survival rates

There is difficulty in determining survival rates because of a lack of suitable databases. For instance one of the main ways of estimating the survival rates of new small business in the UK has been to use VAT registration and de-registration data – although some new businesses do not register for VAT and de-registrations do not necessarily mean that the businesses concerned have closed.

According to this source, the one-year survival rate in 2004 was 92 per cent, which was down slightly on the 2003 figure, and the three-year survival rate was 71 per cent.[38] On this measure there has been a gradual increase in the one-year survival rates over the time period 1995–2004 and in the three-year rate since 1998.

Survival rates differ across the regions, with London having the lowest three-year survival rate at 67 per cent and Northern Ireland having the highest at 79 per cent. The low survival rates in London and the high rates in Northern Ireland may be partly explained by differing start-up rates in both places. In London, business start-up rates as a percentage of the population are high, leading to greater competition and making it more difficult for businesses to survive. In Northern Ireland business start-up rates are relatively low, leading to less competition and hence higher survival rates.

The US Small Business Administration in 2011 quoted the following figures for new employer firms (i.e. excluding one-person businesses)[39] and some European rates are indicated in Table 6.9.

70 per cent survive at least 2 years

50 per cent at least 5 years

33 per cent at least 10 years, and

25 per cent 15 years or more.

(Survival rates were similar across states and major industries)

IN CONCLUSION

The process of starting a business is not a simple one-stage process. If the starting point is a culture which encourages or at least tolerates entrepreneurs, then the successive stages variously involve an inclination to start a business, an opportunity and/or an idea, some assessment of feasibility, and a search for resources and/or the funding to pay for them. Only then can the business start, and success is not guaranteed. Starting a business is risky and businesses do fail, especially at an early stage. Much depends on the entrepreneur, but if the issues that he or she faces are understood, many of the risks can be managed.

☞ THE KEY POINTS OF CHAPTER 6

- Between its conception and eventually its termination a business can go through many stages, although there are no clear boundaries between the different stages.
- Among the first requirements for the development of a business is a culture that encourages, or at least tolerates, business formation and generates a plentiful source of business ideas.
- Another requirement is the entrepreneur who is willing to explore the potential in an idea. However, the entrepreneurs behind small businesses can differ in both their profile and their reasons for going into business.
- The start-up stage is where the business itself is formed. After start-up, survival, consolidation, growth, maturity, decline and eventually termination are all possible stages of business.
- Just as it is wrong to assume that small businesses will behave and respond like big businesses, so too is it wrong to assume that all small businesses are alike. Small businesses in different sectors have their own particular characteristics, as do businesses of different ages and different sizes.
- The growth stage has been of particular interest. Birch and others suggested that most net new jobs were created by small businesses, but further analysis appears to have shown that it is a relatively small proportion of small businesses which grow and create most of those jobs.
- Because of their job creation potential, governments and others saw that there could be economic benefit in supporting small businesses. However, if small business support resources are limited, which is invariably the case, it has been suggested that the way to maximise results is to apply those resources only to growth businesses. Consequently, there has been considerable interest in learning what makes businesses grow and whether such businesses can be spotted at an early stage.
- In the context of small businesses, there are a number of significant influences on growth including the entrepreneur's (or leader's) ambition and desire to grow, the skills of the entrepreneur, and the impact of factors or constraints external to the business. None of these are useful as predictors, especially as chance also appears to be a key factor.

- In the context of the external environment, 'cluster' theory is of interest. It is based on research that shows that internationally successful businesses are often found in geographic clusters where the environment is most advantageous to them; that it is innovation that makes businesses competitive, thus providing the potential for growth; and that it is demanding buyers in the domestic market that can pressure companies to innovate faster.
- Ultimately growth is likely to be dependent upon the interaction of a number of influences, each of which may be important in different combinations for different businesses.
- There are other possible stages of business development as well as start-up and growth which are worthy of attention. All businesses will have static periods and all are likely eventually to decline and to terminate. Understanding and assisting with these stages also could have economic benefits.

✓ ## QUESTIONS, EXERCISES, ESSAY AND DISCUSSION TOPICS

- What do you believe to be the key ingredients of a successful start-up?
- Do small businesses create the majority of jobs in your economy?
- Identify and discuss the key small business statistics with in your region/country. How might they be used to assist research or policy in this field?
- What are the main stages of development of small businesses? Are these categorisations useful and how might they be recognised?
- What are the key variables that affect a small business's chances of surviving three years or more?
- How could more small business growth be encouraged?
- How might growth as an indicator of business success be measured?
- Is the natural tendency for a business to grow or decline? Explain your reasoning.
- Which of the following influences on the growth of the business are likely to be the strongest in their impact: the entrepreneur(s), the business's strategic positioning and operational procedures, or the external environment?
- 'The real barriers to growth are attributable only to managerial weaknesses, everything else is just an excuse.' Discuss.
- What is the role of chance in the growth of small businesses?
- What arguments would you advance for a government-funded scheme to help declining and/or terminating businesses? What assistance should such a scheme offer?

📖 **SUGGESTIONS FOR FURTHER READING**

P. Burns, *Entrepreneurship and Small Business*, 3rd Edition (Basingstoke: Palgrave Macmillan, 2011).

D. F. Kuratko, J. S. Hornsby and D. W. Nattziger, 'An Examination of Owners' Goals in Sustaining Entrepreneurship', *Journal of Small Business Management,* Vol. 35, No. 1, 1997, pp. 24–33.

M. E. Porter, 'From Competitive Advantage to Competitive Strategy', *Harvard Business Review,* Vol. 65, No. 3, 1987, pp. 43–59.

D. Rae, *Entrepreneurship from Opportunity to Action* (Basingstoke: Palgrave Macmillan, 2007).

D. Smallbone, R. Leigh and D. North, 'The Characteristics and Strategies of High Growth SMEs', *International Journal of Entrepreneurial Behavior and Research,* Vol. 1, No. 3, 1995, pp. 44–62.

D. J. Storey, *Understanding the Small Business Sector* (London: Routledge, 1994).

D. J. Storey and F. J. Greene, *Small Business and Entrepreneurship,* (London: FT Prentice Hall, 2010).

P. Urwin, *Self-employment, Small Firms and Enterprise* (London: The Institute of Economic Affairs in association with Profile Books Ltd, 2011).

REFERENCES

[1] S. Shane, *A General Theory of Entrepreneurship* (Cheltenham: Edward Elgar, 2003) pp. 10–11.

[2] S. D. Sarasvathy, *Effectuation: Elements of Entrepreneurial Expertise* (Cheltenham: Edward Elgar, 2008) pp. 10–11.

[3] B. Bolton and J. Thompson, *Entrepreneurs: Talent, Temperament, Technique*, 2nd Edition (Oxford: Butterworth Heinemann, 2004).

[4] P. Drucker, *Innovation and Entrepreneurship* (London: Heinemann, 1985) p. 132.

[5] HM Treasury News Release, 23 June 2000.

[6] D. J. Storey, 'Optimism and Chance: The Elephants in the Entrepreneurship Room', *International Small Business Journal*, Vol. 29, No. 4, 2001, pp. 312, 315.

[7] S. Birley, 'The Start-Up', in P. Burns and J. Dewhurst (eds), *Small Business and Entrepreneurship* (Basingstoke: Macmillan (now Palgrave Macmillan), 1989) p. 16.

[8] S. Birley and S. Cromie, 'Social Networks and Entrepreneurship in Northern Ireland', paper presented at the *Enterprise in Action Conference*, Belfast, September 1988.

[9] M. Moensted, 'Networking and Entrepreneurship in Small High-Tech European Firms: An Empirical Study', *International Journal of Management*, Vol. 27, No. 1, April 2010, p. 16.

[10] Forum of Private Business, 'The Internal and External Problems That Face Small Businesses', paper presented at the *Sixteenth ISBC Annual Conference*, October 1989, p. 6.

[11] M. Scott and R. Bruce, 'Five Stages of Growth in Small Business', *Long Range Planning*, Vol. 20, No. 3, 1987, pp. 45–52, at p. 49.

[12] Forum of Private Business, Op. Cit. p. 6.

[13] Based in part on S. Birley, 'The Way Ahead for Local Enterprise Centres', presentation at Enniskillen, Northern Ireland, January 1988.

[14] P. Burns, *Entrepreneurship and Small Business* (Basingstoke: Palgrave, 2007).

[15] Federation of Small Businesses, *The FSB 'Voice of Small Business' Member Survey*, February 2012, p. 25. Taken from http://www.fsb.org.uk (accessed 6 February 2016).

[16] B Kirchhoff, personal communication.

[17] Ibid.

[18] Ibid.

[19] Ibid.

[20] B. Kirchhoff, 'Twenty Years of Job Creation Research: What Have We Learned?', Proceedings of the *40th ICSB World Conference*, Stockholm, 1995, pp. 195–219, at p. 210.

[21] F. Delmar, A. McKelvie and K. Wennberg. 'Untangling the Relationships among Growth, Profitability and Survival in New Firms', *Technovation*, Vol. 33, No. 8–9, 2013, pp. 276–291.

[22] M. E. Porter, 'The Competitive Advantage of Nations', *Harvard Business Review*, Vol. 68, No. 2, 1990, pp. 73–93.

[23] G. Reid and L. Jacobsen, *The Small Entrepreneurial Firm* (Aberdeen: Aberdeen University Press, 1988) p. 8.

[24] Quoted in D. Deakins and M. Freel, *Entrepreneurship and the Small Firm* (London: McGraw-Hill, 2006) p. 162.

[25] D. J. Storey, Op. Cit. pp. 303–321.

[26] Personal correspondence from David Storey.

[27] D. J. Storey, Op. Cit. pp. 304.

[28] Quoted in D. Deakins and M. Freel, *Entrepreneurship and the Small Firm* (London: McGraw-Hill, 2006) p. 162.

[29] P. Urwin, *Self-employment, Small Firms and Enterprise* (London: The Institute of Economic Affairs in association with Profile Books Ltd, 2011) p. 112.

[30] K. Wennberg and D.R. DeTienne, 'What Do We Really Mean When We Talk About "Exit"? A Critical Review of Research on Entrepreneurial Exit', *International Small Business Journal*, Vol. 32, No. 1, 2014, p. 5.

[31] D. Storey, *Understanding the Small Business Sector* (London: Routledge, 1994) p. 78.

[32] Ibid. pp. 91–104.

[33] T. Mahmood, 'Survival of Newly Founded Business: A Log-Logistic Model Approach', *Small Business Economics*, Vol. 14, No. 2, 2000, pp. 223.

[34] Storey, (1994), Op. Cit. p. 100.

[35] J. Hayton, *Leadership and Management Skills in SMEs: Measuring Associations with Management Practices and Performance*, BIS Research Paper No. 211 (London: Department of Business, Innovation and Skills 2015) p. 7.

[36] X. Huang and A. Brown, 'An Analysis and Classification of Problems in Small Business', *International Small Business Journal*, Vol. 18, 1999, pp. 73–85.

[37] D. Smallbone, D. North and R. Leigh, *Managing Change for Growth and Survival: A Study of Mature Manufacturing Firms in London During the 1980s*, Working Paper No. 3 (London: Middlesex Polytechnic, Planning Research Centre, 1992).

[38] DTI, 'Survival Rates of VAT-Registered Enterprises, 1995–2004: Key Results', URN 07/963.

[39] USA Small Business Administration, Office of Advocacy, FAQs Page 1. Taken from https://www.sba.gov/sites/default/files/sbfaq.pdf (accessed 13 February 2016).

Companion website

Please visit the companion website at www.palgravehighered.com/Bridge-UE-5e for access to additional learning and teaching materials.

Social Enterprise and the Third Sector

CONTENTS

- Introduction
- History of the sector
- Issues of terminology

- The social economy
- Government interest in the third sector
- In conclusion

KEY CONCEPTS

This chapter covers:

- The nature and history of the social economy and why it might have been overlooked in the past.
- Various approaches to the social economy and to its components.
- The nature of social enterprises and their relationship to the social economy.
- The association of the social economy with the concept of social capital, the lack of which has been suggested as factor in social exclusion.
- The wider concept of the third sector, of which the social economy is a significant part.
- The reasons for government interest in this sector.

LEARNING OBJECTIVES

By the end of this chapter the reader should:

- Understand the concept of the social economy, why it might not have been widely recognised in the past and why interest in it is now growing.
- Understand the nature of social enterprises.
- Be aware of the association being made between the social economy and the concept of social capital.
- Understand the concept of the third sector and how it embraces the social economy.
- Appreciate the range of benefits that might be provided by this sector and the reasons for government interest in it.

INTRODUCTION

This chapter concludes Part 1 by exploring an important aspect of enterprise, the potential and contribution of which is now starting to be recognised. Although it would seem that this aspect has always been a feature in economic activity it would appear that, to some extent, it has officially been assumed not to exist.

On the assumption that the two main mechanisms for apportioning resources in human societies are the market and the state, traditional economics have tended to assume that an economy consists of just two sectors: the private sector and the public sector. Thus a recently published book called *Modern Economics* includes the following statement about what is in a mixed economy:

> It is convenient to distinguish between the 'private sector' and the 'public sector'. The former consists of those firms which are privately owned. The latter includes government departments, local authorities, and public bodies such as the Environment Agency. All are distinguished by the fact that their capital is publicly owned and their policies can be influenced through the ultimate supply of funds by the government.[1]

What this statement fails to recognise is that, for as long as there have been distinguishable public and private sectors in an economy, there have also been organisations which belonged in neither sector and did not fit either of the specifications given above. They were not privately owned-firms but equally their capital was not publicly owned and their policies were not necessarily subject to government policy and/or the supply of government funds. Churches are obvious early examples, as are the first schools and hospitals, which were often based on religious bodies. But in England in the 13th century, schools and university colleges were being founded which were secular both in purpose and governance. While much education and medicine has subsequently been taken over by the state and now lies within the public sector, some of the early education bodies still survive and are among the oldest surviving non-governmental organisations. This part of the economy, now sometimes referred to as the 'social economy' or more widely as the 'third sector' (because the organisations in it belong in neither the private nor the public sectors), has often been overlooked, not least because there has not been a suitable vocabulary with which to refer to it. Nevertheless it exists, and Table 7.1 lists just a few examples of the sort of organisations that are in it.

HISTORY OF THE SECTOR

As described in Chapter 2, in the early stages of their existence as a distinct species, human beings were nomadic hunter-gatherers moving around in family bands in search of the food, shelter, warmth and other things that they wanted. In such situations almost everyone engaged in all the work of their society, and trying to separate public and private sector work would have been meaningless.

The next big stage in economic evolution (what Toffler has called the 'first wave') was farming. With the change from hunter-gathering to agriculture, societies became more settled, surpluses could be stored and guarded, and non-food-producing specialists began to emerge, including eventually rulers and bureaucrats. Eventually tribes grouped together as larger units and, once the superior authority of

Table 7.1 Organisations and activities not in the public or the private sector

Amateur dramatic clubs	Mountain rescue services
Building preservation trusts	National Trust
Co-operatives	Oxfam
Donkey sanctuaries	Professional associations
Enterprise agencies	Quakers
Fair trade companies	Rotary clubs
Golf clubs	Scouts
Hospices	Trades unions
Independent schools	University colleges
St John Ambulance	Voluntary Service Overseas
Knights of St Columbanus	Women's Institute
Lifeboat service	Youth clubs

Source: S. Bridge, B. Murtagh and K. O'Neill, *Understanding the Social Economy and the Third Sector* (Basingstoke: Palgrave Macmillan, 2014) p. 4.

kings and other rulers became established, it meant that some activity of, or for, government clearly took place outside the family. This activity of government could be described as work to provide for some of society's needs. It was undertaken separately from the work of providing goods, such as food, for consumption. It is here that the beginnings of distinct public sector activity might be found.

Another feature of agriculturally based societies was the emergence of craft workers, which led eventually to the establishment of specialised businesses. Many of these were relatively small family businesses, but once such ventures grew bigger than the family and had a regular surplus to trade, they could be distinguished as a separate economic activity. The East India Company, which derived its powers from a Royal Charter of 1600, is an early UK example of one such business being established with a distinct and separate legal identity. Consequently, at that stage, a distinction could be made between that economic activity outside the family which was organised for private gain and that which was organised for, or by, the state, even if some of our current terminology for these activities had not yet been established.

At the same time, other organisations were also being established which were neither public sector–led nor profit/private sector–driven. Guilds, trade bodies and other such 'associations' were early examples. Churches, and early schools and hospitals, are further examples which have already been mentioned. What has been lacking until recently, though, has been an encompassing term for such activity.

In 1830 the French economist Charles Dunoyer first used the term *Économie sociale* and from this the term social economy was derived. It has been suggested that the emergence of the social economy as a specific concept, in France and at that time, was the result of institutionalisation and a theoretical assessment of practical experiences.[2] Those experiences might be said to have had their roots in aspects of Egyptian, Greek and Roman life and later in the guilds that appeared in north-west Europe in medieval times when a rich associative life was evident. This was the case in other parts of the world also, including medieval Byzantium, Muslim countries and India, in which 'associations' were formed in order to organise and protect communities of interest.

Moulaert and Ailenei,[3] in a study of the social economy, quote several authors who contend that the social economy has a history of emergence and re-emergence linked to a series of economic and social crises. Many of the guilds and other associations, they suggest, were created to provide assistance, mutual support and charity in the uncertain times of the early Middle Ages. The changes later brought about by the Industrial Revolution led to a decline in craft co-operatives and created renewed interests in 'utopian socialism' and the values of co-operation and mutual support. The French Revolution, it has been argued, fostered political equality but not material equality, and because material inequalities remained, mutual support organisations (*mutuelles*) appeared in the middle of the 19th century. In the last quarter of that century, agricultural and savings co-operatives were formed in response to the needs of small producers affected by increasing agglomeration and the economic power of the bigger businesses thus created. In France, it might be said, republican ideals generated distinctive interests in associations as a buffer between individuals and the state, whereas in England, ideas around communitarianism strongly influenced the co-operative movement.

Although the social economy may have been first conceptualised in the 19th century there have been crises since then which have further stimulated its development. In the 20th century, the economic collapse of 1929–1932 led to the formation of consumption co-operatives for food and housing.[4] Further initiatives in 1970s Europe have been seen, on the one hand, to be a reaction to crises in the mass production system and, on the other hand, to be a response to the overburdening of the welfare state.[5] Indeed Amin *et al.* trace the most recent interest in the social economy to the end of full employment and the crisis in welfare provision which started in the 1970s. This 'post-Fordist' environment, they suggest, was characterised by:

- rising global energy prices
- rising imports from low-wage countries and flexibly organised new economies
- wage drift and sustained opposition from organised labour
- decreasing return on sunk capital
- growth of new technologies and organised principles no longer dependent on economies of scale
- falling demand for mass-produced goods and the rise of customised consumption

- waning support for mass representative democracy
- strains on government to provide expensive welfare services and the rise of new-right market ideas on the management of the relationship between the state and economy.[6]

But this crisis, Amin *et al.* suggest, simultaneously renewed interest in the potential of the social economy as a place of work and provider of welfare services. For instance the European Commission established its Social Economy Unit, within DGXXIII, in 1989, and the importance of the social economy was formally recognised by the European Union in its 1994 White Paper on *Growth, Competitiveness and Employment*. This paper indicated that the EU saw the 'third sector' as a potentially important contributor to the growth of employment and as means of avoiding dual labour markets, twin-speed societies and urban segregation. By the end of the 1990s and into the 21st century attention was being paid to the social economy in many of the EU member states, including the UK, and by different shades of political opinion. It would seem that this re-emergence of the social economy as a subject of interest can be linked to economic and social change resulting, at least in Western Europe, from the late–20th-century 'post-Fordist' changes to manufacturing strength and the welfare state environment.

ISSUES OF TERMINOLOGY

A suggested above, one of the reasons for the low level of recognition for this 'third' sector may have been the lack of an adequate vocabulary with which to describe it. Even today, when interest in it has been stimulated, there still isn't a widely accepted terminology for much of it. Sometimes reference is made to the social economy but this too is ambiguous. As noted above, the term was derived from the French concept of *l'économie sociale*, which came to be seen as encompassing co-operatives, *mutuelles* (mutuals) and associations. The classification *économie sociale* used in some EU member states has specifically included those three categories of organisation, and was expanded in the early 1990s to include foundations also. (These categories are sometimes referred to as CMAFs: co-operatives, mutuals, associations and foundations.)

Often the social economy is more loosely defined. In the UK, a government report suggested that 'the social economy is an imprecise term – but in general can be thought of as those organisations who [sic] are independent of the state and provide services, goods and trade for a social purpose and are not profit distributing'.[7] The European Commission also does not formally define the social economy, but, presumably based on the *économie sociale* classification, it has indicated that:

> The so-called social economy, including co-operatives, mutual societies, non-profit associations, foundations and social enterprises provides a wide range of products and services across Europe, and generates millions of jobs.[8]

These approaches to the social economy are based on including only certain categories of organisation which have a number of shared characteristics. There are many organisations though which, while not belonging to either the public or private sectors, do not share all these characteristics. Therefore, while the term social economy is sometimes used to refer to the whole of the third sector, it is clear that it refers often only to a part of that sector. Alternatively, if the social economy thus defined is indeed a sector in its own right, then there must also be a fourth sector.

Other terms which have been used in a similar context are the third system and the third way, the non-profit or the not-for-profit sector, the voluntary sector and the voluntary and community sector, the community sector or the community economy. Not only have many of these terms at some time been used more or less interchangeably but they also have been used to refer to a sub-sector and at times to the sector overall. The result is that this is often an area in which the terminology can be confusing because there is no accepted standard practice, as the following examples illustrate (italics added):

> In 2003, the *voluntary, third* or *non-profit* sector occupies centre stage in public policy discussions in the UK.[9]

In what might be called the 'community era' we talked of community action, *community enterprise*, and *community business*. Today, in the contemporary 'social era', we are more likely to talk of *social entrepreneurs*, *social enterprise* and *social business*. Is there some serious significance in this shift in vocabulary from community to social? Does it matter?[10]

Social economy refers to a *third sector* in economics between the private sector ... and the public sector.[11]

The *third sector* can be broken down into three sub-sectors: the *community sector*, the *voluntary sector* and the *social enterprise sector*.[12]

Putting all this together to produce a consistent overall picture is not a simple task. One attempt is that of Bridge *et al.* (see Figure 7.1) who have suggested a map of an economy to show the relative positions of the three sectors and of many of their different components from the very small to the very large. No map is a totally accurate representation of reality, but in respect of this map two points may be worth making:

- The lines drawn between sectors to indicate sector boundaries are lines on a map which do not exist in clear form in reality. However, they have led some to view the different sectors as clearly distinct and as the main division on the map.
- The closeness of different components is intended to reflect their degree of similarity, even across supposed sector boundaries. So, instead of sectors, size may be a more meaningful distinction with small organisations in the 'private' and 'third' sectors having more in common with each other than they do with larger organisations supposedly in the same sector.

THE SOCIAL ECONOMY

Although there is a good rationale for it, the term 'the third sector' is a relatively recent introduction and, as indicated above, most people have talked instead about the social economy. Whether this term is

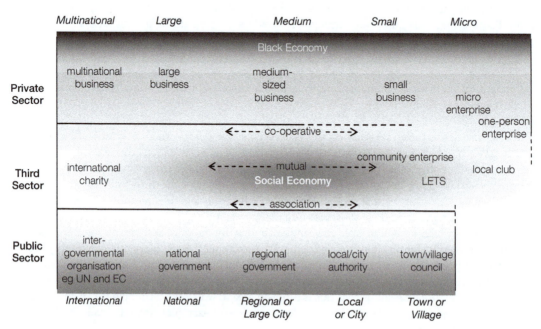

Figure 7.1 *The sectors of an economy*

Source: Based on S. Bridge, B. Murtagh and K. O'Neill, *Understanding the Social Economy and the Third Sector* (Basingstoke: Palgrave Macmillan, 2014) p. 117.

used to refer to a distinct and very significant part of the third sector or to a part of the economy which is itself sufficiently prominent to be considered to be the third sector, it is thought by many people to be very important both economically and socially.

What is the social economy?

Basing descriptions of the social economy on objective assessments of what is in it might appear to be logical, but it is not the sequence that often appears to be followed. Instead assessments of what is considered to be in the social economy are, in effect, based on definitions subjectively derived from the function that it is expected, or hoped, that the social economy will provide.

One of the reasons advanced for the lack of a single, generally accepted definition of the social economy is that this is due, at least in part, to the various different traditions and policy emphases that exist. Amin *et al.*, for instance, have identified 'considerable international differences in the ways in which the social economy and its relationship to market, state and civil society are envisioned'. In the United States, they suggest, which compared with many European countries has a weak welfare state playing a largely residual role, the sector is shaped by 'bottom-up' community development processes fronted by a voluntary sector that is now only loosely connected with political activism. In Western Europe, the tendency towards a withdrawal of state funding has encouraged stronger community economic development and enterprise linked to an expanded role for the third sector more generally. France could be seen perhaps as the paradigmatic model of a state-supported social economy in which the social enterprise has been accorded a specific legal status. But within Europe there are significant variations between a French-German-Belgian tradition of strong social economy providers recognised and regulated by national governments, a weaker Mediterranean model where formal recognition and development of a social economy distinct from strong charities is, at best, embryonic, and an Anglo-Saxon model which has a particular emphasis on tackling social exclusion.[13]

The different definitions officially advanced largely follow the different roles assigned to the social economy and, it is suggested, the argument over the role of the social economy can, at times, be reduced to three broad choices:

- An economic/enterprise approach that sees social economy organisations as 'businesses' that can assist community regeneration and puts an emphasis on their financial sustainability. Social enterprises will function, it is believed, where the private sector won't, at least until some pump-priming has been done by the sector to make it attractive for private interests. It could be argued that the allocation within the UK government of responsibility for the sector at one time to the (former) Department of Trade and Industry indicated a view along these lines.
- A socio-economic policy approach which sees the sector as 'patching up' the inadequacies of the welfare state, while still confining it to a marginal role in the economy. The sector should confine itself to 'the parts that government cannot (or will not) reach' and thus it is characterised as a 'low-cost provider', supplementing rather than complementing the welfare state.
- A political/ideological approach which envisages a social economy sector sufficiently strong to lever institutional change and to promote more democratic structures and citizen participation in decision-making.

Typically an emphasis on the first, or on the second, of these roles will lead to a focus on social enterprises and to definitions of them which emphasise their business attributes. The third one, however, leads to a focus on the social economy and to definitions which emphasise the democratic nature of its components. For instance, the first and second might be associated with what Lloyd, for example, has identified as a US/UK approach and the third as a European approach – two very different schools of thought which he describes. The European approach, he suggests, is a social economy approach which does not hold back from offering a challenge to the post-1980s hegemony of liberal market forces as the only grand narrative and takes a whole society perspective instead of just a business-focused one. In contrast the US/UK approach is a social enterprise approach as it starts with the enterprises of which the social economy is composed, and defines them as businesses operating in a market context but using surpluses to achieve social objectives. Lloyd suggests that this difference reflects a fundamental difference in paradigms between a European political economy approach and the narrow market-based approach arising from Anglo-Saxon neo-liberal traditions.[14]

This could also be construed as representing two opposing desires: to promote the sector on the one hand as an alternative to the supposed inefficiencies of the public sector or on the other hand as an alternative to the supposed anti-social excesses of the private sector. If the private sector is seen as being too focused on pandering to individual greed or if the public sector is seen as being too socialist in imposing big government and stifling individual freedom, then the social economy might be preferred instead. However, there is also a view that sees the social economy, not as an alternative to either of those two sectors, but as a necessary third leg without which the stool is incomplete. Thus, for instance, it is suggested that there has been an increase in social innovation because there are things that neither of the other two sectors do well:

> Why has social innovation moved centre stage over the last decade? The main reason is that existing structures and policies have found it impossible to crack some of the most pressing issues of our times – such as climate change, the worldwide epidemic of chronic disease, and widening inequality. ...

> The classic tools of government policy on the one hand, and market solutions on the other, have proved grossly inadequate. The market, by itself, lacks the incentives and appropriate models to solve many of these issues. ... Current policies and structures of government have tended to reinforce old rather than new models. The silos of government departments are poorly suited to tackling complex problems which cut across sectors and nation states.[15]

The different roles that social enterprises have played, or are expected to play, in these different traditions and approaches not only lead to different definitions reflecting those different roles but also cause some people to focus on the social economy and some on social enterprises. Policy-makers, it has been suggested, generally want to fund social enterprises whereas practitioners often want to develop a social economy.

What is a social enterprise?

The different models of the social economy which are summarised above seem to treat social enterprises differently. The European approach starts with the social economy which, the EU indicates, includes co-operatives, mutual societies, associations, foundations and social enterprises. Thus, by specifying social enterprises alongside co-operatives, mutual societies, associations and foundations, it suggests that organisations in the latter categories, while being at the core of the social economy, are not themselves social enterprises. The US/UK approach, in effect, starts with social enterprises and seems to imply that the social economy amounts to the sum of all the social enterprises within it, which in turn implies that co-operatives, mutual societies, associations, foundations are social enterprises because they are in the social economy.

One way of avoiding the issue of whether social enterprises include co-operatives, mutual societies, associations and foundations is to talk instead about social economy enterprises as a generic term. The European Commission, for instance, under the heading of social economy enterprises, indicates that there are certain common characteristics shared by what it calls social economy entities:

- Their primary purpose is not to obtain a return on capital. They are, by nature, part of a stakeholder economy, whose enterprises are created by and for those with common needs, and accountable to those they are meant to serve.
- They are generally managed in accordance with the principle of 'one member, one vote'.
- They are flexible and innovative – social economy enterprises are being created to meet changing social and economic circumstances.
- Most are based on voluntary participation, membership and commitment.[16]

In 1997 the European Network for Economic Self Help and Local Development analysed the variety of social enterprises in European countries and identified some common principles, which in turn led to working definitions of social enterprises. The common principles were:[17]

- They seek to tackle specific *social aims by engaging in economic and trading activities*.
- They are *not-for-profit organisations*, in the sense that all surplus profits generated are either re-invested in the economic activities of the enterprise or are used in other ways to tackle the stated social aims of the enterprise.
- Their legal structures are such that all assets and accumulated wealth of the enterprise do not belong to any individuals but are held in trust to be used *for the benefit of these persons or areas* that are the intended beneficiaries of the enterprise's social aims.
- Their organisational structures are such that the full participation of members is encouraged on *a co-operative basis* with rights accorded to all members.
- It is a further characteristic of the social enterprise that it encourages *mutual co-operation* between social enterprises and with other organisations in the wider economy.

Other definitions of social enterprises include:

- *UK Government definition.* 'A social enterprise is a business with primary social objectives whose surpluses are principally re-invested for that purpose in the business or in the community, rather than being driven by the need to maximise profit for shareholders and owners.'[18]
- *UK Department for Business, Innovation and Skills (BIS) definition.* BIS has described a social enterprise as 'a business that has mainly social or environmental aims',[19] but it also a more limiting definition which requires that an enterprise should consider itself a social enterprise and it 'should not pay more than 50 per cent of profit or surplus to owners or shareholders and should not have less than 75 per cent of turnover from trading'. In addition, they had to think themselves 'a very good fit' with the following statement:

  a business with primarily social or environmental objectives, whose surpluses were principally reinvested for that purpose in the business or community rather than mainly being paid to shareholders and owners.[20]

- *OECD definition.* 'Any private activity conducted in the public interest, organised with an entrepreneurial strategy but whose main purpose is not the maximisation of profit but the attainment of certain economic and social goals, and which has a capacity for bringing innovative solutions to the problems of social exclusion and unemployment.'[21]

A further way of viewing some of these aspects of social enterprises is provided in Table 7.2, which compares characteristics typical of market-driven private sector businesses with those of many social enterprises.

Key aspects of social enterprises

In reality there is no definitive boundary between many social enterprises and some other small businesses. Many small businesses supposedly in the private sector are not driven principally or exclusively by the desire to maximise profits; often they are started to provide benefits to their founders, and those benefits can include social as well as financial returns. Running social enterprises is not without its problems, however, and is frequently a more complex task than that of running other enterprises. There is the same need to secure income, without which even survival is not possible, but the income generation is not the end in itself and has to be balanced with achieving the delivery of the social

Table 7.2 Comparison of market sector and social economy characteristics

Issue	Market sector characteristic	Social enterprise characteristic
Responds to:	Demand (which generates profit)	Need (which generates sympathy and appreciation)
Objectives:	Profit	Financial and social return
Strategy:	Product/market led	Need/competence/value driven
Organisation structure:	Hierarchical	Flat
Pricing:	What the market will bear	What client can afford
Decision-making:	Quick, one boss, single bottom line	Slow, participative, based on trade offs, multiple bottom lines
Culture:	Stand alone, viability	Dependency, grant driven
Ethos:	Autocratic, effective	Democratic, caring, laid back
Approach to risk:	Managed	Mainly averse
Managerial attitude:	(Get out of) my way	All together, communal, shared approach, shared vision
Business model:	Production (emphasising efficiency and results)	Administrative/strategic (emphasising process and people)

Source: Based on a presentation by P. Quinn to a joint INCORE and Cresco Trust seminar at the Magee Campus of the University of Ulster on 5 May 2006.

purpose. Nevertheless social enterprises do have some particular characteristics and these are to be found, for instance, in:

- *Their founders*: Like the founders of private sector organisations, the founders of social enterprises reveal great heterogeneity, but very often social enterprises are promoted, established and/or directed by groups of people, rather than by individuals.
- *The variety of organisational aims*: Social aims are typically either the primary aims, or are among the primary aims, of social enterprises in what is often referred to as 'the triple bottom line': alluding to social and environmental objectives as well as, and underpinned by, financial objectives. Sometimes an ethical objective is also added, thus making a 'quadruple bottom line'.
- *The possible legal structures*: Third sector organisations have developed differently in different countries, often because of the different regulatory frameworks that exist and the different forms of legal entity that are available. So it is important to recognise that third sector organisations, including social enterprises, are not typically defined by their legal status. A third sector organisation, depending on what sort of organisation it is, may operate as a trust, an industrial and provident society, a co-operative, a company limited by shares, a company limited by guarantee, a public limited company, an unlimited company or a partnership.
- *The concept of ownership*: The concept of ownership of many social enterprises is not straightforward. In the case of a company limited by shares, it is clear that the shareholders are the company's owners with the extent of their ownership being determined by the number (and type) of shares they hold. In the case of a company limited by guarantee, the ultimate authority in the company is its members and it is they who elect its directors, usually on the basis of one vote per member. Those members, while they may control the company in that way, are precluded from selling off the company and/or its assets and keeping the proceeds. In that sense they are not its owners, but then neither is anyone else. Often, however, the people who control social enterprises may be community based – for instance elected community representatives or representatives of other community bodies.
- *Employment profiles*: There can be a perception that jobs in social enterprises are 'low quality' but the meaning of 'low quality' in this context often seems to lack clarity. It appears generally to reflect a perception that many jobs in the third sector have low remuneration and are relatively unskilled, temporary and/or part-time. There is, however, a lack of reliable data upon which to substantiate

or refute such assertions, and it can also be relevant to ask what a 'quality' job is in this context. An indication of a high-quality job might be a low employee turnover rate, which might indicate that the people concerned liked their jobs or at least preferred them to alternatives available.

- *Profitability*: The essence of social enterprises is that they have been established for social purposes and not, or not primarily, to maximise financial returns to their investors. However, they all survive by securing income for the services they provide. Describing these organisations as 'not-for-profit', though, can be misleading. Many of them are actually 'not-for-profit-distribution-to-individuals' (although co-operatives and, at least in the UK, community interest companies can remit profits to their members or investors). But they need to make some profit, or at least to break even over the longer term, in order to survive. The widespread use of the term 'not-for-profit' may have encouraged some groups to pay little attention to generating income and to concentrate instead on the social purpose: a strategy which has on occasion been fatal to the organisation, as the resultant losses meant that it collapsed – and such problems lead some to question the sustainability of the sector. On the other hand there are some organisations in which so much emphasis is placed on achieving financial viability that the overall purpose for which the financial viability is sought is neglected. Nevertheless the longevity of some social enterprises shows that problems of viability can be overcome.

- *Financing*: Social enterprises, like other enterprises, need access to money to start, develop and grow, but the limits placed on their ability to distribute profits to investors preclude them from some forms of finance. There are various ways though in which they can access financial support, including grants, gifts, endowments and commercial loans, and recently there has been a growth in the sophistication of financial support for the sector.

- *Reporting task*: Because of their multiple 'bottom lines', social enterprises often face a complex task in reporting to their stakeholders on their effectiveness and on the success, or otherwise, of their efforts to achieve their aims.

Social capital

Social capital is introduced in Chapter 8 as a key factor in business development, and it is explored further in Chapter 13. However, it is relevant here to reflect that sometimes the common use of the term 'social' has led to social capital being associated particularly with social enterprises and the social economy, along with suggestions that the social economy has a particular potential to help disadvantaged communities. This claim appears to reduce to two assumptions: that for disadvantaged communities social capital is often the key missing ingredient and that social enterprises create social capital. From these assumptions the conclusion is then drawn that social enterprises will help disadvantaged communities. While there are grounds for saying that there is something which is referred to often as social capital which is lacking in disadvantaged communities, whether it alone can effect improvement is much less certain and whether social enterprises necessarily create social capital is also debatable. Indeed a counter-argument is that both financial capital and social capital are needed to start any business, including a social enterprise, and, as disadvantaged communities often lack both, they are not good places in which to start social enterprises. Also the situation may be more complex than the above summary indicates. The vitamin analogy, described in Chapter 13, suggests that there are a number of separate components of what are together referred to as social capital and many of these components cannot usefully be substituted one for the other. Thus, if one component is lacking and another is provided, that might not help, even though both could be described as social capital.

Sustainability

Some criticism of the social economy has focused on its sustainability. It can be argued that, because its main focus is not on profitability, it is likely to lose sight of the need to make money in order to survive. Instead it is sometimes suggested that the term 'social' is a distraction and that social enterprises are essentially enterprises with a great deal in common with other enterprises, including the need to generate funds in order to survive. Supporters of the sector argue, however, that organisations in the sector understand the need to make money to cover their costs but they apply any surplus to their social, ethical and/or environmental purposes, instead of giving it to their owner. They can also point out that some of the oldest surviving organisations, for instance some schools and colleges, are to be found in this sector.

Community enterprise

Despite the counter to the social capital argument, enterprises are on occasion started to try to help particular communities, and may then be referred to as community enterprises. For some communities, the low levels of economic activity they have experienced, associated with high rates of unemployment, often result in a lack of confidence, a lack of relevant skills, a lack of resources and a lack of infrastructure. This can be a vicious circle of deprivation: there is a lack of business tradition, little enterprise and an absence of entrepreneurs. With no role models, a lack of confidence may be reinforced. That is the antithesis of an enterprise culture and it is thought by some that community enterprises can help to counter it.

A community enterprise, however, can relate to any community, not just a disadvantaged one. Community enterprise, if it is distinguished from social enterprise, seems generally to be an enterprise which, while fitting a social enterprise definition, is specifically run for the benefit of a particular community, and often by a group of people from that community. Sometimes individuals acting together as a team or group can demonstrate qualities, command resources and engage in enterprising behaviour in a way that acting individually they would not. Quite often, though, the catalyst for effective community group action is an outsider or enterprising community member who mobilises and releases the latent enterprise in others.

Community and social entrepreneurs

Like other enterprises, social and/or community enterprises are often the creation of entrepreneurs, in this case referred to as social or community entrepreneurs. Of these two terms community entrepreneur is probably the narrower, and various attempts have been made to define it. However, there is general agreement that it is about the use of personal networking, facilitation and resource-accessing skills (that is to say enterprise skills) to improve a local community in both social and economic areas. Community entrepreneurs facilitate community development in the way that the more traditional entrepreneurs facilitate business development. While enterprise in the context of business is seen often in the start-up of new businesses, community enterprise is not generally applied to the start-up of new communities but to the revitalisation of old ones.

Community enterprise is a form therefore of social enterprise, in which the act of forming or growing a social venture is applied in the context of a community. The description of community entrepreneurs, given in comparison with private sector entrepreneurs in Table 7.3, thus also applies to social entrepreneurs, except that their social purpose may not be related specifically to the needs of a particular community.

Government interest in the third sector

While considering the third sector and the social economy it is also relevant to recognise significant levels of government interest in them. Just as there was relatively little interest in small businesses before the 1970s because their economic impact was not widely recognised, so too official recognition of, and interest in, the third sector and the social economy has only followed a wider appreciation of their economic and social impact.

Table 7.3 *Autonomous and community entrepreneurs compared*

Autonomous entrepreneurs	Community entrepreneurs
Aim for the growth of personal resources as the main personal goal	Aim for the development of the community as the main personal goal
Enhance own self-competence	Help to build the self-respect and competence of others
Mobilise resources to build their enterprises	Inspire others to start their own enterprises
Put themselves at the top of the organisation	Regard themselves as the coordinator in a loose federation
See authority and society interest groups as hindrances	See authority and society interest groups as potential supporters and resource providers

Source: Based on B. Johannisson and A. Nilsson, 'Community Entrepreneurs: Networking for Local Development', *Entrepreneurship and Regional Development*, Vol. 1, 1989, p. 5.

Because they focus on wider issues than just enriching their backers, social enterprises and the social economy are seen as having the ability to provide beneficial outputs. As a result, many governments have shown an interest in trying to grow the social economy (and other parts of the third sector – depending on how it is defined) and are prepared to intervene to encourage and support its growth in the sector in order to gain more benefits. These include:

- The provision of goods, services and social benefits which the public sector doesn't adequately provide, and a means for addressing some other problems of the welfare state.
- The provision of jobs for people who might not otherwise be employed.
- The fostering of enterprise and economic competitiveness.
- The promotion of environmental sustainability or ethical operations.
- The creation of social capital and social cohesion. This is sometimes seen as giving it the ability to 'reach parts that other initiatives cannot reach', in particular when trying to tackle disadvantage through urban and rural regeneration projects (but see note on social capital above).
- The promotion of democracy and/or co-operation.

An example of the vagaries of government interest in this area is that of the UK. There, in 2001, a growing interest in strengthening the sector led to the creation in the then Department for Trade and Industry (DTI) of the Social Enterprise Unit tasked with being the focal point 'for strategic decision-making across Government'.[22] Then, in 2008 and 'in recognition of the increasingly important role the third sector plays in both society and the economy'[23] the Unit was absorbed into the newly created Office of the Third Sector within the Cabinet Office. The election of the Coalition government in 2010 with its advancement of the concept of the Big Society led to the Office of the Third Sector being renamed the Office for Civil Society and taking responsibility for charities, social enterprises and voluntary organisations. The Big Society was included as a continuing commitment in the Conservative Party's manifesto for its successful 2015 election campaign with the aim, it was said, of putting more 'power and opportunity into people's hands'.[24] This idea, it was also said, was not new but was something that had been done for centuries and it was about getting local people to make local decisions that affect their local neighbourhood. However, although promoted by the then Prime Minister, David Cameron, the concept subsequently seems to have disappeared from the political agenda. Nevertheless Cameron's successor as Prime Minister, Theresa May, established an Inclusive Economy Unit to promote 'a strong civil society [which] works best when all parts of the economy and of society are being used to their full potential'.[25] However, this Unit was then moved from the Cabinet Office, not into the Department for Business, Energy and Industrial Strategy – a transfer which might have recognised its business links, but to the Department for Culture, Media and Sport – a move which was seen by some as downgrading its importance.

IN CONCLUSION

This review of the third sector, and of the social economy as coincident with it or a component of it, has indicated that it exists, that it is an important part of a mixed economy, and that it provides a number of benefits. Counter to the assumption that the public and private sectors are the only two sectors in an economy worth considering, it reveals that there is a sector which is driven neither by the state nor the market but which nevertheless is believed to have an economic impact. It also counters the assumption that all businesses are exclusively profit-oriented by showing that there are many sustainable organisations run on business lines but pursuing aims which are primarily social, ethical and/or environmental.

☛ THE KEY POINTS OF CHAPTER 7

- Organisations which do not belong in the public or the private sectors of an economy are considered to form a third sector. The social economy can be variously considered to be either a part of this 'third sector' or synonymous with it.
- The social economy has a long history but, until recently, has received relatively little attention for its economic contribution.
- The language with which to describe the social economy and its components has been limited, but is now starting to evolve.
- Different cultures and countries perceive the role of the social economy differently.
- Social enterprises are organisations whose aims include both economic and wider social purposes. They, and the social economy to which they contribute, are concepts that challenge the traditional division of organisational activity into either economic or social categories. Social enterprises include community enterprises in which enterprise is applied specifically for community benefit.
- Nevertheless social enterprises are primarily enterprises and have much in common with other enterprises, including not least the need to generate enough income if they are to survive.
- Because of its economic and social potential, governments have become interested in the social economy and want to encourage and support it.

✓ ## QUESTIONS, EXERCISES, ESSAY AND DISCUSSION TOPICS

- 'A social enterprise is not a real enterprise and does not require the same discipline and purpose.' Discuss.

- Does the language currently available provide clarity or confusion about the social economy and the third sector?

- If the social economy and/or the third sector are so beneficial, why have they been overlooked for so long?

- Is there a better name for the third sector?

- What do you consider to be the critical characteristics of social enterprises?

- What are the types of conflicts that may arise because of the triple bottom line? How might they be resolved?

- Which came first, the public, the private or the third sector?

📖 **SUGGESTIONS FOR FURTHER READING AND INFORMATION**

A. Amin, A. Cameron and R. Hudson, *Placing the Social Economy* (London: Routledge, 2002).

S. Bridge, B. Murtagh and K. O'Neill, *Understanding the Social Economy and the Third Sector* (Basingstoke: Palgrave Macmillan, 2014).

J. Pearce, *Social Enterprise in Anytown* (London: Calouste Gulbenkian Foundation, 2003).

R. Ridley-Duff and M. Bull, *Understanding Social Enterprise* (London: Sage, 2011).

REFERENCES

[1] J. Harvey, *Modern Economics* (Basingstoke: Macmillan, 1998) p. 22.

[2] F. Moulaert and O. Ailenei, 'Social Economy, Third Sector and Solidarity Relations: A Conceptual Synthesis from History to Present', *Urban Studies*, Vol. 42, No. 11, 2005, pp. 2037–2053.

[3] Ibid.

[4] Ibid.

[5] Ibid.

[6] A. Amin, A. Cameron and R. Hudson, *Placing the Social Economy* (London: Routledge, 2002) pp. 3–4.

[7] Policy Action Team 3, *HM Treasury, Enterprise and Social Exclusion*, 1999. Taken from www.hm-treasury.gov.uk/docs/1999/pat3.html (accessed 1 March 2000) paragraph 5.2.

[8] Taken from http://ec.europa.eu/enterprise/entrepreneurship/social_economy.htm (accessed 3 August 2007).

[9] J. Kendall, *The Voluntary Sector* (London: Routledge, 2003) p. 1.

[10] J. Pearce, *Social Enterprise in Anytown* (London: Calouste Gulbenkian Foundation, 2003) p. 66.

[11] From the Wikipedia entry on social economy. Taken from en.wikipedia.org (accessed July 2006).

[12] Taken from www.wikipedia.org/wiki/Social_Economy (accessed 7 December 2006).

[13] A. Amin, A. Cameron and R. Hudson, *Placing the Social Economy* (London: Routledge, 2002) pp. 9–11.

[14] P. Lloyd, *Rethinking the Social Economy*, CU2 Contested Cities – Urban Universities (eds) (Belfast: The Queen's University, 2006) pp. 9–18.

[15] R. Murray, J. Caulier-Grice and G. Mulgan, *The Open Book of Social Innovation* (London: NESTA and the Young Foundation, 2010) pp. 3–4.

[16] Taken from http://ec.europa.eu/enterprise/entrepreneurship/coop/index.htm (accessed 28 March 2007).

[17] European Network for Economic Self Help and Local Development, *Key Values and Structures of Social Enterprise in Western Europe: Concepts and Principles for the New Economy* (Berlin: Technologie-Netwzwerk with 47 European Network for Economic Self Help and Local Development, 1997).

[18] Cabinet Office/Office of the Third Sector, *Social Enterprise Action Plan: Scaling New Heights* (London: Cabinet Office, 2006) p. 10.

[19] BIS Research Paper Number 214, *Small Business Survey 2014: SME Employers* (London: Department for Business, Innovation and Skills, March 2015) p. 35.

[20] Ibid.

[21] Organisation for Economic Co-operation and Development (OECD), *Social Enterprises* (Paris: OECD, 1999) p. 10.

[22] DTI, *Social Enterprise: A Strategy for Success* (London: HMSO, 2002) p. 8.

[23] Taken from http://www.sbs.gov.uk/sbsgov/action/layer (accessed 15 April 2007).

[24] Cabinet Office, *Building the Big Society*. Taken from www.cabinetoffice.gov.uk/news/buiding-big-society (accessed 20 October 2011).

[25] Taken from www.gov.uk/government/news/government-announces-inclusive-economy-unit (accessed 26 February 2017).

Companion website

Please visit the companion website at www.palgravehighered.com/Bridge-UE-5e for access to additional learning and teaching materials.

PART 2:
CHALLENGES TO THE TRADITIONAL VIEW

Enterprise

Entrepreneurs

Small Business

It ain't what you don't know that gets you into trouble. It's what you know for sure that just ain't so.

Mark Twain

In this book Part 1 describes the evolution of our regard for, and understanding of, enterprise and its associated components of entrepreneurship and small business. It refers to what Gibb called 'an explosion of research into entrepreneurship and the small and medium enterprise'[1] and it summarises the conclusions from this research and the main facts about enterprise recorded in papers and books which contribute to the common understanding in this field.

However, Gibb also argued that, 'despite the increase in academic knowledge, indeed perhaps because of it, there has been a growth of ignorance' and 'a major manifestation of this growth of ignorance is the emergence of a number of outstanding "mythical concepts" and "myths" which are considerably influencing the establishment of policy priorities'.[2]

Gibb identified this problem at the turn of the century, and the myths about enterprise and its components to which he referred still persist. They often appear to be related to various assumptions which can be hard to spot because they are often not clearly recorded or even acknowledged and, possibly because of that, are rarely challenged.

Nevertheless these assumptions contribute to a perspective which has become the accepted view of this subject and which it is comfortable to hold because almost all authorities seem to share it. This perspective is widely assumed to provide a helpful picture, not only because it appears to be derived from research and thus to be 'evidence-based', but also because it is more or less universally agreed. It is therefore used by people working in this field and it guides, or at least supports, much entrepreneurship and small business policy.

Thus this perspective has become an example of what J. K. Galbraith called 'conventional wisdom', explaining that:

We associate truth with convenience [and] with what most closely accords with self-interest and personal well-being or promises best to avoid awkward effort or unwelcome dislocation of life. ... Economic and social behaviour are complex, and to comprehend their character is mentally tiring. Therefore we adhere, as though to a raft, to those ideas which represent our understanding.[3]

However, further investigation and fresh thinking suggest that parts of the conventional enterprise wisdom may be misleading because some of the assumptions on which it is based seem to be incorrect. For example in Part 3, Chapter 15 presents evidence that much policy in this area has not worked and the existence of a faulty perspective of entrepreneurship and small business could help to explain why that has happened. However, fresh thinking does not have to depend on new discoveries, but can instead be based on re-interpretations of old ideas. For instance Copernicus's idea that what we now call the 'solar system' was sun-centred, instead of being earth-centred as the then prevailing wisdom maintained, came at least in part from ancient Greek sources. Nevertheless it upset the often strongly held, conventional view and led eventually to the revelations of Newtonian science.

Enterprise is by no means the only field in which knowledge occasionally needs to be re-assessed. Indeed it is now recognised that in other subjects as well as this one, much of our knowledge has a half-life: defined as the period of time over which half of it will be found to be meaningless, partial, irrelevant or even clearly wrong. Science may be supposed to make progress by establishing key principles upon the foundation of which further investigation and/or theory can then be based – such as Newton's laws which helped to establish physics as such a basic deterministic science that it is envied by those labouring in other subjects which appear to lack such a clear underlying structure. Yet eventually even Newton's laws of gravity were found to be less accurate than Einstein's theory, although they may still be good enough for a limited range of applications. Thus, even in subjects like physics, knowledge decays, and in very applied subjects this rate of decay appears to be much faster – branches of medical knowledge are said to have half-lives of ten years or less. And, if the study of enterprise is a science, it is a very applied one and so in it too knowledge might be expected to have a short half-life.

But the idea that knowledge might decay is often resisted, especially by those who owe their position to their fluency in the conventional knowledge, and upsetting strongly held conventional views with new ideas is difficult. As Keynes is reputed to have said: 'the difficulty lies not in the new ideas, but in escaping from the old ones.' That requires a degree of independent thought which does not come easily to people who are in reality very strongly socially influenced. As Mark Earls has commented:

> Independent thinking is to humans as swimming is to cats: we can do it if we have to.[4]

Nevertheless Part 2 presents a critique of the conventional wisdom in this area. It identifies and questions some of the assumptions behind it and revisits some of the earlier observations to show where this conventional view may be wrong, or at least questionable. It introduces other ideas and theories also and provides alternative perspectives to suggest a potentially better conceptual understanding where that seems to be needed. In addition, it considers some lower-level practical applications of this relevant to anyone thinking of, or pursuing, starting or growing a business, or to anyone who might want to advise on or help this process.

The prime focus of the conventional wisdom in this field seems to be the small business – so this part starts, in Chapter 8, by re-assessing the traditional view of small businesses. Then Chapter 9 looks at what has been called 'entrepreneurship' and Chapter 10 at the wider application of enterprise as a part of human life and not just as an end in itself. These chapters suggest where there is new understanding in these areas, and the practical application of this to starting a new venture is considered in Chapter 11 and to operating a business in Chapter 12. Finally Chapter 13 considers the concept of social capital, the relevance of which is increasingly being recognised as an essential supplement to what have been considered traditionally to be the main components of the enterprise mix.

References

1 A. A. Gibb, 'SME Policy, Academic Research and the Growth of Ignorance, Mythical Concepts, Myths, Assumptions, Rituals and Confusions', *International Small Business Journal*, Vol. 18, No. 3, 2000, p. 13.

2 Ibid.

3 J. K. Galbraith, 'The Concept of Conventional Wisdom', *The Affluent Society* (Boston: Houghton Mifflin, 1958) p. 7.

4 M. Earls, author of *Herd: How to Change Mass Behaviour by Harnessing Our True Nature* (Chichester: John Wiley & Sons Ltd: 2009), in an interview on BBC Radio, August 2011.

Rethinking Small Business

CONTENTS

– Introduction
– The 'default' perspective on small businesses

– Examining the assumptions
– Conclusions

KEY CONCEPTS

This chapter covers:

- Some of the assumptions about small businesses which are at least questionable if not wrong but which nevertheless have become part of the conventional wisdom about small businesses.
- However, these assumptions are hard to identify because they are unstated, unrecorded and often not consciously held.
- A suggestion that, nevertheless, these assumptions have contributed to a 'default' perspective which is unhelpful but has become detached from the assumptions – so challenging any of them may not change it.
- The view that small businesses do not behave in the way that these assumptions would suggest.
- An examination of some of the assumptions that have been identified and suggestions for corrections.

LEARNING OBJECTIVES

By the end of this chapter the reader should:

- Understand the danger posed by the conventional wisdom in this area.
- Appreciate the need to try to 're-set' the 'default' thinking.
- Be able critically to assess the main elements in the conventional wisdom about small businesses.
- Understand the reasons for thinking that some of the assumptions which appear to be behind such wisdom are wrong, or at least misleading.

INTRODUCTION

Part 1 of this book describes the evolution of our current interest in enterprise and its supposed components of entrepreneurship and small business and describes why, since the 1970s, there has been significant official interest in the latter in particular. Prompted by a realisation of the economic benefits they appear to offer, governments have attempted to encourage and assist small businesses and this has been supported by efforts to try to understand how they behave and what factors influence their behaviour. Much of the resultant information we now have on small business is summarised in Chapters 5 and 6.

However, as the introduction to Part 2 suggests, there appears to be a set of received assumptions supporting this recorded understanding which also contribute to the perspective many people have on small businesses. A lot of people need and/or want to know about small businesses, often for professional reasons. They include accountants and enterprise agency staff, academics and consultants, policy-makers and evaluators, as well as other small business 'professionals'. Although they may work with small businesses, such people often lack the insight into them which would come from having been a small business owner or otherwise engaging meaningfully in that world. Sharing their problems and rewards, headaches and ambitions, needs immersion, not toe-dipping, and is unlikely to come from courses or reading. Even talking to small business owners may not be enough as they may not fully articulate their experiences, especially when dealing with someone who, however empathetic, sees things in essence from the viewpoint of a different culture.

In any case many 'professional' people have acquired their understanding of enterprise, not from direct experience of starting or running a business or from small business owners, but primarily from their colleagues or from what is taught in business schools or on professional development courses – and that is often based on a big business perspective. Even those people who work in small business often just get on with that work and don't develop their own perspective on its context. As a result many people have come to share a standard 'professional' perspective on business which they often pick up informally and unconsciously. They absorb it rather than learning it in a deliberate manner – and they then apply it to entrepreneurs and small businesses. This received view appears then to become a form of 'default' perspective which is unquestioningly applied whenever businesses are considered. In this it is like the standard 'default' setting on a computer which is adopted automatically each time a programme is used and, while it may be overridden at times for particular applications, will still be reloaded when next operating in that area – unless and until it is deliberately re-set.

This perspective can be very influential, so it is relevant to check its validity. This chapter examines the assumptions on which it is founded, and suggests that many of them are suspect. That means that the perspective many people have of small business can be misleading, which in turn can have an effect, *inter alia*, on small business policy and its implementation. Thus, it is suggested, despite all the accumulated learning about small businesses in the last 30 or so years, there is still a need in some places for significant rethinking.

THE 'DEFAULT' PERSPECTIVE ON SMALL BUSINESSES

A long habit of not thinking something is WRONG, gives it a superficial appearance of being RIGHT, and raises at first a formidable outcry in defence of custom.

Thomas Paine in *Common Sense*

So pervasive is this perspective that sometimes, as suggested above, it seems that it has become the normal 'default'. Thus, even if people may disagree on an intellectual level with some of the assumptions underlying the perspective, many continue to apply the perspective – possibly because they fail to appreciate either the nature of its foundations or the need to replace the 'default' settings. Additionally there can be a natural reluctance to question the comfort afforded by such 'conventional wisdom' (see Illustration 8.1).

What is this perspective?

What this perspective amounts to is a set of loosely connected assumptions about small businesses and the way in which they behave: assumptions which, when taken together, amount to the received wisdom in this area. These assumptions have not evolved separately and are interrelated and often interdependent. But identifying these assumptions is not easy in that, although they have long been held, they are rarely considered or acknowledged. Therefore lists of them cannot easily be assembled

---

ILLUSTRATION 8.1 – CONVENTIONAL WISDOM

It was John Kenneth Galbraith who coined the phrase 'conventional wisdom'. According to him:

> Numerous factors contribute to the acceptability of ideas. To a very large extent, of course, we associate truth with convenience – with what most closely accords with self-interest and personal well-being or promises best to avoid awkward effort or unwelcome dislocation of life. We also find highly acceptable what contributes most to self-esteem. ... But perhaps most important of all, people approve most of what they best understand. ... Economic and social behavior are complex, and to comprehend their character is mentally tiring. Therefore we adhere, as though to a raft, to those ideas which represent our understanding. ...
>
> Because familiarity is such an important test of acceptability, the acceptable ideas have great stability. They are highly predictable. It will be convenient to have a name for the ideas which are esteemed at any time for their acceptability, and it should be a term that emphasizes this predictability. I shall refer to these ideas henceforth as the conventional wisdom.[1]

---

from official or otherwise published sources because they are taken, often unconsciously, as given and not recorded or questioned.

However, to demonstrate that the assumptions exist and should be queried, it is not necessary to list and examine them all. Instead, following the acknowledged scientific method, if a sufficient number of them can be identified and shown to be incorrect, or at least misleading, that should be enough to indicate the need for a re-assessment. Therefore, based on their own experience and observation, the authors suggest that the following narrative is not untypical of such assumptions:

- It is assumed, in trying to understand the business sector (including small businesses) that the business is the natural focus and the key component. Therefore it should be the main unit of analysis.
- It is assumed that the aim of a business is to maximise its profit (and/or its shareholder value). Thus it is assumed that, to achieve its purpose, any business will want to grow in order to make more money. Consequently trying to grow is the natural state for a business and, if that growth imperative is being inhibited, it is likely in many cases to be because of the presence of external constraints such as a lack of one or more of the factors necessary for growth such as skills or external investment. Indeed it is often assumed that finance in some form is the key requirement.
- Because, as noted, profit/shareholder value is deemed to be the business's aim, it is assumed that successful businesses will focus on the bottom line of profitability as the main indicator of success.
- It is assumed that, in general, business decisions will be taken on a logical basis consistent with the above assumptions following a clear rational analysis of the situation and the options available.
- Because all private sector businesses are thought to be profit-focused, it is assumed that there is a clear difference and separation between them and social enterprises, which have a focus on making a social contribution.
- Because all legitimate trading businesses make an economic contribution, it is assumed sometimes that the death of any such business will be damaging to the economy and so should be prevented.

EXAMINING THE ASSUMPTIONS

Because there isn't a definitive list of specific assumptions, it is not appropriate to try to identify and dissect each assumption separately. Instead this chapter seeks to show that they exist by reference to some appropriate quotes and recorded observations and to expose their flaws by demonstrating the validity of a contrary set of propositions on aspects of small business.

PART 2

What should be the focus?

Chapters 2 and 5 indicate that, to a considerable extent, the current interest in small business can be traced back to Birch's report in 1979, which claimed that it was small firms which created the most net new jobs. Before that Penrose had pointed out that small businesses are not small big businesses and Bolton had highlighted some of the other important contributions they make. Nevertheless it was probably Birch who did most to encourage people to look at small businesses by highlighting their key role in job creation.

It appeared that much enterprise research followed this lead in focusing on the small business as, in the mid 1990s, Scott and Rosa pointed out that an underlying assumption in mainstream small business and enterprise research was:

> that the firm is the fundamental unit of definition and analysis, not the entrepreneur. The role of the entrepreneur may be important, but only as the founder of the firm, or as part of the managerial team that grows it. Firm level analysis is paramount and underlies other key assumptions.[2]

Such underlying assumptions, they suggested, had become increasingly unquestioned and self-reinforcing. It is easy to see why this particular assumption would have been made. As indicated above, Birch highlighted small businesses, rather than the entrepreneurs behind them, as the key creators of new jobs. Also it is businesses which are registered and can be seen to start or to end, businesses which have turnovers and employment levels which can be measured, and it is businesses which deliver things people want such as jobs and economic growth. Nevertheless, suggested Scott and Rosa, small businesses are part of the process of wealth creation which is entrepreneur- (not organisation-) based, and 'by using the firm as the unit of analysis the unintended consequence has been the continued invisibility ... of these real wealth-creating activities'.[3]

Like Scott and Rosa, Gibb had earlier highlighted the need, when dealing with small businesses, to understand their owner-managers:

> To many managers the business is the ego. ... Attitudes of owner-managers may therefore not be as objective or impersonal as those of professional managers. ... The business will embody the value system of the owner-manager reflecting his own personal objectives and those of his family. He may not therefore easily identify with the value systems of advisers, accountants, bank managers and professional managers of large companies.[4]

In a small business the ownership often consists of one person or a small group who take an active role in the business. They are much more influential on the business than the shareholder owners of a bigger business who, because they are external and disparate, have less immediate impact. In contrast, suppliers and customers, although they are external, can have a much bigger influence on a small business than a big business. Some reasons for this are that a small business generally has less market influence through pricing or advertising than a big business, and is likely to have fewer customers and suppliers and to work more closely with them. Other external influences on big businesses can include trades unions, public bodies and pressure groups. Small businesses, in contrast, are less likely to be unionised, are more likely to try to ignore regulations, and are a less rewarding target for consumer or other campaigns.

As explained in Chapter 5, in the section on the distinctive characteristics of small businesses, inside a small firm the owner-manager is often all-powerful. While in a big business the chief executive can be very powerful, he or she still has to answer to a chairman and board, and to work with professional senior managers who often have expert knowledge relevant to their particular functions. In big businesses a unionised workforce can have the influence of its combined strength exercised through the union structure. Also, generally, in big businesses professional sources of advice are used. The small business owner-manager, in contrast, has fewer such sources of influence and will be more likely to listen to his or her own inclination, to rely on his or her own experience and to seek advice, if that is needed, from a network of personal contacts. The small business owner-manager, in comparison with the manager of a larger business, often has less general professionalism but more flexibility in, and knowledge of, his or her particular niche.[5]

If small businesses thus reflect the attitudes of their owners, then the key component to consider in seeking to understand small business actions will be the person, not the business. Owners often do not perceive a separation between themselves and their businesses and will make business decisions for their own personal reasons rather than because of any 'business' logic.

The existence of the business as a potential subject for consideration is clearer when the business is a separate legal entity, such as a limited company, and is less clear when the business is the activity of an individual operating as a 'sole trader'. The assumption may have been that the sole trader should be seen as an embryonic limited company which has not yet made it, but the lack of a clear distinction between a sole trader and his or her business points to an important consideration. The business is not only the creation of the person but is also the expression of the person, even when the business is legally separate from that person. A person may start up and close down a business but the person will still continue to exist. The closure of the business is not the end of the matter. It might be followed, as in the case of a 'habitual entrepreneur' (see below), by the setting up of another business and the reason for the closure may lie with the entrepreneur rather than with the business. To make sense of the totality of the entrepreneurial process it is necessary therefore to take the entrepreneur as the focus and prime unit of investigation, not the business.

It is also important to recognise that different owners will have different personal objectives. Chell *et al.*,[6] for instance, in looking at the entrepreneurial personality, reported that there are different types of entrepreneur with different clusters of traits and behaviours. Different types of entrepreneur will have different motivations and these can affect their businesses. Thus a business developed by a sole owner who wants enough income to support his or her lifestyle will differ from a business currently of the same size developed by a group of investors with a view to maximising its future value. Table 8.1 suggests three broad categories of owners' motivation. These can be compared with the three types of business owner shown in Figure 3.1, which also indicates the variety of aspirational differences amongst business owners.

Analysing the small business process from the perspective of the entrepreneur also reveals another potentially useful focus: that of the group, or cluster, of businesses linked together in some way through common ownership and management by an entrepreneur or entrepreneurial team.[7] Owners with more than one business, either at the same time or sequentially, have been referred to as 'habitual' entrepreneurs (and habitual entrepreneurs, with their sub-sets of serial and portfolio entrepreneurs, are explored further in Chapter 9). It has been suggested that, for habitual entrepreneurs, new firm formation within a cluster is a growth mechanism and that while individual firms in a cluster may not grow, the cluster

Table 8.1 *Owners' motivations*

Label	Description
Lifestyle	Lifestyle is the description often given to the motivation of an individual to run a business which not only facilitates, but is also part of, the lifestyle that individual wants to have. Examples of lifestyle motivations are frequently to be found in art or craft businesses where the owner lives to practise that craft rather than only practising that craft in order to live.
Comfort-zone	A comfort-zone motivation typically seeks sufficient returns from a business for the level of comfort in life. Unlike the lifestyle business, the basis of the business is less important than the level of benefit provided. This has been characterised as the 'BMW syndrome' – where the level of comfort desired includes the possession of recognised symbols of success. Once that level of comfort is reached, however, there is little incentive to build the business further.
Growth	The 'growth' motivation is the one that approaches closest to what, for many, is the ideal business approach, namely one where the owner wishes to manage the business to increase its wealth generation. This might be done with a 'professional' motivation to build the organisation to maximise its future earnings potential and/or an 'entrepreneurial' motivation to maximise personal wealth.

does.[8] It may also be relevant to realise that the individual businesses in such a cluster may not, at least under the EU definition (see Illustration 5.1), be considered to be SMEs because they do not satisfy the ownership criterion.

The importance of habitual entrepreneurs was also illustrated further in a study by Carter of rural farmers in a specific area of England (East Anglia) which, at the time of the study, had the fastest growing population of any region of the UK, the lowest levels of unemployment and the highest levels of self-employment.[9] The study demonstrated that there is a core of farmers who have multiple business interests and that these additional business activities made a substantial contribution to both the number of enterprises and employment creation. It is interesting to note that, in presenting her conclusions about East Anglian farmers, Carter commented that within small business studies the conventional use of the firm as the sole unit of analysis appears to have obscured not only the range of activities of individual entrepreneurs, but also their wider economic contribution.[10]

Another relatively common form of very small business is the part-time business. Looked at from the perspective of the business, a part-time business may seem to indicate a lack of seriousness or of application to the business, but from the point of view of the person behind it, it may be a very sensible arrangement. For all the reasons given above, in exploring many aspects of the subject of business development, the fundamental unit to consider should be the entrepreneur, not the firm.

Is there a growth imperative?

> One of the things that most, if not all, businesses have in common is a desire to grow and expand.
>
> An article on business growth in a bank's guide for small businesses[11]

Businesses are inanimate and therefore don't themselves want anything. It is their owners, and other stakeholders, who want things of their businesses and, especially in the case of small businesses, the main requirements of those owners do not necessarily include continued business growth. Nevertheless, as the quote above shows, many people appear to assume that there is a sort of growth imperative – which is sometimes overtly stated.

It is clear that there has been an interest in business growth, particularly by those who want to encourage it, or sell services to it. Thus by 1990 Gibb and Davies were able to report that:

There has been a considerable body of literature embracing very different approaches to understanding the growth process. This can be broadly divided into four categories as follows:

- Approaches exploring the impact of the entrepreneurial personality and capability on growth including the owner-manager's personal goals and/or strategic vision.
- Approaches seeking to characterise the way the small organisation develops and influences, and is influenced by, the owner-manager. These approaches address issues of management style and models of stages of growth.
- Approaches broadly embraced under the term 'business' which focus upon the importance of business skills and the role of functional management, planning, control and formal strategic orientations.
- Approaches which are more macro in scope and which usually have their academic base in industrial economics. These include sectoral approaches pertaining to regional development, a focus upon specific industry sectors or sub-sectors, for example, high-technology firms.[12]

The 2003 edition of this book[13] commented that there are obvious overlaps among these approaches and added that it was interesting to note that much recent economics literature on small firm growth had tended to focus on a combination of a life-cycle effect (young firms grow faster than older firms) and economic variables, especially financial variables, for an explanation of growth. Indeed in modern micro-economic theory there has been allegiance to a model of small firm growth which has led to the 'removal' of the 'human elements'.[14] Thus within economics there is a failing in empirical enquiry to address 'the key questions of entrepreneurial characteristics and motivations and how they may be translated into business strategy'.[15] The earlier edition added, however, that interesting studies by, for example, Barkham *et al.*[16] and Storey[17] have adopted a more comprehensive approach, seeking to bring together research in economics, geography, organisational studies and business strategy to examine the link between entrepreneurial characteristics, business strategy and small firm growth across a wide variety of small firms. Traditionally, however, the unit of study has often been the business, not the entrepreneur. The needs, aspirations and other characteristics of entrepreneurs have been largely ignored by researchers, policy-makers and support agencies.

However, as the earlier part of this chapter points out, to understand small businesses it is necessary to look at their owners. Pink has commented, in the context of the supposed business profit motive, that often business owners 'are purpose maximisers, not just profit maximisers'.[18] This implies that, in order to understand their business intentions, it is necessary to ascertain what their purposes are. In other words, rather than being an end in itself, 'an enterprise is a goal-realisation device'.[19]

Models of business success

What are business goals, the achievement of which might be said to constitute business success? There is a common view that the purpose of a business is to make money, or at least, according to the economist Milton Friedman, the owners of a business will generally want it to make as much money as possible.[20] Therefore, when looking from a business perspective it might be thought that success, or a lack of it, should be obvious, but a failure to appreciate the owner's perspective can lead to a misunderstanding of what is actually happening. The model of success that people have in mind when they talk about small businesses and consider how well they are doing is likely to fall into one of two categories, depending on whether they are looking primarily at the business or at the person behind it:

- *The business professionals' model.* Many business professionals (including business advisers, researchers and professional managers of larger businesses) look primarily at the business and appear to have as their model of the successful, or 'ideal', business one that is achieving its highest potential (which may be assessed in terms of growth, market share, productivity, profitability, return on capital invested or other measures of the performance of the business itself). Professionals may not be conscious that they are adopting this 'default' model, because they may fail to see that there is an alternative. Whether the model is consciously adopted or not, the result is that a business is often judged by how close it comes to what an 'ideal' business might do in particular circumstances. Small businesses often score badly in such comparisons.
- *The small business proprietors' model.* Many owners of small businesses do not share the professionals' model. Their main concern is whether the business is supplying the benefits they want from it. These benefits are often associated with an income level to maintain a satisfactory lifestyle, and if that is achieved then there is no need to grow the business further. Business success for them is being able to reach a level of comfort ('satisficing') rather than achieving the business's maximum potential – a point at which managing the business could become more complex, time-consuming, risky and/ or costly.

This difference of appreciation may be linked to the different ways in which people making the apprecia-tion are connected to the business concerned. Even if the 'professional' is employed as the chief executive of a business, he or she may still see the business simply as a business, and may compare it therefore with the ideal model. Its success or failure may be very important, but 'business professionals' can and do see those aspects of their life that are not involved with the business as being separate. For the small busi-ness owner, however, the business is such a crucial and integral part of his or her life that the business and non-business parts of life are not considered as distinct and separate. Thus the business is seen in terms of life as a whole, including family life, and is subject to more than purely business considerations. The model of an 'ideal' business that the owner has is one therefore that best fits with desired personal goals and values. The stress of further business improvement may be too high a price to pay for a better or bigger business. For example, it may detract from other aspects of life, continuity of employment for well-known employees may be more important than increased efficiency or cost reduction and/or there may be an emotional attachment to a product range or service, the market for which is declining.

The implications of having these two different models is that a professional may see a business as under-performing in terms of its potential as a business, while the owner may see it as successful in terms of what he or she expects from it. In such cases the owner will not automatically share a professional's agenda of pursuing continued business improvement if that involves more time, effort and/or money but has no commensurate increase in perceived benefits.[21]

That does not mean that there will not be motivation and scope for further business improvement, but it should be improvement that increases the returns desired by the owner from the business. Professionals advising small businesses will be puzzled and ineffective unless they understand this. The professionals' business model assumes that growth in a business is almost always automatically positive in its effect: the owners' model may not share that assumption. This means that in the extreme case, which is not uncommon, it may be in the owner's perceived best interests to close the business completely, and that obviously doesn't lead to the business performing better. Such a closure is not a failure, but it would be counted as such on the professionals' model.

One area where this lack of appreciation of two models is very significant is in business accounting. Traditional accounting focuses on money and therefore has a key place in businesses since a lack of money is the final symptom of business failure. Thus it needs to be watched closely, and traditional accounting provides the methods for doing this. However, traditional accounting is often linked to business audits and then to reporting on business success or failure. Here the traditional approach appraises a business in terms of its financial or other tangible returns and not on any other requirements a business owner may have. Provided that is realised and accepted by the appraisers, no problems should emerge. Nevertheless, its very universality of usage means that this model is usually taken as providing the whole picture. See, for instance, the traditional yardsticks for business growth listed in Table 12.1. These are the measures often used to indicate the success of a business, but none of them refer specifically to owner satisfaction. Thus the application of the 'professional' model can leave many business owners feeling that they are perceived to be under-performing, but not understanding why.

If this two-model concept is correct, it suggests that relatively low productivity in small businesses may sometimes be due, not to a failure of management, but to a different vision of what management should be trying to achieve. The 'may' is because there is undoubtedly a considerable amount of management failure in small business, and by no means all of it is due just to differing agenda being pursued by the various stakeholders. Initially, however, it may be hard to distinguish between 'satisficing' and a mere lack of competence.

Thus, by looking at businesses from an owner perspective, it is clear that in many instances growing the business is not an objective. While owners might like to get a greater financial return from their businesses, they may be already getting enough for their purposes and so will not seek more where it requires extra effort. Even when its owners do want a business to make more profit, it seems that focusing primarily on profit can be bad for a business. Kay for instance has reported investigations which suggest that 'the most profitable businesses are not the most profit-oriented' and that 'visionary companies make more money than ... purely profit driven companies'.[22]

What are the constraints on business growth?

One approach to identifying the needs of a growth business is based on different factors of production. As reported in Chapter 2, Adam Smith referred to the 'component parts of price', which he considered to be land or natural resource, labour, and 'capital stock' such as tools, machinery and buildings.[23] Subsequent refinements to this list have included:

- Labelling land and natural resources as *natural capital*.
- Adding *physical capital* to cover things like plant and the built infrastructure.
- Replacing aspects of 'capital stock' with *financial capital* which can be used to buy tools and other purchasable assets.

- Introducing the term *human capital* to include labour and the skills a workforce needs to have.
- Adding *knowledge* or *intellectual capital* to the list to cover ideas and/or know-how, although this can be considered to be a sub-set of human capital.
- Including *social capital* to cover what used to be called 'networks'.
- Suggesting that *entrepreneurial capital* should be included, although some would argue that this is a distinct component of social capital.

One illustration of the application of this 'capitals model' to developmental issues is given in Figure 8.1 (and this topic, in particular the social capital component, is explored further in Chapter 13).

The UK Department for International Development (DFID) developed a 'sustainable livelihoods' model which includes five types of 'capital' asset which have limited substitution potential and all of which are considered to be important in building a strong community. The five-capitals pentagon lies at the core of the livelihoods' framework as it highlights the important inter-relationships amongst the various assets affecting people's quality of life.

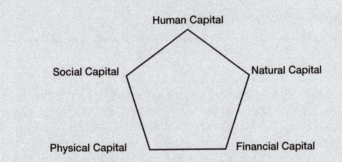

Human Capital:	Human capital represents the skills, knowledge, ability to labour and good health that together enable people to pursue different livelihood strategies and achieve their livelihood objectives. At a household level, human capital is a factor of the amount and quality of labour available; this varies according to household size, skill levels, leadership potential and health status. Human capital appears in the generic framework as a livelihood asset, that is, as a building block or means of achieving livelihood outcomes.
Social Capital:	Social capital is the resources upon which people draw in improving their quality of life and are developed by: - networks and connectedness, either vertical (patron/client) or horizontal (between individuals with shared interests) that increase people's trust and ability to work together and expand their access to wider institutions, such as political or civic bodies; - membership of more formalised groups which often entails adherence to mutually agreed or commonly accepted rules, norms and sanctions; and - relationships of trust, reciprocity and exchanges that facilitate co-operation, reduce transaction costs and may provide the basis for informal safety nets amongst the poor.

Natural Capital:	Natural capital is the term used for the natural resource stocks from which resource flows and services (e.g. nutrient cycling, erosion protection) useful for livelihoods are derived. There is a wide variation in the resources that make up natural capital, from intangible public goods such as the atmosphere and biodiversity to divisible assets used directly for production (trees, land, etc.).
Physical Capital:	Physical capital comprises the basic infrastructure and producer goods needed to support livelihoods. It includes: • Infrastructure consists of changes to the physical environment that help people to meet their basic needs and to be more productive; and • Producer goods are the tools and equipment that people use to function more productively.
Financial Capital:	Financial capital denotes the money resources that people use to achieve their livelihood objectives. The definition used here is not economically robust in that it includes flows as well as stocks and it can contribute to consumption as well as production.

Figure 8.1 *The DFID model of development capital*

Source: Department for International Development (DFID), *Sustainable Development Guidance Sheets* (London: DFID, 1999) p. 5.

The capitals model in Figure 8.1 suggests that if growth is constrained, it is because of a lack of one or more of the identified capitals, rather as plant growth might be constrained by a lack of water, of sunlight, or of mineral nutrients. In other words growth is natural, so if it isn't happening, it must be constrained by a lack of something which, if supplied, will allow growth to happen.

However, another view of the constraints on growth is to look at what might be the natural tendency of the system in question. A consequence of the second law of thermodynamics is that, unless they are maintained, systems tend to increase in entropy and become increasingly disordered and, in this, businesses are probably no different. Thus it might be supposed that, instead of trying to grow, the natural tendency of a business would be to regress, especially under conditions of strong competition. It takes energy and effort to prevent that and to grow instead. There can be positive influences which encourage this, such as the owner's goals or a natural desire to compete. Also government support is sometimes offered to try to encourage business growth.

While it is suggested above that many business owners do not necessarily want growth, they don't necessarily want contraction either. Thus their efforts might act to keep a business where it is by resisting movement in either direction. It is as if a business was on a slope with the natural force of gravity tending to move it downwards, official policy encouraging it upwards, and the friction of owner satisfaction and/or inertia tending, at least for a while, to keep it where it is (as illustrated in Figure 8.2).

One benefit of establishing the totality of influences on a business is that it helps to put any single influence in perspective. Without this there is a tendency to overestimate the effect of any particular one. If, for instance, it is considered that R&D can help to build competitiveness and that a grant scheme would encourage R&D, then it might be thought that such a grant scheme would be a positive influence on a business. It is important, however, to recognise the strength of the influences keeping the business where it is; they may be much stronger than the incentive value of a grant. This can be likened to pushing a heavy object – friction tends to keep it where it is unless the pushing force is raised above a critical point. Consequently attempts to reduce the frictional resistance might be more effective than attempts to increase the amount of external push.

Nevertheless, most small business policy initiatives seem to be based on the assumption that growth is the natural state of a business constrained by one or more factors such as a lack of finance, inadequate

Growth is something of an up-hill struggle:

It might be expected that the natural trend is for a business to contract

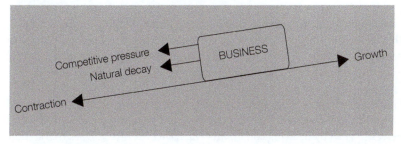

Although there may be some positive influences encouraging growth

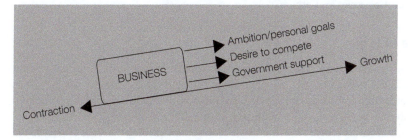

And there are probably also influences which keep a business where it is

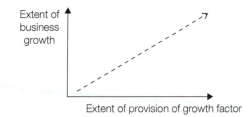

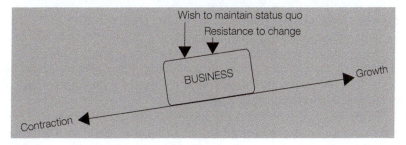

Figure 8.2 *The influences on a business*

information or poor training. So providing more finance, information, and/or training should enable the frustrated growth to proceed. It is as if it was expected that the effect of providing the deficient factor(s) would be as shown in Figure 8.3.

Similarly in horticulture it was thought that plants naturally tried to grow and that, if they didn't, it was due to external constraints such as a lack of warmth and light, a drought or a shortage of nutrients. Thus growth was assumed to be the natural tendency for a plant. However, recent research suggests that growth is restrained by internal inhibitors (arising from parts of a plant's DNA called DELLAs) and therefore non-growth is actually normal. Growth may occur when the conditions are right for the plant to produce hormones which overcome the growth-restraining effects of the inhibitors, but just providing

Figure 8.3 *The supposed effect of the provision of growth support*

PART 2

more sunlight, water and/or fertiliser may not be enough. It is further suggested that this lack of growth can be in a plant's longer-term interest if it prevents it from growing too fast for its conditions.

> And I'm beginning to see the growth of plants as a metaphor for our times. The DELLAs being ... the agents that restrain the rate of growth to a degree consonant with the conditions within which plants find themselves. Lacking DELLAs, a plant becomes insensitive, brash, a fast-liver that is unable to exercise appropriate restraint, and that dies young.[24]

Might businesses also have internal growth inhibitors, with those inhibitors being located in the minds of their owners? If those owners don't want to grow their businesses, then incentives designed to help their businesses to grow by relieving constraints will have little effect. Does this account in part for the commonly reported 'failure' of small businesses adequately to avail of, or benefit from, the services of public support agencies and others?

The role of logic

If, as suggested above, the constraints on small business growth are, to at least some extent, located in the minds of the business owners, then to understand the constraints it is necessary to understand human motivation. Traditional economic theory has assumed that individuals are independent, rational, selfish materialists. Behavioural economists, on the other hand, suggest that this is a distortion of our economic instincts and there are other aspects of human nature which are crucial to understanding our business actions.[25] In particular, it is suggested, we are strongly socially influenced:

> Much of our behaviour is strongly influenced by other people's behaviour. ... Social learning is a process by which we subconsciously take in the behaviour of others to learn how to behave.[26]

Such social influence is not necessarily logical so if, as the argument above suggests, human attitudes are acknowledged to be very relevant to small business behaviour, it cannot be presumed that business decisions will necessarily always be based on logic.

Growth, or its absence, can be attributable therefore to a wide variety of factors. There is no comprehensive theory to explain which firms will grow or how they grow, but various explanatory approaches have been used. Of course, whatever approach or combination of approaches one favours, seeking to distinguish between which businesses will grow and why and which will not is likely to remain an unattainable goal. Indeed, as was said some time ago, most of the research work in this area 'fails to provide convincing evidence of the determinants of small firm growth as a basis for informing policy-makers';[27] and again, 'given the significance of employment created in rapidly growing small firms, it is surprising that theoretical and empirical understanding of the characteristics of these firms remains somewhat sketchy'.[28]

A hierarchy of needs model

Even if an owner is trying to grow, or to start, a business, another complicating factor in assessing what is needed is that different needs may become apparent at different stages, or from different perspectives. It has been observed that, if people who are starting new enterprises are asked what they need to help the process, the answer is very often 'money'; whereas if people seeking to help that process are asked, they will often mention other areas of assistance such as premises, training, advice and mentoring, and some people go as far as to say that money is not the issue. Indeed, not uncommonly, there appears to be a connection between the assistance that those trying to help are best able to supply and what they claim is the main need: trainers for instance often seem to see skills as the key issue while bankers may highlight finance.

So is the main need money or not? What explains this apparent difference of opinion? How is it that different people, each of whom ought to be in a position to know, can provide different answers?

Is it like the case of three blind people each seeking to identify an elephant by what they can feel: they variously describe it as a rubbery hose, a tree, or an unravelled rope, depending on whether they feel the trunk, a leg or the tail.

One model (shown in Figure 8.4) developed to explain the variety of answers obtained to this question borrows a concept from Maslow in his analysis of human needs. He postulated that those needs could be placed in a hierarchy in which lower-order needs are dominant until they are satisfied, whereupon the higher-order needs start to be felt. The higher-order needs are there, but may not reveal themselves until the lower-order needs are satisfied. It has been suggested that a similar hierarchy could apply to enterprise needs, which would explain why they appear differently to different observers. Thus, without an idea, no need is felt for the resources to develop it and, until those resources are provided, no need is often apparent for any extra enterprise skills. Ultimately, if the enterprise is to be a success, it needs an environment which, given a sound approach by the enterprise, is capable of sustaining it.

The model in Figure 8.4 appears, for instance, to work for things like artistic ventures and not-for-profit-distribution enterprises as well as for private sector businesses. For example there is a need for pump-priming support for the artist until he or she can become established, and becoming established can mean earning enough to support the art from direct sales or through some sort of benefaction. Given artistic skill there is still a need for skill in marketing and money control if the venture is to succeed.

In this presentation, money is often a complicating factor. It has not been included in the hierarchy because it is not a direct need but is sought because it can be used to buy what is needed. It is a means not an end. Money is needed at an early stage to buy the resources required for start-up and then it is needed at a later stage to sustain the venture once it is launched. At the later stage the money required should be found mainly from the earnings of the venture itself. These two types of funding can be likened to the flight of a glider. At its launch a glider needs external help to get into the air, but then, if it is successfully launched and piloted, it should itself be able to find enough lift to sustain its flight. But if the glider pilot does not have sufficient skills to do this, the glider will descend and will once again need external help if it is to rise again. It is only after the glider has been launched, however, that such a lack of skills may become apparent. Similarly in enterprise, if some of the higher-order needs are not satisfied, the enterprise will not be operated viably and will need more 'pump-priming' money as a result. Therefore, given an initial idea and some form of start-up finance, failure to meet higher-level needs can appear as a further need for finance.

Given an idea, which is often the starting point without which the needs issue will not arise, the lowest and so the most obvious need is likely to be resources, to which money appears to be the obvious answer. Therefore this hierarchy-of-needs hypothesis explains why the needs of enterprise are, at an early stage, often expressed as a need for money, and why the other needs are hidden until that need is apparently satisfied. Hence it explains why there can be confusion and disagreement about what is the most appropriate assistance to offer. It also explains why, when asked, most people will say that money is the key issue, yet there are other people who will talk not about money but about training and mentoring needs, for example. It also explains why providing more money often does not solve the problem if it is mis-diagnosed.

- An environment which can sustain a well-run enterprise.
- Expert advice and personal support, which can be provided by mentors, advocates, and networks. (*This can be provided by social capital.*)
- The skills needed to advance the enterprise, such as financial and marketing skills. (*This is part of human capital.*)
- Resources for advancing the enterprise, such as equipment, materials, workspace and time. (*These can be purchased with financial capital.*)
- An idea for an enterprise. (*This can be allied to intellectual capital.*)
- Seeing enterprise as a possibility. (*This comes with the right form of social, or entrepreneurial, capital.*)

Higher

Lower

Figure 8.4 *A hierarchy of needs model*

The model can be expanded and explained further. Figure 8.4 shows a level below the idea: it is the need for a culture in which ideas for enterprise can arise and which encourages people to be enterprising, just as to grow a plant there needs to be suitable ground in which a seed can germinate and thrive.

The model also highlights the reason for a not-infrequent temptation to use money as the tool with which to help enterprise. Often bodies which are created to help enterprises are given a budget with which to operate. When they ask those engaged in enterprise what would most help them, they are told it is money. In such circumstances it is very easy to believe that money is the tool to use, instead of seeing that it has to be converted into something else if it is to achieve the desired effect. The model also indicates that anyone seeking to assist the enterprise process should not believe either that it is relevant to try to intervene only at one stage or that one intervention is likely to succeed in addressing all the main needs of enterprise development.

Mixing financial and social aims

If a business's mission is solely to maximise its profitability, then social aims would have no part in this, unless a lack of apparent social responsibility was thought to have an adverse impact on profit. However, as suggested above, many small businesses reflect their owners' goals and will not be focused purely on profit because many owners of private sector businesses have social, environmental or ethical aims, as well as financial ones. Thus many small businesses will have an element of social purpose.

Social enterprises which clearly have an avowed social aim, and are thus presumed not to be in the private sector but in the third sector, are considered in Chapter 7. However, some private sector businesses do acknowledge an element of social responsibility, even if that is sometimes only because it might help to secure their longer-term profit-making future. Indeed it would seem that there is no clear boundary between what might be categorised as socially oriented private sector businesses and business-focused social enterprises. Instead there is a spectrum of different objectives which are often not well reflected in the chosen form of venture incorporation and, even in the private sector, financial and social aims are often intertwined. This is, for instance, recognised in the 'map' of an economy shown in Figure 7.1, which, for smaller organisations, suggests there is no clear boundary between the private and third sectors – and that small enterprises in either sector often have more in common with each other than they do with larger businesses supposedly in the same sector.

Avoiding business deaths

It seems to be logical that, if a business contributes something to an economy, even if it is only one job and its associated expenditure, then the demise of that business will mean a loss to the economy and should be prevented if at all possible.

Viewed from a perspective of trying to achieve economic growth, business deaths may seem like something which is always to be avoided and, from the perspective of the businesses concerned, there may seem to be nothing positive in terminations. However, consider a healthy ecological system such as a forest: if there were no deaths in it, then after a while there would be no space for new growth and no scope for evolution. The deaths of individual trees might initially leave holes in the forest but those holes will fill in time, and without such deaths the forest would eventually stagnate. Having some business deaths may also be natural in a healthy economy and, indeed, necessary for its continued health.

An analysis which treats all business deaths as regrettable usually considers an economy to be ordered and static, instead of alive and dynamic. An ecology in which there were no deaths would also be one in which there was no new growth and no evolution. Like organisms, businesses do not, and should not, live forever. While a business death may be bad in the short term, especially for the business concerned, it is not necessarily bad for the economy in the longer term.

Competition is a key factor in developing an entrepreneurial economy and, as Dennis has stated, 'the link between entrepreneurship and competition is intimate'.[29] But competition produces both winners and losers; it drives innovation but it also means that those who lose the race to innovate may not survive. Indeed, Schumpeter emphasised that economic advancement takes place through a process of creative destruction – a process in which, as he pointed out, entrepreneurs play a key part.

Thus some business deaths are not only an inevitable part of economic development, but even an essential part. If businesses did not occasionally die, there would be no space left for new businesses, whether that is market space, employment space or financial space – and there is evidence that new businesses can drive productivity improvements in their competitors. A low rate of business deaths can also reflect a low rate of business starts, not least because it means that new dynamic businesses are not being created in sufficient numbers to drive out the older, inefficient ones. Therefore, instead of always assuming that business deaths should be prevented, it might be better to assume that some deaths will be both necessary and unavoidable and to help to make those deaths which are unavoidable as easy as possible for all concerned.

CONCLUSIONS

As well as the assumptions outlined at the beginning of this chapter, a further assumption which could be added to the list is that the 'default' view of businesses (which is based on these assumptions) is correct and that there is no other valid position. Instead this chapter indicates that there is an alternative view and suggests why it might provide a more realistic, and therefore a more helpful, perspective on small businesses.

At the start of this book Chapter 1 makes reference to the scientific method and the need, if understanding is to advance, continually to seek contrary evidence with which to test hypotheses. But has that happened in our understanding of small businesses, or has it instead followed the path described by Lunn of the way economics is taught?

> The way economics is taught means that a large number of professionally qualified economists, especially those working outside academia, in private business, in journalism or in government, have at no stage been exposed to any evidence concerning the theories that underpin their professional status. To a scientist, this should be alarming. It is alarming too how many academic economists, including very good ones, have had no exposure to contrary evidence. As an economist, I am ashamed to admit that rather than training sceptical, creative minds, the profession has for years been teaching its practitioners and students to recite doctrine.[30]

Instead of looking for another way, have we all unthinkingly followed the crowd without taking a helicopter view to see if we are going in a helpful direction? In reviewing the key contributions to our understanding of enterprise (see Chapter 2) it is relatively easy to establish what the main contributors have said – but not what they haven't said: the relevant things which, in the light of subsequent understanding, they might have said but didn't. Thus other assumptions have arisen which their input has not denied. Sometimes archaeologists revisit previous digs to see if the evidence should be re-interpreted in the light of subsequently acquired knowledge. Maybe it would be helpful to do more of that in exploring the reality of enterprise.

Nevertheless this chapter has presented an alternative perspective which includes features such as:

- A focus on the entrepreneur – the owner of the business – rather than primarily on the business.
- An understanding that a small business in particular will reflect its owner's (or owners') purposes and limitations or reservations.
- An acceptance that many business owners do not want to grow their businesses. The main constraints to growth may thus be in the owners' minds.
- An acknowledgement that business owners will often be socially influenced. Because of this, and because of the variety of purposes that owners may have for their businesses, the business decisions they make may not always follow 'business' logic. Also because of this social influence, aspects of social capital can be very important to small businesses.

- An understanding that, in practice, even private sector businesses can have a mix of financial and social, ethical and/or environmental aims. This may not, however, be reflected in a business's reported accounts.
- An acceptance that the business sector will not evolve without some business deaths. Therefore, while individual business deaths may often be regretted, overall and in the longer term many of them may be economically beneficial.

This perspective, it is suggested here, is a better foundation for understanding small businesses than the list of assumptions presented at the beginning of this chapter. However, as this chapter seeks to describe, those original assumptions have contributed to a view of small businesses which often continues to be used even if on occasion some of the assumptions which gave rise to it are questioned. That may be either because that questioning is not noticed or because people fail to appreciate that it is on such foundations that their perspective is based. Thus, while showing that at least some of its supporting assumptions are wrong should be enough to indicate the need for a re-assessment of the 'default' perspective, if that 'default' perspective has become disconnected from the assumptions on which it is based, then challenging or even disproving the assumptions will not necessarily change the often subconscious application of that perspective.

Among the implications of changing the received perspective are its application for starting and operating small businesses, which are considered in Chapters 11 and 12, and for enterprise and small business policy, which are considered in Part 3 (see also Illustration 8.2).

ILLUSTRATION 8.2 – A CASE STUDY OF A POLICY BASED ON A FALSE PERSPECTIVE?

In the late 1980s, the government's small business support policy in Northern Ireland included a programme which aimed to encourage businesses to grow by offering them capital grants to assist with the purchase of better production equipment. Although this programme operated over 25 years ago it is used for this case study because it was the subject of some insightful and disinterested evaluation in a way which seems rarely to have happened since. This is a summary of it:

Programme purpose: The purpose of the programme was to stimulate small manufacturing businesses to grow, and thus to increase employment.

Programme rationale: It was assumed that manufacturing businesses wanted to increase productivity and grow but were being constrained by a lack of sufficient accessible and/or affordable finance for investment in the necessary production capacity. Finance was to be provided therefore in the form of grants.

Programme mechanism: Grants of up to 50 per cent of eligible investment in machines and other plant were offered to eligible small businesses. Businesses wanting a grant made applications accompanied by business plans to show what they sought to do and the projected results from doing it.

Feedback from the businesses: The businesses receiving grants were required to submit copies of their subsequent annual accounts to show their progress. These tended to show that, after allowing for a staged release of the grant money, the net worth of businesses had increased (not least because of the increase in their subsidised fixed assets).

Underlying assumptions: This policy looked at businesses, assumed both that they wanted to grow and that they would respond logically if offered the finance they needed to help with that growth. It assumed that the business plans submitted would indicate what the businesses proposed to do and why and that the impact of the scheme on the businesses would be shown in their subsequent accounts.

What did an impartial assessment find? Hitchens *et al.*[31] compared the performance of Northern Ireland businesses with matched counterparts in the then Federal Republic of Germany (chosen as a successful economy). They found that the profitability of the Northern Ireland businesses was similar to that of their counterparts in Germany but, on average, the Northern Ireland businesses had significantly lower levels of productivity. This was attributed mainly to lower wages and to the level of government financial assistance. It was suggested therefore that this assistance (which amounted to around one fifth of manufacturing value added during the 1980s) impeded the efficient operation of some firms by reducing their incentive to conduct essential research and development, training and production innovation.

It was also suggested (in a presentation to one of the authors) that these grants could sometimes have a significant negative longer-term impact on their recipients. If a business could get a large capital grant for the purchase of a new machine, then it would be tempted to buy a better (faster, higher-quality and/or greater-capacity) machine than it needed. If, however, the business did not need the extra speed or capacity that such a machine provided, it would not make full use of that machine. Consequently output would not increase above that which a cheaper machine might have produced. The more expensive machine would, however, probably be more complex and have higher depreciation and maintenance costs (which would not be grant-aided). Thus the business would, as a direct result of the grant, have higher future production costs with no compensating increase in output. This negative impact, being in the future, would not have been reflected in the business's accounts in the short term.

Overall the review suggested that the capital grants programme was failing to deliver its objectives, at least to the extent envisaged. The reason, as described above, was that the programme was based on the assumption that a shortage of capital was constraining business growth and that, if grants were provided to release this constraint, businesses would use the grants to grow their output. The programme thus looked at businesses from a business perspective and assumed a growth-imperative and logical business decision-making.

Instead it seems that many business owners saw the grants, not primarily as a means to help them to achieve a growth aim, but instead as a way of doubling the value of a capital investment and of emulating peer businesses which were acquiring attractive new machines. Thus their motivations for acquiring new machines may have included non-growth objectives such as capital gain, reducing labour problems by substituting machines for people, and the prestige of owning a better machine to 'keep up with the Joneses'. In addition, although it was not raised in the review, it is suggested by the authors' experience that if grants are available, then whether they need a grant or not, business owners will often be tempted to apply because others appear to be doing so and they don't want to feel that they are 'losing out'. Thus they will prepare business plans to justify the grant rather than to reflect the reality of their future intentions.

A conclusion of this study is that the capital grant programme did not achieve its objective of stimulating significant business growth because it was based on a perception that the world of SMEs is a world of logic, objectivity and measurement, as traditional economics assumes – not a world of personality, emotion and feeling, as this chapter argues and as behavioural economics now acknowledges.

☛ THE KEY POINTS OF CHAPTER 8

- There appears to be a 'default' perspective about small businesses which has become the conventional wisdom.
- This perspective is based on a set of assumptions many of which are incorrect or at least questionable.
- Those questionable assumptions include:
  - That the business should be the focus of attention – when focusing on the owner may be much more informative.

- — That businesses have a growth imperative – although actually most owners don't want to grow their businesses if it involves more effort.
- — That businesses focus on the bottom line of profit – whereas business owners are often driven by other motives.
- — That business decisions are made on the basis of business logic – but their owners are often driven by other influences.
- — That financial and social aims do not mix – although in reality many businesses have both financial and social objectives.
- — That business deaths are to be regretted – whereas some business deaths are helpful in a dynamic economy.
- The 'default' perspective may be based on such assumptions but it has become detached from them, so correcting the assumptions may not affect the perspective held.
- Until the 'default' perspective is changed, it will continue to exert a harmful influence on policy and its implementation.

✓ ## QUESTIONS, EXERCISES, ESSAY AND DISCUSSION TOPICS

- Are there any arguments that can be raised to support any of the assumptions identified?
- Can you identify any other questionable assumptions about small businesses?
- If the 'default' perspective is unhelpful and has become widespread, where in the chronology outlined in Chapter 2 did understanding go wrong?
- What might be the consequences if this 'default' perspective continues to go unchecked?

REFERENCES

[1] J. K. Galbraith, 'The Concept of Conventional Wisdom', in *The Affluent Society*, 4th Edition (London: Penguin, 1991) p. 7.

[2] M. Scott and P. Rosa, 'Has Firm Level Analysis Reached Its Limits? Time for a Rethink', *International Small Business Journal*, Vol. 14, No. 4, 1996, pp. 81–99.

[3] Ibid. pp. 81–99.

[4] A. A. Gibb, 'Towards the Building of Entrepreneurial Models of Support for Small Business', paper presented at the *11th National Small Firms Policy and Research Conference*, Cardiff, 1988.

[5] For a discussion on the various sources of influence on organisations, see H. Mintzberg, *Power In and Around Organizations* (Englewood Cliffs, NJ: Prentice Hall, 1983) pp. 32–46.

[6] E. Chell, J. Haworth and S. Brearley, *The Entrepreneurial Personality: Concepts, Cases, and Categories* (London: Routledge, 1991).

[7] P. Rosa and M. Scott, 'Entrepreneurial Diversification, Business-Cluster Formation, and Growth', *Government and Policy*, Vol. 17, 1999, pp. 527–547.

[8] P. Rosa and M. Scott, 'The Prevalence of Multiple Owners and Directors in the SME Sector: Implications for Our Understanding of Start-Up and Growth', *Entrepreneurship and Regional Development*, Vol. 11, 1999, p. 34.

[9] S. Carter, 'The Economic Potential of Portfolio Entrepreneurship: Enterprise and Employment Contributions of Multiple Business Ownership', *Journal of Small Business and Enterprise Development*, Vol. 5, No. 4, 1998, pp. 297–307.

[10] Ibid. p. 297.

[11] *Business Bite*, 2nd Edition (Belfast: Ulster Bank, 2008).

[12] A. Gibb and L. Davies, 'In Pursuit of Frameworks for the Development of Growth Models of the Small Business', *International Small Business Journal*, Vol. 9, No. 1, 1990, p. 16–17.

[13] S. Bridge, K. O'Neill and S. Cromie, *Understanding Enterprise, Entrepreneurship and Small Business*, 2nd Edition (Basingstoke: Palgrave Macmillan, 2003).

[14] H. Barreto, *Entrepreneurship in Micro-economic Theory* (London: Routledge, 1989).

[15] R. Barkham, E. Hanvey and M. Hart, *The Role of the Entrepreneur in Small Firm Growth* (Belfast: NIERC, 1995) p. 2.

[16] Ibid. p. 2.

[17] D. J. Storey, *Understanding the Small Business Sector* (London: Routledge, 1994) pp. 137–143.

[18] D. Pink, Gainful Employment, *RSA Journal* (Spring 2010).

[19] L. Hunter, speaking at University of Ulster seminar on 'Developing a Strategy and Vision for Social Entrepreneurship', 10 September 2007.

[20] See, for instance, M. Friedman, 'The Social Responsibility of Business Is to Increase Its Profits', *New York Times Magazine*, 13 September 1970.

[21] For a discussion on the overlap between personal goals and business goals in SMEs, see R. Goffee and R. Scase, *Corporate Realities* (London: Routledge, 1995) pp. 1–21.

[22] J. Kay, *Obliquity* (London: Profile Books, 2010) pp. 1, 8.

[23] A. Smith, *An Inquiry into the Nature and Causes of the Wealth of Nations*, 1776.

[24] N. Harberd, *Seed to Seed* (London: Bloomsbury, 2007) p. 302.

[25] P. Lunn, *Basic Instincts* (London: Marshall Cavendish, 2008) p. 23.

[26] E. Dawnay and H. Shah, *Behavioural Economics: Seven Principles for Policy Makers* (London: New Economics Foundation, 2005) p. 3.

[27] A. Gibb and L. Davies, 'In Pursuit of Frameworks for the Development of Growth Models of the Small Business', *International Small Business Journal*, Vol. 9, No. 1, 1990, p. 26.

[28] D. J. Storey, Op. Cit. p. 121.

[29] W. J. Dennis, 'Entrepreneurship, Small Business and Public Policy Levers', *Journal of Small Business Management*, Vol. 49, No. 1, 2011, p. 98.

[30] P. Lunn, Op. Cit. p. 257.

[31] D. M. W. N. Hitchens, K. Wagner and J. E. Birnie, *Northern Ireland Manufacturing Productivity Compared with West Germany: Statistical Summary of the Findings of a Matched Plant Comparison* (Belfast: NIERC, 1989).

Companion website

Please visit the companion website at www.palgravehighered.com/Bridge-UE-5e for access to additional learning and teaching materials.

Rethinking Entrepreneurs and 'Entrepreneurship'

CONTENTS

- Introduction
- The received wisdom
- The context for entrepreneurial activity
- How entrepreneurs operate
- The variety of entrepreneurs
- What influences entrepreneurs?
- Reappraising 'entrepreneurship'
- In conclusion

KEY CONCEPTS

This chapter covers:

- Some of the assumptions behind the received wisdom on 'entrepreneurship'.
- Some of the evidence that many entrepreneurs do not behave in the business-focused, homogeneous, financially and logically influenced way that traditional understanding might suggest.
- The reasons to believe that:
  — Entrepreneurs have goals other than making money;
  — Entrepreneurs are heterogeneous;
  — Being human beings, entrepreneurs are strongly subject to social influences; and
  — The word 'entrepreneurship' is not helpful.

LEARNING OBJECTIVES

By the end of this chapter the reader should:

- Be able critically to assess the main elements in the conventional wisdom about entrepreneurs.
- Understand the reasons for thinking that some of the assumptions which appear to be behind such wisdom are wrong, or at least misleading.
- Understand an alternative view of entrepreneurs, seeing them as heterogeneous, as motivated by a wide variety of goals, and as very socially influenced.
- Be aware that 'entrepreneurship' might not exist as the concept we have supposed it to be.

INTRODUCTION

Chapter 8 begins this review of thinking about enterprise, entrepreneurship and small business by examining the 'default' perspective that seems to have developed about small business. That perspective has often taken the business as the key focus for analysis, but decisions in small businesses are made by their owners and/or managers. While the managers of bigger businesses might reasonably be expected to take an objective, professional and business-focused approach to their work, the owner-managers of small businesses are often much more subjective in their approach. Small businesses thus usually reflect their owners' aims and inclinations, rather than a business-focused logic.

Chapter 8 indicates why this 'default' perspective on small businesses needs to be revised, not least because many of the assumptions on which it appears to be based are questionable or even clearly wrong. This chapter follows that by looking more closely at the person behind the business and at the reasons why our received wisdom about entrepreneurs may also be changing.

Chapters 3 and 4 summarise current knowledge about enterprise and entrepreneurship. They consider the various meanings these words have acquired and what research has indicated about the nature of the concepts behind them. It is from such sources that the current received wisdom about entrepreneurs has been constructed. However, current understanding seems to be based on a concept of entrepreneurship, and a number of assumptions about it, which are possibly even less easy to identify and list than the assumptions made about small businesses. Also, as in the case of small businesses, many of these assumptions appear not to be well founded. The result is that conventional wisdom sometimes fails to appreciate, and to allow for, how entrepreneurs actually behave.

Chapter 3 indicates a range of meanings of the words enterprise and entrepreneurship from the very wide, which apply to the application of enterprise attributes in any context (E0 in Table 3.4), to the very narrow, which apply only to the formation and growth of knowledge-based, fast-growth, high-value-added businesses (E4). This chapter, in looking at the received wisdom about entrepreneurs, recognises that they are usually seen as operating in a business context and thus it acknowledges that they are often viewed primarily in the context of the formation and/or growth of any economic venture, including self-employment (E2).

THE RECEIVED WISDOM

As already argued, although there has often been a focus on the business, to understand some key business dynamics it is necessary to look at the entrepreneur and to consider what is motivating him or her. But, as with the default perspective on small businesses, there appears to be a received wisdom about entrepreneurs which is hard to itemise because neither the received wisdom nor the assumptions behind it have been formally recognised or recorded. Nevertheless, the authors suggest, the following might indicate some of them:

- Because the primary focus has been on the business, and entrepreneurs have been viewed from that perspective, the study of entrepreneurs has been seen as a sub-set of the study of businesses – and therefore, for instance, assigned to business schools.
- Similarly there has been an assumption that entrepreneurs are found only in a business context and operate in a business-like way, behaving like other business people, such as the managers of big businesses.
- Further it is assumed that all entrepreneurs have a lot in common with the managers of bigger businesses. For instance, just as professional managers usually only work for one business or employer, it is assumed that entrepreneurs generally only run one business.
- Instead of there being different types of entrepreneur, it is assumed that entrepreneurs are essentially homogeneous and all face similar problems.
- On the basis that businesses are founded primarily to make money, it is assumed that entrepreneurs must be doing it (starting, running and/or growing their businesses) to make money for themselves. Moreover, they would not be doing it unless a logical analysis had indicated that it offered them a better balance of risk and financial return than any available alternative activity.

As with small businesses, this is not a definitive list of such assumptions and, for the same reason, providing documentary evidence for such assumptions is often not possible. Nevertheless, as stated in Chapter 8 with regard to small businesses, if there are grounds for thinking that at least some such assumptions are prevalent, there is a case for examining them. Then, if they seem to be wrong or misleading, there should be an acceptance of the need to change the perspectives to which they contribute.

Therefore this chapter explores aspects of the current understanding of entrepreneurs, and of those small business owners who some might consider not to be entrepreneurs, and indicates where the reality does not seem to conform to the sort of assumptions listed above.

THE CONTEXT FOR ENTREPRENEURIAL ACTIVITY

It is not surprising that entrepreneurs are generally seen only in a business context. As Chapter 2 indicates, the first recorded use of the word in an economic context was by Cantillon and he appears to have used it with a relatively wide meaning. Nevertheless he did introduce it to economics in a business context, and currently the Global Entrepreneurship Monitor (GEM) initiative clearly identifies entrepreneurs as operating within the business sphere. Now, as Chapter 3 indicates, there are contrasting meanings of entrepreneurship – some of which place it only in the realm of business, and some in only relatively small parts of that realm, while others give it a wider meaning. One person who has used a wider meaning is Baumol, whose ideas on the potential for the available entrepreneurial disposition to be applied to productive, unproductive or destructive uses[1] is also summarised in Chapter 3. His hypothesis clearly assumes that this can be applied in non-business contexts, as he offers examples of its unproductive application in politics in Rome and in civic administration in China as well as its destructive application in warfare in middle-age England. Some people may insist on a definition of entrepreneurial activity which limits it only to a business context, but for others, such as Baumol, such behaviour can also be manifest in other situations. Thus, for them, being entrepreneurial is not exclusively a sub-set of business, but an aspect of human behaviour which can be applied in many different situations including, but not limited to, business.

HOW ENTREPRENEURS OPERATE

When their effort is applied to business, how do entrepreneurs operate? To a considerable extent the management and administrative methods and structures of businesses have to be different for different sized businesses. The informal ways in which someone can run a ten-person operation will not work if the business grows much beyond 100 people. The formal procedures necessary for the control and co-ordination of a larger business would be far too cumbersome and expensive for the ten-person business. It is over 50 years since Penrose pointed this out (as noted in Chapter 2) when she said of businesses which grow beyond this stage that it is 'likely that their organisation will become so different that we must look on them differently; we cannot define a caterpillar and then use the same definition for a butterfly'.[2]

Sometimes it seems that this is forgotten and small businesses are treated as if they were small big businesses. Nevertheless a number of authors have pointed out that this is not the case – that the entrepreneurial approach typically found in smaller businesses is very different from the corporatist approach of larger organisations. For instance, Gibb's summary of the differences is shown in Table 9.1 and Stevenson's in Table 9.2.

Gibb points out that a founding entrepreneur is likely to identify closely with his or her business. No matter how dedicated he or she may be, a professional manager employed to run a business is unlikely to identify with that business to the extent many business founders do. The values embodied in a founder-run business will often be those of the owner-founder and can be revealed in the products or services it supplies and its growth orientation, quality standards and employee relations. Where these values of the owner differ from those of business advisers, the input of the latter is likely to be rejected and, indeed, small business owners often lack the confidence to discuss business

Table 9.1 *Entrepreneurial v. corporatist management – some contrasts*

Entrepreneurial management	Corporatist management
Values, beliefs and goals	
Growth by green field management	Growth by acquisition
Short time horizons	Long time horizons
Informal strategic project planning (policy and practice interlinked and changing and emerging)	Formalised planning systems (policy laid before practice)
Failure means missed opportunity	Failure means resource-centred misdemeanour (variance from standard)
Seeks incremental development as a means to reduce risk	Seeks large-scale development with risk reduction by analysis/information
Pursues action strategies with negotiation as and where necessary	Pursues pre-negotiation strategies for decision-making (personal risk reduction)
Management evaluation on task completion	Management evaluation as routine aspect of organisation
Status equals success in the market	Status equals control over resources
Avoidance of overhead and risk of obsolescence by high subcontracting	Seeks ownership of all resources with objective of power and control
Pursues effectiveness in the marketplace	Pursues efficiency information to justify control
Organisational contrasts	
Flat organisational structure	Hierarchical organisation structure
Challenge to owner legitimacy	Clear authority
Need to trust others for reward	Clear reward system defined
Organic relationship emerging	Rational/legal structures

Source: A. A. Gibb, 'Enterprise Culture – Its Meaning and Implications for Education and Training', *Journal of European Industrial Training*, Vol. 11, No. 2, 1987, pp. 21–22.

Table 9.2 *A process definition of entrepreneurs*

Entrepreneur	Key business dimension	Administrator
Driven by perception of opportunity	Strategic orientation	Driven by resources currently controlled
Quick commitment	Commitment to opportunity	Evolutionary with long duration
Multi-stage with minimal exposure at each stage	Commitment process	Single-stage with complete commitment upon decision
Episodic use or rent of required resources	Control of resources	Ownership or employment of required resources
Flat with multiple informal networks	Management structure	Formalised hierarchy
Value-based and team-based	Compensation and reward system	Resource-based, individual and promotion-oriented

Source: H. H. Stevenson, 'Intellectual Foundations of Entrepreneurship' Chapter 1 in H. P. Welsch (ed.), *Entrepreneurship* (London: Routledge, 2004) p. 6.

PART 2

problems with professionals. For these reasons, an owner's support network is likely to be based on personal friendships and contacts, rather than on the formal support network (also see Figure 9.2). 'The business is the ego', Gibb points out, 'and therefore even objective criticism of the business is taken personally'.[3]

These considerations suggest that, even in a business context, the owner-managers of small businesses often do not behave like the professional managers of bigger businesses. The implications of this include:

- A business 'consulting' approach, which attempts to analyse and list what is wrong with a business before suggesting corrective actions, may work for a professional manager. However, a small business entrepreneur is likely to reject it because it is perceived as a personal criticism. Instead, a 'counselling' approach, which seeks to help the owner himself or herself to identify some of the issues, stands a better chance of being accepted and producing change.
- For an entrepreneur, perceived social status or acceptability may be linked to business success. Consequently, indications of business problems may be played down, hidden or even denied, not just in public but also in private, in case they might have an impact on social status (and on self-belief).
- A small business owner may be so committed to a product (range) or service that better opportunities for profitable activity are overlooked. Thus strategic development may be more strongly influenced by personal values and emotions than by logical analysis.
- For small business owners, commitment to family, to the workforce and to the local area may all impact on decisions in a way which is less likely in a big business setting.

THE VARIETY OF ENTREPRENEURS

Chapter 8 refers to the different owner motivations behind lifestyle, comfort-zone and growth businesses, and Chapter 3 (for instance, Figure 3.1) looks at different types of business owners although it suggests that, at least under some definitions, some owners are not entrepreneurs. Thus there are indications that, although they may share the characteristic of operating differently from corporatist managers of big businesses, small business owners are not all the same. Indeed, there can be as great a variety in the nature of entrepreneurial endeavour from the sole trader, to the micro, to the small to the medium-sized business as there is to the large business.

Chapter 5 has a section on the variety of small businesses, and that variety is itself a reflection of the variety of entrepreneurs behind the businesses. Like the businesses they found and run, entrepreneurs are heterogeneous rather than homogeneous. And among the categories sometimes distinguished are habitual entrepreneurs, social entrepreneurs, female entrepreneurs and ethnic entrepreneurs, so these are explored further.

Habitual entrepreneurs

As indicated in Chapter 8, analysing the small business process from the perspective of the entrepreneur reveals groups, or clusters, of businesses linked together in some way through common ownership by an entrepreneur or entrepreneurial team.[4] Owners with more than one business, either at the same time or sequentially, have been referred to as 'habitual' entrepreneurs – as opposed to 'novice' entrepreneurs who only have one business.

The term 'habitual entrepreneur' was coined to describe a person who is not satisfied with starting just one business but who goes on to start others also, either in sequence or simultaneously. He or she was considered to be a special type of entrepreneur, different from the supposedly more common 'novice entrepreneur'. Research, for instance by Scott and Rosa,[5] has indicated that multiple business ownership is more common than had been suspected and they consider it to be 'fundamental to understanding the process of capital accumulation in a free enterprise capitalist economy'.[6]

Scott and Rosa's work on the diversity of business foundations has revealed many differences between entrepreneurs as regards the kind of ventures they started, the strategies they followed and the management practices they adopted, and there is considerable variety even among habitual entrepreneurs. They have, for instance, been subdivided into 'serial entrepreneurs', who start a succession of businesses one after another but only one at a time, and 'portfolio entrepreneurs', who start a succession of businesses and remain actively involved in keeping some or all of them going at the same time.[7]

Rosa and Scott looked at the extent of habitual entrepreneurs in Scotland and found that up to 40 per cent of new limited companies had multiple-ownership and or cross-linkages with other firms.[8] Research by Westhead *et al.*, also into habitual entrepreneurs in Scotland,[9] yielded information on business performance which indicated that the average sales revenues reported by portfolio entrepreneurs were higher than those reported by serial entrepreneurs by a factor of three times, and higher than those reported by novice entrepreneurs by a factor of five times. Marked differences in employment patterns were also detected. In 2001, in terms of total employment, portfolio entrepreneur firms were on average about three times larger than serial entrepreneur firms and about four times larger than novice entrepreneur firms. The authors of the study suggested that such findings highlighted the need for policy-makers and practitioners to target policies towards the varying needs of each type of entrepreneur rather than provide broad 'blanket' policies to all types of entrepreneur.

The Scottish findings seemed to suggest that habitual entrepreneurs learn from their experience and thus their subsequent businesses perform better than their first ones. In contrast, a study of 'the changing nature of entrepreneurship' over a 30-year period (the 1970s, 1980s and 1990s) in the 'low' enterprise area of Teesside found that 'portfolio entrepreneurs performed no better than others who did not own another business' and that 'the performance of serial entrepreneurs was even worse'.[10] The apparent difference between these findings and those of Westhead *et al.* may be due to the nature of the sample used. Teesside is associated with a decline in heavy manufacturing and the subsequent rates of high unemployment, whereas the Scottish study relates to a larger area of the country with a more diverse economic performance and used a different array of research methods. Nevertheless the different findings do suggest that local factors may be important and that the conclusions of such studies might have limited application outside the areas studied.

Storey, who participated in the Teesside study, has returned to this issue of entrepreneurial learning. He reports that the existing literature on this issue, for instance summarised by Harrison and Leitch,[11] 'appears to assume that learning is a continuous, perhaps even cumulative, process'. This, he suggests, would imply that performance would continuously improve over time, or at least not decline. In practice, he finds, the evidence is that, 'small firm performance measured in terms of growth in sales or employment fluctuates considerably over time and, if anything, generally declines or remains constant with age'[12] – and this view is also supported by the work of others such as Rocha *et al.*[13]

Whether or not habitual entrepreneurs learn from their different ventures, it does appear that habitual entrepreneurs are relatively common. In the case of portfolio entrepreneurs this means running several businesses simultaneously – something which the professional manager of a larger business would not be expected to do.

Social entrepreneurs

The Eden Project, in Cornwall, has transformed a disused clay mine into a global garden with the world's largest greenhouse, which is now an important visitor attraction. It includes two large enclosures inside which a tropical environment and a Mediterranean environment are emulated. This informs people about the natural world, creates a learning experience and assists research into plants and conservation. The project is an educational charity and an example of a social enterprise as described in Chapter 7.

The Eden Project was conceived and led by Tim Smit. Despite this, it is not in the private sector but the third sector. So are Tim Smit and people who launch similar ventures (of the kind listed in Table 7.1) not entrepreneurs? They have started businesses, but the prime aim of those businesses is not the making of financial profit for the businesses' owners, and in many cases the businesses concerned have constitutions which preclude this. If entrepreneurs are defined using some of the narrower definitions, such as those covered by the E4 category in Chapter 3, they are not entrepreneurs – but according to most generally accepted definitions they are. They may be referred to as social entrepreneurs, because their main aims are social rather than financial, but they are entrepreneurs nevertheless and serve to disprove the assumption that all entrepreneurs must be starting, running and/or growing their businesses in order to make money for themselves.

Female entrepreneurs

While it might be supposed that gender would have little or no effect on whether a person was enterprising, the specific example of the proportions of female-owned businesses shows that this may not be the case. Historically most entrepreneurs have been men, and those businesses which have been created by women typically have been in a limited range of business sectors. However, in the 1980s and 1990s this picture began to change. Nevertheless (as is described in Chapter 5) although the proportion of female-owned businesses may now be growing, at least in some countries, they are still significantly less numerous than male-owned businesses. (Chapter 5 also indicates some of the differences between those businesses and the issues they face.)

If there are fewer female-owned businesses than male-owned businesses, and if there are some differences between those categories of business other than just the gender of their owners, are there also differences between male and female entrepreneurs? Among the reasons suggested for this are:

- Patriarchal attitudes have existed in countries like Britain, where not so long ago women were required to give up their jobs when they got married or, as exemplified by the airline industry, when they reached the 'advanced' age of 27. Barriers such as this prevented enterprising women from acquiring the essential business knowledge, skills and contacts often necessary for a successful business launch.
- Men and women have had different socio-economic roles. Chell and Baines argue that some feminist literature depicts women and men as biologically different and this might result in different social and economic roles for the sexes.[14]
- Others argue that biological differences are small and conclude that different socio-economic roles arise from social constrictions imposed on entrepreneurial choice by factors such as family, cultural, political and industrial structures, which create and are reinforced by a strongly segregated labour market and occupational structure. Thus women's and men's experiences of occupational choice are different.
- A review of the literature by Ljunggren and Kolvereid suggests that there may well be differences in men's and women's motives.[15] Women seek economic outcomes such as profit and growth but they also seek social and relationship goals. Furthermore, Holmquist and Sundin conclude that women often start a firm to allow them to create their own work places.[16] This allows them to meet both business and family demands. However, Ljunggren and Kolvereid report that there is no consistency in findings about the association between gender and motivation across countries. For example in Norway men were more likely than women to be motivated by a desire to continue a family tradition and to remain at the forefront of innovative technological developments.

Despite these factors, many early studies of female entrepreneurs seemed to depict the male experience as the norm, and this may have led to the conclusion that 'women act from similar motivations and look for similar rewards from entrepreneurship as their male counterparts.'[17] In support of this view, Carter notes that early studies of the stated reasons for business founding reported by women were quite similar to those mentioned by men. From an 11-country study of motivations for starting a business, three broad categories for both genders were identified: challenge, wealth and autonomy.[18] Those studies which used psychological instruments to assess the personal traits of male and female entrepreneurs also found few differences between the genders.[19]

However, a study by Goffee and Scase did indicate that female entrepreneurs were not homogeneous and could be classified according to their attachment to entrepreneurial ideals and conventional female roles.[20] Those women with a strong attachment to both were called 'conventionals', 'domestics' organised their business ventures around the needs of the family, whilst 'radical' women had no strong attachment to either role. It should be pointed out that men who own businesses also experience tension between meeting economic and family needs.

Ethnic entrepreneurs

Like female entrepreneurs, ethnic entrepreneurs have been considered to be a specific category of entrepreneurs but display considerable variety within that category. Ram and Barrett, for instance, comment on the disparity between the circumstances of different ethnic groups in the UK and the different patterns of the self-employed within those groups. They quote figures showing that in 1989–1991 22 per cent of those of Pakistani or Bangladeshi origin were self-employed but only 7 per cent for West Indians or Guyanese. Therefore they explore this contrast.

They refer to cultural arguments that depict South Asians as natural entrepreneurs and African-Caribbeans as uninterested, but they stress, instead, the importance of external factors. They find that two issues predominate in the initial decision to create an ethnic business: structural matters such as the inhospitality of the environment in which ethnic groups are embedded and the advantage conferred on ethnic business by the ethnic resources at their disposal (see also Chapter 13 on social capital). The cultural issue of the relative propensity of certain ethnic groups to become entrepreneurs is, they suggest, a sub-set of the latter.[21] But, whatever the reason for it, this disparity demonstrates that ethnic entrepreneurs are not a homogeneous group.

Entrepreneurs are heterogeneous

These summaries indicate that, in at least some respects, habitual entrepreneurs are different from single entrepreneurs, social entrepreneurs different from private sector entrepreneurs, male entrepreneurs different from female entrepreneurs and some ethnic entrepreneurs different from other ethnic entrepreneurs. However, they also indicate that within these categories there are variations, such as the differences among female entrepreneurs and among ethnic entrepreneurs, which are at least as significant as the distinctions between the categories. Thus even the limited variety of entrepreneurs considered above demonstrate that they are heterogeneous, not homogeneous, and encompass many different people facing different issues and addressing them in different ways.

WHAT INFLUENCES ENTREPRENEURS?

Another questionable assumption about entrepreneurs which seems to persist is the supposition that they are somehow created, or at least influenced, by a condition called entrepreneurship – and therefore, when entrepreneurship is fostered, the people affected will start or grow businesses when logically that is the best thing for them to do. Illustration 9.1 provides some examples of this apparent view, and Bridge, in his assessment of enterprise policy, suggests that this assumption is consistent with many models of the influences on entrepreneurs and that even if not consciously adopted, this assumption has been the foundation nevertheless of much 'entrepreneurship' policy:

> The policies ... pursued have in many cases been consistent with the prevailing models of, and assumptions about, entrepreneurship which tend to suggest that people generally make individual decisions to start businesses, based on a logical assessment of issues such as the perceived desirability of the goal, the ease of pursuing it, the help available and the perceived chances of success. Therefore initiatives such as reducing red-tape, encouraging the availability of more capital, providing business training and mentoring, ensuring the availability of suitable and affordable premises and developing export sales initiatives have been tried. Such steps have been designed to make entrepreneurship

⟳

ILLUSTRATION 9.1 – THE ASSUMPTION OF INDIVIDUAL RISK/RETURN ANALYSIS

The following quotes illustrate the prevalence of the assumption that the entrepreneurial choice is made on the basis of logical risk/return assessments made by the individuals concerned:

> One of the canonical theoretical models in the Economics of Entrepreneurship is of occupational choice. ... Occupational choice models partition the workforce between individuals who do best by becoming entrepreneurs, and those who do best by choosing an alternative occupation, ... (for instance) modelling entrepreneurial choice as trading off risk and return.[23]

> Scholars have generally framed the decision of an individual (*Homo economicus*) to become an entrepreneur in terms of the model of occupational choice, where the income generated is compared to the wage earned as an employee.[24]

> In recent years, most research on entrepreneurship has focused on employment choices and on the alternative motivations that cause some individuals to start new businesses. In these studies, an individual's choice to become an entrepreneur is the result of a decision in which the individual in question compares the returns from alternative income-producing activities and selects the employment opportunity with the highest expected return. In short, the person becomes an entrepreneur because he or she can earn more.[25]

> Individuals are assumed to have a choice between operating a risky firm or working for a riskless wage. There are, of course, many factors which should influence this choice. The most important ones would include entrepreneurial ability, labor skills, attitudes toward risk, and individual access to the capital required to create a firm.[26]

> The entrepreneurial decision, i.e. occupational choice, is made at the individual level. ... An individual's risk–reward profile represents the process of weighing alternative types of employment and is based on opportunities (environmental characteristics, resources, abilities, personality traits and preferences). The occupational choices of individuals are made on the basis of their risk–reward profile of entrepreneurship versus that of other types of employment.[27]

---

more attractive to do by making it easier to do, by increasing the potential return from it, and/or reducing the risk associated with it. They are thus supposedly increasing the likelihood that people will opt for entrepreneurship.[22]

However, as Chapter 17 indicates, there is a lack of evidence that the polices apparently based on such assumptions actually work – which in turn suggests that the assumptions are wrong. So if entrepreneurial activity is neither explained by the phenomenon of entrepreneurship nor the result of individual rational risk–cost–benefit assessments, what does have an impact?

The answer might lie in social influence. As the studies summarised in Illustration 9.2 indicate, social influence is important in many aspects of human behaviour and Bridge suggests that entrepreneurs are no exception.[28] Audretsch and Keilbach have suggested that entrepreneurship capital should be added to the list of factors which drive economic growth, and they describe entrepreneurship capital as 'a milieu of agents and institutions conducive to the creation of new firms ... such as social acceptance of entrepreneurial behaviour, individuals willing to deal with the risk of creating new firms, and the activity of bankers and venture capital agents willing to share risks and benefits.[29] Thus Bridge wonders if social encouragement and approval might be considered to be an element of social capital necessary for many entrepreneurs to thrive (see also Chapter 13).

ILLUSTRATION 9.2 – BEHAVIOURAL ECONOMICS AND THE 'SOCIAL BRAIN'

Traditional economics is said to have developed the concept of *Homo economicus* – a rational being upon whose logical decisions economic models could be based. This assumes that people are rational and always act for their individual benefit. Real humans, however, do not behave like that:

> 'For every problem there is a solution that is simple, clean and wrong,' wrote H.L. Mencken, and the *Homo economicus* model is all that. Unlike *Homo economicus*, *Homo sapiens* is not perfectly rational. Proof of that lies not in the fact that humans occasionally make mistakes. The *Homo economicus* model allows for that. It's that in certain circumstances, people always make mistakes. We are systematically flawed. In 1957, Herbert Simon, a brilliant psychologist/economist/political scientist and future Nobel laureate, coined the term bounded rationality. We are rational, in other words, but only within limits.[30]

Behavioural economics seeks to recognise the reality of human behaviour. It is the subject for which Daniel Kahneman, an Israeli academic at Princeton, won the Nobel Prize in Economics in 2002.

> The award was unusual, indeed controversial, because Kahneman is not an economist but a psychologist. In the 1970s he became intrigued by the list of assumptions traditional economics made, and still makes, about people's nature. As Kahneman put it in the 2003 *American Economic Review*, 'I found the list quite startling, because I had been professionally trained not to believe a word of it.' As a psychologist, instead of assuming how people behave, Kahneman decided to look at how we actually behave ... (and) has become arguably the biggest name in what is now 'behavioural economics'.[31]

Thus, even in economics, it is being recognised that people do not always make important decisions on the basis of rational logical analysis but that, even if only subconsciously, their decisions are influenced by their social surroundings:

> Other people's behaviour matters: people do many things by observing others and copying; people are encouraged to continue to do things when they feel other people approve of their behaviour.[32]

In 2009, the RSA (Royal Society for the encouragement of Arts, Manufactures and Commerce) launched its project 'The Social Brain', designed 'to contribute to constructing the successor paradigm to the individualism of "economic man"'. In introducing the project the RSA explained that:

> in recent years the 'economic man' conception of human decision-making employed in neo-classical economics – a conception where decisions are thought of as only informed and motivated by rational self-interest – has come under increasing pressure. One direction of pressure emanates from the quite dramatic failure of the conception as a short cut for predicting and modelling economic activity. Another comes from new knowledge in neuroscience and the behavioural and social sciences. These two directions are rather obviously connected: the new knowledge shows that the 'economic man' conception provides us with a limited and biased understanding of human decision-making.[33]

The RSA project has, for example, suggested that there are three main strands to the idea that the brain is essentially social:

1. 'The brain, now it is finally beginning to be understood, turns out to unconsciously execute many of the decision-making processes that were previously thought to be self-consciously

produced. The idea that all decisions flow from an executive rational subject, in principle capable of operating in isolation from others, now appears to be at worst false and at best unhelpful.

2. The brain has evolved to develop and function within social networks. For example, a deficit in the neurotransmitter Serotonin (which, amongst other things, enables self-control) will result from unstable social environments lacking in qualities like empathy. Or, another example: mirror neurons are designed to enable (amongst other things) altruistic behaviour that facilitates social cohesion and allows an agent to successfully engage with others (and thus to achieve her own goals).

3. Even when we do make self-conscious decisions these are partly constituted by systematic biases that are fundamentally social. For example, behavioural economists have shown that people often indulge in herd behaviour. Game-theorists have also shown that it can be optimally rational to act altruistically because an agent's good reputation amongst her fellows is massively important for her ability to successfully negotiate the social world. And as neuroscientists like Antonio Damasio have shown, these kinds of socially motivated biases have their basis in the neurology of the brain.'[34]

That leads Bridge to suggest two assumptions which, unlike the assumption of rational risk-benefit assessments, do seem to fit with what is observed in reality:

1. The first assumption it is that, in entrepreneurial terms, a population can be divided into three groups: a group of people who are in practice immune to the temptations of entrepreneurial activity, a group of people who are active entrepreneurs and a third group of people who are 'floating voters' and are susceptible to becoming entrepreneurs under the right circumstances but who might decide not to act entrepreneurially. In other words, instead of assuming that people are either entrepreneurs or not entrepreneurs (a sort of black or white approach consistent with the 'entrepreneurs are born that way' viewpoint) or assuming that everyone has an equal potential to be an entrepreneur (everything is a uniform 'colour'), it is assumed that there is a gradation: a sort of spectrum. At one end of the spectrum there are those who will almost always act entrepreneurially. At the other end those who will almost never act entrepreneurially. Those who might act entrepreneurially sometimes are in the middle. (This model of a spectrum of entrepreneurial potential is also shown in Model C in Illustration 4.1.)

2. Second, consistent with the social influence idea, it is assumed that the major factor that determines whether those in the middle group will act entrepreneurially (i.e. consider starting their own businesses) is not logical, individually made risk/return assessments but the example of whether or not their peers and other influential people are acting entrepreneurially. Thus if, because they see their peers acting entrepreneurially, people in the middle group act entrepreneurially, they will themselves become part of that influence, and a high level of entrepreneurs will thus be self-reinforcing. Alternatively, if those in the middle do not act entrepreneurially, there will not be enough examples of people acting entrepreneurially to persuade others, and the level of entrepreneurs will remain low. Entrepreneurial activity will then be pursued only by that section of the community which was going to do it anyway.[35]

These two assumptions, he indicates, lead to a model in which the key influence comes, not from logical analysis, but from people's social circles. These circles, it might be said, comprise the four Ps of their pals, peers, parents and other persuasive people. In any particular social circle those in the 'middle' group will tend to follow the majority, or a rapidly growing minority. In doing so, they become part of the majority, thus reinforcing its influence. Switching the position of the majority will thus require a sufficient cumulative pressure for change to persuade enough people more or less simultaneously to switch: a sort of critical mass leading to a 'tipping point' – as shown in Figure 9.1.

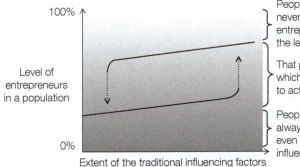

100% ↑
Level of
entrepreneurs
in a population

0%

→
Extent of the traditional influencing factors

People who are probably
never going to act
entrepreneurially, whatever
the level of influence

That part of the population
which might be influenced
to act entrepreneurially

People who will probably
always act entrepreneurially,
even with little or no extra
influence

Figure 9.1 *A possible model of the level of entrepreneurs*

Source: S. Bridge, *Rethinking Enterprise Policy: Can Failure Trigger New Understanding* (Basingstoke: Palgrave Macmillan, 2010) p. 202.

This assumption about the key influence on entrepreneurs is very consistent with Baumol's hypothesis (reported in Chapter 3) that the productive contribution of entrepreneurs to society varies less because of the total supply of entrepreneurs than it does from the way that the available entrepreneurial tendency is applied to productive, unproductive or destructive uses because of the rules of the society in which the entrepreneurs operate.

Bridge and Baumol are both considering the propensity of people to start or run businesses, rather than how they behave if and when they do start a business. Gibb, however, in looking at the way in which entrepreneurs behave (see above), has commented on the influences on the owners of businesses and on the interplay between the different influences. One illustration of some of the influences, and their relative strengths, is shown in Figure 9.2. It was produced by Gibb to indicate the layers of a small business support network and suggests that the closer, more personal and more social layers will usually have a much stronger influence than the outer, more impersonal and more official layers.

Thus there are many indications that humans are very socially influenced in much of what they do. In this it would seem that entrepreneurs are no exception. While some people might do what they want, whether society approves or not, many others will follow the example and/or dictates of their peers and those they aspire to emulate or whose approval they seek. In this it would seem that entrepreneurs are no exception, and despite the conscious assertion by some people that becoming an entrepreneur is a logical response to profitable opportunity, there are clear indications that many entrepreneurs can be more influenced by society than by business logic.

Figure 9.2 *The layers of the small business support network*

Source: A. A. Gibb, 'Towards the Building of Entrepreneurial Models of Support for Small Business', paper presented at the *11th (UK) National Small Firms Policy and Research Conference*, Cardiff, 1988, p. 17.

⊃   ## ILLUSTRATION 9.3 – THE GLOBAL ENTREPRENEURSHIP MONITOR'S ASSESSMENT OF INFLUENCES

One initiative which might have been expected to comment on what influences people to start businesses is the Global Entrepreneurship Monitor (GEM). Its work and results are outlined in Chapter 2 and, while it does not explicitly seek to examine the influences on individuals, one of its three current main objectives is 'to uncover factors determining the nature and level of national entrepreneurial activity'[36] for which the nature of the influences on individuals must surely be relevant.

GEM acknowledges that 'an economy's entrepreneurial energy derives, at least in part, from individuals who perceive opportunities for launching a business', that 'these people are further encouraged by their beliefs in their capabilities for starting the types of ventures they may envisage' and that 'the quantity and quality of the opportunities they perceive, and their beliefs about their capabilities, may be affected by various conditions in their environment: for example, economic growth, culture and education'.[37] It also recognises that, 'over time, societies ... develop particular cultural and social expectations' and 'an entrepreneurial culture may be reinforced by perceptions like the amount of status society confers on entrepreneurs and the extent people think being an entrepreneur is an attractive pursuit'.[38]

Nevertheless GEM suggests that, in considering national rates of entrepreneurial activity, the key relationship is with the level of economic growth. GEM does not find a relationship between numbers of entrepreneurs and aspects of social capital (or entrepreneurial capital) not least because it does not look for it, and neither does GEM look for entrepreneurship outside a business context. GEM is not able, therefore, to indicate whether or not Baumol's hypothesis applies.

GEM does ask questions about issues like people's entrepreneurial intentions, the extent to which people think they have the skills and knowledge needed to start a business, and the extent to which a fear of failure might prevent them from starting a business. However, GEM bases its surveys on direct questions, often put as part of a telephone survey and apparently without any associated probing supplementary questions. As a feature of social influence is that individuals may not be aware that they are following it and tend to rationalise their responses by finding other reasons for them, GEM's surveys may not reveal the importance of any social influence. In his book *Consumer.ology*, Graves suggests a set of criteria for determining how much confidence it might be reasonable to have in consumer research findings. The criteria include whether the analysis is of how consumers actually behave or instead of how they think they behave, what frame of mind the subjects of the study are in, the environment of the study, whether the subjects are aware of the purpose of the study and whether the time-frame for the questions in the study is similar to the time-frame for considering the issues in real life.[39] While these criteria were not designed primarily for assessing the sort of surveys GEM conducts, they do not suggest that a high level of confidence in GEM's findings would be justified.

Therefore, instead of providing results which help to develop new thinking about entrepreneurs, such as is explored in this chapter, GEM seems instead to be an example of the unthinking application of some of the old assumptions.

What the entrepreneur is

The observations summarised in this chapter indicate that aspects of the traditional view of the entrepreneur are due for reappraisal. As one commentator has observed: 'The current generation of entrepreneurship scholars are leaving the entrepreneur out of entrepreneurship'.[40] Contrary to the traditional assumptions described at the start of the chapter, these findings suggest that the entrepreneurs should not be seen as a sub-set of business and that, even when they are in business, they often do not behave like the managers of big businesses. They suggest that, instead of being homogeneous and all doing the same things in the same way, entrepreneurs are very heterogeneous. They differ in where and how they operate, in who they are and the issues they face, and respond differently to opportunities and influences. They also show that entrepreneurs are not all driven by the logic of money making and that, instead, for many of them the main influence is probably their social setting and the perceived views of those around them. Contrary to the traditional economic assumption that people always act logically to maximise their personal benefit (usually perceived in financial terms), recent research has indicated that humans function within social networks. As a result, even when they do appear to make rational, conscious decisions, these are to a greater or lesser extent influenced by systematic biases that are fundamentally social.

Since people are socially influenced, and entrepreneurs are people, they should be considered at least as much from a human and social perspective as a business one. Two illustrations from Gibb, reproduced in Figure 9.3, serve to illustrate this. The first shows how the entrepreneur might look if assembled using traditional assumptions. The second instead models the entrepreneur, not on such theory, but on

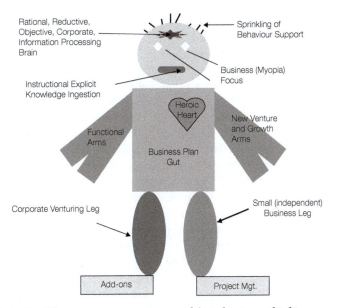

Frank N. Stein – The entrepreneur constructed from business-thinking components

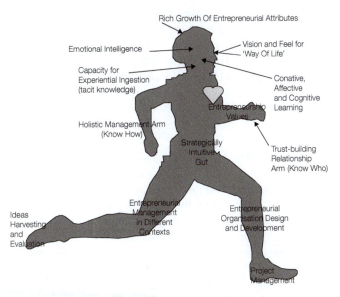

You or Me – The entrepreneur as a human being

Figure 9.3 *Alternative pictures of the entrepreneur*

Source: Based on A. A. Gibb, 'Towards the Entrepreneurial University: Entrepreneurship Education as a Lever for Change', *National Council for Graduate Entrepreneurship Policy Paper 003*, May 2005. Taken from www.ncee.org.

real-life observation. It is therefore suggested that the reality of the second should be recognised and accepted by anyone attempting to understand, work with and/or influence entrepreneurs.

REAPPRAISING 'ENTREPRENEURSHIP'

So far this chapter has largely discussed entrepreneurs, but they and their activities are often referred to collectively as 'entrepreneurship'. This term seems to have been coined in the 1930s although not at that time to have been carefully defined. Since then the term has been taken up and widely used and even studied as an academic discipline. However, Bridge suggests, its academic credibility appears to depend on two assumptions:[41]

- That entrepreneurship exists as a specific, discrete, identifiable phenomenon which somehow produces more and/or better entrepreneurs.
- That this phenomenon is deterministic in that it operates in a consistent way in accordance with 'rules' which can be determined and from which its behaviour can then be predicted.

However, Bridge further suggests, the first assumption is not supported by the evidence. As indicated in Chapter 3, the term 'entrepreneurship' is used with a wide variety of different meanings, not all of which appear to be mutually consistent. Some appear to think that further work will reveal more of the condition of 'entrepreneurship' which will link different uses – rather like the story told in Chapter 8 of the three blind people who identified different parts of an elephant as different objects because they could not see the whole animal. That whole has not, however, yet been discovered, and the contrary suggestion is that the different things labelled 'entrepreneurship' are not any more the same thing than are globe, Jerusalem and Chinese artichokes – which are different parts of very different plants and are only called artichokes because they are supposed to have a similar taste.

Examples of the confusion that can be caused by using the same label 'entrepreneurship' for essentially different things can be found in the field of 'entrepreneurship education'. Among the problems this can cause are those funding the courses may expect them to be about 'enterprise for new venture creation' whereas those participating in them might be better helped by 'enterprise for life' and might be put off by the adverse connotations of entrepreneurship, which is sometimes associated with the baser aspects of capitalism. In any case, if both types of course are just labelled 'entrepreneurship', then the difference is not made clear and one party may not be getting what they want.[42]

Even if a difference is indicated, for instance by labelling one 'for entrepreneurship' and the other 'through entrepreneurship', the use of the word entrepreneurship for both implies a similarity. Therefore because the business plan is often used as the basis for teaching 'for entrepreneurship' (enterprise for new venture creation) it seems to be assumed that it will also be suitable for teaching 'through entrepreneurship' (enterprise for life). If, however, the word entrepreneurship was not used in either case, then that assumption might not be made and a very different syllabus prepared for enterprise for life.

Then the second assumption also appears to lack validity. It assumes determinism and, as Bygrave has indicated, 'classical determinism is one of our basic biases. It implies that a specific set of conditions will produce a specific outcome [and] if these conditions are present, then the outcome is predictable'.[43] Therefore, he suggests, we look for such determinism and, because of that desire, 'management science suffers from some severe cases of physics envy'[44] – at least some entrepreneurship researchers seem to expect or to want entrepreneurship to be as deterministic as physics. Indeed Shane and Venkataraman declare in their paper on the promise of entrepreneurship as a field for research that:

> For a field of social science to have usefulness, it must have a conceptual framework that explains and predicts a set of empirical phenomena not explained or predicted by conceptual frameworks already in existence in other fields.[45]

Shane went on the write a book entitled *A General Theory of Entrepreneurship* to provide such a framework but in it he admitted that development of the theory was still at an early stage and the evidence for it was limited.[46] Further studies still do not appear to have found it, and Bygrave's earlier observation that 'in contrast with physics, entrepreneurship has no great theories'[47] still appears to hold. Bridge asks if the suffix 'ship' implies a deterministic condition and has therefore contributed to this expectation. However, the failure to find a satisfactory theory suggests that entrepreneurship does not exist as the phenomenon it was conceived to be, in which case entrepreneurship would be no more that what entrepreneurs do – which is to act entrepreneurially – and not the thing that causes them to do it.

Because neither assumption appears to be correct, and because of the confusion and misdirection associated with its use, Bridge suggests the word 'entrepreneurship' should be dropped.[48]

IN CONCLUSION

This chapter starts with a list of some of the assumptions which, it is suggested, contribute to the received wisdom about entrepreneurs and entrepreneurship. However, the subsequent sections of the chapter indicate that the reality of entrepreneurial activity is very different from that which some of the assumptions would suggest.

For instance, instead of enterprise and entrepreneurship being a sub-set of business, as appears to be assumed, enterprise is a sub-set of life. It can be realised in business, and especially in new business formation, but many definitions of entrepreneurship fit into the E0 and E1 categories (see Chapter 3), which do not have to be applied only in the traditional business categories. Because entrepreneurs are often viewed within a business paradigm, their existence in other areas has not been studied so much and has often not been seen and/or not been recognised as being part of the same phenomenon. This view of entrepreneurship as a part of life is explored further in the next chapter.

Even when entrepreneurs do operate within a business context, they do not necessarily behave like the managers of bigger businesses. For instance entrepreneurs often see their businesses as extensions of themselves and cannot see them dispassionately, as a hired manager might do. Thus they respond in different ways to advice and suggestions for improvements. Also, while a professional manager might be expected to concentrate on running the one business he or she is hired to run, entrepreneurs can start more than one business and run them simultaneously. Seeing entrepreneurs as professional managers can lead to a failure to understand how they operate and what might help them to do it better.

Exploring different categories of entrepreneurs reveals that there are many different kinds of entrepreneurs starting and running a wide variety of ventures in many different situations. Assuming that all people who might be categorised as entrepreneurs are relatively homogeneous can thus be very misleading. Treating them as a monoculture will be a hit-and-miss affair in terms of gaining their interest, providing them with support and assistance and/or encouraging them to improve their performance.

Another assumption which is often made is that entrepreneurs always follow that course of action that is rationally and logically 'the best'. Thus it is thought that entrepreneurs start businesses because individually made, logical risk–benefit assessments suggest that it is the best way for them to make money and that subsequently in running their businesses they will also follow business logic. This perspective ignores the fact that humans are social animals whose behaviour is often a result of social pressure rather than logic. In business they are no different, and they may not even consider starting a business if it is not socially respectable in their circles. Misunderstanding entrepreneurs' motivations and the influences upon them can lead to a misconceived incentive system which will fail to achieve its purpose.

These are only a few examples of assumptions which are also wrong or misleading but which nevertheless to a greater or lesser extent contribute towards our received wisdom in this area. Relying on such erroneous assumptions, either singly or collectively, can lead to initiatives, incentives and policies which are misguided, ineffective and/or counter-productive. That is why it is important to recognise, to query, and to correct them.

☞ THE KEY POINTS OF CHAPTER 9

- Just as in the case of the received wisdom about small businesses, the received wisdom about entrepreneurs appears to be based on a number of questionable assumptions.
- Many entrepreneurs do not operate in the way that theory might assume:
  - They do not behave like managers of big businesses.
  - They identify closely with their businesses and they view the businesses they create subjectively, not impersonally.
  - Some only run one business, but some run many, either consecutively or in parallel.
  - They are heterogeneous and, for instance, social, female, and ethnic entrepreneurs all often operate differently, not least because they face different issues.
  - They do not respond automatically to opportunities for greater profit and, rather than always responding logically, they are often very socially influenced.
- The entrepreneur is best seen therefore as a human being, responding to many different pressures sometimes in unexpected ways, instead of as the embodiment of traditional economic logic.
- Relying on erroneous assumptions about entrepreneurs, either singly or collectively, can lead to initiatives, incentives and policies which are misguided, ineffective and/or counter-productive.

✓ QUESTIONS, EXERCISES, ESSAY AND DISCUSSION TOPICS

- Although they have their differences, small business owner-managers have more in common with each other than they have with big business managers. Is this true?

- Compare the motivations of ethnic entrepreneurs with those of indigenous entrepreneurs.

- The entrepreneur is the key to the business, and the entrepreneur is a human being, not an automaton. To what extent is accepting that message the key to understanding entrepreneurs?

- This chapter suggests that many of the views identified as the 'conventional wisdom' about entrepreneurs are wrong. Why then do you think they became the conventional wisdom?

📖 SUGGESTIONS FOR FURTHER READING AND INFORMATION

S. Bridge, *The Search for Entrepreneurship: Finding More Questions Than Answers* (London: Routledge, 2017).

A. A. Gibb, 'Towards the Entrepreneurial University: Entrepreneurship Education as a Lever for Change', *National Council for Graduate Entrepreneurship Policy Paper 003*, May 2005. Taken from www.ncee.org.

REFERENCES

[1] See W. J. Baumol, 'Entrepreneurship: Productive, Unproductive, and Destructive', *Journal of Political Economy*, Vol. 98, No. 5, 1990, part 1.

[2] E. T. Penrose, *The Theory of the Growth of the Firm* (Oxford: Basil Blackwell, 1959) p. 19.

[3] A. A. Gibb, 'Towards the Building of Entrepreneurial Models of Support for Small Business', paper presented at the *11th (UK) National Small Firms Policy and Research Conference*, Cardiff, 1988, p. 14.

[4] P. Rosa and M. Scott, 'Entrepreneurial Diversification, Business-Cluster Formation, and Growth', *Government and Policy*, Vol.17, 1999, pp. 527–547.

[5] M. Scott and P. Rosa, 'Has Firm Level Analysis Reached its Limits? Time for a Rethink', *International Small Business Journal*, Vol. 14, 1996, pp. 81–89.

[6] Ibid. p. 81.

[7] P. Westhead and M. Wright, 'Novice, Portfolio and Serial Founders: Are They Different?', *Journal of Business Venturing*, Vol. 13, 1998, pp. 173–204.

[8] P. Rosa and M. Scott, 'The Prevalence of Multiple Owners and Directors in the SME Sector: Implications for Our Understanding of Start-ups and Growth', *Entrepreneurship and Regional Development*, Vol. 11, 1999, p. 21.

[9] P. Westhead, D. Ucbasaran, M. Wright and F. Martin, *Habitual Entrepreneurs in Scotland* (Glasgow: Scottish Enterprise, 2003).

[10] F. J. Greene, K. F. Mole and D. J. Storey, *Three Decades of Enterprise Culture* (Basingstoke: Palgrave, 2007) p. 238.

[11] R. Harrison and C. Leitch, 'Entrepreneurial Learning: Researching the Interface between Learning and the Entrepreneurial Context', *Entrepreneurship Theory and Practice*, Vol. 29, No. 4, 2005, pp. 351–371.

[12] D. J. Storey, 'Optimism and Chance: The Elephants in the Entrepreneurship Room', *International Small Business Journal*, Vol. 29, No. 4, 2011, pp. 303–321.

[13] V. Rocha, A Carneiro and C. A. Varum, 'Serial Entrepreneurship, Learning by Doing and Self-selection', *International Journal of Industrial Organization*, Vol. 40, 2015, pp. 91–106.

[14] E. Chell and S. Baines, 'Does Gender Affect Business Performance? A Study of Microbusinesses in Business Services in the UK', *Entrepreneurship and Regional Development*, Vol. 10, 1998, pp. 117–135.

[15] E. Ljunggren and L. Kolvereid, 'New Business Formation: Does Gender Make a Difference?' *Women in Management Review*, Vol. 11, No. 4, 1996, pp. 3–12.

[16] C. Holmquist and E. Sundin, 'The Growth of Women's Entrepreneurship: Push or Pull Factors?', paper presented to the *EIASM Conference on Small Business*, Durham Business School, 1989.

[17] S. Marlow and A. Strange, 'Female Entrepreneurs: Success by Whose Standards?', in N. Tanton (ed.), *Women in Management: A Developing Presence* (London: Routledge, 1994) p. 173. Cited in E. Chell and S. Baines, Op. Cit.

[18] S. Scheinberg and I. C. MacMillan, 'An 11 Country Study of Motivations to Start a Business', in B. A. Kirchhoff, W. A. Long, W. E. McMullan, K. H. Vesper and W. E. Wetzel (eds), *Frontiers of Entrepreneurship Research* (Wellesley, MA: Babson College, 1988).

[19] S. Cromie, 'Motivation of Aspiring Male and Female Entrepreneurs', *Journal of Organisational Behaviour*, Vol. 8, 1987, pp. 251–261.

[20] R. Goffee and R. Scase, *Women in Charge* (London: Allen and Unwin, 1985).

[21] M. Ram and D. Smallbone, *Ethnic Minority Enterprise: Policy and Practice* (London: DTI, the Small Business Service and Kingston University Small Business Research Centre SME Seminar Series, 2001).

[22] S. Bridge, *Rethinking Enterprise Policy: Can Failure Trigger New Understanding* (Basingstoke: Palgrave Macmillan, 2010) p. 167.

[23] S. C. Parker, 'The Economics of Entrepreneurship: What We Know and What We Don't', *Foundations and Trends in Entrepreneurship*, Vol. 1, No. 1, 2005, pp. 5–7.

[24] D. A. Audretsch, W. Boente and J. P. Tamvada, *Religion and Entrepreneurship* (Germany: Jena Economic Research Papers, 2007-075) p. 4.

[25] M. Minniti, 'Entrepreneurs Examined', *Business Strategy Review*, Vol. 17, No. 4, Winter 2006, p. 79 (London: London Business School).

[26] R. E Kihlstrom and J-J. Laffont, 'A General Equilibrium Entrepreneurial Theory of Firm Formation Based on Risk Aversion', *Journal of Political Economy*, Vol. 87, No. 4, 1979, p. 720.

[27] I. Verheul, A. R. M. Wennekers, D. B. Audretsch and A. R Thurik, *Research Report – An Eclectic Theory of Entrepreneurship: Policies, Institutions and Culture* (Zoetermeer Holland, EIM/Small Business Research and Consultancy, 1999) pp. 15, 67–68; subsequently published as Chapter 2 in D. Audretsch, R. Thurik, I. Verheul and S. Wennekers (eds), *Entrepreneurship: Determinants and Policy in a European–US Comparison* (Dordrecht and Norwell, MA: Kluwer Academic Publishers, 2000).

[28] S. Bridge, Op. Cit. Chapter 11.

[29] D. B. Audretsch, M. C. Keilbach and E. E. Lehmann, *Entrepreneurship and Economic Growth* (Oxford: Oxford University Press, 2006) p. 60.

[30] D. Gardner. *Risk* (London: Virgin Books, 2009) p. 46.

PART 2

[31] P. Lunn, *Basic Instincts* (London: Marshall Cavendish, 2008) p. 42.

[32] New Economics Foundation, *Behavioural Economics: Seven Principles for Policy Makers*. Taken from www.neweconomics.org/publications/behavioural-economics (accessed 9 June 2011).

[33] RSA Projects, Project Briefing, *The Social Brain* (London: RSA, 2009).

[34] Ibid.

[35] S. Bridge, Op. Cit. pp. 202–203.

[36] D. J. Kelly, N. Bosma and J. E. Amorós, *Global Entrepreneurship Monitor 2010 Global Report* (Babson College and Universidad del Desarrollo, 2010) p. 12.

[37] Ibid. p. 19.

[38] Ibid. p. 120–121.

[39] P. Graves, *Consumer.ology* (London: Nicholas Brealey Publishing, 2010) pp. 184–186.

[40] G. D. Meyer, 'The Reinvention of Academic Entrepreneurship', *Journal of Small Business Management*, Vol. 49, No. 1, January 2011, p. 6.

[41] S. Bridge, *The Search for Entrepreneurship: Finding More Questions Than Answers* (London: Routledge, 2017) p. 60.

[42] S. Bridge, C. Hegarty and S. Porter, 'Rediscovering Enterprise: Developing Appropriate University Entrepreneurship Education', *Education + Training*, Vol. 52, No. 8/9, 2010, pp. 722–734.

[43] W. Bygrave, 'The Entrepreneurship Paradigm (I): A Philosophical Look at Its Methodologies', *Entrepreneurship: Theory and Practice*, Vol. 14, No. 1, 1989, p. 14.

[44] Ibid. p. 16.

[45] S. Shane and S. Venkataraman, 'The Promise of Entrepreneurship as a Field of Research', *Academy of Management Review*, Vol. 25, No. 1, 2000, pp. 217–226.

[46] S. Shane, *A General Theory of Entrepreneurship* (Cheltenham: Edward Elgar, 2003) p. 270.

[47] W. Bygrave, Op. Cit. p. 13.

[48] S. Bridge (2017) Op. Cit. p. 74.

Companion website

Please visit the companion website at www.palgravehighered.com/Bridge-UE-5e for access to additional learning and teaching materials.

10 Enterprise and Life

CONTENTS

- Introduction
- 'A goal-realisation device'
- The context for enterprise
- Enterprise as exploration
- The role and forms of enterprise
- In conclusion

KEY CONCEPTS

This chapter covers:

- The relevance of enterprise (and acting entrepreneurially) to a wider range of human activity than just business.
- The reasons people want, or need, to work – and the relevance of enterprise as a work option.
- The relevance of their context to understanding enterprise and entrepreneurs.
- Reasons for viewing enterprise as a form of exploration.
- The different roles, and forms, enterprise can take as a tool for human use.

LEARNING OBJECTIVES

By the end of this chapter the reader should:

- Understand why it can be relevant and helpful to view enterprise and entrepreneurs in a wider context than just business.
- Understand the potential usefulness of enterprise for achieving a wide range of human aspirations.
- Appreciate the role of enterprise in many aspects of life, not just within the business field.

INTRODUCTION

ILLUSTRATION 10.1 – WHAT IS THE AIM OF ENTERPRISE?

A visitor to a Mediterranean country, impressed by the climate and its potential, got into a discussion with a local farmer who was sitting at the side of the road enjoying the sunshine and admiring the view. 'It seems to me', he said to the farmer, 'that, with a little effort, this farm could be so much more successful. You could grow such a variety of crops here.' 'Why', the farmer replied, 'should I want to do that?' 'Because you could invest in more land, grow even more crops and soon you could afford a large house with lots of features such as a terrace and swimming pool.' 'Why would I want that?' 'Because you could then relax and enjoy yourself sitting on the terrace and enjoying the sun and the view.' 'And what do you think I am doing now?' retorted the farmer.

In introducing this book, Chapter 1 points out that there is more to enterprise than just starting, running, or growing small businesses, but acknowledges that its application in a business context is still the prime focus of much of the 'enterprise' and 'entrepreneurship' literature. The narrative in Chapter 2 indicates why this might be the case. It shows that usually enterprise and entrepreneurs have been examined and described from a business perspective. Thus much of the current emphasis on them has arisen largely because of their perceived potential, particularly through the mechanism of small businesses, to contribute to economic development.

However, this chapter seeks to correct the impression that enterprise invariably means business by looking at the broader picture of what enterprise can mean to people's lives. The true spirit of enterprise, it is suggested, is having the inclination and the ability to make one's own choices in life instead of having to follow a path which is in some way predetermined, whether because of tradition, social pressure, lack of other perceived opportunities or apparent lack of appropriate skills – or, in economic terms, being a job maker rather than a job taker.

Governments often consider economic development to be one of their key objectives, although they sometimes appear to view it as an end in its own right rather than as a means of satisfying people's needs. Often, therefore, the focus of official institutions has been on the economy and the businesses within it. As a result, our understanding of enterprise and entrepreneurs has evolved mainly in the context of their application in the world of business – to the extent that it has been assumed by many that enterprise is a sub-set of business and entrepreneurs are found only in a business context.

Chapter 9 does point out the error in this assumption and shows that, instead of being a sub-set of business, enterprise and entrepreneurs are to be found in a much wider range of contexts. While there are some narrower definitions of entrepreneurs (E3 and higher – see Table 3.4) which limit them only to private sector business applications, the wider definitions acknowledge that they can be found in many aspects of life. Even if the narrower definitions are accepted, that does not deny that similar approaches are applied in other contexts – which raises the question of what people should then be called who act entrepreneurially in other contexts.

The 'entrepreneurial method'

The more limited perceptions of entrepreneurs and enterprise have been challenged. Sarasvathy and Venkataraman have suggested that 'scientific progress often occurs through phenomena that do not "fit" dominant wisdom ... [and] Entrepreneurship, in our considered opinion, is proving to be such a beast.'[1] Thus, they wonder:

> What if we have been thinking about entrepreneurship the wrong way? What if we temporarily suspend our thinking of it as a sub-discipline of economics or management, or a subset of courses taught in business schools, and recast it as something as large as a social force – somewhat like democracy in the eighteenth century or the scientific method in the seventeenth? In fact, when we examine the history of the scientific method and its incorporation into basic education, the parallels are uncanny. ... We believe that a similar path of revolutions is waiting in the wings with entrepreneurship.[2]

The scientific method,* they suggest, evolved from early views that only some special people are able to comprehend (super-)natural phenomena. The evolution came through university-based experimentation and on to an agreed method and a belief that anyone can learn to do science, based on experimentation as the dominant logic. Similarly the current understanding of entrepreneurs started with a feeling that some people are able to see, and then to utilise, opportunities while others could not. Again, following considerable, largely university-based, research, the belief evolved that anyone can learn to do it.

In the case of entrepreneurs, however, Sarasvathy and Venkataraman suggest the dominant logic is not the scientific method – but should instead be effectuation. Effectuation is an approach which accepts

---

* 'We simply use the name "scientific method" to capture the notion that the world can be systematically studied and understood in terms that do not include divine revelation or special mystical abilities.'

that the future is uncertain. So it advocates proceeding with that uncertainty in mind – including being on the lookout for other/better opportunities and not risking more than those involved can afford to lose. Sarasvathy found, initially from an examination of business ventures, that this is what expert entrepreneurs do.[3] But, she and Venkataraman argue, the 'entrepreneurial method', as applied through effectuation principles, has a much wider application:

> There exists a distinct method of human problem solving that we can categorize as entrepreneurial. The method can be evidenced empirically, is teachable to anyone who cares to learn it, and may be applied in practice to a wide variety of issues central to human well-being and social improvement.[4]

For Sarasvathy and Venkataraman, therefore, acting entrepreneurially is a sub-set of life, not of business:

> By thinking of entrepreneurship as a subset of other disciplines such as economics or treating it as a setting for testing theories from these disciplines, we may be in danger of falling into a category error. One way out of this error is to reformulate entrepreneurship as a method of human action, comparable to social forces such as democracy and the scientific method, namely, a powerful way of tackling large and abiding problems at the heart of advancing our species.[5]

(For a fuller description of effectuation, see Chapter 11.)

'A GOAL-REALISATION DEVICE'

Consistent with this wider view is the assertion that 'an enterprise is a goal-realisation device'.[6] This suggests that starting or running an enterprise should be seen, not in terms of the (business) field in which it is often practised, but in the context of the goals it can help to realise. Enterprises are created by people and thus it is their goals which matter – so what are the relevant human goals? Maslow[7] suggested that many of our actions are motivated by unmet needs and that these needs can be placed in a hierarchy in which the lower-order ones predominate until they are satisfied whereupon the higher-order ones come into operation.

Building on Maslow's insights, Barrett has articulated some refinements. As well as expanding self-actualisation into four tiers and combining 'physiological' and 'safety' into 'survival', he suggests that, instead of needs as motivating factors, the key drivers come from different levels of consciousness. He lists seven different levels of consciousness – from survival as the lowest to service as the highest (see Table 10.1). He also explains that, even when a need has apparently been met, it can still remain as a motivating factor:

Table 10.1 Barrett's seven levels of consciousness and Maslow's hierarchy of needs

Barrett's Levels of Consciousness		Maslow's Hierarchy of Needs
Service	Engaging in self-less service for humanity and the planet.	
Making a difference	Making a positive difference in the world by collaborating with others.	Self-actualisation
Internal cohesion	Finding a purpose and personal meaning.	
Transformation	Becoming masters of our own destiny.	
Self-esteem	Feeling a sense of personal self-worth.	Self-esteem
Relationships	Feeling a sense of love and belonging.	Belonging
Survival	Feeing secure and safe in the world.	Safety
		Physiological

Source: Based on R. Barrett, *The Barrett Model*, Barrett Values Centre. Taken from www.valuescentre.com (accessed 12 June 2012).

When people have underlying anxieties or subconscious fears about one of their basic needs, their subconscious remains focused on that need. Even though it would appear to an outside observer that they have satisfied that need, they cannot get enough of what they want to assuage their anxiety or subconscious fears.[8]

For some people, that anxiety is money. Many people might say that what they need to be happy is money – although money itself does not feature in either Maslow's or Barrett's lists. That can be explained by assuming that people do not need money itself but instead they need things that money can buy. For instance money can buy food and housing; therefore, it can help to satisfy lower-order needs. The higher the need is in the lists, the less effective money is as a medium of exchange for addressing that need. Indeed at the top, except possibly for philanthropists giving money away, it is hard to see that money can usually buy any degree of self-actualisation directly. Some people might seem to achieve self-actualisation by making lots of money. However, at least in the latter situation, the amount of money they acquire might act as a form of score for their efforts, just as the number of goals can indicate the extent of a football team's efforts. Thus money is still a means to an end, even if that end is in part a higher position in the earnings league.

Those people who inherit, win or marry significant amounts of money, or who are in receipt of an income such as pension or unemployment benefit payments, can use that money to satisfy lower-order needs. For everyone else, satisfying needs requires the expenditure of effort in some form, a process often referred to as work. Even those with money have to work at things like esteem and self-actualisation, although having money can give people more opportunity to concentrate on self-actualisation as they do not have to worry about earning enough to feed or house themselves.

So most people have to work. Given the right conditions, they can satisfy their food hunger by working to hunt or gather enough to eat, by working to grow food, by working to earn money with which to buy food, or by working to steal food. Some of these may be longer-term solutions but they all involve work. Crime may be illegal but it still requires a certain amount of work. Thus people work to satisfy their needs and to try to achieve what they want out of life, whether that is short-term survival or longer-term achievement. People might say that they want happiness but the pleasure and/or contentment that brings happiness usually comes from work in some form.

On the assumption that people generally work to get what they want, what are the things that motivate and direct their working lives? Some possible life goals are indicated in Figure 10.1, which suggests that reaching any of them involves a journey, and it allows for changes of goal as that journey progresses. It also suggests that much of the terrain to be traversed on the journey is as yet unexplored and, while others might suggest routes through it, those routes all involve a degree of uncertainty, not least because the future is always going to hold some surprises.

Ways and means

The alternative routes by which the journey suggested in Figure 10.1 might be accomplished amount to different ways of acquiring the resources needed to reach the chosen goal(s). As noted often that is done by acquiring money with which the necessary resources can then be purchased. Thus among the possible routes are those indicated in Table 10.2 and, like the goals, these routes are not exclusive and more than one can be pursued either in parallel or in succession.

The individual's view of the world suggested in Figure 10.1 does not include entrepreneurial venturing because it is suggested that it is not an objective in its own right. Instead, as Table 10.2 suggests, it can be seen as a form of, or an approach to, work and/or resource acquisition. Therefore, like other work, it is a means to an end. If it were to be added to Figure 10.1 it might be shown as a route or a means of travelling from where someone is to where they want to be. It provides additional choices for that journey.

Not all work is done in order to live, whether that is by working to acquire directly the resources needed to sustain life such as food and shelter or working to earn money to exchange for such things. Some work to satisfy cravings or subconscious fears, as Barrett suggests,[9] and there are many examples of people who seem to want to live in order to work. Many athletes spend a lot of time working hard to

Figure 10.1 *A journey through life?*

Source: Based on S. Bridge, *Rethinking Enterprise Policy: Can Failure Trigger New Understanding* (Basingstoke: Palgrave Macmillan, 2010) p. 90.

Table 10.2 *Some of the means by which people can obtain resources for life*

- Employment
- Entrepreneurial venturing (business ownership and/or self-employment – E2)
- Hunter-gathering – or self-sufficient agriculture
- Inheriting, or marrying, wealth
- Sponsorship
- Unemployment or invalidity benefit payments – or a pension
- Sponsorship, living off friends or relatives – or even begging
- Winning the lottery, or other forms of gambling
- Crime

Source: Based on S. Bridge, *Rethinking Enterprise Policy: Can Failure Trigger New Understanding* (Basingstoke: Palgrave Macmillan, 2010) p. 153.

improve their performance, and there are artists who work hard refining their technique to achieve the effect they are seeking. It has been suggested, for instance, that 'ten thousand hours of practice time is required to achieve the level of mastery associated with being a world-class expert – in anything'[10] and not everyone who aspires to such a level of expertise does it just for the money. Even among those people who can't, or don't, show such levels of commitment there are still many examples of pursuing activities such as art or sport with no expectation of a financial return.

THE CONTEXT FOR ENTERPRISE

Enterprise, and in particular business enterprise, it is thus suggested, should be understood as one of the possible ways by which people can achieve their goals, but how it does this and the form it takes will also depend on its context.

The labour market context

For many people a key aspect of the context has been the labour market. Many people work primarily in order to gain resources for living, and not long ago, at least in the more developed economies, it would have seemed to many people that there was only one practical, available and acceptable resource-acquiring route – which was by working in some form of employment. About 40–50 years ago, when there were relatively high levels of employment, many people in such economies might have expected to have a job for life either in a large private company or in the public sector.

By the time of the 1980s and 1990s, it was clear that the peak of Fordist big business had passed and that the era of the apparently permanent large corporation and its 'jobs-for-life' was ending. In 1990 Charles Handy talked about the 'shamrock organisation' as the organisation form for the future.[11] It had been the assumption, he noted, that an organisation should do as much as possible in-house with its own permanent workforce. Indeed, believing that biggest was best, vertical and horizontal integration was seen as the norm for business development. However, Handy concluded, it was most likely that in future organisations would have three distinct categories of people working for them, like the three leaves of a shamrock. The first category was the professional core, the second was the contractual fringe and the third was the, mostly part-time, flexible labour force. Indeed he pointed out that in the UK already by the end of the 1980s about a third of the paid workforce were part-timers or self-employed, and this could rise to 50 per cent by the end of the century. Subsequent experience has confirmed this trend. The proportion of part-time workers in organisations and self-employed workers contracted to them has increased, with consequent changes in employee loyalty and in expectations about length of service.

According to Handy, we used to work for 47 hours a week, for 47 weeks a year and for 47 years, or about 100,000 hours in a lifetime.[12] But, he foresaw, this might have be halved for someone working $37 \times 37 \times 37$, or it could still be 47 hours a week for 47 weeks a year but only for 25 years in an intense professional job. The 50,000-hour job was just one of the unanticipated outcomes of the shamrock organisation, although with more people living into their eighties and nineties, the pensions 'time bomb' has meant that many people will not be able to afford early retirement and will need to find further employment after their first careers. The employee society has changed fundamentally and is very unlikely to change back. Half as many people in the core of the business, paid twice as much and producing three times as much, may make economic sense for a business, but it does not offer many jobs for life. Other attitudes to employment will be needed. Those not in the core will not have a permanent job but will have portfolio careers moving from job to job or from contract to contract. They will have to find such work, contract to do it, and manage its delivery. Such a situation, even if it amounts to serial employment, will require behaviour that has been described as enterprising.

At the time when, for many people, permanent employment seemed to be the norm, those who couldn't find it, and were thus unemployed, might have considered that they were unlucky. However, in many developed countries, they might also have expected that, if this happened, they would be in receipt of benefits of some kind. Either way, for many people employment or unemployment probably seemed to be the only two alternatives. That view was, in effect, like having an old map of life which suggested that there were only two possible routes to follow, neither of which was entrepreneurial. Therefore enterprise was at one time promoted as representing a third option: that of people doing something themselves to create their own economic activity. In reality, however, as Table 10.2 indicates, there is a much wider variety of possible ways of obtaining the resources needed for a satisfactory life, although all are not necessarily open to everyone. In particular, some of the old ways, such as jobs for life, may now only be available to very few.

Not all the means listed in Table 10.2 necessarily involve a significant amount of work, but those that don't are not available to many people. The point is that for many people life does involve work and enterprise, and being entrepreneurial should be considered in the context of the options for that work.

But there is also work to self-actualise – and for some the form of work chosen might be one that combines resource acquisition with self-actualisation. Even within enterprise there can be different forms with the potential to deliver different proportions of resources (money) and self-actualisation.

The relevance of context

Baumol's observation that society's rules strongly determine how enterprise is applied has already been highlighted in Chapter 3. He contends that the productive contribution of entrepreneurial activity varies more because of how society influences its allocation than because of variation in the total supply of entrepreneurs. Not only does this indicate that enterprise as a concept has been, and is, applied much more widely than in business alone, it also emphasises the importance of context to that application.

If, for whatever reason, people look to their own enterprise as the route to their goals, the form that enterprise takes will be limited by their perception of what enterprise options and opportunities are available. For instance Welter has shown how their context simultaneously provides individuals with entrepreneurial opportunities and sets boundaries for their actions. She quotes the example of Uzbekistan where representatives of local governing councils can assist women in the business registration process, but where local traditions can constrain their entrepreneurial activities. As an example, a young woman might take up gold embroidery and sewing, which could be seen as a low-growth, low-income sector and attributed to a lack of resources for an alternative occupation. However, in rural, post-Soviet Uzbekistan, young women and girls are supposed to stay home until they are married and this traditional craft is one of the few vocational opportunities available to them which could be conducted from home. Hence here context has led this young woman to take up this occupation.[13]

The need therefore, when examining enterprise and entrepreneurs, to consider their context rather than just dissecting the actions taken to pursue them has also been illustrated by Gibb. He quotes the example of a botanist who, when asked to identify a leaf, does not mince it up, put it in the centrifuge and list the resulting molecules. He or she first looks at its structure and considers where it came from, what ecosystem, growing on what soil and in what climate.[14] Thus Gibb proposed the two models in Figure 9.3. The first, the 'Frank N. Stein' model, is constructed from dissected components such as the skills and attributes entrepreneurs are supposed to have and the activities in which they are supposed to engage. It is the model traditionally taught. The second model, the human model, is based on observation of real people operating in a world of uncertainty and complexity to which enterprise can be an appropriate response.

The strength of context

Contributions such as that of Baumol indicate the strength of context and in particular the power of social influence. Others have explored aspects of group influence on human activity and practices (e.g. healthy life-styles), which some might suppose to result mainly from individual choice. To change people's behaviour, it is said, it is better to change their context than their minds.[15] Christakis and Fowler have shown that social networks can spread obesity and (successful) decisions to quit smoking are not solely made by isolated individuals but reflect the choices made by connected groups of people.[16] Thus, it would appear, if someone wants to give up smoking, they should choose to associate with non-smoking friends rather than just trying to apply will-power.

ENTERPRISE AS EXPLORATION

Exploration and scientific discovery are among the reasons why people might want to work. But exploration can be undertaken for reasons other than just a sense of discovery: for instance it can be done to map an unsurveyed area, or to find a way through the unknown to a desired destination. As Illustration 10.2 demonstrates, there is a lot in common between exploration and enterprise as both can involve trying, in uncertain conditions, to find or develop an opportunity for which there should be a commercial or other return to the venturers and their investors. Also both can be helped by the application of the principles of the 'entrepreneurial method', described above.

ILLUSTRATION 10.2 – CHRISTOPHER COLUMBUS: A CASE STUDY OF AN ENTREPRENEUR?

Christopher Columbus (the Anglicised version of his name) was born in Genoa in 1451. He made his living as a sailor and claimed he first went to sea as early as the age of ten. He acted as an agent on behalf of Genoese and then Portuguese interests and, for them, sailed in the Mediterranean and along the European and African Atlantic coasts. It is recorded that he learned Latin as well as Portuguese and Castilian and read widely about astronomy, geography and history.

For a long time Europe had had relatively easy access to the Silk Road – the land route to China and India and their valuable goods. But when Constantinople fell to the Turks in 1453, access to Asia and its markets became much more difficult. Columbus, in common with many educated Europeans, understood that the earth was round and therefore that it should be possible to reach Asia by travelling west. Columbus had calculations of the size of the earth and appears to have concluded that the distance west from the Canary Isles to Japan was only about 3000 Italian miles. That would put it within range of the sailing boats then available, and this estimate persuaded him that the trip should be possible. (Actually Japan is about four to five times as far west from the Canary Isles as Columbus believed – the error apparently arose because the estimate that Columbus had of the size of the earth was too small and the estimate of the length of the eastward journey to Japan too large.)

Knowing that Western European countries were keen to find a better means of accessing Eastern markets and thinking that he had an answer for them, Columbus attempted to raise the support he needed for such a venture. He did manage to line up some private Italian investors but he needed more. He presented his plans to the King of Portugal, to Genoa and Venice and, through his brother, to the King of England, Henry VII. However, none of those pitches produced anything practical and it was the Catholic Monarchs, Ferdinand and Isabella, of Spain, who did agree eventually to provide enough support to let the venture proceed.

The result is well known. Between 1492 and 1504 Columbus made four round trips to the Americas but it is not clear whether, when he died in 1506, he fully accepted that what he had discovered was not Asia but a new continent. He had been promised, if he succeeded, that he would be given the rank of Admiral of the Ocean Sea, that he would be appointed viceroy of any new lands he could claim for Spain, and that he would receive a share of the revenues obtained from them. However, his behaviour in the Americas led to complaints, he fell out with the Spanish authorities, and the deal was not implemented as originally intended.

Columbus saw a possible opportunity to enrich himself by developing a service (in this case a route to Asian markets) which others needed. To realise this, however, he had to raise sufficient funding from investors – a task which proved not to be as easy as he might at first have supposed. But he persevered, and eventually he secured the backing he needed and launched his venture. However, if his goal was to get to Asia by sailing west, he failed; if his goal was to make a lot of money for himself, he also failed. Nevertheless the discovery of the new continent, and in particular its sources of gold, was not unwelcome to Spain – so his backers benefited from their investment in his enterprise.

Both exploration and enterprise involve risk (whether in the sense of known odds or unknown odds) and both might therefore be supposed to appeal to risk-seekers. With both, however, those who succeed, and even those who survive, are likely to be those who, while tolerating an element of risk, don't necessarily like it and seek to avoid, reduce or, at least, manage it. With both, taking a risk may lead to success but taking an unnecessary or unwarranted risk is foolhardy.

Exploration is an example of an activity in which people engage from a sense of curiosity, a desire for adventure or a need for achievement, and not necessarily only for personal financial gain. Enterprise and entrepreneurial ventures can be followed for the same reasons and, because of all these similarities, it can be relevant to see them as a form of exploration – of finding ways around problems and towards opportunities to discover possibilities. In particular early-stage business venturing might be viewed as a sub-set of exploration, as the same guiding principles seem to be relevant. Seeing enterprise as exploration in this way could provide a different perspective from which to view it and would help to highlight some of its key issues and processes.

Seeing enterprise as a form of exploration does not mean that it does not contribute to economic development, but it does help to prevent it being thought of solely in that context and it points to its potential to offer more to life than just business. As explorers engage in exploration because they want to discover things directly, instead of waiting for others to discover things for them, so entrepreneurs engage in enterprise because they want to create benefit directly, instead of waiting for others to do it. Like exploration, enterprise is about people trying to find their own solutions, rather than hoping the solutions will eventually find them.

THE ROLE AND FORMS OF ENTERPRISE

In the context of the journey portrayed in Figure 10.1, enterprise and/or acting entrepreneurially might be seen as exploring one's own route towards one or more life goals instead of hoping to join an expedition led by someone else. Joining someone else's expedition is like working for someone else. It might help you to progress in the way you want but you are not in control. Leading your own venture can seem attractive because you can select your own pace and destination. On the downside, trying to navigate one's own way can be hard work, and sometimes lonely, with the danger of accidents on the way.

Just as there are a number of different possible routes in Figure 10.1, there are different forms of enterprise. Anyone who wants something enough to take significant action to get it, and follow it through to completion and success, might be described as enterprising and fall within the definition of an E0 entrepreneur. That could include action undertaken to help in realising goals in the fields of sport, discovery, learning, the arts, culture, peace-making or many other areas of activity including, but not limited to, work for economic benefit (E1 and higher). Even when applied to work, just as employment can take many different forms, enterprise and/or being entrepreneurial does not have to represent just one way of working. Table 10.3 presents a suggested list of the different kinds of entrepreneur, even within a business context.

Table 10.3 Some different kinds of entrepreneurs

- Academic entrepreneurs
- Classic, or 'heroic', entrepreneurs (Bill Gates, Richard Branson)
- Lifestyle entrepreneurs
- Innovative, growth entrepreneurs
- Intrapreneurs
- Irresponsible and 'casino' entrepreneurs
- Nascent entrepreneurs
- Social entrepreneurs (not-for-profit-distribution, social goals)
- Socially responsible entrepreneurs (Ben & Jerry, Anita Roddick)
- Spin-off entrepreneurs
- Subsistence entrepreneurs (the most common form?)

Source: Adapted from L. Stevenson, presentation to *35th International Small Business Congress*, Belfast, November, 2008.

PART 2

Although some of the activities listed in Table 10.3 might be excluded from the narrower definitions of entrepreneurs considered in Chapter 3, it is generally recognised that entrepreneurs can be found in many areas of life. Other varieties of entrepreneur might also be added to the list such as artistic entrepreneurs, political entrepreneurs or environmental entrepreneurs.

Another aspect of enterprise in the context of progress towards life's goals, and another way in which it resembles exploration, is that essentially it is traversing the unknown. It is not always clear where the enterprising path is going, and often there are no clear distinctions between some of the categories of entrepreneurs listed above. Presenting enterprise as a form or means of work helps to suggest that it need not necessarily be focused exclusively, or even mainly, on making money, although some have tended to see it in that context. Indeed initiatives to introduce entrepreneurship education into university curricula have been resisted at times by those for whom entrepreneurship had adverse connotations associated with the baser aspects of capitalism. However, at least in some cases, once it became clear that it was enterprise for life (E1 or E0) that was being applied, such views have been tempered.[17]

A word of caution

Even when enterprise does lead to the formation of a private sector business, that might be because no other options for a legal organisation were seen, rather than because the founder or founders specifically desired to start a venture which would maximise their own financial returns. Bridge *et al.* use the analogy of mushrooms to suggest that, while ventures might only be noticed when they are legally registered, and often classified according to the form of that registration, there is more to many ventures than their legal status suggests.[18] Just as the mushrooms seen above ground are not the whole of the fungus but only the fruiting bodies of an extensive branched underground mycelium, so the business organisations we encounter are not the totality of the aspirations of their founders (see Figure 10.2). Instead the legally constituted bodies, the existence and activities of which can be reported and recorded, are the result of the interaction of a number of more or less hidden factors including:

- The visions, aspirations, ideas and ambitions of their founders.
- The selection by those founders of methods of operating to realise their purposes.

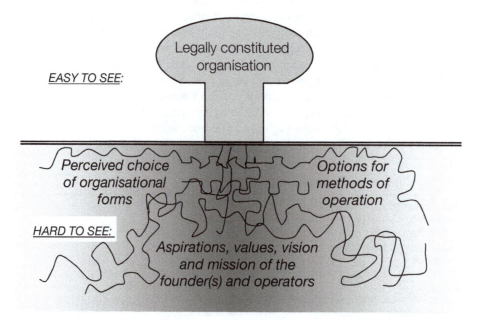

Figure 10.2 *What you see is not everything*

Source: S. Bridge, B. Murtagh and K. O'Neill, *Understanding the Social Economy and the Third Sector* (Basingstoke: Palgrave Macmillan, 2014) p. 103.

- The choice by those founders, from the options perceived to be available, of which legal form to use to give their organisations a legal existence.

Not infrequently, people form judgements about others' entrepreneurial intentions based on long-established preconceptions, and as Chapter 8 suggests, one such preconception is that organisations constituted as private companies limited by shares exist primarily to make money for their founders. Therefore it is also often assumed that that must have been their aim in setting up such companies. The mushroom analogy suggests instead that it is necessary to look beyond that in order to divine the founders' real intentions.

IN CONCLUSION

ILLUSTRATION 10.3 – THE RIGHT TO A JOB

One Saturday one of the authors was having a morning coffee in his favourite café. He happened to know the two people at the adjacent table. He had said 'hello' to them when they came in before resuming his attempts to solve the crossword in the daily paper. Suddenly something one of them said impinged on his consciousness. 'Everyone', she said, 'has the right to a job.' What are the implications of that, he wondered; how can such a right be ensured and how does it fit into an enterprise culture?

There are a number of generally recognised human rights but the one that probably commands the greatest recognition, if not the greatest observance, is the right to freedom. But can a government ensure freedom for its subjects? Good laws, it has been said, can promote freedom, whereas bad laws can restrict it. Despite its recognition as a right, laws cannot, of themselves, ensure freedom; they can only help to set the conditions in which it can exist.

Another human benefit sometimes recognised as a right is an education. Education, however, differs from freedom in that, whether it is seen as a right or not, a government can take steps to provide at least a basic education for all its citizens. An education, it is generally recognised, is within a government's gift.

But can the same be said of work, and is the right to work the same as the right to a job? That 'everyone has the right to work' is enshrined in the Universal Declaration of Human Rights signed by the members of the United Nations. The desirability of full employment as a political objective is often debated, however, not so much because people do not want full employment, but because questions are raised about the practicality of achieving it and the implications it might have. Is employment like health or education, where a government can provide a basic level of service or provision for everyone? Or is it more like freedom, in respect of which a government's powers are more negative than positive, in that it has the power to deny freedom but cannot itself directly provide freedom for everyone? Can a government provide a basic job for everyone who wants one? Governments do create some jobs directly but, at least in Western societies, they are not the main sources of direct employment and they cannot create enough jobs always for everyone who might want one.

> People do realise that job security is gone, but many don't realise what it has been replaced by. The driving force of a career must come from the individual, not the organisation.
>
> Professor Homa Babrami[19]

Although governments may not be able to provide jobs, because they cannot create work at will, often they want to try to ensure that jobs are available for those who want them. Thus enterprise, as Chapter 2 summarises, came to the fore when traditional sources of employment started to disappear. Governments became interested in small businesses, and in the entrepreneurs who create them, when it

Table 10.4 *How enterprise might be viewed from people and venture perspectives*

Issue	Seen from a people perspective	Seen from a venture perspective
Where does enterprise fit in?	Enterprise is one option among several for gaining resources for life and/or satisfaction in life. Enterprise is not an end, but a means to an end.	Enterprise is an essential component of any new venture creation, and its purpose is to create new ventures.
Will anyone be enterprising?	There is no guarantee that people will even consider enterprise.	It is often taken for granted that a new venture is the result of enterprise.
What is the genesis of enterprise?	Enterprise will occur if it is the best route for the individual at that point in time – but only if the individual is looking for enterprise opportunities.	Enterprise will occur when an individual pursues an opportunity.
How will enterprise be assessed?	In assessing enterprise, feelings probably matter more than any logical analysis.	It is presumed that enterprise will be assessed logically.
What is the goal of enterprise?	The goal is generally to realise a life ambition. However this ambition may change – so the goal is moveable.	The goal, which is not expected to change, is generally supposed to be to secure the maximum financial return.
How permanent is the enterprise?	Enterprise will be used only if and when it might be appropriate.	Enterprise is realised in a venture which, once started, is expected to continue.
How valid and desirable are different forms of enterprise?	All forms of enterprise are equally valid, but different forms are appropriate to different aims. The most desirable form of enterprise is that which is most appropriate to the individual's aim at that time.	Some forms of enterprise are more valid than others (at least in the eyes of policy-makers) with private sector business being the most valid and high-tech, high-growth, high-value-added businesses (E4) often being seen as the most desirable.

Source: Based on S. Bridge, *Rethinking Enterprise Policy: Can Failure Trigger New Understanding* (Basingstoke: Palgrave Macmillan, 2010) pp. 157–158.

was realised that they were now the main source of new jobs. That has meant, however, that enterprise and entrepreneurs have often been viewed from a business perspective.

This chapter argues that enterprise and entrepreneurial activity are not just sub-sets of business. It is much more relevant to see them as part of human life, with business being one of the ways in which they can be realised. Instead of assuming that enterprise should be viewed from the perspective of the ventures it creates, which often are businesses, it might be recognised instead for what it can do for people – as Table 10.4 suggests.

☞ THE KEY POINTS OF CHAPTER 10

- Enterprise is relevant to a wider range of human activity than just business, and the 'entrepreneurial method' is useful for problem solving in that wider context.
- People want, or need, to work to achieve their life goals – and enterprise is often a relevant option for achieving those goals.
- To understand enterprise and entrepreneurs it is often relevant to understand their context.
- Enterprise and entrepreneurial activity can be considered to be a form of exploration – an analogy that might help in understanding their processes.

- Enterprise can take different roles, and forms, as vehicles for achieving human aspirations.
- The traditional view of enterprise as a sub-set of business presents a false picture of its usefulness in human affairs.

✓ ## QUESTIONS, EXERCISES, ESSAY AND DISCUSSION TOPICS

- Is the 'entrepreneurial method' as useful as the 'scientific method'?

- Was Columbus an entrepreneur (see Illustration 10.2)?

- This chapter argues that enterprise is a form of exploration. What are the arguments to the contrary?

- How might seeing enterprise as a form of exploration help an understanding of the process of enterprise and the issues faced by anyone undertaking it?

- Is enterprise a sub-set of business – or business a sub-set of enterprise?

- Enterprise and entrepreneurs are better understood if examined in their context rather than through their features. Discuss.

SUGGESTIONS FOR FURTHER READING AND INFORMATION

N. Christakis and J. Fowler, *Connected: The Surprising Power of Our Social Networks and How They Shape Our Lives* (London: Harper Press, 2010).

A. A. Gibb, *Entrepreneurship: Unique Solutions for Unique Environments* (National Council for Graduate Entrepreneurship, Working Paper 038/2006, October 2006).

C. Handy, *The Age of Unreason* (London: Arrow, 1990).

S. D. Sarasvathy and S. Venkataraman, 'Entrepreneurship as Method: Open Questions for an Entrepreneurial Future', *Entrepreneurship Theory and Practice*, Vol. 35, No. 1, January 2011, pp. 113–135.

PART 2

REFERENCES

[1] S. D. Sarasvathy and S. Venkataraman, 'Entrepreneurship as Method: Open Questions for an Entrepreneurial Future', *Entrepreneurship Theory and Practice*, Vol. 35, No. 1, January 2011, p. 113.

[2] Ibid. p. 114.

[3] S. D. Sarasvathy speaking at the Entrepreneurship Day, *RENT XXIV*, Maastricht November 2010.

[4] S. D. Sarasvathy and S. Venkataraman, Op. Cit. p. 125.

[5] Ibid. p. 130.

[6] For instance L. Hunter speaking at a University of Ulster seminar on 'Developing a Strategy and Vision for Social Entrepreneurship', Coleraine, 10 September 2007.

[7] A. H. Maslow, 'A Theory of Human Motivation', *Psychological Review*, Vol. 50, No. 4, 1943, pp. 370–396.

[8] R. Barrett, *The Barrett Model*, Barrett Values Centre. Taken from www.valuescentre.com (accessed 12 June 2012).

[9] Ibid.

[10] David Levitin quoted in M. Gladwell, *Outliers: The Story of Success* (London: Allen Lane, 2008) p. 40.

[11] C. Handy, *The Age of Unreason* (London: Arrow, 1990).

[12] Ibid. pp. 34–35.

[13] F. Welter, 'Contextualising Entrepreneurship – Conceptual Challenges and Ways Forward', *Entrepreneurship Theory and Practice*, Vol. 35, No. 1, January 2011, p. 166.

[14] A. A. Gibb, *Entrepreneurship: Unique Solutions for Unique Environments* (National Council for Graduate Entrepreneurship, Working Paper 038/2006, October 2006) p. 3.

[15] M. Taylor, *Twenty-first Century Enlightenment* (London: RSA, 2010) p. 13.

[16] N. Christakis and J. Fowler, *Connected: The Surprising Power of Our Social Networks and How They Shape Our Lives* (London: Harper Press, 2010) pp. 105–108, 116.

[17] See, for instance, S. Bridge, C. Hegarty and S. Porter, 'Rediscovering Enterprise: Exploring Entrepreneurship for Undergraduates', a paper presented at the *31st Institute for Small Business and Entrepreneurship Conference*, Belfast, November 2008.

[18] S. Bridge, B. Murtagh and K. O'Neill, *Understanding the Social Economy and the Third Sector* (Basingstoke: Palgrave, 2009) pp. 38–39.

[19] Quoted in T. Peters, 'Travel the Independent Road' (*Independent on Sunday*, 2 January 1994).

Companion website

Please visit the companion website at www.palgravehighered.com/Bridge-UE-5e for access to additional learning and teaching materials.

Becoming an Entrepreneur

CONTENTS

– Introduction
– Start-up from an entrepreneurial perspective
– Start-up from a 'professional' perspective – the business plan

– Reflections on the two approaches
– Some implications
– In conclusion

KEY CONCEPTS

This chapter covers:

- How many successful entrepreneurs think and the concept of effectuation.
- The relevance for many new ventures, including many business start-ups, of an accept-uncertainty approach based on effectuation principles.
- The reasons why, nevertheless, the business plan is advocated by so many people.
- The limitations of the business plan as an aid for many start-ups which are, in effect, undertaking a process of exploration.
- Comparisons between an accept-uncertainty, effectual approach and a business plan–based, causal approach.

LEARNING OBJECTIVES

By the end of this chapter the reader should:

- Know the principles of an accept-uncertainty, effectual approach to start-up.
- Understand the limitations of a business-plan approach to start-up, but also understand why it is advocated by many authorities.
- Understand why an accept-uncertainty, effectual approach could, for many people, be seen as a better approach for first and general purpose use, and why a business plan could be seen as a special purpose approach for use in some business circumstances.

INTRODUCTION

The previous chapter looks at enterprise and entrepreneurs in a wider context than the confines of business, which is where they have traditionally been considered to lie. It shows the potential relevance of enterprise to many aspects of people's lives where venturing to overcome obstacles and/or find and realise opportunities can be very beneficial. This chapter considers one practical application of that: the process of starting a new venture, and considers what guidance might be appropriate for this activity. Many people start new ventures but lots of them do it without much guidance. However, especially for those who are thinking of starting a new business, guidance is available from books and the Internet, and often from special agencies and small business start-up support programmes. But is it appropriate guidance?

The traditional view of what is appropriate guidance for a new business venture does not appear to be in accord with how entrepreneurs really think. Therefore this chapter starts with some research into how successful entrepreneurs actually operate – and some of the lessons which might be drawn from it. It then compares this with traditional 'business plan' teaching to show that there is more than one relevant view and that some of the assumptions often made may not be correct.

START-UP FROM AN ENTREPRENEURIAL PERSPECTIVE

Traditionally entrepreneurs have been thought of as people who start and run businesses – and their actions have therefore been viewed from a business perspective. Also most people who have helped, advised, trained, examined or researched them (e.g. academics, accountants, business advisers, bankers, consultants and researchers) have learnt about business fundamentally from a big business perspective, thus their business thinking is essentially big business orientated. Despite the observations of Penrose[1] and others, which might be summarised as 'small businesses are not small big businesses', big business–based thinking is often assumed both to be correct and appropriate to all businesses.

A different view has, however, been advanced by Sarasvathy (see also Chapter 10) who decided to look at the process of new venture formation from the perspective of those doing it. To find what works for entrepreneurs, she studied 27 'expert' entrepreneurs: people 'who, either individually or as part of a team, had founded one or more companies, had remained a full-time founder/entrepreneur for ten years or more and participated in taking at least one company public'.[2] From her findings she concluded that entrepreneurs mainly believed that the future was uncertain and not predictable, and that they broadly followed a set of principles which she labelled 'effectuation'.

The first theme that emerged from the data, she says, was: 'Expert entrepreneurs distrust market research' and they revealed 'a profound distrust of attempts to predict the future'.[3] However, if the future is not predictable, it is not predetermined and so potentially can be shaped by the entrepreneurs' actions. Also, if it is unpredictable, then much market research which attempts to forecast how consumers will react to a product or service offering must be viewed with considerable suspicion – and yet business plans are constructed around such sales forecasts. This view of market research is supported by Graves in his book, *Consumer.ology*, in which he reveals 'why the findings obtained from most market research are completely unreliable' and suggests that 'market research is a pseudo science ... and the beliefs under-pinning it are false'.[4]

The main theme emerging from Sarasvathy's research, however, was that entrepreneurs preferred what she calls an effectuation approach: 'over 63% of entrepreneurs in the ... study preferred effectuation to causal approaches more than 74 per cent of the time'.[5] Traditionally, she suggests, entrepreneurs were thought to pursue a causal approach in which they fix on a target and then try to cause it to happen – like deciding what dish to cook, looking up a recipe, assembling the listed ingredients and then following the recipe to prepare the dish initially chosen. Effectuation, on the other hand, would be to start, not by selecting the target dish, but by considering the ingredients available and then deciding how they might be put together to create a dish, based on the abilities and ideas of the chef. Sarasvathy's five key principles of effectuation are listed in Table 11.1, and some of her reflections on the contrast between it and causation are presented in Illustration 11.1. It is also interesting to compare the contrast between effectuation and causation with the contrast between the entrepreneur and the administrator which is presented in Table 9.2 (and which was originally presented in 1983).

While the effectuation method may have been formulated by Sarasvathy from her research into people who had started businesses, it is not limited to the business field. It has a much wider application. Indeed Sarasvathy herself, together with Venkataraman, has suggested that the 'entrepreneurial method', following effectuation principles, should not be thought of as a sub-discipline of economics, management, or business studies, but should be viewed as something with an application analogous to that of the scientific method.[6] As Chapter 10 suggests, it does seem to have been the approach taken

Table 11.1 *The five key principles of effectuation*

The *bird-in-hand* principle – Effectuation is means-driven, rather than goal-driven. Its emphasis is on creating something new with existing means rather than on new ways to chosen goals.

The *affordable-loss* principle – Instead of making a business plan based on sales projections and trying to raise the investment the expected returns appear to justify, this principle indicates that your commitment to a venture should be limited to no more than you can afford to lose on it.

The *crazy-quilt* principle – Effectuation involves building connections, putting together commitments from stakeholders, and determining the goals based on who comes on board.

The *lemonade* principle – If life gives you lemons, make lemonade.

The *pilot-in-the-plane* principle – Effectuation recognises human agency as the prime driver of opportunity, so the venture should not always stay on a predetermined path and the entrepreneur can, and should, create opportunities and steer the venture accordingly.

Source: Based on S. D. Sarasvathy, *Effectuation: Elements of Entrepreneurial Experience* (Cheltenham: Edward Elgar, 2008) p. 15–16.

by many explorers seeking a way through unknown territory. They cannot plan their route in advance because there are too many unknowns. So when they start they look for a promising path to take them in the direction they want to go, but they are open to apparently better opportunities when they discover them, and they know that they may not discover them until they get started. Additionally, because there is no certain way through, they know that they should not commit more than they can afford to lose to a route which has not yet been proven. Therefore they try to decide which is the most attractive path to take initially from where they are, but remain open to other possibilities and stay flexible so that with relative ease they can go round any obstacles they encounter, or switch paths, or even goals, if that seems more attractive and/or appropriate.

ILLUSTRATION 11.1 – SOME REFLECTIONS ON EFFECTUATION AND CAUSATION

'Causation processes take a particular effect as given and focus on selecting between means to create that effect. Effectuation processes take a set of means as given and focus on selecting between possible effects that can be created with that set of means.'

'Entrepreneurs, it has been said, begin with three categories of "means": they know who they are, what they know and whom they know – their own traits, tastes and abilities; the knowledge corridors they are in; and the social networks they are a part of.'

'One could speculate that effectuation processes are more general and more ubiquitous than causation processes in *human* decisions.' (italics in original)

'Even the generalized aspiration of starting a business is not a necessary starting point for effectuation processes. Several successful businesses and even great companies have begun without any conscious initial intention on the part of the founders.'

'The proliferation of successful nonstarters in human affairs is matched only by sure things that fail disastrously.'

'The theory of effectuation brings another perspective to the table. It suggests we need to give up ideas such as the successful personality or clearly superior characteristics of the successful firm or organisation. Rather, we need to learn to deal with a rain forest of individuals and firms and markets and societies, intermeshed and woven together with completely coherent yet vastly diverse local patterns that add up to a complex, interdependent ecology of human artefacts.'

'Before there are products, there is human imagination, and before there is a market, there are human aspirations. Successful entrepreneurs have long created firms, industries, and even economies by matching up the offspring of human imagination with human aspirations.'

Source: S. D. Sarasvathy, 'Causation and Effectuation: Toward a Theoretical Shift from Economic Inevitability to Entrepreneurial Contingency', *Academy of Management Review*, Vol. 26, No. 2, 2001.

Table 11.2 *What effectuation is not*

Effectuation is not another name for 'anything goes' – It requires a disciplined approach.

Effectuation is not the easy way out – It still requires attention to business essentials like costing and cash flows.

Effectuation is not irrational and intuitive – Effectuation may not deal largely in rational analysis along business plan lines, but it has its own logic.

Effectuation is not charismatic leadership – Expert entrepreneurs may come across as highly charismatic, but they may have got that way through applying an effectuation approach, rather than the other way around.

Effectuation is not passion before all – Effectuation requires the disciplined application of effectual logic.

Effectuation is not an absence of caution – Effectuation does not necessarily mean taking more risks that in a business-plan approach. It requires an awareness of the possibilities of failure if the downside is not to be neglected.

Effectuation is not a bunch of traits – Effectuation requires the learning and application of the effectuation method.

Effectuation is not a recipe for success – It is not a Holy Grail method that will guarantee success.

Source: Based on S. D. Sarasvathy, *Effectuation: Elements of Entrepreneurial Experience* (Cheltenham: Edward Elgar, 2008) pp. 234–236.

Effectuation is not necessarily an easy approach (see Table 11.2) but it can be an effective approach, and in its business application it is an alternative approach to the business plan–based causation approach normally advocated. However, neither effectuation nor causation is appropriate in all circumstances – so the effective entrepreneur will choose his or her approach to suit the task.

Approaches which accept uncertainty

An exploration approach

An approach to new venture formation, based on exploration and effectuation, is suggested by Bridge and Hegarty.[7] Because new ventures are not small big businesses, their founders are more like explorers who know that not every means they try will work and who need to be on the lookout for new possibilities. This approach accepts that the future is uncertain and advocates proceeding accordingly. It does not start with a predetermined target and path to it but involves exploring to find a way to an acceptable result. Rather than fixed steps it can be considered to involve a number of principles:

1. Remember an enterprise is a goal-realisation device – so only engage in a venture if it could help you to achieve your goal(s).
2. Don't commit more than you can afford to lose, whether that is money, time or reputation – and if more is needed find it in other ways.
3. Start from where you are – build on what you have and are.
4. Carry out reality checks and plans – don't be foolhardy, do some basic checks to see if your idea could work, and give some thought to how you might do it, at least initially.
5. The only reliable test is a real one – the only way you will really know if something new works is to try it. If you are producing something, the only reliable way to see if it will sell is to produce it, if necessary on a trial basis, and see if it does sell. Asking hypothetical questions, such as 'would you buy this if I were to offer it', is not reliable research.
6. Get started and get some momentum – too much hesitation can kill a venture and, once started, you will have more incentive to keep going and not to fail (also see Illustration 11.2).
7. Accept that the situation is uncertain and the future may be largely unpredictable, and act accordingly. Proceed cautiously and flexibly and be prepared to alter course if new opportunities or obstacles arise. If the market is predictable, it is fixed in its ways and there isn't much you can do about it. If, on the other hand, it is unpredictable, that suggests that it is not fixed; in that case, what you do might help to change it. So keep your eyes open, look for opportunities (and obstacles) and be ready to respond to them.

8. Look for opportunities and respond to what you find – because many useful opportunities are only revealed by getting started to see what and who is out there.

9. Build, and use, relevant social capital – when working in a human environment, human contacts are vital. But social capital is like financial capital in that you can only use as much as you have acquired. Also it comes in various varieties (see Chapter 13) – so know how to build and use stocks of the sorts you need.

10. Acquire the relevant skills (financial but also marketing/sales and production). Some skills are essential so make sure you have access to them somehow. If you don't have one or more of them, find someone to help you who does.[8]

Lean Start-up

Another approach which accepts that it is not possible to predict in advance how a market will react to an untested offering is Lean Start-up. This approach to business formation and development was formulated by Eric Ries[10] as a development of Steve Blank's Customer Development methodology. Blank found that, instead of incurring all the cost of producing a final fully developed product before exposing it to the market, it was generally better to try an early version of the product on a few customers to get their reaction. That could be very helpful in identifying which features most appealed to customers and which were not appreciated or needed further development.

Lean Start-up relies on a scientific approach to experimentation combined with a series of iterative product releases to gain valuable customer feedback and shorten product development cycles. In this way start-ups can design products or services to meet the demands of customers without requiring lots of initial funding or expensive product launches.

ILLUSTRATION 11.2 – YOU START – AND YOU KEEP GOING

A social entrepreneur

Frances Black is an award-winning Irish singer and social entrepreneur. She set up the RISE Foundation to support families with loved ones in addiction and to change the way people view addiction. She won a Social Entrepreneur of the Year Award and the RISE Foundation won the Vodaphone World of Difference Award. In speaking about her experience of starting the RISE foundation she said:

> I had to do it. I pushed and pushed and pushed. I just kept going. You just keep going and you just keep doing it and you don't stop.[9]

Rock climbers

Some time ago one of the authors read an article about rock-climbing, a sport in which he normally has little interest. What held his attention was the description it gave of rock-climbing practice. As all the easy climbs had been done, harder new climbs were being attempted and, for them, climbers were finding that spending a lot of time looking at the rock before attempting to climb was counter-productive. It tended to present all the obstacles at the same time and make it seem very hard. Instead those climbers who really wanted to do the climb found that a better approach was to get started – because, once started, they had to go forward and tackle the obstacles one by one as they arose.

Does an analogy with rock-climbing have any implications for business?

- Can starting, rather than planning, be the route to success? Starting means that you are in and have the momentum to go on.
- Is it better to be the first up and running, or to be sure first that you are right?
- But is it only for those who have some idea of what they are doing?

Lean Start-up is consistent with, and complementary to, effectuation and exploring, rather than being an alternative to them. It was originally developed in Silicon Valley for high-technology software companies but – not least through the success of Ries's book – the philosophy has since been applied to businesses in other sectors that seek to develop innovative products for the marketplace.

START-UP FROM A 'PROFESSIONAL' PERSPECTIVE – THE BUSINESS PLAN

As Illustration 11.3 shows, to date a lot of start-up guidance has been based on the business plan. However, businesses plans, it has been suggested, were invented by bankers and/or other business professionals,[17] not by business owners – Illustration 11.4 lists the sort of professional business people who advocate them.

Despite some expressions of caution (see Illustration 11.5) many business academics, advisers, agencies and authors do advocate a business plan and/or a deliberate business planning process, for instance

---

ILLUSTRATION 11.3 – BUSINESS PLANS ARE ADVOCATED

Business guides:

> It is essential to have a realistic, working business plan when you're starting up a business.[11]

> Every business needs a business plan ... To do this you'll have to take a long hard look at each element of the plan.[12]

Enterprise text books:

> One of the most important steps in setting up any new business is to develop a business plan.[13]

> It has become accepted that a carefully constructed business plan is important to the survival and successful performance of any business.[14]

Banks and development agencies:

> If you intend to start a business you need to write a business plan.[15]

> Developing a business plan is perhaps one of the most important stages of starting your own business.[16]

ILLUSTRATION 11.4 – WHO ADVOCATES BUSINESS PLANS?

- Bankers – because a business plan can provide the basis for assessing a loan request.
- Business schools – because, as suggested below, developing a business plan provides an exercise which brings together inputs from (almost) all the main areas of business school teaching.
- Business trainers – because the business plan contents offer a seemingly logical framework and approved syllabus for start-up training.
- Business agencies – because a business plan should provide all the key information about the business and its prospects needed to justify their offers of help.
- Accountants and consultants – because business plans are the accepted approach and they can be paid for preparing them.

seeing it as an improvement on previous, less formal, support practice. An example is one text book which states that:

> Many agencies and bankers would say that most new business start-ups are now required to produce a business plan. This is a major advance on what might have existed in the not so distant past, when a person with a business idea could talk it over with their bank manager, produce some rough 'back of the envelope' calculations and walk out of the bank with a start-up overdraft.[18]

The same book concludes its chapter on preparation for business start-up by stressing that:

> The importance of pre-start preparation through market research, competitor analysis and careful planning cannot be underestimated for determining the success of the business start-up process.[19]

However, it is suggested here that this advocacy of business plans is an example of assuming that what seems to be appropriate for bigger established businesses must also be right for new small ones. Therefore many have assumed both that a business plan is the right and essential first step in starting a business and that no alternative method is available which covers the key issues which need to be considered for start-up. However, all those assumptions are now being questioned and, just as Part 2 of this book challenges a number of other assumptions commonly made about entrepreneurship and small business, this chapter suggests that the business plan assumption should be revised also.

The business-plan approach

> I only did it for the bank, and a year later it was obvious that the bank had not looked at it.
>
> (A successful businessman describing his first business plan)
>
> I had to present a business plan for my grant application and now, actually, I find it very useful. At the end of each week, if the sales are above the projected levels, I get a lot of comfort because it means that the business is actually succeeding. If I didn't have that reassurance, I would have a lot of sleepless nights worrying whether the business was a good idea.
>
> (Owner of a recently opened small shop)

For those not familiar with it, the business plan–based approach can be summarised as an example of an overall strategic planning process such as that portrayed in Figure 11.1 and, following this approach, there can be ten steps along the path to new venture creation:

1. Identify a business idea (because it seems promising, trendy, appropriate for you, etc.).
2. Investigate its market – will it sell, in what volumes, under what conditions, and for what price? Also what is the competition and on what basis does it compete?
3. Determine what you will need in the way of premises, equipment, stock, organisation, staff, marketing campaign etc. – and their cost.
4. Plan the sequencing of actions and spends.
5. Prepare financial projections – what level of profit should the venture make, and what investment is required?
6. Write up all that in a business plan (in a form that is ready to present to potential supporters and/or investors).
7. Review your analysis and its conclusions and decide whether or not to go ahead.
8. Raise the investment needed.
9. Start.
10. Follow the plan.

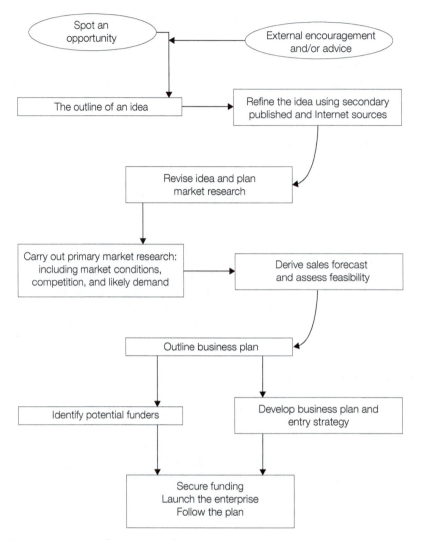

Figure 11.1 *Business start-up: the strategic planning process*

Source: Based in part on D. Deakins and M. Freel, *Entrepreneurship and Small Firms*, 5th Edition (Maidenhead: McGraw Hill, 2009) p. 294.

⟲ ILLUSTRATION 11.5 – BUSINESS PLAN SCEPTICISM

I am more than ever convinced that entrepreneurship cannot be planned to any major extent in advance, and that planning even goes against the entrepreneurial idea. Entrepreneurship is rather about courage and willpower, being venturesome when experimenting and networking, and about exploiting necessary mistakes as moments of learning. (A professor of entrepreneurship who also owns a consulting business)[20]

We have all heard the growing chorus of faculty debating the proper role, if any, for teaching business plans. A valid criticism coming out of this debate is that the way business plans have been traditionally taught results in well-written 'works of fiction'. Students are told to come up with an idea, do extensive research, and write a comprehensive business plan. (An entrepreneurship teacher)[21]

An intense debate emerged recently ... on the value of business planning for established small and especially new firms. (An academic paper on the value of business planning)[22]

My focus ... is on a number of 'elephants in the room' ... such as the worship of the rational business plan in curricula. (An entrepreneurship professor emeritus, author and teacher)[23]

The hegemony of the business plan

The business plan may appear to be a logical and sensible way to proceed but it is essentially a causation approach (and a left-brain approach – see Illustration 11.8) which first selects a target and then tries to cause it to happen. Nevertheless it has gained a position of hegemony (which, according to the dictionary, is associated with leadership, predominance and preponderance[24] – and that is the place which the business plan seems to have assumed in much teaching about the practicality of enterprise). As the quotes in Illustration 11.3 indicate, the business plan is widely advocated as the essential first step in starting a business. Even when a formal written plan is not being suggested, very often the advice and/ or training offered to those starting a business is based on business-plan thinking, apparently assuming, because it is the approved method, that it must cover the relevant issues. But why has the business plan gained this reputation?

It has been suggested that the business plan was invented, not by entrepreneurs, but by bankers and/ or accountants,[25] presumably to provide a logical way of presenting and considering what they thought were the main components of a business proposition. It has been further suggested that it was then taken up enthusiastically by business schools because it unites in one document the main threads of business school teaching: including strategy, marketing, operations, human resources and organisation, management and control, and finance. But, whatever its origins, it is now advocated and/or used by many organisations and people (see Illustration 11.4).

This suggests that the main inventors and proponents of business plan have been professional business advisers and supporters, rather that those actually considering going into business. However, often these professionals don't have the same objectives as those they purport to help. People starting businesses (especially if they follow the affordable-loss principle – see Table 11.1) generally stand to gain more if their venture succeeds well than they might lose if it fails. This is true especially once they have started the venture, as a large portion of any investment is likely by then to be a 'sunk cost'. In this respect they are like someone purchasing a lottery ticket (albeit hopefully with better odds) in that, once the ticket is purchased, there is no more to lose and potentially a lot to win. Success is likely therefore to be their primary aim. Professional advisers, however, unless they have a call on any profits, usually have more to lose if a venture fails than they will gain if it succeeds. That is because, once their input is made (for instance their advice given or their loan terms agreed), if a venture fails the outcome is likely to be a loss of their stake, such as a loan or a grant, and possibly blame for involvement in a failure and a consequent loss of their reputation. If the venture succeeds they will get no extra return beyond their fee, if appropriate. Thus their prime concern will be to avoid failure rather that to achieve success.

Advisers and supporters are likely to be cautious therefore. Taken to extremes, that might mean that they could prefer ventures not to start than have a significant possibility of failure. Consequently the business-plan approach suits them because it involves checks and assessments, because it is based on the apparent reassurance of market research, and because it is the approved and accepted method. After all, if one can't claim non-involvement in the event of a failure, the next best defence is that the laid-down procedure was followed. And it is not only advisers who fear failure in this way, but even those working in businesses. As someone who has held senior marketing positions in several blue-chip companies has put it:

People use different stages of research so that if the initiative is unsuccessful they can say, 'Look how thorough I was. I did my due diligence.' In my experience it comes down to the organisational culture; where there's a fear of failure research is used to avoid getting the blame for a project that fails.[26]

Thus, for many business professionals, business plans can amount to their 'due diligence', which is often done more to provide an umbrella in case of failure than to help to move the business forwards. In addition an emphasis on business plans can mean more work for professionals, as those who need a business plan may well hire someone to do it for them. In any case, with no significant alternative, it has been seen as the business plan or nothing. Thus business plans suit professional advisers who have an interest in establishing formal procedures and who, when it comes to deciding on such 'industry standards', often have a more focused and co-ordinated voice than individual entrepreneurs who tend just to get on with it.

REFLECTIONS ON THE TWO APPROACHES

Are business plans always helpful?

Business plans and a formal business planning approach may suit larger businesses but this is another area in which what is appropriate for larger businesses is not necessarily appropriate for small ones.

Owing, at least in part, to the way it has been presented, many people starting a business often see the business plan primarily as an obstacle – one that they feel they are obliged to address somehow because it seems to be a compulsory part of the process. Professional advisers have told them that they should do it, funders may have indicated that its completion is a precondition for further help, and guidance may have been provided on how to do it. Nevertheless a business plan may still just be seen as an unnecessary chore. Thus, for the person starting a small business, the questions he or she might have about the business plan may not be about how to do it, because they may have some guidance on that, but the reasons for doing it, or even whether to do it at all.

Typically, three ways are suggested in which the preparation of a good business plan can be of very real and direct help to a new business:

1. **Preparation and feasibility**. Advice about business plans may vary but it is generally agreed that one of the most important uses of a business plan, or rather of the process of preparing a plan, is that it can help the business owner to see that all relevant aspects of the potential business are addressed and allowed for. It also provides the basis for assessing the feasibility of the proposition (but that assumes that the projections in the plan are reliable – see Illustration 11.6).
2. **Communication and funding**. Another obvious benefit of a business plan may be its role in 'selling' the business by communicating its merits. Potential investors in the business often need to be persuaded of its worth. A business gets financial support because the providers of that support think that they will themselves benefit from its provision. Banks want to earn interest for an overdraft or loan and grant-givers seek a contribution to the achievement of their targets and aims (often related to improvements in the economy). They don't have to help a business; it is like a supplier–customer relationship: both have to benefit for it to work. In this case, however, the funds have to be provided before the benefits can be delivered, and the investors have to be able to trust the recipients to do that. In such circumstances, the business plan can be an essential tool for persuading investors that if they provide the funds then the business will be able to deliver the benefits and will survive long enough to do so, In effect the business plan is the sales document for the business and, when selling something, an understanding of the benefits the customer is seeking can be helpful:

   - Government agencies want a reliable and lasting contribution to the economy, by means such as increased exports and more jobs. They may use terms such as 'viability', 'additionality' and 'admissibility', so that is what the plan or sales document has to convey;

- Banks want interest on their capital, and eventually their capital repaid, so they will want to see how the business will be able to afford this;
- Business angels and venture capitalists want to see that their investment in the business will increase in value and can be realised subsequently.

3. **Management and control**. Once a business is planned, funded and launched a business plan can help with its subsequent management and control. Monitoring progress against the projections in the plan can show where action is needed, if any, to keep the business on course.

Despite the insistence of some authorities that a business plan is essential, from the above it would appear that if someone starting a business does not need to raise funds from formal sources, and understands enough about what he or she is about to do and the process of doing it, then a business plan may not be needed – although others would suggest that it is still advisable.

Nevertheless, for many people, a major problem with the business plan, at least as it is traditionally presented, is that it seems to be putting the cart before the horse. Many of the things they need to know in order to produce a credible business plan of the sort usually specified cannot realistically be determined until they have been in business for some time, perhaps several years. If the product is a novel one, for example, assessing the likely market may require production of some samples and attempts to sell them, which amounts to starting the business. So, in effect, many people may have to start before they can plan and if, once started, they find that it works, they are unlikely to want to stop again in order to do a pre-start plan.

Unsurprisingly, questions are now being raised about whether business plans are indeed helpful to many entrepreneurs. As the quotes in Illustration 11.5 indicate, business plan–based approaches have had their critics and, while research does not conclusively prove that business plans are detrimental to new ventures, neither does it seem to indicate clearly that they help them. For instance Babson College in Massachusetts, USA, is renowned for its teaching of business and in particular for its pioneering work in studying and encouraging entrepreneurs. Its graduates might be expected therefore to be among those most imbued with the business-plan approach. However, a survey was conducted in 2009 of former students who had graduated between 1985 and 2006 and who had since then founded one or more

ILLUSTRATION 11.6 – THE LIMITATIONS OF MARKET RESEARCH

At the core of the business plan is the sales forecast, which is usually based on some form of market research. It is the starting point for all the subsequent provisions and projections. But how reliable is that foundation? These are some views on it:

There is good reason to be skeptical of data from personal surveys. There is often a vast gulf between how people say they behave and how they actually behave. (In researcher-speak, these two behaviors are known as declared preferences and revealed preferences.)[27]

Philip Graves, one of the world's leading experts in consumer behavior, reveals why the findings obtained from most market research are completely unreliable. Whether it is company executives seeking to define their corporate strategy or politicians wanting to understand the electorate, the idea that questions answered on a questionnaire or discussed in a focus group can provide useful insights on which to base business decisions is the cause of product failures, political blunders and wasted billions.[28]

The fundamental tenet of market research is that you can ask people questions and that what they tell you in response will be true. And yet … this is a largely baseless belief. In fact it turns out that the opposite is far closer to the truth.[29]

As Henry Ford said, 'If I had asked my customers what they wanted, they would have said a faster horse.' Although some may even have balked at that, saying they were very happy with the horse they already had (particularly if they had only just bought it).[30]

> ⊃ | **ILLUSTRATION 11.7 – THE FAILED PLAN**
>
> Sue and Mary were two partners who started a clothing design business with financial backing from their parents, who put up their houses as security. Because they were too busy setting up the business, an adviser prepared most of their business plan for them, including the financial projections. The business looked attractive and the bank supported them. Probably because of their personal appeal and enthusiasm they even won a small business start-up award. Unfortunately the partners had never understood cash-flow forecasts, and the adviser's business plan only served to disguise this. Almost inevitably they lost control of their cash flow, and the business collapsed. The parents of one of them lost their house as a result.

full-time new ventures. It revealed that in only about half of the cases was there a written business plan before the business began operating. Also the survey concluded that the subsequent performance overall of all the new ventures was not related to having such a business plan.[31] While there have also been some positive findings, Honig and Samuelsson examined available studies on planning and its relationship to entrepreneurial performance and concluded that: 'in sum, much empirical research ends up inconclusive as to the effect of business planning in nascent organisations'.[32] Illustration 11.7 gives just one example of a case (based on a real example) where those involved seemed to feel that having a plan was enough, and where having one thus gave them a false sense of confidence. However, they did not understand

> ⊃ | **ILLUSTRATION 11.8 – LEFT- AND RIGHT-BRAIN THINKING**
>
> Recent research and thinking have suggested that some of the conclusions about the division of the brain, which were drawn in the 1960s and 1970s after the first split-brain operations, are wrong. Nevertheless it is clear that the brain is divided and that, to some extent, the left and right hemispheres do different things.
>
> Birds and animals, for instance, seem to use the left side of their brains to focus narrowly on things which they already know to be important, such as identifying food. They use the right side of their brains to be broadly on the lookout for other eventualities, such as the approach of a predator, and to make connections with the world, for instance by communicating with their fellows. Humans apparently do this to an even greater extent, using their left hemispheres for narrow, sharply focused attention to detail and their right hemispheres for sustained, broad, open vigilance.
>
> However, the left hemisphere tends to work on models, not reality, because models are much clearer and abstract, and so from them it can provide the analysis needed to decide on concrete actions. It tends to achieve this clarity and attention to detail by excluding from the models everything that doesn't fit. The right hemisphere sees the world as changing, evolving and inter-connected – but not fully knowable. To manipulate the world, it has been said, we need the left hemisphere; to understand it, we need the right.
>
> *Source*: Based on I. McGilchrist, *RSA Animate – The Divided Brain*. Taken from www.thersa.org (accessed 25 October 2011).

Reflections

To what extent, therefore, is the business plan a construct of the left hemisphere? It presents a relatively clear, simplified picture of the business proposition which can be used as a basis for decisions. It could be said to present a picture which appears to be known, fixed and static, whereas the real world is uncertain, changing and inter-connected. Further its left-hemisphere focus tends to preclude an openness to other possibilities and new opportunities – qualities which are more right-hemisphere based, along with the wider connections and communication needed to prepare for and utilise new eventualities.

Could it be argued that people starting new ventures often do not have sufficient understanding of their situation and market to be able to construct a realistic and meaningful business plan and that they need to be on the lookout for as-yet unforeseen possibilities, opportunities and connections? If so, they need to maintain, or increase, right-hemisphere usage and not focus relatively exclusively on a left-hemisphere view.

the plan or the need to monitor what was happening in the business in order to spot potential problems and take appropriate action.

The two approaches compared

In causal thinking the fixed point is the goal, which is specified, and therefore the focus is on establishing logically the best means by which to achieve it. In effectual thinking the fixed point is where to start, which is based on what the venture is and has (in terms of skills, contacts, experience, etc. – and the affordable loss). The focus then is on exploring what can be done from that starting point exploring possibilities to achieve the benefits the venture desires. These benefits are not fixed in advance, and what is desired may change as the venture proceeds and new opportunities are revealed. This is a process of exploration and is what many explorers do. Some may have looked for a route to particular destination – Columbus was looking for a route to Japan (see Illustration 10.2) – while others have

---

⤴ ILLUSTRATION 11.9 – RISK AND UNCERTAINTY IN ENTERPRISE

La circulation et le troc des denrées et des marchandises, de même que leur production, se conduisent en Europe par des Entrepreneurs, et au hazard.

Translated as: The circulation and exchange of goods and merchandise as well as their production are carried on in Europe by Undertakers, and at risk.　　Richard Cantillon[33]

There are known knowns; there are things we know that we know. There are known unknowns; that is to say, there are things that we now know we don't know. But there are also unknown unknowns; there are things we do not know we don't know.

Former US Defense Secretary Donald Rumsfeld[34]

Uncertainty is inherent in enterprise. Cantillon suggested that the three classes of actor in an economy were the landlords, who owned and rented out the land, the entrepreneurs who often rented the land for their activities, and the hired employees who worked for landlords or entrepreneurs. What distinguished the entrepreneurs from landlords or waged employees was that, whereas the rents or wages due to the latter could be fixed in advance, the returns from the entrepreneurial activity (which for Cantillon included farming) were uncertain because they depended on many factors beyond the entrepreneurs' control. Thus the entrepreneurs operated at a risk. Indeed it has been said more recently that enterprise should itself be spelt R-I-S-K.

> Knight[35] made a distinction between risk and uncertainty with the difference being that for risk the odds are known, or can be predicted with a degree of probability, whereas for uncertainty the odds are not known and cannot easily/realistically be determined. The known unknowns might therefore be converted into risk because, as we know about them, we can try to assess them. Those known unknowns which cannot be easily assessed, along with the unknown unknowns (of which there are many which can face a new business) belong in the realms of uncertainty. If that distinction is used, it would seem that much enterprise is uncertain rather than risky, especially for new enterprise.

sought a specific natural resource, such as deposits of gold. All stood to benefit, however, if they were open to other possibilities which their explorations might reveal. Thus, in causal terms, Columbus might be said to have failed because he did not get to Japan, but in effectual terms he succeeded because he revealed to the Spaniards, and others in Europe, the potential benefits of the Americas, including its stocks of gold.

Which approach is useful depends therefore on the circumstances, but each also requires, or suggests, different attitudes towards goals.

A further key difference between the two approaches outlined above lies in their approach to risk and uncertainty (see Illustration 11.9). The business plan–based approach recognises that the future may be uncertain but seeks to reduce that uncertainty by prior investigation and planning. In particular, for business ventures, it assumes that prior market research can help to indicate what can, or cannot, be sold, in what volumes and at what price (but see Illustration 11.3). By costing what is involved in making the sales and comparing that with the income that might be generated, the profitability of the venture can be assessed against different sales projections. Thus the odds of success can be estimated, and uncertainty changed into risk, so that a risk-benefit assessment can be made as the basis for a decision on whether to proceed. Appropriate dispositions can then be made and the venture, if started, can be controlled or manipulated to follow the route indicated in the plan.

Thus, as Graves reports, 'the notion that risk can be mitigated by soliciting consumer opinion is so tempting that millions of pounds continue to be spent pursuing it'. Yet, he goes on to say, 'it's regularly reported that over 80% of new product launches fail'.[36] The effectuation-based approach acknowledges this and is referred to here as the 'accept uncertainty' approach because that is what it does. It accepts that the future is uncertain and unpredictable and suggests proceeding accordingly. It is consistent therefore with the belief that much market research is unreliable. So instead of trying to plan a particular future route on such forecasts, it assumes that the best way to find routes is to get started and look for them.

Table 11.3 summarises other aspects of a comparison of the two approaches but they are not straight alternatives. They each cover things that the other does not cover and each has its advantages and disadvantages.

Table 11.3 *Comparison of accept-uncertainty and business-plan approaches*

Aspect	Accept uncertainty	Business plan
Philosophy	It is not prescriptive. It entails being flexible and developing through experience an understanding of the territory and of the progression options – exploratory approach in nature.	It is prescriptive. It sets a predetermined path by first researching and developing a business plan which will determine the route to be followed.
Attitude	Reality is uncertain – so proceed with open eyes ready to do what appears to be appropriate as the situation evolves.	First develop a plan and then (just) follow it – trying to do what the plan suggests should be done, although it can be changed.
Mindset encouraged	Encourages exploration, flexibility and responsiveness.	Encourages following a predetermined path.
Environment assumed	Accepts that the environment is uncertain and fluid.	Assumes an environment which is relatively static and predictable.

Starting point	Start from where you are.	Start from where the plan says you should start.
When to start	Start early, because that way you will feel that you are doing something, you will gain confidence and momentum, you will find out what works and you will see more opportunities.	Only start when you have researched your idea, assessed the market, decided what you are going to do, assessed its viability and produced a business plan.
On finding obstacles	If you have built and maintained momentum, it will help you across and/or around obstacles. You may also by then have seen other opportunities.	Follow the plan. If it doesn't work, stop and reassess.
Preparation and planning	Prepare to be flexible.	Plan the venture in detail and then follow the plan.
Resources applied	Invest the minimum amount of resources needed and no more than you can afford to lose.	Try to invest and/or find the resource that the business plan says is needed and justified by the anticipated return.
Route followed	Follow a route as and when you find one going in the direction in which you want to go, and until you find a better one.	Follow the route specified in the plan.
Guidance used	Find an appropriate mentor/expertise.	The plan is your guidance.
Scale of venture	It is often good for small ventures.	Business plans may be helpful for bigger ventures – but the investment needed to produce a plan makes this approach unsuitable for many small ventures.
When to plan	Produce a written plan only when you need one.	Produce a full written plan at the start because that is when (you are told that) you need one.
Approach	Assumes a dynamic situation for which the relevant approach is to have a goal/direction and to be able to steer towards it in a changing environment. In a dynamic situation, movement facilitates control – like riding a bicycle or steering a boat. NB Note Gibb's two diagrams in Figure 9.3: the 'monster' is static and the real person is moving.	Assumes that the situation can be analysed as if it were static and as if the relevant approach would be one of reflective dissection and diagnosis. (Being static may be comforting if you are standing firmly on solid ground, but in a dynamic situation it abrogates control and responsiveness.)
Consistency with the other approach	This approach does not deny that business planning, and the elements within it, may be helpful, but does not insist that they are always essential at the start, especially as sometimes many of them cannot be credibly achieved until later.	Business plan–based approaches usually only cover the components of the traditional business plan and ignore the other key aspects of start-up which are covered by the accept-uncertainty approach.
Resource and cost considerations	Don't put at risk on a venture more than you can afford to lose. But also consider what you will lose if you don't proceed.	Business plans can be relatively expensive to produce – both in time and money – and they can then encourage you to invest what is needed for the plan and justified by the expected return.

Source: Based on S. Bridge and C. Hegarty, 'An Alternative to Business Plan Based Advice for Start-ups?', paper presented at the *34th ISBE Conference*, November 2011.

SOME IMPLICATIONS

For a 'nascent' entrepreneur going into the unknown to achieve his or her aim, what is likely to be the best way to proceed? The three main options for dealing with uncertainty are:

- *Do nothing*. Doing nothing is the only zero risk option. However, while it has zero risk of failure, it also has zero chance of success and may have an opportunity cost.

- *Reconnoitre and plan first.* There is a military saying that time spent on reconnaissance is seldom wasted. If the way forward is uncertain, then prior reconnaissance, such as prototype testing and trial offerings, can be carried out to provide the basis for a proper risk assessment and a plan of how the venture might then be implemented. Some people suggest that only after careful preparation and appraisal of such a plan should the instigator commit to the venture. However, if the venture is relatively small, then the amount of effort involved in testing the market with trial offerings is the same as starting the business on effectuation lines. Reconnoitring is fine if, once you have found a way, you are then going to come back and lead others along it. But if you are the only person involved then what's the point of doing it twice?
- *Accept uncertainty and proceed with caution.* In some situations, where there is uncertainty but prior reconnaissance is unlikely to help, the only way to find a way through is to try. In such circumstances the practical option is to proceed but with caution, following effectuation principles and recognising that the venture is still somewhat experimental.

What therefore is appropriate advice and guidance for someone who wants to start a new venture such as a new business? The default recommendation for a new business enterprise has been based on business-plan thinking. But how appropriate is that approach in reality, rather than just in theory? That may seem to be a relatively simple question but the issues involved are varied – for instance, there can be different areas of advice, different aspects of starting, and different types of venture:

- Different aspects of starting:
  — Where to start?
  — What action is needed?
  — What resources will be needed?
  — Will gaining momentum help?
  — What is the destination?
  — What will be the scale of the venture?
  — To plan or not to plan?
  — Which logic to follow?

- Different areas of advice:
  — How to prepare for it?
  — How to do it?
  — How to teach and/or assist it?

- Different types of venture:
  — Different sorts of activity, from formal incorporated businesses to informal personal or group activity.
  — Different returns sought by the founders, including financial profit, social contributions or a mixture of the two.
  — Different degrees of involvement, from full-time through part-time to minimal.
  — Different sizes of venture, from just self-employment to many employees.

The issues listed above suggest that, because of the variety of the factors involved, there is not going to be one, single, simple approach applicable in all situations – a sort of off-the-shelf one-size-fits-all recipe. Neither an approach based on accepting uncertainty nor an approach based on the business plan will be applicable in all circumstances. An accept-uncertainty approach based on effectuation principles is likely to be of more general use by a wide variety of new ventures, including many in the field of business. A business-plan approach is a more specialised approach relevant for some business situations. Despite that, the traditional approach to people starting new ventures has been to teach, encourage and support then to research and prepare plans following a relatively standard 'business plan' format. However, a re-evaluation of the relevance of the business-plan approach, recognising some of the sort of factors

---

ILLUSTRATION 11.10 – THE 'BEERMAT' PLAN

'Unlike the business plans beloved of MBAs, this plan is simple. It has three things on it:

1 Elevator Pitch
2 Mentor
3 First Customer'

Source: M. Southon and C. West, *The Beermat Entrepreneur* (Harlow: Pearson Education Ltd, 2002) p. 8.

---

considered above, suggests that, for many start-ups, it is not the best way to proceed. Instead an approach based on accepting uncertainty and proceeding accordingly is often more natural and more helpful.

In particular in the case of many small businesses, the amount of work required to produce a full business plan may be the same as, or even more than, the work involved in launching the business. Indeed launching the business is often the only way eventually to produce the information a business plan requires. In other words, it is only by trying it to see if it works that the risks in the apparent uncertainty can be assessed. Therefore in this situation it is not logical to try to produce a formal plan first, and something like the 'Beermat' Plan (see Illustration 11.10) can be all that is needed.

As a start-up guide, the business-plan approach is seriously misleading if it ignores key aspects of start-up such as getting started and gaining momentum and if it encourages people to think of the business plan as the ideal and thus to feel that they are in some way missing an opportunity and/or are at fault unless they have and follow one. An accept-uncertainty, effectuation approach is not second best to a business plan–based, causation approach. For many start-ups it is, on balance, a better approach and it is therefore more logical to follow it.

Nevertheless business plans should not be rejected completely. In some circumstances, they can help. However, they should be seen, not as ends in themselves, but as tools, the components of which are not fixed but should be adapted as appropriate for the context. The activities with which the business plan tool can help include:

- Decision-making by the business owner and by prospective business funders.
- Communication with stakeholders, including especially (potential) funders – such as banks, venture capitalists and support/grant agencies.
- Providing a basis for diagnosing problems.
- Learning some of the principles of establishing a business.

> The plan is nothing: planning is everything.
>
> Napoleon
>
> Whereas anyone can make a plan it takes something quite out of the ordinary to carry it out.
>
> General Sir Frederick Morgan

If an accept-uncertainty, effectuation approach is better for many small businesses, is it also good for larger ones? All business is risky and if the future is uncertain to what extent is it possible to assess and evaluate all the risk beforehand? Is it instead better to minimise any danger in that uncertainty, not by extensive prior analysis, but by proceeding accordingly? In truth, even big businesses have to deal with uncertainty, although they may think they are dealing with risk. Charles Handy, in his book *The Age of Unreason*, points out that getting it wrong is sometimes part of getting it right and that, for instance, oil companies have to accept a high rate of failure in exploratory drilling as they expect to drill nine empty wells for every one that flows.[37] Can such uncertainty be reduced by prior research or should the businesses concerned learn how to proceed in uncertainty? Tesco, for instance, is said to be prepared to try many new ideas on a minimum cost basis expecting that a lot will fail but that it is still the best way to find the successes.

This means that, for those people advising, assisting, promoting, encouraging or teaching start-ups, sticking to the business plan as the only approved method is going to be less than helpful. They should be aware of the alternative approach and recognise that those doing it will have somewhat different priorities than those advising them: achieving success rather than avoiding failure. Basing assistance and teaching only on the business plan formula puts a straight jacket on the syllabus and agenda and unnecessary constraints on thinking about the relevant start-up considerations.

IN CONCLUSION

As explained, the common view of enterprise has been to see it as a sub-set of business. Therefore it has seemed natural to conclude that the business plan was relevant to enterprise. Also the dominance of much of the 'professional' view of enterprise and small business (see Chapters 7 and 8) has meant that enterprise has often been seen as a logical and sequential process of research, planning and implementation – as epitomised by the business plan and its promotion as a key and unavoidable part of the preparation process before a business is started. The emphasis on the business plan appears to have been maintained also because:

- It is what has always been advised.
- It is easy and convenient to describe and teach.
- It provides a logical perspective.
- No alternative approach was known.

However, the business plan has been criticised – for instance because it leaves out some important principles for guiding new ventures, because it is based on a sales forecast which is likely to be very unreliable, and because it encourages an unhelpful mindset. Many people coming afresh to enterprise need to get started and to get a feel for their market before they can complete a meaningful business plan. Also, after investing in the effort of producing a business plan, there is a temptation to stick to the chosen method, both because that has been the focus of attention and because so much work has been invested in its determination.

That does not mean that people should leap into a new venture without looking at all, but that the level of planning should be appropriate to their circumstances and not dictated by 'professional' views of what a start-up business plan should be. This is not advocating going from one extreme to another: from insistence on going from full business plans in every case to no planning at all. It is suggesting instead an interim position with planning being no more than giving some thought to what might be done, without trying to structure and record the future according to a prescribed template.

Also if enterprise is seen, not as a sub-set of business, but essentially as a process of exploration, which can sometimes but not always take place in a business context, it is less likely that the business plan will automatically be thought to be relevant – not least because effectuation can be a much better guide for exploration. For exploration, people need to engage the right side of their brains, whereas the business plan tends to encourage and/or reinforce left-brain thinking. An effectuation, accept-uncertainty approach is not a lazy alternative – it is different but still requires a disciplined application of its principles if it is to be successful.

Both those starting new ventures and those advising and/or assisting them, need to understand both approaches and when to apply each of them. Despite this, often the business plan–based approach – the more specialised tool – is the only one advised or taught, with the result that it is often tried in circumstances for which it is not really appropriate. Using such a 'specialist' tool, especially when a more general tool would be better, can have unforeseen adverse side effects. For instance producing a business plan for a possible direction or opportunity changes it into a discrete venture which, if it doesn't work, becomes a failure. Instead the effectuation approach, as in any exploration,

↻ | ## ILLUSTRATION 11.11 – THE ESTABLISHMENT OF A SMALL CONSULTANCY BUSINESS

This case is based on a real situation familiar to the authors and concerns the establishment of a small consultancy business providing services to other small businesses (e.g. help with business plans, grant applications, and strategy and organisation reviews). At the time of writing, the business had been in existence and meeting its founder's aims for over 15 years.

Earlier in his life the thought of having his own business had never occurred to the founder and only arose later in a theoretical way when he accepted a job in a small business support agency which tried to help people to start and grow their own businesses. However, a re-structuring of the agency led to him being made redundant. As a result of his recent efforts to encourage others to start businesses, he felt obliged to try it himself – although he did also keep an eye on the local job market in case any attractive jobs were advertised.

During his time in the small business agency two colleagues in sister organisations had started their own consultancy businesses and this was something he thought he could try also. So when he was approached, separately, by two clients of the agency for which he had worked asking if he could help them to prepare their applications to the agency, he was interested. He checked with his former colleagues in the agency. They encouraged him to go ahead, pointing out that they wanted to assist these clients but needed business plans with their submissions and he should be able to write plans which met all the agency's requirements.

He started working from home using his home phone and desk-top computer. At this stage he also made an application himself to the agency for support for his business start-up. Because it was only a one-person business, at least at this stage, a formal business plan was not required, just a cash-flow forecast, which he knew had to demonstrate that that support was needed if he was to get a grant. The cash-flow forecast and supporting assumptions were tuned therefore to the task of justifying the application rather than to providing a realistic projection of the business prospects. This forecast was, however, the closest he got to producing a business plan for his own business.

The next stages in developing the business included selecting an accountant, ordering business cards and headed paper, registered for self-employment national insurance, and advertising his services in general terms in Yellow Pages.

His main sources of customers were networking and word of mouth. These, however, not only produced other prospective customers but also indications of other services which he might offer and other potential collaborators. Thus the business prospered to the extent that he stopped looking for other possible employment. As the service he offered depended largely on his own contacts, experience and knowledge, he remained a one-person business but he did sometimes collaborate with other self-employed people to work on larger projects. After a while his turnover grew to the level at which he needed to register for VAT, and after a couple of years, and at his accountant's suggestion, he formed a limited company which took over the business's activities and acquired its goodwill. He officially became the sole employee. (It is interesting to note that in doing this he had to de-register and then re-register for VAT – despite there being no actual change in the business's activities.)

Relatively early in this process he was asked in a survey of new small businesses what his business aims were. This made him think about them and he recorded them as follows, and in no particular order. He has not seen the need subsequently to change them:

- To generate enough income to maintain his standard of living.
- To make a contribution to the local community.
- To enjoy his business activity.

Which approach would have been best for this business – business planning or accepting uncertainty – and why?

sees a possible opportunity in the context of alternative avenues to be explored if a successful venture is to be developed. Thus finding that an apparently possible opportunity is something of a dead end is not failure but part of the normal exploration process. Another implication is that before business advisers insist on advocating business plans, they should consider the impact that such an approach can have upon the development of the entrepreneurial person as well as the entrepreneurial venture. Could it be that advocating an essentially cautious, reflective, research-and-planning approach, especially at a stage when there is inevitably a lot of uncertainty, may have the unintended consequence of stifling enterprise and reducing the momentum which might be necessary for success?

☛ THE KEY POINTS OF CHAPTER 11

- For many new ventures, including many business start-ups, an accept-uncertainty approach based on effectuation principles can be helpful.
- However, the business plan is advocated by many people as an essential aid for start-ups.
- There may have been some good reasons for this advocacy but it reflects the view that enterprise is just a sub-set of business.
- There are significant limitations to the business plan as an aid for many start-ups which are, in reality, undertaking a process of exploration.
- Professional advisers can have somewhat different aims which are more likely to be assisted by a business-plan approach.
- An accept-uncertainty, effectual approach can be seen as a general purpose guide applicable in many situations including business, whereas a business-plan approach can be seen as a specialised guide applicable only to some situations within business. Teaching, or advocating, only the specialised approach many not be helpful and it may even reduce a venturer's chances of success.

✓ QUESTIONS, EXERCISES, ESSAY AND DISCUSSION TOPICS

- 'The plan is nothing – planning is everything.' Does this mean that the standard business plan–based approach is not helpful and, if not, why not?

- Luck favours the bold and unless you try something, despite the uncertainty, you will never succeed in doing anything. To what extent is this a relevant consideration when starting a business? Which is the greater danger: paralysis by analysis, or becoming extinct by instinct?

- Getting it wrong can be part of getting it right. Failure can lead to opportunity, experience, learning and improvement. Is this true in business and, if so, how can the downside of failure be minimised?

- Effectuation or the business plan – with which approach are you most comfortable? With which approach is the person to whom you are trying to communicate your business idea most comfortable? Is the business plan the language a right-hemisphere person needs to employ to communicate with a left-hemisphere person?

- The following are the chapter headings in a guide to starting a business:[38]

    Introduction

    Starting a business

    Forming a business

    Marketing and sales

    Managing your money

    Where to work

The legal bit

Selling yourself

Mentors and role models

Going for growth

Writing a business plan

Consider this list in the context of the traditional business plan–based approach and the accept-uncertainty, effectuation approach. How well does it help with each approach? What is missing from it?

SUGGESTIONS FOR FURTHER READING AND INFORMATION

S. Bridge and C. Hegarty, *Beyond the Business Plan: 10 Principles for New Venture Exploration* (Basingstoke: Palgrave Macmillan, 2013).

P. Graves, *Consumer.ology*, (London: Nicholas Brealey Publishing, 2010).

S. Reid, S. Sarasvathy, N. Dew, R. Wiltbank and A.-V. Ohlsson, *Effectual Entrepreneurship* (Abingdon and New York, NY: Routledge, 2011).

S. Sarasvathy, *Effectuation: Elements of Entrepreneurial Experience* (Cheltenham: Edward Elgar, 2008).

REFERENCES

[1] E. T. Penrose, *The Theory of the Growth of the Firm* (Oxford: Basil Blackwell, 1959) p. 19.

[2] S. D. Sarasvathy, *Effectuation: Elements of Entrepreneurial Experience* (Cheltenham: Edward Elgar, 2008).

[3] Ibid. p. 24.

[4] P. Graves, *Consumer.ology* (London: Nicholas Brealey Publishing, 2010) dust jacket and p. 2.

[5] S. D. Sarasvathy, *Effectuation*, Op. Cit. p. 131.

[6] S. D. Sarasvathy and S. Venkataraman, 'Entrepreneurship as Method: Open Questions for an Entrepreneurial Future', *Entrepreneurship Theory and Practice*, Vol. 35, No. 1, January 2011, pp. 113–135.

[7] S. Bridge and C. Hegarty, *Beyond the Business Plan: 10 Principles for New Venture Exploration* (Basingstoke: Palgrave Macmillan, 2013).

[8] Based on S. Bridge and C. Hegarty, Op. Cit.

[9] F. Black speaking at the Richard Cantillon Summer School (held in Tralee, Ireland, September 2010) about her experience of starting the RISE foundation.

[10] E. Ries, *The Lean Start-Up: How Constant Innovation Creates Radically Successful Business* (London: Penguin, 2011).

[11] Business Link, Prepare a Business Plan. Taken from www.businesslink.gov.uk (accessed 6 July 2010).

[12] Harvard Business School Press, *Creating a Business Plan* (Boston, MA: Harvard Business School Publishing, 2007), back cover.

[13] P. Burns, *Entrepreneurship and Small Business*, 3rd Edition (Basingstoke: Palgrave, 2011) p. 365.

[14] D. Deakins and M. Freel, *Entrepreneurship and Small Firms*, 5th Edition (Maidenhead: McGraw Hill, 2009) p. 316.

[15] HSBC, *Quick Start Business Plan*. Taken from www.tsbc.co.uk/sbo/hsbckn/viewlesson.aspx?lid=35 (accessed 31 January 2011).

[16] Invest Northern Ireland, *Starting Your Own Business*. Taken from www.goforitni.com (accessed 20 November 2010).

[17] A. A. Gibb, *Towards the Entrepreneurial University: Entrepreneurship Education as a Lever for Change* (National Council for Graduate Entrepreneurship Policy Paper 003, May 2005).

PART 2

[18] D. Deakins and M. Freel, Op. Cit. p. 295.

[19] Ibid. p. 275.

[20] B. Bjerke, *Understanding Entrepreneurship* (Cheltenham: Edward Elgar, 2007) p. viii.

[21] J. Cornwall, *The Entrepreneurship Educator Newsletter June 2010*. Taken from www.planningshop.com (accessed 29 June 2010).

[22] J. Brinckmann, D. Grichnik and D, Kapsa, 'Should Entrepreneurs Plan or Just Storm the Castle?' *Journal of Business Venturing*, Vol. 24, 2010, p. 24.

[23] G. D. Meyer, 'The Reinvention of Academic Entrepreneurship', *Journal of Small Business Management*, Vol. 49, No. 1, Jan 2011, p. 1.

[24] The Compact Edition of the Oxford English Dictionary (Book Club Associates, 1979).

[25] A. A. Gibb, Op. Cit. p. 2.

[26] Tim Dewey quoted in P. Graves, *Consumer.ology* (London: Nicholas Brealey Publishing, 2010) p. 3.

[27] S. D. Levitt and S. J. Dubner, *SuperFreakonomics* (London: Allen Lane, 2009) p. 7.

[28] P. Graves, *Consumer.ology* (London: Nicholas Brealey Publishing, 2010) – from the dust jacket.

[29] Ibid. p. 4.

[30] Ibid. p. 167.

[31] J. E. Lange, A. Perdomo and W. D. Bygrave, 'Do Actual Outcomes Justify Writing Business Plans Either for Educating Students or For Starting Real Ventures?', paper presentation to *6th AGSE Conference* (Australia: Adelaide, 2009).

[32] B. Honig and M. Samuelsson, *Business Planning and Venture Level Performance: Challenging the Institution of Planning* (Swedish Entrepreneurship Forum working paper, 2011).

[33] R. Cantillon, *Essai sur la nature du commerce en général*, edited with an English translation and other material by H. Higgs (London: Frank Cass & Co Ltd, 1959 – reissued for the Royal Economic Society) p. 46.

[34] US Department of Defense, News Transcript: News Briefing – Secretary Rumsfeld and General Myers, 12 February 2010.

[35] F. H. Knight, *Risk, Uncertainty and Profit* (Boston, MA: Hart, Schaffner & Marx; Houghton Mifflin, 1921).

[36] P. Graves, *Consumer.ology* (London: Nicholas Brealey Publishing, 2010) p. 29.

[37] C. Handy, *The Age of Unreason* (London: Arrow Books, 1990) p. 55.

[38] The Prince's Trust, *Make It Happen: The Prince's Trust Guide to Starting Your Own Business* (Chichester: Capstone Publishing Ltd, 2011).

Companion website

Please visit the companion website at www.palgravehighered.com/Bridge-UE-5e for access to additional learning and teaching materials..

Running a Small Business

CONTENTS

- Introduction
- The traditional view
- The official support view

- The owner's view
- Implications

KEY CONCEPTS

This chapter covers:

- The view traditionally taken of established small businesses and the problems they face.
- The way that official support tends to be based on a business growth aim and/or a component-based perspective.
- The perspective of many small business owners, which is usually a holistic one focused on day-to-day issues and not necessarily on growth.
- The differences between these perspectives and the consequent limitations in much official support for small businesses.

LEARNING OBJECTIVES

By the end of this chapter the reader should:

- Understand some of the different issues likely to face small business owner-managers.
- Appreciate the difference in the perspective likely to be taken by official sources of advice and support and that of the small business people they are supposed to be helping.
- Understand some of the likely consequences of that difference in perspective and, in particular, the limitations in support.

INTRODUCTION

Chapter 11 looks at the process of starting a new venture, particularly a new business, and considers what guidance might be appropriate for this activity. It concludes that, although this process has traditionally been seen as a sub-set of business, and as requiring the logical and sequential research and preparation of a business plan, in many situations an alternative approach of exploration based on 'effectuation' principles might be more helpful.

But once ventures have been started, no matter how successfully, they do not run themselves. Even if the founder is already an experienced business manager, such as a habitual entrepreneur, it is likely that, in trying to run a new business, new situations will be encountered. Many people will probably be inclined just to persevere and try to work it out for themselves. Others may seek advice or guidance, often from relevant friends or people like their accountant (see Figure 9.2), but some may go to an official support network.

It is therefore important to recognise, as with start-ups, that many sources of help, especially official ones, will not necessarily share the same goals as those they are supposed to be assisting. That means that the advice and/or support they supply may not always be the most appropriate. This chapter considers the practical issues involved in running a business at its various stages and explores the different perspectives of those officially engaged to encourage and assist the process as well as those who are actually trying to do it.

THE TRADITIONAL VIEW

This exploration of operational small business issues involves two dimensions: one being the different stages through which a business might go and the other the different views that advisers and participants might have of what is involved in, or relevant to, those stages. To put this into context, this chapter starts with a summary of what has generally and traditionally been said about some of the key issues in running a business. The subsequent sections contrast that view with an adviser's perspective and an operator's perspective before identifying some of the issues arising from the differences revealed.

The seven stages of business

As Chapter 6 indicates, a business does not usually remain unchanged; it does not remain in the state it is in immediately after it is formed. Instead, like the seven ages of man identified by Shakespeare, once there is an intention to start a business, seven stages can be determined in its life. However, just as individuals are unlikely to distinguish in their own lives all of Shakespeare's seven stages, so individual business owners are unlikely to distinguish clear stages in their businesses. In any case, like the ages of man – and the colours of the rainbow – the division of the development of a business into seven stages is somewhat arbitrary. In the main, the stages are not clearly separate events with distinct boundaries but are areas with some common features which can have sub-categories but which can also merge one into another. Furthermore all the stages do not necessarily apply to every business and, unlike the ages of man, neither do they always occur in the same order. Nevertheless, in considering a business, it can be useful to consider the following stages (although there are other lists with different categorisations of stages such as those in Figure 6.1 and Table 12.2):

- Idea
- Preparation
- Inception
- Static (including early survival and consolidation and, later, comfort and maturity)
- Growth (and expansion)
- Decline
- Termination.

As this chapter considers the progress of a business after its inception, it is the last four of these stages which are relevant here. They provide a context for the chapter, but it is important to realise that they are more apparent when a business is viewed from an external perspective rather than from an internal one. Thus business advisers may perceive them but not necessarily business owners. Those owners will be more interested in the specifics of operating their own businesses than in generalisations about the progression of all businesses. Nevertheless these stages matter, as the key issues involved can change between the stages and because there can be different views on which constitute the priority stages. For instance:

- Survival is probably the main concern of many, if not most, small business owners. If the business is providing them with enough benefits to justify their investment of time and money, they may not have an overwhelming wish to grow it further but equally they may not want to see it regress. Thus for them the '**static**' stage is the best compromise.

- In contrast **growth** is almost certainly the main focus of many business advisers and supporters. Whether that is because they see growth as the natural state of a business (see Chapter 8) or because their main aim or wish is economic development for which business growth is crucial, or both, they often assume that the aim of their involvement is to help the business concerned to grow.

- It might be thought that neither advisers nor owners would want to see businesses **decline**, but that should not be a reason not to think about this stage. The possible causes of decline need to be understood if decline is to be avoided, corrected if it does occur, or understood and the effects of it minimised if it is inevitable.

- As with decline, if not more so, the **termination** of a business might appear to be something to be avoided at all costs. However, as Chapter 6 points out, if termination is inevitable (and some business deaths are necessary in a healthy economy), then easing its progress can be an advantage. Also, for those business owners who started businesses with the intention that it should have a limited life, for instance to provide them with an income until they retire, termination at the due time is actually a sign of the success of their ventures, provided they do it in an orderly fashion.

ILLUSTRATION 12.1 – ASPECTS OF GROWTH

For many people growth might be the key or most desirable state for a business and so it might be supposed that there would at least be agreement about what business growth is. Nevertheless, while the concept of business growth might seem quite straightforward, in practice it has a number of complications.

First there is the question of the dimension by which growth is to be measured. Turnover is a measure traditionally used, as are profitability and market share, but often firm size is assessed by the number of its employees, especially as this is the measure preferred by those who see employment as the key contribution of a business to an economy. For government support agencies, for instance, straightforward growth in employment (or at least an overall improvement in the economy) may be the requirement. This is most likely to come from a growth in exports or a replacement of imports, which may lead to a growth in employment.

Although, as noted by Smallbone and Wyer, 'a number of studies have demonstrated the close correlation that exists between employment growth and sales growth in small firms over a long period of time ... [nevertheless] increased employment is less clearly related to a growth in profitability'.[1] Some analysts may in addition interpret growth in the context of a broader product range, or an increased number of patents or of customers, none of which necessarily imply greater turnover, profitability or employment.

People with a financial interest in small businesses often want to see an increase in the value of their investments by growth in shareholder value, which implies a growth in business earnings and net assets, which themselves may be achieved by growth in turnover and/or profitability (or the potential for it). Employment, therefore, is not necessarily a growth goal for them, but may be a by-product of it.

Many business owners, however, have other criteria which they value. These can include having a comfortable life, job satisfaction, customer service, innovation or product quality. If the relevant criteria can be improved without the bother of having to do more work or employ more people to increase sales, then these forms of growth might actually be preferred to those which meet the more traditional criteria.

Then there can be the case of businesses which grow in one dimension but shrink in another. Can a business be said to have grown if it has increased its turnover but reduced its employment, as might happen if it invests in robotic production?

A further complication is the time for which growth has to be maintained, or the timescale over which growth is to be measured, if a business is to be considered to be a growth business. Growth, when is does occur, is often sporadic; very few businesses grow continuously. And for how long after it last grew should a business still be considered to be in the growth category?

In Chapter 9 it is also suggested that some habitual entrepreneurs appear to grow their business portfolios by starting new businesses rather than growing the businesses they already have. Thus there might be overall growth in the portfolio – but not in any existing business.

Therefore it is important to realise that, while people might want to see growth, it will mean different things to different people. For many people, growth in employment will generally be the primary goal. For those managing economies and balances of payments, growth in export turnover, or in import substitution, is critical. For shareholders, profitability as a route to enhancing dividends and share value is likely to be predominant. The individual small business owner, however, as noted above, may have one or a number of aspirations. These might include providing local employment, creating wealth, building a large income, being seen as innovative or providing jobs for the family. Many of these will be derived from, or be facilitated by, growth in aspects of the business.

While researchers frequently measure growth in terms of employment, its potential to signify different things to different people means that care must be taken in describing it. Unless its meaning in a particular situation is clear, misunderstandings may arise. It may also be necessary to remember the distinction made between forms of growth, and the different yardsticks used to measure growth, some of which are indicated in Table 12.1.

Table 12.1 *Yardsticks for business growth*

Share value	Return on investment	Market share
Net worth	Size of premises	Exports/imports substitution
Profit	Standard of service	New products/services
Employment	Profile/image	Innovations, patents, etc.
Turnover	Number of customers	Added value

Running a business

Because of the desire by many people, although not necessarily by business owners, that businesses should grow, not least in terms of their employment, businesses have often been assessed in terms of their potential growth. Thus, while other stages are recognised, when businesses are examined it is the growing business which is the ideal model with which they are compared and it is the growth stage which receives most attention. The following are among the factors which are thought to be relevant for growth.

Management performance

Many would argue that the motivation (see next section) and ability of a firm to grow rests with the owner and his or her management team. Such an approach recognises that growth is related to a business's performance in the marketplace, and in particular to its ability to make rational (profitable) decisions about its products and/or services in the context of market development. In short, a condition of growth is the ability of management to plan and implement the firm's growth in both strategic and operational terms. In this context it is instructive to note that a European Observatory for SMEs identifies four weaknesses of smaller businesses[2] (albeit it combines causes and effects):

- High mortality rates
- Weak market orientation due to lack of strategic marketing approaches and to operating in small segmented markets
- Low productivity of labour leading to high unit wage costs
- Low equity–debt ratio and difficult and costly access to financial markets.

All of these weaknesses can be related to management inadequacy (as indeed can almost all aspects of small business performance). Even difficulty in raising finance can be attributed to a 'failure' of management adequately to search for sources, build networks, prepare suitable proposals or share ownership and control.

Evidence concerning the impact of a selection of firm-specific elements attributable to the performance of the management team is summarised by Storey.[3] These elements include management recruitment and training, workforce training, technological sophistication, market positioning, market adjustments, planning, new product introduction, customer concentration, exporting (information and advice) and external equity. The list of elements reflects research which has been done, and is not necessarily an exhaustive list of management-related issues.

Unfortunately, the findings are not conclusive. Taken together, good performance of these elements is conventionally seen to be the basis of good management. So it seems to be counter-intuitive that proper practice in many of these elements is not found as yet to be correlated with growth in businesses. It is, however, suggested that three aspects of management do appear to be the most closely linked with growth, as opposed to size (an important distinction): these are market positioning, new products and management recruitment.

- **Market positioning.** A key decision for any business is the definition of its market and where it perceives itself to be in relation to its competitors. While it is difficult to define precisely, market positioning has to do with notions of who the customers are, competitive advantage, product and service range and the role of quality, service and price. It would appear that the ability to know, and take advantage of, market positioning (in other words, to determine one's niche) is related to growth success.
- **New products.** The development and introduction of new products are related to market positioning. There is some evidence, but it is by no means conclusive, that new product introductions are associated with faster growth. Introducing new products is usually seen in much of the literature as part of the process of innovation, which is seen as the engine driving continued growth. Nevertheless, definite conclusions in this area are difficult to draw from empirical studies, although the OECD expresses a commonplace view in suggesting that 'A businessman's attitude to using new technologies to ensure or increase competitiveness ... appears extremely significant'.[4]
- **Management recruitment.** Common sense dictates that, as a firm grows, it becomes more dependent on its management team. A CBI (Confederation of British Industry) report revealed that there is a 'greater awareness of management weaknesses among growth firms', and that 'recruitment of outside managers also tends to increase with growth'.[5] There is much other research evidence to show that not acquiring the right management expertise and not building the appropriate structure are amongst the main reasons why growth-orientated firms fail to achieve their objective of growth.
- **Other factors.** Overall, one cannot deduce that other firm-specific factors are not important for growth, just that, so far, there seems to be an absence of adequate evidence to demonstrate a causal relationship.

Management skills

In Chapter 6 (see Table 6.4) it is suggested that there can be four dimensions of management ability which apply even to small businesses: functional knowledge and skills, generic management knowledge and skills, business and strategic awareness, and personal competencies.[6] Further, as has been suggested above, in the area of functional ability, all businesses need the ability to manage in three, or sometimes four, key areas if they are to operate successfully. The three areas which apply to all businesses have traditionally been identified as production, marketing and money[7] – the fourth, which applies to all except the smallest businesses, is people (although other models may offer different terminology).

Discussion of management ability often blends into issues of leadership. For many, however, it is not a question of developing either leadership or management ability, but rather of recognising that both leadership and management are essential and must be present simultaneously. Indeed it is argued that the coexistence of both visionary leadership and sound management processes and practices is a defining feature of the best performing businesses.

From entrepreneur to leader

Nevertheless the evolution of business leadership is a relevant factor in business growth. Some growth models have been presented in Chapter 6 and implicit in them is a recognition that the role of the entrepreneur will and should change if the organisation is to grow successfully. This change is often described as moving from entrepreneur to (strategic) leader. For many this is not an easy transition and, the more rapid the growth, the more difficult it is.

In the early stages, the entrepreneur will play the key role in attracting resources such as money, people and customers. He or she must be the marketing, sales, finance operations and people manager all rolled into one. Responsibilities will quickly switch from the strategic to the operational as decisions on products and markets give way to replacing a faulty part on a machine or unblocking the drains. As the business grows, tasks will be differentiated. Not only will the qualities and the skills needed change but the application of the functional disciplines will change (see above). Roles become more specialised and delegation of responsibilities occurs. Greater formalisation is necessary while not giving way to a bureaucratic structure. The entrepreneur should relinquish participation in operational activities and concentrate on managing the business as a whole. He or she should put in place a management team and work as part of this team. Many entrepreneurs do not find the transition to a leadership role, where the development of the organisation is dependent on the development of the people within it, an easy one. This can be because of their lack of skills or their entrepreneurial character, which can reveal itself in a reluctance to relinquish control and share decision-making.

Kets de Vries contended that the typical entrepreneurial traits can lead to entrepreneurs seeking to exercise too much control over their businesses – becoming 'control freaks'.[8] This is less of an issue for a micro-business where the founders may do everything for themselves – indeed it is often essential. It is as the business grows that it becomes a problem which may constrain growth.

The Churchill and Lewis and other models in Chapter 6 seek to summarise the key factors which affect the success or failure of a business distinguishing between the attributes of the entrepreneur and resources. In essence, the challenge for the entrepreneur is to become the leader of a management team. Burns[9] identifies the following five elements as key to successful leadership:

- Having vision and ideas.
- Being able to undertake long-term strategic planning.
- Being able to communicate effectively.
- Creating an appropriate culture within the firm.
- Monitoring and controlling performance.

In conclusion

Many familiar with micro- and small-firm behaviour will recognise that the 'informal and intuitive' dominates over formal planning procedures and is at least equally effective – the existence of a business plan should not be confused with planning. The OECD reports in its study on globalising SMEs that 'successful small firms often do not rely on formal strategic planning although they are very conscious of what they want to achieve'.[10] Overall, however, it might be foolish to deny the significance to business growth of product and/or market-related decisions, cost/price decisions and constraint decisions (including time and finance) taken by a strategically aware management team, despite the absence of appropriate evidence. Barkham *et al.* found that four business aims stated by owner-managers were significantly associated with growth: expansion of profits, improving margins, having a marketing strategy and improving the production process.[11] It is interesting to note that a study of 179 super-growth companies in the United States resulted in the identification of five factors leading to a 'winning performance'.[12] These were:

- Competing on quality not prices.
- Domination of a market niche.
- Competing in an area of strength.

- Having tight financial and operating controls.
- Frequent product or service innovation.

Barkham *et al.*'s results indicate that it is the characteristics of the entrepreneur and the strategies he or she adopts which largely determine the growth of the small enterprise.[13] Company characteristics, including size, location and sector, appear to be influential but in a relatively minor way. To a large extent growth in small firms derives from the skills, values and motivations of the entrepreneur and the strategies adopted with regard to innovation, marketing and market research.

This approach to exploring small business growth by identifying the key management aims and/or actions reflects what Gibb and Davies described as an 'organisational development' approach, emphasising the development sequence of a firm as it passes through a series of stages in its life cycle.[14] (Some of these 'stages of growth' models are described in Chapter 6.) The different stages require different roles for the development of the business, as suggested in Table 12.2, which also draws a parallel between the management roles needed by a developing business and Maslow's hierarchy of needs – reflecting a possible change of emphasis from lower- to higher-order needs as a business matures.

The role of intention and motivation

A final issue to be considered in this review of the traditional view of business development is the part played by the owner's (or owners') intentions for the business. Intention is, for instance, clearly related to ambition, but there can be people who might have the ambition or desire to grow their business without ever clearly forming an intention so to do, and this is unlikely to lead to the desired result. Thus it has been suggested that growth ambition is best defined as wanting to, desire to or willingness to grow the business.[15]

It will also be apparent that the will or motivation to grow is important but by no means guarantees growth. Nevertheless a growth model that focuses on the individual entrepreneur as the key to the growth process must also take into account aspects of the individual's motivation, as well as other factors such as their traits, behaviour and resources.

However, even willingness and wanting to grow have slightly different meanings. Wanting to grow may imply a readiness to be somewhat more proactive to achieve growth. It is suggested that it can be helpful to divide attitudes to growth into separate categories:[16]

- **Proactive Growers.** These are seen as more actively seeking out opportunities. They explore different growth paths. They view the world through opportunistic lenses. They are believed to be less risk averse then average and to be more concerned with business profit rather than simply family income. It is suggested they are somewhat more likely to achieve growth.
- **Reactive Growers.** These are willing to grow but do not seek out opportunities. Growth requires an external trigger (e.g. by a customer, someone else's idea/push). They are more risk averse and concerned with a satisfactory income level.
- **Must Growers.** These are those who have to grow the business (or go out of business) because without growth the business is not viable. Hence this willingness to grow is driven by economics (e.g. minimum efficient scale) rather than anything to do with ambition.
- **Non-Growers.** Perhaps having reached a given size, these make a positive decision to grow the business no further.

Table 12.2 *The roles needed for business development at different stages*

Business stage	Related role	Maslow's hierarchy
Maturity	Leader	Self-actualisation
Expansion	↑	Esteem
Growth	Manager	Belonging
Survival	↑	Safety
Start-up	Entrepreneur	Physiological

⊃ | ## ILLUSTRATION 12.2 – MOTIVATION AND THE THEORY OF PLANNED BEHAVIOUR

Considerations of planned behaviour followed from the failure of trait theory to provide reliable predictors of behaviour. In theory personality traits, which might be defined as relatively enduring behavioural dispositions, should help to predict behaviour in a variety of different situations. Thus, for instance, it was suggested that individuals who cheat on their income tax are dishonest and might be supposed therefore to have a dishonesty trait which would lead them to be dishonest in other situations. Research has not found this to be the case, and people who do cheat on their taxes do not appear to be more likely than non tax-cheats to shoplift or to lie to their friends. Also personality traits might be supposed to be related to attitudes, but when attitudes are assessed through questionnaires they do not seem to correlate closely with observed behaviour.

The thinking behind the planned behaviour approach was not that traits are irrelevant, but that there are other factors which also influence behaviour. Ajzen, in developing his Theory of Planned Behaviour,[18] suggested that, of all the behavioural dispositions, it is intentions which are most closely linked to the corresponding actions. According to his theory a person's intentions are assumed to capture the motivational factors that have an influence on that person's behaviour. Those factors act directly to determine intentions which in turn affect actions and thus, although there is a connection between the factors and the actions, it is indirect. Further, intentions do not necessarily lead to immediate action, and intentions, once they are formed, initially remain as behavioural dispositions until, given an appropriate time and opportunity, they translate into actions.

Others who have explored this area in the context of business growth have concurred and suggest that ambition, motivation, aspirations and/or intent are linked and are good predictors of subsequent growth. As an example, Miner *et al.* looked at 59 technology innovative firms over a period of five years and found that the overall task motivation of their entrepreneurs was correlated with the success of their firms.[19]

Source: Based, in part, on S. Bridge, *Rethinking Enterprise Policy: Can Failure Trigger New Understanding?* (Basingstoke: Palgrave Macmillan, 2010) p. 207.

In this context it may also be relevant to note the suggestion by Storey that existing theories of new and small businesses do not capture their temporal diversity. They explain only those businesses which do grow and not those which decline, and they explain why some businesses have grown but don't forecast which ones will grow. Instead he suggests that business growth may be better seen as a combination of chance and optimism, with the latter factor being relevant because optimists are more likely to try again if, by chance, an earlier attempt does not succeed.[17]

THE OFFICIAL SUPPORT VIEW

As indicated in the section above and in Illustration 12.3, the view of business development held by many business support agencies and business advisers appears to be heavily biased towards the growth stage. If, as Chapter 14 explains, official support is often offered with the aim of securing growth, and if, as Chapter 8 indicates, that desire for business growth is also accompanied by a belief that businesses have some form of growth imperative, then the official view of businesses will often have a strong growth focus. It will concentrate more or less exclusively on businesses which are growing or might soon grow, or offer advice which is specifically designed to help them grow.

The adjustments required

However, most small business owners do not share this focus and, while they might like their businesses to earn more money or other benefits for them, they are not necessarily always trying to grow them.

ILLUSTRATION 12.3 – CRITERIA FOR ASSISTANCE

What follows illustrates how one business support agency, on its website and in its literature, made clear its assumptions and its criteria for supporting existing businesses:

Already in business: Our tailored solutions help you to grow your business.

If you've already been in business for a few years you'll be looking to take the next step to grow your business, improve profitability and exploit opportunities in markets outside Northern Ireland.

You will need to demonstrate that now, or over the next three years, your business will have:

— total sales of over £100,000 per year; and
— export sales greater than 25 per cent of turnover, or greater than £250,000 a year.

Source: Based on Invest NI criteria. Taken from www.investni.com (accessed 17 November 2011).

Therefore, if advisers are to relate better to their clients, they need to move outside the perspective of the 'professional' model and its supporting assumptions (see Chapter 8). Success will derive from being able to see the world and the business through the owner-manager's eyes – otherwise any support provided is likely to be inappropriate.

It is also valuable to recognise that a business is seen too often as the sum of its parts. When diagnosing its problems, therefore, there is a tendency to look for issues in its different aspects and components. Business owners are not inclined to see their businesses in that formulaic and/or templated way. They are much more likely to see a business as a whole – as a single and continuous process aiming cost-effectively to meet customer expectations. This different perspective also applies to some of the diagnostic tools that might be considered, as they are too often based upon formulaic business plan–based models.

Thus the official view tends to assume both a growth aim and the validity of rational diagnostic analysis, where the reality is that growth is often not the aim and a component-based diagnosis is not understood. It may be that small business owner-managers need to stand back a bit from a fixation with day-to-day immediate problems, to take a wider view and learn about generic problems and their resolution if they are to improve – but their advisers can assist the process by using, as the learning vehicle, a practical business issue/problem which the entrepreneur currently faces. As it is being resolved, the underlying theories and concepts can emerge and be understood so that they can be successfully transferred for application elsewhere. Bringing out the theory from resolving problems – starting with the specific and recognisable and moving to the general rather than the other way around – is much more readily comprehended and capable of ensuring engagement by the entrepreneur than the reverse.

Moreover, it is usually the case that owner-managers will only take purposeful and sustainable actions for significant change when they 'feel' the need to do so and when they genuinely accept ownership of the change process. Emotional involvement is essential. It is necessary, therefore, for any adviser to be sensitive to the extent of personal ownership that the owner-manager experiences towards any actions for change which he or she might suggest. To seek to pursue recommendations for change which do not engage the owner, no matter how logical or sensible they may seem, will lead too often to superficial assent but ultimately active or passive resistance, if not alienation. An effective approach taken towards intervention recognises the need to 'engage them in their world', the adviser working in harmony with the owner and his or her informed priorities, so gaining their confidence and increasing the likelihood of 'unwanted' changes being adopted. As has been observed:

The essential difference between emotion and reason is that emotion leads to action while reason leads to conclusions.[20]

THE OWNER'S VIEW

Chapter 6 summarises some current concepts and understanding about the process of small business development, but theory often appears to be of little relevance to practitioners because what they experience tends to be the pressure of subjective daily reality rather than the abstraction of objective analysis. Theory may try to explain what might be happening in a business, but that is very different from actually experiencing it, and although the theory may be helpful in finding longer-term solutions, often learning it will seem to be a distraction from the business of addressing immediate problems.

Herzberg suggested that in their working lives people experienced two sets of factors: hygiene factors, which, if not addressed, can lead to dissatisfaction, and motivator factors, which, if they are pursued, can lead to satisfaction.[21] Perhaps it might help to see the activity of managing a business as including the hygiene-like factors of day-to-day problems and the motivator-like factors of achieving the aims of the business, but with the 'hygiene'-like factors often seeming to predominate.

That does not mean, however, that the only relevant help for small business managers should focus on solving the immediate day-to-day issues. Often such day-to-day issues arise because of longer-term factors which have to be addressed if the shorter-term issues are not constantly to re-occur. Those trying to manage a business will do better therefore if they both understand the nature of the problems they are likely to encounter and appreciate that they probably need to acquire, or otherwise have access to, the requisite business skills and knowledge.

Chapter 8 introduced the analogy of a glider for the process of launching and then sustaining the progress of a business. As well as illustrating the need for external help to launch the venture, this analogy also indicates the need, even in favourable conditions, for the pilot to have sufficient skill to sustain the glider's flight once launched. The difference is that, while very few people would attempt a solo flight in a glider alone before they had received any training, many people will launch a business first and worry about controlling it later.

All that, however, presupposes that business owners know what they want of their ventures and/or where they want it to take them.

What do business owners want of their businesses?

> If growth of any kind is to be achieved it is important for the entrepreneur to be clear about their ambition for the business. Do they want to run a nice lifestyle business that could give them a good living for 20 years? Do they want to build the business up rapidly to sell it within five to ten years? Or do they want to build it piece by piece over time to pass it on? There is nothing wrong with any of these ambitions. They each can give the entrepreneur guidance on what risks they should be prepared to take and what they need to do to be successful in terms of the ambition they have for the business.
>
> Chris Gorman (Portfolio Entrepreneur)[22]

As noted above, business owners do not necessarily think in terms of the stages of development outlined at the beginning of this chapter. It is relevant, nevertheless, once their businesses are up and running, for them to ask themselves what they now want of them and what they need to do to get it. As also explained, it has often been assumed that business owners want to grow their businesses and that growth, or at least trying to grow, is the normal state. As Storey reports, however, the reality is that over time the typical business contracts rather than grows.[23]

Storey is reporting what actually happens, but not what was hoped for by the relevant business owners. While it does not seem credible that all business owners want their businesses to contract, it is equally incredible that they all want them to grow, especially if growth has undesirable trade-offs such as the need for a great input of time or money into the business or a greater risk of loss (see Illustration 12.4). Because he was not in a position to establish what the businesses covered by the surveys were actually trying to do, it is not possible to say to what extent the performance he observed was in line with the owners' requirements and/or expectations.

Similarly Storey suggests that the facts of business performance support the assumption that 'the outcome of business ownership is strongly influenced by chance'. However, he adds, the evidence does not appear to support the assumption that, in second and subsequent attempts to start businesses, 'business performance is enhanced by owner learning'[24] because there does not appear to be any overall improvement in business performance:[25]

> Do those with prior business experience perform better either than novices or better than they did previously as a business owner? The answer from large datasets is No to both questions.[26]

However, while Storey does not find support for the assumption that business owners do learn from experience, that does not mean that they cannot learn. In other words what appears to be an indication that business performance is not improved by owner learning could be because most owners do not try to learn how to improve their businesses rather than because they are unable to learn in a useful way. It could also be that the owners do learn in some relevant dimensions (see Table 6.4) but not all of them.

What can business owners do?

It has been suggested that the key constraints on business growth by micro-entrepreneurs are a lack of business skills, a lack of adequate information and a lack of money.[28] They are probably the needs that are most likely to apply to a struggling small business at any stage and may help to indicate what those entrepreneurs might do to improve their position.

Acquiring skills

It might seem that skills, information and money are three keys things that official supporters of small businesses most often seek to provide, or at least in some way to make available, at least for the growth businesses they try sometimes to target. However, again a failure to understand the reality of small business life can lead to such support failing to engage properly with small business owners. In the case of skills, for instance, there are a number of ways in which small business can avail of the business skills they need: the owner-managers can endeavour to acquire the skills themselves by learning them; they can seek to find partners, advisers or mentors with the skills that are needed; they can try to bring the skills in-house by hiring employees with the appropriate skills; and they can try to use the services of relevant consultants.

Those options do not, however, often appear to be stated or analysed, and the assistance advertised often seems to assume which option will be followed – such as when management training schemes

---

ILLUSTRATION 12.4 – WHY BUSINESS OWNERS MIGHT NOT WANT TO GROW THEIR BUSINESSES

Some studies, such as that by Wiklund *et al.*,[27] have examined the attitudes of business owner-managers towards growth and found that individuals do not share the same view on the effects or consequences of growth and often they do not want to grow. The apparent reasons for this can include:

- While many believe that growth would have a neutral or positive effect on their income, some believe it would have a negative effect.
- Some believe growth would have a negative effect on other aspects of their business, including on its 'atmosphere', on their control of the business, on their independence and on issues such as their expected workload and the stability of the business.
- In the majority of cases, even those who think that growth would have a positive effect on their income think that this is not the important factor. They perceive that the negative consequences of growth would outweigh the positive benefits.

⊃ | **ILLUSTRATION 12.5 – HOW OWNERS LEARN**

Just as theoretically trained advisers and consultants tend to see a business as the sum of its parts, so trainers can see business skills as having a number of components which can be taught separately. However, a small business person with a problem can be like a medical patient experiencing a pain. Such a patient usually wants to stop the pain as soon as possible and does not want to have to learn about the different aspects of medicine first. Thus much teaching has been unhelpful because it has started with separate components – such as marketing, operations management, finance, book-keeping, etc. – before seeing how they might be put together to address problems.

There is evidence that many business owners learn best, not from theoretical abstractions, but from practical examples – from relevant case studies and stories which relate to the business as a whole and which might then justify and show the need for some subject theory.

So the owner is likely to see problems, not concepts, but may need to learn something about the concepts in order to resolve the problems. Nevertheless training which recognises the likely mindsets of owners is more likely to be effective than training based on a theoretical division of the matter into its separate component parts.

are launched or management salary grants offered. Indeed, often when training is offered there seems to be confusion about what sort of training is appropriate, whether it is training in functional knowledge and skills, or strategic and leadership development, for example, and how it is best delivered (see Illustration 12.5).

Finding information

Gaining access to relevant information can be one of the key components of social capital (see Chapter 13), but often official sources of help seem to concentrate on supplying the information, rather than on showing business owners how to find it for themselves by developing and using appropriate contacts. Further the official sources of information may not always come with an appropriate cautionary advice and may therefore be given undue weight by those encouraged to rely on them.

However, when seeking external guidance, especially from formal sources, the use of language can be a problem. There is inevitably a tendency by those who have been formally or officially taught to use 'technical' language which may convey a distinct meaning in academic and/or professional circles but may not be understood in practical business circles. Terms such as 'marketing strategies' may be in regular use by consultants but may mean little to the small business person.

Sourcing money

In Chapter 15 there is a section which describes why financial support often forms a key part of the assistance made available to small businesses. There are strongly held views on this issue, with the relationship between banks and small businesses under strain and scrutiny for some time.

On the one hand, it is contended that it is not primarily a supply-side problem and that there is no overall shortage of finance (except perhaps as a consequence of the banking collapse in some Western countries in the last decade) and instead the issue is about the appropriate means of focusing that finance and avoiding an over-reliance on overdrafts and security-based lending.

On the other hand, there are those who support the view that any problems that may arise lie on the demand-side. They will point to the failure of business owners to give sufficient thought to how best to approach banks and make the case for additional finance. It is also pointed out that owners of under-capitalised businesses are often reluctant to dilute their equity stake – the price to be paid usually for the involvement of business angels or venture capitalists.

While the UK has introduced a wide variety of government-inspired funding initiatives (see Chapter 15), it remains the case that too often they remain unknown or unused by their target market due to inadequate communication of their existence and/or what are perceived as overly bureaucratic application procedures followed by overly lengthy decision-making periods. The problem of effective two-way communication is not assisted by the failure of those working with small businesses such as bankers, accountants and advisers to keep abreast of support initiatives.

For a small business owner seeking finance, it is important to remember that there is no right to funding and it will only be provided if the funder also benefits from the transaction. Therefore two pieces of preparation can be important:

- Finding out what are the relevant sources of finance and understanding what they are looking for as a return from their funds.
- Becoming 'investor ready' and able to 'sell' the proposal by communicating the key points of the funding proposition (and that is one area where a formal business plan can help).

IMPLICATIONS

Official policy often seeks to encourage more business start-ups, and so support is provided for start-ups even if, as suggested in Chapter 11, it is not necessarily always the best or most appropriate support. Nevertheless for start-ups support in some form, even if only through guide books and websites, is relatively widely available.

The same does not apply to existing businesses. Less attention seems to be given to them – as if start-up was seen to be the difficult bit and after that they can be left to their own devices. The official policy for existing businesses is generally to encourage them to grow, not least through exporting, and so the officially available information is very growth focused. For those business owners who do not aspire to grow their businesses, therefore, the reality is often that there is little understanding of the issues they face and little help is available to them.

If this chapter is not as clear, or as definitive, as some others, that may be because this area of small business activity has received less attention than other aspects. There is less understanding and there are fewer theories to report. However, this chapter does challenge some aspects of the traditional view on running businesses. In particular it questions the emphasis on business growth as if that were, or should be, the aspiration of most businesses. It suggests that, while a 'professional' approach to diagnosing business problems might produce a correct diagnosis, it may not help to communicate to a business owner what he or she should do.

Such issues mean that there is often a lack of available and relevant support for many businesses. There is, of course, no absolute requirement that all businesses should be offered help, or should seek it. However, if those trying to offer help fail to share the business owners' perspective, and if business owners fail to accept the need for some longer-term analysis and thinking, it may mean that many small businesses will fail to deliver as much benefit as either their owners or their supporters would like.

☛ THE KEY POINTS OF CHAPTER 12

- Business can go through a number of different stages between start-up and eventual closure. Because of an apparent assumption of a growth imperative and/or a desire for the economic benefits of business growth, most observers and supporters tend to focus on the growth stage.
- Official support in particular tends to be growth focused.
- Often business owners are not aiming to grow their businesses, especially if it involves extra effort, money and risk without sufficient compensatory benefits. Nevertheless they often face real problems in their businesses.
- Small business owners tend to see their businesses holistically, and not as a collection of functional departments as advisers are prone to do. This can lead to misconceptions in understanding how to interpret the causes of, and solutions to, problems.

- Small business owners tend to learn by moving from problem to conceptualization and not vice versa. Problem- or issue-based approaches will tend to engage their interest much more than traditional academic approaches.
- This difference of aims and perspectives may help to explain why many small business owners think there is little meaningful support from agencies.

✓   QUESTIONS, EXERCISES, ESSAY AND DISCUSSION TOPICS

- Are there relatively simple things that could be done to support existing businesses?

- What single extra piece of assistance would be of most benefit to established businesses?

- Would it be worthwhile to provide publicly funded support for businesses which are not planning to grow?

- What assistance do you think should be made available to established businesses – and why would that be justified?

- Could business owners and the advisory network ever see eye-to-eye? And, if so, what could be done to facilitate that communication?

REFERENCES

[1] D. Smallbone and P. Wyer, 'Growth and Development in the Small Firm', in S. Carter and D. Jones-Evans (eds), *Enterprise and Small Business: Principles, Practice and Policy* (London: Financial Times/Prentice Hall, 2000) p. 410.

[2] European Network for SME Research, *The European Observatory for SMEs: First Annual Report* (Zoetermeer: EIM Small Business Research and Consultancy, 1993) p. 24.

[3] D. J. Storey, *Understanding the Small Business Sector* (London: Routledge, 1994) pp. 144–154.

[4] OECD, *Small and Medium-Sized Enterprises: Technology and Competitiveness* (Paris: OECD, 1993) p. 21.

[5] CBI, *Managing to Grow* (London: CBI, December 1995) p. 11.

[6] Based on R. E. Boyatzis, *The Competent Manager: A Model for Effective Performance* (New York, NY: Wiley, 1982).

[7] See, for instance, E. Sirolli, *Ripples from the Zambezi* (Gabriola Island: New Society Publishers, 2005) p. 92.

[8] M. F. R. Kets de Vries, 'The Dark Side of Entrepreneurship', *Harvard Business Review*, Vol. 63, No. 6, 1985, pp. 160–167.

[9] P. Burns, *Entrepreneurship and Small Business* (Basingstoke: Palgrave Macmillan, 2011) pp. 441–442.

[10] OECD, *Small and Medium-Sized Enterprises*, Op. Cit. p. 9.

[11] R. Barkham, E. Hanvey and M. Hart, *The Role of the Entrepreneur in Small Firm Growth* (Belfast: NIERC, 1995) pp. 16, 39.

[12] Quoted in P. Burns, *Entrepreneurship and Small Business* (Basingstoke: Palgrave (now Palgrave Macmillan), 2001) p. 272.

[13] Barkham *et al.*, Op. Cit. pp. 15–18.

[14] A. Gibb and L. Davies, 'In Pursuit of Frameworks for the Development of Growth Models of the Small Business', *International Small Business Journal*, Vol. 9, No. 1, 1990, pp. 15–31.

[15] R. Hakkert and R. C. M. Kemp, *An Ambition to Grow* (Zoetermeer: EIM, 2006).

[16] Based on Ibid. pp. 27–28.

[17] D. J. Storey, 'Optimism and Chance: The Elephants in the Entrepreneurship Room', *International Small Business Journal*, Vol. 29, No. 4, 2001, pp. 303–321.

[18] See, for instance, I. Ajzen, 'Attitudes, Traits, and Actions: Dispositional Prediction of Behaviour in Personality and Social Psychology', *Advances in Experimental Social Psychology*, Vol. 20, 1987, pp. 1–63.

[19] J. B. Miner, N. R. Smith and J. S. Bracker, 'Role of Entrepreneurial Task Motivation in the Growth of Technological Innovative Firms: Interpretation of Follow-Up Data', *Journal of Applied Psychology*, Vol. 79, No. 4, 1994, pp. 627–630.

[20] D. Calne, Donald Calne, Wikipedia (accessed 2 August 2011).

[21] F. I. Herzberg, 'One More Time: How Do You Motivate Employees?', *Harvard Business Review*, Vol. 65, No. 5, September/October 1987, pp. 109–120.

[22] Chris Gorman, Lecture to University of Stirling students, 2006.

[23] D. J. Storey, 'Optimism and Chance: The Elephants in the Entrepreneurship Room', Op. Cit. p. 304.

[24] Ibid. pp. 312, 315.

[25] See also V. Rocha, A. Carneiro and C. A. Varum, 'Serial Entrepreneurship, Learning by Doing and Self Esteem', *International Journal of Industrial Organisation*, Vol. 40, 2015, pp. 91–106.

[26] D. Storey, personal communication to the authors, 19 January 2016.

[27] J. Wiklund, P. Davidsson and F. Delmar, 'What Do They Think and Feel about Growth? An Expectancy–Value Approach to Small Business Managers' Attitudes toward Growth', *Enterprise Theory and Practice*, Vol. 27, No. 3, 2003, pp. 247–270.

[28] R. Chandy and O. Narasimhan, 'How Micro-Entrepreneurs Could Change the World', *Business Strategy Review: Special Edition 2011* (London: London Business School, 2011).

Companion website

Please visit the companion website at www.palgravehighered.com/Bridge-UE-5e for access to additional learning and teaching materials.

PART 2

Social Capital and the Enterprise Mix

CONTENTS

- Introduction
- Our evolving understanding of social capital
- Social capital and enterprise
- The nature of social capital
- Suggestions for a 'vitamin' model
- The implications for entrepreneurs
- What next?

KEY CONCEPTS

This chapter covers:

- Why social capital has been overlooked and what it is now understood to be.
- The relevance of social capital to enterprise and entrepreneurs.
- The nature, and different forms, of social capital.
- The theory that social capital might be considered to be like vitamins in that its different forms each have different applications which cannot be substituted for by other forms, and why it is helpful, therefore, to find the particular form(s) needed for a particular application.
- Some guidance on how to acquire and/or develop social capital.

LEARNING OBJECTIVES

By the end of this chapter the reader should:

- Understand what social capital is and why its relevance may have been overlooked.
- Appreciate the relevance of social capital.
- Understand the 'vitamin' theory about the nature of social capital and, in particular, of its different forms, and why it is advantageous to know which forms are needed for a particular application.
- Understand how social capital can be acquired and/or developed.

INTRODUCTION

Social capital might be described as the overlooked component in the enterprise mix because, despite its importance, it rarely features in things like enterprise training and business plans. Some people may associate social capital particularly with social enterprises (see Chapter 7) but the reality is that it is very relevant to almost all businesses. However, possibly because it is not as tangible as other 'capitals', it has often been ignored. This chapter seeks to correct that omission.

Adam Smith's identification of the 'component parts of price' is mentioned in Chapters 2 and 8. According to Smith the price of every commodity 'resolves itself immediately or ultimately into the same three parts of rent, labour and profit',[1] and it seems to have been from such considerations that economists have traditionally identified three main factors of production:

- Labour/human resources.
- Natural resources: land and raw materials.
- Manufactured resources.[2]

Those factors are now sometimes labelled 'capitals', and, since Smith's day, other factors have been suggested for inclusion in the list. Thus the manufactured resources are now sometimes called 'fixed' or 'physical capital', or 'working capital' if they consist of stocks of finished or part-finished goods, and 'financial capital' is recognised as the money invested, or available for investment, in the business. Chapter 8 introduces the DFID (Department for International Development) model, which suggests five different types of capital, including social capital (see Figure 8.1). More recently other capitals have been suggested such as 'knowledge capital' and 'intellectual capital'; with the former referring to the skills and knowledge and the latter to, *inter alia,* copyrights and patents which help to protect parts of this knowledge from use by other businesses. Also, as Chapter 9 notes, the addition of 'entrepreneurship capital' has been suggested. It appears to be related to social capital but it seems to be less easy to pin down what entrepreneurship capital and social capital cover and what the relationship is between them, possibly because their meanings are still evolving.

Just as, if they are to thrive, people need food – which is a mixture of components such as proteins, carbohydrates, fats, fibres and vitamins – so businesses, whether they are starting or running, need a mixture of capitals. Chapters 11 and 12 look at some of the issues involved in actually starting or running a small business – so why should they be followed by a chapter devoted just to social capital? Of the capitals described, all businesses, new or established, need some financial capital and most of them need to use some form of physical capital. All of them also need human capital, even if it is only the skills and/or knowledge of their owners, and many depend on or use natural capital. Although these capitals are important, social capital has been selected for special treatment in this chapter for the following reasons:

- Human beings are essentially social animals, and social capital, or at least aspects of it, is very relevant to business as a human activity. For instance Chapters 8 and 9 both emphasise that starting and running small businesses are activities performed by people who are generally much more influenced by perceived social pressures than by logic, and the model in Figure 8.1 itself suggests that social capital must be included in any list of relevant factors.
- A case can be made that social capital is the least well understood of the five capitals covered in Figure 8.1. There is still debate about its nature and it appears to lack a single, clear and widely accepted definition.
- Possibly because of this lack of clarity about its nature, social capital is often not covered in business assessments (for instance it is not a defined section in the standard business plan format) – so often a lack of it may not be identified as an issue.
- If and when a lack of social capital is diagnosed as a problem, there are few sources of assistance in finding, acquiring and/or accessing it. If financial (and physical) capital is needed there are sources of assistance such as banks, venture capitalists and even development agencies and grant schemes; if help is needed in acquiring and/or building aspects of human capital there are training providers, employment agencies and HR consultants. But who provides, or helps people to access, social capital?

So, although social capital is important, it does not often feature in formal business assessments, and if business owners need it, they probably have to identify and remedy the problem themselves. Understanding what social capital is and how to access and apply its various aspects is often at least as important as knowing how to find and use the other capitals which are often perceived to be in the enterprise mix, not least because those others are much more likely to be covered by assistance agencies and business guides.

OUR EVOLVING UNDERSTANDING OF SOCIAL CAPITAL

Although it refers to a long-standing aspect of human relationships, social capital is, if not a new concept, at least a relatively new label. The first recorded mention of the term is ascribed to Hanifan in 1916,[3] but the key promoters of the concept have been people like Pierre Bourdieu, James Coleman and Robert Putnam who published mainly in the last quarter of the 20th century. However, their work has not produced a uniform understanding of what social capital is.

Bourdieu, for instance, defined social capital as 'the aggregate of the actual or potential resources which are linked to possession of a durable network of more or less institutionalized relationships of mutual acquaintance or recognition'.[4] He connected social capital to both cultural and material economic assets and to links between individuals, between institutions, and between individuals and institutions. This suggests that it has two dimensions:

- First, it is a resource that is connected to group membership and social networks, and the volume of social capital possessed by an individual depends on the size of the network created; and
- Second, it is about the quality of these relationships and especially the capacity of the groups to mobilise resources in their own interests.[5]

Coleman also saw different aspects in social capital which, according to him:

is defined by its function. It is not a single entity, but a variety of different entities having two characteristics in common: They all consist of some aspect of social structure, and they facilitate certain actions of individuals who are within the structure.[6]

He added that:

like physical capital and human capital, social capital is not completely fungible, but is fungible with respect to specific activities. A given form of social capital that is valuable in facilitating certain actions may be useless or even harmful in others.[7]

Few seem to have done more to highlight the value of social capital as a concept than Putman, and in much of his writing he appears to treat social capital as sufficiently homogeneous as to constitute a single dimension. He has defined it as 'the networks, norms and trust that enable participants to act together to effectively pursue shared objectives'.[8] In his influential book, *Bowling Alone,* which was published in 2000 following an earlier article with the same name, he talks of social capital as 'social networks and the associated norms of reciprocity [which come] in many different shapes and sizes with many different uses',[9] and he refers to a growing body of evidence that such civic connections 'make us healthy, wealthy and wise'.[10] Social capital, he suggests:

- 'Allows citizens to resolve collective problems more easily.'
- 'Greases the wheels that allow communities to advance smoothly.'
- 'Widens our awareness of the many ways in which our fates are linked.'[11]

In *Bowling Alone* Putnam measures the average level of social capital in the different states of America by compiling a single 'index of social capital' from a number of independent measures, but he states that:

These fourteen indicators of formal and informal community networks and social trust are in turn sufficiently intercorrelated that they appear to tap a single underlying dimension. In other words, these fourteen indicators measure related but distinct facets of community-based social capital, and we have combined them into a single Social Capital Index.[12]

○ | **ILLUSTRATION 13.1 – THE POWER OF SOCIAL CAPITAL – A SINGLE-DIMENSION VIEW**

In his book *Outliers,* under the heading of 'The Roseto Mystery', Gladwell describes the town of Roseto in Pennsylvania and the puzzle, which became apparent in the 1950s, of why it had significantly better levels of health than the USA as a whole, including having roughly half the average death rate from heart disease than that of neighbouring towns. This could not be accounted for by factors such as smoking, diet or exercise as, in these respects, the practices of the people of Roseto did not seem to be significantly different from those of their neighbours.

Halpern, among others, has reported the deduction that the reason for the good health of the inhabitants of Roseto was the nature of the relationships within that community. Roseto was named after a town in Italy from which the ancestors of many of its residents had once come, and the relationships between the residents were still like those of the Italian town and very different from those of neighbouring towns in Pennsylvania. People in Roseto talked more to their neighbours, they still often had three generations living together, they attended church regularly and there were at least 22 civic organisations in a town of just under 2000 people. In other words it was Roseto's social capital in the form of the totality of their personal relationships which made its citizens healthier.

Sources: M. Gladwell, *Outliers* (London: Allen Lane, 2008) and D. Halpern, *Social Capital* (Cambridge: Polity Press, 2005).

He uses this single index to indicate a correlation between the level of social capital and aspects of the fabric of social life such as the level of crime, the level of child welfare, the equality of income distribution and the level of civic equality. Thus, in order to show the effects of social capital, Putnam assumes the validity of a single-dimensional index as if, despite 'the different shapes and sizes' of social capital, they all ultimately contribute to the same effect. In that case, each variety of social capital must either be fungible – that is capable of mutual substitution – or be so closely linked to other varieties of social capital that they are interdependent. However, in the same book Putnam acknowledges that this is not always the case when he describes the differences between bonding and bridging social capital, because he states that 'some kinds of bonding social capital may discourage the formation of bridging social capital and vice versa'.[13]

Other authors have added to the confusion about the nature of social capital but, in view of its relative newness as a concept, it may not be surprising that no single clear, widely accepted description seems to have been established. Schuller *et al.* have commented, for instance, that 'the relative immaturity of social capital as a concept ... (and its) rapid proliferation has allowed a diversity of approach' and, in summary, they suggest that:

> Social capital has several adolescent characteristics: it is neither tidy nor mature; it can be abused, analytically and politically; its future is unpredictable; but it offers much promise.[14]

So while few deny that social capital exists, when it comes to defining it and determining what it does and whether all its forms are fungible, there is still considerable disagreement. That does not mean that it is not an important and useful concept. Because human beings are social animals, it is clear that in their activities, including business activity, social relationships matter:

> The durability of social capital in the vocabulary of the social sciences does not, therefore, depend on people agreeing on a single and unequivocal definition, but in the way in which different researchers can profitably make use of it as an intellectual tool, giving us a grip on the world we inhabit.[15]

PART 2

SOCIAL CAPITAL AND ENTERPRISE

Putnam and many of the others who promoted the concept of social capital have highlighted its relevance to a range of social issues and thus to how we live our lives. Consistent with the view that enterprise is itself a part of life, rather than something separate from it, the relevance of social capital to entrepreneurs and business has also been identified, although it has not always been called 'social capital'. For instance over 30 years ago an examination of new ventures observed that 'as the venture evolved it became apparent that "who you know" was as important as "what you know"' and that 'the key to developing support appeared to lie in the strategies used by entrepreneurs to develop rapport with their network contacts'.[16] Thus 'networking' was recognised as an important need for business start-up – as Figure 13.1, which represents a model used at the time, indicates.

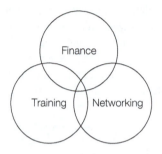

Figure 13.1 *The perceived key business start-up needs (circa 1985)*

Source: S. Bridge, *Rethinking Enterprise Policy* (Basingstoke: Palgrave Macmillan, 2010) p. 39.

It was also in the 1980s that Peterson and Rondstadt identified the importance for entrepreneurial endeavour of what they called 'know-who' and indicated this in their formula: 'Entrepreneurial Success = New Venture Idea + Entrepreneurial Know-how + Entrepreneurial Know-who'.[17]

Since then Fukuyama, in his book *Trust,* has identified trust between people not linked by family relationships as a key factor in economic development. He suggests that this trust is needed for enterprises to develop and that 'it would appear to be no accident that three high-trust societies, Japan, Germany and the United States, pioneered the development of large-scale, professionally managed enterprises'.[18] More recently still, Harford, when considering some countries which have very under-developed economies, has taken Cameroon as an example and observed that:

> We still don't have a good word to describe what is missing ... but we are starting to understand what it is. Some people call it 'social capital', or maybe 'trust'. Others call it 'the rule of law', or 'institutions'. But these are just labels. The problem is that Cameroon, like other poor countries, is a topsy-turvy world in which it's in most people's interest to take action that directly or indirectly damages everyone else.[19]

Thus, through terminology such as 'networking', 'know-who', and 'trust', the concept of social capital, which was developed primarily for other disciplines, is being applied to enterprise. Svendsen and Svendsen, for instance, even define social capital as 'the presence of entrepreneurship and trust in a society',[20] and in 2007 the *International Small Business Journal* dedicated an entire edition (Vol. 25, No. 3) to the connection between social capital and entrepreneurship. In their introduction to this edition, Cope *et al.* start by acknowledging that, although the concept of social capital is widely used in the social sciences, its precise meaning is elusive. Nevertheless they point out that, 'since the 1980s, ... the importance of social contacts and networks to entrepreneurship and entrepreneurial performance has been more widely recognised' and that 'relationships clearly matter to entrepreneurs but understanding how they function requires an appreciation of social capital'.[21] Casson and Della Giusta argue that different types of networks are needed to support entrepreneurial activity at different stages of development and these are evident at the local, regional, national or global level.[22] The other contributions also value the quality of networks and relationships as a resource and asset which could help to explain the performance of entrepreneurs.

The edition includes reviews of relevant books and its contents serve to demonstrate that, although there is no single widely accepted definition of social capital or even agreement on just what it entails, it is increasingly being recognised as an important factor in enterprise.

Entrepreneurship capital

It was Audretsch and Keilbach who proposed that 'entrepreneurship capital' should be added to the list of factors which drive economic growth. They acknowledge that there is a large and compelling literature which has emerged linking social capital to entrepreneurship, but they suggest that what has been referred to in this literature as social capital may actually be a more specific sub-component which they call 'entrepreneurship capital'. They emphasise that entrepreneurship capital should not be equated to social capital and that:

> The major distinction is that, in our view, not all social capital may be conducive to economic performance, let alone entrepreneurial activity. Some types of social capital may be more focused on preserving the status quo and not necessarily directed at creating challenges to the status quo. By contrast, entrepreneurship capital could be considered to constitute one particular sub-set of social capital. While social capital may have various impacts on entrepreneurs, depending on the specific orientation, entrepreneurship capital, by its very definition, will have a positive impact on entrepreneurial activity.[23]

Using the number of start-up businesses in a region relative to its population as an indicator of the level of entrepreneurial capital, Audretsch and Keilbach found that in Germany there is a positive link between entrepreneurship capital and regional economic performance, measured by labour productivity. However, they reported that their findings do not enable them to shed any light on what exactly constitutes entrepreneurship capital, although they speculate that it 'would include a broad spectrum of institutions, policies, historical, social and cultural traditions, as well as personal characteristics associated with the particular region'.[24] Subsequently Audretsch and others have described entrepreneurship capital as 'a milieu of agents and institutions conducive to the creation of new firms ... such as social acceptance of entrepreneurial behaviour, individuals willing to deal with the risk of creating new firms, and the activity of bankers and venture capital agents willing to share risks and benefits'.[25]

This introduction of the concept of entrepreneurial capital is not therefore an attempt to re-label or replace social capital but instead a suggestion that there is a sub-set of social capital which, unlike some other types of social capital, has a very positive effect on entrepreneurial activity.

THE NATURE OF SOCIAL CAPITAL

The suggestion that entrepreneurship capital is a sub-set, or sub-component, of social capital and that it has different properties from those of other sub-components, implies that social capital is not a single factor but more a collection of components or factors with distinct effects.

At least some early writings about social capital seem to have implied that although it might have different forms or components, those forms all had similar effects and could all be treated therefore as being part of one factor. This, for instance, is the view of social capital taken in Illustration 13.1, which assumes that the effect of social capital is proportional to the total amount of it, and therefore increasing the total amount will increase the effect. Attempts to measure the amount of social capital thus depend on the assumption made about its nature. In *Bowling Alone* Putnam describes how he produced a single-dimensional index of social capital by combining different aspects of social capital to produce a single meaningful total. However, as noted earlier, in the same book, he indicates that bonding and bridging are forms of social capital that cannot meaningfully be included in one total. Additionally, in

Table 13.1 *The 'Conscise' project and the elements of social capital*

The 'Conscise' project attempted to identify the elements of social capital. It encapsulated the key parts of various definitions of social capital under six headings and then suggested that these six elements themselves fell into three categories:

Headings	Categories
Trust	Trust, social networks and reciprocity/mutuality are about relationships between individuals and organisations.
Formal and informal social networks	
Reciprocity and mutuality	
Shared norms of behaviour	Shared norms of behaviour and shared commitment and belonging are about more than one individual and/or organisation sharing values and ways of thinking.
Shared commitment and belonging	
Effective information channels	Effective information channels permit individuals and organisations to access information from outside and within their community.

Source: Based on A. Kay, 'Social Capital in Building the Social Economy', in R. Pearce, *Social Enterprise in Anytown* (London: Calouste Gulbenkian Foundation, 2003) p. 74–75.

their introduction to *Democracies in Flux*, Putnam and Goss, after alluding to the debate about whether physical capital was sufficiently homogeneous to be added up in a single ledger, comment that 'a dentist's drill, a carpenter's drill, and an oil rigger's drill are all examples of physical capital, but they are hardly interchangeable'. They then state that: 'The same is true of social capital – it comes in many forms that are useful in many different contexts, but the forms are heterogeneous in the sense that they are good only for certain purposes and not others'.[26] Coleman also suggested that social capital is not completely fungible,[27] and Table 13.1 and Illustrations 13.1 and 13.3 support this view because they too suggest that different forms can have different effects – in which the aggregate effect will not be proportional to an overall total. The irrelevance of a single total has also been emphasised by Smith:

> The notion of social capital is a useful one in evaluating the resources to be found in a place [but it is] totally impossible and probably misguided to reduce the concept of social capital in its many varied forms to a single measurable index.[28]

⊃ ILLUSTRATION 13.2 – THE POWER OF SOCIAL CAPITAL – A MULTI-DIMENSIONAL VIEW

Illustration 13.1 presents the case of Roseto as an example of a situation in which it is apparently claimed that social capital has a significant impact on the health of a town. The suggestion being that it was because Roseto had so much social capital, assessed on a single dimension, that its citizens were healthy.

A different example of the potential health impact of social capital has been described by Campbell.[29] According to her:

> health-related behaviours, such as smoking, diet, condom use, and exercise, are determined not only by conscious rational choice by individuals on the basis of good information, as traditional health educational approaches assumed, but also by the extent to which broader contextual factors support the performance of such behaviours.

In other words those health-related behaviours are socially influenced in that, for instance, we tend to smoke less if there is general social disapproval of the habit of smoking. However, in this case, what apparently matters is not simply the overall amount of social contact, as in the case of Roseto's health (see Illustration 13.1), but whether that social contact approves of smoking or not. Thus adding a set of social contacts who disapproved of smoking to a set of contacts who approved of, or at least tolerated, smoking, would not enhance this effect of the social capital and instead the different varieties would tend to cancel each other out. One part of the social capital would not be interchangeable with the other part, and Putnam's single-dimensional measurement methods would not be relevant in such a case.

Different forms of social capital

Although there is evidence that social capital has a variety of different forms or components, that does not mean that is it easy to list them. Entrepreneurship capital has been suggested as a component, or a sub-set of components. Bonding and bridging capital have already been mentioned, and linking capital can be added to that list. Illustration 13.3 describes an attempt to identify different components of social capital used in the start-up of a social enterprise which suggests at least five different non-substitutable aspects of social capital. The Conscise project (see Table 13.1) looked at different definitions of social capital to identify elements under six headings which fell into the three categories of trust and reciprocity, shared norms of behaviour, and effective information channels – and the five aspects from Illustration 13.3 between them cover at least four of the Conscise project's six headings and all of its three categories. Other contributions include that of Gibb who has identified 'abundant positive role images of successful independent businesses' as a key aspect of an enterprise culture[30] and Krueger who has suggested that 'perceived social norms' are a key influence (see Figure 4.1).

ILLUSTRATION 13.3 – IDENTIFYING DIFFERENT FORMS OF SOCIAL CAPITAL

The Old School in Holywood, County Down, was built in 1845 to provide a National School for the town. After about 30 years a bigger school was built, but the Old School was put to other uses including housing a local scout troop. It is one of the older surviving buildings in Holywood but, after about 160 years, its condition had deteriorated to the extent that it was no longer used by anyone and, although listed, was thought to be under threat of demolition. The Holywood Old School Preservation Trust was formed to save the building. In this it has had two objectives:

- A conservation objective, which is to retain as much as possible of the original fabric of the building and to conserve both its outward and inward appearance.
- A viability objective, which is to find a sustainable use, or mix of uses, for the building which would be both consistent with the conservation requirement and of direct benefit to the community in Holywood.

The Trust was incorporated as a company limited by guarantee in 2004 and accepted by the Inland Revenue as a charity for tax purposes. The Trustees first looked at the feasibility of a restoration project and established that the building could be restored and that it should then be able to raise enough income from its users to cover its operating costs. They decided therefore to proceed and next addressed the task of raising the money necessary for the restoration work. This took about two years. The restoration work itself took a further year to complete, and the completed building was finally handed over to the Trust in April 2008. Since then it has earned its keep by providing premises for a variety of community and local activities.

  Studying the process of forming and operating the Trust suggests that it included many examples of the application of social network resources, including the following:

(a) ***Contact within the local community.*** Within the local community there was a regard for the building and a clear appreciation of the need to do something to preserve it. This was also manifest in:
- Contacts between like-minded people willing to be involved by becoming trustees.
- Support from local schools for a logo designing competition.
- Support from the local printer who provided promotion leaflets.
- A good response to local fund-raising efforts.
- Identifying well-known local people to lend their support as patrons and several local artists who agreed to give sketches or paintings of key local buildings for an associated heritage education project.

(b) ***Contact outside the local community.*** Relevant contacts outside the local community included:
- Contact with other examples of building preservation trusts which had successfully restored old buildings for active use.
- The visit to a neighbouring building preservation trust which provided the Trustees with an understanding of what such a venture might involve and of its possible feasibility.
- A Trustee with experience of both sides of the grant system who thus knew how to communicate with grant-giving bodies.
- People to advise on which conservation architects to invite to bid for the task of being the Trust's professional advisers and how to specify and manage that tendering process.
- Obtaining advice from PR experts.

(c) ***Obtaining relevant information.*** Contacts which provided the Trustees with key relevant information included:
- A contact who was able to advise the Trustees on how much grant they might realistically ask for from a key funder.
- A contact who was able to advise the Trustees on a contract of employment and a staff handbook and who helped in the process of recruiting a caretaker.
- A contact who was able to provide the Trustees with an example of an 'invitation to tender' which allowed them to recruit professional advisers for the first stage of the process without precluding them from obtaining grants for their professional advice in the second stage of the process.

(d) ***Trust and vouching.*** The Trust was able to obtain an overdraft facility from a local bank branch without the need for personal guarantees. It is understood that the reputation several of the Trustees had established through personal banking at that branch helped the branch to vouch for their *bona fides* and credibility as Trustees.

(e) ***Encouragement of specific behaviours.*** Local approval was expressed in a number of ways for the formation of the Building Preservation Trust and for its attempts to save the building. This helped to reinforce the commitment of the Trustees to their task.

The analysis suggests that the interactions included in each of the five categories listed above were beneficial to the venture and do seem to be social capital or sub-components of social capital, as recognised by at least some commentators. However, at least four of the interactions appear to represent specific applications of social capital which are not transferable or substitutable for each other. For instance:

- Contacts within and contacts outside the local community were both valuable – but a shortage of one could not have been addressed by more of the other.
- Contacts which were able to provide specific information were very helpful and this could not have been found from general contacts whether within or outside the community.
- The trust established by the Trustees with the bank was dependent on their specific dealings with the bank. If they had not built up this reputation it could not have been provided in other ways.

Thus the study suggests that the Holywood Old School Preservation Trust benefited from a number of specific, non-substitutable aspects of social capital and that, if any of these had been missing, a general provision of more social capital of another sort may not necessarily have helped.

Source: Based on S. Bridge and S. Porter, 'Social Capital: Protein or Vitamins in the Enterprise Mix?', a paper presented at the *33rd ISBE National Small Firms Conference*, London 2010.

A link with social enterprise?

Several writers have looked at the relationship between social capital on the one hand and the social economy and social enterprise on the other. As it is suggested that social capital is a necessary factor for any enterprise, and as social enterprises are indeed enterprises, it should not be surprising that they too rely on social capital. However, possibly because they both contain the word 'social' in their labels, sometimes it seems to be assumed that there is some sort of special connection between social capital and social enterprise. Indeed, social enterprises are sometimes established to try to help disadvantaged people and/or communities, and a lack of social capital has sometimes been diagnosed as being a factor in that disadvantage. For instance:

> In terms of social capital, deprived neighbourhoods with relatively stable populations may have levels of intra-community 'bonding' social capital that are equal to, or above, that of more affluent districts. The downside of heavily bonded communities is an insular and exclusionary local culture which limits connections to external networks. There is often an absence of extra-community 'bridging' social capital, which connects different groups and individuals to a wider range of social networks that extend beyond their community.[31]

However, as noted by Bridge *et al.*,[32] there have been suggestions that the social economy has a particular potential to help disadvantaged communities through the mechanism of social capital. Such claims are summarised by Birch and Whittam, for instance, who report that:

> [Addressing] the lack of social networks, usually referred to as social capital, has been highlighted within both policy and academia as the main method to empower communities. The social economy is supposed to be a means to encourage the development of social capital by encouraging mutualism amongst communities through grass-roots empowerment based on 'active participation' and a 'stakeholder society'. In a somewhat circular conceptualisation, social entrepreneurship is supposed to provide the means to achieve this mutualism through the social economy.[33]

This claim, in effect, reduces to the two assumptions that for disadvantaged communities the key lack is often social capital and that the social economy creates social capital. From these two assumptions the conclusion is drawn that the social economy will help disadvantaged communities. Although the town of Holywood would not generally be considered to be disadvantaged, it may still be relevant to consider the extent to which the social enterprise described in Illustration 13.3 – the Holywood Old School Preservation Trust – created social capital or instead used the social capital which already existed in the town to achieve its objectives. As Bridge *et al.* suggest:

> All enterprises can create social capital, just as all businesses can create financial capital, but they can also lose it and generally they only create it when the conditions are particularly favourable. Examined in this way therefore the 'social economy helps disadvantage' claim does not seem to be particularly strong. Indeed a counter argument is that, just as financial capital is needed to start businesses, so too is social capital needed to start enterprises, including social enterprises and, as disadvantaged communities often lack social capital, they are not good places in which to start social enterprises.[34]

Social capital contradictions

This review of aspects of the nature of social capital suggests that there is a lot in common amongst the various statements that have been made about it, but also a number of uncertainties or contradictions. In particular there seems to be a lack of agreement about whether social capital is essentially one factor in development, or the collective name for a group of factors each of which have their own particular applications.

One issue complicating the situation is exemplified by the example of Roseto quoted in Illustration 13.1 because it found a correlation between social capital and a health effect, but not a clear mechanism for the connection between the two. The analysis of social capital quoted in Illustration 13.3 identified different conscious uses of social capital where the relevant contacts between people could be linked to each different effect. That, however, was not the case in Roseto where the inhabitants were not consciously using their social capital. Instead, according to Christakis and Fowler, behaviours can spread from person to person – a bit like germs – and behaviour can have a big effect on health.[35] 'When people are free to do as they please, they usually imitate each other',[36] and so if people associate with fat people, they become fat also. In this way, obesity is contagious.

SUGGESTIONS FOR A 'VITAMIN' MODEL

The introduction to this chapter suggests that the mixture of capitals needed for the development of an enterprise is rather like the mixture of food components such as proteins, carbohydrates, fats, fibres and vitamins needed in a healthy diet. Using the diet analogy, and following the example of Halpern,[37] Bridge has suggested that social capital acts in the enterprise mix like vitamins in a diet.[38] Vitamins are necessary if the body is to use the other components of a diet, but there are different vitamins which cannot be substituted one for another. Further, once enough of a vitamin is present, more is of no extra value; indeed, in excessive amounts, some vitamins can be poisonous. Studies such as that described in Illustration 13.3 indicate that social capital does have components which can be essential for enterprise but which cannot be substituted one for another. Further, once there is enough of a particular form of social capital, more is of no extra help.

An alternative view could be that, if the suggested components of social capital have different, non-fungible effects, then only one of those components is actually social capital and the rest are something else. That would maintain the position that social capital can be totalled validly into a single-dimension index, but it does not help in identifying the other components – which are still necessary for enterprise and have been identified as forms of social capital by many commentators.

Suggesting that social capital includes a variety of different non-fungible components does not actually make it different from many of the other suggested 'capitals'. While financial capital may be like protein in that if a business is short of financial capital, the different forms of shares, loans, overdrafts and seeking extended credit can all help to address the problem, those different forms can have different effects and conditions. Physical capital, as Putnam and Goss have pointed out, is often not fungible, and neither is human capital: skills and knowledge are specific in their application, and while some people can be given training in new skills and can acquire new knowledge, that takes time. Thus it would seem that different non-fungible forms of the 'capitals' are the norm and not the exception.

But, if this is the case with social capital and if, like vitamins in a diet, it comes in different forms from somewhat different sources and with different applications, does that contradict the one-dimensional index of social capital Putnam uses in *Bowling Alone*?[39] It might appear so – because different aspects working in different ways cannot usefully be all be added together in a one-dimensional measure. However, if, instead, what Putnam was measuring for his index was not the total amount of social capital itself, but the volume of the media through which it is acquired and exchanged, then his index would be consistent with a 'vitamin' model.

Applications

The vitamin model as an analogy for the role of social capital has a number of potentially relevant applications.

Identifying forms. Once the existence and role of vitamins was discovered it took quite a long time to identify all the different relevant vitamins. The first vitamin to be identified was Vitamin A in 1909, but Vitamin B_9 was not discovered until 1941. The naming of vitamins with a mixture of letters and numbers, with some renaming and some gaps in the series, is also a result of this prolonged discovery time with its occasional false leads and slowly revealed relationships. If social capital follows this example, then it might be expected that it will take some time for all its variations and components to be identified.

Addressing deficiencies. A protein deficiency can be addressed by adding more protein of any useable form, whereas a vitamin deficiency can be addressed only by identifying and supplying the specific vitamin which is missing. Could that difference also apply to the role of social capital in economic development? If development is being hindered by a lack of social capital, then it will be very important for policy-makers to know whether the protein analogy applies and the deficiency can be addressed by a general increase in social capital, or whether, instead, the vitamin analogy is more appropriate and only very specific forms of social capital will help.

The need for supplements. Most vitamins are normally present in a fresh-food diet, although some can come from other sources, for instance vitamin D can be synthesised in the body in sunlight. Thus experiences such as long ocean voyages with plenty of preserved food but without access to fresh fruit and vegetables resulted in deficiency diseases and thus led to the discovery of vitamins. In the case of capitals, could it be that other capitals often come with an element of social capital and it is only when these are provided in a refined, arm's-length form that any attached social capital is removed and thus needs to be supplemented? For instance recently some banks have been providing non-financial services to SME clients, which could be interpreted as an attempt to provide formally the social capital (advice and guidance) which had been provided informally by bank managers when funding requests were dealt with face-to-face at a local level.[40]

Enough is enough. Once enough of a vitamin is present in a diet, more of it adds no extra benefit. While extra financial, human and physical capital might be used by a business to enable it to grow more, once it has enough of the relevant forms of social capital, it does not need, and cannot use, more.

THE IMPLICATIONS FOR ENTREPRENEURS

So far this chapter has explored the evolution of the concept of social capital – but what does that mean for anyone involved in starting a new venture or running an existing one, or in trying to help or encourage either of those activities? The 'adolescent characteristics' of the concept of social capital have been acknowledged, which means that its nature is not yet completely established and some of its features may not yet be fully obvious. Nevertheless it is much too promising to ignore. Therefore, in seeking to draw from all this some lessons about social capital and its implications for enterprise in particular, this section makes some suggestions which are possibilities rather than proven fact.

Despite such reservations, the main conclusion to be drawn from all that has been said about social capital might be summarised as 'networks work'. This observation is applicable to both practising entrepreneurs and those seeking to advise or assist them. It acknowledges not only that in business, as in other aspects of life, human beings are social animals and connections amongst them are important and can deliver many benefits, but also that some of those connections are essential if thriving ventures are to be established and operated sustainably.

Understanding the nature and importance of those connections is likely to be very helpful therefore, even if they are not yet fully determined. Although it is clear, at least for its application to enterprise, that different aspects of social capital have different applications, all the different possible parts, and all their various applications, have not yet necessarily been identified. Nevertheless here is a possible list, based on an identification by Coleman of three forms of social capital: 'obligations and expectations, information channels and social norms'[41] (which are similar to the categories in Table 13.1 of trust, social networks, and reciprocity; effective information channels; and shared norms of behaviour).

Obligations and expectations. The concept of social capital embraces a set of mutual relationships between individuals and organisations based on established trust and which, depending on their nature, can deliver benefits such as:

- **Advocacy and mentoring**. Those who can vouch for a person or group or act as their advocates.
- **Introductions and links**. Those who can make introductions, such as to potential partners, suppliers or customers, or even become patrons themselves. This can also include introductions to people or groups with whom the subject might not normally come into social contact (bridging) or to people at different levels in status (linking).
- **Partnerships**. Those who can be partners in ventures, either formally or informally.
- **Other assistance**. People who are prepared to offer help or assistance: contributions in cash or kind varying from simple advice through to meaningful financial investment.
- **Bridging and linking**. Included in the above can be introductions made to people or groups with whom the subject might not normally come into social contact (bridging) or to people at different levels in status (linking).

Information channels. The links provided by aspects of social capital can help individuals and organisations to access information from within or from outside their organisations or communities. In a business context this information can include:

- Where to find things such as suppliers, customers or sources of finance.
- The requirements of particular markets or customers, or the legal requirements for certain activities.
- How to do things like word a contract, conduct a job interview, or write a funding application.
- To whom to go for advice or guidance on specific issues.

Social norms. A particularly strong aspect of social capital can be its ability to encourage individuals and/ or organisations to share values and ways of thinking including the imposition and/or reinforcement of commitments and/or norms of behaviour. This aspect of social capital can be seen, for instance, in a relatively mild form in the influence of role models and in a stronger form in the sort of 'society rules' which Baumol (see Chapter 3) suggests direct any entrepreneurial tendencies people have towards productive, unproductive or even destructive applications. It is this promotion of shared norms which features in Krueger's model (see Figure 4.2), and the peer influence which Bridge (see Chapter 9 and Figure 9.2) has suggested has a significant impact on whether people consider becoming an entrepreneur. This aspect of social capital can thus influence whether people start a new business or how they behave once they are in business. It features in Audretsch and Keilbach's entrepreneurship capital and it provides the 'social glue' (bonding) which can be found in family or ethnic groups. Illustration 13.4 provides an example of how a micro-social group (see Figure 17.3) can influence the enterprise of a member of the group.

⊃ | **ILLUSTRATION 13.4 – AN EXAMPLE OF THE INFLUENCE OF SOCIAL GROUP NORMS**

David (not his real name) came from very humble roots; he was brought up in an impoverished working class estate and although he served his apprenticeship as a joiner he found himself out of work still living at home with an unemployed father and brother and a very sick mother. To try to use his own initiative to start a business that would bring in money, he started a gardening business on a shoe string. His grandmother gave him a mobile phone and his girlfriend managed to get some flyers produced which he distributed. Directly after this David started to get a lot of calls on his work line in the middle of the night and when he answered it the phone went dead. He told me about these phone calls and how worrying they were because his mum was in hospital and each call filled him with dread. David confided that he thought it was 'some of his mates just having a laugh'. I replied that it wasn't funny and they were not good mates. I explained they were men who wanted David to stay their little friend; they didn't want him to better himself or outgrow them. They were happy with the unemployed David they knew and were trying to keep the situation unchanged and in effect were holding him back. I advised that he should keep his business life very separate from his social life and stop discussing and confiding in these guys because they wanted to maintain the status quo at the expense of his business.

His business did well, he started to employ his brother as a casual self-employed person whenever he needed it and kept it all above board. However, some months later I received a call from David out of the blue asking for my advice regarding the following situation. He was sorting out a garden for a girl and her dog bit him. The girl naturally was very upset and (as she knew me) confided in me that she was embarrassed and very upset, not only did her dog bite David but he never returned. This worried the girl as she didn't know how he was, the extent of his injuries and if he was even prepared to finish the garden.

David's phone call clarified things for me. He was fine but his friends wanted him to sue (I think the phrase they used was 'take a claim' meaning to take legal action for monetary recompense) – they said he would be mad not to do so, that he could make a packet. He wasn't sure about this. He felt that he shouldn't, but they advised so vociferously he thought he better run it by me. I told him that if he took her to court, that would be the last money he would ever make because no one would employ him (including me and my friends). He agreed. He followed my advice and texted his client to say 'apologies in the delay in getting back to you, bite now a distant memory – no scarring, no pain, will return to complete gardening at your convenience. Please advise.' I went on to advise David that again he should keep his social and business life separate, but for such a guy its always going to be a struggle and perhaps not one he will win without changing his friends!

Source: Based on personal communication from David's mentor to the author.

Implications for (potential) entrepreneurs

For people in, or proposing to be in, enterprise, the implications could be:

- The need to be aware of the potential in social capital and the variety of benefits its different aspects can provide and try to diagnose which bits are needed.
- The relevance of learning how to acquire and use the relevant aspects of social capital and even, in some cases, learning how to un-acquire it. If, for instance, someone has social contacts who don't approve of people being entrepreneurial, it might be necessary to learn how not to be affected by their views and to develop links instead with people who will provide encouragement – just as someone trying to give up smoking might try to avoid socialising too much with dedicated smokers.

Implications for enterprise supporters

For people seeking to support enterprise, the implications might include:

- Recognising how social capital is normally provided and trying not to reduce it by de-personalising contact and forms of assistance too much.
- Not applying or relying on one-dimensional measures of social capital and instead recognising the potential need for a selection amongst its many varieties.

- Trying to encourage the supply and/or acquisition of supplementary social capital where and when necessary to address specific deficiencies.
- In the case of shared norms of behaviour, being aware of what norms they themselves are encouraging and, if necessary, trying to determine how a perception of positive social engagement can be encouraged.

Available guidance

If social capital is important for enterprise, then it might be thought that guides to its use would be widely available – but this is not the case. There are guides for finding financial capital and guides for aspects of human capital – such as recruiting, training, and managing people – but social capital does not yet seem to have had this level of recognition (although Illustration 13.5 presents some advice on networking suggested in the 1980s). Entrepreneurs wanting to improve their uses of social capital, or enterprise supporters seeking to help with this process, have to try to work it out for themselves.

ILLUSTRATION 13.5 – SOME THOUGHTS ON NETWORKING FROM THE 1980S

SOME OF THE BENEFITS AVAILABLE FROM NETWORKS

- *Information*. Entrepreneurs use their social networks to signal their intentions and to gather information about potential opportunities.
- *Sponsorship and support*. Family and friends will not only provide introductions into appropriate networks, but will also offer emotional and tangible support.
- *Credibility*. Membership of the network gives added weight to the evaluation of skills. Family and friends can provide credibility in areas unfamiliar to the entrepreneur.
- *Control*. Membership of the network, and assistance from it, require certain standards of behaviour. Owner-managers who do not conduct their business in a way that is acceptable to the community will quickly find themselves, and their businesses, isolated.
- *Business*. There are market networks of customers, suppliers and partners as well as production networks of subcontractors, consultants and service suppliers. In addition, there are networks of firms that may work together on projects on a basis of collaboration. This structure can provide all the components necessary for a project without the need for 'vertical integration'.
- *Resources*. Friends and family can also be sources of resources for a new small business, and many businesses are assisted by the informal venture capital market that their owners access through their networks.

Source: Based in part on M. S. Greico, 'Social Networks in Labour Migration', *Industrial Relations Journal*, December 1985 quoted in S. Birley and S. Cromie, 'Social Networks and Entrepreneurship in Northern Ireland', paper presented at the *Enterprise in Action Conference*, Belfast, September 1998.

Some 'Rules Of The Road' For Networking

1. Accept that entrepreneurial know-who is as important as entrepreneurial know-how.
2. Be systematic, explicit and proactive in managing your network.
3. Identify the central core of your own personal distinctive entrepreneurial competence.
4. Your personal network is unique.
5. Personal networks of entrepreneurs should include different actors and types of linkages depending on the type of ventures being pursued.
6. Locate your business venture geographically as close as possible to existing support services provided by the personal networks of successful entrepreneurs.
7. Be alert to different cultural and contextual norms of other actors.

8. Remember that reciprocity is a universal cultural norm.
9. Use your network. The strengths and weaknesses of your personal network become apparent only when it is used.
10. Identify and communicate continuously with the gatekeepers in your network.
11. Contact more than one individual in your network to check qualitative data and opinions.
12. Be careful not to divulge confidential information that may harm you or your network members.
13. Be cognizant of the relative power relationships within your network.
14. Look at the contacts within your network as linkages that are negotiated using a win–win strategy.
15. Assess your personal network periodically in terms of the entrepreneurial support it is supposed to give.
16. Finally, don't spend too much time on managing your network.

Source: Based on R. Peterson and R. Rondstadt, 'A Silent Strength: Entrepreneurial Know Who', *The 16th ESBS/EFMD/IMD Report* (1986/4).

WHAT NEXT?

If social capital is relevant to enterprise, then there are aspects of its use which might benefit from further exploration. This chapter has looked primarily at what it is, because there appears to be little information available on how it can best be used and how its use can be learnt. Also, if social capital is an essential part of the enterprise recipe, policy-makers will want to know how it can best be stimulated and how the relevant aspects of it can be measured in order to recognise when levels are low and extra provision is needed. However the lack of such knowledge should not be a reason for ignoring social capital. It does exist, it appears to be important, and those who want to succeed in enterprise are recognising this (as shown for instance in Illustration 13.6).

PART 2

ILLUSTRATION 13.6 – ACCESSING SOCIAL CAPITAL THROUGH THE DRAGONS' DEN

Is the *Dragons' Den* programme on television primarily about money – or is it actually more about social capital? Are the Dragons trying to make arm's-length investments – or seeking profitable opportunities for hands-on involvement? Therefore are the participants, or at least those participants who understand what is on offer, just seeking financial support for their business ideas, or are they really looking for the right mix of social capital to supplement their ideas and enthusiasm?

Descriptions of the programme state that it is about entrepreneurs pitching for investment to venture capitalists willing to invest their own money in exchange for equity. The rules of the competition specify that the competitors have to state how much money they are seeking and do not succeed unless they persuade the Dragons to offer at least that amount.

It is very apparent that the Dragons are seeking to make hands-on investments. They expect to support any investment they may make with their industry knowledge and contacts. In other words, they have relevant social capital and it is that social capital which often makes the deal attractive. The competitors might be able to get money elsewhere, but not with such useful social capital attached. Some competitors realise this and pitch for it, targeting particular Dragons who they think have the social capital for which they are looking.

Thus the difference between a Dragon and a bank is that a bank will want to know if it will get its money back, plus interest – so it will look at things like ability to pay and security. A Dragon, on the other hand, will want to know if the mixture of the competitor's idea – and anything else the competitor brings with it such as time and money – together with the Dragon's investment backed by his or her commercial, business and sector knowledge and contacts, is likely to be a winning combination. And what will make it a winning combination is most likely to be the Dragon's social capital at least as much as any financial capital that might be invested.

↻ ILLUSTRATION 13.7 – SOCIAL CAPITAL IN ETHNIC NETWORKS

Ram *et al.* discuss the ethnicity of entrepreneurs in the UK and refer to 'the apparent entrepreneurial flair of some ethnic groups, noticeably South Asians, and the below-average propensity for self-employment among other communities, in particular African-Caribbeans'.[42] Carter *et al.*, in looking at barriers to ethnic minority and women's enterprise, indicate that in the UK 'entrepreneurial ambitions ... are unevenly distributed across social groups'.[43] Examinations of relatively high rates of enterprise in ethnic groups usually compare them with the general small business population and do not explain why there is such a variation between different ethnic communities.

Nevertheless some authors do acknowledge a cultural influence – which would appear to be an example of the suggested social norm category of social capital:

> The creation of wealth is roundly applauded in the Asian culture. Temples, gurdwaras (Sikh temples) and mosques are richly decorated; the use of gold and precious gems in these places of worship is legendary. The communities are extremely generous and communal money has made many advances. This society equates wealth with success and sees it as nothing to be ashamed of. The basic driver is to succeed in life with dignity and respect, and to provide for the family. If you can help relatives and friends too, then your status is further enhanced. Wealth enables you to give.[44]

☛ THE KEY POINTS OF CHAPTER 13

- What is now being referred to as social capital may have been overlooked in the past as an important economic component.
- Social capital has not (yet) been consistently defined, but it is the label now often given to aspects of human networking and social connections.
- Social capital, at least in one of its forms, is relevant to enterprise and entrepreneurs as it appears to be an essential component in business formation and growth.
- There appear to be different forms of social capital which are not substitutes one for another. It has been suggested therefore that social capital might be considered to be like vitamins: its different forms each have different applications and it is helpful to find the particular form(s) needed for a particular application.
- Guidance is rarely available on how to acquire and/or develop social capital.

✓ QUESTIONS, EXERCISES, ESSAY AND DISCUSSION TOPICS

- Is social capital just a fancy new name for networking?
- How many different, non-substitutable forms of social capital can you identify?
- Is social capital the missing ingredient in many failed attempts to generate more enterprise?
- What arguments can you advance for and against the 'vitamin' theory of social capital?
- If an enterprise lacks social capital how might that need be diagnosed and how might the deficiency be rectified?

📖 **SUGGESTIONS FOR FURTHER READING AND INFORMATION**

S. Bridge, *Rethinking Enterprise Policy: Can Failure Trigger New Understanding?* (Basingstoke: Palgrave Macmillan, 2010) Chapter 11.

International Small Business Journal (Vol. 25, No. 3) 2007 – special edition on social capital and entrepreneurship.

R. D. Putnam, *Bowling Alone* (New York, NY: Simon & Schuster, 2000).

F. Fukuyama, *Trust* (London: Hamish Hamilton, 1995).

REFERENCES

[1] A. Smith, *The Wealth of Nations* – first published 1776 (London: Penguin, 1986) p. 153.

[2] J. Sloman, K. Hinde and D. Garratt, *Economics for Business* (Harlow: Pearson Education/Prentice Hall, 2010) p. 19.

[3] L. J. Hanifan, 'The Rural School Community Centre', *Annals of the American Academy of Political and Social Science*, Vol. 67, 1916, pp. 130–138.

[4] P. Bourdieu, 'The Forms of Capital', in J. G. Richardson (ed.), *Handbook of Theory and Research for the Sociology of Education* (New York, NY: Greenwood Press, 1986) p. 248.

[5] F. Sabitini, *Social Capital, Public Spending and the Quality of Economic Development: The Case of Italy* (Milan: Fondazione Eni Enrico Mattei, 2006).

[6] J. S. Coleman, *Foundations of Social Theory* (Cambridge, MA: Belknap Press of Harvard University Press, 1990) p. 302.

[7] Ibid.

[8] R. Putnam, '*E Pluribus Unum*: Diversity and Community in the Twenty-first Century The 2006 Johan Skytte Prize Lecture', *Scandinavian Political Studies*, Vol. 30, No. 2, 2007, pp. 137–174.

[9] R. D. Putnam, *Bowling Alone* (New York: Simon & Schuster, 2000) p. 21.

[10] Ibid. p. 287.

[11] Ibid. p. 288.

[12] Ibid. p. 291.

[13] Ibid. p. 362.

[14] T. Schuller, S. Baron and J. Field, 'Social Capital: A Review and Critique', in S. Baron, J. Field and T. Schuller (eds), *Social Capital: Critical Perspectives* (Oxford: Oxford University Press, 2000) pp. 24, 35.

[15] D. Castiglione, J. W. Van Deth and G. Wolleb (eds), *The Handbook of Social Capital* (Oxford: Oxford University Press, 2008) p. 9.

[16] I. C. MacMillan, 'The Politics of New Ventures', in *Frontiers of Entrepreneurship Research*, Proceedings of the *1981 Conference on Entrepreneurship* at Babson College.

[17] R. Peterson and R. Rondstadt, 'A Silent Strength: Entrepreneurial Know Who', *The 16th ESBS/EFMD/IMD Report* (86/4) p. 11.

[18] F. Fukuyama, *Trust* (London: Hamish Hamilton, 1995) p. 338.

[19] T. Harford, *The Undercover Economist* (London: Little Brown, 2006) p. 201.

[20] G. L. H. Svendsen and G. T Svendsen, *The Creation and Destruction of Social Capital* (Cheltenham: Edward Elgar, 2004).

[21] J. Cope, S. Jack and M. Rose, 'Social Capital and Entrepreneurship: An Introduction, *International Small Business Journal*, Vol. 25, No. 3, 2007, p. 214.

[22] M. Casson and M. Della Giusta, 'Entrepreneurship and Social Capital: Analysing the Impact of Social Networks on Entrepreneurial Activity from a Rational Action Perspective', *International Small Business Journal*, Vol. 25, No. 3, 2007, pp. 220–244.

[23] D. S. Audretsch and M. Keilbach, 'Does Entrepreneurship Capital Matter?', *Entrepreneurship Theory and Practice*, Vol. 28, No. 5, 2004, p. 420.

[24] Ibid. p. 424.

PART 2

[25] D. B. Audretsch, M. C. Keilbach and E. E. Lehmann, *Entrepreneurship and Economic Growth* (Oxford: Oxford University Press, 2006) p. 60.

[26] R. Putman and K. Goss, 'Introduction', in R. Putnam (ed.), *Democracies in Flux* (Oxford: Oxford University Press, 2002).

[27] J. S. Coleman, *Foundations of Social Theory*, Op. Cit. p. 302.

[28] G. Smith, 'A Very Social Capital: Measuring the Vital Signs of Community Life in Newham', in B. Knight *et al.* (eds), *Building Civil Society: Current Initiatives in Voluntary Action* (West Malling: Charities Aid Foundation) p. 67.

[29] C. Campbell, 'Social Capital and Health: Contextualising Health Promotion within Local Community Networks', in S. Baron, J. Field and T. Schuller (eds), *Social Capital: Critical Perspectives* (Oxford: Oxford University Press, 2000).

[30] A. A. Gibb, 'Enterprise Culture – Its Meaning and Implications for Education and Training', *Journal of European Industrial Training*, Vol. 11, No. 2, 1987, p. 14.

[31] D. North and S. Syrett, *The Dynamics of Local Economies* (London: Department for Communities and Local Government, 2006) p. 9.

[32] For instance in S. Bridge, B. Murtagh and K. O'Neill, *Understanding the Social Economy and the Third Sector* (Basingstoke: Palgrave Macmillan, 2009) pp. 206–207.

[33] K. Birch and G. Whittam, 'Social Entrepreneurship: The Way to Sustainable Regional Development?', *ISBE Conference*, November 2006, p. 5.

[34] S. Bridge, B. Murtagh and K. O'Neill, *Understanding the Social Economy and the Third Sector* (Basingstoke: Palgrave Macmillan, 2009) p. 207.

[35] N. Christakis and J. Fowler, *Connected* (London: Harper Press, 2010) pp. 105–111.

[36] E. Hoffer quoted by N. Christakis and J. Fowler, *Connected* (London: Harper Press, 2010) p. 112.

[37] D. Halpern, *Social Capital* (Cambridge: Polity Press, 2005) p. 35.

[38] S. Bridge, *Rethinking Enterprise Policy* (Basingstoke: Palgrave, 2010) p. 187.

[39] R. D. Putnam, *Bowling Alone*, Op. Cit.

[40] International Finance Corporation, *Why Banks in Emerging Markets Are Increasingly Providing Non-financial Services to Small and Medium Enterprises* (Washington, DC: International Finance Corporation, undated but probably 2012).

[41] J. S. Coleman, 'Social Capital in the Creation of Human Capital', *American Journal of Sociology*, Vol. 94, 1988, p. S95.

[42] M. Ram, G. Barrett and T. Jones, 'Ethnicity and Entrepreneurship', in S. Carter and D. Jones-Evans (eds), *Enterprise and Small Business*, 3rd Edition (Harlow: Pearson Education, 2012) pp. 199–217.

[43] S. Carter, S. Mwaura, M. Ram, K Trehan and T. Jones, 'Barriers to Ethnic Minority and Women's Enterprise: Existing Evidence, Policy Tensions and Unsettled Questions', *International Small Business Journal*, Vol. 33, No. 1, 2015, pp. 49–69.

[44] S. Dhaliwal, *Making a Fortune – Learning from the Asian Phenomenon* (Chichester: Capstone - John Wiley and Sons, 2008) p. 98.

Companion website

Please visit the companion website at www.palgravehighered.com/Bridge-UE-5e for access to additional learning and teaching materials.

PART 3: ENTERPRISE POLICY AND GOVERNMENT INTERVENTION

The earlier parts of this book explore the current understanding of enterprise, 'entrepreneurship' and small business and consider the evolution of that understanding and areas where it is changing, together with its application to the practicalities of new venture formation and development.

Along with this evolution in knowledge about them, government interest in enterprise and small business has also grown, not least because of the indicated links between small businesses and job creation. Governments, especially in times of high unemployment, want more jobs; therefore, many governments attempt to intervene in the economic process in order simulate more enterprise and support more small business activity.

For many people a key feature of the communist-inspired systems of government was that they guaranteed a job for everyone. Actually, it would seem that was not really the case; it might be more accurate to say that they provided everyone with an employment position and a wage, whether or not they really had a full job to do. But to achieve even that required centrally controlled economies, which are now largely deemed to have failed. Nevertheless a job for everyone who wants one remains a very desirable aspiration.

Earlier in the last century, after the upheavals of the Industrial Revolution and the First World War, there did seem to be some prospect that a job for everyone might become the norm. Then, in the Western world at least, there were the traumas of the 1930s. Following the Wall Street crash in 1929 it appeared that there were indeed fundamental problems with the structure of capitalist economies in maintaining full, or nearly full, employment. However, by the end of that decade major job creation initiatives had produced significant reductions in unemployment, and John Maynard Keynes had, at least in theory, suggested how unemployment might continue to be controlled. Then there was another war, which increased the demand for armaments and other requirements for the military struggle and brought an end to the remaining unemployment.

After that war economic prospects seemed to be much better. Keynesian economic theory appeared to be working, the experiences in the 1930s of practical employment creation seemed still to be valid, and in Britain unemployment remained relatively low at about a quarter of a million. This was a manageable figure, which offered support to the view that full employment was realistically achievable. But (as explained in Chapter 2) by the end of the 1960s this figure had doubled to about half a million (see Figure 2.1). Although history is lived forwards, it is viewed backwards, and it is only in retrospect that it would now seem that this was a turning point. Half a million now looks like a relatively small figure and it was during the 1970s, when the figure grew to one and a half million, and the 1980s, when it rose again, to 3 million, that notions about the practicality of achieving sustained full employment appeared finally to be shattered.

People like Handy and Toffler saw that the nature of much employment was changing. Many large organisations began to decline and, in Britain, since the early 1970s the aggregate profits from the service sector had exceeded those from manufacturing. This meant that some new jobs were being created but the generation of those new jobs did not seem to be keeping pace with the demand for jobs, whether because other jobs were ending or there was a growth in the available labour force.

In this situation there was a natural tendency to look back to the 1930s when job creation measures had worked and to try to repeat that prescription. A number of solutions were proposed. Expanding the business sector was one solution considered, although to an extent business output was already expanding, but primarily through increases in productivity not in jobs. Some businesses were simultaneously increasing output and shedding jobs – a phenomenon referred to as 'jobless growth'. Other suggestions included expanding government employment to take up the slack in jobs – a Keynesian type of solution that required increased government spending on infrastructure, health and education. That looked problematic, however, because of the numbers who would have to be employed, the cost and the potential impact on inflation.

Governments struggled to find something that might work but, at least initially, they were not looking at small businesses. The 'Bolton' Committee of Inquiry on Small Firms was set up in 1969 because small businesses were seen as a 'vanishing breed' and there were worries about their survival. So government support for small businesses in the 1970s was often designed to protect them from 'unfair' competition from bigger businesses. However, it was the work of Birch in particular in identifying small businesses as an important source of net new jobs that did much to focus official interest on this sector, especially at a time when it fitted so well with the political approaches of Thatcherism and Reaganism and their emphasis on 'the role of the individual'.

Thus governments wanted more jobs for people but recognised that it is businesses, and apparently small businesses in particular, that create most jobs. However, what governments can do is encourage and incentivise people and businesses to create jobs, try to provide a supportive environment for the creation of jobs, and legislate for people to have an equal opportunity to get the jobs that do exist. It is the first two of these possibilities which are a key driver for much enterprise policy.

Part 3 of this book looks at this intervention: intervention which cannot of itself create enterprise but, at least in theory, can promote it. It is people who can act in an enterprising way and it is people who can start and develop small businesses. Intervention can seek to encourage them to do it more and to make it easier or more rewarding for them. That is what is meant by promoting enterprise.

However just wanting to promote more enterprise is not enough: that desire has to be given effect through policy. Chapter 14 starts, therefore, with a model of the different possible components of policy, from drivers through to delivery agents. It explores in more detail the drivers – the reasons for government interest in this area – and their translation into objectives and targets. It also reviews some of the arguments against intervention.

Chapter 15 follows this with a review of policy methods: the possible areas for intervention and the forms it might take. It considers the different approaches that policy in this field can use to achieve its purposes and the different instruments or sorts of assistance that are made available. It concludes with a look at some of the issues affecting how such assistance is delivered.

Although it seems that part of the reason for policy can be a desire to be seen to be doing something, the variety of interventions that are practised raises the question of how successful they are. Therefore Chapter 16 considers policy evaluation and the question of how successful enterprise policy is. Evaluating enterprise intervention is not easy and there is relatively little reliable evidence about it – but what there is does not seem to indicate that much policy is working as intended.

That conclusion may be controversial, but Chapter 17 nevertheless ends this part by considering the implications of the apparent policy failure. If current approaches are not working because the assumptions on which they are based are questionable, what alternative theory can be advanced as a guide to policy which might work? Areas where research and policy attention might be focused more usefully are suggested.

Why Governments Intervene: The Aims of Enterprise Policy

CONTENTS

- Introduction
- Intervention policy: components and considerations
- Policy drivers: the reasons for government interest
- Policy objectives (and targets)
- Policy justification: the rationale for intervention
- Why not? The arguments against intervention
- In conclusion

KEY CONCEPTS

This chapter covers:

- The desire of governments to intervene to encourage and/or support enterprise, entrepreneurship and small business – which means that there will be policy in this area.
- A model framework for the components of such policy.
- The policy drivers – the reasons why governments want to intervene.
- The objectives of policy, for which the main underlying themes appear to be start-ups (birth-rate policy), business growth and employment.
- The justifications given for interventions, including addressing market and other failures and removing barriers faced by particular groups.
- Some of the arguments against intervention.

LEARNING OBJECTIVES

By the end of this chapter the reader should:

- Understand the reasons why governments want to intervene to support entrepreneurship and/or small business, and therefore why they do intervene – whether it is justified or not.
- Be aware of the different components, features and stages needed for a credible intervention policy.
- Be aware of the main objectives often set, or implied, for policy in this field.
- Understand the main reasons that can be advanced to justify intervention policy.
- Be aware of some of the main arguments against such intervention.

INTRODUCTION

Throughout the world, governments and governmental organisations intervene in the economies of their countries at national, regional and local levels. In the context of this chapter, intervention is taken to be the attempt by a governmental or other body to affect the behaviour of an economy, or to improve an input to an economy, in a way which is intended to produce an economic benefit which would not have happened had it been left solely to market forces.

No matter how much market forces may be praised, and laissez-faire economics promoted, no government appears able to resist the pressure to intervene in some way to promote or protect the economy for which it is perceived to be responsible. That intervention may not always be effective, or may have effects contrary to what was intended, but there is still always a pressure to do something, or at least to be seen to be doing something.

Some of this economic intervention is intended to have the effect of promoting more enterprise, usually in the form of business and often small business. For instance:

- In the UK the Richard Report commissioned by the Shadow Cabinet concluded in 2008 that 'total public expenditure spent on small businesses support is now more correctly estimated to be over £12 billion' and 'this accounts for over 2 per cent of all Government expenditure'.[1]
- 'The goal of the Dutch Ministry of Economic Affairs is to help establish and maintain a prosperous, sustainable and enterprising country; an open country that is an integral part of the global economy. The Ministry has set itself the additional goals of encouraging more entrepreneurs in the Netherlands and of supporting a higher quality of entrepreneurship.'[2]
- 'Creating a business friendly environment for existing small and medium-sized enterprises (SMEs) and potential entrepreneurs is one of the EU's main objectives.'[3]
- 'Small business is America's most powerful engine of opportunity and economic growth. That's where SBA [Small Business Administration] comes in. SBA offers a variety of programs and support services to help you navigate the issues you face with your initial applications, and resources to help after you open for business.'[4]

Intervention exists

A pragmatic view of intervention is to recognise that it exists and will, in some form or another, continue. One form of intervention is laws and regulations to control business: such as laws that require businesses to be registered, laws that seek to control monopolies and laws that stipulate permitted labour practices.

However, there is an almost irresistible temptation for governments to intervene further. If it is understood that small businesses create jobs, and if significant numbers of people are unemployed and want jobs, then government will find that intervention to promote small business will be a popular option. Politically motivated behaviour is also prevalent in conditions of uncertainty. The SME area is complex and there is still only limited knowledge about the connection between policy and its outcomes. In this context few governments will wish to irritate electorates with subtle arguments on the pros and cons of intervention – action will take priority.

There are many advocates of a laissez-faire economic policy, but no government appears to have adhered strictly to such a policy. Governments intervene in numerous ways to manage their economies and redistribute wealth. As the editors of *Business Week* have noted, the most successful economies, in spite of huge differences among them, all have 'broad support throughout their societies for basic national economic goals and for measures of industrial policy to achieve them'.[5] In many respects, therefore, the debate about intervention is not about the principle of intervention but about the means that are to be used.

Part of the debate should be about the effectiveness of those means, but the sheer size of the small business sector makes it very difficult for governments to ignore its real or perceived needs. Also, there has been a paucity of sophisticated, systematic evaluations of specific interventions aimed at enhancing the achievements of small businesses (see Chapter 16). The result is that many uncertainties arise in connection with the usefulness of various policies. These uncertainties permit, or even encourage, a political dimension to policy to develop. There are many people in the 'small business support industry', and any apparent willingness to promote small businesses, especially when combined with any uncertainty surrounding policy objectives, provides them with ample opportunity to use their creativity in providing and developing small business support services. If actions appear to look good and there is no clear evidence for what they achieve, or fail to achieve, then the actions may be pursued, not for the results they bring, but for the credit that applying them will earn for those responsible.[6]

The call for intervention will also continue to be made because of the number of groups which have a vested interest in it – researchers, policy-makers, support agencies and SME groups.

> Providers of business information, support and training rely heavily on programmes – the jobs of policy-makers and officials ultimately revolve around designing, developing and managing support programmes. A large part of the role of SME membership bodies is concerned with lobbying government to introduce new forms of support.[7]

It is not surprising therefore to discover that so much of the literature in this field is focused on the 'how' as opposed to the 'why' of SME policy.

INTERVENTION POLICY: COMPONENTS AND CONSIDERATIONS

A policy framework

While there may be a temptation, if such intervention is thought to be necessary, simply to implement what appear to be good ideas, at least in theory such intervention should be thought through, planned and justified if it is to offer good value for its cost. That process can have a number of different components between which the links may not always be obvious. A theoretical framework, showing the links, is presented in Figure 14.1, and its components are expanded upon in Table 14.1. In practice the situation may not be this clear and one or more components may seem to be missing. Nevertheless the model is offered as a framework for exploring and analysing policy discussions.

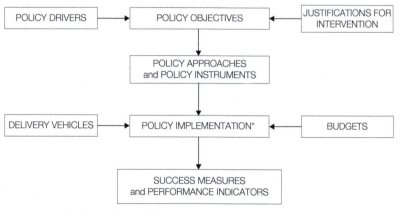

* Also referred to as 'policy delivery' – the terms are sometimes used interchangeably.

Figure 14.1 *A diagram of a policy framework*

Source: Based on S. Bridge, B. Murtagh and K. O'Neill, *Understanding the Social Economy and the Third Sector* (Basingstoke: Palgrave Macmillan, 2014) p. 222.

Table 14.1 *The possible components of a policy framework*

Policy drivers
The policy drivers can be interpreted as the overall political reasons for having a particular policy, although these are rarely highlighted. Reducing unemployment, for instance, could be a policy driver.

Policy objectives
The policy objectives are the overall aim(s) of the policy in question and they can be stated qualitatively or quantitatively. Sometimes, however, the overall aim is described in a vision or mission statement while the term objectives is instead applied to a set of quantified targets for the policy. Having more and/or better small businesses could be a policy objective.

Justification for policy intervention
Although a government may identify certain objectives, intervention to achieve them may, overall, be counter-productive unless there is a good rationale for it. The justification frequently used (whether adequately assessed or otherwise) is that of 'market failure' in that, without intervention, deficiencies in the normal working of the market will preclude the desired outcomes.

Policy approaches and instruments
To achieve the objectives of enterprise intervention a number of broad approaches are generally available, with two being the most common. One (sometimes referred to as an entrepreneurship approach) concentrates on the creation of an environment favourable to the establishment and growth of enterprise, and the other (sometimes referred to as a small business approach) supports more directly the actual start-up and growth of individual enterprises. Within each approach a number of specific instruments can be used. These approaches need not be mutually exclusive and both lie behind the policy instruments adopted in the UK. (Some instruments are highlighted in the next Chapter in Table 15.1.)

Delivery vehicles
In order to undertake the work of implementing its policy, a government needs delivery vehicles: agents or initiatives which will undertake or host the work required to implement the policy.

Budgets
Implementing the policy is also likely to require a budget to pay for it.

Policy implementation
Having put all that together, policy implementation should then take place, and that can happen at national, regional and/or local level and through a wide variety of delivery organisations.

Success measures and performance indicators
The effectiveness of that implementation can then be assessed through success measures and/or performance indicators. In order to be able to determine if and when the policy achieves its objectives, and therefore accomplishes its mission, actual performance needs to be measured and compared with predetermined objectives and with targets for each policy instrument.

Source: Based on S. Bridge, B. Murtagh and K. O'Neill, *Understanding the Social Economy and the Third Sector* (Basingstoke: Palgrave Macmillan, 2014) pp. 222–225.

Policy features

It is also relevant to note that, as well as having a good rationale, objective(s) and approach, if it is to be effective a policy needs to be applied in the right way. For instance Stevenson suggests that a good entrepreneurship policy should have:

- A clear, high-level statement about the importance of business dynamics to economic renewal and growth.
- A plan for accelerating entrepreneurship activity presented in one policy framework.
- A rationale, objectives, explicit targets, set policy lines of action, policy and programme priorities and measures.
- Reinforcement in other government policy documents.
- Performance indicators (e.g. for improved culture, climate, conditions for new entries, entrepreneurial activity levels) and quantified targets.
- A specific budget allocation.
- Clear responsibility for the implementation of the policy framework.[8]

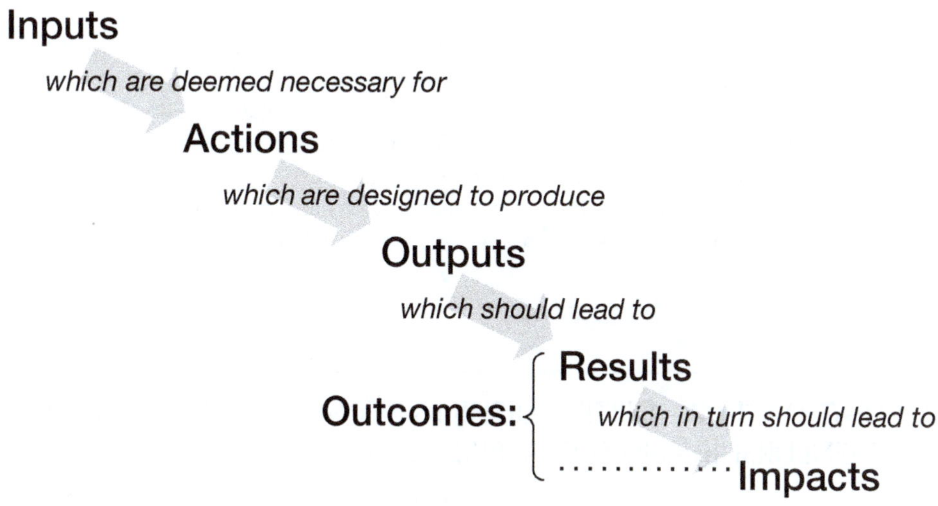

Inputs

which are deemed necessary for

Actions

which are designed to produce

Outputs

which should lead to

Outcomes: $\Big\{$ **Results**

which in turn should lead to

Impacts

Figure 14.2 The sequence from inputs to impacts?

Policy sequence

Unlike the possibilities offered in magic and fairy tales, policy is not a matter of making a wish and waiting a short while for it to come true. Instead it is necessary to do something to achieve what is desired. Figure 14.1 indicates the main components of a policy framework but, even when it gets to the action part, it is important to appreciate that policy action rarely delivers the desired benefits directly: there are likely to be intermediate means for getting to the desired end and it is important to distinguish between them. Therefore, when designing, or considering the effectiveness of, a project, making a distinction in its 'outturns' between 'outputs' and 'outcomes' can be very helpful. In this terminology the 'outputs' are those things which are within the ability of a project to deliver, whereas the 'outcomes' are those things which it is hoped and/or expected will happen as a result of the outputs but which may also be subject to other influences beyond the direct control of the project. These outcomes can be divided further into shorter-term 'results' and longer-term 'impacts'. This sequence is illustrated in Figure 14.2, and an example of the relevance of this distinction is described in Illustration 14.1.

ILLUSTRATION 14.1 – AN EXAMPLE OF OUTPUTS AND OUTCOMES

A project in a remote farming community in Northern Ireland illustrates the difference between outputs and outcomes and demonstrates why the distinction can be important in assessing a project when things don't quite go according to plan.

In this community, farm incomes were low and, as a result, young people were leaving the area. To encourage them to stay and thus to keep the community alive, a scheme was devised to improve farm incomes by improving the quality of the calves the farms produced.

Therefore the output of the scheme was to be better-quality calves, and the outcomes hoped for were that farm incomes would increase and that more young people would stay in the area to take over the farms. Thus the increase in farm incomes was the anticipated result and the retention of young people was the impact which it was hoped this would have.

To improve the quality of the calves produced, the project employed a variety of means including higher-quality artificial insemination, better feeding and better winter accommodation for the cattle in calf. The outturn of this was that the farms in the scheme did produce better-quality calves: an output which was shown by veterinary inspections and the fact that they sold in better-quality markets. Therefore the scheme delivered what it was contracted to deliver. However, farm incomes did not increase as a result because, in the meantime, the BSE problem had arisen and depressed the price for all cattle. The scheme could not be blamed for this, but it did mean that the hoped-for result was not achieved. Nevertheless there was some evidence that more young people were staying on the farms, possibly because they saw that some attention was now being given to the area. So the desired impact was, to some extent, happening.

However, without making the distinction between outputs and outcomes – and within outcomes, between results and impacts – it would not have been possible to analyse properly the effectiveness of the project.

ILLUSTRATION 14.2 – DISTINGUISHING BETWEEN SMALL BUSINESS, ENTREPRENEURSHIP AND ENTERPRISE POLICY

It is possible, and indeed helpful, to distinguish, between enterprise, entrepreneurship and small business policy although, as a consequence of the lack of clear definitions of these words, there is often confusion about what is meant by such policies. They can be perceived as interchangeable, overlapping or quite separate, and distinctions which might be possible in theory may not be made in practice. As a result, important policy differences can often be obscured or ignored.

Lundström and Stevenson, for instance, developed Figure 14.3 to illustrate the interrelated, but at the same time distinctive, policy domains of entrepreneurship and small and medium-sized enterprise (SME) policy.

Because it separates entrepreneurship policy from small business policy, this terminology facilitates a distinction which is important because these policies require very different approaches. It has been suggested that policies which try to cover both are likely to fail to do either. A small business policy should be about business development, while policies for entrepreneurship should be about wider personal, social and economic development. If enterprise policy is the label given to wider policies in this area, then there are three broad distinctions which can be made:

- *Small business (or SME) policies*, which are policies for stimulating growth of already established small businesses, variations of which have also been called 'growth' or 'business growth'

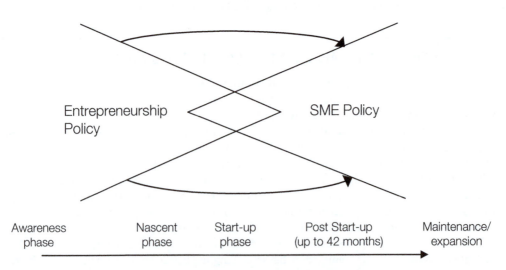

Figure 14.3 *The interface between entrepreneurship policy and SME policy*

Source: L. Stevenson and A. Lundström, *Beyond the Rhetoric: Defining Entrepreneurship Policy and Its Best Practice Components* (Stockholm: Swedish Foundation for Small Business Research, 2002) p. 27.

policies and 'backing winners' policies. This sort of policy tends to focus on the businesses and what will help them to grow, not the entrepreneurs behind them (an approach which is challenged by the arguments advanced in Chapter 8).

- *Entrepreneurship policies*, which are policies for encouraging and facilitating more people to create their own businesses. These policies are centred on people and on what will persuade or help them to start businesses, although they can be referred to as 'business start' or 'business birth-rate' policies.
- *Enterprise policies*, which are policies for encouraging enterprise in its broad sense, much but not all of which may be manifest as new business starts. These policies are clearly focused on people, both as individuals and in groups, and seek to develop skills and attitudes likely to assist people to be more successful in any chosen career or endeavour.

The policy reality

What is described in the section above may be the theory about policy development, but often the reality is different. The general picture may be one of confusion because steps in the theory are missed, rationales or objectives are not clear, and linking intention to effect is very difficult. Nevertheless the frameworks and distinctions are explained above because they can help both with the development of better policy and with the evaluation of current and past policy.

'A COHERENT FRAMEWORK?'

Given the large number of small businesses in England, the many sectors in which they operate and the variety of economic, social and government influences to which they are subject, any moves to improve small business performance are inherently complex. In an effort to reduce that complexity and help deliver quality support to all small businesses, the SBS created a performance framework bringing together multiple objectives, targets and strategic themes. Unfortunately, the resulting performance framework is complex. In particular, it has been difficult to see how success with the strategic themes would lead to the achievement of the targets, and how achieving targets would, in turn, satisfy the government's aims and objectives.

Source: House of Commons Committee of Public Accounts 'Supporting Small Business', 11th Report of Session 2006–07. HC262 6 February 2007, p. 3.

POLICY DRIVERS: THE REASONS FOR GOVERNMENT INTEREST

As the introduction to Part 3 explains, governments and other organisations do intervene to try to encourage enterprise, and they often spend relatively large amounts of money on this. The reasons for this relatively high level of government interest in enterprise in many countries are introduced in Chapter 2. Nevertheless the main themes are summarised here because, in the terms used in Figure 14.1, they are the 'policy drivers'.

Employment

Small firms were the source of the majority of net new jobs created between 1969 and 1976 in the USA.
David Birch[9]

The UK results are broadly similar to those of the United States ... indicating that smaller firms provide a disproportionate share of new job creation.
Colin Gallagher[10]

PART 3

> Small firms play an important role in the economy, in creating jobs, in innovation and in regenerating regions.
>
> Andrea Westall and Marc Cowling[11]
>
> There was a net gain of 800 thousand jobs, in the period (1995–1999), and small businesses accounted for around 70 per cent of this.
>
> Small Business Service[12]
>
> Any honest conversation about creating jobs in the United States must include the role played by small business. Collectively, these businesses create the lion's share of new jobs.
>
> Ty Kiisel[13]

The need for jobs and thus for businesses to create jobs, and for entrepreneurs to create those businesses, is often a policy driver. Faced with a serious unemployment problem, such as that in the UK in the 1980s and 1990s, and apparently persuasive evidence that small businesses are effective as job creators and are particularly resilient in an economic recession, it is easy to see why there has been a strong *prima facie* case for government intervention in support of small businesses with the creation of more employment as an objective. Although small businesses provide other social and economic benefits, jobs have often been quoted as the justification for intervention to promote enterprise.

Economic growth

The employment argument for supporting small businesses is now relatively well established – and entrepreneurship is encouraged because it generates the people who will in turn create those small businesses. But there are also theories linking the rate of entrepreneurship to the rate, or stage, of economic growth.

GEM (see Chapter 4) is one example of a project which has established and is exploring a correlation between entrepreneurship and economic growth, but it has not yet determined just what the link between them is. Nevertheless, if economic growth is an objective, then an apparent relationship between entrepreneurship and economic growth might suggest that an entrepreneurship policy may have relevance.

Economic and political health

In any case there are a lot of small businesses: up to 99 per cent of all businesses in developed Western economies.[14] So they are a very significant part of an economy – their health will have big impact on the economy's health, and they are a significant part of the electorate to which democratic governments will want to appeal.

Regeneration and social inclusion

As well as being of general benefit to an economy, enterprise has also been seen as a way of helping to regenerate deprived communities and of increasing the social inclusion of the people in them. For instance in 2008 the UK government, in setting out its 'renewed vision to make the UK the most enterprising economy in the world', also indicated that:

> The Government's vision is, through enterprise, to bring significant social and economic benefits to more deprived parts of our country and those groups in the population heavily represented there.[15]

POLICY OBJECTIVES (AND TARGETS)

The sort of benefits identified above indicate the reasons why governments and others intervene to encourage and support entrepreneurship and small businesses but alone they do not give enough focus for individual policies. The benefits considered are generally the impacts sought from policies; however, as Illustration 14.1 demonstrates, while the output of policies may often be an essential component of the process, the final desired outcome may come later and also be subject to other factors. Therefore, to check that the policies are working, intermediate objectives are often specified (which, in the terminology of Figure 14.2, may be either outputs or results).

Despite their apparent relevance to policy formulation, the objectives of entrepreneurship or small business policies are often not made clear because policy is rarely described with such clear distinctions. In 1994, for instance, Storey observed that:

> There has been no UK White Paper about the objectives and targets of public policy towards SMEs. Instead, policies have been introduced on a piecemeal basis, often in response to pressure from small firm lobby organisations and to changes in the macroeconomy. It is therefore necessary to guess at the objectives of policy, rather than being able to view each initiative as clearly fitting into an overall conceptual framework.[16]

According to Storey,[17] the objectives of government SME policies* – intermediate and final, stated and unstated – are likely to be one or more of the following:

Increase employment.

Increase number of start-ups.

Promote use of advisers.

Increase competition.

Promote 'efficient' markets.

Promote technology diffusion.

Increase wealth.

Get elected.

In the terminology of Figure 14.1, Storey's list includes actions, outputs and outcomes. An official list, which also includes both outputs and outcomes, was provided when, in 2003, a UK government action plan for small business was developed which was 'based around seven themes identified as key drivers[†] for economic growth, improved productivity and enterprise for all:

Building an enterprise culture.

Encouraging a more dynamic start-up market.

Building the capability for small business growth.

Improving access to finance for small businesses.

Encouraging more enterprise in disadvantaged communities or under-represented groups.

Improving small businesses' experience of government services.

Developing better regulations and policy.'[18]

Other objectives which are encountered include:

Promoting the start-up and growth of high-tech businesses – because they are expected to have high value added and to be less susceptible to competition.

---

* Here this includes the full range of policies including those for both entrepreneurship and small business.
† Terminology can be a problem in this area as it is not used consistently by everyone. These themes were labelled 'drivers' in the action plan, but in the usages of Figure 14.2 they are the outputs expected from policies which are in turn expected to lead to the hoped for results of 'economic growth, improved productivity and enterprise for all'.

Promoting the use and spread of innovation and technology.

Exporting.

Improving supply chains.

Increasing consumer choice.

Revitalising traditional sectors.

Key themes

Although the lists quoted above indicate a wide range of possible objectives, the core objectives of much enterprise, entrepreneurship and small business policy can be summarised in just three themes:

Start-up objectives

There is a theme of encouraging more business start-ups – which would include building an enterprise culture and facilitating a more dynamic start-up market. These objectives are generally pursued because more small businesses are supposed to lead to more employment, and more entrepreneurship is supposed to lead to economic growth.

Often policies which are designed to encourage more business start-ups are called birth-rate policies and the arguments for them include:

- Start-ups are the seedbed for growth. This argument is summarised in the view that, without a healthy and quality stock of new businesses, the future supply of 'winners' or growth businesses will be curtailed. Not to support them, therefore, would be to reduce the pool of potential 'winners'.
- Market failures constrain start-up rates. This argument seeks to highlight barriers to start-up which are attributable to organisational or institutional deficiencies. These 'market failures' are seen as impacting disproportionately on new and small businesses, disadvantaging them. The barriers include cultural/social values, difficulties in financing, legislative and administrative burdens, including reporting requirements as well as access to information.
- The quality, volume and viability of new business starts can influence the strength and competitiveness of the small business sector. This in turn is at the root of the creation of an economy which not only generates jobs but also contributes to the achievement of wider economic and social goals, including productivity, living standards, price stability, diversity, choice and personal opportunity. It is suggested that three key questions need to be asked when considering the part that start-ups play in an economy:
  - Are there enough of them?
  - Is the quality of the stock of new and small businesses adequate?
  - Are start-up rates, and net additions to the business stock, rising or falling?

However arguments are also advanced against birth-rate policies. For instance it has been suggested that:

- There can be too many business start-ups and, instead, there is a desirable equilibrium rate. Supporting start-ups can distort the market if it acts counter to the market mechanism.
- Start-up policies waste resources because many people thus targeted do not start businesses and many of the businesses which do start do not thrive.[19]
- Such policies can encourage ill-prepared individuals to take a risk and actually make their own position worse.[20]
- The link between general firm creation rates and economic development remains unproven. Business creation rates fall as economic development increases in low-income countries, and in middle- and higher-income countries higher rates of enterprise creation may be an effect, rather than a cause, of increased wealth.[21]

Growth objectives

Once they have been launched, small businesses can be divided into three broad groupings. First, there are many small businesses that have a short life. There is a second large group of businesses that, although surviving, remain small. The third group is by far the smallest: it consists of those businesses that achieve rapid growth. These groups have been referred to by Birch as 'failures', 'mice' and 'gazelles' and by Storey respectively as 'failures', 'trundlers' and 'fliers'; and it is on the gazelles or fliers that much attention has been focused.

As noted in Chapter 5, it was in 1994 that Storey claimed that in the UK 'over a decade, 4 per cent of those businesses which start [at the beginning of the decade] would be expected to create 50 per cent of employment generated'[22] and in 2015 Hart and Anyadike-Danes found 'that typically [in the UK], over a three-year period, high-growth SMEs represent less than 1 per cent of established businesses, but generate 20 per cent of all job growth amongst established businesses which grow'.[23] Other findings help to confirm the view that in the UK a small number of businesses have a disproportionate impact on job creation and the US experience is broadly similar. For example, a study of new firm growth in Minnesota found that 9 per cent of new firms formed in the 1980s provided over 50 per cent of employment after two to seven years.[24] While there are particular criticisms that can be made of these findings, the general picture, which is probably reasonably accurate, is that a relatively small proportion of all small businesses accounts for the major part of the small business contribution to new jobs. However, it is important to note that demonstrating that, in any cohort of businesses, a few will create most jobs is not the same as demonstrating that, in any one year or combination of years, the greatest overall net job creation comes from the fastest-growing businesses in those years.

Nevertheless the idea that only 4 per cent of the businesses create 50 per cent of the jobs in a cohort has led to the suggestion that, instead of offering support to all businesses, it would be much more productive if it was given only to the 4 per cent of 'fliers' or 'gazelles'. Hence there has for some time been a desire to focus assistance on 'growth businesses' or 'winners'. However, as well as arguments for this view, arguments are also advanced against it (see Illustration 14.3).

ILLUSTRATION 14.3 – ARGUMENTS FOR AND AGAINST TARGETING GROWTH BUSINESSES

Arguments for. A number of arguments have been advanced for targeting growth businesses:

1. *Growth businesses provide economic benefit*. It is those businesses which grow which provide the extra economic benefit such as employment.

2. *Targeting increases the effectiveness of support measures*. There is evidence which suggests that, over time, a proportionately small number of firms will create a large proportion of new jobs. Therefore, it is argued that targeted support for these 'growth' businesses should be more effective in promoting jobs than more generalised support because the former has a clear focus and concentrates resources where they are most needed and where they can produce the best results.

3. *Targeting minimises support requirements*. By applying support only to growth businesses, the total support requirement, and its cost, is reduced. Indeed with many hundreds of thousands of businesses starting each year, it is not feasible to deal with them all and make a sufficient impact with limited resources.

4. *Targeting encourages a clearer focus on the needs of growth businesses*. Targeting growth businesses forces small business support organisations to identify more clearly how to support such businesses and to develop appropriate strategies for such support. It also helps agencies to develop a better understanding of the processes of growth in the target market and how best to assist such processes. High levels of expertise are thus more likely to be developed.

5. *Targeting is inevitable*: Smallbone and Massey have observed that:

> Targeting is inevitable (and indeed sensible, given the constrained resources available to the agencies responsible for economic development) [although] the way in which it ... is operationalised could be improved.[25]

Arguments against. There are also arguments against targeting growth businesses:

1. *The difficulty of identifying growth businesses*. It is very difficult, if not impossible to identify growth businesses before they grow. The process of picking winners has been likened to selecting a potentially good wine. It is viewed as more of an art than a science and is the preserve of a tiny group of cognoscenti with exceptional 'noses' and 'palates'; it is a skill that takes years of training and experience to acquire, and not everyone can do it even then. (Even the wine cognoscenti generally only make predictions for wines with a good pedigree, with the result that most of them missed the potential of the 'New World' wines.) It is not something therefore that can be systemised in business agencies. As Birch said:

> I haven't figured out a way [to anticipate which firms will be the gazelles and which will end up the mice]. In fact, one of the fascinating things about the gazelles is that they sometimes appear to be mice for long periods of time.[26]

And as Smallbone and Massey have concluded:

> In this context, two of the main empirical findings have important potential implications for the implementation of targeting for growth by public agencies. The first is that even where growth occurs in small firms it is typically discontinuous. ... The second key finding is that most of the descriptive (or easily verifiable) profile characteristics used for targeting, such as size or age of firm, sector, and whether it is innovating or exporting, did not consistently distinguish growth firms from their weaker performing counterparts.[27]

2. *Growth policy is usually one-dimensional*. Dennis's typology (see Figure 17.2) suggests that both the institutional and cultural dimensions may be relevant to enterprise policy, but growth policies generally only try to operate in, and address, the institutional dimension.

3. *Targeting growth businesses is misguided and/or is too simplistic*. There are a number of reasons for suggesting that such a growth strategy is misguided:

- *Chance is the major factor in growth*. According to Storey a major factor in growth is chance:

> 'Growth is the least likely outcome and ... continuous growth is truly exceptional' and 'in practice ... small firm performance measured in terms of growth in sales or employment fluctuates considerably over time and, if anything, generally declines or remains constant with age.' 'Existing theories of the performance of new and small firms ... suffer major limitations ... [and] key empirical regularities among new and small firms are explained more insightfully by elevating the role of chance and combining it with optimism of the business owner.'[28]

- *Growth businesses are not the main source of jobs*. According to Botham new firms create lots of jobs, but the majority are in start-ups which remain small in the short to medium term. Therefore high-growth start-ups are not the main source of new firm job creation. Also:

> The evidence presented here poses a serious challenge to entrepreneurship strategies which aim to increase the number of high growth new starts without simultaneously seeking to increase the overall business birth rate.[29]

- *The growth process is complex.* Hynes, in reviewing research into growth businesses, concluded that it was difficult from this to extract 'a single comprehensive perspective of the phenomenon or construct a profile of the higher growth small firm'.[30] Mole *et al.* also suggest that the process has not been understood:

  > Our research suggests that understanding a complex process like growth needs to examine the structural, cultural constraints and the way that the small firm managers deal with them. However, this depends upon their ultimate concerns. The key role for the manager in the small firm allows them great latitude in their ambitions for the firm. A major reason for our failure to understand firm growth is that this aspect has been underplayed.[31]

4. *Providing support is not like providing venture capital.* The venture capital industry would pride itself on picking winners, and needs to pick them to survive. However, it only needs to select a few winners that would be enough for its own purposes, and it would acknowledge that it still selects a majority of 'dogs' that have to be compensated for by the occasional correctly chosen 'star'. Public support policy, in contrast, would seek to back all the winners and avoid any losers so as to avoid the charge of wasting or losing public money.

5. *Growth businesses are the wrong target.* Instead of trying to identify and target specific growth businesses, what is needed is an enterprising culture which encourages more businesses activity. This set of arguments revolves around the view, explored in Chapter 4, that cultural values supportive of entrepreneurial activity and entrepreneurs can be considered a major influence on the level and success of start-up and subsequent business activity. In consequence it is argued that an investment needs to be made in building support and stakeholder networks positively disposed towards start-ups and growth rather than in direct intervention in growing businesses.

6. *Targeting growth businesses doesn't work.* This point is pursued further in Chapter 16.

Employment objectives

As well as often being a policy driver, more employment can also be an overt policy objective, particularly in policies for disadvantaged areas and communities. Such an objective is often expressed in terms of a 'job creation' aspiration as if the policy itself could actually create jobs, instead of recognising that it has to be done by businesses. This may just be careless drafting but it could serve to disguise the need to consider how such an objective is actually going to be achieved.

Pursuing employment objectives through small business policy can also have other drawbacks. Many jobs in small businesses may be the result of transfers of work from bigger businesses due for example to contracting out, which in turn may have resulted in efficiency gains but may not lead to net job creation. Productivity gains in bigger businesses can result in greater output but fewer jobs.

Therefore the existence of figures showing net job creation in smaller businesses does not necessarily mean that they are better wealth creators. Indeed a strong emphasis on jobs in economic interventions may result in a bias against improvements in productivity, because such improvements, which can benefit an economy, may actually result in net job losses. Also, it can be argued from an economic development perspective that employment creation should be seen as a result of business growth rather than as a prime policy objective.

These are not criticisms of small businesses, and do not mean that they are not important. It is just a caution that small business development need not inevitably result in net economic growth, and that increases in employment in some small businesses do not necessarily mean more jobs overall. However, at times the 'more small businesses equals more jobs' approach would seem to be accepted so readily that often it appears to be followed without further exploration or consideration.

Targets

> Too often the target is anything you happen to hit.
>
> David Storey[32]

If there is a difference between objectives and targets it is that an objective indicates what a policy is trying to do, whereas a target specifies how much of it is required. However, while there may be a range of objectives which are generally agreed, it is unusual for governments to set targets for their (enterprise) policies in the sense of measured outputs to be achieved within a given time-frame. Some would argue the need for such targets if government's attention is to be adequately focused on what it is trying to achieve and how it expects to do so. On the other hand it is problematic to argue for targets for interventions when it is not known whether they will work, how they work, within what timescales they will achieve what outputs, or how those outputs will in turn lead to the desired outcomes. To be able to predict outcomes in a system requires knowledge not just of its inputs but also of the process which links them to outputs and in turn to the outcomes. This process is often not sufficiently understood in the field of enterprise development, it is suggested, for it to be possible to predict outcomes accurately.

Nevertheless governments have been attracted occasionally to setting targets for programmes as, without them, it is argued that 'If you don't know where you are trying to go, any road will take you there'. Intermediate targets, or 'milestones', can also provide a form of progress measurement. An example of the problems inherent in setting targets was in Scotland where, early in the 1990s, Scottish Enterprise embarked on a 'business birth-rate strategy'.

This strategy reflected what was felt to be an entrepreneurial deficit in Scotland compared with the most prosperous areas of the UK, and sought an increase in the country's historic rate of new firm formation. The target set was that this rate should be increased by a factor of 3.5. This was not, in the event, achieved, leading many people to regard the strategy itself as a failure. However, an alternative view was that it appeared to have been more successful in changing attitudes to enterprise and entrepreneurship in a positive direction than in increasing the business birth-rate within the relatively short timescale originally set. Scotland's experience showed a downside of setting targets when the socio-economic dynamics are not fully appreciated and of setting too ambitious a timescale for achieving them. Nevertheless the public sector environment is such that similar targets are set. For instance, the former Welsh Development Agency had set itself a target of a 65 per cent increase in the rate of new firm formation, and Northern Ireland declared that it sought to bring its start-up rate up to the UK average – because they were also seeking to overcome what they regarded as an 'entrepreneurial deficit' in similar ways to Scotland.

It should be recognised that seeking a more entrepreneurial economy requires the changing of attitudes to entrepreneurship and other fundamental changes which themselves are long term and will not be apparent solely in the number of new firms (or jobs) created – and that even these may take many years to be realised. Inevitably, measurement of deeper changes will take time and involve other indicators. When setting performance targets, governments and agencies appear to rely often on short-term indicators to measure what is inevitably long-term change. This can be counter-productive when there is also a tendency towards policy and programme implementation being 'target driven' to achieve an easily measurable definition of success in the shorter term.

A source of confusion?

There is another problem which, at least in the UK, can make it hard to identify objectives. It was articulated by Perren *et al.* as:

> a plethora of organisations and initiatives that have been identified as having some part to play in this area. ... The continuing churn and name changes adds [sic] to the challenge.

The majority of the organisations identified and many of the initiatives are funded through the public purse, either fully or through part subsidy. Therefore the government is largely responsible for the volume and fragmentation of organisations and initiatives in the area. Indeed the inflexibility of funding regimes often appears to encourage the development of new initiatives even if there are similar schemes already in operation. The aim may have been to respond to perceived needs, but ... it appears to have resulted in a tangled and confusing assortment of dislocated organisations and initiatives. ... Many organisations in the area appear to be driven by government agendas and funding rather than any direct demand from SMEs themselves.

Informants, and by implication their organisations, appear to have a relatively narrow sphere of knowledge and relationships. ... They can be seen as occupying micro-worlds that are embedded within a wider system of which they have partial knowledge. No single organisation emerges as providing a central bridge between the various ... worlds. The inevitable consequence is that any new initiatives run the risk of being developed in isolation from what presently exists.[33]

While it might seem surprising that apparently little regard should be paid in this way to the consumers' needs, it is yet another example of market forces. If the government is funding the initiatives, then the government is the customer. It is not surprising therefore that the organisations delivering initiatives pursue the money and follow the customer's agenda, not that of the consumers. In part the result has been a small-firms policy (and it is still largely about small businesses) that has been described as 'an excess of loosely connected and apparently uncoordinated policy initiatives shooting off in all directions, generating noise and interest, but not commensurate light.'[34]

In a similar vein, Arshed *et al.* report that in England 'the implementation process of enterprise policy initiatives is complex and confusing, with fragmented relationships between the actors involved. The abundance of enterprise policy initiatives being delivered at the time, the absence of clearly defined objectives, the limited emphasis on the delivery of business support and the lack of measurement and evaluation combined to create an unnecessarily complicated process of enterprise policy implementation which, in turn, reduced its effectiveness.'[35]

POLICY JUSTIFICATION: THE RATIONALE FOR INTERVENTION

Intervention to promote more enterprise, more entrepreneurship and/or more growth in small businesses is proposed because these are thought to be beneficial. However, intervention should only be considered if it will enhance the quantity and/or quality of their impact and deliver the benefits sought. The argument that it will do so is generally that there are obstacles and barriers preventing their development, that these obstacles and barriers occur through a failure of some sort, and that intervention can correct this failure. Whether the failure is in the market, in governance, or in economic systems, will determine what sort of intervention should be considered but, the argument goes, if there is no failure there is no justification for intervention. The various forms of failure are examined below.

Market failure

It is argued that SMEs face particular challenges compared to larger businesses. They face size-related discriminatory barriers that prevent a 'level playing field', and these are generally classified as 'market failures'.[36] According to neo-classical economic theory there is a tendency towards perfect markets. Attempting to intervene in a perfect market would not result in any improvement in that market. The value of any apparent benefits in one area would be outweighed by the cost of displacement effects elsewhere, and there would be no net economic benefit. However, after a disruption in the market, there may be some factors that delay the return of the market to perfection. Therefore intervening to address these inherently temporary factors could produce benefits. Such factors are market failures in that they represent a failure of the market to perform perfectly.

The term 'market failure' can mean different things to different people. To the neo-classical economist, if it exists it is only a temporary phenomenon that will eventually go. If it is not temporary, it is not a market failure, and trying to address it will not result in a net benefit. To others, however, a market failure is potentially a permanent feature, which will continue to disrupt unless addressed. They point out that the neo-classical perfect market is a myth and that many of the assumptions about markets made by neo-classical economists do not hold true. There are always imperfections in markets. Many organisations have the power to dominate markets, and use it. Large corporations dominate markets, product differentiations by means of marketing manipulations are manifold, and predatory practices are commonplace. The result is many 'market failures' which place small businesses at a disadvantage and are likely to be permanent unless steps are taken to address them.[37] (See also Illustration 14.4 and Table 14.2.)

Table 14.2 *Market imperfections, their causes and the actions needed*

Market gap	Cause of market gap	Action needed
Supply of entrepreneurs	Social and economic bias in favour of employment rather than self-employment	Social security system Education Tax system
Supply of innovations	Inadequate R&D	Education and research policy
		R&D expenditure
		Tax system
Lack of capital	Distortions in capital markets	Tax system
		Subsidised lending
		Monopoly policy
		Credit guarantees
Labour shortage	Imperfections in the labour market	Social security system
		Social environment
		Housing policy
		Training and education
		Monopoly policy
		Labour relations policy
Lack of premises	Imperfections in property market	Urban redevelopment
		Planning regulations
		Infrastructure investment
		Tax system
Bureaucracy and compliance costs	Growth of government	Simplification, exemption, changes in local taxation
		Reorganisation of central and local government
Purchasing	Imperfections in supplier markets	Monopoly policy, tax system
Marketing	Imperfections in seller markets	Government, 'crowding out'

Sources: Developed from D. Keeble and S. Walker, 'New Firms, Small Firms and Dead Firms: Spatial Patterns and Determinants in the United Kingdom', *Regional Studies*, Vol. 28, No. 4, 1994, pp. 411–427; and P. Westhead and A. Moyes, 'Reflections on Thatcher's Britain: Evidence from New Production Firm Registrations 1980–88', *Entrepreneurship and Regional Development*, Vol. 4, No. 1, 1992, pp. 21–36.

ILLUSTRATION 14.4 – POLICY RATIONALE: AN OECD VIEW

'It is often argued that governments should promote SMEs because they face special challenges, as well as special opportunities, compared to larger firms. SMEs have been shown to be important for the economy, particularly for job creation. But is this sufficient justification for special treatment or schemes for smaller firms? Policies and measures targeted on SMEs should be adopted only to the extent that there is a clear rationale for doing so, particularly in terms of market and other failures. In addition, there is a broader, wide-ranging set of government policies (competition, fiscal, and so on) which affect SME performance, and these must also be reviewed in terms of their implications for smaller firms.

'Traditional market failure arguments, when cited in the case of SMEs, usually concern problems related to economies of scale, asymmetric information and imperfect appropriation of returns. Smaller firms generally have fewer financial, human and technical resources which constrains their ability to take advantage of given opportunities, particularly those associated with economies of scale. Small firms also suffer more from information gaps and have difficulty evaluating the benefits of, for instance, adopting new technologies or entering distant markets. SMEs may be at a disadvantage in adopting new technology due for example to greater dependence on external sources of scientific and technological information and the need for tailored technical responses. With regard to financing, small firms have more problems obtaining bank loans and other capital due to a lack of collateral, unproven track record and risk-averse investors; at the same time, they may lack information on alternative financing sources. In general, the social returns of SME activities are higher than the expected private returns, but more difficult to appropriate, resulting in under-investment by the market.'

Source: OECD, *Working Paper On the Role of SMEs: Findings and Issues* (Paris: OECD/DSTI/IND, 2000) p. 7. Personal communication from members of The Working Party on SMEs.

Government and systemic failures

Much attention has been given to market failure as a justification for intervention but, it would seem, there has been less recognition of the problems of relevant 'failure' in areas such as government and economic systems. Initiatives have been introduced to try to correct market failures but, the Organisation for Economic Cooperation and Development (OECD) argues, this has often been a piecemeal development of policy measures and 'insufficient co-ordination between different government bodies and policies has reduced the efficiency of SME policies and thus limited their potential to fuel economic growth'.[38]

On the same theme, the Chief Executive of the UK's Small Business Service claimed:

> to pursue needs of small business and to bring some intelligence and rationalisation to Government's efforts, all of which stand up in their departmental silos – but when taken in the round and viewed from the customer's point of view – do not necessarily add up. ... [I]t is a similarly complex problem to what we are trying to do with the simplification of business support. Successive governments have created and presided over such complexity.[39]

Johnson offers a number of other theories that are also used to explain the existence and nature of policy interventions. These are the public choice model, the economic theory of bureaucracy and the more radical approaches focusing on the power relations between different interest groups and those which emphasise the ideological dimension of SME policies:[40]

- *Public choice and the role of politicians.* Underlying this model is the argument that politicians will maximise their own welfare and so will 'instigate and promote policies that will maximise their chance

PART 3

of remaining in office through re-election'.[41] What can be called their 'rent-seeking' behaviour may improve economic welfare but need not, for two reasons. Their time horizons are limited to the election cycle and so they will favour short-term gains but will also consider the gains to only that part of the electorate to which they hope to have appeal. Following such a logic will not necessarily correct market failures or increase economic welfare.

- *The economic theory of bureaucracy.* Another tradition focuses upon government officials and their motivations. It is recognised that state bureaucrats also have vested interests which can mean that they wish to be associated with prominent and apparently successful initiatives. While they are not subject to re-election, power, job prospects, remuneration and other benefits can flow from association with what is perceived to be successful. The results of pursuing their own welfare can be 'more resource intensive programmes ... over-bureaucratic management and control structures, reluctance to undertake robust evaluations and a reluctance to curtail ineffective programmes for fear of loss of power or status'.[42]

- *Power relations, pressure groups and ideology.* This approach emphasises the power relations within society and suggests that it is 'the outcome of conflict between powerful groups in society that ultimately determine (sic) the direction of public policy'.[43] Some would base their views on the Marxist concept of a class struggle with the state supporting specific ideologies which support the status quo – with SMEs representing the free market capitalist economy, for example. Others perceive a thriving SME sector as essential to a healthy democracy. Indeed in the United States the role of the Small Business Administration was seen as supporting small business as, *inter alia*, essential to the 'security of this Nation'.[44] In this type of model, one looks to the relative strength of groups in their abilities to influence government policies. Johnson notes that 'it is puzzling to observe that SME policy has been particularly prominent in the UK since the early 1980s, whereas SME organisations have only appeared to be in positions of influence in relation to government since ... 2000'.[45] He suggests on such evidence that power relations between business groups can only be a small part of the continuing popularity of SME policies across Europe and the world.

- *Conclusion.* Johnson concludes that: 'Market failure alone does not justify or explain the existence of SME policy in most countries of the world, nor does it explain why these policies differ over space and time.' It is impossible to ignore that issues of equity, the self-interest of politicians and government officials, political lobbying, societal power structures and ideological considerations all play a role in making and shaping SME policies.[46]

Examples of market failure?

Of the varieties of market failure in which it is argued that small businesses are at a disadvantage, two of the most common relate to the advantages of big business and the need for external support.

The advantages of big business

There are multinational firms with turnovers that exceed the gross national product of most nations. The sheer size and economic power of such firms allow them to dominate consumer and factor markets. They can use huge advertising and marketing expenditure to make it very difficult for new entrants to gain a foothold in their markets. They can benefit from economies of scale. In the procurement field, large firms can secure discounts and organise just-in-time contracts that shift the burden of stockholding to their suppliers. In the labour market they can attract the best staff with their competitive remunerative packages and career prospects for employees.

Some of the reasons for their advantages are as follows:

- Larger businesses may have higher fixed costs but they can spread them over a larger output. Also such costs tend to increase in discontinuous steps that are proportionately higher for small producers than for larger ones.[47]

- Large businesses can often use the capital market with greater facility than small businesses. Indeed, it has long been argued that an equity gap exists for small businesses which cannot find market sources for the type and amount of capital they need.[48] Many small businesses are unquoted companies and, for them, the divestment and exchange of information are time-consuming and costly for both the small businesses and the sources of capital involved.[49]

- It is also argued that small firms are at a relative disadvantage when complying with a range of statutory and administrative regulations imposed by government.[50]
- Entrepreneurialism is concerned with spotting and realising opportunities, but small firms rarely have sufficient resources to exploit them, particularly those openings which offer economies of scale.

A counter to this is the argument that in many cases large firms have earned these cost advantages. Developing a business can require considerable skill and capital, and cost advantages are the reward for this endeavour. In this sense these are not market failures. It can also be pointed out that large firms are currently breaking themselves up into smaller strategic business units and are reducing the size of these units by outsourcing services. If this trend continues, then some of the benefits of size may no longer be available to large firms.

The need for external support

Businesses, if they are to develop, need access to a range of skills and abilities in areas such as organisation, management, production, marketing, selling, strategy, finance and law. Bigger businesses can have all of these competencies in-house, but smaller businesses must inevitably depend on external agencies to provide at least some of them. It has been argued that if the felt need for services is great enough, then small businesses will seek out the services on offer and pay the market price for them. However:

- The need for support is not appreciated. It can be difficult to analyse fully the complexities of a business organisation and identify needs precisely.
- Owners fear that exposing their efforts to others may lead to their ideas being stolen.
- There is a reluctance to approach experts because owners fear that the experts may despise their efforts and because they believe that they do not have the interpersonal and technical skills to deal with sophisticated advisers.
- Perceptions of how consultancies approach assignments is off-putting to many small businesses.
- They do not have sufficient information about the availability and cost of services to make a rational choice.
- They feel that the available support is not appropriate to their needs.
- They might also be discouraged by the price of advice.

A counter-argument might be that making a special case for small business support is a paternalistic approach. Business founders have to learn to stand on their own feet, and in doing so will develop an invaluable set of skills and contacts. Gibb argues that the development of transactions with the suppliers of needed services is a crucial aspect of entrepreneurial learning.[51] Owners must understand their environments and learn how to acquire resources on favourable terms. Services from accountants, market researchers and consultants are commercial offerings and there are adequately developed markets in these areas. It could also be pointed out that there is no overwhelming demand for the services of small business support agencies, and that this might well be because there is little need for the services.

Overcoming other barriers

Government and economic system failures do exist, but they apply across wide areas and do not explain, for example, the variations in business start-up between different regions in the same jurisdiction. Market failure may explain part of this variation but that applies to the narrow aspect of enterprise as small business. There are other barriers that are more apparent when the development of enterprise in its broad sense of an enterprise culture is considered, and these will be relevant when an 'entrepreneurship'

⊃ | **ILLUSTRATION 14.5 – 'SMALL BUSINESS GROWTH STUNTED BY RELUCTANCE TO SEEK ADVICE'**

Survey finds biggest barrier to advice is a psychological one

The vast majority of the UK's small businesses do not ask for business advice because they don't think they need it. According to leading psychologist, Dr. Peter Collett, entrepreneurs are less likely to ask for advice due to their psychological make-up.

A survey of small businesses conducted by NOP and commissioned by Business Link, the information and advice service for small businesses, found that 82 per cent of businesses said the reason that they do not seek business advice was because they didn't need it. Surprisingly this ranked way above other barriers to advice like cost, which was stated by 5 per cent of respondents, and lack of time which was cited by only 1 per cent of the sample.

Dr. Peter Collett, a psychologist specialising in culture and management style, believes that attitudes have to be changed to encourage people to ask for advice. He explains:

> People who run their own business are usually extremely confident and self-assured: they need to be in order to survive. But they sometimes feel hesitant about asking for help, particularly if they feel they ought to know the answer. What makes them so effective up to now often prevents them from being even more successful in the future.

David Irwin, Chief Executive of the former Small Business Service, the agency within government tasked with managing Business Link, said:

> There is a common misconception that you only need to ask for advice when your business is in trouble. It is our job to challenge this view and ensure that UK businesses benefit from the wealth of expertise that Business Link has to offer.

During his analysis of the results, Dr. Peter Collett identified the following types of business that appear to be most in need of advice:

1. Small businesses that have just started up and which need to learn the ropes.
2. Those that have been in existence for a long time and which have become set in their ways.
3. Small businesses with a small turnover, which are particularly vulnerable.
4. Those that don't have many employees, and which therefore have less internal expertise and diversity of opinion.
5. Those that don't get a lot of advice from institutions like banks.

On this basis one would expect to find that these five types of business ask for advice more often. The survey results indicate that the opposite is true – those that are most in need of advice are least likely to ask for it.

Source: Business Link Press Release, 8 October 2001.

Points raised

This report is a reminder that meeting an apparent need is not always a straightforward process.

---

as opposed to a 'small business' policy is being considered. Barriers of culture or of education exist that prevent people from starting businesses, or even thinking of starting them, as well as from being enterprising in the broad sense, and intervention might be considered to address these also.

Cultural barriers

In some situations, where there is not a tradition of independent small businesses, the option of entrepreneurship as a form of employment may not be commonly recognised. People may see only two economic possibilities: if they are lucky they can have a job working for someone else, or if they are unlucky they will be unemployed and reliant on social security benefit payments. In this, and in other situations of economic and social deprivation with second- and third-generation unemployment, the facilitation of the entrepreneurial process could be viewed as one means of overcoming social disadvantage. However, it is not easy: the problems are long term and are likely to require long-term solutions, and many government activities in this sphere are viewed with suspicion because they can have strong political overtones.

Thus certain areas or countries appear to be more enterprising and entrepreneurial than others. Many factors create an enterprise culture, and the values, beliefs and assumptions that are widely shared by members of a community will not be the same in Britain, in Scandinavia and in Eastern Europe, and even in different regions of the same country. Economic theory suggests that a market-driven reduction in wage rates and other costs, plus the exit of firms from certain industries, would provide opportunities for profit in some areas and therefore encourage an influx of entrepreneurial firms. However, economic forces alone are unlikely to redress the balance between regions.[52] That implies that if an imbalance is to be redressed, then intervention of some sort will be necessary.

Barriers for ethnic and women-owned ventures

It is argued by some that ethnic businesses and firms owned by women face discriminatory barriers (see Chapter 5) and that special support should be offered to help them overcome these. Although many people from immigrant communities do start businesses this may be, at least in part, not because they find it a particularly easy thing to do but because they have little choice. They may perceive that language problems, a lack of recognised qualifications, glass ceilings or just racism reduce their chances of otherwise finding suitable employment. It was a cultural norm in many Western societies until recently that women and ethnic groups played subordinate roles, and over recent years support agencies in Britain have been keen to assist where possible in the formation and development of ethnic business enterprises. Interestingly, Phizacklea and Ram report that when the director of a business start-up agency in France visited England, he was impressed by the 'proliferation of business agencies which specifically target ethnic minority populations, not just at the inception but by providing business support services as well'.[53] Help is offered but there is a low take-up of support, and studies of ethnic firms in Britain have given the following reasons for the reluctance to use formal support services:[54]

- Language difficulties.
- 'I started on my own therefore I don't need help.'
- 'Agencies are only interested in larger firms.'
- 'I can't afford the time to attend meetings and courses.'
- 'West Indians are stereotyped as incapable of running a firm.'
- 'We are discriminated against for being Nigerian.'

Ram approached the topic of under-use from the perspective of providers and concluded that problems arose because:[55]

- There were no precise data about ethnic entrepreneurs.
- Providers were unsure of the rationale for intervention.
- There was competition between the agencies.
- It was more important to meet 'targets' than specific needs.
- Providers perceived themselves as marginal.

Just as some people feel that it is important to assist ethnic entrepreneurs, so some feel that women entrepreneurs face particular obstacles and should be assisted. Additional business obstacles may exist for women entrepreneurs if they cannot acquire resources as easily as men, if their work and life experiences have not allowed them to develop entrepreneurial competence, or if they face gender discrimination. We should note, however, that some recent studies on discrimination against women in acquiring start-up capital, for example, point to the complexity of the topic.[56] Further Carter *et al.*[57] draw attention to studies suggesting the 'gendering' of structure is itself a gender effect, and Walker and Joyner argue that women's difficulties in getting business finance can arise because of pure gender discrimination, institutionalised gender discrimination, statistical gender discrimination or economic gender discrimination.[58]

Pure gender discrimination occurs when women are offered different financial terms simply because they are women. Institutional gender discrimination occurs when it is presumed that a woman is less likely to operate a firm successfully. Statistical gender discrimination occurs when women as a group are offered different terms based on statistical averages. Economic gender discrimination occurs when a woman does not meet the criteria for financing simply because she is a woman. These authors point out that various forms of government assistance have different impacts on these four kinds of discrimination. For example, in the United Sates, government procurement programmes which ration contracts on the basis of gender can remove pure and institutional discrimination but not statistical and economic discrimination. On the other hand business counselling and training can reduce all four kinds of discrimination.

WHY NOT? THE ARGUMENTS AGAINST INTERVENTION

> It is almost universally accepted among politicians that more small enterprise is unquestionably beneficial to the economy. Yet this can be questioned. ... Several frequently offered justifications for policies appear dubious. For example, the alleged existence of shortages of start-up finance or the negative impact of employment legislation on small business expansion and job creation have been overwhelmingly rejected by research. Yet Conservative and Labour administrations [in the UK] have continued to cling to these assumptions and policy continues to be influenced by them strongly.
>
> James Curran[59]

Economic arguments justify intervention in a market economy when there is market failure. Some economists, however, maintain that market failure, although a necessary condition, is not alone a sufficient condition for intervention. There must in addition be evidence that the overall welfare improvements resulting from the intervention will be sufficient to justify the cost of that intervention and that there is no better way of achieving the same improvements.

It might be expected that attempts to promote enterprise and entrepreneurship would find favour in most quarters, but this is not necessarily the case. It is said that enterprise thrives in a free enterprise economy, and many advocates of this economic system caution against interference with market forces. These people argue that the laws of supply and demand, operating through the price system, send signals to interested parties who respond to market opportunities and threats. Those persons who are able to interpret market forces accurately will reap economic rewards, and this pursuit of self-interest leads to the most efficient utilisation of economic resources. Enterprising individuals are inclined to be energetic, forward-looking people who take bold steps to realise opportunities, and it can be seen that free enterprise economic systems are an attractive milieu for enterprising individuals to display their skills. It is argued therefore that there is no point in promoting entrepreneurship and enterprise: the enterprising will avail themselves of opportunities, and the aggregate outcome of their decisions will produce greater welfare than decisions made by central authorities.

This argument assumes perfectly competitive markets, yet many maintain that markets are far from competitive. Nevertheless, it is still contended that there is no generalised market failure in the small business sector. Bennett, like Gibb, points to the size and growth of the sector as evidence of advance.

He argues that, when asked about those factors that inhibit the development of small businesses, owners comment on general economic and regulatory factors such as the condition of the economy and the inhibiting impact of statutory regulations. Where specific needs are highlighted they arise in areas such as venture capital, marketing advice, training and cash flow problems: 'areas where well developed markets already exist'.[60]

Two comments in particular may be made in response to these views. First, many small businesses may be unaware of the immense power of large corporations and their subtle ability to inhibit competition. Those small businesses may occupy niche markets where, unless they threaten industrial giants directly, they may be tolerated or, with the advent of strategic outsourcing, they may be positively welcomed by some large businesses. Second, the methods used by those who seek to identify the problems experienced by small firms rarely delve, in a detailed way, into the problems small firms experience. Researchers commonly present entrepreneurs with lengthy lists of problems and ask them to say which of the problems apply to them. Just as Bennett argues that it is only by means of in-depth discussion with small business owners that the effectiveness of policy initiatives can be judged, so it can be argued that quantitative studies of the problems faced by small businesses will merely elicit pre-programmed responses. It is important to understand how entrepreneurs perceive and construct problems, and there may also be a tendency for small business owners to project their problems away from themselves towards more distant perceived impediments such as the government, the European Commission or the economic environment.

On the issue of the provision of needed services, such as information, advice and training, Bennett argues that if the felt need of businesses is great enough, then they will pay the market price for the consultancy services on offer. As mentioned above, however, economic reasoning ignores many of the personal and interpersonal aspects of seeking external advice, whether it is from consultants, counsellors or mentors. Many owners have a real need for such assistance but lack the information and confidence needed to identify, approach, and if necessary negotiate terms for, suitable help.

IN CONCLUSION

The fact is that intervention exists – like it or not, and as Arshed and Carter have summarised, 'enterprise policy is the main mechanism used by governments to stimulate economic growth, employment and international competitiveness'.[61] Despite that, this chapter suggests that wanting to intervene is not enough. If intervention policies are to be effective they have to be justified and have clear purposes and objectives. Establishing what intervention is supposed to achieve is often difficult. In 1994, for instance, Storey pointed out that in Europe there was a wide range of policy initiatives to assist small businesses, but that the governments concerned had yet to formulate a coherent policy towards the sector. What he said still appears to be largely true today:

> In no country, as far as we are aware, is there the equivalent of a 'White Paper' which articulates the range of public policies towards smaller firms which currently exist, which provides a justification for the existing configuration of policies, and which provides criteria for judging whether or not policies are successful.[62]

But, whether there are such clear criteria or not, there is intervention and the next chapter looks at the next stages in the framework: the methods employed to give effect to intervention policy.

☞ **THE KEY POINTS OF CHAPTER 14**

- Because governments want to intervene to encourage and/or support enterprise, entrepreneurship and small business there are policies in this area.
- A model framework for constructing a policy is suggested as an aid to understanding the relationship between different policy components.

- Among such components are, or should be:
  — Policy drivers – the reasons why governments want to intervene.
  — Policy objectives – of which the ones most often advanced appear to be start-ups (birth-rate policy), business growth and employment.
  — Policy justifications, including market and other failures and barriers faced by particular groups.
- Despite the various reasons advanced for policy there are also arguments against intervention.

✓ QUESTIONS, EXERCISES, ESSAY AND DISCUSSION TOPICS

- Is government intervention to increase the amount of enterprise ever justified?

- How do you distinguish between policy drivers, objectives, targets and justifications?

- If governments are going to intervene anyway, what is the point of trying to record policy drivers and distinguish policy objectives?

- On balance, do you think policy can usefully target growth businesses?

SUGGESTIONS FOR FURTHER READING AND INFORMATION

R. Blackburn and M. Schaper (eds), *Government, SMEs and Entrepreneurship Development* (Farnham: Gower, 2012).

A. Lundström and L. Stevenson, 'Patterns and Trends in Entrepreneurship/SME Policy and Practice in Ten Economies', Vol. 3 of the *Entrepreneurship Policy for the Future* Series (Stockholm: Swedish Foundation for Small Business Research, 2001).

D. J. Storey, *Understanding the Small Business Sector* (London: Routledge, 1994).

D. J. Storey and F. J. Greene, *Small Business and Entrepreneurship* (Harlow: Pearson Education Ltd, 2010) Part 6.

REFERENCES

[1] D. Richard, *Small Business and Government: The Richard Report* (London: NESTA, 2008) pp. 9–10.

[2] *Entrepreneurship in the Netherlands*, 10th Edition (Zoetermeer: EIM Business and Policy Research, 2009) p. 9.

[3] Taken from http://ec.europa.eu/growth/smes/business-friendly-environment/index_en.htm (accessed 4 May 2016).

[4] Taken from http://www.sba.gov/about-sba (accessed 4 May 2016).

[5] Business Week Editors, *The Reindustrialisation of America* (New York, NY: McGraw-Hill, 1982), cited in K. Vesper, *Entrepreneurship and National Policy* (Chicago, IL: Heller Institute for Small Business Policy Papers, 1983) p. 74.

[6] See H. Mintzberg, *Power In and Around Organizations* (Englewood Cliffs, NJ: Prentice Hall, 1983) pp. 171–183, for a discussion of the conditions that favour political behaviour in organisations.

[7] S. Johnson, 'Public Policy and the Small Firm' book proposal reviewed by authors (2006), Chapter 2.

[8] L. Stevenson, in *Fostering Entrepreneurship: A Seminar Organised by Invest Northern Ireland* 14 March 2007, report by S. Bridge. Taken from www.isbe.org.uk (accessed 16 October 2008).

[9] D. Birch, cited in D. J. Storey, *Understanding the Small Business Sector* (London: Routledge, 1994) p. 161.

[10] C. Gallagher, cited in D. J. Storey, *Understanding the Small Business Sector* (London: Routledge, 1994) p. 165.

[11] From the back cover of A. Westall and M. Cowling, *Agenda for Growth* (London: Institute for Public Policy Research, 1999).

[12] Small Business Service, *A Government Action Plan for Small Business: The Evidence Base* (Department of Trade and Industry, 2004) p. 15.

[13] T. Kiisel, 'Small Business, Job Creation, and Why We Should Lend to Young Companies', *Forbes*. Taken from http://www.forbes.com/sites/tykiisel/2015/06/17/small-business-job-creation-and-why-we-should-lend-to-young-companies/#7305581b789a (accessed 14 May 2016).

[14] R. Bennett, 'SME Policy Support in Britain since the 1990s: What Have We Learnt?', *Environment and Planning C: Government and Policy*, Vol. 26, No. 2, 2008, p. 375.

[15] Department of Business, Enterprise and Regulatory Reform, *Enterprise: Unlocking the UK's Talent – Summary* (London: HM Treasury, 2008) p. 23.

[16] D. J. Storey, *Understanding the Small Business Sector* (London: Routledge, 1994) p. 257.

[17] D. J. Storey, 'Six Steps to Heaven: Evaluating the Impact of SME Policies', paper presented to *23rd ISBA Small Firms Conference, Leeds*, 1999; also published in D. L. Sexton and H. Landstrom (eds), *Handbook of Entrepreneurship* (Oxford: Blackwell, 2000) pp. 176–194.

[18] Small Business Service, Op. Cit. p. 4.

[19] S. Singer, J. E. Amoros and D. Moska Arreola, *Global Entrepreneurship Monitor 2014 Global Report* (London: Global Entrepreneurship Research Association, London Business School, 2015) p. 68.

[20] Ibid.

[21] Ibid.

[22] D. J. Storey, *Understanding the Small Business Sector*, Op. Cit. p. 115.

[23] M. Hart and M. Anyadike-Danes, *Contribution to Job Creation by High Growth SMEs* (Birmingham: ERC Insight, Enterprise Research Centre and Aston Business School, Aston University, July 2015) p. 1.

[24] E. Garnsey, 'A New Theory of the Growth of the Firm', in Proceedings of the *41st ICSB World Conference*, Stockholm 1996, p. 126.

[25] D. Smallbone and C. Massey, 'Targeting for Growth: A Critical Examination', paper presented at the *33rd ISBE National Small Firms Conference*, November 2010.

[26] Extract from an interview in 'The Job Generation Process Revisited', *ICSB Bulletin*, Spring (1995).

[27] D. Smallbone and C. Massey, Op. Cit. p. 52.

[28] D. J. Storey, 'Optimism and Chance: The Elephants in the Entrepreneurship Room', *International Small Business Journal*, Vol. 29, No. 4, 2011, pp. 303–321.

[29] R. Botham, 'Regional Variations in New Firm Job Creation: The Contribution of High Growth Start-ups', paper presented at the *33rd ISBE National Small Firms Conference*, November 2010.

[30] B. Hynes, 'Endeavouring to Profile Higher Growth SMEs – The Debate Continues', paper presented at the *33rd ISBE National Small Firms Conference*, November 2010.

[31] K. F. Mole, S. Roper and M. Levy, 'Small Firm Growth in the Combined ASBS Database: The Impact of Family Business, Women-Leadership and BME Leadership', paper presented at the *33rd ISBE National Small Firms Conference*, November 2010.

[32] D. J. Storey, 'Six Steps to Heaven', Op. Cit.

[33] L. Perren, M. Davis and R. Kroessin, *Mapping the UK SME Management and Leadership Development Provision* (London: Council for Excellence in Management Leadership, 2001) p. 14.

[34] J. Curran and D. J. Storey, *Small Business Policy: Past Experiences and Future Directions* (The Small Business Service and Kingston University Small Business Research Centre SME Seminar Series 'Linking Research and Policy', DTI Conference Centre, December 2000) p. 2.

[35] N. Arshed, C. Mason and S. Carter, 'Exploring the Disconnect in Policy Implementation: A Case of Enterprise Policy in England', *Environment and Planning C: Government and Policy*, published online before print 27 January 2016.

[36] OECD, *The Role of SMEs: Findings and Issues* (Paris: OECD/DSTI/IND, 2000) p. 7.

[37] See H. Mintzberg, *Power In and Around Organisations* (Englewood Cliffs, NJ: Prentice Hall, 1983) p. 636, for a discussion of the fallacy of economic markets.

[38] OECD, Op. Cit. p. 2.

[39] Committee of Public Accounts, Oral Evidence on 19 June 2006 on Report by the Controller and Auditor General, 'Supporting Small Business', HC962.

[40] S. Johnson, *Public Policy and the Small Firm*, Op. Cit. Chapter 2.

[41] Ibid. p. 17.

[42] Ibid. p. 18.

[43] Ibid. p. 18.

[44] G. Bannock, *The Economics and Management of Small Business: An International Perspective* (London: Routledge, 2005) p. 111.

[45] S. Johnson, Op. Cit. p. 17.

[46] Ibid. p. 19.

[47] See W. R. Scott, *Organisations* (Englewood Cliffs, NJ: Prentice Hall, 1992), Chapter 10, for a discussion of the impact of size on organisations.

[48] C. Mason, R. Harrison and J. Chaloner, *Informal Risk Capital in the UK* (Southampton: Venture Finance Research Project, 1991).

[49] M. B. Slovin and J. E. Young, 'The Entrepreneurial Search for Capital: An Investment in Finance', *Entrepreneurship, Innovation and Change*, Vol. 1, 1992, pp. 177–194.

[50] G. Bannock and A. Peacock, *Governments and Small Business* (London: Paul Chapman, 1989).

[51] A. A. Gibb, 'SME Policy, Academic Research and the Growth of Ignorance: Mythical Concepts, Myths, Assumptions, Rituals and Confusions', *International Small Business Journal*, Vol. 18, No. 3, 2000, pp. 13–35.

[52] H. Mintzberg, *Power In and Around Organizations* (Englewood Cliffs, NJ: Prentice Hall, 1983) p. 636.

[53] A. Phizacklea and M. Ram, 'Ethnic Entrepreneurship in Comparative Perspective', *International Journal of Entrepreneurial Behaviour and Research*, Vol. 1, 1995, pp. 48–58.

[54] A. Fadahunsi, D. Smallbone and S. Supri, 'Networking and Ethnic Minority Enterprise Development: Insights from a North London Study', *Journal of Small Business and Enterprise Development*, Vol. 7, 2000, pp. 228–240.

[55] M. Ram, 'Unravelling Social Networks in Ethnic Minority Firms', *International Small Business Journal*, Vol. 12, 1994, pp. 42–53.

[56] S. Carter and P. Rosa, 'The Financing of Male- and Female-Owned Businesses', *Entrepreneurship and Regional Development*, Vol. 10, 1998, pp. 225–241.

[57] S. Carter, S. Mwaura, M. Ram, K. Trehan and T. Jones, 'Barriers to Ethnic Minority and Women's Enterprise: Existing Evidence, Policy Tensions and Unsettled Questions', *International Small Business Journal*, Vol. 33, No. 1, 2015, pp. 49–69.

[58] D. Walker and B. E. Joyner, 'Female Entrepreneurship and the Market Process: Gender-Based Policy Considerations', *Journal of Developmental Entrepreneurship*, Vol. 4, 1999, pp. 95–116.

[59] J. Curran, 'What Is Small Business Policy in the UK For? Evaluation and Assessing Small Business Policies', *International Small Business Journal*, Vol. 18, No. 3, 2000, pp. 38, 42.

[60] R. J. Bennett, 'SMEs and Public Policy: Present Day Dilemmas, Future Priorities and the Case of Business Links', paper presented at the *19th ISBA National Small Firms Policy and Research Conference*, Birmingham, 1996, p. 6.

[61] N. Arshed and S. Carter, 'Enterprise Policy Making in the UK: Prescribed Approaches and Day-to-Day Practices', in R. Blackburn and M. Schaper (eds), *Government, SMEs and Entrepreneurship Development* (Farnham: Gower, 2012) p. 61.

[62] D. J. Storey, *Understanding the Small Business Sector*, Op. Cit. p. 253.

Companion website

Please visit the companion website at www.palgravehighered.com/Bridge-UE-5e for access to additional learning and teaching materials.

Enterprise Policy: Approaches and Implementation Methods

CONTENTS

- Introduction
- Policy approaches
- Forms of assistance – policy instruments

- Policy implementation
- In conclusion
- Annex – A taxonomy of enterprise initiatives

KEY CONCEPTS

This chapter covers:

- The different approaches which can be taken to achieve enterprise policy objectives, including those which:
  - Focus on individual people and businesses.
  - Endeavour to improve the institutional environment.
  - Try to make the cultural environment more encouraging.
- The different forms which assistance can take – the policy instruments that give effect to policy.
- Some of the issues relevant to policy implementation.

LEARNING OBJECTIVES

By the end of this chapter the reader should:

- Understand that, to achieve policy objectives, it is necessary to select approaches, instruments and delivery agents.
- Understand the different approaches which can be taken: in particular the difference between approaches which seek to alter the general business environment and those which seek to help individual people and/or businesses.
- Be aware of some of the many different forms that assistance can take.
- Know about the key agencies which have been formed to deliver policy in the UK.

INTRODUCTION

Chapter 14 explores the reasons why governments, governmental organisations and sometimes other organisations want to intervene to encourage and support more enterprise, entrepreneurship and/or small business. It also considers the objectives that are often set for policies in this area and the justifications that can be offered for such intervention. Those considerations cover the top line of the framework introduced in Figure 14.1 (and repeated as Figure 15.1), and this chapter follows the sequence of that framework by looking at the methods used: the policy approaches and instruments that are employed to try to achieve the desired objectives as well as some of the issues that can arise in policy delivery (the boxes shaded in grey in Figure 15.1).

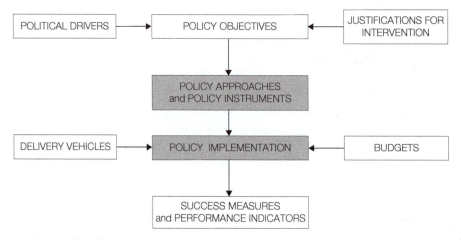

Figure 15.1 *(repeated) A diagram of a policy framework*

It might be thought that the methods chosen would be designed to give effect to strategies but often the strategies appear to be missing. For instance, despite a multitude of initiatives in the UK since the end of the 1970s, an overall strategy, in the sense of a coherent set of objectives and associated means of achieving them, was lacking at least until 2002. The Small Business Service then produced a paper setting out the measures the government was putting in place.[1] Until that time, the last real attempt in the UK to articulate a coherent SME policy in a single document, some claim, was the Bolton Report on Small Firms in 1971.

Nevertheless, because of the perceived importance of smaller firms for economic development, virtually every country in the world now intervenes in some way to promote enterprise skills, to encourage more entrepreneurs and to grow more indigenous businesses. But choosing appropriate methods by which to achieve policy objectives in this area is not simple, even when those objectives are clearly specified, because there appears to be such a wide range of possibilities. There are many different factors which are supposed to have an influence on enterprise, entrepreneurship and small businesses. Also there are often different ways in which each factor might be used in order to apply its supposed influence in the direction desired, and different routes through which that influence might be delivered.

POLICY APPROACHES

As Figure 14.1 suggests, once the objective of a policy has been determined, it is necessary to think about how that objective might be achieved. Policy approaches and instruments refer to the ways in which policy might be put into effect. Approaches can refer to the overall methods used and instruments refer to the tools applied for each method; however, as the term approaches can be used to embrace instruments, and as other terms can also be used, this distinction is not always clear.

Approaches to achieving enterprise policy objectives, however ambiguously those objectives are stated, can be divided into the following broad categories:

- *Addressing individuals and businesses.* The more obvious, and sometimes also the commonest, approaches are those which endeavour to support the start-up and growth of businesses by providing direct assistance to the individuals or businesses concerned.
- *Addressing the institutional business environment.* There are also approaches which try to create a favourable environment for business creation and growth. Such approaches seek to stimulate a positive climate for enterprise or apply measures, often delivered by the institutions of government, to liberalise trade, to deregulate, to reform legal and taxation regimes, or to facilitate the acquisition of the relevant skills.
- *Addressing the cultural environment.* It is increasingly being recognised that social attitudes affect people's willingness to engage in business – but few approaches yet appear to address this.

The 'map' presented in Figure 15.2 is one attempt to show, within these categories of approach, the variety of different fields, or sub-approaches, of enterprise (including entrepreneurship and small business) policy.

These approaches are not mutually exclusive, and in nearly all countries they are adopted simultaneously. This was specifically acknowledged, for instance, in the UK by the former Department of Employment, which stated:

> There are three strands in the Government's approach to small firms. First, and of most importance, the role of the Government is to ensure that small firms can flourish in conditions of fair competition and to create space and incentives for enterprise by minimising taxation, regulations and red tape. Second, the Government strongly supports and reinforces the change to more positive social attitudes towards the small business sector. Third, the Government helps to fill gaps in the supply side by providing commercial services for small firms, largely to improve their access to finance, information, professional advice and training. Wherever possible the Government's approach is provided in partnership with the private sector.[2]

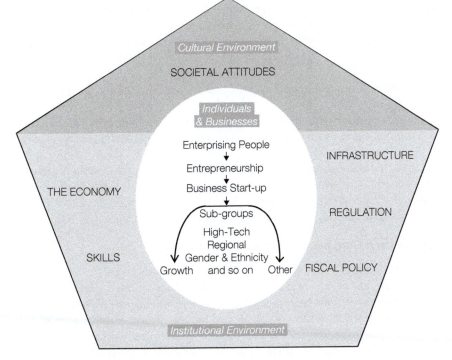

Figure 15.2 Enterprise policy map

PART 3

A multi-strand approach is not universally favoured, however. It has been argued by many, on the basis of numerous surveys, that the main factors which restrict the growth of businesses relate to the macro-economy. For instance in 1996 the Confederation of British Industry's (CBI's) SME Council claimed that:

> It is through the creation of a healthy economy and conditions for growth that employment will be generated. ... The CBI therefore believes that Governments should focus on creating the right conditions for SMEs to start and grow rather than introducing individual policy objectives aimed at market distortions.[3]

Another way of categorising some of the approaches can be by their intended effect, and the instruments which are often adopted seem to be designed to do one of the following:[4]

- *Risk reduction:* the use of macro-economic policies (e.g. taxation, interest rates) to stabilise the economy and reduce uncertainty.
- *Cost reduction:* the use of grants, subsidies or low-cost loans to reduce the cost of inputs to the business. These can be targeted (e.g. a grant to a specific business) or general (e.g. to reduce energy/fuel costs or labour costs).
- *Increase the flow of information/advice:* to make information more readily available on trends in international markets, national/local issues and government programmes for small business. This can be through targeted supports (and information services) or general publicity.

Individuals and businesses: assisting the enterprise process

The first broad approach listed above is that of promoting the enterprise process by interventions targeted at the level of the individual business or at the person preparing to start a business. This is in contrast to 'environmental' interventions, which are at the meso- or macro-economic level – although there is no clear division between where one approach ends and the other begins.

These interventions, which are aimed at individual people or businesses, generally target segments or sub-groups of the population categorised by stage of business development, by business sector, by geographic region, by market area or by type of owner: categories where unique sets of problems and/ or opportunities are perceived to exist. Some of these categories, which are described further below, include:

- The development of enterprising people (in the broad sense) and the supply of entrepreneurs who start businesses.
- Assisting the start-up business in its birth stages and subsequent aftercare. Such assistance is often viewed as critical not only to survival rates but also to the quality and quantity of the subsequent growers.
- Removing the barriers and giving incentives to established businesses wishing to grow. The growth of businesses is often perceived as central to policy, and support for it is now quite common. Less common is support for the other, non-growing businesses although they are still considered by some as potential growth businesses and therefore worthy of some attention.

Pre-start-up – enterprising people and entrepreneurship

The pre-start-up stage could be perceived as including anyone who might start a business, including those who so far have not even considered self-employment or business creation as a valid option. Influencing the perspectives of the latter is considered under the subheading 'The cultural environment for enterprise – societal attitudes'. Attention is focused here on those who, having thought about it, are working to try to become entrepreneurs. There are interventions to help such people including business skills training in its various forms, but there are also interventions to assist and guide market research, programmes to help with early product and/or service development and initiatives that try to help inventors with potential new business ideas.

Variations of intervention help with the sourcing, identification and development of business ideas, and with the formation of enterprise teams to combine the different strengths of individuals in order to promote one successful venture.

Business start-up

While a healthy rate of start-ups is thought to be essential for new ideas, innovation, competitiveness and the overall vibrancy of the economy, in the UK policy emphasis throughout recent decades has fluctuated: at times focusing not on the quantity of start-ups but on their perceived quality (e.g. their potential for growth or for exporting). It has been argued that non-discriminating support to start-ups is counter-productive because many will fail, and that this implies that a more selective approach to business support should be adopted. Thus in Britain the support infrastructure has sometimes been tasked to offer most support to firms with the motivation to grow and at other times adopting a more balanced approach (see Policy Implementation below).

Interventions in the start-up field have included financial assistance, training, networking, information, advice and counselling. They have also included the provision of workspace geared specifically to meet the needs of small businesses. This has taken the form of managed workspace (MWS) – often on attractive leasing terms and typically with the availability of central services such as secretarial support and business advice. In addition, there have been variations on the business incubator concept and special initiatives encouraging start-ups to become e-enabled.

High-tech, high-growth businesses

General issues relating to targeting growth businesses are considered in Chapter 14, but one particular aspect of this is businesses in the high-tech category. These businesses – typically small entrepreneurial firms which are knowledge-based or involved in the commercialisation of knowledge – have been subject to a range of targeted policy initiatives since the 1980s. Such businesses are believed to have high growth potential but also to face particular problems needing tailored solutions. Thus specific support for them is now a strong feature in many countries because of their contribution to innovation and their potential for growth, and because they are likely to be the seeds for the new industry sectors of the future. Their particular needs are seen to arise from the relatively high cost of research and development and its associated risks, which makes them unattractive to conservative or risk-averse lending institutions. Their potential for fast growth can mean that the need for finance will be even greater. Such problems are frequently compounded by other aspects of these businesses, for example:

- A value which is often linked primarily to longer-term growth, based on scientific knowledge and intellectual property.
- A lack of tangible assets in their initial development to use as collateral when significant up-front investment may be needed (and little evidence that the businesses can trade profitably).
- Products with little or no track record, untested in the marketplace and possibly subject to a high rate of obsolescence.
- The funders' lack of understanding of the potential of the products or processes, which is due very often to their specialist nature.
- Their owners' frequent failure to pay enough attention to communicating meaningfully in a non-technical way.

The overall result is that funders have difficulties in assessing the viability of the proposals, particularly in terms of judging the technology, estimating prospective demand and quantifying the risks. Since the 1980s, therefore, in the UK a range of schemes have been introduced to help high-tech businesses financially and in other ways. Examples of such help are shown in Illustration 15.1.

⊃ | **ILLUSTRATION 15.1 – INITIATIVES FOR HIGH-TECH BUSINESSES**

Various ways have been tried, in different parts of the world, to encourage and support the start-up and growth of high-tech businesses. In the UK they include initiatives such as:

Clustering: Clustering is encouraged because US high-tech companies are believed to have benefited greatly from the grouping of firms and finance providers together as, for example, has happened in Silicon Valley.

Business incubators: Incubators have been viewed as an effective means of encouraging innovation and the wider dissemination of technology, although some now query this.

The UK Innovation Investment Fund (UKIIF): The fund was announced in June 2011 'to drive economic growth and create highly skilled jobs by investing in businesses where there are significant global opportunities'. UKIIF will operate on a Fund of Funds structure which means it will not invest directly in companies, but rather invest in a small number of specialist, private sector funds. Such funds are then obliged to invest in technology-based SMEs in strategically important sectors.

The Business Angel Co-investment Fund: This fund was set up in 2011 with £50 million government funding from the Regional Growth Fund and £100 million from the British Business Bank. Its aim is to invest in 'high potential SMEs' and to encourage the UK business angel market.

The Enterprise Capital Fund programme (ECFs): This programme was launched in 2005 to 'address a market weakness in the provision of equity finance to SMEs by using government funding alongside private sector investment to establish funds that operate within the 'equity gap'. It replaced the *Regional Venture Capital Funds*.

The Capital for Enterprise Fund: This fund was established in 2008 to provide equity and mezzanine investments for high-growth companies struggling to raise finance because of the credit crunch. On 1 April 2008, responsibility for the management of ECFs and the Small Firms Loan Guarantee Scheme (SFLG) was transferred to a new body, Capital for Enterprise Limited (CfEL), which was 'aimed at improving the selection and management of the funds, but did not change the nature of the funds or their policy objectives'.[5] CfEL was also responsible for the management of the Enterprise Finance Guarantee (EFG) – the replacement for the SFLG Scheme. It ceased operating independently on 1 October 2013 and became part of the British Business Bank (see below).

The Help to Grow programme: The programme was launched in 2015 to provide up to £200 million of loans to small businesses to encourage growth and innovation. Administered through the British Business Bank, it aims to address the financing needs of smaller businesses which are struggling to raise sufficient senior debt to fund their growth opportunities.

Tax credit for R&D: An R&D tax credit for SMEs based on the total cost of their R&D expenditure was introduced in 2000. By helping to reduce some of the financial risk for technology businesses, the government hopes to accelerate their development.

Exporters

There is thought to be a danger that support for many small businesses will result in displacement of other local business activity and so will not result in net local benefits. If the businesses assisted are exporting, this danger will be largely avoided. Because of this, and because of their growth potential, there have been a variety of incentives to encourage greater export performance by the small firm sector, mainly through financial subsidies and information-based assistance (such as travel and trade show subsidies, export credit guarantees, subsidised market research, free access to databases, and information on trends, market requirements and potential contacts). Growth has become associated, in the minds of many, with the need to export, and such businesses are finding an increasing amount of support from the private sector, as well as from the public sector.

Regional – geographical areas of disadvantage

Policies have been adopted to assist in the regeneration, through enterprise and small business development, of areas of special disadvantage. Deprivation is a complex issue and the nature and extent of its impact vary, not least between urban and rural areas:

> Deprived areas have particular features which include high mortality rates, poor physical environment, low levels of educational attainment and participation, high crime rates, and poor housing. The promotion of enterprise can play an important role in addressing social exclusion. It should not, however, be viewed as a panacea for social and financial exclusion. High levels of displacement of existing businesses, the risks involved in setting up in business and the propensity to create marginal businesses are potential limitations to the contribution of small firms in deprived areas.[6]

On the other hand, run-down inner cities and depressed rural areas have benefited from initiatives designed to promote social enterprises, such as 'community enterprises' and co-operatives. In addition, managed workspace has been publicly funded in whole or in part in an attempt to provide localised support that is relevant and real (and visible).

This latter provision often takes the form of local enterprise agencies, which can become the centrepiece of policies to create a focus for urban or rural regeneration involving local people in their management and activities. Such local roots can strengthen the ability of local agencies to be meaningful centres and role models for stimulating a local enterprise culture. As well as premises, they can offer various other forms of business support – particularly training, advice and information – and can be vehicles for moulding regional programmes to meet local needs. Some UK initiatives are described in the next section.

Population sub-groups, including genders and ethnic groups

Efforts to encourage the population in general, and certain sub-groups in particular, to become more aware of and receptive to the possibilities of enterprise have already been referred to in earlier chapters. A variety of (usually business start-up) programmes have targeted graduates, youth, the unemployed, corporate employees, ethnic minorities, women and the disabled. Across Europe, it is perceived that an effective enterprise policy will seek to improve the start-up rate among some or all of such sub-groups, for instance 'improving the start-up rate among women, young people and unemployed'.[7] Indeed, the Global Entrepreneurship Monitor (see Chapter 4) identified three main demographic characteristics as impacting on entrepreneurship, of which one was 'the level of female participation in entrepreneurial activity', women being the largest 'sub-group' in the population.[8] This has led to special funding from the European Union and a range of national and transnational programmes to help women to increase their participation rates.

The institutional environment for business

The individual approaches listed above are like the medical services provided by GPs and hospitals which seek to help individual patients. Environmental approaches, however, are like health schemes which try raise everyone's health by means such as better sewers, less pollution and improved health education.

Improving the business environment is the second of the three broad approaches to small business support described earlier. Although the business environment affects the performance of all firms, not just small businesses, and many initiatives in this area will affect all businesses, some interventions are designed to address distortion or market failures which affect small businesses disproportionally. However, Bannock argues that, rather than focusing on specific policies and programmes for small businesses, it is more productive to concentrate on improving what he calls the framework conditions for all enterprises, as these will often have a disproportionately beneficial effect upon small enterprises.[9]

Figure 15.2 suggests that policy does, or could, address five key areas of the institutional business environment, but other interpretations could produce different categorisations. Nevertheless these five are described here:

The economy

Most governments strive for stable growth, low inflation, low interest rates and a steady exchange rate as the economic backcloth against which it is thought that businesses can plan effectively in the context of reasonable certainty about future trading circumstances. It is thus supposed that the impacts of taxation and public spending are critically important policy intervention measures. Indeed the effects of trade cycles upon the rates of birth, death and growth of all businesses may generally override the impact of all interventions.

Fiscal policy

There are various fiscal measures which can be applied with the aim of helping the growth and survival of small businesses. These range from a reduced rate of corporation tax to inheritance tax concessions and extended value added tax (VAT) exemption thresholds, as well as tax incentives for business angels and investors.

Although, when asked, small business owners might indicate that lower taxes would encourage them to do more because it would raise the amount of reward they would thus gain from additional enterprise, the relationship between lower taxes (more disposable income) and economic activity does not appear to be straightforward. For example, Rees and Shah investigated the hours worked by self-employed persons and found that personal and family factors like age and number of children were key determinants.[10] However, when these variables were controlled, they found that the number of hours worked fell when personal taxation rates fell, presumably because with lower rates of taxation less work could generate the same level of after-tax income.

Skills

The business need for labour market skills is apparent at all levels from management to operative. The ability to access appropriate skills at affordable prices is an essential ingredient in any supportive economic environment. Small businesses, especially growing ones, would appear to have more acute difficulties in accessing skills. Indeed, small firms would appear to experience genuine problems in dealing with the formalities and legalities of recruitment in an increasingly sophisticated environment. In particular, there is evidence that the small business sector has been reluctant to recruit graduate labour and has difficulty in doing so. Changes in the tax treatment of share options in the UK, however, has allowed many more firms, and particularly small high-growth companies, to use them as a carrot to attract key staff.

Infrastructure

An efficient and effective infrastructure is needed, including appropriate transportation systems and networks, communication networks and an adequate supply of business premises, appropriately located. Indeed, with the knowledge economy becoming all-pervasive, speedy and reliable transfer of more and more information has put increasing pressure on regions and nations to ensure that they are abreast of the latest developments in information and communication technology (ICT) and have the infrastructure to support it.

(De)regulation and administrative simplification

We need to tackle regulation with vigour to free businesses to compete and create jobs, and give people greater freedom and personal responsibility ... I want us to be the first Government in modern history to leave office having reduced the overall burden of regulation, rather than increasing it.

UK Prime Minister's letter to all Cabinet Ministers, 6 April 2011[11]

The cost of compliance for the UK's 1.2 million micro, small and medium-sized employers is £20 billion in terms of actual costs. The perceived costs (including opportunity costs) are £41 billion when senior management time devoted to administration instead of pursuing growth opportunities are allowed for.

Based on Forum of Private Business press release, 17 July 2015[12]

Often, when surveys are made either of the problems of small businesses or of the constraints on their growth, issues of 'red tape and bureaucracy' tend to come at or near the top of any list. Clearly, a certain level of regulation is needed to create a healthy business environment and a 'level playing field'; adequate standards are needed in the areas of health and safety, data protection, employment rights, environmental protection and reducing anti-competitive practices, and, as is often claimed, one man's right is another man's burden. Nevertheless, it has been argued that statutory regulations in the above areas and in taxation, statistical reporting and company registration are disproportionately burdensome for small businesses. However, it has been suggested that, while these and other burdens have been identified by lobby groups as barriers to small business development, they are not necessarily perceived as such by all small businesses.

Governments across the world pay lip service at least to reducing the burdens on small business. Listing all examples would be a very lengthy process, but, as an illustration, in the UK there has been increasing emphasis on deregulation since the publication of the White Paper *Lifting the Burden* in 1985. The Deregulation Unit was established within the Department of Trade and Industry (DTI) in 1985, and in 1994 the Deregulation Task Force was set up. In 1997 it was renamed the 'Better Regulation Task Force' and subsequently it became a Better Regulation Executive within the then Department for Business, Innovation and Skills (BIS). A Regulatory Delivery directorate was launched by BIS in 2016 which brought together the Better Regulation Delivery Office (BRDO) and the National Measurement and Regulation Office (NMRO) to focus on regulation and enforcement. A year earlier a Regulatory Policy Committee (RPC) was appointed by the government to act as the independent verification body as set out in the Small Business, Enterprise and Employment Act (2015). In this role the RPC is required to verify the costs and benefits to business and civil society organisations of regulatory provisions. Also, since January 2013, as part of what is called the Red Tape Challenge government departments have been expected to offset any increase in the cost of regulation by finding deregulatory measures of at least twice the value (known as the One-In-Two-Out rule).[13] These and other initiatives imply that attention is being paid to:

- Measuring the impact of new regulations on small businesses.
- Critically examining existing legislative measures affecting business with a view to eliminating many of them.
- Increasing emphasis on making regulations 'goal-based' and not over-prescriptive (that is, in enforcement procedures, emphasising outcomes not processes).

Thus, while some observations might suggest that the UK is not doing well in this, comparative assessments such as that reproduced in Table 6.7 present a somewhat different picture. There may still be burdens in the UK but they appear to be relatively less onerous than those in many other countries.

The cultural environment for enterprise – societal attitudes

The third area of the framework suggested in Figure 15.2 is the cultural environment: the informal set of social norms and incentives which represent society's attitudes to entrepreneurial activity. Although the influence of social rules has been recognised (for instance by Baumol – see Chapter 3) and since the 1980s, at least in the UK, there has been talk of encouraging an 'enterprise culture', few specific initiatives have directly sought to address societal attitudes. Nevertheless they are included in the environmental field in Figure 15.2 because there are some initiatives in this area.

Possibly the main focus has been in the field of education. The view is often articulated that the supply of entrepreneurs will ultimately be increased more if awareness of the feasibility and desirability of starting a business is established at a young age. Thus the education system has often been encouraged and assisted to foster, support and facilitate those interested in knowing what it is like to run a business. In 2002 the Enterprise Directorate-General of the EU claimed that general knowledge about business and entrepreneurship needs to be taught right through primary, secondary and tertiary education, 'yet many [school leavers] know little of enterprise and almost nothing of the opportunities offered by entrepreneurship'.[14] A Danish report sums up the views of many as follows:

> The experts in each one of the 21 GEM (Global Entrepreneurship Monitor) nations consistently placed the provision of individuals with high-quality entrepreneurship education as a high priority. Danish experts do not believe that the current education system provides adequately for the promotion of entrepreneurship. They believe that the education system does not focus sharply enough on entrepreneurship and that there is a paucity of formal courses in the subject. Furthermore, they were of the opinion that the quality of both teachers and the material taught in entrepreneurship is low. According to the experts, there are more opportunities for entrepreneurship in Denmark than there are people equipped and skilled to take advantage of them.[15]

Consequently in many countries enterprise education programmes are now being delivered:

- Young Enterprise, a mostly privately funded charity founded in 1963 and based on the USA's Junior Achievement organisation, is the leading provider engaged in this process in the UK. Its aim is to develop 'enterprise skills', and currently its flagship programme involves setting up and running mini-businesses. Each year it helps '250,000 young people learn about business and the world of work'.[16]
- Also in the UK the then Department for Business, Innovation and Skills funded and managed initiatives to encourage young people and give them the skills to set up their own business, including:
  - 'recruiting young business owners to volunteer as enterprise champions who will go into schools and talk to young people about running their own business,
  - working with schools and colleges to encourage the use of schemes, for example "Tenner", which gives £10 to each student to start a business and "Enterprise Village", to help schools to set up businesses'.[17]

Some of the education provision is thus about how to be an entrepreneur and start a business – but some is more about the cultural aspects and 'being entrepreneurial'. For instance a literature review of articles on 'entrepreneurship' education published in 2010 found that:

> Scholars in this field of study, though differing in a number of definitive issues, are converging towards a single framework of entrepreneurship education. There is a shift from a start-up view to an attitude-changing perspective. [However,] there is still a non-alignment between what educators and other stakeholders wish to achieve in educating for entrepreneurship with the applied pedagogical approaches, and success indicators.[18]

ILLUSTRATION 15.2 – POLICY ANALYSIS: AN EXAMPLE FROM DENMARK

Denmark is a member of the International Consortium on Entrepreneurship (ICE), which is a group of leading entrepreneurship countries working to improve the analytical foundation for entrepreneurship policies. Working closely with the OECD, Denmark has endeavoured to identify

Figure 15.3 *Simple form of the OECD Framework for Entrepreneurship Indicators*

Source: N. Ahmad and A. Hoffman, 'A Framework for Addressing and Measuring Entrepreneurship', *OECD Statistics Working Papers*, No. 2008/02 (Paris: OECD Publishing, 2008), DOI: http://dx.doi.org/10.1787/243160627270, p. 10.

the key factors conducive to entrepreneurship and, in an attempt to give some structure and rigour to guide policy-makers, has developed a general policy framework for entrepreneurship.

The Danish model, and its OECD derivation, are based on the conceptual framework which is illustrated in its simplest form in Figure 15.3. This framework was initially developed to encompass five factors which, 'according to both the theoretical and empirical literature, constitute the five pillars of entrepreneurship: (1) entrepreneurship skills, (2) access to capital, (3) access to markets, (4) entrepreneurship incentives, and (5) entrepreneurship culture and motivation'. It is suggested that: 'not all factors conducive to country entrepreneurial performances may be altered using policy instruments. However, most factors can be influenced directly or indirectly by government policy.'[19]

The list of factors has been expanded subsequently into the following six determinants, each of which, the framework then suggests, 'is comprised of a number of policy areas believed to have an impact on these factors and therefore (on) entrepreneurship: regulatory framework; market conditions; access to finance; R&D and technology; entrepreneurial capabilities; and culture'.[20]

Combining an examination of entrepreneurial policies in the top-performing countries with the theoretical correlation between policy and entrepreneurship has produced the various areas for policy application such as:

For the regulatory framework: Administrative burdens for entry and growth, product, market, safety, health and environmental regulations, and bankruptcy rules.

For market conditions: Anti-trust and competition laws, market access requirements, public procurement.

For access to finance: Access to debt finance, business angels, access to venture capital, stock markets.

For R&D and technology: University/industry interfaces, technology co-operation and diffusion, broadband provision.

For entrepreneurial capabilities: Business and entrepreneurship education (skills), immigration.

For culture: Society attitudes to risk and towards entrepreneurs, mindsets and a desire for business ownership.[21]

The other components of the model in Figure 15.3 were also expanded. Entrepreneurial performance was to be considered based on the dimensions of firms, employment and wealth – with a wide range of possible indicators listed for each dimension: for instance the dimension of 'employment' could include as indicators the proportion of high-employment-growth firms, the rates of self-employment and/or start-up ownership and the amount of employment in different age ranges of firms. Impact was then expected to be indicated by job creation, economic growth, poverty reduction and/or formalising the informal sector.

The intention was that further analysis should then be done 'to determine ... the significance of each supposed determinant in creating or hindering entrepreneurship and entrepreneurs and their relationship to the specific entrepreneurship performance indicators', and it is anticipated that this might lead to 'a reduction in the number of indicators included in the framework (if some ... have no or very marginal impact on performance'.[22]

'Ideally', it is suggested, 'a perfect correlation between the indicators for entrepreneurial performance and impact would exist. Countries aiming at increasing GDP growth, for example, should be able to pick a few performance indicators and expect that an increase in those performance indicators will lead to higher GDP growth.'[23] The initiative has tried therefore to establish internationally comparable indicators for the policy areas so that it should be possible for policy-makers to establish which policy areas score highly in countries with high levels of the outcome they want as well as how their own policy areas compare with those high-scoring ones. Denmark, for instance, decided that it wanted more high-growth firms, and in the analysis for this initiative 'entrepreneurship is defined as the entry and creation of high growth firms'.[24]

Its authors explained the concept behind the framework by referring to the following travel analogy:

> For simplicity however, and to assist interpretation, the basic idea behind the Conceptual Framework can be illustrated by means of an analogy. Passengers want to get from A to B by time t (reflecting the policy objective, *Impact*). There are various means of transport available, some more costly than others, with each means having many variants (engine size, fuel consumption etc, which collectively form the *Determinants*). During the journey, passengers are informed whether they are heading in the right direction and on time via speedometers and GPS readings (the *Performance* indicators). Different passengers (policy-makers) will, of course, want to go to different places and get there at different times (different Impacts), using, whether by design or necessity, a mode of transport (Determinant) that reflects the price they're willing to pay for a certain level of comfort.[25]

The above quote suggests overtly the intention that this model, once completed, should provide a good guide to effective policy. The implication is that the model could help policy-makers in two ways. First, to decide which 'determinants' (i.e. policy fields/approaches and instruments) will best serve their purpose by achieving the impact they want at a price they are willing to pay. Second, through performance indicators, it could provide them with feedback on how well their policies are doing. That assumes, however, that the determinants indicated are indeed capable of delivering the entrepreneurial performance sought and, through it, of achieving the desired impact. It is thus testing the assumption that at least some current entrepreneurship policies both can and do work; an assumption which is examined in Chapter 16.

FORMS OF ASSISTANCE – POLICY INSTRUMENTS

The fields of intervention considered above can generally be considered to be approaches: that is the broad methods within which a number of different instruments might be applied. The instruments are thus the tools used to give effect to the approaches and, when it comes to selecting the instruments by which to deliver policy, there is a much greater choice. Table 15.1 presents a list of instruments which have at some stage been used by the UK (and many other) governments.

Such lists make no real attempt to relate intervention measures to the stages in the growth of a business, as described in Chapter 6. Therefore, to illustrate the variety of the possible fields and instruments available for the different stages of business development, Annex A is provided. It suffers from the limitations associated with such modelling, and certain measures (e.g. information and counselling, finance and training) are often made available throughout most or all of the development stages of a business – although both the nature and extent of the delivery mechanisms can vary for different stages.

The lists in the tables mentioned above cover instruments for a variety of approaches. They relate mainly, however, to institutional approaches to the business environment and to the provision of assistance to individuals or businesses. Elaboration on some of the instruments used for such approaches is offered below.

Financial assistance

Since 1931, when the Macmillan Committee reported and identified what has since been known as the 'Macmillan Gap', shortage of finance has been one of the central issues in discussions of the support

Table 15.1 *UK government SME policies*

Macro policies
- Interest rates
- Taxation
- Public spending
- Inflation

Deregulation and simplification
- Cutting 'red tape'
- Legislative exemptions
- Legal form

Sectoral and problem-specific policies
- High-tech firms
- Rural enterprises
- Social enterprises/social economy
- Ethnic businesses
- Women-owned businesses

Finance assistance
- Tax incentives for investors
- Government-backed loan guarantees
- Venture capital funds
- Grants

Other assistance
- Export guarantees
- Premises and business incubators

Indirect assistance
- Information and advice
- Training
- Consultancy, counselling/mentoring
- Network development (for example for owners and business angels)

Source: Based on D. J. Storey, *Understanding the Small Business Sector* (London: Routledge, 1994) p. 269.

needs of small firms. The 'gap' refers to a situation where a firm has profitable opportunities but there are no, or insufficient, funds (from internal or external sources) to exploit the opportunity. This need was reiterated in the Bolton Report (1971) and in numerous other reports and papers since.[26] Burns presents the problem thus:

> The question remains as to whether there is a funding gap – defined as an unwillingness on the part of suppliers of finance to supply it on terms and conditions that owner-managers need. Owner-managers who are unsuccessful in obtaining finance will always say that there is. Survey after survey of owner-managers will reveal this to be a major 'barrier to growth'. However, just because the owner-manager might want finance – on specific terms – does not necessarily mean that it should be provided, either for the good of the owner-manager, the financier or the economy as a whole.
>
> Economists would criticise the use of the word 'gap' and prefer to use the term 'market failure' or 'credit rationing' because there may be a 'gap' even in a perfect market simply because, for example, an owner-manager is unwilling to pay higher rates of interest or investors judge a project to be too risky. … 'Gaps' can easily arise, largely as a result of information asymmetry, the fixed costs of providing small amounts of capital, and the requirement of bankers for collateral. Also there is the inherent reluctance of the owner-manager to share equity in their business. The question is, however, whether there is evidence that the gap actually exists.
>
> On the one hand there is the evidence of numerous surveys which ask owner-managers what they perceive to be barriers to the growth of their firm. Almost inevitably lack of appropriately priced finance will be cited as a major constraint, particularly for fast-growing and newer firms. However this proves nothing – perception is one thing and reality another. Even if accurate, the lack of appropriately priced finance for certain projects may actually indicate that the market is working perfectly well.[27]

⊃ | **ILLUSTRATION 15.3 – THE CRUICKSHANK REVIEW**

The Cruickshank Review posed two main questions relating to SMEs:

- Whether they had access to appropriate external finance?
- Whether there was effective competition in the provision of banking services?

As far as equity finance was concerned, the Review highlighted some key barriers to entry in the SME equity markets, including asymmetric information, and confirmed the existence of an equity gap for firms who seek to raise between £100,000 and £500,000. It also criticised the Small Firms Loan Guarantee Scheme for not addressing these market imperfections.

On banking services, the Review pointed out that there was a limited number of suppliers and very few new entries into the SME banking services market. It also suggested that the banks were making excess profits in the SME market but concluded that there was no evidence to suggest that SMEs then had difficulty accessing debt finance from banks.

Source: Based on Bank of England, *Finance for Small Firms: An Eighth Report* (London: Bank of England, 2001) pp. 63–64.

Burns goes on to claim that numerous surveys 'have been unable to objectively establish that a "gap" exists in any systematic way'.[28] But, despite his conclusions and the availability of other sources of finance, the issue continues to be central to many intervention strategies. There is, at least in some economies, a strongly held view that the major problem now for the funding of small businesses lies not in an overall shortage of finance, but in the appropriate means of focusing that finance (and avoiding, for instance, an over-reliance on overdrafts and security-based lending). As a result, in the UK, the relationship between banks and small businesses has been under strain and scrutiny for some time, and the subject has probably been the single most prominent issue in the small business literature over many years. It led in part, in 1998, to the commissioning of a review chaired by Don Cruickshank which resulted in the publication of Competition in UK Banking in March 2000. Key elements of this report (called the Cruickshank Review) are shown in Illustration 15.3.

Cruickshank's findings triggered a Competition Commission inquiry which found 'a complex monopoly' which distorted price competition in banking services to small businesses from within the 'Big Four' (clearing banks) which controlled 90 per cent of the UK market.[29] Although the Labour government had commissioned the Cruickshank Review, and both it and the Competition Commission warned of the danger of loose regulation, the government did not impose more restrictions on the banks.

A renewed surge of interest in this field began when the financial crisis in 2007/8 led to restricted lending by banks. The 2010 Coalition government responded by setting up 'Project Merlin' with the four major UK banks to produce a series of reforms aimed to improve both the stability and competition between UK banks. Efforts also included the encouragement of a range of new ('challenger') banks offering competition to the biggest banks in the industry and the creation of the British Business Bank in 2012. The latter is a state-owned economic development bank whose aim is to increase the supply of credit to SMEs as well as provide business advice services. Governments have tended to focus on both the demand and supply sides of the issue, promoting both the knowledge of and ability to access finance, and the availability of finance as the following paragraphs illustrate.

Reducing late payment of debts

Late payment by customers can be a severe handicap to small businesses, and the consequent adverse effect on cash flow and viability has been a constant complaint by small firms and their representative organisations. Various initiatives have been identified to address this. In December 2008, the Department for Business, Innovation and Skills, together with the Institute of Credit Management, launched a prompt payment code to tackle again the issue of late payments given the background of the difficult economic climate at the time. By signing the code, an organisation commits to paying suppliers on time and according to their agreed terms, to give clear guidance to suppliers and encourage good practice through the supply chains.

Based on a commitment in the Small Business Act, the European Commission put forward proposals in April 2009 seeking changes to the Late Payment Directive of 2000. It aimed to help businesses (especially SMEs) by tackling a culture of late payments particularly within the public sector. The EU decision-making process was concluded in January 2011 with a new directive which allowed member states two years to transpose it into national law (Directive 2011/7/EU on Combating Late Payment in Commercial Transactions). The UK introduced its changes through its Late Payment of Commercial Debts Regulations 2013, which requires that debtors should be forced to pay interest and reimburse the reasonable recovery costs of the creditor if they do not pay for goods and services on time (60 days for businesses and 30 days for public authorities). (For a summary of the outcome of an evaluation in 2015 of the EU Directive, see Chapter 16.)

Start Up Loans

Start Up Loans is a scheme launched by the UK government in 2012 initially aimed at young people. However, the age restrictions have now been lifted and any UK resident over 18 is theoretically eligible. The average loan is about £6000, but larger amounts can be accessed, and by 2014 finance had been supplied to over 25,000 firms with overall lending reaching £129m.

The Seed Enterprise Investment Scheme (SEIS)

Designed to de-risk investments in new businesses, SEIS allows individuals to back companies up to £100,000 and provides them with 50 per cent tax relief. Furthermore, profits made from the sale of equity are exempt from capital gains tax, whereas losses can be potentially offset against it. The scheme is designed for those thinking of investing in new tech start-ups and other higher-risk categories. Investors can take no more than 30 per cent of the business and the companies must be unquoted, have fewer than 25 employees and assets worth no more than £200,000.

The Regional Growth Fund (RGF)

The Regional Growth Fund is a £1.4bn (expanded to £3.2bn) competitive fund operating across England since 2011 with a similar initiative in Scotland. It supports projects and programmes that lever private sector investment to generate economic growth and sustainable employment. It aims particularly to help those areas and communities currently dependent on the public sector to make the transition to sustainable private sector–led growth and prosperity. It seeks in part to substitute for the nine English Regional Development Agencies (RDAs), which were replaced in March 2012 by smaller Local Enterprise Partnerships (LEPs).

The Enterprise Finance Guarantee (EFG)

The Enterprise Finance Guarantee is a targeted measure introduced in 2009 to replace the Small Firms Loan Guarantee Scheme, which was introduced in the UK as a pilot in 1981. The EFG opened the scheme to a wider number of businesses, with the specific objective of facilitating new bank lending in response to the credit crunch. Under the measure, as with the SFLG Scheme, the government provides a guarantee to the banks (or other approved institutions) of a percentage (variously between 70% and 85% and currently 75% for the EFG) of specified loans.

Enterprise Investment Scheme (EIS) and Venture Capital Trusts (VCTs)

The Enterprise Investment Scheme and its precursors, the Business Start-Up Scheme (BSUS) and Business Expansion Scheme (BES), were introduced in the UK to increase the supply of relatively small amounts of equity capital to mainly manufacturing and tradeable service businesses. EIS, introduced in 1993, provides tax relief to individuals (business angels) investing in qualifying unquoted companies. Unlike its predecessors, EIS allows the investor to be a manager or director of the businesses concerned. The venture capital trusts (VCTs) introduced in 1995 are a pooled investment mechanism to enable private investors to spread the risk of investing in private companies. They aim to increase the supply of risk capital for businesses with growth potential. As with EIS, tax relief (on income and capital gains tax) is a prime incentive, but the investors are also expected to benefit from the greater marketability of their shares as VCTs are quoted companies.

Alternative Investment Market (AIM)

Replacing the Unlisted Securities Market (USM) in the UK, the Alternative Investment Market was introduced by the Stock Exchange, in 1995, as a second-tier market to target small or young companies whose shares are not publicly traded. It provides easier entry requirements and less rigorous continuing obligations than the main market, thereby encouraging smaller companies to access public equity. However, 'costs are considered by some companies to be not much lower than those required for a full listing'.[30]

Business angel networks

'Business angels' is the term often used for informal investors in small businesses who tend to operate on the basis of personal knowledge and contacts rather than through formal equity markets. These high-net-worth individuals invest risk capital (up to £100,000 typically) in small, unquoted companies. Angels invest their own funds, unlike venture capitalists who pool the money of others in a professionally managed fund. They provide not only capital but often experience and advice to assist the company. In the UK, groups of potential business angels have been developed by the former Business Links, banks and others through a variety of local and regional networks. However, many business angels wish to remain anonymous, making it difficult to measure their overall impact.

It has been estimated that there are between 20,000 and 40,000 business angels in the UK investing £500 million to £1 billion annually, mostly for start-up and early-stage finance (many of whom will use the Enterprise Investment Scheme as a tax-efficient vehicle for their investments).[31] The government sought to strengthen the UK informal investment market by, for example, support for the former National Business Angel Network (NBAN) — replaced by the UK Business Angels Association. It is a national trade body representing angel networks which act as conduits for matching investors and investees. Such initiatives aim to promote more investment, cut the costs of finding suitable partners and make the process speedier and more efficient.

Grants and loans

As well as schemes of the kinds considered above, there is a wide variety of direct grant-aid schemes to encourage business development. Often such support is targeted to try to increase competitiveness through improvements in key areas of the business such as management, marketing, design, production, research and development, quality systems and training. Grants may also be available to assist with the cost of capital acquisitions such as premises, machines and equipment.

There is an impression that in many cases grants were introduced because government wanted to assist small businesses, and a financial budget was the facility it could most easily make available to the relevant agencies. Agencies therefore gave out money in the form of grants, but such grants have been suspected of inducing a dependence on them. Instead of grants, assistance may sometimes be provided in the form of subsidised low-interest loans ('seedcorn' loans). The costs of administering such funds may be subsidised, but usually interest and repayments are expected to provide a continuing source of revolving support without the need for additional capital injections.

Enterprise Zones

Enterprise Zones (EZs) are part of the government's strategies to encourage investment outside London. In 2016 there were 25 EZs in England (and a target of 44) and 7 in Wales. Businesses that choose to locate in these areas get relief from business rates and enhanced capital allowances as well as other incentives such as access to incubators and infrastructure advantages. EZs are typically sector-specific and tend to focus on industry and technology designated as an EZ with 26 sites earmarked, covering a range of industries.

Scotland has its own scheme, with 15 areas focused on life sciences, low carbon and manufacturing, with similar incentives to the English scheme.

Exporters

Small exporting businesses have had difficulty in acquiring attractive credit insurance from the private sector. The causes of this were noted in a Bank of England report and, while new products have been introduced, take-up was low.[32] In 2000 the DTI's Export Credits Guarantee Department (ECGD) announced a new export credit package for SMEs, indicating that it would work with other government agencies to give export advice to SMEs. Subsidised trade fairs and outward missions as well as funds to develop specific overseas markets have been given a particularly strong emphasis in an attempt to increase the exporting performance of SMEs. Then in 2011, the Export Enterprise Finance Guarantee (ExEFG) was introduced on a pilot basis. Similar to the Enterprise Finance Guarantee (see above) it facilitated the provision of commercial export finance to even smaller businesses. Currently a range of schemes, which complements the private market, provides assistance to exporters and investors, principally in the form of insurance and guarantees to banks.

Support for particular sub-groups

Support for ethnic minority businesses (EMBs)

The prevalence of self-employment amongst some ethnic minorities is an important feature in the labour markets in many countries. There is a recognition that ethnic minority businesses have special financing needs, given that they can face 'difficulties in raising external finance [which] can be more acute' than for small businesses as a whole.[33] Many EMBs have benefited from using their own community finance schemes instead of, or in addition to, bank finance. For example, 'partnering schemes' which involve members paying an agreed amount of savings into a mutual savings fund are important for African-Caribbean businesses. The success of many UK-based Asian business start-ups can be put down, at least in part, to the 'flexible' repayment conditions set by the often extended family group, removing the normal bank lending repayment pressures on a new business.

There has been concern that the take-up of official business support by EMBs is lower than for other businesses, with both demand- and supply-side factors being used as explanations. This problem leads some to question the 'capacity of mainstream business support agencies to cater adequately for the needs of ethnic minority firms'.[34] An Ethnic Minority Business Forum was set up in 2000 to highlight issues of concern to EMBs and to consider how government policies might meet them. It was disbanded in early 2007, and was succeeded by the Ethnic Minority Business Task Force, which was in turn disbanded in November 2009.

Any real problems of discriminatory practice become mixed up with issues such as the disproportionately high representation of EMBs in inner-city areas, and in rented accommodation, and a tendency towards concentration in sectors with above-average failure rates (such as catering and retail). There is evidence which suggests that 'as a group EMBs are not disadvantaged in terms of start-up capital from banks and other formal sources' and that there is more variation 'within EMBs (as a group) than with white-owned firms'.[35] On the other hand, there is continuing concern about 'circumstances which raise suspicion of racist discrimination and negative stereotyping'.[36]

Support for women-owned businesses

Women-owned businesses are another sub-group which may need special forms of support (see also Chapter 5). Relative to other high-income countries, UK rates of female business ownership have been persistently low. However, recent statistics reveal that the number of women in self-employment is increasing at a faster rate than the number of men. In 2014 'women made up just under one third of the self-employed (1.4 million). Since 2009 the number of self-employed women has increased by 34%. By comparison over the past five years the number of self-employed men has risen by 15% to 3.1 million in 2014. Despite the rise in women being self-employed, men still make up 68% of self-employed workers.'[37]

Also, as with EMBs, issues of discrimination in relation to bank finance become intermingled with 'factors such as lower expected, and actual, turnover and a greater desire to work part-time which might reduce the ability of women-owned businesses to raise finance'.[38] However, there was no national strategic approach to the development of women's enterprise in the UK until the government launched the Strategic Framework for Women's Enterprise (SFWE) in 2003. From this a range of initiatives to support female entrepreneurship evolved, including the Regional Women's Enterprise Initiatives. In 2005, a major report on the state of women's enterprise[39] concluded that there was a growing realisation of the economic contribution to be made by women's enterprise but there was still a lack of understanding and articulation of the contribution to be made by women in many circumstances. Also, in 2006, a Women's Enterprise Task Force (WETF) was established for a three-year period to champion women's enterprise and to increase the quantity, scalability and success of women-owned businesses in the UK.[40] The Task Force produced its final report in 2009 and was disbanded.

Support for deprived areas

Various initiatives have been launched to try to provide financial support for enterprise in disadvantaged areas (and see Enterprise Zones above). In the UK, for example, following the establishment of the UK government's Social Exclusion Unit in 1997 (closed in 2006 and transferred to the Social Exclusion Task Force, itself disbanded in 2010), a report was published entitled *Enterprise and Social Exclusion*. It focused on access to finance and support services by small firms in deprived areas. It called upon the Bank of England to report on a regular basis on finance for business in these areas. The Bank accepted this remit, citing several factors that may limit lending by external agents such as a 'lack of business experience, lack of collateral and personal equity; concentration in business sectors subject to higher failure rates; remoteness; small and localised markets and high crime rates'.[41] The Bank followed up with a special report in 2003, *The Financing of Social Enterprises*.[42] The report found that 'Social enterprises are more likely to have been rejected for finance, although the majority of those rejected by one lender appear subsequently to be successful with another'.

Recognising the potential of a strong community development sector to promote enterprise in deprived areas, a Social Investment Task Force was established in 2000 (and disbanded in 2010). It was independently managed by the UK Social Investment Forum in partnership with the New Economics Foundation and the Development Trusts Association (the Treasury had an observer role), and its purpose was to explore suitable ways in which social investment and financing might be developed. It made five recommendations that it suggests would create the environment in which a 'vibrant, entrepreneurial community development sector' could emerge. The proposals were for:

- A community investment tax credit.
- Community Development Venture Funds.
- Disclosure of individual bank lending activities in under-invested communities.
- Greater latitude and encouragement for charitable trusts and foundations to invest in community development initiatives.
- Support for Community Development Financial Institutions (CDFIs).[43]

All of these recommendations were implemented to at least some extent. For example Community Development Finance Institutions were launched in 2001. They are social enterprises providing finance (usually loan but sometimes equity) to individuals, businesses and social enterprises which cannot access all or part of their financial needs from mainstream sources such as banks. There are currently in excess of 70 CDFIs operating in the UK, and it is contended that a major advantage of using money available through the CDFIs is that they don't take into account credit history, they look at applications on a case-by-case basis and they tend to cover all sizes of business – from the sole trader looking to boost cash flow to a multimillion-pound concern set on expansion. As yet they have not acquired the level of business anticipated for them.

Community and group self-help schemes

An alternative to externally supplied grants or loans for small businesses may be found, in various parts of Europe, in community or group self-help financing schemes such as credit unions and mutual credit guarantee schemes. The logic behind such schemes is that each individual in a community may be able to save a small amount, and if these amounts are pooled they are together much more effective than they would be separately. Alternatively, shared resources can be used to guarantee a bigger loan than any one person could manage alone. Mutual credit guarantee schemes apply the same principle to small businesses, which combine into self-help groups to pool their financial resources in order to fund, or secure credit for, significant projects for the member businesses as appropriate. Thus, one or two at a time, the members can afford to undertake projects they could not have afforded on their own. Such schemes apply ideas similar to those on which the early building societies were based. Intervention may help to get them started by providing encouragement and by making available information on how to set up and run a mutual credit guarantee scheme.

Microfinance schemes have also been popularised in recent times with Grameen Bank often being highlighted as an example of what can be achieved (see Illustration 15.4). Microfinance is the provision of financial services to low-income clients or solidarity lending groups including consumers and the self-employed, who traditionally have difficulty accessing banking and related services.

Summary

Governments are tending to focus on both the demand and supply sides of the financing issue. On the demand side, the major approaches seek to improve the information flow between SMEs and investors and to provide counselling services to SMEs to improve their willingness and ability to find and secure debt and equity financing. On the supply side, the major approaches have been to encourage banks to do more small business lending and make them accountable (through loan guarantees, statistical reporting

---

ILLUSTRATION 15.4 – THE GRAMEEN BANK

The Grameen Bank is reputed to be the world's first microfinance lender and community development bank. It was started by Muhammad Yunus in Bangladesh in 1976, and in 1983 it was transformed into a formal bank. It makes small loans (known as microcredits) to the rural poor. It is owned by the borrowers of the bank who are mostly women and who own about 95 per cent of the total equity of the bank, with the remaining 5 per cent owned by the Government of Bangladesh.

Grameen Bank does not require any collateral for its loans. Although each borrower must belong to a five-member group, the group is not required to give any guarantee for a loan to its member. Repayment responsibility solely rests on the individual borrower, while the group and the centre oversee that everyone behaves in a responsible way and none gets into repayment problem. There is no form of joint liability. Grameen Bank finances 100 per cent of its outstanding loan from its deposits, over half of which come from the bank's own borrowers. The bank has made a profit in almost every year in which it has operated, and its success has inspired similar projects in more than 40 countries around the world.

Source: www.grameen-info.org (accessed 6 December 2011).

For completeness it should also be noted that Grameen Bank has had its detractors. In 2011 the Government of Bangladesh announced that Muhammad Yunus had been sacked from the bank, and there have been suggestions that some of the bank's affairs were not in order. While the government opposition to Muhammad Yunus and his associates may be politically inspired, such controversies have done little to enhance the overall reputation of the microcredit concept around the world, with some micro-financial institutions being criticised for exorbitant interest rates and alleged coercive debt collection.

and setting minimum targets for SME loans), to provide tax incentives for equity investments, and to provide government financial assistance programmes (such as micro-loans, subsidised interest rate loans and R&D funds).

Other assistance

Although financial assistance may be the most obvious, there are many other types of assistance measures. Subsidised provision of various forms of information, advice, training and counselling is a very large and fast-growing part of attempts to improve the internal efficiency of small businesses. Together they are often referred to as 'soft' support as opposed to the 'hard' support of finance, premises and plant. Some soft forms of assistance are described below.

Counselling, information and advice

Small businesses are believed to be at a disadvantage relative to larger ones because of their limited ability to scan the environment and filter for information relevant to their progress. Indeed it can be argued that a lack of relevant and timely information, delivered in a manner which can be quickly and easily absorbed and used, is a critical problem for most small businesses. This example of market failure in access to information should be addressed if small businesses are to realise their potential. Consequently, the major part of the remit of the network of business support agencies is to remedy this information gap. With the huge expansion of the Internet as a means of communicating vast amounts of data, this medium has assumed a significant role in providing information for SMEs. International, national, regional and local agencies as well as private sector organisations are developing websites and knowledge portals dedicated to supplying information believed to be useful for SMEs.

StartUp Britain is a (2011) private sector initiative with government support. It describes itself as a response from the private sector to the government's call for an 'enterprise-led' recovery and aims 'to celebrate, inspire and accelerate enterprise in the UK'.[44] It seeks to pull together a range of practical resources to help people to start up and develop a business – from advice on marketing and practical help with legal issues, to discounts on the materials needed to start a business.

Another method has been the use of personal business advisers (PBAs) offering person-to-person and face-to-face communication, which is an approach preferred by many business owners. Subsidised consultancy can also enable businesses to engage professional specialists to help them to analyse their situations and prescribe improvement actions. Another type of special initiative relies on experienced business people acting as 'mentors' to selected local businesses. The UK initiated a Business Volunteers Mentors Association, and in the Republic of Ireland the government's business support agency, Enterprise Ireland, has delivered the Mentor Programme nationally to SMEs for over 20 years. The UK government, in co-operation with the private sector, launched mentorsme.co.uk in 2011 as its new national mentoring gateway to a network of volunteer business mentors, replacing the paid PBAs who had been employed by the former Business Links. Mentoring programmes can be found in many other countries, often using retired business people. Prominent amongst these has been the SCORE programme in the USA supported by its Small Business Administration.

Skills-management and workforce development and training

Support for management development in small businesses has developed rapidly over the years, as both the private and the public sectors have identified a gap in the market. It is well known that the right mix of management skills is important for any business and is critical if a business is to grow successfully. Yet a consistent finding of research on training provision in developed countries is that workers (managers and employees) in small firms are less likely to be in receipt of formal training than those in larger enterprises. For instance:

- A report by the Department for Business, Innovation and Skills found that 32 per cent of SME employers provided training for managers in the year 2011–2012 and 28 per cent for employees only. Of those who did not provide training for managers, 14 per cent had considered it but had not done so.

The main reason for not providing management training was that it was not considered a priority (58% of SME employers), followed by a lack of money (8%).[45]

- A recent Federation of Small Business survey found that 'while three fifths of small business owners (59%) say they update their business knowledge and skills at least once a year, specific management training is often lacking. What's more, only a quarter of small firms questioned (25%) had undertaken management training in the last 12 months, and a similar proportion (26%) had never undergone any form of management training at all.'[46] It also found that 'few smaller businesses seek external management training for staff, with just a fifth (19%) offering such training to their employees'.[47]

Bannock notes that, while 'survey results vary according to sample composition and how questions are phrased and, in particular, to how training is defined', nevertheless 'there is no doubt that SMEs carry out less training (as conventionally defined) for all their staff'.[48] Kitching and Blackburn record in their analysis of training that established staff are most commonly trained in working methods, IT and product knowledge; for the owner-manager the content was working methods, IT and health and safety.[49] Training in general management processes and techniques and finance were much lower. Table 15.2 indicates some of the possible reasons for a reluctance to train.

Government intervention over many years has been designed to enhance management and workforce training in small businesses (perceiving a market failure to exist in that small businesses do not see the benefits of training). Others, like Bannock, will argue that there is much more on-the-job informal training going on in SMEs than is appreciated. 'It is not possible to capture fully the training and learning that actively goes on.'[50] In the 1980s, Business Growth Training in the UK offered a consultant paid from public funds to train and develop management in small firms. Small Firms Training Loans were introduced in 1994 to help pay for training by subsidising the interest payments on bank loans which

Table 15.2 Barriers and incentives to training

Barriers	Incentives
Cost implications • Time is the most valuable and precious resource and time spent on training is considered to be a cost not an investment • Time training is time not working • Much training is not relevant • Much training is not effective	*Value* • Courses of real current relevance that require minimal time off the job, and have identified early benefits *Funding available* • Grant assistance available to help with the cost
Attitude • Bad experiences of formal training, e.g. at school • Failure to perceive the need and the potential benefits • A belief that the benefits will not last	*Content* • Trainers with business credibility • Training itself promotes further training • Process counselling will be accepted but not expert consultancy
Lack of relevance • No desire to improve or grow the business • Want solutions to yesterday's problems today • Not prepared to look ahead	*Promotion* • Peer business managers will be believed • Influencers will be listened to, but not 'officials' • Mail shots don't work • 'It's about increasing profits' • Through networks of contacts
Promotion of training • The word 'training' is a turn-off • Suggestions of paternalism • Government initiatives are distrusted	
Apprehension • Too many courses on offer • Too many agencies • They may be sold something they don't need • It's an admission of defeat • Exposes oneself and one's business	

small firms took out to invest in training, but awareness and take-up were low. In 2000, the then DfEE/DTI in a joint initiative established a Council for Excellence in Management and Leadership. It aimed 'to develop a strategy to ensure that the UK has the managers and leaders of the future to match the best in the world'. It further sought, in the context of SMEs, 'to establish a coherent approach to the confusing plethora of management and leadership development initiatives' and to introduce schemes which offer entrepreneurs 'a range of solutions which work with the grain' and mimic their informal procedures. Subsequently there has been strong encouragement for smaller firms to engage in Investors in People (IIP). A more recent government initiative in 2011 from the Department of Business, Innovation and Skills – entitled Business Coaching for Growth – is aimed at new and established businesses capable of fast growth. It is worth noting that, although management competence is perceived as vital to business success, Storey concluded in 2004 that 'econometric methods linking training participation to small firm performance produce weak findings [which] suggests that the relatively low take up of formal management training is an informed decision on the part of the small firm owner/manager'.[51] On the other hand a study by McKinsey & Company and the Centre for Economic Performance found that 'better management practice ... is correlated with a range of corporate performance metrics ... [and] improving management is also related to increases in productivity and output'.[52]

Market, product and process development

Small businesses may have difficulty finding and researching new markets, especially export markets. Equally, in the longer term the survival and growth of businesses will require the constant development of new or improved products or services. Various programmes of support to help businesses in these areas have been devised. They include R&D assistance, export marketing grants, trade missions and shows, market intelligence reports and export credit guarantee schemes, as well as assistance with the development and production of sales literature and advertising materials. Productivity increases through, for example, process development are encouraged by assisting benchmarking studies, quality initiatives and best-practice visits. The linking of markets and products – or services, suppliers and customers – has also been facilitated by the Internet and e-commerce, and therefore there have been various initiatives to promote and assist increased small business connectivity.

Procurement

Considerable attention has, and continues to be, focused on the role of central and local government in ensuring that SMEs are not discriminated against in the process of tendering for public procurement contracts. It is a widely held belief amongst SME owners and their representatives that the bureaucratic requirements, minimum quantities required and risk-averse nature of public servants mitigates significantly against smaller businesses winning a 'fair share' of public sector contracts. Thus quotas and other incentives have been applied in a number of countries to assist SMEs in overcoming some of these barriers. For instance in the UK, the Conservative Party Manifesto in 2015 stated that it would 'raise the target for SMEs' share of central government procurement to one-third'[53] by 2020.

The European Commission notes that SMEs are 'underrepresented in public procurement (at least in procedures above the EU thresholds) compared to their overall weight in the economy'.[54] It has therefore encouraged 'Member States to share their good practices in facilitating SMEs' access to public procurement and stimulate the innovation and growth potential of SMEs'.[55]

Technology

The importance of technology in stimulating innovation, competitiveness and growth of businesses is well understood. It is believed, however, that the potential of many smaller businesses to identify and exploit new and existing technologies is limited by lack of information on their availability and potential, or by cost factors (another example of 'market failure'?). A wide range of schemes exist to ensure that the process of technology transfer is enhanced. The former Business Links offered an Innovation and Technology Counselling Service, and Innovate (UK), formerly the Technology Strategy Board, supports various forms of knowledge transfer including the Knowledge Transfer Partnership – a scheme which brings SMEs and universities/FE colleges into co-operative alliances through (up to) three-year placements for highly qualified graduates. It also provides a range of support for R&D and innovation, including grants as well as a network of Technology and Innovation Centres (TICs) and Catapult Centres to commercialise R&D in new and emerging technologies.

POLICY IMPLEMENTATION

An important distinction also has to be made between the formulation of small business policy and its implementation. In the UK formulation of such policy is very largely determined at the level of central government, while its implementation is achieved through a network of regional agencies. Within the overall framework of policy, these agencies can, and indeed are often expected to, alter the emphasis and priorities of implementation according to local needs and circumstances. In the UK, for the most part, the public sector business support structure has often undergone re-structuring and refocusing. This constant process of change, which is intended to produce greater effectiveness and efficiency in support, is viewed by some as self-defeating in that structures are not allowed to settle. Before April 2001 the situation which prevailed was one which included such agencies as the Training and Enterprise Councils (TECs) in England and Wales and the Local Enterprise Companies (LECs) in Scotland. In addition regional and local authorities contributed a network of support services, while Scottish Enterprise (SE) in Scotland and the Welsh Assembly government in Wales had countrywide jurisdictions and Northern Ireland had its own small business agency: the Local Enterprise Development Unit (LEDU), which was absorbed in 2002 into the newly created Invest Northern Ireland (Invest NI).

The TECs and LECs were complemented in Great Britain by the establishment of the DTI-initiated Business Links in England, by Business Connect in Wales and by Business Shops in Scotland. Business Links were funded by the DTI, but this funding came through the TEC network, which was the responsibility of the then Department for Education and Employment. TECs and Business Links found themselves therefore under the direction of two different government departments.

In April 2000 the UK government established a new Small Business Service to provide a single organisation within government dedicated to promoting the interests of small firms. Its chief executive reported to the Secretary of State for Trade and Industry. In addition, the chief executive was supported by a Small Business Council and a Small Business Investment Task Force, but both were subsequently disbanded. The Small Business Service itself became the Enterprise Directorate of the Department for Business, Enterprise and Regulatory Reform (BERR), which then became the Department for Business, Innovation and Skills. In 2016, BIS was merged with the Department of Energy and Climate Change (DECC) to form the Department for Business, Energy and Industrial Strategy (BEIS).

The business support landscape was also altered in England in 2001 by the creation of business-led RDAs and the Learning and Skills Council for England (LSC), while greater powers were also devolved to the Scottish Parliament and Welsh Assembly. The RDAs were an attempt to give greater influence at a regional level to economic policy. The LSC was the leading body in post-16-years learning and skills development and operated through 47 local arms known as local LSCs. They had a key role in human resource development for small businesses and replaced the Training and Enterprise Councils. The LSC closed in March 2010 and was replaced by the Skills Funding Agency and the Young People's Learning Agency – although the latter was abolished in 2012.

Business Link and most business development initiatives were devolved to RDAs from 2005, with the result that different 'business support' strategies operated within each region of England as well as Scotland, Wales and Northern Ireland. The role of Business Links and their counterparts was to create partnerships of providers of small business services in their regions to ensure that the small business consumer was presented with a seamless collection of services accessed through 'one-stop shops', or through 'first-stop shops'. However, the RDAs and Business Links ceased to operate in 2011 and LEPs were created in their stead. The LEPs are voluntary partnerships between local authorities, businesses and other relevant public, private, voluntary and community bodies and it appears that each LEP is taking its own development path.

One-stop shops?

> The notion of a one-stop shop is, for serious entrepreneurial regions, simply untenable.
>
> Ron Botham[56]

Although greater efficiency, professionalism and quality of impact are believed to be possible where services are concentrated, it is difficult and very unusual to bring individuals and organisations offering support services into close physical proximity. Mostly, what is achieved or sought is in fact a 'first-stop shop' where users can receive advice and information from a range of services immediately available and can be signposted to those others believed to be most useful to them.

Two different approaches actively evolved for such networking: Business Links in England aimed to be 'one-stop shops', while Business Shops in Scotland are based on a 'first-stop shop' approach. The distinction between the concept of a 'one-stop shop' and a 'first-stop shop' is often missed, however. While both derive from a desire to reduce proliferation and dispersal of support services and to make accessing them easier and less confusing for the potential user, the 'one-stop shop' approach aims to concentrate them, or at least their representatives, into one location. On the other hand the 'first-stop shop' concept assumes that it will often not be feasible to concentrate all the relevant sources of support in this way. Instead it is suggested that there should be initial contact points, the 'first-stop shops', which will either offer assistance directly if they can, or will be able to signpost the inquirer to the right place for specific assistance. The aim is that the knowledge throughout the network about the other organisations in it should be such that an inquirer to one, if he or she does not get the right place initially, will be so directed that his or her second stop will be correct. (The right place might be the second place to be contacted, which is why this approach is also sometimes referred to as the 'second-stop shop' concept.) This is a different approach from a 'one-stop shop', and indeed it has been further observed that one does not get a 'second-stop shop' by aiming at a 'one-stop shop' and missing.

Disconnected implementation?

It might seem inevitable that the variety and change in this process would not be helpful. Arshed *et al.* have specifically examined enterprise policy implementation in England but they note that, across the UK, government spending in this area has resulted in over 800 different sources of support for start-ups and SMEs (reduced from over 3000 support schemes since 2003).[57] The findings of their exploration, which are also summarised in Figure 15.4, are that:

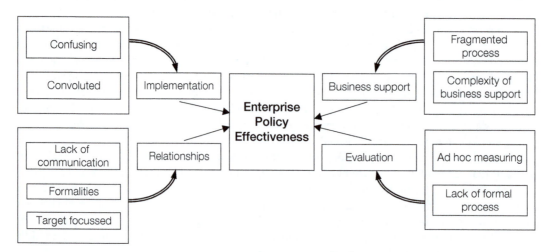

Figure 15.4 *Aspects of enterprise policy implementation in the UK*

Source: N. Arshed, C. Mason and S Carter, 'Exploring the Disconnect in Policy Implementation: A Case of Enterprise Policy in England', *Environment and Planning C: Government and Policy*, Vol. 34, No. 6, 2016, p. 1593.

The implementation process of enterprise policy initiatives is complex and confusing, with fragmented relationships between the actors involved. The abundance of enterprise policy initiatives being delivered at the time, the absence of clearly defined objectives, the limited emphasis on the delivery of business support and the lack of measurement and evaluation combined to create an unnecessarily complicated process of enterprise policy implementation which, in turn, reduced its effectiveness.[58]

IN CONCLUSION

Presenting a comprehensive picture of policy approaches, instruments and delivery mechanisms is not easy because there are so many different initiatives which, at least in the UK, seem to be in a constant state of change. Nevertheless overall the characteristics of the UK approach to small business support may be summarised as:

- Creating a healthy business environment, with increasing emphasis on deregulation and reduced and simplified administrative burdens.
- Selective intervention where market failure can be demonstrated.
- Developing forms of support geared to improving the competitiveness and export performance of small firms, emphasising marketing, quality, productivity, benchmarking, product development, management and workforce skills.
- Encouraging greater private sector involvement in the delivery of services through 'partnership' arrangements.
- Decentralised delivery combined with variations in the priorities and scope of support services to cater for differences in local and/or regional needs.

The reality, however, is that in the UK national and regional governments have not usually looked to small business for a significant contribution to economic renewal and development – despite much lip-service being paid to that concept. Attracting inward investment has been seen as a much more fruitful focus for support.

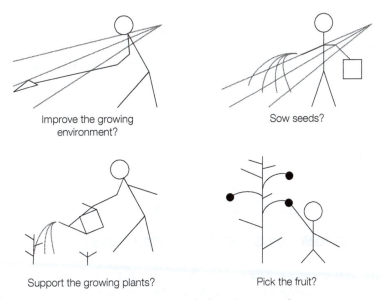

What is the best thing to do if you want to harvest more?

Improve the growing environment?

Sow seeds?

Support the growing plants?

Pick the fruit?

Figure 15.5 Applying limited resources to maximise the benefit returned

PART 3

☛ THE KEY POINTS OF CHAPTER 15

- To achieve policy objectives, it is necessary to select approaches, instruments and delivery agents.
- Different approaches can be taken to achieve enterprise policy objectives, including:
  — Focusing on individual people and businesses.
  — Improving the institutional environment.
  — Stimulating a more encouraging cultural environment.
- Within each approach assistance can take different forms. Thus a wide variety of policy instruments have been tried to give effect to policy.
- Not least in the UK there have also been a variety of policy delivery agents as different governments have devised different structures.

✓ QUESTIONS, EXERCISES, ESSAY AND DISCUSSION TOPICS

- Which is likely to be more effective: environmental approaches or approaches addressing individual people or businesses? Why?

- Summarise the arguments for and against targeting support on individual people and businesses.

- What policy stages can you distinguish – from identifying a need to confirming that it is being addressed?

- Can support for particular sub-groups be justified in economic development terms?

- Does the number of different forms of support available in the different areas indicated by Figure 15.2 indicate differences in the importance attached to each of the areas?

📖 SUGGESTIONS FOR FURTHER READING AND INFORMATION

BIS Analysis Paper Number 2, 'SMEs: The Key Enablers of Business Success and the Economic Rationale for Government Intervention' (London: Department for Business, Innovation and Skills, 2013).

R. Blackburn and M. Schaper (eds), *Government, SMEs and Entrepreneurship Development* (Farnham: Gower, 2012).

A. Lundström and L. Stevenson, *Entrepreneurship Policy for the Future* Series (Stockholm: Swedish Foundation for Small Business Research, 2001).

D. J. Storey and F. J. Greene, *Small Business and Entrepreneurship* (Harlow: Pearson Education Ltd, 2010) Part 6.

Websites

www.gov.uk/browse/business

www.business.scotland.gov.uk

www.business.wales.gov.uk

www.nibusinessinfo.co.uk

ANNEX – A TAXONOMY OF ENTERPRISE INITIATIVES

The list below attempts to enumerate the main instruments that have, at one time or another, or in one place or another, been deployed to address perceived enterprise needs. If it is compared with the overall framework presented in Figure 15.2 it is apparent that, in practice, most instruments have been deployed to address the perceived or expressed needs of individuals and businesses at the various stages of business development. Some attempt to improve the different aspects of the institutional environment but only a few try to change societal attitudes in the cultural environment.

Table 15.A1 *Taxonomy of enterprise initiatives*

Overall approach (and component or stage of business)	Policy field or need	Instrument
Individuals and Businesses:		
Pre-start	Ideas	Spin-off ideas Technology transfer Ideas generation workshops and publications
	Small business know-how (accounts, finance, selling, marketing and so on)	Small business skills training Training trainers
	'Know-who' networks	Networking advice Network access points, for both business and technical assistance
	Advice	Pre-start counselling/mentoring
Start-up: external	Customers	Purchasing initiatives
	Suppliers	Local sourcing initiatives Trade directories
	Advice/consultancy: business	Business expertise available Coordination of third party provision (Local Enterprise Partnerships) Training, counselling and mentoring Websites
	Advice/consultancy: technical	Technical advice, research and so on
	Networks	Business clubs Export clubs
	Information	Databases Internet portals
	Producing the business plan	Business plan services, including 'investment ready' plans
	Premises	Incubation centres Managed workspaces Business/science parks
Start-up: internal	Finance	Grants, loans, loan guarantee schemes Business angel networks
	Market expertise Administration expertise Financial management Employment expertise Company formation	Training services Advice/counselling Mentors
Established	Ideas	Ideas generation workshops Spin-off ideas Technology transfer programmes
	Encouragement	Guidance services, including 'one-stop shops'
	Specialist guidance	Banks, accountants
	Investment	Solicitors

Growth	Market opportunities, including exports	Trade missions Market visits Export development advisers Export credit insurance Market information: trends, contacts and so on
	Product development	Technical advice/support for product development
	Strategic approach	Development courses
	Management skills	Salary support Subsidised staff attachment programmes Benchmarking
	Finance	Grants and loans Business angel networks
Decline	Confidence	Mentors
	Customers	
	Money	
	Strategic review and planning	Advice and guidance
Termination	Legal and other advice	Provision of advice and counselling
Other dimensions	Business sector	Sector initiatives, including sector-based training
	High-tech Regions Gender and ethnicity	Special support schemes targeted on particular types of business, regions or groups of people

Environment – Institutional:

Infrastructure: physical	Premises, communications and transport facilities	Business parks Providing broadband coverage
Infrastructure: financial	Supply of credit and investment funds	Tax incentives and lending targets
Regulation	Minimal 'red tape'	Deregulation, legislative exemptions
Fiscal policy	Low taxation for higher returns	Small Profits Rate
	Investment in capital equipment	Accelerated capital allowances
Skills	Increased capability and competence	Graduate employment programmes Training programmes
The economy	Information on small business needs and behaviour	Research coordination, databases and centres
	General information and advice	Internet portals and other online assistance

Environment – Culture:

| Societal attitudes | A positive, encouraging and supportive environment | Media advertising
Capacity-building
Role models
Enterprise in education |

REFERENCES

[1] Small Business Service, *Enterprise Britain: A Modern Approach to Meeting the Enterprise Challenge* (London: HM Treasury, November 2002).

[2] J. Stanworth and C. Gray, *Bolton 20 Years On: The Small Firm in the 1990s* (London: PCP, 1991) p. 20.

[3] CBI SME Council, Internal working paper (unpublished).

[4] R. J. Bennett, Chapter 4 'Government and Small Business', in S Carter and D. Jones-Evans (eds), *Enterprise and Small Business*, 2nd Edition (London: Prentice Hall, 2006) p. 60.

[5] Taken from www.bis.gov.uk/policies/enterprise-and-business-support/access-to-finance/enterprise-capital-funds (accessed 13 September 2011).

[6] Bank of England, *Finance for Small Firms: An Eighth Report* (London: Bank of England, March 2001) pp. 63–64.

[7] Commission of the European Communities, *Towards Enterprise Europe: Work Programme for Enterprise Policy 2000–2005*, Commission Staff working paper, Brussels 08.05.2000, SEC(2000)771, p. 7.

[8] M. Hancock, K. Klyver and T. Bager, *Global Entrepreneurship Monitor: Danish National Executive Report* (Prepared at the University of Southern Denmark, for the Danish Agency for Trade and Industry, Danish Ministry for Trade and Industry, 2000) p. 59.

[9] G. Bannock, *The Economics and Management of Small Business: An International Perspective* (London: Routledge, 2005) p. 134.

[10] H. Rees and A. Shah, 'The Characteristics of the Self-Employed: The Supply of Labour', in J. Atkinson and D. J. Storey (eds), *Employment, The Small Firm and the Labour Market* (London: Routledge, 1993) pp. 317–327.

[11] BIS, *Better Regulation Framework Manual: Practical Guidance for UK Government Officials*, BIS/13/1038 (London: Department for Business, Innovation and Skills, March 2015) p. 4.

[12] Taken from https://www.fpb.org/press/UK-Economy-Loses-41bn-to-Red-Tape (accessed 29 May 2016).

[13] BIS: Better Regulation Executive, *The Ninth Statement of New Regulation*, BIS/14/P96B (London: Department for Business, Innovation and Skills, December 2014).

[14] Commission of the European Communities, Op. Cit.

[15] M. Hancock, K. Klyver and T. Bager, *Global Entrepreneurship Monitor: Danish National Executive Report* (Prepared at the University of Southern Denmark, for the Danish Agency for Trade and Industry, Danish Ministry for Trade and Industry, 2000) p. 22.

[16] Taken from www.young-enterprise.org.uk/about_us (accessed 4 December 2011).

[17] Taken from https://www.gov.uk/government/publications/2010-to-2015-government-policy-business-enterprise/2010-to-2015-government-policy-business-enterprise (accessed 4 June 2016).

[18] E. S. Mwasalwiba, 'Entrepreneurship Education: A Review of Its Objectives, Teaching Methods, and Impact Indicators', *Education + Training*, Vol. 52, No. 1, 2010, pp. 20–47.

[19] National Agency for Enterprise and Construction, *Entrepreneurship Index 2005: Entrepreneurship Conditions in Denmark*, October 2005. Taken from www.foranet.dk (accessed 16 March 2009) p. 25.

[20] National Agency for Enterprise and Construction, *Entrepreneurship Index 2006: Entrepreneurship Conditions in Denmark*, November 2006. Taken from www.foranet.dk (accessed 16 March 2009) p. 24.

[21] OECD, *Entrepreneurship at a Glance 2011* (OECD Publishing) DOI: 10.1787/9789264097711-en, p. 9.

[22] N. Ahmad and A. Hoffman, 'A Framework for Addressing and Measuring Entrepreneurship', *OECD Statistics Working Papers*, 2008/2 (Paris: OECD Publishing, 2008) DOI: 10.1787/243160627270, p. 20.

[23] Ibid. p. 17.

[24] A. Hoffman and H. Gabr, *A General Policy Framework for Entrepreneurship* (FORA, April 2006) p. 5. Taken from www.foranet.dk (accessed 16 March 2009).

[25] N. Ahmad and A. Hoffman, Op. Cit. p. 10.

[26] See Wilson Committee 'The Financing of Small Firms: Interim Report of the Committee to Review the Function of the Financial Institutions' (London: HMSO, 1979).

[27] P. Burns, *Entrepreneurship and Small Business* (Basingstoke: Palgrave Macmillan, 2011) pp. 275–276.

[28] P. Burns, *Entrepreneurship and Small Business* (Basingstoke: Palgrave Macmillan, 2011) p. 276.

[29] Patrick Tooher, *Financial Mail on Sunday*, 27 January 2002.

[30] Bank of England, Op. Cit. p. 54.

[31] C. Mason, 'Venture Capital and the Small Business', in S Carter and D. Jones-Evans (eds), *Enterprise and Small Business*, 2nd Edition (London: Prentice Hall, 2006) p. 364.

[32] Bank of England, *Small Exporters: A Special Report* (London: Bank of England, January 1998).

[33] D. Smallbone, R. Baldock, M. Ram and D. Deakins, 'Access to Finance by Ethnic Minority Businesses: Some Results from a National Study', Proceedings of the *24th ISBA National Small Firms Policy and Research Conference*, November 2001, pp. 1115–1136, at p. 1134.

[34] M. Ram, G. Barrett, and T. Jones, Chapter 10 'Government and Small Business', in S. Carter and D. Jones-Evans (eds), *Enterprise and Small Business*, 2nd Edition (London: FT Prentice Hall, 2006) p. 205.

[35] Bank of England (March 2001), Op. Cit. p. 76.

[36] M. Ram, G. Barrett and T. Jones, Chapter 10 'Government and Small Business', in S. Carter and D. Jones-Evans (eds), *Enterprise and Small Business*, 2nd Edition (London: FT Prentice Hall, 2006) p. 204.

[37] 'Self-employed Workers in the UK – 2014' (London: Office for National Statistics, August 2014) p. 10. Taken from http://webarchive.nationalarchives.gov.uk/20160105160709/, http://www.ons.gov.uk/ons/dcp171776_374941.pdf (accessed 23 July 2016).

[38] Bank of England, *Finance for Small Firms: An Eighth Report* (London: Bank of England, March 2001) p. 2.

[39] R. Harding, *The Regional State of Women's Enterprise in England*, (Norwich: Prowess, 2006).

[40] Women's Enterprise Task Force (WETF) report, *Greater Return on Women's Enterprise* (GROWE), Final Report and Recommendations (2009). Taken from www.womensenterprisetaskforce.co.uk (accessed 28 January 2012).

[41] Bank of England, *Finance for Small Firms: An Eighth Report* (London: Bank of England, March 2001) p. 64.

[42] Bank of England, *The Financing of Social Enterprises, A Special Report by the Bank of England* (London: Bank of England, Domestic Finance Division, May 2003).

[43] HM Treasury/Cabinet Office, 'The Future Role of the Third Sector in Economic and Social Regeneration: Final Report', CM7189 HM Treasury (July 2007) p. 79.

[44] Taken from http://www.startupbritain.org (accessed 29 October 2011).

[45] BIS Analysis Paper Number 2, *SMEs: The Key Enablers of Business Success and the Economic Rationale for Government Intervention* (London: Department for Business, Innovation and Skills, 2013) p. 24.

[46] A. Peate, *Policy Blog: FSB – Leading the Way on Leadership and Management*. Taken from http://www.fsb.org.uk/resources/blogs/site-blog/2016/03/07/policy-blog-fsb-leading-the-way-on-leadership-and-management (accessed 25 July 2016).

[47] Taken from http://www.fsb.org.uk/media-centre/latest-news/2016/03/03/leadership-skills-shortfall-holding-back-uk-economy (accessed 25 July 2016).

[48] G. Bannock, *The Economics and Management of Small Business: An International Perspective* (London: Routledge, 2005) p. 147.

[49] Ibid. p. 148.

[50] Ibid. p. 154.

[51] D. J. Storey, 'Exploring the Link, among Small Firms, between Management Training and Firm Performance: A Comparison between the UK and Other OECD Countries', *International Journal of Human Resource Management*, Vol. 15, No. 1, 2004, p. 112.

[52] BIS Analysis Paper Number 2, *SMEs: The Key Enablers of Business Success and the Economic Rationale for Government Intervention* (London: Department for Business, Innovation and Skills, 2013) p. 20.

[53] Taken from https://s3-eu-west-1.amazonaws.com/manifesto2015/ConservativeManifesto2015.pdf (accessed 25 July 2016) p. 21.

[54] PwC, ICF GHK and Ecorys (the Consortium), a study commissioned by the DG Internal Market and Services, the European Commission, *SMEs' Access to Public Procurement Markets and Aggregation of Demand*

in the EU (Brussels, February 2014) p. 5. Taken from ec.europa.eu/DocsRoom/documents/15459/attachments/1/translations/en/.../native (accessed 25 July 2016).

[55] Taken from http://ec.europa.eu/enterprise/policies/sme/business-environment/public-procurement (accessed 22 October 2011).

[56] R. Botham of the Training and Employment Unit, University of Glasgow, speaking at a Scott Policy Seminar in Belfast, 12 November 2001.

[57] N. Arshed, C. Mason and S. Carter, 'Exploring the Disconnect in Policy Implementation: A Case of Enterprise Policy in England', *Environment and Planning C: Government and Policy*, Vol. 34, No. 6, 2016, p. 1586.

[58] Ibid. p. 1583.

Companion website

Please visit the companion website at www.palgravehighered.com/Bridge-UE-5e for access to additional learning and teaching materials..

Does the Policy Work?

CONTENTS

- Introduction
- Policy evaluation

- Evaluation evidence
- Evaluation conclusions

KEY CONCEPTS

This chapter covers:

- The process, which is often called evaluation, for assessing the results and impacts of programmes or policy.
- The many factors that have to be taken into account in evaluation, including additionality, deadweight and displacement.
- Other issues which can affect evaluations include objectivity versus the involvement needed for insight and the difficulty of maintaining impartiality.
- Summaries of some evaluations of individual programmes and some overall assessments.

LEARNING OBJECTIVES

By the end of this chapter the reader should:

- Understand the need for evaluations and the processes involved in conducting them.
- Appreciate some of the difficulties in evaluations and the various factors that have to be taken into account.
- Understand the reasons why some evaluations may not be as impartial and objective as might be desired.
- Be aware of the sort of results reported by evaluations of specific programmes and the verdicts of some overall assessments.
- Be aware that there appears to be no strong evidence for policy success and a number of studies which, on balance, indicate failure.

INTRODUCTION

It might be expected that intervention by governments and others to encourage and support an activity should be justified by the results it achieves. While there may be some circumstances where being seen to intervene is itself thought to be important, most people would expect that, if intervention is to continue, there should be clear evidence that it achieves its purpose. If that is so, the fact that many governments across the world, including that of the UK, devote substantial resources to assist enterprise, entrepreneurship and small business development suggests that the results are indeed positive.

That might be the theory but there is mounting evidence that the practice is often different. It is in the outputs of programme or policy evaluation that the evidence for effectiveness might be found. However, evaluation is not easy and is not always done well, or even done at all. There are many factors which can prevent the emergence of a clear and/or accurate picture, including ambiguity, complexity, confusion, inconsistency and self-interest.

As a result, reliable evaluations may be few but they do suggest that, in this field, the evidence for positive results is not as clear as might be expected. Unambiguous evidence of direct positive outcomes appears to be sparse, and increasingly it seems that the balance of the available evidence is that those enterprise policies which have been assessed are not achieving their main purpose.

So, if many of those evaluations which are done credibly do not produce consistent evidence of policy success, then there is a case for an equally rigorous approach to evaluation of the many policies and their programmes which are not well evaluated. The requirements for the measurement and assessment of results, the development of rigorous and comprehensive evaluation criteria, the methods available, and the problems that these entail, all need to be considered. Finally the results obtained need to be examined, conclusions drawn and the implications of policy failure considered. These issues form the subject of this chapter.

POLICY EVALUATION

Appraisal, monitoring and evaluation

In this context evaluation is the process whereby the achievement of a policy, programme or project can be assessed. However, in the field of evaluation, as in many of the subjects covered in this book, the terminology can be confusing not least because some of the words used can have narrow specialist meanings. Therefore it may be helpful to start a section on evaluation with a brief guide to the difference between it and the associated concepts of appraisal and monitoring.

According to the official UK government guide[1] appraisal is the process of defining objectives, examining options and weighing up the costs, benefits, risks and uncertainties before a decision is made (and see Illustration 16.1), whereas an evaluation is the retrospective analysis of a project, programme or policy to assess how successful or otherwise it has been and what lessons can be learnt for the future (see Illustration 16.2). Other sources suggest that the timing of an evaluation 'is not fixed [and] it can be undertaken at an early stage in policy implementation, or after its completion'[2] (see Figure 16.1 – also Figure 14.2 and Illustration 14.1).

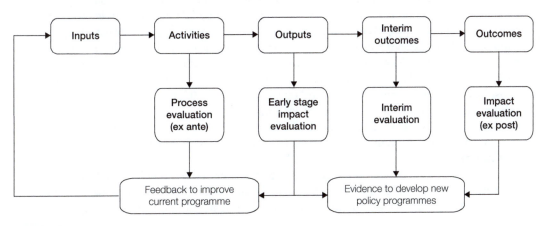

Figure 16.1 *Possible evaluation stages*

Source: Adapted from W. K. Kellogg Foundation by P. Cowie, 'SME Policy Evaluation: Current Issues and Future Challenges', chapter in R. Blackburn and M. Schaper (eds), *Government, SMEs and Entrepreneurship Development: Policies, Tools and Challenges* (Farnham: Gower Publishing, 2012) p. 246.

In his work in this field, Scott emphasised the distinction between monitoring and evaluation, because these concepts are often confused with each other.[3] Monitoring has narrower objectives than evaluation. It is limited to observing and recording partial indicators of inputs and outputs. Typical inputs would be that conditions of assistance have been met, a description of the programme of assistance and the scope, level and types of activity undertaken. These findings would usually be rounded off with some partial indicators of outputs such as jobs created or qualifications gained.

Evaluation is broader and usually has two primary aims:

- An improving and learning aim, to provide information that will help those involved to learn and so improve the design, operation and outcomes of policy initiatives. (This can be done in real time through monitoring as well as through after-the-event evaluation.)
- A proving aim, to examine what difference the policy initiative has made to the individuals or firms or to the wider economic and social parameters it seeks to influence.

Evaluation studies will have additional benefits if they also indicate how and why initiatives have their effects. Such learning enables initiatives to be enhanced in an informed way. This can be particularly valuable when more than one initiative is aimed at a particular objective. In this case, it may be important to analyse not only individual impacts but also whether the combined effects are greater than the sum of those individual impacts.

Evaluation objectives

Many people would like to know the results of intervention programmes, not least those responsible for their design and implementation. What they would like to know, however, is often not just a simple yes or no in answer to the question of whether the programme hit its target, but also the accuracy and/or degree to which the target was hit, or the closeness of any misses. It is also important to establish what lessons can be learnt from the experience and, not least, what improvements should be made to future

---

↻ **ILLUSTRATION 16.1 – ECONOMIC APPRAISALS**

Although a prior appraisal of a project is not an evaluation of its eventual results, there is a connection in that the issues raised in the appraisal are likely to influence the agenda for a subsequent evaluation.

In the UK at least, the established government system for the prior appraisal of projects is essentially an economic one. *The Green Book*[4] produced by HM Treasury to guide government departments in project appraisal describes a method of economic appraisal based on a comparison of net present values.* Those values can only include items to which a monetary value can be assigned. The book does acknowledge that, in making a choice among options, there will frequently be a need to consider factors that cannot usefully be valued in money terms. However, by concentrating primarily, and in some detail, on the more easily appraised economic aspects, it can have the result of encouraging appraisers to ignore the other factors, or at least to treat them as if they were less important. This is particularly serious when the other factors are the main point of the project, or where they could be the deciding factor in prioritising projects.

It is only to be expected that the issues raised by the appraisal are then likely to feature in the requirements set for monitoring during the project, which will in turn influence the subsequent evaluation. A limited, and biased, agenda will have been set, even if only subconsciously.

* The net present value of a project is defined as the difference between the present value of its stream of benefits and of its stream of costs. The present value of a stream of benefits (or costs) is the projected values at the time when the benefits (or costs) will occur, discounted at an appropriate rate.

efforts, whether in the form of better methods or better delivery. Providing meaningful information about results therefore is not just a simple matter of measurement.

Who will be interested in the results, and what do they want, or need, to know? The stakeholders in intervention include those who initiated it, those who paid for it, those who delivered it and those who consumed, received or were affected by it. Even assembling such a list can be difficult. Often, in intervention of this sort, there is a temptation to mislabel the components: for instance to describe the consumer of the intervention as the customer. This may be done because it is hoped that it will lead to the consumer being treated with the deference that typical businesses are supposed to afford their customers. But frequently there is a fundamental difference in that the consumer does not pay for the intervention, or only pays a relatively small portion of the cost, with the major share of the cost being borne by government and therefore ultimately by the taxpayers. Thus the government, on behalf of the taxpayer, is the customer, and the consumer is not, because what matters is not the label but the money and the direction in which it flows. In such cases using the word customer to describe non-paying consumers usually only leads to confusion. It is government which has a legitimate interest in knowing what it is getting for its money – and the voters and taxpayers in whose name the intervention is made.

What do these stakeholders want to know? For government, at least in the UK, there is a desire for evaluations to provide answers to major policy questions, some of which are listed in Table 16.1. For other stakeholders the position is often less clear, although they will generally share the same concerns.

Answering the questions in Table 16.1 requires rigorous and comprehensive evaluation criteria and methods: the 'what' and the 'how' of measurement. The question of what to measure itself raises a number of other questions, such as:

Table 16.1 *Major UK enterprise policy questions**

- What is the appropriate balance to be accorded to assisting start-ups, existing businesses and growing businesses? Is there a case for a selective targeting and, if so, on what basis should it be undertaken?
- If there is a desire for more start-ups, how can the business birth rate be increased, especially that of fast-growing, knowledge-based businesses with international market potential?
- If the aim is to stimulate more growth in existing businesses how can that be achieved – and can such efforts be targeted on businesses which might have the greatest economic impact?
- Will the policy implementation system prove effective in generating a meaningful demand for, and a supply of, services to small business?
- What form and structure should business support take?
- Is the current analysis of the financial needs of new and growing firms correct?
- How critical is the role of management training and development in the small firm sector?
- How can the sector be facilitated to expand its exports and keep abreast of technological developments?
- Should policy-making and its implementation be more, or less, centralised?
- Which interventions 'work' (however defined) and which don't? Are any of the interventions indicated above justified by their results and/or impacts?
- If the results and/or impacts of any policies, programmes or projects are not as good as was expected/planned/hoped, what, if anything, can be done to improve the initiative concerned? Is it the objectives, the methods or the delivery mechanisms which need to be changed?
- If the results and/or impacts of any policy, programme or project are good, can the initiative concerned be transferred to other places?
- Who should pay: the client or the provider/government?
- What is the role of publicly-funded business support?

---

* In theory these questions should be asked by policy-makers but in practice some of them may not be emphasised, or at least not in an unbiased way. For instance, some policy-makers may not want to learn that their policies are failing so they look for evidence that their policies are working, while trying to avoid or minimise any indications to the contrary.

- What are the links between enterprise, jobs and other benefits?
- With what should the results be compared? What results might be expected (benchmarks) and how do these compare with the results required and achieved?

- Over what timescale is it reasonable to expect and measure results?
- What value could or should be attached to results which cannot easily be measured (due to their intangibility or difficulties in isolating cause-and-effect relationships)?
- To whom do the benefits or the drawbacks accrue (the 'stakeholders') and who bears the costs?

Of the two main aims of evaluation indicated earlier, it is that of proving – examining the difference made by an intervention – that is often the more difficult. Seeking to examine the impact of a policy requires knowing what would have happened in the absence of the initiative in question and then determining what has changed as a result of the initiative. The changes considered should not be restricted to the direct recipients of assistance only, but should also embrace the effects on the wider economy, community and society (for instance on the other businesses that did not receive assistance). This implies clearly identifying the stakeholders interested in changes or, more importantly, affected by them.

Different individuals, groups or organisations in society may well seek different outputs or combinations of outputs from policy interventions. These outputs can range broadly across economic, social and political aspirations, with the different stakeholder interests not infrequently being incompatible or in conflict. Therefore a conclusion such as 'the policy worked' often raises the question: 'In whose terms?' The need to take a wide view of the effects is reinforced by the current emphasis on the concepts of social accounting and the social audit. Traditionally, recorded effects have tended to be limited to the direct and easily measurable effects, especially those that could be expressed in money terms. Now, with increasing concern for the environmental and social impact of policies and the functioning of organisations generally, wider measures, new measures and new measuring techniques are becoming imperative. Traditional accounting systems are too narrow in scope to deal with many of the complexities and interest groups in the modern world. Even if financial assessments of some effects were possible, such an assessment might be too costly, too uncertain or could take too long. Projects which target social need, for example, will have a number of objectives, the achievement of which will be evidenced not only in some economic measurements but also in other qualities or values that cannot be added together and then scientifically compared.

Evaluation processes

Because of the variety of policies, projects, programmes and purposes for which an evaluation might be required, there is no such thing as a one-size-fits-all evaluation process. Nevertheless some guides are available (see Illustration 16.2) and some general principles can be enunciated:

1. Clearly understand the objectives of the initiative, so that an evaluation can be related as closely as possible to them. (But, as noted in Chapter 14, determining the objectives of policy initiatives is often very difficult, because they may not be made explicit.)
2. Look for, and record, not just intended effects but other effects as well, both direct and indirect. This may mean broadening the scope of the evaluation study. Policy initiatives can have effects beyond those intended, both positive and negative. For instance, will an increase in business start-ups reduce the growth prospects of some existing businesses? Moreover, as already noted, the scope of an evaluation may need to embrace social and environmental as well as economic effects.
3. Record the effects as they impact on the various stakeholders.
4. Have common measures of the effect so that comparisons can be made across different initiatives.
5. Determine the basis upon which the effect of any initiative is to be judged. Is it to be compared with the situation in the absence of that initiative? Is it to be compared with the effect of a previous initiative or a (future) alternative initiative? Or is it to be compared with the effects of the best parallel initiative elsewhere (a benchmark)? In short, it is necessary to determine whether there are better ways to achieve similar results.
6. Determine what the effects of more, or less, expenditure on the initiative might be, not just the effect of all or nothing.
7. Determine whether the policy initiative would be more effective if it were implemented within a different institutional framework and delivery mechanism.

The core of an evaluation should be the extent of the net benefit, or additionality, attributable to the intervention in question. Implicit in the foregoing, however, are two concepts that are often ignored in evaluation studies of small business policies: the deadweight and displacement effects, which have the effect of reducing the net benefit of interventions. Multiplier effects, on the other hand, enhance the benefits and should also be considered, while effectiveness, efficiency and economy are measures of different aspects of the process.

- *Additionality*: This is the measure of the net benefit: the benefit which accrued as a result of the measure, whether intended or not, which would not otherwise have accrued.
- *Deadweight*: This is a measure of 'what would have happened anyway' without the measure. Because of deadweight, even the direct effects alone of intervention are often not easy to ascertain. It may be possible to show that a business has received assistance and has subsequently improved; but to what extent is that improvement due to other factors and so would have happened in any case, even had there been no intervention?
- *Displacement*: This is a measure of 'how much of the gain in one area is offset by losses elsewhere'. It may be that a business directly benefits from intervention and increases its employment as a result. However, if the employment in a rival business is reduced because the first business takes its market, then the total employment between the two may not increase and, unless redistribution is helpful, overall there may be no benefit. While, superficially, improved small business creation and growth may appear to be beneficial, this is so only if there is net growth and wealth creation (as opposed to redistributing existing wealth) and there are no adverse effects on non-economic benefits. (In addition the benefits of a measure should exceed the cost of the measure.)
- *Multiplier effects*: There can be additional benefits from the indirect or side effects of intervention. If an increase in activity in a directly affected business results in an increase in activity in another business, for instance because it is a subcontractor, that is a beneficial multiplier effect which increases the extent of the additionality.
- *Effectiveness, efficiency and economy*: This is a trio of measures concerned with value for money. Effectiveness is the extent to which an intervention achieved its aims; efficiency measures the amount of direct output that the inputs achieved; and economy is concerned with the cost of those inputs.

Observance of the principles described above, coupled with a practical and useful evaluation method, would provide a sound basis for determining the value for money of an economy's (or region's) support programmes. It strongly suggests that the implications of enterprise development polices have to be examined in a wider framework than has traditionally been the case.

ILLUSTRATION 16.2 – TWO GUIDES TO EVALUATION

Two guides to evaluation, which between them indicate some of the principles to be applied, are outlined here:

The Green Book. The official central UK government guide to evaluation is *The Green Book*[5] and, according to it, an evaluation is a 'retrospective analysis of a project, programme or policy to assess how successful or otherwise it has been, and what lessons can be learnt for the future'. It involves comparing the results of the project both with what was targeted for the project and with what might have happened should the project not have been implemented. It should seek to draw lessons from this comparison and present, in its findings, the results and recommendations arising from this. The evaluation, it suggests, 'should normally follow this sequence:

(a) Establish exactly what is to be evaluated and how the past outturns can be measured.
(b) Choose alternative states of the world and/or alternative management decisions as counterfactuals.

(c) Compare the outturn with the target outturn, and with the effects of the chosen alternative states of the world and/or management decisions.

(d) Present the results and recommendations.

(e) Disseminate and use the results and recommendations.'[6]

David Storey's Six Steps. *The Green Book* does not go into a lot of detail about how appropriate counterfactuals might be selected and compared. They are important because the counterfactuals include what else might have been done or what would have happened if the project had not been run. In a scientific experiment it is generally advisable to run a control group but often that may not be practical in the enterprise field. Consequently some other way has to be found to show what effect an initiative had or whether any improvement observed would in all probability have happened anyway. It has been suggested by David Storey that, for many small business support programmes, there can be six steps in an evaluation and that the meaningful evaluations are those which go as far as the sixth step. In this sequence it is Steps III to VI that establish the counterfactual position but, Storey suggests, in most OECD countries evaluation rarely passes Step III and in many instances does not pass Step I. The steps are:

Step I	Take up (the numbers)
Step II	Do they like it? (the happy sheets)
Step III	What difference did it make?
Step IV	Compare the assisted businesses with 'typical' non-assisted businesses.
Step V	Compare the assisted businesses with 'match' non-assisted businesses (because assisted businesses are not 'typical').
Step VI	Compare the assisted businesses with 'match' non-assisted businesses taking account of sample selection.

Sources: HM Treasury, *The Green Book: Appraisal and Evaluation in Central Government* (London: TSO, 2003).
D. J. Storey, 'Six Steps to Heaven' in D. L. Sexton and H. Landström (eds), *Handbook of Entrepreneurship* (Oxford: Blackwell, 2000) pp. 176–194.

Other evaluation issues

Despite the apparent clarity with which some guides to evaluation explain the process, it is unusual to find evaluation studies that observe the principles of evaluation fully. This might be:

- Because a rigorous study would be too expensive (especially if the effort needed to establish fully all the results is likely to cost more than the original initiative or its benefits).
- Because in some situations it is argued that there are so many variables at work that it is not possible in practice to isolate the effects of one or two.
- Because it is argued that many of the effects of an initiative can be intangible and therefore difficult or impossible to measure.

There are a number of other factors which can reduce the reliability and credibility of evaluations, including the following, which are considered in more detail below:

- The difficulty of balancing the need for objectivity with the need for insight.
- The conflicts of interest that can arise when the evaluators are reliant on the policy-makers or deliverers for some or all of their funding.
- The problems that can arise in quantifying outputs and outcomes.

- The difficulty in establishing the direction of causation.
- The time needed for some of the impacts to develop and become apparent.

Objectivity and insight

Research is often supposed to be better if done impartially and objectively, but a researcher also needs to have insight into the subject of the research if he or she is going to understand what to look for. As Gibb has suggested, without insight into the process, researchers might conclude that revision causes exams[7] and insight is also needed if the traps of the 'default' assumptions described in Chapters 8 and 9 are to be avoided. The trouble is that it is hard to get insight without involvement, but with involvement also comes partiality and subjectivity.

He who pays the piper

According to Curran, the evaluation of small business policies in the UK has been of two main kinds:

- 'Evaluations sponsored by government funding departments and/or agencies delivering the policy, conducted by private sector for-profit bodies. Most small business support evaluations in the UK are probably of this type and often the results never enter the public domain.
- Evaluations by independent (usually academic) researchers on a not-for-profit basis, sponsored by others than those funding or delivering the initiative. ... The results are normally made public with the aim of promoting constructive discussion.'[8]

Wilful blindness is a term used in legal circles under which 'you are responsible if you could have known, and should have known, something which instead you strove not to see'.[9] As most evaluations are carried out by, or for, those responsible for funding or running the policies or programmes in question, there is a strong temptation, consciously or unconsciously felt, for the evaluators to avoid seeing negative evidence. Therefore, because it is human nature often to succumb to such weakness, positive evaluations can be inherently suspect.

It is natural that funders or implementers would wish to see a positive verdict on their efforts; however, this often means that, instead of wanting to be told whether an initiative has worked or not, they want to be told that it has worked. That desire, even if not overtly expressed, can influence evaluators who might hope for repeat business. Also if, despite their wishes, an evaluation is still negative it may not be published – which is a further reason why published reports are likely to provide a positive bias.

The distinction between Curran's two kinds of evaluation is important. The first kind is much more likely to be favourable to the policy or programme than the second kind. Where those conducting the evaluation are dependent on the initiator or deliverer for their fees and future similar work, there will be pressures to be less critical. This is less likely if evaluation is by researchers not reliant on policy-makers or deliverers for their funding and the results are open to peer scrutiny. One result of these pressures is that small business initiatives in general probably receive more favourable recognition than they merit. It is not always obvious where there might be bias as authors of such reports do not have to indicate the extent of their interest(s) in the subject.

Quantification

Many people like to see quantified targets and outputs/outcomes because their measurement seems to be clearer and more 'scientific'. However, problems arise when the outcomes sought are real and relevant but not easily quantified. If, for instance, measurable indicators are used as proxies for the real objectives of a policy, those executing the policy may try only to address the indicators. As an example, if a measurement of the time spent on hospital waiting lists is used as a proxy for the level of patient care, hospital administrators may try to reduce reported waiting times, for instance by restarting the clock each time a patient is seen, rather than by speeding up the process. The quantification problem is also recognised in the McNamara fallacy (see Illustration 16.3).

PART 3

⊃ | ## ILLUSTRATION 16.3 – THE McNAMARA FALLACY

'The first step is to measure whatever can be easily measured. That is OK as far as it goes. The second step is to disregard that which can't easily be measured or give it an arbitrary quantitative value. This is artificial and misleading. The third step is to presume that what can't be measured really isn't important. This is blindness. The fourth step is to say that what can't be easily measured really doesn't exist. This is suicide.'[10]

Or, as Einstein is reputed to have said: 'Not everything that counts can be counted and not everything that can be counted counts!'

Cause and effect

If a correlation can be demonstrated between inputs and outputs, it does not necessarily imply causation, or clarify its direction. Gibb's observation, reported above, that without insight researchers might conclude that revision causes exams illustrates the difficulty of establishing cause and effect, because even an apparent sequence in time is sometimes not enough to establish the direction of causation.

Timing

The timing of evaluations is often a problem. The cost of an evaluation may be included in a programme or project budget which has to be spent within the time set for the initiative in question. This timing is also consistent with the need to carry out the evaluation sufficiently in advance of the scheduled expiry of an initiative for a renewal or extension to be considered, should the evaluation results justify it. For this and other reasons, such as a political desire to proclaim a success, there is often pressure for an evaluation to be completed early.

It might be possible at a relatively early stage to see whether an initiative is being implemented as it should be and whether the planned outputs are being achieved. However, the anticipated results and impacts of the initiative, which are the reasons why it was launched, often take far longer to become apparent and it is often difficult to determine how long this might be and when they should be assessed. Thus evaluations are, in practice, often carried out before it is actually possible to ascertain if they are delivering the benefits sought.

EVALUATION EVIDENCE

One of the embarrassing truths of modern innovation and entrepreneurship policy is that surprisingly little policy is backed by hard evidence.[11]

What does evaluation tell us about the effectiveness of enterprise (and entrepreneurship and small business) policy? The previous section describes why evaluating a policy may often be a complex procedure; nevertheless, feedback on policy effectiveness is still important if resources are not to be wasted on unproductive, or even counter-productive, effort. Evaluation is necessary therefore, but because it can be difficult to do well and can be subject to distorting influences, frequently its conclusions are not as clear as might be hoped.

Despite the importance of evaluation, many programmes are not evaluated properly, the results of many evaluations are not made publicly available and, for the reasons indicated above, many evaluations which are published might be expected to be unduly favourable to the programme in question. Therefore any attempt to draw conclusions from the evidence that is available is not necessarily going to provide a scientific, accurate and/or objective assessment – but it is all that is available. What follows is a sample of what has been said about some individual programmes, some methods and areas of intervention and some overall assessments of the effectiveness of enterprise intervention.

Some individual schemes

UK Small Firms Loan Guarantee Scheme

Before the Small Firms Loan Guarantee Scheme was replaced by the Enterprise Finance Guarantee (see Chapter 15) it was the subject of several evaluations:

- In 1990 National Economic Research Associates concluded that the impact of the Scheme on the small business sector was negligible, although it may have had some initial effect 'in providing a demonstration to the clearing banks that there were opportunities for profitable lending in the small business sector'.[12]
- An independent evaluation of the scheme by KPMG in December 1998 suggested that it continued to play an important role in businesses that lack a track record or collateral.
- Nevertheless in 2001 the Cruickshank Review recommended that the government 'should progressively switch financial support away from the scheme and instead focus on market imperfections in the provision of small-scale risk capital to certain segments of the SME population'.[13]
- The results of the Graham Review[14] of the scheme were published in September 2004, as a result of which the scheme was focused on start-ups and young businesses, two groups viewed as suffering most from the lack of collateral and a business track record. Subsequently, the Public Accounts Committee referred to the Graham Review and its estimate 'that the Scheme has a default rate of 35 per cent compared with a commercial default rate for small business of 4 per cent', adding that the default rate 'is partly attributable to intervening when the market will not but, with a default rate so much higher than the commercial rate, it is questionable whether the Scheme is best calculated to promote the generation of viable businesses'.[15]
- An evaluation of the scheme by Cowling in 2010 concluded that the scheme was well targeted with high levels of self-reported additionality and that the overall benefits outweighed the cost to the economy. It also shows that there were other economic benefits attributable to the scheme which appears to be a particularly cost-effective way of creating additional employment.[16] Nevertheless the report does add a significant caveat that it is:

> important to note that this evaluation relies on business owners self reported outcomes and assessment of scheme's impact rather than using administrative measurements of business performance. It is acknowledged that business owners may not be able to give an accurate assessment, but this issue is common in all business support evaluations and careful questionnaire design attempts to minimise this.[17]

As an overall comment, however, Parker finds loan guarantee schemes generally 'to be, at least ineffective: while they do not do much obvious harm they do not appear to do very much good either'.[18]

Trade credit and late payment

The Late Payment of Commercial Debts (Interest) Act (see Chapter 15) took effect in the UK in 1998 and introduced the statutory right to interest on late payments of debt:

- In 2001 a Bank of England report noted research which claimed to show that 'over 90 per cent of small businesses have not noticed any improvement in late payment since the introduction of the Act'.[19]
- In October 2006, the Credit Management Research Centre (CRMC) released data to suggest that late payment by UK companies was higher than when the Act was introduced, and this despite further European Late Payment legislation introduced in 2002.[20] In examining the SME position, it noted that:

> 'large firms are currently receiving more credit than they are extending and SMEs are being forced to extend more credit than they are receiving', adding that 'the clear imbalance could be evidence

that large firms use their dominant position at the expense of the small firm. While a fairer comparison would be SME indebtedness to large firms now as against their indebtedness in 1998, nevertheless there appears to be little of significant gain for the sector overall.'

- In 2009 the UK government in its Impact Assessment of the Directive of the European Parliament and of the Council on Combating Late Payment concluded that 'with limited exceptions, there is no appetite for further legislation in the UK from business organisations. Current legislation is rarely utilised given the long-standing nature of the majority of supplier-customer relationships.'[21] In supporting the case for the European Directive, the government offered as evidence, *inter alia*, that the CBI (Confederation of British Industry) notes that:

> UK legislation is rarely utilised – [while] 72% of SMEs are aware of the legislation only 7% of SME employers had used it to take legal action; and 'believes a far more comprehensive strategy that addresses the full range of drivers of late payment should be developed'.[22]

The inference is that UK legislation had been so ineffective that additional measures were justified. In addition, an evaluation of the overall impact of the 2011 EU Directive itself was published in 2015 and it concluded that:

> There is little evidence that the Directive has had an impact on payment behaviour and the practice of late payment to date. Furthermore, exercise of the rights conferred by the Directive is not widespread due to fear of damaging good business relationships. Rather than legislation, business culture, economic conditions and power imbalances in the market are the driving factors of payment behaviour.[23]

UK Enterprise Investment Scheme/Venture Capital Trusts

The UK's Enterprise Investment Scheme (EIS) was introduced in 1994 to promote access to risk capital for certain types of smaller companies by providing private individuals with tax relief on their direct investments. Venture Capital Trusts (VCTs) were introduced in 1995 and promoted indirect investment into similar companies through a managed fund structure for private individuals.

A recent and rigorous evaluation (using matched samples) of the EIS and VCTs, published in 2008, failed to find evidence of meaningful impact or, indeed, of sufficient impact to justify their continuation without further study. It concluded:

> In future, however, a rather longer time-series aspect to the dataset used here may allow us to be more definitive about the overall impact of EIS and VCT on recipient company development and performance. Such a study should also be able to better examine the equally fundamental question of whether the schemes benefit UK economic performance overall – whether outcomes in terms of company performance justify the transfer payments of tax receipts foregone.[24]

In Europe generally, the various incentives offered by such schemes have been criticised as having been 'insufficiently targeted, or at least ineffective in getting funds into new-technology based enterprises or into depressed regions'[25] with venture funding having a bias towards expansion and buy-in–buy-out finance. Bannock further argues that the most fundamental criticism of the schemes is that they 'provide no help for SME owners, who are invariably forced to invest personal funds in their own business out of taxed income',[26] while tax relief is offered on investment in their pension funds (which rarely invest in SMEs).

Swedish Innovation Centre financial support programme

Norrman and Bager-Sjögren investigated the impact of a Swedish financial support programme 'directed to supporting early stage innovative ventures'. Their hypothesis was that supported firms would perform better than those firms which were not supported, and that firms that received multiple support would perform better than those that applied and gained support only once. However, they found that:

The evidence of an impact of the support to early stages ventures given by the public programme ... is weak or non-existent ... [and] our test of the projects that programme officials considered to be most promising did not support their belief.

and added:

The fact that no additionality resulting from the programme has been detected is serious. However, it does not necessarily imply programme failure but instead that further research ... is necessary to find explanations.[27]

Scottish Intermediate Technology Initiative

A significant recent programme by Scottish Enterprise was the Intermediate Technology Initiative. Described as 'arguably, the UK's most ambitious ever "systemic" policy instrument',[28] it was launched in 2003 as a ten-year programme with the objective of identifying emerging global market opportunities in life sciences, ITC and digital media, and energy. It had a separate Intermediate Technology Institute (ITI) for each of these three areas tasked to 'foresight' (identify new) areas of unexploited research potential, commission research programmes to develop new platform technologies, and commercialise the technology through new venture creation or licensing.

However, the programme was effectively terminated after only seven years of operation. By then it had expended a budget of £231 million (equivalent to about one third of Scotland's annual business expenditure of research and development – BERD) but had produced just five new technology-based firms (NTBFs). This 'massive failure'[29] has been attributed, at least in part, to its use of an outdated linear view of innovation – 'the dominant, linear logic of UK technology and innovation policy as a whole'.[30]

Perhaps not surprisingly there is very little information about the Intermediate Technology Initiative on Scottish's Enterprise's website. However, it was researched by a team from three Scottish universities who also noted that:

Policy failures are rarely acknowledged and even less likely to be the subject of analysis, preventing the opportunity for learning. Markusen notes that despite the fact that technology policy failures are 'numerous and costly', remarkably little research examines such failures. She claims it is often implicitly deemed to be less promising than examining successful ventures.[31]

Other examples of intervention

There are studies, or summaries of other evaluations, which look at different types of intervention.

Grant schemes

Grants are, at least in the eyes of many recipients, a popular way of intervening to promote small business development and the resultant job creation. The job creation aspect is frequently seen, by those awarding the grants, to be crucial. Therefore the amount of grant awarded was often reported in terms of grant-cost per job promoted (created or maintained), because what is known at the time the grant is awarded is the number of jobs planned, or at least indicated in the business plan on which the grant award is typically based. If the plan works, which is not always the case, the jobs will be created later. However, while the number of jobs promoted can be recorded at the time the grant award is made, the number of jobs actually created will not be known until sometime later. Therefore evaluations of grant programmes should consider both the cost per job promoted, and the proportion of jobs thus promoted which were subsequently created.

Another significant issue with grants is additionality: the extent to which the benefits, such as the jobs created, were attributable to the grant support and would not have happened anyway. Those applying for grants and those awarding grants usually know that if the projected benefits are not going to be additional, the grants should not be awarded. Both parties will be motivated therefore to record a strong case for the additionality which subsequent evaluations may not counter.

The evidence for the success of grants is mixed. Owen, who examined state aid to small businesses in three areas of Europe (South Yorkshire in England, Nord-Pas-de-Calais in France and the Hainault region of Belgium), found that in all three areas the provision of grants led to additional economic activity.[32] However, a report by Hitchens *et al.* on Northern Ireland's industrial productivity compared with West Germany's found that Northern Ireland firms, despite lower productivity, were at least as profitable as their German counterparts and this was attributed in a large part to lower wages and to the level of government financial assistance.[33] It was suggested that the level and nature of such assistance (which in Northern Ireland in the 1980s amounted to about 20 per cent of manufacturing GDP) impeded the efficient operation of some local businesses by reducing their incentive to carry out essential research and development, training, and product innovation and design (and see Illustration 8.2). In effect, the grant tended to become almost a direct supplement to the firm's profit (although, it is argued, it has sometimes led to lower, and therefore subsidised, pricing).

This work was instrumental in triggering a change in the emphasis of Northern Ireland's grant strategy away from capital grants towards assistance with planning, product development, marketing, strengthening management and applying quality standards, as well as training and development of staff. A subsequent study in Northern Ireland appeared to be much more positive about the effectiveness of grants. Scott's work used control groups in Leicestershire in England and in the Republic of Ireland to demonstrate the effect of the work of the government-funded Northern Ireland small business agency, LEDU (which was subsequently absorbed into Invest Northern Ireland).[34] He found that LEDU-assisted businesses had higher employment-growth rates than comparable non-assisted businesses and that the cost per job year was estimated at between 3 per cent and 5 per cent below the estimate for the Regional Investment Grant in Great Britain.

Counselling, information and advisory services

Counselling has been a popular area of small business support. Evaluations of such services tend to typify the superficial nature of studies in this area because often they concentrate on headcounts (how many use the service) and satisfaction indicators (how many clients say they find it useful). Instead the critical question is how the service affects the performance of the business in terms of employment, turnover, profitability or other measures.

On the issue of satisfaction indicators it would appear that reaction is largely positive from clients of these services. However, some studies reveal that small businesses found greater satisfaction with their banks and accountants than with public support services.[35]

Early evaluation of the impact on business performance appeared to be inconclusive. Relatively little research was done in this area, and most of what was done did not stand up to rigorous critical analysis. The conclusion of Storey was that 'We are not aware of any studies which demonstrate that the provision of information and advice is a significant factor influencing the survival of the business.'[36] It must be remembered, however, that the absence of proof does not mean that the influence of this form of support is not positive in terms of business performance; it may merely remain to be demonstrated.

A 2007 study by Bennett shows government advice services to be strongest where the SME clients are most focused in what they seek and where the quality expectations are not too demanding.[37] He concluded that Business Link should 'focus on the primary aim of specialist advice links to subsidised services, primarily with a skill or other technical focus'. Bennett further added that about 79 per cent of clients report they are fully or partly satisfied with the service they receive – which fell short of the 90 per cent target sought by the DTI (Department of Trade and Industry).[38] Moreover while the DTI has a strategic objective that 50 per cent of businesses should improve productivity or competitiveness after receiving advice, small businesses themselves use it for 'softer' outcomes such as reassurance, confirmation of prior expectations, and adding value to management's skills/knowledge base, rather than providing an immediate impact on the bottom line.[39]

Bennett also stated that 'government targets are not very relevant to SMEs' and that Business Link needed 'to be far more sensitive to client needs, and to be client-driven, rather than policy or political-driven'.[40]

Another study into the impact of Business Link assistance was published in 2008 by Mole *et al.* who found 'no significant effects on growth from other assistance but ... positive and significant employment growth effects from intensive assistance' although no associated growth in sales was found. This, they surmise, could be due to 'a type of restructuring effect in which assistance encourages the firm to explore new opportunities which require new employees, but which take some time to have a sales or productivity benefit'.[41]

(NB – As previously noted, Business Link (BL) no longer exists. The BL regional advisory service was abolished in November 2011 along with the Regional Development Agencies (RDAs). Instead, Local Enterprise Partnerships (LEPs) are expected to drive regional economic growth.)

Management and workforce training and development

The conclusions about counselling, advice and information apply also to management training and development. Improving the quality of management is self-evidently the *sine qua non* of improved business performance, but to what extent does management development lead to improved management and therefore to improved business performance?

While a great deal of research has been carried out in the field of management development, its value is limited. The research tends to confirm the importance of developing management, especially in the growing firm, but it does not isolate the benefits either of management development in general or of different types of management development appropriate to the particular circumstances.

Storey and Westhead concluded that there was 'little evidence that management training programmes clearly led directly to better performance amongst participating SMEs', and also criticised most studies as methodologically flawed.[42] However, an analysis by Fraser *et al.* of the impact of the Small Firms Training Loans Scheme did find that it enhanced business performance.[43] This latter finding was not supported in the major study, undertaken for the British Bankers' Association, of the Golden Key Package training scheme.[44] While reaction to the scheme by the parties involved was positive, there was no statistically significant impact on business performance.

On the subject of workforce training, an overview of existing studies by Collier *et al.* comments that:

> Remarkably little is known about the impact of employer training, or of human capital generally, on the financial performance of companies. Moreover, few existing studies directly examine the longer term impacts of training. In view of the importance of this empirical issue, this knowledge gap in the research and policy-making community might seem surprising, leading one to ask why more is not done to investigate the issue more comprehensively.[45]

The reasons for the lack of useful research evidence in the areas of advice, information, training and consultancy, and indeed other areas, are essentially twofold:

- There is a lack of rigour in much of the research, and the methodology adopted is inappropriate to the objectives of the research (in so far as the objectives are genuinely to assess impact). There are various reasons for this, including a failure to distinguish between the training of managers and that of other employees, the timescales not being adequate, the sample sizes being too small, the impact of multiple variables not being allowed for, and the absence of control groups for comparisons.
- The area of training and advice is a very complex one. It can be difficult to demonstrate clearly the benefits of management development. Distinguishing between correlation and causality, and knowing the direction of causality, is particularly problematic. Moreover, the effectiveness of management development activity in any business is subject to many influences, not least the size and structure of the management team itself, the nature of its products or services, its stage of development and, of course, the quality of the management development input provided.

Support for women-owned businesses

As noted in Chapter 15, it was not until 2003 that a national strategic approach to the development of women's enterprise in the UK began to appear. As with other efforts to stimulate enterprise, a piece-meal approach had been predominant. Despite developments, a government commissioned report on support for women's initiatives in this field concludes with a familiar message. It states on evaluation that:

> Within a growing body of knowledge on good practice and learning outcomes, evaluation evidence for the efficiency, effectiveness and value for money of women's enterprise initiatives remains limited. Policy and programme development of women's enterprise will struggle to move forward on a sure footing without the development of appropriate evaluation frameworks, monitoring and outcome data, and impact assessment, including female business sustainability.[48]

ILLUSTRATION 16.4 – WHY WORKERS IN SMALLER BUSINESSES ARE LESS LIKELY TO RECEIVE TRAINING

A consistent finding in research on training provision in developed countries is that workers in small firms are less likely to be in receipt of formal training than those in larger enterprises.[46]

Two explanations are advanced for this. The first is that small firm owners are unaware of the benefits to their enterprise of the provision of training. Storey and Westhead refer to this as the Ignorance Explanation: that is, small firm owners are, for some reason, less aware than those managing large firms of the benefits which training provides for their enterprise.[47] There is evidence that government certainly appears to believe small firm owners underestimate (are ignorant of) the benefits of training. Thus the official Investors in People (IIP) literature highlights the benefits which firms themselves will gain from enhanced workforce procedures. It seeks to show that firms which have participated in the past have obtained 'bottom line' benefits. A similar pattern is observed in the promotional literature on Small Firms Training Loans (SFTL).

Government support for these initiatives, which focused on smaller firms, appears to be based on persuading firms that there are tangible benefits from the firm's training provision and, by implication, that the small firm owner is imperfectly aware of these benefits.

In contrast, the second explanation does not imply imperfect knowledge on the part of the small firm owner. Instead it assumes the small firm owner-manager makes a (fully) informed judgement but is more likely than a large firm counterpart to conclude that the benefits of training are insufficient to offset the costs.

To some extent these explanations are open to empirical assessment. It is possible to assess whether small firms which train, in some sense, perform better than otherwise compatible firms which do not. If there is no evidence of enhanced performance on the part of the firm training then this would favour the second explanation over the first.

Source: Based on: S. Fraser, D. Storey, J. Frankish and R. Roberts, 'The Relationship between Training and Small Business Performance: An Analysis of the Barclays Bank Small Firms Training Loans Scheme', paper presented at the *23rd ISBA National Small Firms Policy and Research Conference*, Aberdeen, 2000, pp. 1–2.

Points raised

The fact that there is a diagnosed need for training does not mean that training will be consumed if it is supplied, even when it is subsidised. This extract explores some of the issues behind the observed lack of training up-take (see also Table 15.2).

Delivery vehicles

As is highlighted in Chapter 15, policy effectiveness depends not just on good policy formulation but also on good implementation. Also, as noted in Chapter 15, a wide variety of delivery vehicles have been employed to give effect to policies and related initiatives. Indeed one of the most dominant trends over the past decade and earlier has been the trend towards regional and local delivery vehicles. These have been favoured on a number of grounds – not least that the services provided may be tailored to the particular needs of an area, typically in partnership with other local organisations.

Bennett reviewed the history of such forms of delivery in England through the experiences of local chambers of commerce. He suggests that, if such partnerships are to work better, there needs to be a recognition that there will be difficulties because different fields of business activity are developed to varying degrees, but that this 'can be best overcome by support for association self-development to improve their capacity where they have lowest coverage'. However, he argues that government is tempted:

> to believe that it is necessary for it to intervene directly to have a uniform system everywhere ... The outcome is a sort of equality of mediocrity, where everyone gets something rather unsatisfactory but that may meet government targets for what it believes it wants. This is usually an expensive solution with many perverse outcomes, and difficulties of engaging with businesses. It also leads to public sector competition with associations which is pure deadweight and destructive of business voluntarism and self-supporting initiative.[49]

More recently Arshed *et al.* considered enterprise policy implementation in England and concluded that 'the process of translating enterprise policy from policy-makers to delivery bodies has also had adverse effects on its effectiveness. The evidence highlights that the implementation process is complex, fragmented, unpredictable and weak.'[50]

Some overall assessments

Finally some reviews and commentators have reported on the overall effectiveness of interventions.

- Using GEM data (see Chapter 2) Reynolds has examined the extent to which rates of 'entrepreneurship' have changed in countries over time. Despite government policies to raise these rates he found little movement:

> While much attention has been given to the dramatic global diversity in business creation – some countries have over 10 times the activity of others – there has been less attention to the year-to-year consistency found in individual countries. This stability has occurred despite considerable government efforts to increase the level of activity.[51]

- After reviewing the effectiveness of 'entrepreneurship' policy, Ramlogan and Rigby report that 'overall we find that recent policy initiatives in this area have not been evaluated ... [and] the growing interest in entrepreneurial education has not been matched by sound evaluation evidence'.[52]
- Brown and Mason suggest that 'current regional industrial and enterprise promotion policies in the UK are poorly equipped to help firms grow rapidly'.[53]
- Bennett concluded from his research that 'successful government intervention is difficult to make effective at realistic cost–benefit ratios' and 'if a market gap existed in the past, it is no longer apparent'. He added, 'Over the period 1991–2004 there is little to indicate the overwhelming success of government SME support policies, particularly at the level of cost that they now involve'.[54]
- Greene *et al.* looked at entrepreneurship over a 30-year period in an area of 'low' enterprise in the NE of England. They concluded in 2008 that:

PART 3

'whilst it has been a laboratory for enterprise culture experiments for 30 years, it has not resulted in any clear acceleration of entrepreneurial activity'[55] and 'along with every other UK region remains in the same relative position as it did 10, 20 and probably 30 years ago'.[56]

- In 2007 the Richard Review on (UK) Small Business and Government stated that:

  There is a general lack of hard evidence about the impact of different types of programme and intervention ... [and] genuine economic evidence of the impact (or otherwise) of assistance to small businesses is hard to find. The Government has been reluctant (or unable) to publish any and has restricted itself to anecdotal or survey-based data. These clearly *do* demonstrate that Government support does and can assist individual companies. But, given the scale of expenditure, does this add up to a real impact on regional economies?[57]

- Huggins and Williams reviewed UK government intervention in the period from 1997 to 2007. Although they indicated that steps were taken 'to tackle barriers to enterprise and entrepreneurship by addressing economic, political, legal and cultural issues' they concluded that 'there has been little improvement in start-up rates or other entrepreneurship indicators'.[58]
- The National Audit Office, in reviewing the performance of the UK government's own Small Business Service, reported that the UK 'government spends over £2.6 billion [in 2003–4] in providing support to small business ... [but] SBS is not able to establish the overall impact of either its or wider Government activity on small business'.[59]

And a more general comment was provided by Bannock who, writing in 2005 from an international perspective on small business economics, reported:

Our review of business policy instruments indicates that, with few exceptions, results are unimpressive. ... [E]ven for the exceptions, they are fairly marginal in their effects. There is no reason to suppose that if most subsidy and assistance programmes were abolished altogether, it would make a significant difference to the shape and prosperity of the SME sector anywhere.[60]

He also added that:

All governments recognise the importance of SMEs and wish to promote them ... [but] most instruments used by governments to promote SMEs fail to achieve their objectives, or have only a very minor impact.[61]

EVALUATION CONCLUSIONS

Policy-makers would like to know how effective the possible forms of intervention are in order to select the ones that will be most cost-effective in achieving their purposes. Due to reasons such as the complexity of the subject area and the time it would take any results to become clear, as well as to avoidable shortcomings in evaluations, the evidence available to them is often imperfect, ambiguous and even contradictory. Nevertheless there appears to be no strong body of evidence to say that intervention has worked and a number of studies, some of which are reviewed above, suggest that so far much intervention has failed.

The evidence available does not conclusively prove that, overall, the usual methods of intervention do not work. But it does suggest that there is *prima facie* evidence that at least some schemes haven't worked as they were intended and that there is an absence of the meaningful supportive endorsements which might have been expected if, in general, intervention was effective. Although there may be limited findings that cast doubt on the effectiveness of interventions, there appears to be significantly more reliable evidence for such a view than for the contrary belief that intervention has worked.

It seems reasonable to conclude, from the evidence overall, that the methods so far applied have not worked in that they have not had the effect intended in improving rates of entrepreneurship or levels of business performance. Despite the similarity of policies and interventions across the world, there are few proven examples of successful 'best practice'. The adoption of interventionist policies appears to be due more to a 'me too' approach than any rigorous examination of their impact. If governments still want to intervene, and they will, and if they want to achieve more than just being seen to do something, they will need to recognise that just doing more of the same is unlikely to yield significantly different results.

These conclusions do not question the policy drivers and objectives but they do suggest that those objectives are not being achieved by the current methods. It appears that the case for intervention, at least in its common forms, is not proven and there is sufficient evidence of policy failure to indicate the need for new approaches. In this sense, much of the policy which has been followed for a quarter of a century and more is not working – and that raises a number of questions, including:

- Why has the policy failed?
- What does this failure say about the assumptions on which policy is based?
- What might now be done to institute better policy?

Answering these questions is attempted in the next chapter.

☛ THE KEY POINTS OF CHAPTER 16

- Evaluation is the process of assessing the results and impacts of projects, programmes or policy.
- Evaluation is not easy as many factors have to be taken into account, including additionality, deadweight and displacement.
- Other issues which can affect evaluations include objectivity versus the involvement needed for insight and the difficulty of maintaining impartiality.
- The result is that there are not a lot of reliable evaluations. Those evaluations of individual programmes summarised are mixed and overall assessments generally negative.
- The conclusion is that there is no strong evidence for policy success and instead clear indications of policy failure.

✓ QUESTIONS, EXERCISES, ESSAY AND DISCUSSION TOPICS

- Outline the key requirements of a policy evaluation.

- What are the purposes of an appraisal and an evaluation?

- Is it easy to produce an unbiased, reliable and informative evaluation? If not, why not?

- Is it fair to conclude, on the basis of the evidence offered in this chapter, that enterprise policy hasn't worked?

- The McNamara fallacy (see Illustration 16.3) suggests that there is a tendency to think that that which can't be measured is unimportant and to ignore it. Are there important aspects of enterprise which can't be measured? If so, how can they be assessed in evaluations?

PART 3

📖 **SUGGESTIONS FOR FURTHER READING AND INFORMATION**

N. Arshed, C. Mason and S. Carter, 'Exploring the Disconnect in Policy Implementation: A Case of Enterprise Policy in England', *Environment and Planning C: Government and Policy*, Vol. 34, No. 8, 2016, pp. 1582–1611.

R. Blackburn and M. Schaper (eds), *Government, SMEs and Entrepreneurship Development* (Farnham: Gower, 2012).

A. Lundström and L. Stevenson, *Entrepreneurship Policy for the Future* (Stockholm: Swedish Foundation for Small Business Research, 2001).

For more on evaluations see:

J. G. Potter and D. J. Storey, *OECD Framework for the Evaluation of SME and Entrepreneurship Policies and Programmes* (Paris: OECD, 2008).

For some developments in assessing the benefits of training see:

W. Collier, F. Green, Y-B. Kim and J. Peirson, *Education, Training and Economic Performance: Evidence from Establishment Survival Data*. Taken from http://ideas.repec.org/p/ukc/ukcedp/0822.html (accessed 12 December 2011).

REFERENCES

[1] HM Treasury, *The Green Book: Appraisal and Evaluation in Central Government* (London: TSO, 2003).

[2] P. Cowie, 'SME Policy Evaluation: Current Issues and Future Challenges', in R. Blackburn and M. Schaper (eds), *Government, SMEs and Entrepreneurship Development: Policies, Tools and Challenges* (Farnham: Gower Publishing, forthcoming).

[3] R. Scott, personal correspondence based on work for Northern Ireland's Department of Economic Development.

[4] HM Treasury, Op. Cit.

[5] Ibid.

[6] Ibid. p. 12.

[7] A. A. Gibb in a conference presentation.

[8] J. Curran, 'What Is Small Business Policy in the UK For? Evaluation and Assessing Small Business Policies', *International Small Business Journal*, Vol. 18, No. 3, 2000, pp. 38–39.

[9] M. Heffernan, *Wilful Blindness* (London: Simon & Schuster, 2012) p. 1.

[10] D. Yankelovich, quoted in C. Handy, *The Empty Raincoat* (London: Hutchinson, 1994) p. 219.

[11] G. Mulgan and A. Bravo-Biosca, *Bringing Experimentation and Evidence to Innovation Policy* (London: Nesta News, 3 May 2016).

[12] D. J. Storey, *Understanding the Small Business Sector* (London: Routledge, 1994) p. 227.

[13] Bank of England, *Finance for Small Firms: An Eighth Report* (London: Bank of England, March 2001) p. 29.

[14] HM Treasury, 'The Graham Review of the Small Firms Loan Guarantee' (London: 2004).

[15] House of Commons Committee of Public Accounts, 'Supporting Small Business', 11th Report of Session 2006–7 HC262 (February 2007) p. 5.

[16] M. Cowling, *Economic Evaluation of the Small Firms Loan Guarantee Scheme* (Brighton: Institute for Employment Studies, 2010) p. 6.

[17] Ibid. p. 45.

[18] S. C. Parker quoted in F. J. Greene, K. F. Mole, and D. J. Storey, *Three Decades of Enterprise Culture* (Basingstoke: Palgrave Macmillan, 2008) p. 153.

[19] Bank of England, Op. Cit. pp. 30–31.

[20] Taken from http://www.cmrc.co.uk/october_2006.pdf (accessed 10 February 2008).

[21] Department of Business, Innovation and Skills, *Impact Assessment of Directive of the European Parliament and of the Council on Combating Late Payment*. Taken from www.bis.gov.uk/files/file53264.doc (accessed 6 November 2011).

[22] Ibid.

[23] P. Hausemer, J. Rzepecka, F. Lofstrom, P. Eparvier, L. Rivoire, C. Gallo and N. Maroulis, *Ex-Post Evaluation of Late Payment Directive*, ENTR/172/PP/2012/FC – LOT 4 for Directorate-General for Internal Market, Industry, Entrepreneurship and SMEs (Luxembourg: Publications Office of the European Union, 2015) p. 6.

[24] M. Cowling, P. Bates, N. Jagger and G. Murray, *Study of the Impact of the Enterprise Investment Scheme (EIS) and Venture Capital Trusts (VCTs) on Company Performance* (London: HM Revenue & Customs, Research Report 44, 2008) p. 72.

[25] G. Bannock, *The Economics and Management of Small Business: An International Perspective* (London: Routledge, 2005) pp. 124.

[26] Ibid. p. 124.

[27] C. Norrman and L. Bager-Sjögren, 'Entrepreneurship Policy to Support New Innovative Ventures: Is It Effective?' *International Small Business Journal*, Vol. 28, No. 6, 2010, p. 615–616.

[28] R. Brown, G Gregson and C, Mason, 'A Post-Mortem of Regional Innovation Policy Failure: Scotland's Intermediate Technology Initiative (ITI)', *Regional Studies*, Vol. 50, No. 7, 2016, p. 1269.

[29] Taken from www.deadlinenews.co.uk/2015/01/19/67370 (accessed 22 August 2016).

[30] R. Brown et al., Op. Cit. p. 1269.

[31] Ibid. p. 1262.

[32] G. Owen, *Aid Regimes and Small Business in the UK, France and Belgium*, EFMD report to ESRC (Brussels: EFMD, 1992).

[33] D. M. W. N. Hitchens, K. Wagner and J. E. Birnie, *Northern Ireland Manufacturing Productivity Compared with West Germany* (Belfast: Northern Ireland Economic Research Centre, 1989).

[34] R. Scott, 'Does a Regime of Intensive Grant Assistance to Small Firms Create Jobs?', paper presented to the *23rd EFMD European Small Business Seminar*, Northern Ireland, September 1993.

[35] R. J. Bennett, 'SMEs and Public Policy: Present Dilemmas, Future Priorities and the Case of Business Links', keynote address to the *19th ISBA National Small Firms Policy and Research Conference*, Birmingham, November 1996.

[36] D. J. Storey (1994), Op. Cit. p. 290.

[37] R. J. Bennett, 'Expectations-Based Evaluation of SME Advice and Counselling: An Example of Business Link Services' *Journal of Small Business and Enterprise Development*, Vol. 14, No. 3, 2007, pp. 435–457.

[38] See also R. J. Bennett, 'SME Expectations from Business Link Services: How Are They Met?', paper presented at the *28th Institute for Small Business and Entrepreneurship Conference*, Blackpool, 2005.

[39] Ibid. pp. 439, 454.

[40] Bennett, 2007, Op. Cit.

[41] K. Mole, M. Hart, S. Roper and D. Saal, 'Assessing the Effectiveness of Business Support Services in England: Evidence from a Theory Based Evaluation', *International Small Business Journal*, Vol. 27, No. 5, 2009, p. 571.

[42] D. J. Storey and P. Westhead, *Management Training and Small Firm Performance: A Critical Review*, working paper No. 18 (Coventry: Warwick University Centre for Small and Medium-Sized Enterprises, 1997) p. 1.

[43] S. Fraser, D. Storey, J. Frankish and R. Roberts, 'The Relationship between Training and Small Business Performance: An Analysis of the Barclays Bank Small Firms Training Loans Scheme', paper presented to the *24th ISBA National Small Firms Policy and Research Conference*, Hinkley, November 2001.

[44] Cambridge University *et al.* for The British Bankers' Association, *The Evaluation of the Golden Key Package Component of the Small Business Initiative* (London: The Association, April 2001).

[45] W. Collier, F. Green and Y-B. Kim, *Education, Training and Establishment Survival, Draft* (Canterbury: Department of Economics, University of Kent, November 2007) p. 8.

[46] For the US: L. M. Lynch and S. E. Black, 'Beyond the Incidence of Employer Provided Training', *Industrial and Labour Relations Review*, Vol. 52, No. 1, 1998, pp. 64–81. For the UK: A. L. Booth, 'Job Related Formal

PART 3

Training: Who Receives It and What Is It Worth?', *Oxford Bulletin of Economics and Statistics*, Vol. 53, No. 3, 1991, pp. 281–294.

[47] D. J. Storey and P. Westhead, 'Management Training in Small Firms: A Case of Market Failure?' *Human Resource Management Journal*, Vol. 7, No. 2, 1997, pp. 61–71.

[48] GHK Consulting Ltd in association with Bren and Partners, *The Regional Women's Enterprise Initiatives: Final Report* (London: Department of Business, Enterprise and Regulatory Reform, *2008*). Taken from www.bis.gov.uk/files/file45553.doc (accessed 12 December 2011) p. viii.

[49] R. J. Bennett, 'Using the Relation between Business Associations and SMEs as a Policy Tool: From History to LEPs', paper presented at *34th ISBE Conference, Sheffield*, November 2011, p. 1.

[50] N. Arshed, C. Mason and S. Carter, 'Exploring the Disconnect in Policy Implementation: A Case of Enterprise Policy in England', *Environment and Planning C: Government and Policy*, Vol. 34, No. 8, 2016, p. 1603.

[51] P. D. Reynolds, 'Business Creation Stability: Why Is It So Hard to Increase Entrepreneurship?', *Foundations and Trends in Entrepreneurship*, Vol. 10, No. 5–6, 2014, pp. 321–475.

[52] R. Ramlogan and J. Rigby, *The Impact and Effectiveness of Entrepreneurship Policy* (Manchester: Manchester Institute of Innovation Research, University of Manchester, August 2012) p. 30.

[53] R. Brown and C. Mason, 'Raising the Batting Average: Re-orienting Regional Industrial Policy to Generate More High Growth Firms', *Local Economy*, Vol. 27, No. 1, 2012, p. 33.

[54] R. J. Bennett, 'SME Policy Support in Britain since the 1990s: What Have We Learnt?' *Environment and Planning C: Government and Policy*, Vol. 26, 2008, pp. 375–397.

[55] D. Storey, in an e-mail communication about Greene *et al.*, 21 January 2008.

[56] F. J. Greene, K. F. Mole and D. J. Storey, *Three Decades of Enterprise Culture* (Basingstoke: Palgrave Macmillan, 2008) p. 245.

[57] *Richard Review on Small Business & Government*, Interim Report, March 2007. Taken from www.conservatives.com/pdf/richardreport-interim-2007.pdf (accessed 17 October 2009) pp. 33, 37.

[58] R. Huggins and N. Williams, *Enterprise and Public Policy: A Review of Labour Government Intervention in the United Kingdom*, The University of Sheffield Management School Discussion Paper No. 2007.03, August 2007.

[59] National Audit Office, *Supporting Small Business* (London: The Stationery Office, ordered by the House of Commons to be printed on 23 May 2006) p. 5.

[60] Bannock, G. (2005) *The Economics and Management of Small Business*, Op. Cit. p. 133.

[61] Ibid. p. 194.

Companion website

Please visit the companion website at www.palgravehighered.com/Bridge-UE-5e for access to additional learning and teaching materials.

What Might Work?

CONTENTS

- Introduction
- Facing the facts
- The implications of policy failure
- Is there an evidence base for policy?

- An alternative perspective
- Changing the culture
- In conclusion

KEY CONCEPTS

This chapter covers:

- Why a failing enterprise policy might have been pursued for so long.
- The implications of that failure for assumptions behind policy and the theories consistent with it.
- The potential importance of the 'cultural' dimension of influence and the differences between it and the 'institutional' dimension.
- The possibility that, if it is to succeed, enterprise policy needs to stimulate positive social influence.

LEARNING OBJECTIVES

By the end of this chapter the reader should:

- Be aware of some of the implications of the apparent failure of much enterprise policy.
- Understand the relevance of the 'cultural' dimension of influence and how it differs from the 'institutional' dimension.
- Recognise the potential of social influence to encourage or discourage entrepreneurship, and the need to recognise this if enterprise policy is to succeed.

INTRODUCTION

So far, in Chapters 14 and 15, this part of the book describes the current state of enterprise policy: its drivers, aims and objectives; and its approaches, instruments and delivery mechanisms. Chapter 16 continues this exploration of the present position by assessing whether the policy works and examining the evidence for its effectiveness.

Chapter 16 concludes by suggesting that, overall, the evidence is that the enterprise policy methods so far applied have not worked in that they have not had the effect intended in improving rates of business creation or levels of business performance. This conclusion does not question the policy drivers and objectives, but it does suggest that those objectives are not being achieved by the current policy, approaches, instruments and/or delivery. If this is correct, and therefore if much of the policy which has been followed for a quarter of a century and more is not working, it raises questions about a number of aspects of policy, including:

- Why has the policy failed, and why has the policy which fails been pursued for so long?
- What does this failure say about the evidence, assumptions and/or theories on which policy is based?
- Are there alternative policy approaches which might work?

These questions and the issues associated with them are pursued in this chapter, thus concluding this review of intervention policy and Part 3. Moreover, by examining the reasons for that policy failure and from a basis of the fresh thinking outlined in Part 2, it suggests what might be tried instead.

FACING THE FACTS

> The first thing in science is to face the facts; making sense of them has to come second.
>
> A comment on the report from CERN in September 2011 that some experiments appeared to show particles travelling faster than light, which, according to prevailing theory, should be impossible.

Chapter 16 indicates both that there is not a lot of reliable and available evidence about the effectiveness of much enterprise policy and that the evidence that is available is not conclusive. Nevertheless it clearly suggests that the balance of probability is that if the aim of the policy is to stimulate higher rates of business start-up and/or small business growth, then it is not working because business start-up and growth rates are not increasing in a way that might have been expected.

That view gives rise to a number of questions such as why has it taken so long to come to this conclusion, why haven't more questions been raised about policy effectiveness, and what does this policy failure say about the assumptions, theories and models on which it is based. It also leads to questions about the implications of this for both policy and research (e.g. What policy approaches might work? Are the relevant policy objectives, in practice, unattainable?).

Just because it is clear that something has failed, it does not mean that it is obvious what should be done instead. The 'scientific method' (see Figure 1.2) suggests proceeding from facts to theory, to experiment and to observation; and then, if necessary, to refinement of the theory and trying again. The effectuation approach, outlined in Chapter 11, advocates starting where you are, accepting the reality of the situation as you find it, and looking for other opportunities to proceed.

But where can one look for other opportunities? A medical analogy might suggest that, if a supposed cure isn't working, this could be because:

- The diagnosis is wrong – a patient usually presents with a symptom or symptoms, but the nature of the problem causing them may not have been correctly diagnosed.
- The prescription is wrong – the problem may have been correctly identified but the cure then suggested may not be appropriate for that condition.
- The application is wrong – the cure may be appropriate but the treatment prescribed to deliver the cure may not be administered to the patient in an effective way.

It is, of course, also possible for a patient to get better despite one (or more) of these mistakes having been made. That was the case, for instance, when bleeding was widely applied to cure fevers: modern medical knowledge suggests it was actually harmful, nevertheless many patients recovered.

If this analogy is applied to the case of enterprise policy, the patient has been the economy and a key symptom has been high levels of unemployment which, together with other conditions such as low taxation revenues and/or low levels of exports, are thought to arise because the economy is unhealthy. The diagnosis has been that this ill-health is the result of low levels of enterprise, so the cure prescribed to restore economic health has been to apply more enterprise (with an increasing focus on high-growth/

high-tech enterprise). Therefore the enterprise policy adopted has generally been to apply a variety of methods which are supposed to increase levels of enterprise.

The evidence presented in this book suggests that, in this case, those methods have failed and the patient has not received the additional enterprise prescribed, and consequently has not been able to benefit from it. It does appear that recently in countries like the UK levels of self-employment have risen. For instance according to Henley, 'by the end of 2014 there were almost three quarters of a million more self-employed in the UK workforce than at the start of the global financial crisis in early 2008'.[1] However, a lot of this self-employment appears to be free-lancing or one-person businesses, and it has not generally been prevalent in the sectors or geographic areas most targeted by policy. In any case, it does not seem to have had the desired impact on the economy, which overall does not seem to be as healthy as is desired, and the level of unemployment has not reduced to that pertaining in the 1950s and 60s (see Figure 2.1).

Whether more enterprise of the type sought would improve the economy is a different point which will not be tested until that enterprise is delivered – but this book suggests that the policies being followed are not doing that. If that is the case, and the conclusion of Chapter 16 is accepted, then the next question is why has policy which fails to deliver more enterprise been pursued for so long? Several reasons can be suggested, but often they act in combination:

- Policy formulation and implementation are disorganised.
- Observing the results and impact of policy is difficult.
- Evidence of poor results and impacts is often not welcome – and so it is avoided if possible.
- There is failure to accept responsibility for connecting policy and research results and thinking.
- The research results, theories and models which might guide policy are not known or understood, or are wrong.

It has already been pointed out that, in the UK as elsewhere, there is often an absence of explicit statements of objectives and targets to guide the development of policies to encourage and support small business. This situation has led, *inter alia*, to a piecemeal development of policies, lacking cohesion and synergy. Moreover, the review and evaluation of existing support measures has often been narrow in scope, lacking in rigour and superficial. The explanations for this state of affairs are often complex and include reactions which range from 'it is very difficult', 'the data aren't there' and 'lack of resources' to 'the political will is lacking'. Another factor to consider is that policy-makers can be reluctant to accept that their policies are not working. Thus, consciously or unconsciously, evidence of a lack of success is not sought or is sought only from those who might not find or report it. Certainly much more can be done, and until it is, our knowledge of policy effects will be limited and policy itself will be 'hit and miss'.

The criticism has been made that 'too often public policy is made without regard to empirical research but in conformity with a misconceived conventional wisdom or ideological fixation'.[2] Indeed, early policies seem to have been based not on evidence about what had worked, but on assumptions that providing the help that people apparently said they needed would work. Those assumptions appear not to have been changed subsequently.

Similar problems were highlighted by Stevenson in explaining the difficulties of formulating and implementing an Entrepreneurship Development Strategy in the Atlantic Region of Canada.[3] She listed the following obstacles:

- *Lack of existing comprehensive models*: It is argued, in essence, that few if any models of entrepreneurship development exist that are based on a comprehensive, integrated and well-researched strategy. Because of this, 'there was a great deal of risk in the initiative.'
- *Lack of clarity about what entrepreneurship development is*: It is claimed that 'there is confusion in the minds of policy-makers and practitioners alike' about the meaning of entrepreneurship development, about its relationship with small business, about how to stimulate new ventures and growth of existing ones, and about how to determine priorities.

- *Prevailing myths*: Attention is drawn to the 'born not made' ('nature versus nurture') argument about entrepreneurs. 'There are still a number of government officials, policy-makers and business leaders who do not accept that the supply of entrepreneurs can be increased.'
- *Adapting to the paradigm shift in regional development policy*: It is argued that entrepreneurship development requires a different approach to economic development – the emphasis needs to be on 'community animation' rather than on the traditional 'industrial development' approaches of developing economic infrastructure, undertaking macro-economic planning or evaluating investment projects.

This message had also been echoed by the OECD, which, for instance, in a paper on 'Fostering Entrepreneurship and Firm Creation as a Driver of Growth in a Global Economy' emphasised that:

> To design programmes and support policies in a cost-effective way, governments need a good empirical understanding of the linkages between, *inter alia*, entrepreneurial environment factors, entrepreneurial activity, social factors and the entrepreneurial contribution to outcomes. Currently, many major gaps exist in the current empirical knowledge and there is a need to strengthen the factual and analytical basis for policy-making so that policy-makers, having a better understanding of the processes and the trade offs, can make decisions in an informed manner based on empirical evidence.[4]

THE IMPLICATIONS OF POLICY FAILURE

The above analysis suggests that, in terms of the components of policy indicated in Figure 14.1, the problem lies, not in the drivers and objectives, or even in the delivery drivers and implementation, but in the approaches and instruments. So why have approaches and instruments which don't appear to work been pursued for so long?

The diagnosis offered by the authors, based on their own experience and other inputs is that, despite the apparent rationale of diagrams like Figure 14.1 and the output from 30 years or more of entrepreneurship research, enterprise policy has mainly continued to follow an unchanged course. Essentially the methods being used now are still the same as those adopted up to 30 years ago and since then, despite all the research, there has been very little input from critical and/or alternative views. Many policy-makers seem to consider copying 'international best practice' to be the cheapest and quickest route to success. Doing their own research, or accessing the research done by others, and using the results to devise their own policy would be slower, significantly more expensive, and riskier because it might not work in the end. Copying what is reputed to be the best existing international policy, which is available and apparently tried and tested, seems to be the obvious course and the one for which it is much more likely approval can be secured.

However, a careful examination of much 'international best practice' in enterprise suggests that it is often recycled old policy because it too is based on copying others, although often it is repackaged – and then hyped because those responsible want it to appear to be working. Thus it appears to others as new and successful and so is copied in turn. In this way what is essentially the same basic policy recipe is circulated perpetually. Once it has been adopted and used, it is then natural to prefer the familiar and to want to do more of the same. New may sometimes be unavoidable, but it is awkward and requires new justification and possibly new structures – whereas continuity can be very desirable once the appropriate methods, organisations and budgets have been approved and put in place. So there is a temptation, once a policy is in place, to welcome any indications that it is working but to avoid, or ignore, any contrary indications. As a result, reporting on the policy can involve a selective and uncritical focus on any feedback which appears to support a success hypothesis.[5]

IS THERE AN EVIDENCE BASE FOR POLICY?

Thus the combination of the lack of cohesive objectives, an adherence to conventional wisdom, and inadequate review has led to a situation where, it is suggested, policy is formulated, and support maintained too often on the basis of assumption and/or 'pressure from small business lobby groups, short-term fluctuations in macro-economic conditions and political expediency'.[6]

A popular claim is that policy is 'evidence based' – but what does that mean? It should mean that policy is based on good evidence for what works and confirmed by good evidence that it does work, but it seems that this is rarely the case. In the UK in 2004, for instance, the UK government's Small Business Service (SBS) published *The Evidence Base*[7] for a government action plan for small business which purported to ensure that all decisions which affect small business are only taken after reviewing the evidence. Despite this, the document presented information about the policies that were being followed and some related findings but not why they were being followed. It did not, for instance, present evidence to show:

- Why enterprise and/or small businesses should be promoted.
- How enterprise/entrepreneurship and/or small business can be promoted.
- That enterprise/entrepreneurship and/or small business are being successfully promoted.

Who should connect policy and research?

As has been reiterated in this book, for at least the last 35 years there has been a significant growth of official interest in enterprise, entrepreneurship and small businesses which has prompted and often funded a significant growth of academic interest and research. Also, as reported in Chapter 2, Gibb has indicated that:

> Since the 1980s ... there has been an explosion of research into entrepreneurship and the small and medium enterprise. This is reflected in a substantial growth in both the academic literature and in the grey literature of the press, journals and consultant reports. Combined with ease of access to information through the new international information technologies the growth in 'knowledge' has been exponential.[8]

It might have been thought that, as a result of this research, the sort of problems with evaluations just discussed would have been resolved, or that, because of this research and the information it should have produced, evaluation evidence would be less critical to our understanding of this subject. This seems not to be the case, however, and Gibb goes on to say:

> Despite the increase in academic knowledge, indeed perhaps because of it, there has been a growth of ignorance. ... A major manifestation of this growth of ignorance is the emergence of a number of outstanding 'mythical concepts' and 'myths' which are considerably influencing the establishment of policy priorities.[9]

Instead of the availability of an increasing amount of information about enterprise, entrepreneurship and small business bringing the understandings of researchers and policy-makers (and also practitioners) closer together, Bridge[10] has referred to a research – policy gap, or divide. Despite occasional attempts from both sides to link policy and research, he suggests that the relationship between the two remains more like a division than a bridge. A number of reasons are likely to contribute to this lack of connection, including:

- *Different aims*. Policy-makers, researchers and actual entrepreneurs have different aims. Policy-makers seek things like more enterprise, more business start-ups and more growth in existing businesses. Academics seek things like PhDs and publications. Entrepreneurs want to run their businesses with minimum interference but maximum support. Also what entrepreneurs want from running their businesses, and thus how they should run them to achieve that objective, will differ from business to business. Thus governments may fund small business support schemes because they want fast-growing businesses, whereas business owners want help with their individual businesses but are not necessarily trying to grow. A medical analogy could be that what individuals want from a medical system will be treatment and cures when they are ill and for that they look to doctors and hospitals, whereas a government may want a healthier population and for that measures such as better health education, providing a good water supply, and reducing pollution by maintaining a good sewerage system could be a much more cost-effective option than funding more hospitals. Moreover research will follow the funding so the allocation of funding is likely to determine what is researched, instead of research determining what should be funded.

- *Different processes.* Two successive processes are involved in developing research-based policy or practice: first the research and then the development of the research output into something useful for people such as practitioners and/or policy-makers. They are different processes, and those doing the first are often not the best positioned or motivated to do the second. This has been likened to a cow being good at producing milk but not then able to convert that milk into butter (or double cream, yoghurt or cheese as the consumer requires).[11]

- *Different understanding.* Policy-makers are rarely experts on the subject for which they are making policy, Therefore they would like to establish in relatively simple form the key facts about the subject to form a base upon which they can make their policy assumptions. They also want to be assured that it is the generally accepted understanding and isn't going to change significantly. As a result of this, policy-makers like to acquire, and in all probability will then defend, the conventional wisdom (see Illustration 8.1), whereas some researchers may be more willing to challenge it.

There have also been other influences on policy formulation, some of which are suggested in Chapter 14 in the section on government and systemic failures. They support the view that often policy has not been based directly on research findings. To suggest that the failure of policy indicates that there

---

ILLUSTRATION 17.1 – THE CONTRIBUTION OF GEM

Reference is made to the Global Entrepreneurship Monitor (GEM – see Chapter 2) when citing evidence to justify aspects of enterprise policy, and GEM has clearly been influential not least because of its wide coverage and its apparent acceptability. GEM might appear to be an example therefore of research influencing enterprise policy.

GEM originally set out to explore, on a cross-country basis, a number of questions which are very relevant to the wider study of entrepreneurship and how to promote it, but it has not answered all of them. GEM has assembled a considerable amount of data about entrepreneurship in a wide range of countries, and its studies to date indicate that the level of entrepreneurship differs considerably across countries. GEM is not claiming to have found any causal relationship between the level of entrepreneurship and the level of, or rate of increase in, a country's GDP or per capita income. GEM is also refraining from suggesting what might determine the level of entrepreneurship in a country. Also, despite the apparent relevance of its initial questions to entrepreneurship policy, GEM does not now seem to offer much policy advice.

A problem with GEM might be that it is used because it appears to be authoritative and to be established practice. Also it does appear, sometimes, that GEM information is quoted selectively to justify policy, but not as the basis for its original formulation. But the GEM information may not be appropriate. For instance the TEA rates indicating levels of entrepreneurship are assessed by country, or sometimes by region, and imply a uniform rate across the country or region because it does not reflect any variances within it. Also sometimes GEM information is used to suggest that a country may have a higher than average 'fear of failure', but the question on which that assessment is based is often put in a telephone interview with no follow-up or probing of the answers. Further the question appears to follow one which asks respondents if they think they have the skills necessary to start a business. Thus, if people feel they don't have the necessary skills, they may think they are more likely to fail for that reason and not because they have a general fear of failure.

is a disconnect between policy and research evidence implies that there was a connection at some stage in the past. Suffice it to say that, because of the way policy has often been developed, there appears to be a lack of meaningful interchange between policy-makers and recent enterprise thinking. Instead, as Chapter 8 and in particular Illustration 8.2 indicates, if policy is based on any sort of theory or evidence, it is based on the 'conventional wisdom' and the old ideas and assumptions behind it. It also appears not to have observed its outcomes nor recognised its lack of success.

Because models of the influences on enterprise often appear to share many of the same assumptions, it seems that much policy has evolved alongside, and is consistent with, traditional theory instead of being developed from it. For instance the logic behind early policy, and thus still behind a lot of current policy, appears to assume that people make individual and logical risk-cost-benefit assessments; the same assumption seems to be behind much theory. Thus, following that assumption, enterprise policy seeks to affect the enterprise decision made by:

- reducing the risk, for instance by providing business training and information/advice, by improving the regulatory environment and by using macro-economic policies to stabilise the economy;[12]
- reducing the costs, for instance by reducing the red tape, providing subsidised premises and/or making it cheaper to find finance; and/or
- increasing the expected level of return, for instance by reducing taxes on business profits.

As many models and theories seem to support this approach, then the failure of policy apparently based on it must raise questions about the validity of those models and theories. A better understanding of the influences on enterprise, entrepreneurship and small business is needed therefore because, without a new approach, policy is likely to continue to follow the old methods and continue to fail.

AN ALTERNATIVE PERSPECTIVE

Much current enterprise policy seems, if not to be based on the conventional wisdom of what influences enterprise and entrepreneurship, then at least to be consistent with it. Chapter 9 raises a number of queries about that conventional wisdom. In particular it suggests that, instead of always responding logically, as traditional economic theory assumes, enterprise and entrepreneurship are often very socially influenced. Thus policies which essentially seek to present a logical case for entrepreneurship (often through attempts to alter the enterprise environment so as to reduce risk, reduce cost and/or increase returns) may fail because such incentives may not persuade more people to act entrepreneurially.

These policy attempts might be described as institutional because institutions of state are usually given responsibility for their design and delivery. Implementing the policies generally involves trying to make the thinking and actions of those institutions more supportive of entrepreneurship. So, instead of passing laws making it difficult to start a business (or, as was apparently the case in some communist regimes, making private business illegal), regulations should be relaxed, bureaucracy and relevant taxes reduced, and appropriate business support offered. In these ways the official institutional 'rules' are made (more) positive.

Interestingly some, but by no means all, models of the influences on entrepreneurship also acknowledge a cultural influence. The diagram reproduced in Figure 17.1 is an attempt to summarise some of the main influences suggested by a variety of sources and it includes the 'socio-cultural environment'.

Institutional and cultural dimensions

The influence of culture is also acknowledged by Dennis who suggests that the two key factors in achieving economic change are institutions (formal rules) and culture (informal rules), each of which can be either favourable or unfavourable:

> Favorable and unfavorable are positioned as independent entities, but in reality, they more closely resemble a sliding scale. Many public policies affect the overall entrepreneurial climate, whereas many

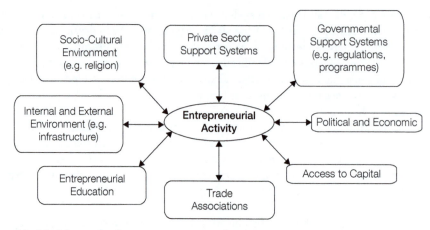

Figure 17.1 *Model of factors leading to entrepreneurial activity*

Source: J. Kim, A. G. Weinstein, S. E. Shirley and I. Melhern, 'Toward a Comprehensive Model of Global Entrepreneurship', a paper presented and the *ICSB Conference at Seoul*, Korea, in June 2009.

cultural norms and traditions serve the same function. The result within each political jurisdiction or area within one is a unique mixture of institutional and cultural constraints that shape the incentive structure. If the incentive structures are different, it is reasonable to expect that economic outcomes over time will also be different.[13]

Favourable institutional support would, for instance, include tax breaks, the minimum of 'red tape' and support schemes for entrepreneurs, whereas unfavourable institutional support would include high entry barriers, high taxes for businesses, no official support and even making self-employment illegal. Favourable cultural support would be a social environment which encourages people to engage in entrepreneurship because it is a socially approved and lauded activity, whereas an example of unfavourable support would be a society which shuns entrepreneurs and instead accords much higher respect to people with careers in other occupations such as the legal profession, medicine and/or the civil service.

However, instead of placing institutional and cultural factors in the same list, and thus encouraging a belief that their impacts are cumulative, Dennis, in the typology reproduced in Figure 17.2, suggests that 'institutions' and 'culture' are different dimensions of influence:

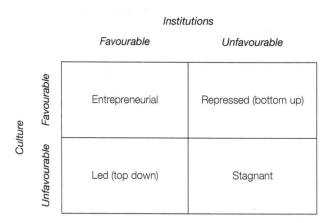

Figure 17.2 *Institutional and cultural dimensions*

Source: W. J. Dennis, 'Entrepreneurship, Small Business and Public Policy Levers', *Journal of Small Business Management*, Vol. 49, No. 1 (published by John Wiley & Sons, 2011) p. 96.

An implication of Dennis's presentation is that, by showing institutional and cultural influences in different dimensions, it suggests that they are different and act in different ways. It raises questions therefore about the nature of that difference and what happens when the two influences act in opposing ways: when one is favourable but the other unfavourable.

What are the dimensions?

Dennis explains the institutional dimension as involving 'government structures, such as legislative bodies, court systems and constitutions ... that create and enforce the formal "rules of the game"'.[14] There are many things that can be done in this dimension to make it more favourable towards entrepreneurship. They include regulatory changes such as relaxing any laws that constrain the starting of businesses and reducing business registration requirements; economic and fiscal changes such as providing a favourable tax regime; and business promotion changes such as increasing the training, financial support (including grants) and advice made available to individual businesses. As all of these can be changed in small ways, it is possible therefore to make incremental changes to the overall institutional position which can vary from very unfavourable to very favourable across a wide spectrum of different intermediate positions. This is indicated, for instance, in attempts to score or rank institutional favourability to entrepreneurship, such as that shown in Table 6.7. It shows that many countries are neither very favourable nor very unfavourable but can be found in various intermediate positions.

Dennis does not closely define 'cultural support' in his typology, although he indicates that it includes the 'cultural norms and incentives handed from generation to generation that constitute the "informal rules of the game"'.[15] The cultural dimension is taken, therefore, to lie in the social influence on people which comes from the shared values, beliefs and accepted ways of behaviour within their social circles. These informal rules often come from a different source of authority than that responsible for the formal rules, but both establish the constraints shaping the incentive structure. A further reflection of this is seen in Baumol's suggestion, summarised in Chapter 3, that the productive contribution of entrepreneurs to society varies less because of the total supply of entrepreneurs than it does from the way that the rules of the society encourage their application to productive, unproductive or destructive activities. By looking at historical evidence from ancient Rome, early China, the Middle Ages and Renaissance Europe, he shows that the role entrepreneurs play is influenced by the society in which they operate.

Highlighting the importance of the cultural dimension in this way is consistent with studies of human nature which emphasise that human beings are very social animals and that their actions have to be viewed in their social context. Consequently, when people change their minds about something, they often do it together. Ball,[16] in exploring this aspect of human behaviour, has likened it to the way that physical substances change their state. While the freezing point of water in normal conditions is zero degrees, if there are no impurities water can be super-cooled below this point and still remain liquid. However, when it does freeze, all the individual molecules in the water freeze at the same temperature as if they are all affected by the behaviour of the others. If the water is heated again, it will not change back to liquid at the temperature at which it froze but wait until a higher temperature when again all the molecules change together. This sort of phase change, Ball suggests, can also be seen when people resort to crime. Quoting some work by Campbell and Ormerod, Ball suggests that many people will tend to follow the example of the people around them: so, if few people are resorting to crime, they won't, but if lots are, then they will join in – a phenomenon which can be seen in riots and looting (and this suggestion led Bridge to formulate Figure 9.1).

Another aspect of the cultural dimension could also be the extent to which the thinking which guides economic development, and thus also the institutional response, is still based on an outdated paradigm. In their analysis of the entrepreneurial economy Audretsch *et al.* describe the shift from what they refer to as the managed economy to the entrepreneurial economy. In support of this, they suggest, the focus should not be on developing entrepreneurship policy, with 'its focus on promoting new firms and small firms', but rather on 'policy for the entrepreneurial economy'.[17] They ask whether many of the institutions and policies 'created during the era of the managed economy may actually contribute to the knowledge filter and pose barriers to entrepreneurship in the entrepreneurial economy'.[18]

For instance how much of the thinking behind career advice, industrial relations and business regulation is still based on an assumption that the big business is the ideal and/or the norm? Is there still a belief in some quarters that employment for life in such businesses is the norm and that it is the role of the state to apply limits to the otherwise unrestrained economic power of big corporations? Therefore does income tax policy assume employment, rather than self-employment, and does employment legislation assume that employees need to be protected from large monopolistic employers trying to drive down prices, and maximise profits, through economies of scale, minimal wage rates and poor working conditions? In effect does such policy seek to operate, police, and ensure fair play in a system which pertained in the middle of the 20th century but which is now ceasing to be as relevant?

If it does, it would not be surprising. It took some time for legislation to catch up with Fordism, and some of the effects of the shift to an entrepreneurial economy have yet to become apparent. Nevertheless this view does suggest that one aspect of the relevant cultural dimension is the thinking which informs and guides the institutions and their response.

The nature of the difference

Chapter 9 suggests that it is the assumption of many authorities that individuals opt for entrepreneurship on the basis of individually made, logical assessments of issues such as the perceived desirability of the goal, the ease of pursuing it, the help available and the perceived chances of success. Therefore many 'institutional' initiatives appear to be designed to increase the likelihood that people will opt for entrepreneurship by making it easier to do, by increasing the potential return from it, and/or reducing the risk associated with it. Such initiatives seem to be designed to influence people through conscious business logic.

In contrast, cultural factors do not appear to act through logic, or even through conscious means. 'Culture' is usually absorbed unconsciously, although actions taken under the influence of 'culture' may, if queried, subsequently be rationalised, because people like to think they act for logical reasons. Further, as Ball has suggested, not only are things like resorting to crime very socially influenced but, when they change, they change in discrete jumps – from few people doing it to lots of people doing it with no stable intermediate point.

It seems likely that this would apply to the cultural influences on entrepreneurship, but few surveys have attempted to measure this, not least because asking people directly is unlikely to work if they do not realise the extent to which they are so influenced. As Graves comments, in reviewing the unreliability of much market research:

> The nature of a conscious response says much about a respondent's conscious values and how they would like to perceive themselves, but can reveal very little about what really has driven their behavior in the past or what they will do in the future.[19]

Based on the work of Cova on tribal marketing,[20] Earls[21] indicates that there three main levels at which human behaviour might be understood (see Figure 17.3). He suggests that Anglo-Saxons (North Europeans and their trans-Atlantic cousins) attempt to understand human behaviour either at the individual level or at the macro level of society at large and ignore the intermediate micro level of actual social groupings (such as the tribe). Yet it is influence at the micro level which might explain why immigrant communities, for instance, can often be well disposed towards entrepreneurship, even if others around them are not. It might also explain why Audretsch and Keilbach,[22] when looking at the capacity to create new firm start-ups within different regions in Germany, found that it appeared to be a very localised phenomenon. Whether they were looking at knowledge-based entrepreneurial new ventures or low-tech entrepreneurial new ventures, they found that 'entrepreneurship capital shows significant spatial autocorrelation and does not spill over into neighbouring regions'. However, these differing levels within a country or region will not be picked up by surveys such as that of GEM, which does not examine small enough groupings.

If the key level for social influence is the micro level, and if what matters is the perceived majority view in a social circle at this level, changes in cultural movement at that micro level will often appear as a discrete step-change (and not on a sliding scale as Dennis indicates). Thus, within those social circles and given a build-up of sufficient reason for change, the apparent majority view might flip relatively suddenly between unfavourable and favourable. However, measurements at a national level might still

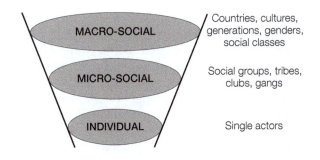

Figure 17.3 *Levels of observation*

Source: Adapted from B. Cova, and V. Cova, 'Tribal Marketing: The Tribalisation of Society and Its Impact on the Conduct of Marketing', *European Journal of Marketing*, Vol. 36, No. 5/6, 2002, p. 601.

suggest an intermediate average position (just as a mixture of black and white dots can appear to be grey when viewed from a distance). Building up sufficient pressure or critical mass for change might take time, but then, when it happens, change will be relatively sudden and significant – not steady and incremental – and, if so, that is an important difference from the institutional dimension.

What happens when the institutional and cultural influences are opposed?

Dennis presents the interplay between these influences in the diagram in Figure 17.2 – which suggests some interesting reflections. Could it, for instance, highlight the potential for some people to be responsible for contrary influences? Is it possible that on occasion the same public servants who, in their nine-to-five jobs, are responsible for implementing policies to make institutional support more favourable are at the same time, in their five-to-nine lives, reinforcing unfavourable cultural stereotypes by encouraging their children to see careers in the law, medicine and/or even the civil service as much more acceptable?

Institutional factors (including both wider regulatory and fiscal measures and narrower business support measures) are formal and overt and are presumed to affect entrepreneurship through a consciously applied business logic. It seems to be assumed that, if the measures are favourable, they will make it more likely that start-up or growth will be seen as the logical thing to do because it will be seem as likely to be less risky, less costly and/or more profitable. The evidence presented in Dennis's paper suggests that so far, in efforts to promote, stimulate and encourage entrepreneurship, there has been a tendency to focus only on this institutional dimension – possibly because that is what governments can do, what they know, what they are used to considering, and what is easier for them to observe and measure.

In contrast, cultural factors are not formally expressed and their influence is often subconsciously felt. They do not act through any conscious logic, but are absorbed through social interaction. Nevertheless actions which are taken under the influence of culture may subsequently be rationalised – because people like to think they act for logical reasons and often don't realise the unconscious influence. The apparent failure of much entrepreneurship policy based largely on institutional factors, together with insights such as those of Baumol about the power of society's 'rules', suggest that often the cultural dimension is crucial to entrepreneurship. The cultural dimension may be 'sticky' in that change in it is not smooth and incremental but happens relatively suddenly, and in jumps, when sufficient social momentum builds up. A failure to recognise this may explain the apparent lack of success of many efforts to date to encourage more entrepreneurship, because they have tried to improve the institutional factors without also trying to unstick the social reservations.

This in turn suggests that where institutional improvements have not led to more entrepreneurship, it is because the countries are in the 'led' quadrant in Dennis's typology – where the institutional dimension is relatively favourable but entrepreneurship is being constrained by the cultural dimension. In those circumstances further institutional improvement is likely to have very little effect because cultural change is the key. Changing the cultural dimension may not be easy, but it is not necessarily impossible. It would require the application of new thinking if change is to be effected. Thus those countries and regions which do want to be more entrepreneurial should neither give up if their (institutional) efforts to date haven't succeeded nor continue only to apply the same methods hoping eventually to get a different result, but instead they should explore the cultural dimension.

As indicated, there seems to be a paucity of examples of a significant change in the level of entrepreneurship being occasioned anywhere by changes in the institutional dimension, despite the effort that has been put into it. One example of a clear change seems to be China, where recently there has been a significant rise in the levels of entrepreneurship, shown, for instance, in the number of businesses being founded. Yet this has happened at a time when China appears to have had few, if any, of the institutional conditions which were thought to support or encourage entrepreneurship. Gibb and Li, for example, have argued both that there was very significant growth in the GDP of China between 1980 and 1995 and that, 'in an economy known for state ownership, remarkably this growth has been led by the non-state sector composed of community/collective enterprises, co-operatives, individually owned businesses, private corporations, and foreign joint ventures'.[23] They suggest that this was despite the absence of factors which were thought to underpin Western economic development such as private property rights, clear forms of ownership, a clear regulative environment, an adequate banking system and a government small business support agency[24] (and the position of China in the OECD assessment in Table 6.7 would seem to support this view). Could it be, instead, that what has led to the rise of entrepreneurship in China is a cultural shift in at least some elements of Chinese society which makes entrepreneurship socially acceptable despite a lack of significant institutional incentives?

⟳ ILLUSTRATION 17.2 – A STUDY IN GOVERNMENT ENTERPRISE POLICY

The Labour government which came to power in the UK in 1997 believed that enterprise was crucial to the country's economy. According to Gordon Brown, then Chancellor of the Exchequer, 'the central economic policy issue will be widening and deepening the enterprise culture'.[25] As a result, the government took steps 'to attempt to tackle barriers to enterprise and entrepreneurship ... in order to boost rates of entrepreneurial activity'.[26] It had, it said, 'an ambitious vision – that, by 2005, the UK will be the best place in the world [in which] to start and grow a business'.[27]

It is noticeable that the UK government did not declare that it wanted the UK to be the place in which most people wanted to start a business – just that, if they did so wish, it should be easy to do it. It thus expressed its ambition in terms consistent with an institutional rather than a cultural approach, and its plans indicated that the steps taken to achieve its aim would include institutional means such as:

- school initiatives 'promoting an enterprise society';
- establishing better macro-economic conditions;
- 'rewarding enterprise' by reducing tax rates;
- promoting competition;
- regulatory reform;
- improving access to finance;
- raising standards of business advice;
- training and skills; and
- supporting innovation and R&D.[28]

Thus, in carrying out its plans, the UK government took action to improve the institutional dimension and Table 6.7 indicates that the UK has achieved a very high ranking for the ease of starting a business within its jurisdiction. However, when Huggins and Williams reviewed the effect of UK government intervention in the 1997–2007 period (the first ten years of the Labour government), they concluded that 'across the UK as a whole, there has been little improvement in business start-up rates or other entrepreneurship indicators':[29]

> In terms of headline indicators, the impact of Labour government policy on enterprise development appears limited. ... Business start-up rates across the UK actually fell between and 1997 and 2004, with no UK region showing any marked improvement in their business start-up rate. Similarly, self-employment rates ... are the same in 2005 as they were in 1997, with many regions seeing little growth in the number of firms per head of population. At the international level, the Global Entrepreneurship Monitor (GEM) measures annual entrepreneurial activity across a number of nations, and ... it shows that the UK's rate fell from 7.7% in 2001 to 5.8% 2006. However, it should be noted that many of the other G8 nations saw even more dramatic falls, which can mainly be attributed to the post-2000 economic downturn. Nonetheless, such indicators do little to suggest that policy intervention has positively impacted on enterprise development in the UK.[30]

In this case the UK government indicated that its objective was a higher rate of entrepreneurial activity and that, to achieve this, its overall approach focused on the institutional dimension and the specific methods it used were also institutional. However, any subsequent institutional improvement appeared to have had no effect on business start-up rates, which, instead of rising, as had been the aim, appear to have fallen slightly over the relevant period.

Institutions and culture – a summary

This review suggests that what Dennis has labelled culture is important but acts differently from institutional influences, which is why it can be considered to be a different dimension of influence. For example:

- Cultural influence often has a subconscious effect, whereas institutional interventions generally seek to influence conscious business logic.
- Because institutional influences are varied (e.g. regulation, fiscal policy and support provision) and many of these can change incrementally, there can be wide variety of different institutional positions. But, because cultural movement often produces a discrete step-change in attitudes, it is likely to be either clearly favourable or unfavourable.
- Cultural influence may be stronger than that of institutional factors.

This suggests that, despite the apparent attraction of trying to influence entrepreneurship through institutional improvements – because they are both more familiar and apparently easier to do – they may not be effective if the cultural influence is unfavourable. It is the 'cultural' influence perhaps which may be the key to changing levels of entrepreneurship.

CHANGING THE CULTURE

Governments generally want economic growth, and so they endeavour to encourage more entrepreneurship to deliver more business start-ups and more business growth. This has usually been done through institutional means and it hasn't worked. If that conclusion is accepted, then instead of just trying more of the same, it would appear that a different approach is required. Further, the analysis summarised above suggests that if institutional means aren't effective, that might be because the cultural dimension is more influential. If, as Earls suggests, 'we do what we do because of *other people and what they seem to be doing*',[31] then, if more enterprise is still needed, social influence might be the key.

It would appear that this is being recognised in other areas of public policy. The 'zero tolerance' approach to crime reduction is designed to develop a situation in which even relatively low-level crime such as fare-dodging and graffiti is stopped, because if they are allowed to continue they give the impression that crime in at least some forms is acceptable. Also campaigns to reduce the incidence of drunken driving and littering now put less emphasis on the penalties and the chances of detection and instead focus on presenting such behaviours as socially unacceptable.

The importance of social example is also recognised by those who try to market fashion goods. Gladwell likens examples of the spread of both fashion and crime to epidemics. Given the right conditions, he suggests, a tipping point is reached at which a critical mass of social influence develops enough momentum to continue without any further external stimulus.[32]

There have been some aspects of enterprise interventions which have attempted to influence attitudes to enterprise, but not many, and none seem to have reached epidemic proportions, possibly because they have tried to influence people directly rather than through social influence. The Annex to Chapter 15, for instance, lists over 60 examples of intervention instruments, but only 4 might be considered to be addressing culture – and they are not mainstream initiatives.

As well as a preference for institutional measures and a lack of recognition of the potential impact that social influence might have on entrepreneurship, a further reason for not pursuing cultural initiatives is that this area is still largely unexplored. Without information about what might be done and the best ways of doing it, it is not possible to devise relevant policy instruments. Consequently there is plenty of scope for research.

IN CONCLUSION

The evidence presented in Chapter 16 seems to indicate that enterprise policy needs to change if it is to succeed. 'Cultural' influence may not be proven to be the decisive factor, but it would seem that continuing the old, mainly 'institutional' approach is not working and culture seems to offer a promising alternative.

Increasingly the strength of group influence is being recognised in many aspects of human life. It appears to affect rates of obesity and other health issues such as smoking. It may explain why rates of crime vary between different areas. Networks, it seems, can spread altruism and happiness, whereas having poor social connections appears to be linked to inequality in other areas also.[33] It therefore seems reasonable to think that social influence and example could also affect people's attitudes to, and engagement in, enterprise and entrepreneurial activity.

However, 'cultural' approaches will require different understandings and perspectives, in both research and policy. If cultural factors do not influence logically, they cannot be deployed or steered through logic. That is not to say that social influence cannot be steered, or nudged, but that steering social influence requires an understanding of its nature, how it works and of how it is possible to use it to achieve the effect sought.

☛ THE KEY POINTS OF CHAPTER 17

- The failure of much enterprise policy has a number of implications worth highlighting, including:
  - As policy appears to follow old ideas and assumptions, those ideas and assumptions must now be questioned.
  - There has been a failure to connect policy with evidence and some recent thinking.
  - Without a new approach policy is likely to continue to fail.
- 'Cultural' and 'institutional' influences on enterprise are very different and can be seen as acting in different dimensions.
- What governments have done is largely institutional, and that has not had the overall impact to the extent desired and apparently expected.
- The strong influence of social/group connections on human activity is recognised in the 'cultural' dimension, which can be stronger than the institutional dimension, which appeals more to reason than emotion.
- Making the 'cultural' dimension more positive might be a policy approach which could work, but more exploration of the nature of social influence on enterprise might also be needed.

✓ ## QUESTIONS, EXERCISES, ESSAY AND DISCUSSION TOPICS

- If similar enterprise polices have been pursued for over 25 years but are being seen to have failed only now, what implications does this have for:
  - The rationale for those policies?
  - The thoroughness of policy evaluation?
  - Current theories of the influences on enterprise?
  - The extent of communication between policy and research?

- In what ways might 'institutional' and 'cultural' factors influence enterprise either favourably or unfavourably?

- How might you investigate the extent of the influence of social factors on enterprise?

- What policies might be suggested to make cultural factors more positive?

📖 ## SUGGESTIONS FOR FURTHER READING AND INFORMATION

S. Bridge, *Rethinking Enterprise Policy* (Basingstoke: Palgrave Macmillan, 2010).

N. Christakis and J. Fowler, *Connected* (London: Harper Press, 2010).

W. J. Dennis, 'Entrepreneurship, Small Business and Public Policy Levers', *Journal of Small Business Management*, Vol. 49, No. 1, 2011, pp. 92–106.

M. Earls, *Herd: How to Change Mass Behaviour by Harnessing Our True Nature* (Chichester: John Wiley & Sons Ltd, 2009).

J. Kay, *Obliquity* (London: Profile Books, 2010).

R. H. Thaler and C. R. Sunstein, *Nudge* (London: Penguin, 2009).

REFERENCES

[1] A. Henley, 'The Post Crisis Growth in the Self-Employed: Are They a Volunteer Army?', paper presented at the *38th ISBE Conference*, Glasgow, November 2015, p. 2.

[2] R. Taylor, *Britain's World of Work – Myths and Realities* (Swindon: Economic and Social Research Council, 2002) p. 23.

[3] L. Stevenson, *Lessons Learned from the Implementation of an Entrepreneurship Development Strategy in Canada: The Case of the Atlantic Region*, April 1996 (unpublished) p. 2.

[4] OECD, 'Fostering Entrepreneurship and Firm Creation as a Driver of Growth in a Global Economy', a paper prepared for the *2nd OECD Conference of Ministers Responsible for Small and Medium-sized Enterprises (SMEs)* in Istanbul, Turkey, 2004, p. 7. Taken from http://www.oecd.org/cfe/smes/31917899.pdf (accessed 6 September 2016).

[5] For instance see Case 4.1 in S. Bridge, *Rethinking Enterprise Policy: Can Failure Trigger New Understanding?* (Basingstoke, Palgrave Macmillan, 2010) pp. 68–70.

[6] D. Storey, quoted in D. Smallbone, 'Policies to Support SME Development: The UK Experience', paper presented at a *Conference in Novara*, Italy, June 1995, p. 3.

[7] Small Business Service, *A Government Action Plan for Small Business: The Evidence Base* (Department for Trade and Industry, 2004). Taken from http://www.sbs.gov.uk.

[8] A. A. Gibb, 'SME Policy, Academic Research and the Growth of Ignorance, Mythical Concepts, Myths, Assumptions, Rituals and Confusions', *International Small Business Journal*, Vol. 18, No. 3, 2000, p. 13.

[9] Ibid. p. 13.

[10] S. Bridge, *Rethinking Enterprise Policy: Can Failure Trigger New Understanding?* (Basingstoke, Palgrave Macmillan, 2010) pp. 137–142.

PART 3

[11] F. Kitson, *Low Intensity Operations* (London: Faber and Faber, 1971) pp. 95–96.

[12] R. J. Bennett, 'Government and Small Business', in S. Carter and D. Jones-Evans (eds), *Enterprise and Small Business: Principles, Practice and Policy* (London: Prentice Hall, 2006) p. 60.

[13] W. J. Dennis, 'Entrepreneurship, Small Business and Public Policy Levers', *Journal of Small Business Management*, Vol. 49, No. 1, 2011, p. 95.

[14] Ibid. p. 95.

[15] Ibid, p. 95.

[16] P. Ball, *Critical Mass: How One Thing Leads to Another* (London: Arrow Books, 2004).

[17] D. B. Audretsch, A. R. Thurik and E. Stam, *Unraveling the Shift to the Entrepreneurial Economy* (Zoetermeer: EIM, December 2011) p. 24.

[18] Ibid. p. 4.

[19] P. Graves, *Consumer.ology* (London: Nicholas Brealey Publishing, 2010) p. 18.

[20] For instance B. Cova, and V. Cova, 'Tribal Marketing: The Tribalisation of Society and Its Impact on the Conduct of Marketing', *European Journal of Marketing*, Vol. 36, No. 5/6, 2002, pp. 595–620.

[21] M. Earls, *Herd: How to Change Mass Behaviour by Harnessing Our True Nature* (Chichester: John Wiley & Sons Ltd, 2009) pp. 95–96.

[22] D. B. Audretsch and M. Keilbach, 'The Localization of Entrepreneurship Capital – Evidence from Germany', Jena Economic Research Papers, 2007 – 029. Taken from www.jenecon.de.

[23] A. A. Gibb, and J. Li, 'Organising for Enterprise in China: What Can We Learn from the Chinese Micro, Small, and Medium Enterprise Development Experience', *Futures* 35, 2003, p. 403.

[24] A. A. Gibb, comments made by Gibb when making a presentation on Gibb and Li (2003) on 20 April 2004.

[25] Gordon Brown, then the UK Chancellor of the Exchequer, in an interview in May 2001 ahead of the publication of the Labour government's business manifesto.

[26] R. Huggins and N. Williams, *Enterprise and Public Policy: A Review of Labour Government Intervention in the United Kingdom*, The University of Sheffield Management School Discussion Paper No. 2007.03, August 2007, p. 2.

[27] SBS, *SBS Strategy 2001/04* (London: Small Business Service, 2001) p. 3.

[28] HM Treasury, *Enterprise Britain: A Modern Approach to Meeting the Enterprise Challenge* (HM Treasury, 2002) pp. 3–4. Taken from http://www.hm-treasury.gov.uk/media/5/3/adentbrit02part1-373kb.pdf (accessed 25 September 2011).

[29] R. Huggins and N. Williams, Op. Cit. p. 23.

[30] Ibid. p. 6.

[31] M. Earls, Op. Cit. p. 5.

[32] M. Gladwell, *Tipping Point* (London: Abacus, 2001).

[33] N. Christakis and J. Fowler, *Connected* (London: Harper Press, 2010).

Companion website

Please visit the companion website at www.palgravehighered.com/Bridge-UE-5e for access to additional learning and teaching materials.

Afterword: The Impact of Change

CONTENTS

- This book
- Challenging conventional wisdom

- The implications of the new paradigm
- Agenda for the future

It ain't what you don't know that gets you into trouble. It's what you know for sure that just ain't so.

Mark Twain

THIS BOOK

As Chapter 2 indicates, interest in enterprise, 'entrepreneurship' and small businesses grew significantly in the 1980s, stimulated by the findings that small businesses, as a sector, were the net creators of jobs. Consequently, there was considerable interest in learning more about them, what led to their creation and how they operated. The drive was to explore them and to discover what wasn't known about them.

Part 1 of this book presents a summary of the understanding that came from that exploration. It indicates how, and why, the current understanding has evolved. This understanding might be described as the received wisdom about enterprise: it is what sometimes we seem to think we 'know for sure'.

But, as the exploration continues, things are learnt which do not conform to earlier assumptions. Part 2 highlights some of those assumptions about small business and entrepreneurship and suggests that at least some parts of the apparent corpus of knowledge 'just ain't so'. It suggests alternative views which accord better with observed reality and explores the application of some of those alternative views to improve the way we practise, or help, enterprise.

Part 3 recognises that much of the stimulus for the current interest, and much of the budget behind it, has come from governments. So it explores why governments have sought to engage with enterprise, what they have they been doing to encourage and support it, and whether that works. The finding that much of it doesn't work reinforces the view that there are problems with the current wisdom since the policy that is failing often appears to be supported by that wisdom.

CHALLENGING CONVENTIONAL WISDOM

This book is suggesting that, in the area of enterprise, 'entrepreneurship' and small business, much of what we thought we knew is wrong or misleading. But that should not be very surprising. The history of science indicates that knowledge like this grows episodically, with many initially promising paths becoming blind allies and false directions along the way. This process does not stop: there isn't a final end point at which everything is finally known 'for sure'. The concept of the 'half-life of knowledge' acknowledges this in its suggestion that in almost any area of human learning some of what we think we know will, over time, turn out not to be correct. It should be expected, therefore, that some earlier assumptions would eventually be found to be incorrect – so a quizzical reassessment of previous learning is appropriate and should continue.

As explained earlier, to a large extent the trigger for the present interest in enterprise occurred at the end of the 1970s when Birch demonstrated that the earlier received wisdom about the supply of jobs in an advanced economy 'just wasn't so'. In saying, at least in the USA, that it was small businesses and not big businesses which were the main creators of net new jobs, he was not saying that it had always been the case – just that it was so in the period he examined. In retrospect it seems that what was happening in the 1970s was that signs were emerging that Toffler's 'second wave' had peaked and the third wave was starting to supersede it. The second wave can be seen as a process that began with the Industrial Revolution and led to the emergence of big conglomerates pursuing the benefit of economies of scale – with such success that it seemed to many that they were unstoppable. Thus initiatives such as setting up the Bolton Committee in the UK to examine the position of small businesses, and the establishment of the Small Business Administration (SBA) in the USA, were conceived, not because small businesses were thought to be important for the economic future, but through a concern that, at least in some sectors, they might disappear altogether with a consequent loss of those benefits they did provide.

In retrospect is seems clear that, by the time Bolton was appointed and the SBA established, the relative decline of small businesses had already halted. The main indication of this came at the end of the 1970s with Birch's findings. This was, in effect, an early signal that, at least in the USA and Western Europe, the big-business-is-the-future paradigm was ending, if not already over. Writers like Toffler and Handy also recognised this. As Handy, from an employee's perspective, said:

> It was during the 1970s ... that the familiar scenery of our working lives began to show visible changes. The large employment organisations which have been day-time houses for so many people all their lives began to decline.[1]

Toffler called the new paradigm that was then emerging in its place the 'third wave', because it came after the first two waves of the agricultural and the industrial revolutions. Audretsch *et al.* suggest that it is leading to the 'entrepreneurial economy', after the 'managed economy' of the era of big businesses with their economies of scale and 'routinized production'.[2] But, whatever name it is given, it does represent a change from what had seemed to be in many countries the economic norm.

That does not mean that there was a sudden switch to a new norm. The change was not instantaneous, even if it has happened more quickly than the industrial and agricultural revolutions. It has been a gradual process of economic change which is likely still to be continuing. Further the perception and understanding of what is happening is likely to lag the reality and, as the historical review in Chapter 2 indicates, our understanding of entrepreneurs has been evolving for over 250 years. So there is no reason to think we have come to the end of that process. Entrepreneurs and small businesses may be more relevant in an entrepreneurial economy, but that does not necessarily mean that they are better understood.

Enterprise and small businesses comprise what is still a relatively new and emerging field of knowledge. Also, like any other such field of study, it should not be expected that all the initial guesses, assumptions and theories will endure. It is now over 35 years since Birch's findings triggered an 'explosion of research into entrepreneurship and the small and medium enterprise'[3] so, instead of just looking for new information, it is appropriate also to re-assess some of the assumptions made earlier and the conclusions reached. The process of checking received wisdom, even if it is only recently established wisdom, is relevant and should continue. That is how knowledge advances.

Therefore, in presenting and reviewing received wisdom about enterprise, entrepreneurship and small business, this book also indicates areas where a re-assessment does appear to be needed. Some of these are listed in Table 18.1.

Table 18.1 *Some of the challenges to conventional enterprise wisdom*

Assumptions challenged	Alternative view (and its implications)
The assumptions underpinning the 'professional' perspective of small businesses.	Small businesses are not small big businesses. Small businesses should be seen as they are – not as they are supposed to be. So there is a need to discard big business–based assumptions.
Entrepreneurship is a real, discrete, identifiable condition which somehow produces more and/or better entrepreneurs.	Entrepreneurship is an invented concept which does not actually exist as we have conceived it.
Enterprise is a sub-set of (private sector) business.	Enterprise and entrepreneurs are a part of life and can be wider than just profit-oriented business. So think of enterprise as a form of exploration.
The business plan is an essential first step when starting any business and all the key issues are covered in the standard business plan menu.	Issues like the importance of social capital, the need to accept uncertainty, the relevance of gaining momentum and the need to explore and expect some dead-ends are very relevant but are not included in the business plan menu. So it is important to recognise that an effectuation approach will often be much more relevant and will be a better tool to use.
High-growth, high-tech entrepreneurs can be cultivated separately.	Entrepreneurial activity has common roots – and it may not be possible to cultivate some varieties separately at an early stage. Policy shouldn't be based on wishful thinking.
(Business) logic is the main influence.	In most cases cultural influence is very important in determining who engages in productive enterprise. Thus it is important to recognise the role and forms of social capital and the influence of social groups.
Current policy works.	Much current policy doesn't appear to work and so its budgets are wasted. New policy is required and for that new insights are needed.
The second wave/managed economy is the appropriate basis for much economic thinking.	The third wave/entrepreneurial economy is already upon us and is the future. However, much policy is still based on second wave/managed economy thinking. So it needs to be changed if progress is to be made.

THE IMPLICATIONS OF THE NEW PARADIGM

If the new paradigm is not yet fully established, at least the old one is being discounted. It had seemed that all 'developed' countries were converging toward second wave 'managed' economies dominated by a few large enterprises, 'constrained only by the countervailing powers of the state and workers'[4] (see Illustration 2.2). Now many signs indicate that that is no longer the case – but what are the implications of this shift?

Implication for governments

A clear implication, and one of the first to be identified, is that big businesses have ceased to be the main net creators of jobs. Instead, what had seemed to be an inevitable decline in the population of small businesses has been reversed as some of the economic advantages of size have been negated. The competitiveness of small, knowledgeable, innovative, flexible businesses with speedy responses has meant that often they can be more suitable for the needs of the market. So they have created jobs and, in consequence, governments and others have turned to the small business population as the new source of employment and of other economic benefits.

Although its employment-creation effects may have encouraged interest in the new economy, its key feature is its wealth-creation potential. There will still be big manufacturing businesses, just as agriculture was still needed after the rise of industry. But the entrepreneurial economy provides opportunities for wealth creation based on other criteria. In particular it relies for its competitiveness on the application of knowledge, rather than on the effective and/or or cheap application of labour. It makes different demands therefore on its supporting environment.

That supporting environment can be very relevant to the economic health of the businesses established in it. Using a horticultural analogy it can be likened to the soil in which plants grow – because a soil prepared for one type of plant may not be the best for a different crop. The newer businesses that epitomise the entrepreneurial economy are very different from the old, larger, economy-of-scale businesses of the managed economy, and they need different supporting conditions. Are we trying to plant entrepreneurial seeds in ground which is ill-prepared for it? They will not necessarily thrive well in the wrong conditions – just as alkali-liking plants will not grow well in the more acid soil liked by, and thus prepared for, other garden arrangements.

It is therefore relevant to ask if even the current 'institutional' environment is suitable for the new entrepreneurial businesses, or whether it has, to at least some extent, been prepared for the older economies-of-scale businesses. To what extent are many of the employment laws enacted by states, and the policies followed by unions, still based on the assumption that, in a managed economy, there is convergence towards domination by a handful of powerful enterprises. As a result does the need continue to be perceived for countervailing powers, or at least restraints: Galbraith's 'big business' balanced by 'big labor' and 'big government'?[5] Thus Audretsch *et al.* argue, not for entrepreneurship policy which encourages more entrepreneurs, but for a 'policy for the entrepreneurial economy'[6] which involves a re-assessment of incumbent institutions and practices based on the needs of a previous era.

Implications for people

One of the obvious implications for many people in the move to an entrepreneurial economy is the change in employment prospects, at least. In the conditions that seemed to prevail in a managed economy it appeared that big businesses were destined to last for a long time, and could be expected therefore to provide jobs for life. But it is now recognised that, like human beings, businesses do not survive forever and generally they die at an earlier age than humans. Lifetime employment is not to be expected in those circumstances, and employment might be viewed, not as just one event, but as a potential series of different manifestations, perhaps a bit like the way Buddhists view existence.

Should it be expected that, when one form of employment ends, there will be others? In a situation where change is the norm, economic security will increasingly depend, not on long-term employment contracts, but on being able to respond to change: on having the skills, ideas, and the ability to learn and to adapt to meet changing requirements – which are key attributes of enterprising behaviour. That means having people who are enterprising and entrepreneurial, and there is an interest therefore in building an enterprise culture in which people feel that they can and should use their own initiative to secure their economic future.

This represents a challenge that is social as well as economic. It had been observed that in the United States, 'the nature of work has changed, but the nature of education has not. ... Global competition and new technology are overthrowing the assumptions behind mass production and, simultaneously, the lessons taught in American classrooms.'[7] People need a different approach: an enterprising approach.

Other paradigms?

In considering paradigm shifts, thus far this book has pointed mainly to the change from second to third wave thinking. However, from a perspective of looking back from the future, it might be apparent that other changes are also happening. Could the resurgence of interest in social enterprise, reported in Chapter 7, be part of a paradigm change which increasingly recognises that there is no clear division between private sector businesses whose primary pursuit is profit and third sector businesses with social, environmental and/or ethical aims? Is there instead, in the emerging ideas of 'conscious capitalism', a realisation that business is a form of human social activity which is likely to be more sustainable in the longer term if it pursues both profit and wider benefits and seeks to satisfy all its stakeholders including, but not limited to, its financial backers? Such a paradigm would be relevant to big businesses as well as small ones and has echoes in Kay's comment that often 'the most profitable businesses are not the most profit oriented'.[8] Recognising that would change a lot of perceptions, such as the view sometimes held that all entrepreneurs are only interested in building their own wealth at the expense of others. And there could be other changes underway of which we are not yet conscious.

AGENDA FOR THE FUTURE

Where are we now in our understanding of enterprise and entrepreneurship and their manifestation in small business? This book recognises that the desire to learn about these subjects has arisen because of a change in the economic situation. In much of the 'developed world', there is a shift from the supremacy of big businesses, whose competitiveness came largely from economies of scale, to the emerging world of small businesses which compete on the basis of knowledge and/or flexibility. This change has not finished and our understanding of it is still incomplete. We should expect the change to continue, so our learning about it and its impact also needs to continue and, on occasion, to be re-assessed.

It is already appreciated that, in the more advanced economies, the old 'second wave' businesses are no longer the main source of new jobs – so we have started looking for new sources of employment among the 'third wave' businesses that will replace them. But, if we want to encourage these new businesses, our thinking, programmes, institutions and systems need to be appropriate – and they won't be if they remain in essence oriented to the old 'managed economy'. Do we need a policy to change our approach, therefore, from one based on 'second wave' assumptions to one appropriate to the third wave? Or will we instead try to grow new plants in old soil?

To a considerable extent this is a book about change and in particular:

- The change from managed economies to entrepreneurial economies.
- The resultant change in the economic relevance of small business and enterprise.
- The associated increase in research into small business and enterprise, leading to changes in knowledge about them.

All those changes are still continuing. This book indicates areas where, in consequence, our thinking may also need to change. For instance recognition of the changes and their consequence raises many questions, not only about enterprise and entrepreneurs themselves, but also about their wider role in an economy and how they can be promoted.

Should enterprise and entrepreneurs be seen, not just as a sub-set of business, but as a part of wider life? Have they been considered to be aspects of business, at least in part, because it was expected that they would provide economic benefits? Has thinking about them as a part of business led to assumptions that they respond to the same influences and logic that are supposed to influence bigger business? Has that precluded recognition of their social context and the strong social influence upon them?

Recognising their social dimension, in turn, has implications for efforts to help or encourage enterprise, entrepreneurs and small business. Have many efforts to date, although well-meaning, essentially been misguided and even ultimately counter-productive – rather like bleeding people to cure them of infectious diseases? Has current understanding about 'entrepreneurship' been followed without checking its underlying assumptions and seeing if it corresponds with how successful entrepreneurs actually behave?

It might have been expected that research would have answered some of these questions, so is research another area where change is needed? And the divide between research and policy – can it be reduced? Alternatively, should the reality of the divide be accepted and the consequent need to construct communication bridges across it?

Which brain side should dominate in seeking to explore and explain this field of study? Should it be the rational left or the imaginative right? Has the left side, in practice, come to dominate with its apparent logic but its consequent staleness in thinking – whereas a full understanding (and the flexibility to recognise and respond to change) requires the joint application of both sides?

How those questions are answered will determine the future direction of our evolving understanding of enterprise.

📖 SUGGESTIONS FOR FURTHER READING AND INFORMATION

D. B. Audretsch, A. R. Thurik and E. Stam, *Unraveling the Shift to the Entrepreneurial Economy* (Zoetermeer: EIM, December 2011).

C. Handy, *The Future of Work* (Oxford: Basil Blackwell, 1984).

A. Toffler, *The Third Wave* (London: Collins, 1980).

REFERENCES

[1] C. Handy, *The Future of Work* (Oxford: Basil Blackwell, 1984) p. ix.

[2] D. B. Audretsch, A. R. Thurik and E. Stam, *Unraveling the Shift to the Entrepreneurial Economy* (Zoetermeer: EIM, December 2011) p. 3.

[3] A. A. Gibb, 'SME Policy, Academic Research and the Growth of Ignorance, Mythical Concepts, Myths, Assumptions, Rituals and Confusions', *International Small Business Journal*, Vol. 18, No. 3, 2000, p. 13.

[4] D. B. Audretsch and A. R. Thurik, 'What's New about the New Economy? Sources of Growth in the Managed and Entrepreneurial Economies', *Industrial and Corporate Change*, Vol. 10, No. 1, 2001, p. 268.

[5] J. K. Galbraith, *American Capitalism: The Concept of Countervailing Power* (Boston, MA: Houghton Mifflin, 1956).

[6] D. B. Audretsch, A. R. Thurik and E. Stam, Op. Cit. p. 4.

[7] M. Prowse, 'Is America in Decline?', *Harvard Business Review*, Vol. 7, No. 4, 1992, pp. 34–45, at p. 44.

[8] J. Kay, *Obliquity* (London: Profile Books, 2010) p. 8.

Companion website

Please visit the companion website at www.palgravehighered.com/Bridge-UE-5e for access to additional learning and teaching materials.

Index

In this index figures are indicated by f., illustrations by i., and tables by t. (e.g. Asia 28(i.2.2) indicates that Asia is mentioned on page 28 in Illustration 2.2). Published documents are presented in italics.

A

academic spin-outs   92–93
Accelerating Entrepreneurship
    Strategy   47–48
accept uncertainty approach   208–209,
    218–222, 359(t18.1)
achievement motivation/
    orientation   43(t3.2), 58–59, 61,
    92 see also NAch
Acs, Z. J.   48
additionality   214, 325, 329, 331
adoption rate   112(t6.2)
advocacy   254
Africa   27, 101, 118(t.6.7)
Ahlstrom Corporation   89, 97
Ahmad N.   299(f15.3)
Ailenei, O.   138
Alternative Investment Market   304
Amin, A.   139, 141, 149, 154
Anderson, A.   70/1
Armington. C.   80
Arshed N.   277, 285, 312(f15.4), 335,
    338
Asia   28(i2.2), 198(i10.2)
associations   25, 137(t7.1), 138/9,
    142, 335, 348(f17.1)
Atlanta   27
attributes/attributes and
    resources   22, 35, 42, 43(t3.2),
    45(i3.2), 46, 50, 61–68, 65(f4.1),
    66(f.42), 73(f4.4), 113–116, 122,
    141, 197 see also entrepreneurial
    attributes
Audretsch, D   25, 27–28(i2.2), 247,
    254, 349–350, 358, 360, 362
Austin   27
Australia   17, 118(t6.7), 131,
autonomy (including need for
    autonomy) 43(t3.2), 58(t4.1), 60,
    111(f6.3), 178

B

Babrami   201
Babson College   22, 215
backing winners see winners
Bager-Sjögren, L.   330
Baines, S.   178
Ball, P.   349–350
Bangladesh   101, 179, 307(i15.4)
Bannock, G.   295, 309, 330, 336
Barclays Bank   334(i16.4)
Barkham, R.   159, 232–233
Barrett, G.   179
Barrett R (Levels of consciousness)
    193(t10.1)
Barriers
    cultural   282–283
    for ethnic and women-owned
        ventures   178, 258(i13.7), 283–284
    to advice/training   115, 282(i14.5),
        309(t15.2)
    to enterprise/entrepreneurship/
        SMEs/ start-up   37, 117, 121,

272, 277, 281–282, 336, 349,
    352(i17.2)
    to entry   90, 101, 302(i15.3), 348
    to growth   21, 277, 292, 297, 301,
        310
Baumol, W. J.   49–50, 51(t3.4), 53,
    174, 183, 184(i9.3), 197, 254,
    297, 349, 351
Bayh-Doyle   92
'Beermat' plan   221(i11.10)
behavioural economics   99, 164,
    169(i8.2), 181(i9.2)
Belgium,   23, 118(t6.7), 332
Bellinger, G.   4(f1.1)
Bennett, R. J.   284–285, 332, 335
BERR, see Department for Business,
    Enterprise and Regulatory Reform
Better Regulation Taskforce/
    Executive   297
Big Society   147
Birch, D. L.   15, 18–20, 34, 48,
    51(t3.4), 78–82, 86, 124, 132,
    156, 262, 269, 273–274, 358
Birch, K.   251
Birley, S.   256(i13.5)
birth-rate policy/strategy   269(i14.2),
    272, 276
BIS, see Department for Business,
    Innovation and Skills
Black, F.   209(i11.2)
Blackburn, R. A.   26(t2.3), 286, 309,
    314, 321(f16.1), 338
BMW syndrome   157(t8.1)
Bolton Report (also Bolton, J. E. and
    the Bolton Committee)   14–16,
    15(t2.1), 29, 73(f4.4), 74, 78, 85,
    87, 88, 156, 262, 290, 301, 358
Bolton W. K.   12
born or made   45(i3.1), 67–73, 182, 344
    (and see nature and/or nurture)
Botham, R.   81, 274, 312
Bourdieu, P.   244
Boyatzis, R.   64, 114(t6.4)
Boyd, N. C.   63, 64
Brain – left, right thinking   213,
    216(i11.8), 222, 361
Branson, R.   3, 67, 73, 75, 199(t10.3)
Brazil   118(t6.7)
Bridge, S.   22(i2.1), 48, 50, 51(t3.4
    f3.2), 53, 69, 81, 137(t7.1),
    140, 140(f7.1), 149, 179, 180,
    182, 183(f9.1), 186–187, 188,
    195(f10.1, t10.2), 200(f10.2),
    202(t10.4), 208, 219(t11.3), 225,
    234((i12.2), 246(f13.1), 251(i13.3),
    251–252, 254, 259, 265(f14.1),
    266(t14.1), 345, 349, 355
Britain   13, 26, 36, 78, 100, 101, 129, 178,
    261–262, 283, 293, 308, 311, 332
British Business Bank   294(i15.1), 302
broad approach – to defining
    entrepreneurship (see narrow
    approach)

Brown, Gordon   36, 352(i17.2)
Bruce, R.   116(t6.6)
Burns, P.   103, 131(f6.8), 134, 232,
    301–302
business
    angel   27, 119(f6.5), 120, 215,
        238, 294(i15.1), 296, 299(i15.2),
        301(t15.1), 303, 304, 315
    birth-rate policy/strategy (see
        birth-rate)
    failure   127–131, 131(f6.8), 160 (see
        also models of business failure)
    formation/founding   36, 45, 49–50,
        51(t3.4, f3.2), 68, 74, 109, 130, 157,
        173, 187, 200, 206, 208–209,
        276
    incubation/incubator   293,
        294(i15.1), 301(t15.1), 304, 315
    plan   117, 130, 168–9(i8.2),
        185(f9.3), 186, Chapter 11
        passim, 227, 232, 235, 239, 242,
        243, 315, 331, 359(t18.1)
    hegemony of   213
    professionals' model   159–160
    proprietors' model   159
    school/studies,   6, 21, 21–22(i2.1),
        38, 154, 158, 173, 192, 206,
        210(i11.4), 213
    start-up rate   23, 132, 272, 276,
        295, 336, 353(i17.2)
    survival rates   80, 97, 130,
        131–132, 292
    termination   9, 88, 109–110,
        110(f6.1), 124, 126–129,
        128(f6.7), 166, 228, 229, 316 (see
        also business survival rates)
Business Connect   311
Business Expansion Scheme   303
Business growth, yardsticks for   160,
    230(t12.1)
Business Link(s)   304, 308, 310–312
Business Start-up Scheme   303
Business Shops   311–312
Bygrave, W.   4, 5(f1.3), 112(t6.2),
    186–187

C

Cambridge phenomenon
    27, 28(i2.2)
Cameroon   246
Campbell, C.   248(i13.2)
Campbell, M.   349
Canada   22, 118(t6.7), 343
Cantillon, R.   12–13, 22(i2.1), 29, 34,
    35, 48, 57, 78, 174, 217(i11.9)
capabilities   13, 46, 58, 184(i9.3),
    299(i15.2)
Capital for Enterprise   294
Capital for Enterprise Limited (CfEL)
    294
capitalism/capitalist   13, 16, 17, 19,
    176, 186, 200, 280, 360
Caribbean   179, 258(i13.7), 305

Carnazza, G.   127(t6.9)
Carter, S.   75, 90, 99, 100, 103, 158, 178, 258(i13.7), 284, 285, 312(f15.4), 338
Casson, M.   246
Castro, R.   4(f1.1)
causation/causal *see* effectuation
CBI-SME Council *see* Confederation of British Industry
CERI   42
change management   131
characteristics of small businesses   17, Chapter 5 *passim*,   156
Christakis, N.   197, 203, 252, 355
Chell, E.   50, 53, 59–62, 67, 74, 157, 178
China/Chinese   49, 101, 118(t6.7), 174, 186, 189(i10.2), 349, 352
Churchill, N. C.   109(t6.1), 121(f6.6), 132
churn   80, 276
cluster(s) *and* cluster effect   81, 122, 157, 294(i15.1)
CMAFs   139
cognitive approaches/concepts/ theories   59, 63–66
cohort analysis   80
Coleman, J.   244, 248, 254
Collett, P.   282(i14.5)
Collier, W.   333, 338
Columbus Christopher   198(i10.2), 217–218
comfort zone   120, 157(t8.1), 176
commercialisation   38, 92, 293
Committee of Public Accounts, *see* Public Accounts Committee
communist   261, 347
community business/enterprise/sector Chapter 7 *passim*,   295, 352
Community Development Finance Institutions (CDFIs)   306
community entrepreneur   146, 147(t7.3)
competence/competency   38–39, 45(i3.2), 63–64, 99, 114(t6.4), 115, 121, 130, 231, 281, 284
Confederation of British Industry (CBI)   231, 292, 330
conscious capitalism   360
Conscise project   248(t13.1), 249
Conservative (party / government)   19–21, 37, 147, 284, 310
consolidation *see* stages of small business development
conventional wisdom (*and* received wisdom).   xi, 5–6, 18, 29, 122, 151–152, 154, 155(i8.1), 173, 187, 343, 344, 346–347, 357–358, 359(t18.1)
Co-operatives   25, 130, Chapter 7 *passim*,   295, 352
Cope, J.   246
corporate entrepreneurship   22, 49
Cotton, J.   43(t3.2)
Council for Excellence in Management and Leadership   310
Cova, B. and V.   350, 351(f17.3)
Cowie, P.   321(f16.1)
Cowling, M.   270, 329
craft businesses   89, 94, 157(t8.1)
creative destruction   16–17, 34, 49, 167
credit unions   307
Cromie, S.   99, 256(I13.5)
Cruickshank, D. and Cruickshank Review   302, 302(I15.3), 329

culture
  cultural influence   258(i13.7), 347–354, 359(t18.1)
  enterprise/entrepreneurial   xi, 19–20, 36, 39, 112, 146, 184(i9.3)), 201(i10.3), 249, 271–272, 281, 283, 295, 297, 336, 352(i17.2), 360
Cunningham, J. B.   40(t3.1)
Curran, J.   26(t2.3), 284, 327

D
Davies. H.   46
Davies, L.   158, 233
deadweight   325, 354
Deakins, D.   67, 212(f11.1)
decline stage   126 (*see also* stages of small business development)
definitions
  of enterprise – broad or education   39–45
  of enterprise – narrow or economy   39–45, 47–49
  of small business   85–88
delivery vehicles   265(f14.1), 266, 335
Della Giusta, M.   246
Delmar, F.   61, 63–67, 122
Denmark/Danish   22, 47, 118(t6.7), 298–300(i15.2)
Dennis, W. J.   166, 274, 347, 348(f17.2), 349–351, 353, 355
Department for Business, Energy and Industrial Strategy (BEIS)   37, 147, 311
Department for Business, Enterprise and Regulatory Reform (BERR)   37, 311
Department for Business, Innovation and Skills (BIS) 37, 38, 86(i5.1), 97, 99, 124, 143, 297, 298, 302, 308, 311
Department for Education and Employment (DfEE)   310–311
Department for International Development (DFID)   161, 162(f8.1), 243
Department of Trade and Industry   20, 37, 141, 147, 297, 305, 310–311, 332
dependency   36, 144(t7.2)
deregulation   16(t2.2), 297, 301(t15.1), 313, 316
Deregulation Unit/Taskforce   297
DfEE, *see* Department for Education and Employment
Directorate-General (DG) Enterprise and Industry   36, 298
displacement   277, 294, 295, 325
division of labour   102
Dragons' Den   257–258(i13.6)
Drakopoulou Dodd, S.   70–71
Drucker, P. F.   2, 59, 112
DTI, *see* Department of Trade and Industry
due diligence   119, 213–214
Dunbar's Number.   86
Dunn, B.   97
Dunoyer, C.   25, 138
dynamic analysis   19, 80
dynamic capitalism   120

E
E-numbers   50–51, 50(t3.4, f3.2)
Earls, M.   152, 350, 353, 355

East Anglia   158
Eastern Europe   xi, 283
economic appraisal   322(i16.1)
economic growth   xi, 19, 22–24, 29, 35, 38, 47, 78, 92, 120, 129, 156, 166, 180, 184(i9.3), 247, Chapters 14 and 15 *passim*,   333, 353
economic theory of bureaucracy   279–280
économie sociale   25, 138–9
economies of scale   13–14, 26, 27–28(t2.4), 78, 84, 122, 129, 138, 279(i14.4), 280–281, 350, 358, 360–361
education approach *see* enterprise, education school
effectuation/effectual   192–193, 206–210, 207(t11.1, i11.1), 208(t11.2), 218, 220–222, 225, 342, 359(t18.1)
Einstein   4, 152, 328(i16.3)
employment/job creation   15, 19, 34, 38, 41, 78–82, 85, 86, 119, 132, 156, 261–262, Chapter 14 *passim*, 299, 331, 357, 359
England   11, 12, 38, 49, 93, 137, 138, 158, 174, 198, 269, 277, 283, 303, 304, 311, 312, 332, 335
Enterprise Allowance   20
enterprise attributes *see* attributes
Enterprise Capital Fund programme (ECFs)   294
enterprise competency *see* competency
enterprise culture   xi, 19, 20, 36, 39, 112, 146, 201(i10.3), 249, 271, 272, 281, 283, 295, 297, 336, 352(i17.2), 360
Enterprise Directorate-General (of the EU)   298, 311
enterprise, economy school of (narrow definition)   41, 52
enterprise, education school of (broad definition)   41, 52
Enterprise Educators UK   38
Enterprise Finance Guarantee (EFG)   87(i5.1), 120, 294, 303, 305, 329
Enterprise Fund (The)   294
Enterprise in Higher Education   38
Enterprise Initiative   20, 37, 306, 334
Enterprise Investment Scheme   303–304, 330
Enterprise Ireland   308
enterprise needs hierarchy/ model   164–165, 165(f8.4))
Enterprise Northern Ireland   38
Enterprise Zones   304, 306
enterprise policies   xi, 19, 36, 179, Part 3 *passim*
enterprising acts   45–46(i3.2)
enterprising/entrepreneurial behaviour   12, 23, 35, 42, 43(t3.2), 52, 57–58, 61, 62, 66, 67, 70–73, 113, 146, 180, 247, 360
entrepreneurial
  attributes *see* attributes
  behaviour *see* enterprising/ entrepreneurial behaviour
  capital   161, 165(f8.4), 184, 247
  culture   36, 184(i9.3)
  economy   27–28(i2.2), 34, 166, 276, 349–350, 358–360, 359(t18.1)
  self-efficacy *see* self-efficacy
entrepreneurs
  stellar   3, 67–68, 71, 73, 73(f4.4)

lifestyle 50, 199((t10.3)
nascent 91, 199(t10.3), 219
entrepreneurship policy 49, 51(t3.4),
    179, 266, 268(i14.2), 270, 328,
    354, 346(i17.1), 351, 360
Environment
    institutional 274(i14.3), 291(f15.2),
        295–296, 300, 315–316, 347–354,
        348(f17.2), 353(i17.2), 360
    cultural 274(i14.3), 283, 291(f15.2),
        291(f15.2), 292, 297–298, 315,
        347–354, 348(f17.2),
equilibrium level/rate of
    entrepreneurship 272
equity averse 119
ethnic
    businesses 89–91, 96–102, 179,
        283, 301(t15.1)
    enterprise/entrepreneurship/
        entrepreneurs 62, 91–92,
        101–102, 176, 179, 283
    minorities/groups 63–64, 91–92,
        101–102, 179, 254, 258(i13.7),
        283, 295, 305
    minority businesses (EMBs) 91,
        101, 305
European Commission (EC) 78, 139,
    142, 285, 303, 310
European Observatory for SMEs 230
European Union (EU) 25, 35, 36, 78,
    86, 87(i5.1), 139, 142, 158, 295,
    298, 303, 310, 330
evaluation Chapter 16 *passim*,
Evidence Base 344–345
Export Enterprise Finance Guarantee
    (ExEFG) 305
external equity 231

F
factors of production 12, 25, 58, 160,
    243
failure / business failure 18–19, 71,
    98, 100, 112, 119, 127–131,
    131(f6.8), 160, 213, 219, 305–306
    see also market failure
family business/firms 11, 46, 63,
    89–90, 96–99, 102, 138
fear of failure 184, 214, 346(i17.1)
female enterprise/entrepreneurs/
    entrepreneurship 90, 99–102,
    176, 178–179, 305–306 *see also*
    women/women-owned businesses
female-owned businesses *see* women/
    women-owned businesses
Finland 22, 89, 97, 118(t6.7)
first-stop shop 311–312
fiscal policy 291(f15.2), 296, 316,
    353
Ford, H. (Fordist and Fordism) 13–14,
    19, 26, 26(t2.3), 28–29, 78,
    138–139, 196, 215(i11.6),
foreign direct investment, *see* inward
    investment
foundations 25, 139, 142, 209
Fowler, J 197, 203, 252, 355
France 12, 22, 26, 35, 118(t6.7),
    127(t6.9), 138, 141, 332
Fraser, S. 333, 334(i16.4)
free enterprise 176, 284
Friedman, M. 159
Freud, S. 62
Fukuyama, F. 246, 259
funding gap *see* Macmillan Gap

G
G7 countries 22
Galbraith J. K. 14, 151, 155(i8.1), 360
Gallagher, C. 269
Garnsey, E. 110(f6.2)
Gates, Bill 3, 73, 199(t10.3)
gazelles 48, 51(t3.4), 81, 273–274
gender 64, 90–91, 99–100, 102, 130,
    178, 284, 291(f15.2), 295, 316,
    351(f17.3)
Germany/German 22, 57, 118(t6.7),
    127(t6.9), 141, 169, 246–247,
    332, 350
Gibb, A. A. 21, 35, 42, 43(t3.2),
    44(t3.3), 50, 151, 156, 158, 174,
    175(t9.1), 176, 183, 183(f9.2),
    185(f9.3), 188, 197, 203,
    219(t11.3), 233, 249, 281, 284,
    327, 328, 345, 352
Gladwell, M. 245(i13.1), 354
Global Entrepreneurship Index 48
Global Entrepreneurship Monitor
    (GEM) 22, 35, 174, 184(i9.3),
    295, 298, 346(i17.1), 353
Gorman, C. 236
Goss, K. 248, 242
Government Action Plan for Small
    Business 271, 345
Grameen Bank 119, 307(i15.4)
Graham Review 329
Graves, P. 184, 206, 215(i11.6), 218,
    225, 350
Gray, C. 63
Green Book 322(i16.1), 325–326(i16.2)
Greene, F. 92, 134, 286, 335
Greiner, L. E. 111(f6.3)
growth
    barriers/constraints/restrainers 21,
        121, 123, 160–164, 301
    imperative 158, 170, 239
    jobless 262, 270
    model 111(f6.3)
    stage 109(t6.1) *see also* stages of
        small business development

H
habitual entrepreneur 121, 157–158,
    176–177, 179, 227, 230
Handy, C. 26, 71, 196, 203, 221, 262,
    358, 362
Hanifan, L. J. 244
'hard' support 308
Harford, T. 246
Hart, M. 103, 273
happiness 194, 354
Hegarty, C. 208, 219(t11.3), 225
heroic entrepreneurs 3, 58, 67, 70–73,
    88, 199(t10.3)
Herzberg, F. I. 236
hierarchy of needs model 164,
    165(f8.4), 193(t10.1)
hierarchy of sciences 5(f1.3)
high technology/high-tech
    businesses 3, 48–50, 51(f3.2),
    52, 93, 115, 158, 202(t10.4), 210,
    271, 291(f15.2), 293, 294(i15.1),
    301(t15.1), 316, 343, 359(t18.1)
Higher Education Innovation Fund
    (HEIF) 92
Hitchens, D. M. W. N. 169, 332
Hoffman A. 299(f15.3)
Holland *see* Netherlands
Holmquist, C. 178

Holywood Old School 249–251(i13.3),
    251
Hornaday, R. W. 44(f3.1), 73
Hornsby, J. S. 134
Huggins, R. 336, 352
human capital 25, 102, 161,
    161(f8.1), 165(f8.4), 243–244,
    256, 333
Hungary 23

I
ignorance explanation 334(i16.4)
ignorance, growth of 151, 345
immigrant 91, 102, 283, 350
incubation/incubator *see* business
    incubation
India/Indian 101, 118(t6.7), 138, 198
industry sectors 88, 158, 293
influences
    on entrepreneurs / on the
        entrepreneurial decision 9,
        61–74, 70(f4.3), 176, 179–186,
        183(i9.3), 197, 254, 254(i13.4),
        258(i3.7), 347–354, 348(f17.2),
        359(t18.1)
    on a (small) business 90–92, 98,
        120–124, 129–130, 132, 156, 162–
        164, 163(f8.2), 167, 237, 243, 361
information and advice 117, 231,
    282(i14.5), 301(t15.1), 308, 316,
    332
information and communication
    technology (ICT) 28(i2.2), 296
innovation 11–12, 15(t2.1), 17, 19,
    20, 24, 26(t2.3), 27(i2.2), 28(t2.5),
    34, 40(t3.1), 44–45(f3.1), 46, 48,
    57–58, 59(t4.1), 78, 79(t5.1), 120,
    122, 126, 133, 142, 166, 169(i8.2),
    229(i12.1), 231, 233, 270, 272,
    293, 294(i15.1), 310–311,
    328, 330–332, 352(i17.2)
intellectual capital 25, 161, 165(f8.4),
    243
intentions model 65(f4.1)
International Consortium on
    Entrepreneurship (ICE) 298(i15.2)
International Small Business
    Journal 246, 259
Internet 112(t6.2), 206, 212(f11.1),
    308, 310, 315–316
intervention Part 3 *passim*
intrapreneur/intrapreneurship 22, 24,
    40(t3.1), 199(t10.3)
invention 17, 44(i3.1)
Invest Northern Ireland / Invest NI
    47, 51(t3.4), 235(i12.3), 311, 332
inward investment 313
Ireland 23, 308, 332
Irwin, D. 282(i14.5),
Israel 22, 118(t6.7), 181(i9.2)
Italy 22, 118(t6.7), 127(t6.9),
    245(i13.1)

J
Jacobsen, L. 123
Japan 22, 28(i2.2), 118(t6.7),
    198(i10.2), 217–218, 246
job creation *see* employment/job
    creation
job quality 144–145
Johnson, S. 279–280
Joyner, B. 284
Junior Achievement 38, 298

K

Kahneman D   181(i9.2)
Kay, A.   248(t13.1)
Kay, J.   160, 355, 361
Keeble, D.   278(t14.2)
Keilbach, M.   25, 180, 247, 254, 350
Kets de Vries, M.   62, 71, 232
Keynes, J. M.   18–19, 152, 261–262
Kim. J.   348(f17.1)
Kirzner, I.   58
Knight, F. H.   57, 218
know-how   93, 113(f6.4), 114–115,
    161, 246, 256, 315
know-who   113(f6.4), 115, 246, 256,
    315
knowledge capital   25, 243
knowledge economy   296
knowledge – half-life   xii, 5, 152, 357
Knowledge Transfer Partnership (KTP)
    92, 310
Kolvereid, L.   178
Korea   101, 118(t6.7)
Krueger, N. F.   65–66, 65(f4.1), 249, 254

L

Labour (party / government)   20–21,
    37, 284, 302, 352–353(i17.2)
large business   3, 9, 14, 15(t2.1), 17,
    26, 28(t2.5), 57, 79(t5.1), 80,
    82–85, 86(i5.1), 88, 117, 122,
    129–130, 140(f7.1), 156, 159,
    166, 174, 196, 214, 277–278,
    280–281, 329–330, 334(i16.4)
late payment   100, 123(t6.8),
    302–303, 329–330
latent enterprise   146
Latin America   27
Learning and Skills Council   311
legal form/structure (of a business)   88,
    113(i6.1), 121, 143–144, 201
Leibenstein, L.   17
Lessem, R.   114(t6.3)
Levels of observation – macro-social,
    micro-social, individual   350,
    351(f17.3)
Lewis, V. L.   109(t6.1), 232
Li, J.   352
Li, Y.   93
lifestyle business   50, 157(t8.1), 236
Lisbon   36
Lischeron, J.   40(t3.1)
Ljunggren, E.   178
Lloyd, P.   141–142
Local Enterprise Agency (LEA)   38, 295
Local Enterprise Company   311
Local Enterprise Development Unit
    (LEDU)   311
Local Enterprise Partnership   38, 303,
    315, 333
Local Exchange Trading Schemes/
    Systems (LETS)   140(f7.1)
locus of control   43(t3.2), 59(t4.1)
    59–60, 69, 92
Lundström, A.   268(i14.2), 286, 314, 338
Lunn, P.   167

M

Macmillan Committee   300
Macmillan Gap   300
managed economy   27–28(i2.2), 349,
    358–361, 359(t18.1)
managed workspace (MWS)   293,
    295, 315

Management Charter Initiative   64
management development   114(t6.4),
    308, 333
management recruitment   231
management team   84, 93, 98–99,
    230–233
market failure   266(t14.1), 272,
    277–281, 279(i14.4), 284, 295,
    301, 308–310
market position   95, 109(t6.1), 121,
    231
market research   27, 116(t6.6), 125,
    130, 206, 211, 212(f11.1), 213,
    215(i11.6), 218, 233, 292, 294, 350
Marshall, A.   16
Maslow, A.   165, 193–194, 193(t10.1),
    233(t12.2)
Mason C.   312, 335, 338
maturity stage (of a business) *see* stages
    of small business development
McClelland, D. C.   58–59
McGilchrist, I.   216(i11.8)
McNamara fallacy   328(i16.3)
mentors/mentoring   164–165, 179,
    219(t11.3), 221(i11.10), 237, 254,
    285, 301(t15.1), 308, 315
Mexico   101, 118(t6.7)
micro-finance   307
Mills, A.   4(f1.1)
Miner, J. B.   45(i3.1), 234(i12.2)
Mises, L. von   58
models of (small) business
    success   159
Moensted. M.   115
Mole, K.   275, 333
Morgan, Sir Frederick   221
Moulaert, F.   138
Murtagh, B.   137(t7.1), 140(f7.1), 149,
    200(f10.2), 265(f14.1), 266(t14.1)
Mutuals/Mutuelles   25, 139,
    140((f7.1), 142–143

N

NAch (Need for Achievement)   40(t3.1),
    58–59, 59(t4.1), 61, 92, 199
narrow approach (to defining
    entrepreneurship) *see* enterprise-
    economy school
National Audit Office   336
National Economic Research
    Associates   329
nature and/or nurture Chapter 4
    passim
necessity entrepreneurship   23–24
need for achievement *see* NAch
need for autonomy   59(t4.1), 60 *and
    see* autonomy
Nelson, D.   123
NESTA   81
net new jobs   19, 78, 80–82, 132, 156,
    262, 269, 358
Netherlands   23, 118(t6.7), 264,
network(s)/networking Chapter 13
    passim,
New Economics Foundation   306
new economy   25–26, 27(t2.4), 359
Newton, I.   4, 152
Nicolaou, N.   69, 70(f4.3)
Nilsson, A.   147(t7.3)
Norrman, C.   330
Northern Ireland   35, 38, 131–132,
    168–169(i8.2), 235(i12.3),
    267(i14.1), 276, 311, 332

Norway   118(t6.7), 178
novice entrepreneur   176–177

O

Odle, C.   80
OECD   39, 42, 80, 143, 231, 232,
    279(i14.1), 298–299(i15.2),
    326(i16.2), 344, 352
old economy   27(t2.4)
O'Neill, K.   137(t7.1), 140(f7.1), 149,
    200(f10.2), 265(f14.1), 266(t14.1)
one-stop shop   311–312, 316
opportunity entrepreneurship   23–24
Ormerod, P.   349
outputs/outcomes   41, 57, 147,
    267(f14.2), 267–268(i14.1), 271,
    276, 321(f16.1), 322, 324, 326–328
Owen, G.   332
Oxford Economics   96
owner types   44(i3.1), 67, 73, 157,
    176

P

Paine, T.   154
Pakistan   101, 179
Parker, S. C.   329
Pearce, R.   149
Penrose, E. T.   17, 78, 82, 156, 174, 206
perfect market   277–278, 301
Perren, L. G.   276,
personal business advisers   308
personality approaches, personality
    theory/traits   58–62, 65,
    180(i9.1), 234(i12.2)
Peterson, R.   113(f6.4), 246, 257(i13.5)
Phizacklea, A.   283
picking winners *see* winners
Pink, D.   159
planned behaviour, theory of   64–65,
    234(i12.2),
Poland   118(t6.7)
policy framework   265–267,
    265(f14.1), 266(t14.1), 299(i15.2)
Porter, M. E.   122, 134
Porter, S.   251(i13.3)
portfolio career   196
portfolio entrepreneur   157, 177, 236
Portugal   18(t6.7)
power relations   257(i13.5), 279–280
problem-solving   43(t3.2), 83, 193
prompt payment code   302
psychodynamic approach   61–62
Public Accounts Committee   329
public choice model   279
Putman, R.   244

R

Ram, M.   179, 258(i13.7), 283
Reagan, R.   20
received wisdom *see* conventional
    wisdom
Rees, H.   296
Regional Development Agencies (RDA)
    38, 303, 333
Regional Growth Fund (RGF)
    294(i15.1), 303
Reid, G.   123
resistance to change   163(f8.2)
Richard, D *and* the Richard Report/
    Review /   264, 336
risk averse/risk avoidance   233,
    279(i14.4), 293, 310
risk capital   304, 329, 330

risk-taking propensity   40(t3.1),
  58–59, 59(t4.1), 92
Roberts, A. K.   63
Roberts, R.   334(i16.4)
Rondstadt, R.   113(i6.4), 246,
  257(i13.5)
role models   92, 124, 145, 225, 254,
  295
Rosa, P.   81, 115, 156, 176–177
Roseto   245(i13.1), 248(i13.2), 252
Rotter, J.   59
'Route 128'   27
RSA   181(i9.2)
rural areas/business/farmers   79(t5.1),
  93–94, 130, 158, 197, 295,
  301(t15.1)

S
Sarasvathy, S.   112, 192–193, 203,
  206–208, 207(t11.1, i11.1),
  208(t11.2), 225
Say, J-B.   12–13, 58
Scase, R.   178
Schuller, T.   245
Schultz   58
Schumpeter, J. A.   16–17, 19, 34, 49,
  57–58, 167
Science Enterprise Challenge   38
science park   315
scientific method   4–6, 4(f1.2), 155,
  167, 192–193, 206, 342
SCORE   308
Scott, M.   81, 116(t6.6), 156, 176–177
Scott, R.   322, 332
Scotland   37, 177, 276, 303, 305,
  311–312, 331
Scottish Enterprise   35, 37, 276, 311,
  331
Scottish Intermediate Technology
  Initiative   331
second stop shop   312
Seed Enterprise Investment
  Scheme   303
self-actualization   29, 193–194
  193(t10.1), 197, 233(t12.2)
self-confidence   38, 41, 42, 43(t3.2),
  52, 59(t4.1), 60–61, 66(t4.2), 99,
  113, 131
self-efficacy   64–66, 65(f4.1), 91
self- employed/employment   13,
  22, 35, 41, 46, 49, 50, 51(t3.4,
  f3.2), 63, 67, 73(f4.4), 88–90,
  94, 99, 101–102, 128, 173, 179,
  195(t10.2), 196, 220, 223(i11.11),
  255, 258(i13.7), 278(t14.2), 292,
  296, 299(i15.2), 305, 307, 343,
  348, 350, 353
serial entrepreneur   177
Shah, A.   296
shamrock organisation   196
Shane, S.   21(i2,1), 35, 61, 68, 69,
  70(f4.3), 72, 111, 186–187
Shaw, E.   90
Silicon Valley   27, 28(i2.2), 210,
  294(i15.1)
Simon, H.   181
Singapore   23, 118(t6.7),
Small Business Administration (SBA)
  16, 79(t5.1), 80, 87(i5.1), 88, 132,
  264, 280, 308, 358
Small Business Council   311
Small Business Investment Task
  Force   311

small business/firms/SME policy   16,
  151, 154, 168, 168(i8,2), 265,
  268(i14.2), 280, 282, 290, 311
Small Business Service (SBS)   20, 270,
  279, 282(i14.5), 290, 311, 336,
  345
Small Firms Loan Guarantee Scheme
  (SFLGS)   87(i5.1), 294,
  302(i15.3), 303, 329
small firm(s) policy *see* small business
  policy
Small Firms Training Loans   309, 333,
  334(i16.4)
Smallbone, D.   131, 134, 229(i12.1),
  274(i14.3)
SME Observatory, *see* European
  Observatory for SMEs
SME policy *see* small business policy
Smith, Adam   12–13, 25, 160, 242–243
Smith, G.   248
social capital   25, 92, 102, 115, 145–
  147, 152, 161, 161(f8.1), 165(f8.4),
  167, 180, 184(i9.3), 209, 238
  Chapter 13 *passim*,   359(t18.1)
social economy   9, 25, Chapter 7
  passim, 251, 301(t15.1)
Social Economy Unit   139
social enterprise   24–25, 39, 50,
  51(t3.4), 94, Chapter 7 *passim*,
  155, 166, 177, 242, 249, 251, 295,
  301(t15.1), 306, 360
social entrepreneurs/
  entrepreneurship   39, 50,
  51(t3.4), 140, 146, 176–179, 199,
  209(i11.2), 251
social exclusion   46, 141, 143, 295,
  306
Social Exclusion Unit/Taskforce   306
Social Investment Task Force   306
social norms   64, 65(f4.1), 249, 254,
  258(i13.7), 297
social objectives   142–143, 170
social-psychological approaches   61–2,
  74
societal attitudes   45(i3.2), 64, 280,
  291(f15.2), 292, 297, 315, 317
sociological approaches   62–63, 65
'soft' assistance/support   308
sole trader   88, 90, 97, 121, 157, 176,
  306
South Korea *see* Korea
Southon, M.   221(i11.10)
Soviet Bloc   27
Spain   118(t6.7), 127(t6.9), 198
stages of entrepreneurship/small
  business development   50, 85
  Chapter 6 *passim*, 164, 223
  Chapter 12 *passim*,   246, 292,
  300, 315–317
Stanworth, M. J. K.   63
Starship Enterprise   39
StartUp Britain   308
Start Up Loans   303
start-up stage *see* stages of business
  development
static analysis   80
stellar entrepreneurs   3, 67–68, 71, 73,
  73(f4.4)
Stevenson, H. H.   174, 175(t9.2)
Stevenson, L.   199(t10.3), 266,
  268(i14.2), 286, 314, 338, 343
Storey, D. J.   16(t2.2), 34, 81, 93,
  115, 123, 129–130, 134, 159,

  177, 231, 234, 236–237, 271,
  273, 274(i14.3), 276, 285, 286,
  301(t15.1), 310, 314, 326(i16.2),
  332–333, 334(i16.4), 338
succession planning   126, 98
Sundin, E.   178
support agencies   115, 130, 159, 164,
  223(i11.11), 229(i12.1), 234,
  235(i12.3), 265, 281, 283, 305,
  308, 352
support measures/services   256,
  264–265, 273, 283, 306, 311–313,
  332, 343, 351,
Svendsen, G. L. H. and G. T.   246
Sweden   118(t6.7), 122
Swedish Innovation Centre   330
systemic failure   279, 346
Szerb, L.   48

T
targeting growth businesses
  273–275(i14.3), 293, 323(t16.1)
taxonomy (of enterprise initiatives)
  314
Technology and Innovation Centres
  (TICs)   311
Teesside   177
termination stage, *see* stages of small
  business development
Thatcher. M. / Thatcherism   19–20
third sector   9, 25, 39, Chapter 7
  passim,   166, 177, 360
Thurik, A. R.   28(i2.2), 49, 362
Toffler, A.   25–26, 28, 137, 262, 358, 362
Total Entrepreneurial Activity (TEA)
  23–4, 346
Training and Enterprise Council (TEC)
  311
traits   40(t3.1), 58, 59(t4.1), 61,
  65, 67–70, 73, 92, 157, 178,
  180(i9.1), 207(i11.1), 208(t11.2),
  232–233, 234(i12.2)
Twain, M.   151, 357

U
UK   xi, 11, 14, 16–20, 18(f2.1), 22, 25,
  27–29, 28(i2.2), 36–38, 43, 47,
  63–64, 78–81, 86, 86–87(i5.1),
  88–92, 94, 96–97, 99, 102, 117,
  124, 131, 138–139, 141–143,
  145, 147, 158, 161, 179, 196,
  238, 258(i13.7), 264, 266(t14.1),
  269–271, 273, 276, 279, 280,
  282(i14.5), 284, 290–291, 293,
  294(i15.1), 295–298, 300,
  301(t15.1), 302–306, 308–313,
  312(f15.4), 320–323, 322(i16.1),
  323(t16.1), 325(i16.2), 327,
  329–331, 334–336, 343, 345,
  352–353(i17.2), 358
UK Innovation Investment Fund
  (UKIIF)   294(i15.1)
United Nations (UN)   140(f7.1), 201
Unlisted Securities Market (USM)   304
Urwin   81, 89, 103, 124, 134
US/USA/United States   16, 18–20, 22,
  26–27, 28(i2.2), 38, 78, 79(t5.1),
  80–81, 86, 87(i5.1), 88–89,
  92, 96–97, 99–101, 112(t6.2),
  118(t6.7), 119, 119(f6,5),
  123, 132, 141–142, 215, 232,
  245(i13.1), 246, 269–270, 273,
  280, 294(i15.1), 308, 358, 360

V

VAT (*including* registration and deregistration)   87(i5.1), 88, 128(f6.7), 128, 130–131, 223(i11.11), 296

Venkataraman, S.   21(i2.1), 186, 192–193, 203, 206

venture capital (*including* funds, venture capitalists and trusts)   48, 115(t6.5), 120, 180, 215, 221, 238, 243, 247, 256, 257(i13.6), 275(i14.3), 285, 294(i15.1), 301(t15.1), 303–304, 330

Vietnamese   101

vitamins   243, 252–253

Vohora, A.   93

voluntary sector   25, 139–141, 147

Vozikis, G. S.   63–64

W

Wales/Welsh   93, 304, 311

Walker, D.   284

Walker, S.   278(t14.2)

Walras, L.   16

Wealth of Nations   12–13

Welsh Assembly   311

Welsh Development Agency   276

Welter, F.   197

Wennekers, S.   49

West. C.   221(i11.10)

West Indian   101, 179, 283

Westall, A.   270

Westhead, P.   177, 278(t14.2), 333, 334(i16.4)

Whyte, W. H.   14

Williams, M.   100

Williams, N.   336, 352(i17.2)

Winfrey, O.   67

winners (*including* backing winners *and* picking winners)   123–124, 166, 269(i14.2), 272–273, 274–275(i14.3)

wisdom, the transition route from data   4(f1.1)

women/women-owned businesses/ enterprises/firms/ventures (inc female-owned)   50, 62, 89–91, 96, 99–102, 176, 178–179, 283–284, 295, 301(t15.1), 305–306, 307(i15.4), 334

Women's Enterprise Task Force (WETF)   306

Winter, S.   123

Wyer, P.   229

Y

yardsticks for business growth   160, 230(t12.1)

Young Enterprise   38, 298

Young, Lord   20, 29, 36–38

Yunus, M.   307(i15.4)

An Intro **LAB for** Behavioral Researchers